$tripers

$tripers

The Economic Value Of the Atlantic Coast Commercial and Recreational Striped Bass Fisheries

Edited by
Virgil Norton, Terry Smith and Ivar Strand

Contributors

Jon Conrad
Cornell University

Leon Abbas
North Carolina State University

Marilyn Altobello and Norman Bender
University of Connecticut

Virgil Norton, Terry Smith and Ivar Strand
University of Maryland

A Maryland Sea Grant Publication
University of Maryland
College Park

Publication Number
UM-SG-TS-83-12

Copy editors: Michael W. Fincham
Mark E. Jacoby

Designer: Sandy Harpe

Cover illustration: Sandy Harpe

Copies of this publication are available from:

Sea Grant Program
University of Maryland
1224 H. J. Patterson Hall
College Park, MD 20742

UM-SG-TS-83-12

The publication of this report is made possible by grant NA81AA-D-00040, awarded by the National Oceanic and Atmospheric Administration to the University of Maryland Sea Grant Program.

Contents

Preface   *vii*

Acknowledgements   *ix*

Introduction   *x*

The Commercial Fishery   *2*

The Recreational Fishery   *26*

Economic Value of the Striped Bass Fisheries   *32*

Economic Impact of the Striped Bass Fisheries   *46*

Summary   *53*

References   *55*

Table Index   *57*

Preface

DECLINING STOCKS OF North Atlantic striped bass prompted legislators and management agencies to seek information concerning the economic importance of striped bass. One of the questions legislators and managers need answered is whether the resource has sufficient economic importance to warrant government expenditures on research, regulation of harvest, or augmentation of stocks through hatchery programs.

In generating the information necessary to address this issue, over 1500 industry participants were interviewed concerning their activities associated with striped bass. Existing commercial and recreational data were also obtained. As with most studies, data perfectly suited to our needs did not always exist and collection of such data would have required expenditures well beyond available funds. In these cases, the best available or affordable information was used.

This report is also a culmination and digest of individual studies at the participating universities. The material presented herein is only a portion of the information generated during the study. Those interested in economic information on subjects not dealt with in this document should contact individual contributors from the region of interest. The reader should recognize that this report is basically a snapshot of the industry as it existed during 1979 through 1980. Changes have occurred in the industry since 1980, especially in response to changes in legislation. Because of the time needed for data gathering, analysis and publication, implications of some recent changes are not incorporated into this report.

The contents of this report, however, should contribute some of the information needed by policy makers. Descriptions of the commercial and recreational harvesting sectors by regions are presented first. Highlighted are the economic characteristics of these users along with other information of general interest. Following these descriptions are analyses emphasizing the economic value and activity generated by striped bass fishermen. The economic value section addresses the dollar value of the benefits arising from the recreational and commercial uses of stripers. Economic activity analysis estimates how much economic activity striped bass fishing creates, in terms of dollar volume of goods and services as well as employment. The analysis is based on three scenarios: activity associated with the current level of landings, activity implied by the high level of landings in the early 1970s, and activity under proposed managment regulations. The information presented should help provide an understanding of the industry and some background for the discussion involved in the management process.

Acknowledgements

SEVEN INVESTIGATORS FROM four Sea Grant universities participated in the economic analyses required for the assessment. This report contains the findings of these analyses. Many individuals assisted the investigators during the study.

Field interviews to obtain primary data were conducted by Laurie Bates in New England; Jim Sieber and Ben Muse in New York and New Jersey; Jim Adriance, Rod Brennan and Brett Snyder in New Jersey, Delaware, Maryland and Virginia; and Mike Principe, Marcus Hepburn and other interviewers working on an allied study, "Recreational Fishing in the Sounds of North Carolina," in North Carolina, headed by Peter Fricke.

The efforts of all of the federal and state officials who provided data are appreciated. We also thank the many recreational and commercial fishermen; fish wholesalers, retailers and suppliers; and the restaurant, club and hotel operators who took time to answer questions related to their operations.

Support for the study was provided by the Sea Grant Programs and Agricultural Experiment Stations of each university; the U.S. Department of Commerce, National Sea Grant program and National Marine Fisheries Service (NMFS); and the U.S. Department of Interior, Fish and Wildlife Service.

This report represents scientific Article No. A-3691, Contribution No. 6667, of the Maryland Agricultural Experiment Station and Scientific Contribution No. 1030, Storrs (Connecticut) Agricultural Experiment Station. Computer support was also provided by the University of Maryland Computer Center.

Leon Abbas
Marilyn Altobello
Norman Bender
Jon Conrad
Virgil Norton
Terry Smith
Ivar Strand

Introduction

AMERICANS HAVE BEEN catching and eating and arguing about striped bass for centuries, but seldom in our history has this popular fish caused as many controversies as it has during this last decade.

The cause of those controversies is scarcity. Commercial catches have been declining dramatically since 1974 when 14.7 million pounds of striped bass were reported caught and sold by commercial fishermen working rivers, estuaries and coastal waters from North Carolina to Maine. By 1980 the commercial catch for these same states totaled less than 5 million pounds. Similar catch declines—though less easily documented—were reported by sport fishermen.

We now have an estimate of the cost of that decline—at least, the cost in dollars and cents and jobs. Resource economists Virgil Norton, Ivar Strand and Terry Smith organized a three-year, 10-state study of the economic impact and value of the commercial and recreational striped bass fishery along the northeast Atlantic Coast. With their report, we have our best estimates to date of the economic structure and potential of the fishery that once flourished and of the fishery that still exists today—though in diminished form.

The seven participating economists found that:

• The decline in commercial and recreational catches since 1974 has cost the region 7,500 lost jobs and $220 million in lost economic activity.

• Though much is lost, much remains. In 1980, the current commercial and recreational fishery was supporting 5,600 jobs, causing $90 million in annual spending and creating $200 million in related economic activity in the coastal areas of the states.

• The economic impact of commercial and recreational fishing extends beyond the coastal counties of these 10 states. For every six dollars generated in coastal areas because of striped bass fishing, another one dollar's worth of output is created in inland counties. Similarly, for every five coastal jobs created, one inland job is generated.

• For society in general, the net economic value of commercial and recreational striped bass fishing is not the dollars people *actually* spend or make; it's the amount they are *willing* to spend above what they *have* to spend. This net value is estimated to be $11.5 million annually, the value that federal planners might best use in evaluating the use of federal funds for maintaining or increasing a fishery that is so popular with so many people.

• To increase recruitment of new fish, the Atlantic States Marine Fisheries Commission has recommended that state legislators and fishery agencies impose greater restrictions on current harvesting practices. If those restrictions increase future stocks and harvests as predicted, then economic output in the region could grow by $3.8 million and 63 new jobs.

• The cost of that improvement comes high in some regions. The size restrictions proposed for striped bass catches in the spawning rivers of the Chesapeake Bay will annually cost Maryland and Virginia $6 million in lost economic activity and 250 lost jobs, while providing an immediate boost to harvests in the northern states. If the decline in striped bass stocks is not reversed, however, future losses to the Chesapeake could be even greater.

The study that produced these findings began with federal legislation known as the Chafee Bill or Emergency Striped Bass Act, an effort to encourage and coordinate striped bass research. Funds for the project originated with the National Marine Fisheries Services of the U.S. Department of Commerce and the U.S. Fish and Wildlife Service of the U.S. Department of the Interior. Staff for the multi-state project included economists from the University of Maryland, the University of Connecticut, Cornell University and North Carolina State University. The Sea Grant Programs and Agricultural Experiment Stations of these universities provided additional support.

The study is designed to help resource managers, state legislators, and even the U.S. Congress—all of whom are pressed by pleas to restore a fishery that apparently carries considerable emotional and economic value in the 10-state north coastal region. This report includes economic information on the structure and potential of the striped bass fishery, information that can be applied to the difficult social and political questions raised by the striped bass decline. Some of the major questions are:

• Is there sufficient economic impact to justify government expenditures on research, regulation of harvest and possibly replenishment of stocks through hatchery programs?

• How much public money should be spent maintaining the fishery?

• What would be the economic loss caused by additional catch restrictions?

• Should management efforts focus on the commercial fishery or the recreational fishery?

That last question remains one of the most difficult. Because striped bass is such a popular gamefish, charterboat captains, surfcasters, and a variety of rod and reel clubs have lobbied strenuously and successfully for anti-netting laws that have nearly eliminated commercial fishing in many states and severly restricted it in others. In Maryland and New York, regulations are expected to cut commercial catches significantly over the next several years. The state of Rhode Island, after a decade of debate, has proposed a complete ban on the catching, buying and selling of striped bass by both commercial and sports fishermen.

The issues are complex, the decisions difficult. Whether careful research can isolate the causes of decline, whether hatcheries can replenish the fishery, whether management can conserve the existing stocks, no one can predict. With this report, however, it is clear that restoring the striped bass fishery—a diminished fishery—is still worth considerable effort and expense.

—Michael W. Fincham
Communications Coordinator
Maryland Sea Grant College

$tripers

The Commercial Fishery

STRIPED BASS HAS historically been an important commercial species along the Atlantic Coast. It has been harvested in every state from Maine to North Carolina. Although there have been year-to-year fluctuations in annual landings, there was a general increase in commercial landings during the period 1924-1973 (Strand et al. 1980). Atlantic Coast commercial landings reached an all time high of 14.7 million pounds in 1973. Since then there has been a steady and precipitous decline in the catch of commercially harvested striped bass. The 1980 catch, according to NMFS preliminary data, was 4.5 million pounds, and had an estimated value of $4.9 million.

In order to understand the nature and economic effects of the decline in commercial catch, the distribution of landings, the methods of harvest, and the marketing of striped bass were examined. The distribution of landings offers a general indication as to which states are most directly influenced by striped bass production. Analysis of harvest methods reveals the specific technology adopted because of existing physical conditions or state regulations. Information on costs indicates how much expense each technology requires in the production of striped bass. Finally, information on marketing shows the distribution routes, product forms, and price received for striped bass as it is moved from the waterman to the consumer.

Distribution of Landings

It is convenient to categorize the eastern coastal states in which striped bass harvest occurs according to four regions: New England (Maine, New Hampshire, Massachusetts, Rhode Island and Connecticut), Mid-Atlantic (New York, New Jersey and Delaware), Chesapeake (Maryland and Virginia) and South Atlantic (North Carolina). To a large degree, this regionalization corresponds to different fisheries, each of which is discussed below.

The regions have contributed varying amounts to Atlantic landings since 1929 (Figure 1). The Chesapeake region accounted for about two-thirds of total landings from 1929 to 1973; the New England, Mid-Atlantic and South Atlantic regions contributed 7 percent, 14 percent and 14 percent, respectively. For the period 1974-1980, the Chesapeake's share declined to about 48 percent, while the New England, Mid-Atlantic and South Atlantic shares changed to 20, 19 and 13 percent, respectively. (See Strand et al. 1980 for additional information on the relative catch of striped bass by region and state.)

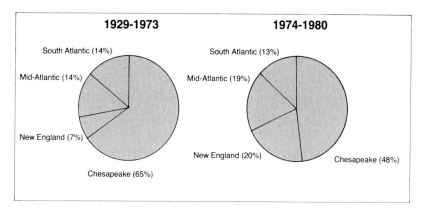

Figure 1. Commercial striped bass landings, by region

Massachusetts is the major striped bass harvesting state in New England, with Rhode Island accounting for most of the other landings (Figure 2). Connecticut has reported a small share in some years (it is now illegal to land commercially caught striped bass in Connecticut), while the Maine and New Hampshire landings have been less than one percent of the New England striped bass harvest.

Among the three states in the Mid-Atlantic, most striped bass are landed in New York. New Jersey has contributed about one-fifth of the harvest, while the Delaware share in recent years has been below one-tenth (Figure 3).

Maryland has accounted for about two-thirds of the commercial land-

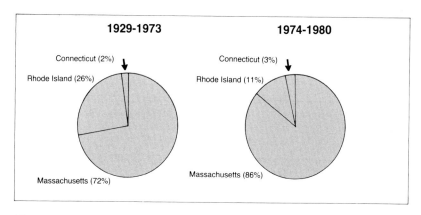

Figure 2. Commercial striped bass landings in New England, by state.

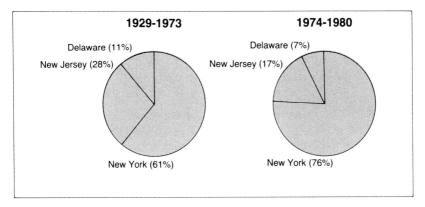

Figure 3. Striped bass landings in the Mid-Atlantic region, by state.

ings of striped bass in the Chesapeake region (Figure 4). Although the relative share of the Chesapeake landings in Maryland and Virginia has not changed greatly, the decline in harvest by fishermen in Maryland and Virginia has been dramatic. In 1973, the commercial catch was 7.9 million pounds. During the past three years, the annual harvest diminished to well below three million pounds.

For several decades prior to the mid-1960s, the annual commercial harvest of striped bass in North Carolina remained relatively stable. In 1966, landings of .66 million pounds were reported. In 1967, the harvest increased to over the million pounds. Landings remained high until 1978 when the annual harvest dropped back to near the 1966 levels.

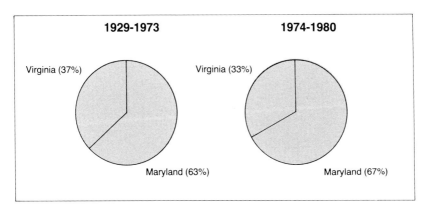

Figure 4. Striped bass landings in Chesapeake Bay, by state.

Seasonality in Landings

According to Berggren and Libbermann (1978), there are three major coastal stocks of striped bass along the U.S. Atlantic Coast. The Chesapeake stock accounts for 80 percent of the coastal migratory population, with migratory stocks from the Hudson and Roanoke rivers accounting for the balance. Since the Chesapeake stock is the largest, the seasonal harvesting pattern in each region is determined primarily by the migratory pattern of this stock. Young, sexually mature fish, predominately females three to four years of age, and a portion of the older population, migrate out of the Chesapeake Bay in April and May and move northward along the coast (Kohlenstein 1980). Some of these fish appear as far north as Cape Cod by early summer and remain off the coast of Massachusetts and Rhode Island until fall. A reverse migration begins in October along the northern part of their range. These fish return to the Chesapeake Bay in November and December. This migration is repeated each year and leads to a consistent seasonal pattern in commercial landings in each region. As a result, the majority of landings in New England and the Mid-Atlantic occur in the period from early summer to October. Maryland and Virginia landings peak in the spring and increase again in November and December. Most striped bass landed in North Carolina are caught in the early spring and late fall.

Harvesting Methods[1]

As was pointed out by Strand et al. (1980), the methods of harvesting striped bass differ within and among regions. Three methods, however, account for most of the Atlantic Coast landings of striped bass. These are hand lines (or hook and line), set and drift gill nets.

New England

The major gear types used in harvesting striped bass in New England in 1980 were hook and line, floating trap and otter trawl. The Massachusetts fishery is entirely hook and line as a result of a law passed in 1945 making

---

[1]Much of the information used in this and the following sections of this report was obtained through field interviews necessary to supplement published and unpublished data from national and state agencies and other sources. More than 1500 personal contacts were made along the coastal area from North Carolina to Maine with sport and commercial fishermen, wholesalers, retailers and restaurant operators. Details of the interviews, including copies of the questionnaires used, sample distributions, and other information, are available on request.

it illegal to harvest striped bass by any other means. Gear is also restricted to hook and line in Maine and New Hampshire.

Most striped bass in Rhode Island are commercially harvested using hand lines. Floating traps and otter trawls are also used in the Rhode Island commercial striped bass fishery. Since the mid-1970s, a shift toward greater use of hand lines has occurred. In 1974 approximately 49 percent of total catch was taken by hand lines and 48 percent by floating trap. In recent years hand lines have accounted for over two-thirds of the catch.

Floating traps are designed for harvesting species such as scup, butterfish, squid, and fluke, and landings of striped bass by this gear are considered incidental catch. During 1980 special permits were issued by the Rhode Island Department of Environmental Management for each trap location, and are valid for up to three years. In 1980, approximately six Rhode Island firms had permits for about 50 locations. Up to 25 locations are used in a season with 8 to 10 traps in place at any one time.

Summarized in Table 1 are characteristics of the typical New England hook and line operation. Major items of capital equipment are a skiff of 14 to 19 feet in length, a pickup truck and the hook and line gear. As was indicated above, striped bass occur in New England waters primarily during the summer and early fall. Tidal conditions, winds and currents affect the size of the striped bass harvest. Commercial fishermen fish about 80 days per year for this species, while fishing about 140 days for other species.

In 1980, the typical commercial hook and line fisherman in New England landed approximately 3,300 pounds of striped bass valued at about $6,350. The price received averaged $1.92 per pound. Expenses incurred

Table 1: Characteristics of commercial striped bass harvesters using hook and line gear, Massachusetts and Rhode Island, 1980

	Average	Range
Vessel Length (ft.)	17	14–19
Percent of Fishing Income from Striped Bass	40	10–100
Days Fished for Striped Bass	80	45–150
Days Fished for Other Species	140	0–300
Pounds of Striped Bass Harvested	3,300	200–10,000
Sales receipts from Striped Bass	$6,350	$350–$20,000
Striped Bass Size Distribution:		
Small (< 5 lb.)	10%	0–20%
Medium (5–10 lb.)	13%	0–65%
Large (>15 lb.)	77%	35–100%

SOURCE: Survey data from University of Connecticut

in harvesting striped bass are shown in Table 2, along with a relative breakdown of expenditures by category. Major items include expenditures for fuel, wages and tackle. Based on average catch and expenses, a pound of striped bass costs $1.71 to produce by hook and line in New England.

Table 2: **Average annual expenditures attributable to striped bass, by Massachusetts and Rhode Island hook and line fishermen, 1980**

Item*	Average Annual Expense	Range	Relative Expense
Fuel	$ 900	$ 225–2,700	16%
Wages	2,000	1,650–3,750	35
Nets	25	0–125	1
Lines/Ropes	10	0–45	1
Tackle	900	0–3,000	16
Truck Repair	100	0–450	2
Equipment Repair	360	0–1,200	6
Ice	11	0–50	1
Shipping	20	0–120	1
Supplies	215	0–1,000	1
Insurance	155	37–325	3
Interest	90	0–540	2
License Fees	20	8–80	1
Depreciation	300	0–1,500	5
Taxes	110	0–690	2
Dock Fees	130	0–450	2
Other	300	60–1,500	5
Total	5,646		100%

SOURCE: Survey data from University of Connecticut

*Does not include electronic equipment

Summarized in Tables 3 and 4 are characteristics and estimated expenses for a typical fish trap striped bass operation. Wages make up the largest expense, followed by fuel and tackle. Based on the average catch and expenses, a pound of striped bass costs $1.38 to harvest. Because much of the catch is incidental, the expense data are likely to have large variation and the cost per pound figure may also vary widely among fishermen.

Mid-Atlantic

A summary of unpublished NMFS 1980 landings data for New York State, excluding the Hudson River, indicates that 93 percent of the report-

Table 3: Characteristics of commercial striped bass harvesters using fish traps, New England, 1980

	Average
Vessel Length (ft.)	70
Percent of Income from Striped Bass Harvest	43
Days Fished for Striped Bass	90
Days Fished for Other Species	120
Pounds of Striped Bass Harvested	70,000
Sales receipts from Striped Bass	$129,500

SOURCE: Survey data from University of Connecticut

Table 4: Average annual expenditures attributable to striped bass, by New England fish trap fishermen, 1980

Item	Average Annual Expense	Relative Expense
Fuel	$ 1,960	2%
Wages	40,142	41
Nets	14,700	15
Lines/Ropes	6,000	6
Floats/Leads	5,000	5
Equipment Repair	5,000	5
Insurance	8,400	9
License Fees	840	1
Depreciation	2,100	2
Taxes	12,600	14
Total	$96,742	100%

SOURCE: Survey data from University of Connecticut

ed landings occurred in Suffolk County, with the remaining 7 percent from Nassau and Kings Counties (Table 5). The majority of fishing activity for striped bass in Suffolk County occurs along the southern coast of Long Island from Shinnecock Inlet eastward to Montauk Point. Table 5 also shows the 1980 striped bass landings by gear type.

Unfortunately, the small number of completed interviews, together with high variability in operations and confidentiality requirements, preclude presentation of data on economic activity by gear type for fishermen operating in New York. For the haul seiners, however, sufficient data exist to state they receive approximately $2.00 per pound. The haul seine share system implies that wages vary directly with profits. Net revenues are first calculated and then divided equally among the crew. In one instance, there was another share which went to the boat owner. Striped

Table 5: Striped bass landings in New York by county and gear, 1980

Gear Type	Suffolk	Nassau and King	Total	Percent of Total
Drag Netters	65,628 lbs.	4,311 lbs.	69,939 lbs.	12%
Trappers	95,051	0	95,051	17
Handlines	178,148	36,349	214,497	37
Gill Netters	112,905	0	112,905	20
Haul Seiners	79,651	0	79,651	14
Total	531,383	40,660	572,043	
Percent	93	7		100

SOURCE: NMFS Office in Patchogue, New York

bass were important components of revenues in the April-though-June and September-through-November periods.

New Jersey's commercial fishery has been declining in recent years, due in part to the laws prohibiting the use of particular gear in certain state waters.[2] Commercial fishermen landed 40,000 pounds of striped bass in 1979 and about 25,000 pounds in 1980. Striped bass commercially harvested in 1980 came principally from by-catches of offshore draggers and from gill netters in Delaware Bay. As a result, the New Jersey counties reporting landings were, in order of increasing importance, Cape May, Ocean, Cumberland and Monmouth.

The seasonal variation in landings relates primarily to the migratory habits of the bass. The spring northern migration is harvested by the inshore (Cumberland County) gill net operations, whereas the fall/winter southern migration is taken by the offshore trawlers (Ocean and Cape May counties).

Otter trawls, gill nets and pound nets are the primary gear types used by New Jersey commercial fishermen who land striped bass. The average number of days fished by gill netters was reported to be 210, while that for trawlers was 260. The gill netters operate small boats and incur relatively small costs for fuel. For the larger trawlers (60 to 120 feet), however, fuel costs were reported to be as high as $50,000 in 1980.

Large expenditures were also made for crew wages, equipment and repairs. It is important to note, however, that striped bass landings by these large trawlers are mostly incidental catch, and only a small portion of total expenses can be attributed to striped bass. Expenditures by har-

---

[2]Since 1952, netting in the territorial waters of New Jersey's Atlantic Ocean has been prohibited. In 1981, netting in all New Jersey waters was prohibited.

vesters for fuel, equipment, maintenance, and most other expenses are generally made within the county of operation. A notable exception to this is nets, which are often purchased directly from large net manufacturers located in Tennessee.

There are four ports in Delaware where most of the striped bass harvests are landed—two in Kent County (Port Mahon and Bowers Beach) and two in Sussex County (Misspillon and Indian River). The majority of the 1980 harvest was taken in March and April with the remainder harvested between November and January. Gill netting is the only gear type used to harvest commercially marketed striped bass. A typical Delaware netter uses a mid-sized (18-32 feet) work boat with an outboard motor and open bridge. One or two smaller (14-16 feet) skiffs are towed and used to lift the nets and store the fish. The boats are operated close to port. Delaware netters (estimated to consist of 32 crews) set about 25,000 yards of gill net in 1980.

The greatest concentrations of Delaware striped bass harvesters are found in Kent County followed by the northern section of Sussex County with a few in the upper bay area of New Castle County. Interview data indicate that Delaware gill netters fished an average of 200 days for finfish, including striped bass, in 1980, but none of those responding fished primarily for striped bass.

A sample of Delaware gill netters showed an average 1980 fuel expenditure attributable to striped bass of about $400. This figure represents about 10 percent of gill netter's total 1980 fuel expenditures. The average expenditures in major expense categories attributable to striped bass effort in the Delaware gill net fishery during 1980 are given in Table 6.

Table 6: Average annual expenditures attributable to striped bass, by Delaware gill netters, 1980

Item	Average Annual Expense	Relative Expense
Fuel	$ 393	10%
Nets	1,533	39
Lines & Ropes	263	7
Floats & Leads	1,221	31
Equipment Repair	107	3
Other	411	10
Total	$3,928	100%

SOURCE: Survey data from University of Maryland

The operations normally have only one man and thus no wage figure is shown. Expenditures in most of the categories are made within the county of operation, with the exception of nets, which are purchased from manufacturers in Tennessee.

Chesapeake

The middle and upper Chesapeake Bay areas are the primary producers of striped bass in Maryland, accounting for nearly 72 percent of the total 1980 Maryland landings. The seasonality of striped bass landings varies in different parts of the state. The higher landings in the middle and upper bay counties are in part due to the location of spawning grounds and the extended season in the upper bay area. Landings in the lower bay and Potomac River regions occur principally in the late fall and early spring.

Gill netting is Maryland's primary commercial striped bass fishery, accounting for 97 percent of the total 1980 commercial striped bass landings. Anchor, drift and staked gill nets are used throughout the state, depending on the season, water conditions and legal restrictions. Boats used by Maryland gill netters range in size from large bay boats (30 to 50 feet) to small wood or fiberglass skiffs. Crew sizes vary from two to seven. Interview data suggest that about one-fourth of the 1,555 registered Maryland gill netters are part-time fishermen. Most full-time fishermen who fish for striped bass are also involved in crabbing, oystering, or fishing for other finfish species. Full-time fishermen annually averaged about 240 days on the water. Table 7 shows the characteristics of part-time and full-time fishermen.

Table 7: Average characteristics of all gill net operations (part-time and full-time) in Maryland, 1980

	Part-time Fishermen	Full-time Fishermen
Vessel Length (ft.)	23	35
Percent of Income from Striped Bass Harvest	27	46
Days Fished for Striped Bass	91	125
Days Fished for Other Species	15	115
Pounds of Striped Bass Harvested	4,970	18,866

SOURCE: Survey data from University of Maryland

Expenses incurred by Maryland gill netters for fuel, wages, equipment, and other items vary in different parts of the state. In Kent County, where the largest striped bass fishing operations are located, fishermen's average fuel costs attributable to striped bass were nearly double the state average. Table 8 shows average expenses attributable to striped bass for the part-time Maryland gill net operations as well as those for the full-time fishermen. The average expense per pound landed for the full-time fishermen was $1.20.

Table 8: Average annual expenditures attributable to striped bass, by the part-time and full-time fishermen using gill nets in Maryland, 1980

Item	Part-time Fishermen Expense	Relative Expense	Full-time Fishermen Expense	Relative Expense
Fuel	$1,279	23%	$ 2,550	11%
Wages	1,557	28	11,577	51
Nets	596	11	2,832	12
Lines and Ropes	313	6	694	3
Floats and Leads	261	5	837	4
Truck Repair/Rental	86	1	548	2
Equipment Repair	394	7	1,022	5
Other	1,030	19	2,657	12
Total	$5,516	100%	$22,717	100%

SOURCE: Survey data from University of Maryland

The contributions to income from striped bass fishing also vary widely geographically. In general, harvesters in the middle and upper bay counties rely more heavily on striped bass and other finfish than on shellfish. Many of the large Kent County harvesting operators told interviewers that the further decline of striped bass could force them to lay off entire crews and to seek employment elsewhere.

Virginia's striped bass landings are concentrated in the northern counties in an area lying between the Potomac and Rappahannock rivers known as the Northern Neck. This area produced nearly 95 percent of Virginia's 1980 reported striped bass landings. The Eastern Shore peninsula, made up of Accomack and Northampton counties, accounted for the remaining landings.

Seasonal fluctuations in landings coincide with the striped bass migration in the early spring and late fall. Landings in March and April accounted for 36 percent of the total 1980 Virginia landing, with another 47 percent landed during October, November and December.

During 1980, 82 percent of Virginia's striped bass landings were caught in drift, anchor and staked gill nets. The type of gill net used depends on weather, water conditions and legal restrictions. In most areas, legal restrictions apply only to the size of the net and not to the type. Other gear types landing striped bass in Virginia include pound nets, otter trawls and handlines.

An estimated 761 full-time gill netters work in Virginia waters, with an additional 2,000-3,000 part-time or casual netters. Many of the part-time gill netters focus effort specifically on the striped bass because of the high ex-vessel price. Full-time netters, however, find that they cannot rely solely on the scarce and often unpredictable availability of striped bass. In northern counties, the striped bass accounted for 10 to 50 percent of gill netters' total 1980 seafood sales. In southern counties (south of the York River) less than one percent of harvesters' total seafood sales were from striped bass. Typical expenditures by Virginia striped bass fishermen for fuel, wages and other items are given in Table 9. The share of cost associated with wages was the lowest state average encountered in our interviews, representing only 20 percent of all costs.

Table 9: Average annual expenditures attributable to striped bass by Virginia fishermen, 1980

Item	Average Annual Expenditures	Relative Expense
Fuel	$ 304	13%
Wages	484	20
Nets	482	20
Lines & Ropes	140	6
Floats & Leads	140	6
Truck Repair	58	2
Other	807	33
Total	$2,415	100%

SOURCE: Survey data from University of Maryland

Virginia fishermen, especially those in northern counties, said the further decline of striped bass would hurt them economically, some to the extent of being forced out of fishing completely. All Virginia fishermen interviewed expressed the hope for an increased abundance of striped bass, and many indicated they would switch out of other fisheries and direct effort on the striped bass if stocks increased.

South Atlantic[3]

Striped bass in North Carolina are harvested by a variety of gear. Prior to 1967, the primary gear types for the capture of the species were pound nets, gill nets and haul seines, accounting for approximately 92 percent of the total harvest. Pound nets, used on the inside waters of the sounds, particularly in Albermarle Sound, on the average accounted for 37 percent of the total harvest. Gill nets (anchored) used in Albemarle Sound and its immediate tributaries, as well as in Pamlico Sound, contributed an additional 31 percent. Haul seines used on the outer beaches and at selected locations on Albemarle Sound and its tributaries or on Pamlico Sound provided 24 percent of the catch.

During the period 1967 through 1973, when the striper landings reached all-time highs, there were some significant changes in gear contributions to the annual harvests. Otter trawls, which had contributed little to the harvest in previous years, accounted for approximately 15 percent of the total landings. Gill nets were the primary gear used during the 1967-1973 period, comprising 45 percent of the total harvest. Haul seines came into increasing use, accounting for 29 percent of the harvest.

In the post-1973 period, the dominant gear types have been haul seines and gill nets, with the latter increasing in importance and dominating the fishery in recent years. Seines accounted for 43 percent of the total harvest in 1974. By 1978, following legislation restricting seine use in coastal waters, harvest by seines had decreased to only 3 percent of the total harvest. By 1980 they were no longer used.

The only other gear of note is the trawl, which continued to be used during the 1974-1980 period. As with seines, however, the catch dropped off drastically. By 1980, the trawl contributed only 4 percent to the harvest, even though it was ranked second behind the gill net for its overall contribution to the fishery, and gill nets contributed 87 percent of the total harvest for the commercial landings of striped bass.

North Carolina striped bass fishermen earn three-fourths of their income from fishing. In 1980, an average of 93 days were devoted primarily to effort on striped bass (Table 10).

The cost structure of North Carolina gill netters (Table 11) is similar to that found in Virginia, with fuel, wages and nets representing approximately 60 percent of total annual costs. The total cost is also similar and yielded an average cost of $1.38 per pound.

---

[3]Since North Carolina was the only state in this region to report significant striped bass landings, any South Atlantic region reference refers only to the State of North Carolina.

Table 10: Characteristics of striped bass harvesters in North Carolina, 1980

	Average
Vessel length (ft.)	16
Days fished for Striped Bass	93
Days fished for Other Species	163
Pounds of Striped Harvested	1,477
Sales Receipts from Striped Bass	$1,724

SOURCE: Interview data from North Carolina State University

Table 11: Average annual expenditures attributable to striped bass, by North Carolina gill netters, 1980

Item	Average Annual Expense	Relative Expense
Fuel	$ 404	20%
Wages	500	25
Nets	467	23
Lines & Ropes	65	3
Floats & Leaders	29	1
Truck Repair and Rental	82	4
Equipment Repair & Maintenance	177	9
Shipping	30	2
Supplies	15	<1
Insurance	28	1
Interest	14	<1
License Fees	7	<1
Depreciation	20	1
Federal Tax	145	7
State Tax	38	2
Dock Slip Fees	1	<1
Miscellaneous	13	<1
Total	$2,035	

SOURCE: Interview data from North Carolina State University

The large mesh gill net fishery for striped bass in the eastern area of the sounds of North Carolina is of recent origin. The former fishery for striped bass on the Outer Banks (north of Cape Hatteras, southward to Ocracoke) was a haul seine fishery operated on the outside beaches in late winter. Following legislation that restricted the operation of haul seines on the outside beaches, the number of crews dwindled. In the winter of 1980, one crew from Buxton (Cape Hatteras) introduced a large mesh gill net to the winter striped bass fishery. The gear proved to be successful and by the 1981 season there were six crews operating the large mesh gill nets for striped bass in the Cape Hatteras to Ocracoke region. The fish caught are primarily larger females migrating into the embayed water in mid to late winter for spawning. The gill nets used in this fishery are constructed of monofilament webbing with nine and one-half-inch stretched mesh (four and one-quarter-inch bar). The nets are 80 to 120 yards in length and are fished as anchor gill nets. They are anchored along the inside waters usually within a range of five miles of the inlets and are set perpendicular to the tidal current running down the channels. The depths fished range from four to twelve feet or more. Once set, the nets are allowed to stand and fish overnight. They are marked with buoys at either end and the float line remains visible above water.

Crews of one or two per boat operate the fishery and may fish ten or more nets. The boats used in this fishery are 20 to 30 feet in length. Since the boats are used in other fisheries during the rest of the year, no special design features have developed. They are wooden or fiberglass semi-displacement hulls with inboard automobile or marine engines. Several of the smaller boats use outboard engines. Hydraulic net haulers or other specialized gear are not used.

Individuals engaged in this fishery are primarily full-time commercial fishermen. During other times of the year they participate in a variety of other fisheries such as the shrimp fishery, the hard crab fishery and gill-netting operations for other species.

Marketing

The marketing of striped bass on the Atlantic Coast involves a complex structure of intermediate and direct activities covering local and central market outlets. This structure and the related product flow are affected by state laws such as those regarding gear type, the selling of recreationally caught fish, closed seasons and the size of fish that may be landed in certain areas. Also important are the availability of striped bass, as influenced by stock size fluctuations, and the market quantity and prices of other species. Estimation of economic impacts and values of striped bass related activities requires an understanding of, and data on, the complex striped bass marketing structure along the Atlantic Coast.

A general indication of the flow of striped bass is given in Figure 5. Watermen sell striped bass to primary wholesalers, who sell to local

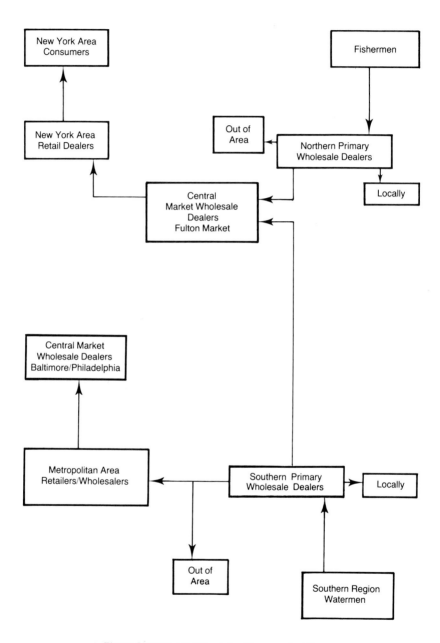

Figure 5. North Atlantic striped bass market flow.

outlets, to central market wholesalers, or to buyers outside the region (see Adriance 1982, for details on market flows). The volume passing through the Baltimore and New York (Fulton) central markets represented about 65 percent of the reported landings from 1972 to 1978. These central markets are key establishments for distribution of striped bass as well as for determining market prices.

New England

Wholesale dealers and fishing cooperatives are important to the market flow of striped bass in New England. There are approximately 60 such establishments, most of which function as primary wholesalers. In the Boston area, however, there are eleven secondary establishments which purchase significant quantities of striped bass from other establishments rather than directly from fishermen. The terms "primary" and "secondary" refer to the first and second handlers, respectively.

The primary wholesalers purchase from commercial or sport fishermen and ship to regional secondary markets in Boston or New York. These primary wholesalers also distribute striped bass locally to retail stores, restaurants, and other final markets.

Little processing of striped bass is done before it reaches the retail outlets. Most of the wholesalers only box, ice and ship the striped bass. This is in contrast to the filleting and other processing that takes place for many other species. This practice adds little value to the product and hence reduces the local economic impact relative to that associated with a product that is locally processed.

Approximately two-thirds of the striped bass handled by Massachusetts wholesalers in 1980 was purchased by them directly from commercial or sport fishermen. Barnstable County establishments handled the largest amount of striped bass relative to other counties in Massachusetts. Most of their purchases were from fishermen, although they did purchase some striped bass from wholesalers in Plymouth County. Bristol County wholesalers were second in volume to those in Barnstable County. Bristol County firms purchased primarily from fishermen, with about 10 percent of their product coming from Connecticut and Rhode Island fishermen. In Suffolk County, wholesalers bought striped bass from local fishermen as well as from the New York Fulton Market, Maryland wholesalers and Plymouth County wholesalers. Wholesalers in four other Massachusetts counties (Essex, Plymouth, Nantucket and Dukes) purchased from local fishermen.

Interviews with New England wholesalers indicated that their usual marketing margin or mark-up is between 10 and 20 percent of the price paid to fishermen. This price is determined primarily by the Fulton Market situation. The mark-up, which usually amounts to 15 to 50 cents per pound, covers the cost of ice, packing materials, labor, shipping and return on investment.

Many retail establishments in New England sell striped bass. These range from small seafood speciality outlets to large supermarkets. Retailers generally purchase from local or central market wholesalers but occasionally (especially the smaller retail firms) purchase directly from fishermen. In some instances, wholesalers also perform retail services. Retailers generally buy striped bass whole and sell whole, filleted, or steaked products.

About three-fourths of the New England 1980 retail sales of striped bass flowed through Massachusetts outlets. Connecticut retailers accounted for about 20 percent with Rhode Island retail outlets making up the remaining 5 percent of New England sales. In addition to these retail sales, almost 300,000 pounds of striped bass were shipped by wholesalers in Suffolk County to supermarket chains outside of New England.

There are two basic pricing policies at the retail level. The retail mark-up on whole striped bass ranges from 10 to 50 percent. Fillet prices are established according to the rule "two and one-half times the knife," which means 2.5 times the cost of the fish to the retailer.

In 1980, over ten percent of the total New England product flow of striped bass was sold through more than 300 restaurants. Approximately 40 percent of the restaurant trade was in Massachusetts, 25 percent was in Rhode Island, and about 35 percent took place in Connecticut. At least 35,000 pounds of striped bass were shipped by wholesalers to restaurants outside the New England area.

Counties with large concentrations of restaurants serving striped bass in 1980 were: Barnstable and Suffolk, with 60 percent of the Massachusetts total; Providence and Newport, with 73 percent of the Rhode Island total; and Fairfield County, Connecticut, with 52 percent of the state's total. Restaurants do not carry a large inventory of striped bass at any time and usually offer it as a specialty entree. Restaurants generally purchase large whole striped bass from local fishermen, regional or local wholesalers, or from the Fulton Market. They then fillet or steak the fish and serve it baked, broiled, or poached.

Over two-thirds of the striped bass handled by Massachusetts restaurants in 1980 was purchased from primary or secondary wholesalers and distributors within the state. In Rhode Island, only one-fifth of the striped bass handled by restaurants was purchased directly from fishermen with most being purchased from primary wholesalers within the state and from the Fulton Market. Striped bass served in Connecticut restaurants were generally purchased from the Fulton Market.

Most restaurants offering this item on their menus are the more expensive "white table cloth" type of eating establishment. Entree prices in 1980 for striped bass in New England ranged from $6.00 to $12.00, with $10.00 representing the average.

Mid-Atlantic

The most important striped bass wholesale location in the Mid-Atlantic region is New York's Fulton Market. Striped bass are shipped to the Fulton Market by fishermen and wholesalers from Maine to North Carolina. The percentage of mark-up used by the wholesalers ranges from 10 to 15 percent, depending on the market situation. The range of wholesale prices observed during the 1980 survey was between $2.00 and $3.50 per pound. Table 12 illustrates the movement of striped bass from Fulton wholesalers to various destination points. Retail seafood outlets account for the largest proportion of sales by the wholesalers. Restaurants indirectly represent a greater quantity than is apparent from Table 12 because purveyors (who are buyers for specific enterprises) primarily supply restaurants.

Table 12: Distribution of striped bass by five Fulton Market wholesalers

Fulton Market Wholesalers	Destination			
	Restaurants	Retailers	Wholesalers	Purveyors
Wholesaler 1	20%	60%	—	20%
Wholesaler 2	—	75	10%	15
Wholesaler 3	50	50	—	—
Wholesaler 4	25	50	—	25
Wholesaler 5	10	30	20	40

SOURCE: Interview data from University of Maryland

Table 13 shows relative revenue from striped bass, the price and the substitutes for striped bass for five large retail seafood outlets in Manhattan. Four retail oulets preferred 2-4 pound striped bass and sold striped bass whole and in fillets. The other preferred 25-30 pound striped bass since sale was in the form of steaks. All retail outlets surveyed base selling price on a fixed percent markup over the wholesale purchase price.

Table 13: **Contribution to total sales revenues, 1980 price per pound, and main substitutes for striped bass at five Manhattan retail seafood outlets**

Outlet	Percent of Total Sales	1980 Price Per Pound	Main Substitute
Retail 1	5%	$3.00–5.00	Sea Bass
Retail 2	5	3.00–4.00	none specified
Retail 3	1	3.00	Tilefish
Retail 4	1	5.99–6.50	Tilefish
Retail 5	2	4.50	Snapper

SOURCE: Interview data from Cornell University

The restaurant respondents carrying striped bass obtained their product primarily from seafood purveyors. Medium to large sizes of over five pounds are preferred by the restaurants contacted. The amount carried per year depends on the class and size of the restaurant. The low- to medium-price establishments carry striped bass only when the wholesale price is low. Substitutes are widely used, the most frequently mentioned being tilefish. The medium- to high-price restaurants are less vulnerable to fluctuations in the striped bass price. These establishments generally carry striped bass at all times. The potential substitute most often mentioned was salmon.

Responses from two private club restaurants in New York City were similar to those of other restaurants. The respondents felt that their sales volume for striped bass was lower than that for some public restaurants due to the menu variety required for their repeat club members. These clubs purchased their striped bass from purveyors. Size preferences were for the 5-10 pound fish and tilefish was considered the primary substitute for striped bass.

New Jersey wholesalers interviewed in Cape May and Cumberland counties bought striped bass from both commercial and recreational fishermen. Interviews with southern New Jersey wholesalers indicated that the inflow of recreationally caught striped bass into New Jersey markets is significant. Harvesters (commercial and recreational) bring their fish to wholesalers, who in turn sell to retail outlets or central markets.

Interviews with wholesalers and fishermen indicated that most commercially landed striped bass are bought by large wholesalers, boxed in ice and shipped directly to New York or Philadelphia markets. Wholesalers in Cape May, Cumberland, and Atlantic counties generally ship to the nearby Philadelphia markets, while those in Ocean and Monmouth counties ship to New York's Fulton Market. Striped bass not sold to central markets (about 10 percent of total landings) is generally sold whole to local retail outlets.

A sample of New Jersey restaurant and retail outlets handling striped bass in 1980 revealed that 50 percent of the restaurants and 30 percent of the retail outlets purchased their striped bass from wholesalers. The remainder purchased directly from commercial or recreational fishermen.

In Delaware striped bass move from the fishermen to small wholesalers, who in turn may act as middlemen for restaurants and larger wholesalers, or in many instances sell through their own local retail outlets. The local wholesalers often sell to large wholesalers who market in Philadelphia, Baltimore, or New York. In some instances local Delaware wholesalers buy from a central market and sell to restaurants.

Chesapeake

Wholesalers operating within Maryland vary widely in the amount of striped bass they handle. Interview data indicated that 95 percent of Maryland's striped bass landings flow to wholesalers; of this, three-fourths is handled by wholesalers in the northern Chesapeake area (north of Annapolis) and the remainder goes to southern bay wholesalers.

The destination of striped bass landed in Maryland is, to a large extent, determined by the size of the fish. A small percentage of commercially harvested striped bass flows directly to local restaurants or retail outlets. Those which measure less than 16 inches are generally sold to large Eastern Shore or Baltimore wholesale markets for distribution in Maryland, Delaware, or Virginia. The larger fish (greater than 16 inches) are sent primarily through Eastern Shore wholesalers to the Fulton Market.

Buyers of the striped bass are located throughout the coastal areas of the state. The largest markets for striped bass are located in Kent, Dorchester and Anne Arundel counties, as well as in the Baltimore City Fish Market. Fish are generally paid for with cash and shipped by truck to large wholesalers or to the Baltimore market. Wholesalers in Kent County attributed 77 percent of their 1980 finfish revenues to striped bass sales, while those in Wicomico and Worcester counties attributed only a small amount to striped bass.

Striped bass leaving Maryland wholesalers flow to a variety of users including restaurants, retail outlets and the large central markets. The destination is primarily determined by the size of fish and seasonal retail demand. Figure 6, compiled from wholesale interviews, shows the flow of striped bass from wholesalers to various destinations.

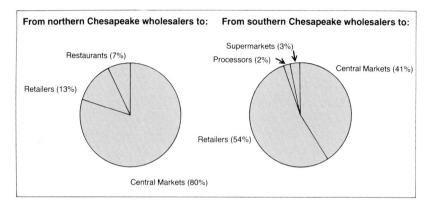

Figure 6. Flow of striped bass from Maryland wholesalers.

Interviews with restaurants throughout Maryland showed an average striped bass use of 2,634 pounds in 1980. Of the 50 seafood and French restaurants contacted, 60 percent handled striped bass at some time during 1980, generally serving it as an off-menu (Fish of the Day) special. The greatest concentrations of restaurants handling striped bass were found in the Washington, D.C. and Baltimore metropolitan areas. Restaurants serving striped bass in the Baltimore metropolitan area had an average entree price of $10.35, while the state average was $8.80. Comparisons made with prices of other entrees served in Maryland restaurants indicated that in most restaurants striped bass is served as a premium item. Restaurant proprietors indicated they would handle much more striped bass if it were more available at lower prices.

Maryland wholesalers, retailers and restaurant proprietors indicate a greater dependence on the striped bass relative to other states—though this dependence varied geographically and seasonally. Wholesalers, particularly in northern Maryland, indicated that the disappearance of the striped bass would have a marked effect on their economic stability, forcing some to lay off personnel and significantly scale down operations. Retail and restaurant establishments in the northern counties also stated that they would be hurt by further declines in commercial striped bass availability.

Interviews with Virginia wholesalers indicate that about 90 percent of the commercially landed striped bass leaves the state for markets in Baltimore, New York, North Carolina and as far south as Florida. A significant amount of striped bass also flows into the state from large Maryland markets in order to meet seasonal retail demand. This flow pattern occurs because the local demand for striped bass in Virginia is strongest in the late spring, summer and early fall when the tourist trade is flourishing. Virgina landings, however, occur primarily in the late fall and early spring.

Virginia retailers and restaurants dealing in striped bass responded similarly to those in Maryland regarding the economic effect of the decline of striped bass.

South Atlantic

In North Carolina, striped bass are harvested by many small independent fishermen selling primarily to wholesalers. The wholesalers sort the whole fish by size, rebox, ice and ship the fish north by truck. The trucks are owned by the wholesalers or by independent truck lines. The smaller wholesalers tend to transfer the fish to other buyers who ship the fish in their trucks for a fee but who do not have ownership of the fish. Nearly all fish caught move through wholesalers to the northern markets. Most retailing of striped bass is done by wholesalers, but a small number of retail fish markets sell striped bass.

Some restaurants replied that they did not now serve striped bass due to its high price. They indicated striped bass would be put back on the menu if the price were lower (less than $2.00 per pound) and if they could find a reliable supply.

The inlet gill net fishery of eastern North Carolina Sound represents a specialized fishery and therefore a somewhat specialized market process. Once caught, the fish are kept in boxes or on the decks of the boats. Most of the fish are large females in the 40-50 pound range. The local dealers who handle the catches are often unable to handle more than several hundred pounds of fish. Thus, a single fishing operation is faced with the situation of selling to several dealers to market their catch. As one fishermen stated, it is "... kind of like dropping a fish off here and a fish off there...." The local market for the striped bass is severely limited because the market links that existed in the past years to handle the substantially larger catches from the haul seine crews no longer seem to exist.

The Recreational Fishery

RECREATIONAL FISHING FOR striped bass has long been a popular sport along the East Coast. As the number of participants has increased and the catch declined, recreational fishermen have become more vocal in support of fisheries management for striped bass. Unfortunately, the fishery management agencies have had to work without estimates of the economic impact and value of this recreational fishery. To analyze the economic impact and value of the recreational fishery it was first necessary to estimate the annual East Coast recreational catch and then determine the direct total expenditures on recreational fishing. This study indicates that the recreational catch of striped bass by sportsmen fishing the coastal waters of the northeast United States often rivals or exceeds the reported catch of commercial fishermen working those same waters.

Methods

The analysis of recreational striped bass fishing is based on estimates of total effort (trips), catch rate and total catch, mean and total expenditures, and the central tendency or "norm" for the striped bass fishing trip. These estimates are based on the 1979 Marine Recreational Fishery Statistics Survey conducted by the National Marine Fisheries Service and on a separate survey conducted in 1980 by personnel working on this project.

Data from the 1980 NMFS survey were not yet available when this project began. This necessitated the use of data from two different years, 1979 and 1980. Recreational catch and effort were estimated from the 1979 NMFS survey data.[4] These estimates are presented in this chapter. The expenditure data collected in 1980 were used to generate estimates of out-of-pocket expenses by type of expenditure (e.g., restaurant food purchases) of recreational striped bass fishermen; these numbers were used as input to the impact model described later.

The NMFS survey is based on a dual-frame sampling approach first described by Hiett and Ghosh (1977). The approach uses two independent surveys.[5] The first is a field survey of recreational fishermen (also known as a creel census), wherein fishermen are interviewed at the completion of their fishing trip by interviewers trained in fish identification. During this interview, information is collected on the catch for this trip, the type of trip and the total expenditures. Catch rates for striped bass for the type of trip are estimated from this survey.

---

[4] The similarity of the 1979 and 1980 participation rates was later borne out by analysis of the entire 1980 survey data.

[5] See Hiett and Ghosh (1977) or McConnell and Smith (1979) for a more detailed explanation.

The second survey is an independent random telephone survey of households located in the coastal zone of each state. Each household contacted is asked if members have participated in recreational fishing in the prior two months. If the answer is "Yes," members of the household are interviewed to obtain specific trip information. The data collected from the telephone survey allow the estimation of participation rates per household (trips per household per two month period for the same categories of trips as in the field survey). These participation rates are multiplied by the total number of households from U.S. Bureau of Census data to produce estimates of total trips.

The final estimation step is to derive the total catch and total expenditures by multiplying the trip estimates by the mean catch rate or the mean expenditure estimates (from the field survey), respectively.

The 1979 NMFS survey collected information on 24,773 recreational fishing trips in the regions from Maine through North Carolina. Of these, 1,818 were seeking striped bass.[6] The National Marine Fisheries Service also surveyed 44,325 households (Maine to North Carolina) by telephone. In addition to these data, the survey conducted by project personnel collected information on 505 striped bass fishing trips.

An important part of determining the economic activity associated with striped bass fishing is the analysis of a set of characteristics which represent the central tendency or "norm" of the group of fishermen. This offers guidance as to how the angler behaves on an average trip.

Averages for certain characteristics of striped bass trips are presented in Table 14. These data are derived from the 1979 NMFS survey. The mean catch rate for striped bass for all recreational fishing trips that involved the seeking or catching of striped bass was 0.54 fish per trip, or one fish in every 1.85 striped bass trips. Catch rate was lowest in New Jersey (one fish per 12 trips) and highest in Connecticut, New York and Maryland. Out-of-pocket expenditures ranged from $20 in New Jersey to $78 in Massachusetts.

Total Catch, Effort and Expenditures

The level of striped bass trips is determined by the overall effort level, i.e. the number of all recreational fishing trips. Total finfish trips were

---

[6]A striped bass trip is defined as a trip where the fisherman either stated he was seeking striped bass or had caught striped bass.

Table 14: Characteristics of the mean striped bass trip, 1979

	Average Expenditures ($)[1]	Average Catch Rate (fish per trip)[2]
New England	49.41	0.36
Maine	—	0.74
New Hampshire	26.67	—
Massachusetts	78.28	0.26
Rhode Island	22.58	0.24
Connecticut	48.13	0.96
Mid-Atlantic	58.79	0.48
New York	77.42	0.68
New Jersey	20.26	0.07
Delaware	87.93	0.33
Chesapeake	24.41	0.70
Maryland	23.54	0.71
Virginia	57.13	0.38
South Atlantic	46.33	0.35
North Carolina	46.33	0.35
Overall	41.14	0.54

SOURCE: Derived from data in table 15

[1]Total trip expenses divided by total trips.
[2]Striped bass per striped bass trip calculated as total catch divided by total trips.

estimated from the 1979 NMFS telephone survey as described above. Striped bass trips were estimated by multiplying this number by the 1980 proportion of striped bass trips in each state.

According to this approach, there were more than two million trips directed toward striped bass in 1979. Maryland, New York and Massachusetts, were the centers of activity. Total estimated catch for the East Coast was about 1.2 million fish. Maryland's high catch rate (Table 14) and high effort levels (Table 15) resulted in the largest estimated state catch, 649 thousand fish. The next most important harvest contributor was New York.[7]

---

[7]Catch is estimated using the 1979 NMFS survey because it is the only published information. Unofficial communication with NMFS personnel suggests that the 1980 striped bass catch is lower than the numbers shown in Table 15.

There are several important caveats to remember in considering these estimates of fishing effort. In many states, separating recreational and commercial fishing effort proved difficult during data collection. In some northern states, particularly Massachusetts and Rhode Island, the predominant commercial harvest comes from hook and line fishing—the

Table 15: Recreational trips, catch and expenditures, the striped bass recreational fishery, Maine to North Carolina, 1979

	Trips (000)	Catch (numbers of fish) (000)	Expenditures ($000)
New England	517	185	$25,547
Maine	23	17	—[1]
New Hampshire	17	—	456
Massachusetts	227	59	17,723
Rhode Island	181	44	4,119
Connecticut	67	65	3,249
Mid-Atlantic	610	290	35,863
New York	408	276	31,570
New Jersey	199	13	4,038
Delaware	3	1	255
Chesapeake	934	658	22,861
Maryland	910	649	21,467
Virginia	24	9	1,394
South Atlantic	109	38	5,051
North Carolina[1]	109	38	5,051
Total	2,170	1,171	$89,262

SOURCE: Based on 1979 NMFS recreational survey

[1]North Carolina trips and expenditures were estimated from an independent survey of North Carolina recreational fishermen because the 1979 NMFS survey intercepted no fishermen seeking or catching striped bass in North Carolina.

same technique used in most recreational fishing. Since commercial landings are usually estimated from weigh-out slips of fish wholesalers and from port sampling, it is conceiveable that many recreationally caught fish are counted in the commercial sampling. Similarly, recreational sampling techniques—on-site interviews of returning fishermen—may also include commercial fishermen in the recreational fishing sample. The effect from these two potential sources of error is unknown.

Economic Value Of the Striped Bass Fisheries

ECONOMIC INFORMATION NECESSARY for an economic evaluation of the importance of striped bass has been examined by Strand and Norton (1980). From a national perspective, it is useful to have the net economic benefits or values attributable to a resource and to understand how these values change with federal policy. This need stems from the federal interest in national well-being. On the other hand, a state perspective is likely to focus on the local economic activity or impact generated by the resource and policies affecting it. The state interests stem from local and regional development goals. This chapter contains information relevant to the net economic benefits or values generated on the East Coast by striped bass fishing. The next chapter pertains to the income and employment activity associated with striped bass.

Net economic benefits are the value of consumption in excess of the opportunities foregone in production. Commercial and recreational users of striped bass receive satisfaction from consumption, the recreational experience, or income from harvest and marketing. Willingness to pay for the good is the dollar measure of the satisfaction to the purchaser of the product.[8] Costs of production are the dollar measure of the opportunities foregone in its production.[9] The difference is net economic benefit or what is referred to as the economic value of striped bass.

Although this definition is consistent for both recreational and commercial uses of striped bass, the fact that recreational fishermen are both producers and consumers of striped bass raises measurement problems and requires analytical techniques sufficiently unusual to warrant separate treatment of the two harvesting groups.

Recreational Benefits

The Measurement Concept

The usual procedure for measuring the "value" of any good, such as fish, is to use competitive market prices and quantities. If a sportfishing market existed, one could obtain market data on price, number of customers and number of fish landed per customer. With information from this private activity, a demand curve and supply curve for the fish could be estimated. The demand and supply curves (Figure 7) would show the

---

[8]Other benefit measures (e.g. willingness to sell) are assumed to be of similar magnitude to the willingness to pay. For the conditions necessary for the assumption to be valid, see Willig (1976).

[9]No consideration is given to the external costs of use (Scott, 1955). Measurement of these were beyond the scope of the report. Nor was an attempt made to estimate option or preservation values (see Strand and Norton 1980, for a discussion of these concepts).

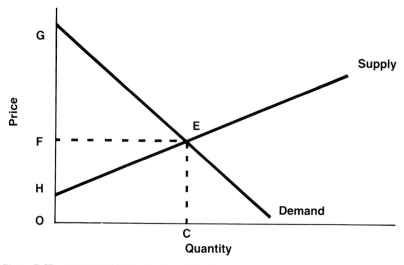

Figure 7. The conceptual basis for the estimation of net market value of sportfishing.

market revenue (FECO), the consumer surplus (net consumer benefit, GFE) and the producer surplus (net producer benefit, EFH) at equilibrium.

Usually, however, sportfishing does not take place in the limited access private market situation. Atlantic coastal states allow sportfishermen access to fishery resources without fees and thus there is not a direct access price associated with either the entire fishing trips or the fish. Therefore, implicit or derived prices must be used to determine the demand function. The most common approach to estimating the demand for sportfishing is through the use of trip costs. Variations in trips taken and cost of trips are used to examine implicitly how prices might influence trips.

For example, if striped bass fisherman A fishes five times a year and his trip costs are $5 per trip, and striped bass fisherman B fishes two times when his trip costs are $12 per trip, it is concluded from the travel cost approach that a fee of $7 per trip imposed on fisherman A would reduce his trips from five to two. Such a comparison is warranted if A behaves like B when "price" is the same. This will occur only if A and B have the same tastes and income and face the same price for substitutes, and if other demand determinants are the same for each. Of course, these factors are not equal in practice and therefore the analysis must suitably account for these individual variations.

The consumer of the sportfishing trip is also the producer of the trip, and the estimated demand curve has both costs and willingness to pay considered. The supply curve is normally assumed to be the average travel cost, and the area under the demand curve and above the supply curve is used as the measure of net benefits associated with the trip (Figure 8).

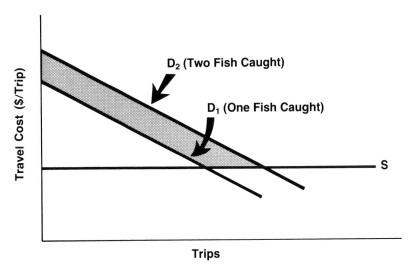

Figure 8. Benefits from additional catches per trip.

The problem remains, however, of determining what proportion of the benefits arise from catching the fish as compared to other desirable attributes of the fishing trip. One conventional method is to include the catch rate for the species along with cost in estimating number of trips. By observing how the demand curve shifts as catch rate changes, the researcher can determine how benefits change in response to catch rate changes. The area between the two curves in Figure 8 illustrates the increase in net benefits associated with a catch rate increase. One can thus determine how a change in creel limits (say from 2 fish to 1) will change the fisherman's net benefits from fishing or how much the catching of each fish is worth. Unfortunately, the number of fish caught during a trip is normally uncertain to the fisherman before the trip. The fisherman, therefore, must use an expectation of catch in making the decision of whether or not to go fishing. The expectation incorporates a subjective probability of catch, the accuracy of which depends mostly on the previous experience of the participant. If estimated actual catch is used to shift the demand curve shown in Figure 7, and the individual's expectation of catch is lower than actual catch, the measure of surplus is too low.

Estimated Net Value

Estimates were determined for the average recreational consumer surplus per trip for four regions: New England, Mid-Atlantic, Chesapeake and South Atlantic (see Snyder 1983, for details). The regions represent different types of fishermen. In New England, a summer/fall fishery exists in which many sportsmen sell their catch. The Mid-Atlantic fishery tends to be supported by a fall/spring migratory stock with shore fishing most prevalent. The Chesapeake is a year-round boat fishery with the large stripers not available in the summer and fall.

Table 16 contains the estimates of average daily consumer surplus per striped bass trip by region for 1980. The values ranged from $169 per trip in the Mid-Atlantic to approximately $39 per trip in the Chesapeake area. The representative New England and South Atlantic fisherman received a surplus of about $86 and $115 per trip, respectively. Differences relate to socio-economic characteristics, the type of fishing, the size of fish caught and other factors.

Table 16: **Average consumer surplus per trip and marginal willingness to pay for the recreational experience of catching striped bass, by region, 1980[1]**

Region	Consumer Surplus per Trip	Marginal Willingness to pay for a Striped Bass per Trip
New England	$ 86	$2.23 (12.63)[2]
Mid-Atlantic	169	7.44
Chesapeake	39	5.30
South Atlantic	115	1.34

[1]Excludes sales value. See text for explanation and derivation of actual willingness to pay.
[2]Adjusted value, see text for explanation.

Also shown in Table 16 is the marginal willingness to pay for an additional striped bass per trip. These are the values that the sportfishermen would be willing to pay to have one additional fish on each trip. The value is derived by determining the individual's value of trips with the 1980 catch rate and with a marginal increase in the catch rate.

The rather low estimated value per fish in New England is not consistent with other information obtained in the analysis. The likely reason for this is related to the fact that many sport fishermen in New England sell their catch. The percentage of fishermen who reported selling their catch ranged up to 90% in certain local geographic areas. The $2.33 net value per fish estimated for New England fishermen may reflect only the recreation value associated with the fish. This is because the fishermen may discount the potential sales value of their catch when deciding to take the recreational trip. The uncertainty of catching fish may preclude sales considerations in the decision. Therefore, the actual net value associated with the recreational catch of striped bass in New England can be estimated as the net "sport value" plus the actual income from sales. Based on the survey, we estimate that up to approximately 60 percent of the fish caught by "recreational fishermen" in New England are sold. Considering an average weight of approximately 14.3 pounds per fish and a sales price of $1.20 per pound, the additional weighted value per fish would be .6 × 14.3 × $1.20 = $10.30. This, when added to the recreation value of $2.33, gives a total net value in New England of $12.63 per striped bass.

Although some of the recreational catch in other regions is sold, the survey results indicated the proportion of fish sold is likely not high enough to significantly affect the estimated net values. Therefore, no adjustments are made in the net value estimates for the other regions.

Total value of striped bass trips by state is shown in Table 17. These values are derived by multiplying the average consumer surplus of a striped bass trip from Table 16 by the estimated number of trips in the various states (Table 15). Based on value, the leading states are New York, New Jersey and Maryland. New York and New Jersey have relatively high numbers of trips and a large value per trip ($169). On the other hand, Maryland has nearly twice as many trips as the next closest state but has a relatively low value per trip. In all, the 2 million striped bass fishing trips produced slightly under $200 million dollars of net value or an average of about $100 per trip.

These figures represent the value of trips taken by persons seeking or having caught striped bass. Sportfishermen often seek more than one species and gain satisfaction from boating and the outdoor aesthetics associated with the trips. To attribute the entire value of the trips to striped bass might seriously overstate the recreational benefits associated with only the catching of fish. To obtain an estimate of the value generated by the use of the resource, the marginal willingness to pay for striped bass (Table 16) was multiplied by the number of striped bass caught in the state (Table 15). The number reflects the catch in a state and the responsiveness of trips to catch. Because of the method used to estimate recreational demand, the recreational benefits vary proportionally to the catch (kept and released). This is important as the data on catch are not avail-

Table 17: Recreational trips and net value of striped bass sportfishing trips, by state and region, projected for 1980

	Trips[1] (000)	Value of Striped Bass Sportfishing Trips ($000)
New England	517	$ 44,456
Maine	23	1,983
New Hampshire	17	1,498
Massachusetts	226	19,481
Rhode Island	182	15,694
Connecticut	67	5,800
Mid-Atlantic	610	103,089
New York	408	68,923
New Jersey	199	33,682
Delaware	3	484
Chesapeake Bay	934	36,131
Maryland	910	35,188
Virginia	24	943
South Atlantic	109	12,536
North Carolina	109	12,536
Total	2,170	$196,212

[1]Based on 1979 total trips and 1980 striped bass participation rates.

able for 1980. We thus used the 1979 published catch data. There are indications that the 1980 catch is substantially lower. When the NMFS publishes the official 1980 data, the recreational benefits can be adjusted by multiplying the 1979 benefits by a ratio of 1980 to 1979 catch.

Using the published information, the Chesapeake Bay and Mid-Atlantic regions received the most benefits with striped bass generating the largest recreational values in Maryland and New York. In all, $8 million in net value can be directly attributed to recreationally caught striped bass (Table 18).

Commercial Benefits

The Measurement Concept

The same basic concepts described above can be applied to measure the benefits from commercial fishing, even though the marketing system

Table 18: Recreational catch and net value of striped bass caught, by state, 1979

Region State	Estimated Recreational Catch ($000)	Estimated Net Value of Catch ($000)
New England	185	$2,337
Maine	17	215
Massachusetts	59	745
Rhode Island	44	556
Connecticut	65	821
Mid-Atlantic	290	2,157
New York	276	2,053
New Jersey	13	97
Delaware	1	7
Chesapeake	658	3,487
Maryland	649	3,440
Virginia	9	47
South Atlantic	38	51
North Carolina	38	51
Total	1,171	$8,032

is more complex. For each marketing level (i.e., ex-vessel, wholesale and retail), a demand and supply curve could be estimated. The net value of the product to the demanders (i.e. ultimate consumers or middlemen) is the area under the demand curve but above the market price. This is shown as a consumer surplus, GFE, in Figure 7 on page 34.

It is possible that commercial fishermen gain net income from striped bass production and this is also considered. In Figure 7, when C pounds of fish are placed on the market, a price of F is negotiated. This results in consumers' surplus of GFE and watermen's revenues of FECO. In general, the watermen's surplus would be FEH. When watermen have a constant average expense per pound of striped bass harvested of F, there is no surplus to the watermen. A constant marginal cost less than F, would result in a positive producer surplus.

The Marketing Situation

As discussed earlier, institutional considerations are important in marketing striped bass and must be considered when estimating benefits.

Striped bass are obtained from the fishermen by local wholesalers and many are sold on consignment in the Fulton or Baltimore wholesale markets. Together, Baltimore and Fulton marketing represent about two-thirds of the reported commercial striped bass landings (Adriance 1982). Moreover, the industry in general uses either the Baltimore or Fulton market price to establish ex-vessel price for watermen (Yamashita 1982). Thus, events in the Baltimore and Fulton markets cannot be overlooked.

A second institutional factor is the market segmentation according to the size of fish. The Fulton Market has a 16″ minimum size requirement and tends to receive the large striped bass. The Baltimore market, on the other hand, accepts 12″ bass but cannot legally transfer striped bass that exceed 32″. It, in general, receives small striped bass.

In the southern region (Delaware to North Carolina), primary wholesalers take fish on consignment and sell them to local retailers or to the central wholesalers in the Baltimore or Fulton market. Size and volume of the catch, and the availability of local markets are prime determinants of how much product is distributed to the various wholesale markets. The product then flows through retailers to the consumers. Small volumes in New York are processed (filleted or steaked) but the majority of New York retailers and nearly all Baltimore retailers sell whole (gutted/scaled) fish. The northern (north of Delaware) landings move in a similar pattern except the Baltimore market is not a primary market for the product. Volume not sold locally goes through the Fulton Market before reaching the consumer. The central markets both facilitate transfer of the product and provide a mechanism through which prices are established.

Through discussion with numerous fishermen and dealers, a model of price determination was derived. Monthly landing are considered a function of factors (e.g. seasonal availability) not related to price. The sales to wholesale markets primarily are a function of fish size and location of landings. Price determination appears to occur in the following manner:

• Quantity landed—(predetermined) based on factors such as weather, previous investments, work habits or availability of fish, rather than striped bass prices

• Wholesale market quantity—based on landings and size of fish

• Retail price—based on consumer preferences, retail quantity, substitute price, and income

• Wholesale price—based on retail price, wholesale quantity and availability of other fish

- Ex-vessel price—based upon wholesale prices, landings and availability of local market alternatives.

The Statistical Model

In order to test whether this abstract system as shown is a reasonable description of short run behavior in the market, monthly data were gathered to determine whether these relationships were statistically significant. Baltimore and Fulton receipt data, as well as landings and landed value data, all collected by NMFS, were used. Seemingly unrelated regression was used to estimate coefficients of the model.

The results of the estimated system are shown in Tables 19 and 20. Quantity received in the Fulton Market from the northern region (north of Delaware) is correlated with landings in the region as are southern receipts and southern landings (Table 19). Prices at the various levels of marketing appear to be strongly influenced by sales within the market and the price established in the next higher market (Table 20). For southern ex-vessel price for the period 1976-1979, the Fulton wholesale price was a stronger determinant than was the Baltimore wholesale price. For a longer period (1972-1979), however, Baltimore prices were influential in determining southern ex-vessel prices. The difference may relate to the changing age structure of the striped bass population.

The coefficients shown in Tables 19 and 20 were used to estimate the commercial consumer and producer surplus generated by East Coast striped bass. An application of the theory of multi-market welfare[10] was carried out based on the above estimates. When the price in the next higher level market is included as a right hand side variable in estimating a given market level price (e.g the Baltimore wholesale price equation which has the Baltimore retail price in it), the area, GEF in Figure 7, represents the surplus to the buyers in *that* given market level. For price equations in which the next higher market price is not included, an area analogous to GEF represents surplus to participants in *all* market levels from buyers in that market up the chain. Thus, the Fulton price equation captures surpluses of both the ultimate consumer and retailer whereas the Baltimore wholesale price equation captures only the retailers' surpluses. To get consumers' surpluses in Baltimore, the retail price equation must be used.

The reported preliminary landings for 1980, which totaled 4,566 thousand pounds, were used to determine surpluses in the Fulton and Balti-

---

[10]See Just et al. (1982) for a complete discussion of multi-market welfare.

Table 19: Regression results for monthly quantity received in the Fulton and Baltimore markets, as related to regional landings, 1976–1979

Market	Dependent Variable (000's)	Constant	Independent Variables		
			Northern Landings (000's)	Southern Landings (000's)	Summer Dummy (1 = summer mos.)
			Estimated Coefficients		
Fulton					
	Quantity Received from Northern States	51.6	.26 (5.73)[1]		148.8 (6.63)
	Quantity Received from Southern States	6.54		.43 (18.37)	
Baltimore					
	Quantity Received from Southern States	16.2		.18 (14.11)	

[1]t—Values shown in parentheses

more markets. Equations in Table 19 were used to predict that, out of the 4,566 thousand pounds, there would be a flow of 543 thousand pounds to the Baltimore market and 2,857 thousand pounds to the Fulton market. For the Baltimore market, this generated surpluses of $179 thousand to retail consumers and $82 thousand to retailers. The volume passing through the Fulton market is estimated to have generated $1,260 thousand to retailers and consumers in 1980. The total benefits therefore of the 3,400 thousand pounds going through these two markets is $1,522 thousand. These fish represented 74% of the total 4,566 thousand pounds harvested.[11]

The remaining 1,166 thousand pounds are not accounted for in the model because data do not exist on their ultimate use and price. The

---

[11]Ex-vessel price equations indicated there were no surplus profits to the wholesalers of striped bass.

Table 20: Regression results for striped bass price equations for various market levels, 1976–1979

Dependent Variable- Deflated Price (1967 $/lb)	K	Market Sales (000 lbs)	Baltimore Retail Price ($/lb)	Fulton Wholesale Price ($/lb)	Spring Dummy (1-Spring)	Income ($000/ CAP)	Substitute Good Price (Index)
				Independent Variables			
				Estimated Coefficients			
Baltimore Retail	1.18	−.0035 (5.15)¹			.29 (3.23)		
Baltimore Wholesale	.52	−.0016 (7.15)	.18 (4.58)				
Southern Ex-Vessel	.04			.53 (12.08)			
Fulton Wholesale	−.83	−.0015 (8.45)			.006 (.12)	.49 (1.98)	.00030 (.29)
Northern Ex-Vessel	.18			.38 (5.78)			

¹t—values shown in parenthesis
K = Constant

equation for northern shipments to Fulton accounts for nearly all northern landings and therefore, the remaining volume in considered to be landed by the southern states. These are either marketed in other central markets such as Philadelphia or Newport News or in local retail outlets. Using the Baltimore retail price coefficient (− .0035) and assuming these fish go through one market in the same seasonal distribution as southern landings, we calculated benefits of $1,191 thousand.[12] The total benefits to consumers, retailers and wholesalers generated in 1980 reported landings is therefore $2,713 thousand.

[12]An alternative assumption concerning disposition and surplus of these uncounted fish is that they yield the same average surplus per pound as fish passing through the Fulton and Baltimore markets. In this case, the benefits from these fish are calculated to be $521 thousand.

The only remaining group to be considered is the commercial fishermen. The cost and revenue data of the Commercial Fishery chapter show
that fishermen in southern states reported no revenues in excess of total
costs. No surplus profit to fishermen is therefore estimated for southern
fishermen. The hook and line fishery of New England, however, reported
approximately $.21/pound surplus. This figure is used to calculate surplus
generated by the reported northern landings (1475 thousand pounds) as
$772 thousand in 1980.

The total net economic benefits from reported 1980 landings is estimated to be $3,485 thousand (Table 21). The total is distributed to various

**Table 21: Recreational and commercial net value of striped bass use by
state and region, 1980**

Region/State	Recreational Value[1] ($000)	Commercial Value ($000)	Total Value ($000)
New England	2,337	842	3,179
Maine	215	—	215
Massachusetts	745	780	1,525
Rhode Island	556	19	575
Connecticut	821	43	864
Mid-Atlantic	2,157	580	2,737
New York	2,053	547	2,600
New Jersey	97	22	119
Delaware	7	11	18
Chesapeake Bay	3,487	1,747	5,234
Maryland	3,440	1,410	4,850
Virginia	47	337	384
South Atlantic	51	316	367
North Carolina	51	316	367
Total	8,032	3,485	11,517

[1]Recreational value based on 1979 catch.

states on the basis of landings and therefore is not necessarily of benefit to
those states' residents. That is, many New York City or Connecticut consumers receive benefits from landings in the Chesapeake and in Table 21
these benefits are attributed to the Chesapeake, where landings occurred,

not where the benefits were derived. The fishermen benefits were distributed only to the northern states because no surpluses were observed for the southern fishermen.

One must recall, however, that the reported landings in 1980 were only a third of the reported record landings in 1974 of 14.7 million pounds. To show the benefits associated with a record year, we determined benefits in the Baltimore market for 1974 reported shipments. The Baltimore market benefits in 1974 were $6.4 million or nearly 25 times the benefits estimated for 1980. This figure alone represents 50 percent of all 1980 recreational and commercial benefits.

Table 21 also summarizes the total net benefits generated by recreational and commercial users. On a regional basis, the New England and Mid-Atlantic areas each generated about 25% of the total. The Chesapeake region represented about 45-50% of the total, and the South Atlantic about 5%. The contribution of each region's sector was reasonably consistent. For example, recreation in the Chesapeake Bay contributed 43% of the total recreational benefit whereas commercial Chesapeake production represented 50% of the entire commercial benefits. The total net benefits to users of striped bass is estimated to be $11.5 million in 1980.

The authors recognize the potential for underestimating landings and landed value due to possible under-reporting or the lack of coverage in all areas. The commercial benefits derived, therefore, are possibly underestimated and care should be taken when comparing recreational and commercial data.

Economic Impact
Of the
Striped Bass
Fisheries

THE GENERAL CONCEPT of regional economic impact analysis is based on determining both the interrelationships among industry or economic sectors in a given geographic area, and the interaction between economic activity in that area and economic activity outside the area. The objective of regional impact analysis is to determine the change in total economic activity that is generated from an initial change in expenditure.

Some key considerations in measuring economic activity changes are:

- What is the initial change in expenditure?

- In what economic sector(s) does the change in expenditure take place?

- What is the rate of spending by the economic sector(s) in the geographic area of interest as compared to "leakages" or expenditures outside the area?

- How is the spending by the initally affected sector(s) distributed among all economic sectors in the area?

The completed regional economic analysis, then, yields the estimated dollar amount of economic activity changes after all the effects of an initial change in expenditure are dissipated throughout the economy of the geographic area.

For example, assume a sport fisherman who is from a non-coastal area travels to a coastal area to fish for striped bass. While he is in the coastal area he buys $20 worth of gasoline for his car from a local service station. This $20 can be considered as an initial increase in expenditure in the coastal area. Assume further that the service station operator re-spends the $20 dollars as follows:

a. Eleven dollars for the gasoline to a wholesaler/refinery located outside the coastal area

b. Two dollars to hired workers who live in the local area

c. One dollar for upkeep on the station (to a local painter and a local plumber)

d. Two dollars to a local utility company

e. One dollar to the local landlord who owns the service station property

f. One dollar for federal and state taxes

g. Two dollars to the local grocery store for groceries for his family

Now it can be seen that of the $20 initial increase expenditures, $12 (a and f) will immediately flow outside of the local area as "leakage. The remaining eight dollars (b,c,d,e and g) have been respent in the coastal area and are available to those represented in b,c,d,e and g for further respending. Some of the further respending will be in the local area, and the remainder will flow outside of the area.

At this point, considering only the first set of responding activity by the station operator, we can see that the initial $20 increase in expenditure has resulted in total spending in the local area of $28 (the initial $20 plus the $8 respent in the area by the operator). Therefore, even at this early stage of the spending and responding that will take place as a result of the initial change in expenditure, the multiplier effect is 1.4. The multiplier is derived by dividing the initial change in expenditure of $20 into the total new economic activity at this point of $28.

Of course, additional responding will take place with the eight dollars still remaining in the local area. The initial $20 could generate $25, $30 or even $40 more in additional economic activity. This would represent multipliers of 2.25, 2.5, or 3.0 respectively. The higher the multiplier, the greater the effect an initial expenditure will have on the local community.

It is clear that the total economic effect (as expressed through the multiplier) of an initial change in expenditures depends greatly upon the "leakage" out of the local area. In the example above, if the wholesaler/re-finery in (a) is located in the local coastal area, a much larger proportion ($19 of the $20) of the initial expenditure would remain in the local area to be used for stimulating local income and employment.

Methods

The purpose of the impact phase of this study was to measure the economic activity, as described above, associated with the existence of the striped bass commercial and recreational fisheries. The study covered the 10 coastal states from Maine through North Carolina. The states were divided into coastal and non-coastal areas. The coastal area was specified as the two-county wide band of counties along the coast. This resulted in two areas (coastal and non-coastal) in all states except Rhode Island and Delaware, which are defined as coastal in their entirety.

The approach used for the analysis was the "Harris Model" (See Harris 1973; and Harris and Norton 1978). As indicated in Harris and Norton, the principal driving force of the model is a set of industry location equations that explain changes in output by county. The explanatory variables are: a partial measure of location rent, which accounts for the marginal transportation cost of shipping goods out of each region, the marginal transportation costs of obtaining inputs at the place of production, the cost of labor, the value of land, prior investment, prior production, demand and input scarcity. Included are equations to explain population migration, with the explanatory variables being wage rates, changes in employment and the amount of labor surplus or deficit. Based on these parameters, the changes in income, employment and output resulting from an initial change in economic activity can be estimated.

In order to use the model, it was necessary to obtain extensive information through personal field interviews and published and unpublished data. It was necessary to identify not only the amount of expenditures associated with the striped bass commercial and recreational fisheries but also where (coastal vs. non-coastal) and in which economic sectors it was spent. The expenditures derived from the field interviews were classified and divided among eleven economic sectors: fishery, hotels and other lodging, personal and repair service, amusements and recreation, water transportation, food stores, gas stations, eating and drinking establishments, miscellaneous retail stores, state and local government, and federal government.

As implied by the latter two sector categories, it was necessary to obtain estimates of state and federal administration, research and enforcement expenditures on the striped bass resource.

Estimated Impacts

For the purpose of this analysis the economic impacts associated with three alternative situations were estimated:

Scenario I: The commercial and recreational striped bass fisheries as they existed in 1980

Scenario II: The commercial and recreational striped bass fisheries as projected to result from the management changes recommended in the Atlantic States Marine Fisheries Management Plan for Striped Bass

Scenario III: The hypothetical commercial and recreational fisheries that could have existed in 1980 if the striped bass stock size would have been as large as it was in the early 1970s

The economic activity in terms of generated output and employment changes was estimated for each of these scenarios.

Scenario I

The basis for this scenario was the striped bass commercial and recreational fisheries as they existed in 1980. The recreational and commercial fishery data from the previous chapters formed the primary input for this analysis. Specifically, we used the recreational trip expenditures calculated from our 1980 supplementary survey, and commercial value of the harvest by county as reported by the National Marine Fisheries Service and supplemented by information for state agencies.

Table 22 is a summary of the estimated economic impact in the coastal areas of the commercial and recreational striped bass fisheries in 1980. Total direct expenditure associated with these fisheries was about $90 million in the coastal areas of the 10 states covered in this study. It is difficult to specify the breakdown of these expenditures between commercial and recreational fisheries because of the sharing of port facilities in some areas, and primarily, because in some areas recreationally caught fish are sold and therefore enter the commercial channels, creating income and employment in the commercial fisheries sector.

Table 22: Estimated coastal area economic impacts of striped bass commercial and recreational activity: Scenario I.

Region	1980 Expenditures ($000)	Associated Total Output ($000)	Economic Activity Multiplier	Jobs	Expenditure per Job Created
New England	$26,630	$ 60,775	2.29	1,888	$14,105
Mid-Atlantic	36,259	82,323	2.20	2,245	16,151
Chesapeake	23,993	48,706	2.03	1,214	19,764
South Atlantic	2,946	8,491	2.88	330	8,927
Total	$89,828	$200,295	2.24	5,677	$15,823

As is indicated in Table 22, the initial expenditures of $90 million in the coastal areas of these 10 states generated a total of over $200 million of economic output and employment of more than 5600 people. The economic activity multiplier ranges from 2.03 in the Chesapeake region to 2.88 in North Carolina. The relatively low multiplier in the Chesapeake may be a reflection of the fact that there are no major refineries in Maryland and thus much of the fuel expenditures flow directly out of the state to other regions. The multipliers indicate that each dollar spent by sport or commercial fisheries generates a total of two to three dollars of additional economic output in the coastal areas of the states covered in this study.

The last column in Table 22 indicates that increase in expenditures on striped bass necessary to create one more job in the coastal areas. The expenditure required ranges from about $9,000 to $20,000.

If the expenditures on the striped bass commercial and recreational fisheries in 1980 had somehow been eliminated, total output in the coastal areas of the four regions could have been diminished by $200 million, and up to 5677 people would have lost their jobs in the sectors affected by the striped bass fisheries.

There are additional effects on the non-coastal areas. Under Scenario I, these non-coastal generated effects were estimated to be $32.7 million of output and 1050 associated jobs. Therefore, in general, for the 10 states considered in this study, the non-coastal effects on ouput and jobs was about 20% of the coastal area effects. This means that for every six dollars generated on the coast, an additional one dollar of output is generated in the non-coastal areas. Similarly, for every five jobs generated in the coastal counties by the existence of the striped bass fisheries, an additional job is generated in the non-coastal counties. Even though the economic activity associated with striped bass is primarily concentrated in the coastal areas, the non-coastal areas of the states derive considerable economic activity from the striped bass fisheries.

Scenario II

The analysis for Scenario II was based on the Striped Bass Management Plan adopted by the Atlantic States Marine Fisheries Commission. The principal changes are in the minimum size of striped bass commercial and recreational fishermen may keep. The purpose of the increased minimum sizes is to allow more fish to spawn in the hopes that the overall stock size will increase. The management plan specifies the general effects the new regulations are expected to have on recreational and commercial catches in the Chesapeake and non-Chesapeake regions. Using these changes and the implied effects on expenditures, the Harris Model was re-run to reflect this scenario. As is indicated in Table 23, the overall effect of the proposed management plan, assuming a new equilibrium is established, will be an increase in output of almost four million dollars in the 10 states and an increase in employment of 63 people. The positive changes in the New England, Mid-Atlantic and South Atlantic regions come at some expense to the Chesapeake region. However, it is important to note that if the proposed plan is necessary to protect and preserve the existence of striped bass commercial and recreational fisheries in the Chesapeake, this region is better off with the plan results than with no striped bass fisheries.

Table 23: Differences in estimated economic impact for alternative scenarios

Region	Effects of Management Plan[1]		Effects of Larger Striped Bass Population[2]	
	Impact ($000)	Jobs	Impact ($000)	Jobs
New England	+ 4,580	+ 151	+ 78,119	+ 2,477
Mid-Atlantic	+ 4,427	+ 159	+ 105,238	+ 2,974
Chesapeake	− 6,080	− 257	+ 24,074	+ 1,607
South Atlantic	+ 931	+ 10	+ 11,065	+ 438
Total	+ 3,858	+ 63	+ 218,496	+ 7,496

[1]This is the estimated economic impact of changes in catch predicted by the Atlantic States Marine Fisheries Commission if the Proposed Commission Striped Bass Management Plan is adopted (see Appendix A of the Commission Plan).

[2]This is the estimated additional output and jobs generated if the striped bass commercial landings and recreational trips had been in 1980, what they were in 1974.

Scenario III

As is indicated in Table 23, if the Striped Bass stock level had been in 1980 what it was in the early 1970s, the four regions would have gained $220 million in output and 7500 jobs. These numbers can be used as a general indication of the loss in economic activity as a result of the decline in the striped bass resource since the early 1970s.

Summary

THE RESULTS OF a comprehensive review and analysis of the 1979-1980 North Atlantic striped bass fishery indicate a wide breadth of activity associated with an economically valuable resource. Harvest seasons, methods and costs illustrate the geographic diversity in commercial production. The predominant summer and early fall catches in New England are accomplished with hook and line and cost approximatly $1.70 per pound. Peak harvests in late fall, winter and spring by Chesapeake gill netters cost approximately $1.20 per pound. Chesapeake commercial catch is generally comprised of smaller fish than occur in New England. Additionally, the recreational fishery captures substantial numbers of stripers from a variety of access points including private and party boats. The distinction between commercial and recreational fishing is obscured in New England and parts of the Mid-Atlantic due to the large percentage of "recreationally caught" striped bass which are sold to wholesalers and therefore enter the commercial market channels.

The economic benefits generated from 1980 commercial and recreational harvest of striped bass were substantial, even for the relatively low stock levels during that year. For the ten states from Maine to North Carolina, a total net economic value of nearly $12 million was generated. Slightly over two-thirds of the total was associated with recreational harvest while the remainder arose from commercial harvest. Care must be exercised in comparing commercial and recreational benefits, however, because the commercial harvest data are reputed to be substantially underreported, leading to potential underestimates of commercial benefits.

It was also found that consumer benefits in the Baltimore market were nearly 25 times larger in 1974 than in 1980, even though the annual marketings were only three times larger. This suggests substantial returns from policies or research which increases production.

In addition to the net benefits generated for society in general, the striped bass fisheries produce important income and employment opportunities in the coastal areas. The 1980 commercial and recreational striped bass fisheries resulted in $90 million direct expenditures in the coastal areas of the 10 states. These direct expenditures generated a total direct and indirect contribution in the coastal areas of over $200 million in economic output and employment for over 5600 people.

Although most economic impacts occur in the coastal counties, the study shows that there are also important non-coastal area impacts. For every six dollars of output and five jobs created in the coastal counties, striped bass fishing creates an additional one dollar and one job in the non-coastal areas.

The study indicates that up to $218 million of economic activity and 7500 jobs may have been lost to the coastal areas of the 10 states as a result of the decline of the striped bass resource since the early 1970s. Furthermore, although other regions gain relative to the Chesapeake regions as a result of the proposed Atlantic State Marine Fisheries Commission Striped Bass Management Plan, there is a net gain in economic activity and jobs in the four regions combined.

References

ADRIANCE, J.G. 1982. A Market Model for the North Atlantic Striped Bass Industry. M.S. Thesis. Department of Agricultural & Resource Economics, University of Maryland.

ATLANTIC STATES MARINE FISHERIES COMMISSION. 1982. Interstate Fisheries Management Plan for the Striped Bass of the Atlantic Coast from Maine to North Carolina. Prepared by the State of Maryland, Department of Natural Resources.

BERGGREN, T.J. and J.T. LIBBERMAN. 1978. Relative Contribution to Hudson, Chesapeake, and Roanoke Striped Bass, *Morone saxatilis*, Stocks to the Atlantic Coast Fishery. U.S. Fish. Bull. 76:335-345.

HARRIS, C.C. 1973. The Urban Economics, 1985: A Multiregional, Multi-Industry Forecasting Model. Lexington Books, Lexington, Mass.

HARRIS, C.C. and V. J. NORTON. 1978. The role of economic models in evaluating commercial fishery resources. Am. J. Ag. Econ. 60(5): 1013-1020.

HIETT, R.L. and D.N. GHOSH. 1977. A Recommended Approach to the Collection of Marine Recreational Finfishing and Shellfishing Data on the Pacific Coast. Human Sciences Research, McLean, Va.

JUST, R.E., HUETH, D.L. and A. SCHMITZ. 1982. Applied Welfare Economics and Public Policy. Prentice Hall. Englewood Cliffs, N.J.

KOHLENSTEIN, L.C. 1980. Aspects of the Population Dynamics of Striped Bass (*Morone saxatilis*) Spawning in Maryland Tributaries of the Chesapeake Bay. Ph.D. Dissertation JHU. JHU/PPSE T-14.

MCCONNELL, K.E. and T. P. SMITH. 1979. Marine Recreational Fishing in Rhode Island. University of Rhode Island Marine Memorandum 62, Kingston, R.I.

NATIONAL MARINE FISHERIES SERVICE. 1980. Marine Recreational Fishery Statistics Survey, Atlantic and Gulf Coasts, 1979. Current Fishery Statistics Number 8063.

SCOTT, A. 1955. The fishery—the objectives of sole ownership. J. Pol. Econ. April:116-124.

STRAND, I.E. and V. J. NORTON. 1980. Economic Information Needs in the Management of the Striped Bass Resource. Reprint to the Northeast Regional Office of the National Marine Fisheries Service, Gloucester, Mass.

STRAND, I.E., V.J. NORTON and J. ADRIANCE. 1980. Economic Aspects of Commercial Striped Bass Harvest. In H. Clepper ed. Fifth Annual Marine Recreational Fisheries Symposium. Boston, 1980. Sport Fishing Institute.

SNYDER, R.R. 1983. Specification Errors and Surplus Values for Recreational Striped Bass Fishing. M.S. Theses. Department of Agricultural & Resource Economics, University of Maryland.

WILLIG, R.D. 1976. Consumer surplus without apology. Am. Econ. Rev. 66(4):589-597.

YAMASHITA, V.F. 1982. Marketing of Striped Bass in the Chesapeake States of Maryland and Virginia. M.S. Thesis. Department of Agricultural and Resource Economics, University of Maryland.

Table Index

		Page
Table 1:	Characteristics of commercial striped bass harvesters using hook and line gear, Massachusetts and Rhode Island, 1980	7
Table 2:	Average annual expenditures attributable to striped bass by Massachusetts and Rhode Island hook and line fishermen, 1980.	8
Table 3:	Characteristics of commercial striped bass harvesters using fish traps, New England, 1980.	9
Table 4:	Average annual expenditures attributable to striped bass by New England fish trap fishermen, 1980	9
Table 5:	Striped bass landings in New York, by county and by gear, 1980	10
Table 6:	Average annual expenditures attributable to striped bass by Delaware gill netters, 1980	11
Table 7:	Average characteristics of all gill net operations and all full-time gill net operations in Maryland, 1980	12
Table 8:	Average annual expenditures attributable to striped bass by the part-time and full-time fishermen using gill nets in Maryland, 1980	13
Table 9:	Average annual expenditures attributable to striped bass by Virginia fishermen, 1980	14
Table 10:	Average annual expenditures attributable to striped bass by North Carolina gill netters, 1980	16
Table 11:	Characteristics of striped bass harvesters in North Carolina, 1980	16
Table 12:	Distribution of striped bass by five Fulton Market wholesalers	21
Table 13:	Contribution to total sales revenues, 1980 price per pound, and main substitutes for striped bass at five Manhattan retail seafood outlets	22
Table 14:	Characteristics of the mean striped bass trip, 1979	29
Table 15:	Catch, effort and expenditures, the striped bass recreational fishery, Maine to North Carolina, 1979	30
Table 16:	Average consumer surplus per trip and marginal willingness to pay for the recreational experience of catching striped bass by region, 1980	36
Table 17:	Estimated trips and value of striped bass sportfishing trips by state and region, projected 1980	38
Table 18:	Estimated recreational catch and value of catch by state, projected 1980	39
Table 19:	Regression results for monthly quantity received in the Fulton and Baltimore markets as related to regional landings, 1976–1979	42
Table 20:	Regression results for monthly striped bass price equations for various market levels, 1976–1979	43
Table 21:	Recreational and commercial net value of striped bass use by state and region, 1980	44
Table 22:	Estimated coastal area economic impacts of striped bass commercial and recreational activity: Scenario I	50
Table 23:	Differences in estimated economic impact for alternative scenarios	52

"Grandpa, were you a hero in the Meme Wars?"

And Grandpa said, "No..."

"...but I served in the company of heroes."

Dedicated to all the Anons
and all the Legionaries who fought with me in the trenches…
Dedicated to all my loyal readers
who supported my efforts on the front lines…

And to my father.
Without him and his steadfast support and influence,
this book simply would not exist.

Contents

Preface vii

Chapter One: Nothing Will Stop What is Coming............................. 1

Chapter Two: The President Needs Your Help 11

Chapter Three: How Do You Defuse a Bomb? 39

Chapter Four: You Are Taking Back Control.................................. 115

Chapter Five: How About a Nice Game of Chess 171

Chapter Six: Canis Lupus 229

Chapter Seven: The Same Sick Cult 265

Chapter Eight: Pain Comes in Many Different Forms 379

Chapter Nine: The Shot Heard Round The World.......................... 427

Epilogue: WE, THE PEOPLE!.. 471

Preface

By the time this book is released and in wide circulation, the political landscape of the nation and indeed, the world, will look vastly different from the one people have known for decades prior. If the predictions of the mysterious figure known as "QAnon" are to be believed, at some point great crimes will be exposed to the American people of such a scale, of such depravity, of such pervasiveness, that it will strike at the very heart of the nation and turn the power structures around the world upside-down and inside-out. Soon people everywhere will begin to understand just how close we came to the collective brink of worldwide destruction.

Of course this will not be an easy thing for most to comprehend, at least at first. Because the Cabal (as I've come to call them over the past year and a half, investigating their history and writing about their activities on my site, www.NeonRevolt.com) has its tentacles spread throughout halls of power, the media, big business, and overseas—many in the general public will have been programmed to riot and rebel. What else will they do when they see their previous political saviors, their ideological idols, and their favorite media mouthpieces swept up and whisked away to detention centers in the middle of America while they await criminal processing? I'm reminded of what Q said all those months ago:

"Estimated 4-6% we consider 'hopeless' and forever brainwashed."

Doubtless the cries of "Death Camps" and analogies relating Trump to "Hitler" will flow freely. The good news is that former statistic still leaves upwards of ninety-four percent of the population as reachable and teachable, and if you are reading this book, the chances are high that you are among that greater percentage.

Reaching people with Q's message: that's been the purpose of my online efforts for quite some time now. In the wake of finding myself banned, censored, and de-platformed on mainstream platforms like Twitter and Facebook (which may not exist by the time this book is in wide circulation, given their own crimes), I've since spent countless hours crafting hundreds of articles—almost five-hundred at this point—all full of startling information and disclosures the likes of which the world has never seen before. What started as a mere meme page on Facebook, borne out of my frustration with the rabid, politically correct culture that was spreading across social media like the Marxist cancer it was, soon became so much more to me, and somewhat unexpectedly, to so many out in the real world. What was once a place where I could have a good laugh, vent my frustrations, and connect with like-minded peers, soon morphed into something much bigger and much more important as I began to understand the immensity of what was transpiring in the world. I came to see, with what little access I had; the shape of the invisible war that had been raging around us for so many years. It is no exaggeration to say that my little corner of the internet, where I finally unleashed the voice that had been previously beaten and shamed into silence by the Cultural Marxists and self-appointed gatekeepers of our culture, soon became a major battleground in the fight for our very lives and the continued existence and prosperity of the United States.

But to really understand what's happened, we have to go back to the beginning. Back to where it all started. Back… to the trenches of the information war. Think of this book as something akin to a war-journal—complete with harrowing tales of adventure, wartime companions, hard-fought battles won, and terrifying villains—all written by, if you'll allow me the temporary and somewhat embarrassing indulgence of applying the label to myself, a "digital soldier."

Because, make no mistake, if there's any metaphor that's appropriate for what's about to happen, and what's been happening… it is _**War!**_

And hopefully, by the time you're reading this, the good guys will have won.

CHAPTER 1

"Nothing Will Stop What is Coming"

—November 6, 2018 From Qdrop #2442

Q !!mG7VJxZNCl No.422 📁   **2442**
Nov 6 2018 16:16:21 (EST)

History is being made.
You are the saviors of mankind.
Nothing will stop what is coming.
Nothing.
Q

"How long will you lie down, O sluggard? When will you arise from your sleep?"
—Proverbs 6:9

Realistically speaking, the chief problem I have to overcome with this book is information asymmetry.

If I had to boil it down to just one issue, that would be it.

There's so much I have to tell you, and so little time it seems, for things could start really hitting at any moment. We're at the edge of a precipice, and the dominoes could start falling at any day now. And once that cascade starts, there's truly no stopping it.

But I want to know…

Has President Trump answered "the question" yet?

"What question?" you may be wondering.

The question as to whether or not the figure known as "QAnon" is real.

Maybe you've heard the name by now. Maybe you've never heard it mentioned at all—which, if that's the case, that's not surprising either. Don't worry, you're going to get to learn more than you probably ever wanted to know about this mysterious figure, in short order.

But as for we researchers, we "Anons," as we've been dubbed…we have known for months the answer President Trump will give when the time comes:

"Where we go one, we go all."

The phrase was pulled by Q himself from the 1996 Ridley Scott film named *White Squall,* wherein Jeff Bridges' character unites a rowdy bunch of young men and turns them into efficient sailors in order to travel half-way around the world. But that's before they are overtaken by a sudden and severe storm, a storm known to veteran sailors as the titular "white squall." The storm would be so huge, so devastating, it would put their skills, their resolve, and their ability to work as a team to the ultimate test.

"Where we go one, we go all."

That's been the rallying cry for Anons since Q introduced the phrase to our collective consciousness. The only difference is, instead of trying to save a ship, we're trying to save America, and indeed, the entire world. Q has been working for over a year now to train us, to whip us in to shape and give us the skills necessary to endure what we know is inevitably coming.

And if Trump has answered the question, we Anons already know…

The Storm is now upon us.

Q !CbboFOtcZs ID: 03ac69 No.1953310 ☐ ▶   **1644**
Jun 28 2018 23:59:18 (EST)

> Anonymous ID: ffd993 No.1952748 ☐ ▶
> Jun 28 2018 23:25:43 (EST)
>
> >>1952583
> I almost hope they don't ask. It would be fun to watch them try
> to manage the spin when 90% of the country is aware of you and
> all that you've been shining a light on, while the MSM still can
> acknowledge it.
> I can see them squirming now..

>>1952748
It must happen.
Conspiracy no more.
Think of every post made.
It would force us to prove everything stated to avoid looking crazy,
correct?
What do they fear the most?
Public awakening.
If they ask.
They self destruct.
They know this is real.
See attacks.
The build is near complete.
Growing exponentially.
You are the frame.
You are the support.
People will be lost.
People will be terrified.
People will reject.
People will need to be guided.
Do not be afraid.
We will succeed.
Timing is everything.
Think Huber.
Think DOJ/FBI reorg.
Think sex/child arrests / news.
Think resignations (loss of control).
How do you remove evil in power unless you reveal the ultimate
truth?
It must be compelling to avoid a divide (political attack/optics).
We are the majority (growing).
WW.
Sheep no more.
TOGETHER.
Q

The build is near complete.
Growing exponentially.
You are the frame.
You are the support.
People will be lost.
People will be terrified.
People will reject.
People will need to be guided.
Do not be afraid.
We will succeed.

"So… I'm part of the frame, it seems…"

That's what I keep telling myself as I undertake this massive task; the task of trying to explain everything that's happening right now, to you, in anticipation of what we Anons know is going to happen. I don't know when you, the reader, will be picking up this book, but if it's close to the time it's originally published, it's probable that you came looking for answers.

I'll try to give them to you as clearly and as cleanly as possible. But understand, what you're going to read is not always going to be easy to comprehend. Such is the nature of the evil we're dealing with. Though I've tried my best to keep this as engaging and explanatory as possible, much of what you're about to hear will turn your stomach when you learn of it for the first time. You may experience denial, anger, rage, and a host of other negative emotions when you first come to understand all that I'm truly trying to communicate here, but like a foul-tasting medicine you take to cure a worse sickness, you're going to have to tough it out and stomach it for a bit.

For the rest who will get here later, after the dust has settled, I want this to stand as a testament to what happened, so that future generations won't repeat the same mistakes, or be deceived in the same manner by a group you'll soon learn all about: what I call "the Cabal."

Obviously, I won't be covering *everything* I possibly could cover. Many of these topics spiral out well beyond what could be covered in any one volume, and in such intricacy and detail that one could easily get lost in all the resulting confusion. Rather than getting mired in endless details, my larger goal is to help people see the forest for the proverbial trees. People will be writing about these events for *years* to come, but I'll do my best to distill this down to the most essential parts, so that when the Storm finally hits, you won't get swept away by deceptions, half-truths, or drown in the resulting torrent.

Information asymmetry…

That's what I've got to overcome.

Because it's no exaggeration to say that we've been kept in the dark our whole lives.

It's like Plato, and his Allegory of The Cave.

The allegory says that we've all been trapped, imprisoned in a cave, only allowed to see the passing of distorted and twisting shadows dancing across a cave wall. It's so dark, we can't see anyone else, nor can we see the chains binding us, but we can feel them, and we can hear and bump into other unfortunate souls trapped in the cave alongside us. We try to remember how we got here, but the truth of the matter is that all of us were born here, in this prison, and just as soon as we were able to comprehend our position, we found ourselves bound and unable to escape.

But in our version of the story, a few of our fellow prisoners, through sheer brilliance, ingenuity, and strength of character, have figured out how to escape from this infernal cave, and have since come back, bringing news of a wide world beyond; a world of amazing wonders that can barely be described to those who have been kept in the dark all their lives. It's a world kept from us by others who wished to keep us bound, enslaved, and systematically exploited our whole lives. In short: it's a world that has to be seen to be believed.

And that is exactly why these brave warriors have decided to come back and try to help free everyone trapped in this infernal cave. This isn't mere wishful thinking, or utopian delusion, but the very reality we could realize within our lifetimes if only we would arise, and together, break off the shackles that have kept us bound for so long.

You would think everyone would jump at the chance, but the truth is, many aren't too keen on leaving the cave. It's… well, it's not freezing in the cave. And it may not be dry, but at least it's not raining, right? Plus, some have really grown accustomed to the mashed cockroach gruel delivered by the caretakers each morning. And besides, haven't you heard? The "outside world" is just a "Far Right conspiracy" peddled by crackpots!

Which is to say, some will need more convincing than others. They need access to real knowledge, to real truth.

But how do you begin to describe something like *color* to someone who has only seen shadows their whole life? How would you describe a tree to someone who has no notion of what a tree even is? How do you set someone free who has decided he "prefers" his chains?

The answer is actually, surprisingly simple.

You have to bring a little of that outside light into the cave.

Q has often described what will happen as a "Great Awakening;" a moment when the truth will shine forth so plainly as to be undeniable, and inspire an almost religious fervor among the people. There will be no debate, because you can't debate against the truth. You can't negotiate terms with the truth. The truth will present itself so forcefully as if to say, "I am here! Behold me!" And there will be no arguing with it at that stage in the game.

I have, at times to myself, jokingly referred to this moment as the "Rude Awakening" for some, because it will become instantly clear in that moment how much of our public discourse, how many of our allegiances, how much of our very history has been based on lies. The people will see the liars and deceivers, truly, as our jail keepers (if you'll allow me to extend the cave analogy a bit further), and the truth will be so disturbing, so distressing, that many will want to reject it outright.

That's what happens when the cave gets flooded with light.

Q !CbboFOtcZs ID: 97de56 No.1843055 📎   1585
Jun 21 2018 01:01:30 (EST)

> Q !CbboFOtcZs ID: 97de56 No.1842740 📎
> Jun 21 2018 00:35:10 (EST)
>
> >>1842655
> We told you proofs were going to be important very soon.
> New eyes.
> Be ready.
> 5:5?
> We thank you for your service.
> Q

>>1842740
We stand.
We fight.
TOGETHER.
Organized riots being planned.
Counter measures in place.
Resistance far smaller than portrayed by MSM.
Attacks will intensify.
You, collectively, are a massive threat.
Censorship applied to scale down impact/reach.
It's failing.
Trust yourself.
Public awakening.
Q

It takes a moment for our eyes to adjust.

No, my bet is that if this book has found its way into your hands, something *massive* has just taken place in the United States; something the likes of which we've never seen before. On the surface, it may look like an incumbent president is using his powers to round up his political opponents and throw them in jail. Cries of "dictator" are probably ricocheting across the airwaves (if the TV, radio, and internet are all still functioning at this point), but believe me when I say, that couldn't be further from the truth. If I'm correct (and I think, by the end of this, you'll see there's good reason to believe I am), Hillary Clinton, Bill Clinton, Barack and Michelle Obama, and so many others will have already been arrested on charges of treason. Many are already on their way to prison at Guantanamo Bay, or other sites around the nation.

Emergency messages will be sent to people's cell phones through the emergency broadcast protocols President Trump tested out earlier in 2018. Perhaps the long-awaited "HRC Vid" will have finally been released—a video whose contents remain mysterious even to most Anons, though Q assures us, are damning to the ultimate degree. (Some Anons believe the video to be of Hillary conspiring to commit treason. Others think it's a video of her participating in some of the most dreadful and heinous acts imaginable—though personally, I don't think such a video would be made public by President Trump and his team.) There's also the photo that's slated to be released of Obama, in full Muslim garb, wielding an AK and firing at, well… it's up for debate at this point though there seems to be two competing theories: either an American flag… or a captive American.

More on that, later.

The point is, Anons have been prepared for this moment for well over a year now; possibly two or more by the time all this starts to really cascade. We know better than most what to expect, and for good reason.

The general public?

Not so much. So it's hard to predict what the people's collective reactions will be.

Those on the Conservative side of things may welcome this; those well acquainted with these particular individuals' past crimes, who refused to turn a blind eye to their injustices over all these years.

Those on the Left?

I'd wager they're having a much harder time processing what's going on right now, seeing as many don't even know the first thing about, for instance, the trail of bodies that have been left in the wake of the Clintons over the past few decades. So common has this occurrence been, it's even got its own name now: Arkancide (that's Arkansas homicide, for those playing along at home).

There will probably be attempts by the media and by various "grassroots" groups to exploit this imbalance and get people who have long considered themselves Democrats, or politically Left to riot, though that kind of message might only be broadcast sporadically, as many of those who would usually stir up such action will have probably also been arrested once all this goes down. Not to mention the mass arrests of those in the media who are themselves guilty of participating in this treason.

Oh, and believe me, they are guilty.

Really, what they want from the Left when this all goes down is for them to be their good little foot-soldiers; to cause as much civil unrest as possible while they try to escape the justice that is coming for them. To those who consider themselves "liberal" or "left-of-center" who may be reading this, I would say this:

Don't be someone else's useful idiot. Don't be someone else's cannon fodder; a mere pawn to be sacrificed by elites on the altar of their agenda. I believe most good Americans want the truth and not a mere agenda. It's just a matter of coming to an understanding of the real truth of the situation, now.

Make no mistake, what I'm going to explain to you throughout this book is not going to be easy to hear, but it's going to be necessary. And as Q has said, the farther we go down the rabbit hole the more "unrealistic it all becomes." I've spent the past year-and-a-half trying to come to grips with everything that's now unfolding, and writing about all things-Q-related during that whole time, so there are few better positioned to try and lay it all out for you and make some semblance of sense out of the now over 3000 drops Q has left for us. But that doesn't mean it's going to be easy. Some of the things I have to tell you are so unbelievable, no person in their right mind would ever want to believe them. Some things are so challenging to comprehend, I can almost guarantee that you're going to feel like your brain is melting at some point. And yet, it is the truth.

Everything I'm about to tell you is all true, to the best of my knowledge. (And while I know there are some wild claims out there, I've done my best to be very "Conservative," and disclose to you, the reader, when I'm speculating on a subject.)

But the simple reality is this: Whether you decide to get onboard with Q, or join some armed Anti-Trump resistance group roaming the sewers of DC, plotting paramilitary strikes on strategic targets… I want you to know the truth first, before you act. Its only in the light of truth that you can act appropriately.

And you're on the side of truth, aren't you?

Besides, there's no harm in hearing me out. At least this way, you'll know the claims you're dealing with here.

If Q is true, the events you'll see unfolding around you will be the culmination of decades of work by good men and women embedded throughout the various strata of our government and society; a sort of underground coalition of good guys, working together, often in secret, to ensure the safety and security of the citizens of the United States. Right now, as of this writing, there are over one-hundred--thousand sealed indictments waiting to be unsealed at a moment's notice. When that happens, a cascade of arrests will begin, the likes of which the world has never seen before. Thousands upon thousands of individuals will be caught up in this operation, which is the result of law enforcement officials and a team of 470 investigators working inside the Department of Justice in conjunction with Military Intelligence (MILINT), at the behest of President Trump. This has been planned with military precision, and no details surrounding the specifics of this investigation have been leaked to the public.

The individuals slated for arrest are also spread out through our society. Some are from government. Some are from the private sector. Others are TV personalities and talking heads; people whose faces we've seen in our living rooms millions of times. Some are moguls. Others are base criminals. Still, others are judges, who will be ripped out of the court system and suddenly called into judgment themselves. No matter where they come from, all these individuals will be tried and processed in a series of military tribunals.

As a result, many, if not most, will be sentenced to serious jail time.

But for the worst, they will be sentenced to death. Oh, and it will be a death most deserved, for if once exposed, the government did not carry out such a sentence, the People most assuredly would.

So why all these arrests, and why now?

Buckle up, because this is where things start to sound crazy.

For centuries, the world has been ruled by an ancient and secret death cult. Throughout my intensive study about who these people are, how they function, and how they retain their power, I've come to call this group, simply, the Cabal. The Cabal is a hierarchical organization that, at its core, is Satanic in origin. We'll get in to the specifics in a later chapter, but the short of it is that they are an occult group that leverages institutions like banking, media, governments, as well as blackmail, pedophilia, human sacrifice, and even cannibalism in order to achieve their goals. Nothing is off the table, so long as it accumulates power for themselves. They've embedded themselves in the halls of power all over the world, and use whatever means they have at their disposal to retain that power. The depths of evil in which they are willing to engage reveal their fundamental depravity. And the insidious thing about them is that, just like snakes in the grass, they are experts at hiding in plain sight.

Many, if not most of the people who will be arrested and tried are all members of the Cabal.

And really, this isn't as foreign as it seems. How many household names have been exposed in public now for their past transgressions. There was a time when Bill Cosby was the ultimate TV father figure. He was a good guy, right? And then Harvey Weinstein—but Hollywood would have you believe he's just the exception to the rule, correct? Oh, but what about Kevin Spacey? And Bryan Singer? And…

They all seem so *normal*, for lack of a better term. Barack Obama, he was the "cool" president, right? Hillary? Well, isn't it just so admirable how she forgave Bill all those years ago? And she was, as the media line went, the most experienced person (forget woman; the most experienced *person*) to ever run for office! It was her turn and Trump *STOLE* that election by colluding with those Russians!

…Right?

I'm sorry to be the one to have to tell you this, but these are all finely-crafted illusions, brought to you by their media lapdogs; all members of the Cabal themselves. These men and women have been tasked with the explicit mission of promoting Cabal candidates and ensuring public opinion swayed in whatever direction the Cabal deemed fit. The mainstream media is mostly a tool of the Cabal, leveraged to sway public perceptions and accumulate power by programming the people with, well, their "programming."

The real truth, which the talking heads intentionally keep from you, is that the likes of Obama and Hillary had nothing but the destruction of the United States as their goal. And no, I'm not talking about mere economic ruin, or problems due to mass immigration. Those were aspects of it, yes, but I'm talking about nuclear catastrophe and the initiation of World War III. The sheer scale of evil here is so massive, it's almost unbelievable. It was called "The 16 Year Plan" and we'll get to the specifics later.

But the scary part?

The *really* scary part..?

…Is how *close* they came to fulfilling their plans.

The money had already changed hands. Deals were made for the uranium, and the Cabal-affiliated assets planted in secret bases around the world were already hard at work designing the bombs that they were planning to one day rain down upon our heads, with the intention of turning our loved ones into little more than heaps of ash and utterly erasing our way of life from the face of the planet.

See, it wasn't enough for them just to use and exploit the American people for years. It wasn't enough just to keep us all locked up as prisoners inside the cave.

They wanted us dead because they needed us out of the way in order to bring their ultimate plans for the world to fruition. Their goal was the wholesale slaughter of the United States. Once you come to understand the insidious extent of their plans, you'll begin to see all these modern events in a new light.

But trust me when I say it gets so much worse than that. Not everyone reading this book will be able to handle everything I will explain all in one dose. Just like how a starving person needs to be nursed back to health using simple, digestible liquids before they can handle solid food again, just like how eyes kept in darkness their whole life will blink and strain even under dim lights, not everyone will be able to process everything I will divulge here right away. We'll work up our tolerance as we go, but understand this: it's taken me years to process some of what I'm about to tell you. There were times I would be awake into the late hours of the night, and my body would be involuntarily shaking from what I was reading and researching. I'm sure I earned more than a few gray hairs digging into the kind of raw information I was seeing at the time, but that was several years ago now. I'll do my best to pace things out for my readers. If you'll allow me one more analogy, I'll play Virgil to your Dante, guiding you through the many circles of this nightmarish Hellscape, while doing my best to make sure the devils don't drag you down with them in the process.

Information asymmetry…

That is the fundamental imbalance you need to understand if we're to succeed in this endeavor.

See, information asymmetry is how they maintain their power. The ancient Greek word *gnosis*, meaning "knowledge," (and from which we derive the term "Gnostic," as in Gnostic mysteries) is most often used to connote *hidden* knowledge; things which are kept only for a *select few*. Why is this done? The answer is simple. When you know what others don't, you have a distinct advantage over them. You can maneuver and position yourself more effectively, always aligning yourself in the most advantageous way, while the hapless rubes scramble for cover below. An imbalance in knowledge allows you to exploit others weaknesses and failings. In short, information asymmetry grants the Cabal power over *others*. This has been the main advantage The Cabal has leveraged over these many centuries (and possibly even millennia—as we'll explore later).

I don't mean to sound like a killjoy, either. No, if there's one thing we Anons know, it's how to have fun and laugh. I fully intend to make this as entertaining and compelling for you, the reader, as possible. But I do want to impress upon you the importance of what I'm saying, precisely because I already know—thanks to Q—what kinds of challenges the world is going to be facing very soon, and how many will react to the events unfolding before their very eyes. I hope that in writing this, people will find comfort in these words, that they will bring solace and a degree of understanding to those who need it, and that it will help chart a path forward for all patriots.

And so, my fellow Americans—and indeed, all freedom-loving people of the world:

To shift the balance of power, things which have been hidden must now come to light. To accomplish that, we now have to capture some of that light and bring it down to our level, so all can see.

I was lucky enough to encounter someone who helped me find the way out of the cave a long time ago. And now, I've written this to help you find your way out if you would so desire such freedom for yourself.

Friends, we've been kept in the dark for far too long.

It's time to step out of the dark and into the light.

CHAPTER 2

"The President Needs Your Help"

—November 5, 2017 From Qdrop #96

Donald J. Trump ✓
@realDonaldTrump

Follow ⌄

Very little reporting about the GREAT GDP numbers announced yesterday (3.0 despite the big hurricane hits). Best consecutive Q's in years!

5:22 AM - 28 Oct 2017

Anonymous ID: BQ7V3bcW No.147012719 ☑ ▮   **1**
Oct 28 2017 15:44:28 (EST)

> Anonymous ID: gb953qGI No.147005381 ☑ ▮
> Oct 28 2017 14:33:50 (EST)
>
> >>146981635
> Hillary Clinton will be arrested between 7:45 AM - 8:30 AM EST on Monday - the morning on Oct 30, 2017.

>>147005381
HRC extradition already in motion effective yesterday with several countries in case of cross border run. Passport approved to be flagged effective 10/30 @ 12:01am. Expect massive riots organized in defiance and others fleeing the US to occur. US M's will conduct the operation while NG activated. Proof check: Locate a NG member and ask if activated for duty 10/30 across most major cities.

Even as I am sitting down to start writing this particular chapter, it's 10:43 p.m. Eastern, on May 25, 2018. Q's last drop was three days ago—almost four at this point—and it read:

Q !CbboFOtcZs ~~ID: fe402e~~ No.1509322 🗗 📑   1439
May 22 2018 16:29:23 (EST)

UNITY NOT DIVISION.
Last post was simply for IDEN_reconf.
http://www.foxnews.com/politics/2018/05/22/fbi-doj-to-brief-
lawmakers-on-handling-russia-probe-on-thursday.html 🗗 📑
Who is missing from the scheduled meeting?
[RR]
Who is Ed O'Callahan?
"Acting"
[Ed]
DECLAS_
Pain.
Enjoy the show.
Q

And we Anons are waiting... Waiting for Q to return to bring us more intel drops.

Waiting for Q to drop intel is akin to waiting for manna to fall from Heaven. And just like the Israelites in that story of old, we too, finally have some hope as we follow our leader into a brighter future—a future we can have, if only we will fight for it. The atmosphere is electric. The anticipation is almost overwhelming. There's a tangible sense among the dedicated Q-followers that something has finally shifted in America; more than most people currently realize, and that we will once again be truly free and truly prosperous.

But for right now, we still have a long way to go before that dream is realized.

We are the Anons, an army of "digital soldiers," all of equal rank and stature, who populate the message boards known collectively online as "the Chans." Actually, I might irritate some Anons by calling them message boards—which I only do for the sake of those who might have no prior exposure to such sites. The Chans are more properly labeled imageboards, and unlike most online forums that require users to register with a screen-name and an e-mail, imageboards allow anyone to post just about anything, anonymously—so long as the content is legal. And because posters are anonymous when speaking to each other, the users of these sites naturally refer to each other as Anons.

The Chans first started as mere textboards, like as the Japanese site Ayashii World, where users could only post text; no images. The general idea was copied across other communities at the time, but the format really came into its own when image posting was added to the likes of 2chan (a Japanese-speaking site), and subsequently, 4chan (an English-speaking clone). Today, there are many such Chans, and these sites are usually subdivided into separate "boards," organized by topic, and can get incredibly niche in their focus. So if you wanted to talk about TV and movies, you might go to 4chan.org/tv/. Or if you want to get ripped and learn how to work your way up to a five-hundred pound deadlift, you might go to 8ch.net/fit/. The boards themselves are often insular, unruly, and have their own distinct memetic culture that might seem inexplicable and impenetrable to outsiders, but frankly, that's the way Anons like it. "Normies get out" is the common refrain among Anons. You are not welcome here! And that may seem harsh, but in a world where identity isn't a factor, it has had a way of preserving a distinct culture; a culture so organic and engaging, that it often percolates up, across the web, onto other more mainstream sites where the masses could laugh at the jokes being cracked on the Chans as well, albeit weeks or months after the fact, and without ever actually realizing their true point of origin.

Beyond that, there's a level of coordination and expertise fostered on the boards rarely seen anywhere else online. Because you don't know who you're talking to, the only way to back up your words is by demonstrating your expertise in a way that others can understand. The Anonymity bit significantly reduces the influence of ego on the matter, as well. Either you contribute something significant, something of value to the conversation, or you're ignored. Depending on area of interest, this could be as simple as posting a collection of your favorite music albums from the last month, or as big as entire data dumps containing earth-shattering, never before seen information on a public figure. Such is the nature of the Chans.

But in case it isn't clear by now, the number one rule online is that you never, **ever** mess with the Chans. There's a reason it's been called "the internet hate machine" over the years. I don't care who you are, or how important you think you are; when you come to the boards, you are Anon. You could be the wealthiest person in the world, or the most famous, or you could be the front-runner for leader of the free world, supported by a vast network of media personalities and corrupt institutions. It does not matter. If you mess with the Chans, you will get wrecked. Case in point: the utter and gleeful demolition of Hillary Rodham Clinton's presidential prospects in 2016 (and, if this pans out the way I think it will) her inevitable execution following a military tribunal exposing her many murderous crimes to the world.

But I'm getting a bit ahead of myself in my attempt to give you the lay of the land, and you might not be ready to even entertain such a possibility as of right now. When it comes to the Q saga, even if you've never seen a Chan before in your life, there are a few boards you should be aware of, for these form the backdrop of our story. So keep in mind, these boards are:

/pol/ or Politically Incorrect

/cbts/ or Calm Before the Storm

/thestorm/

/qresearch/

/GreatAwakening/

/PatriotsFight/

and the most recent edition, a sort of 8chan training ground known as:

/PatriotsAwoken/

These are the boards across which the incredible drama of Q was staged. These would become the digital battlefields where White Hat would clash with Black Hat, where privileged insider would come to expose the perversions of the rich and powerful, and where Anon would go toe-to-toe with gloating, global elites. These were the gathering points for Anons across the nation and indeed, the world, where they could come and meet with that one Anon who somehow rose above the entire crowd and captured the attention of so many. We are, of course, talking about QAnon. No, to call this anything other than a battleground, and to understand what has transpired here as anything other than a revolution, is to completely misunderstand what happened across these sites.

And the most amazing thing about all this… is that most people in the world had no idea any of this was going on until after the fact.

(At least, not until a certain tipping point was reached, when Q hit critical mass and simply became too big to ignore.)

See, we had—and potentially still have—a major problem in America, and it's the simple fact that the average American voter is not well-informed—Not that it is entirely their fault. After all, we live in an age of information overload, and rely heavily on all sorts of authorities and information-filtering methods to arrive at some semblance of understanding the truth of our reality. We also expect these authorities to be (mostly) honest. Do you see the problem, though? This kind of system is ripe for abuse and manipulation. Despite Jefferson's vehement warnings about the importance of having a well-informed citizenry, the average American has been, for at least the last half-century, a plaything for the "Mockingbird Media" and the Cabal. I'm even going to make the somewhat contentious statement that the common man is more easily manipulated through modern-day propaganda than at any other time in history. And that's not necessarily because we've become less intelligent, but it's because propaganda didn't stop evolving with the fall of Nazi Germany or Soviet Russia and their distinct war posters and propaganda films. No, new methods and avenues for propagandizing the people were created, discovered, and exploited. Mouthpieces were selected from the top of their classes at Langley and groomed for a life in front of the public eye. Stories were coordinated via Central Intelligence and distributed across clandestine electronic distribution systems every day at 4 a.m. Entire systems of narrative control were perfected by rogue intelligence agencies over decades, and the average citizen remained blissfully unaware as they went about their own business and concerns. Edward Bernays could have never anticipated such a heinous and insidious system, not even in his worst nightmares.

Understand, I'm not just speaking in generalizations here. Many of my longtime readers who have followed my site for the past year or more will know *exactly* what I'm talking about when I mention these things, but the casual reader just picking up this book for the first time may have no idea that, for instance, Anderson Cooper (of CNN fame) spent considerable time at Langley and is, in fact, actually a bloodline Vanderbilt—heir to a vast fortune from one of the wealthiest families in the world. He or she might also not realize that the father of MSNBC personality, Mika Brzezinski, is none other than Zbigniew Brzezinski, Jimmy Carter's national security adviser. Zbigniew helped the CIA and ISI coordinate together on a secret program in the 80s called SOVMAT, which sought to buy AK-47s from Eastern Europe and import them into Pakistan and Afghanistan with the help of a particular Pakistani arms dealer—last name: Siddiqui.

But wait, it gets better.

That arms dealer? He was the father of Sohale Siddiqui who was... are you ready for it? Barack Obama's college roommate (and yes, you can see many photos online of them together, including one where many Anons now believe a turtleneck was drawn on Obama's chest in what looks like sharpie marker, in order to cover up whatever he was wearing (or perhaps, what he wasn't wearing) underneath:

And so, this future president and the son (who just so happened to be his roommate) of a Pakistani arms dealer (who was working with the CIA and Brzezinski at the time), visited Karachi, Pakistan together in 1981. It's no small coincidence then, that Karachi was also where the AK-47 hit the Pakistani markets for the first time, spreading throughout the Middle East as a result. That's right, all those images of jihadi terrorists wielding AKs? Those didn't exist before Obama and his friends arrived on the scene. And those are just the facts that are available, out in the open, for public consumption. We're not even in any kind of real "conspiracy" territory yet. What's actually *more* shocking in this particular case is that most Americans simply don't know about this—which goes to demonstrate the point I was trying to make earlier: we're intentionally kept in the dark by a media that has a vested interest in perpetuating the power structure of the Cabal.

It should surprise no one that former CIA Director, closeted Wahhabi Muslim, and walking human canker sore, John Brennan, was also reportedly on the scene around that same time. And I realize I'm repeating myself yet again, but I want to get this through to people: Q has even told us that at some point in the near future there will be a photo released of Barack Hussein Obama dressed in full Muslim garb, wielding an AK-47.

"Big deal," you might be thinking. "He's holding a gun. So what?"

Except, Q told us it's not so much what he's holding; it's *who* he's aiming the gun at. And he gave us three words to consider when thinking about the target:

"Red, White, and Blue."

Though we do not yet (as of this writing) have the photo in our possession, there has been much speculation that this photo shows former president Obama killing an American citizen during this time, perhaps as a demonstration of the weapon's "effectiveness." We will only know for sure once that photo—possibly from a series of photos—is released to the general public. And of course, as I mentioned earlier, this will be complimented by the release of the HRC video. But already, the Mockingbird Media has been at work, prepping people's minds to doubt the veracity of these impending releases by implanting seeds of doubt when and where they would be beneficial to the Cabal. Don't believe me? Take a look at how many articles have been published on "Deepfakes" over the past year and a half. Deepfakes, for those unaware, are essentially "Photoshopped" videos, wherein a computer analyzes the face of someone, say, Barack Obama, and overlays Obama's face over an actor's face in a photorealistic manner. The end result would be a video looking like "Obama" is saying or doing something he never actually said or did. It's freaky, but imperfect tech right now—and there are often tell-tale signs which accompany deepfaked videos (all manner of glitches and imperfections). The point is, the mainstream media (MSM) has been leveraged to prepare people's minds to repeat the false narrative that the HRC video is actually just deepfake propaganda, when in reality, it's very real and very devastating to the Cabal.

As I alluded to earlier, this kind of narrative is manufactured every single morning at 4 a.m. by intelligence agencies like the CIA, and distributed to their media partners as an extension of an old CIA project called Operation Mockingbird. Most recently, the CIA was using a system called SecureDrop (securedrop.org), a program ostensibly designed to allow journalists and whistleblowers to communicate through secure, encrypted channels, in order to distribute and coordinate their messaging to nearly every single media outlet in America, every single day. (The side-benefit of using this program was that it allowed the CIA to scoop up information about potential whistleblowers under the guise of helping them connect with the press, and effectively silence them before they could make so much as a peep, if they really needed to.)

It's also why, occasionally, you'll notice patterns like those on the following page:

To be clear, I'm not suggesting all of these outlets are Cabal affiliates. At a certain point, the narrative they establish takes root and self-perpetuates among "journalistic" types, so there's a bit of a feedback loop being created, to be sure. And while the above may seem like a rather innocuous example—after all, that's just *Star Wars* we're talking about here—what happens when you leverage that kind of coordinated media assault against, say:

A presidential candidate?

What about a sitting president?

What about a "conspiracy theory," like QAnon?

…

See the problem?

Messaging like this is, of course, at its most effective when the populace doesn't even realize it's happening. Indeed, the term "propaganda" is almost anachronistic these days. You say it, and it conjures images of Hitler screaming from a podium, or the obvious manipulation of old film reels from the USSR. It's one thing to plaster a stylized poster of an idealized soldier in the public square in order to stir up nationalistic feelings among the people, and maybe make their boys sign up to go die in a god-forsaken trench in some foreign land. (Why, it's almost quaint compared to what's going on today!) It's another thing entirely when propaganda is being spread through almost every single mainstream media outlet in existence, at the behest of puppet-masters operating from within the shadows of the intelligence community, unbeknownst to the general public.

This kind of invisible power allows them to present opinions, but more often outright lies, as clear and obvious truths. Each new article, each new story reinforces the narrative someone else chose for us. In fact, Q has disclosed the internal term used for the people subjected to this system: "flies." Specifically, "feeders."[1] I speculate on the true nature of what this means[2] on my site, but the short of it is, "What do flies eat?" The answer is, excrement, manure, disgusting filth. If you're a liar feeding someone else lies, and you *know* you're feeding them lies, you're not giving them good, nutritious mental food. You're feeding them a four-letter word that begins with S, ends with T, and rhymes with "grit," all the while laughing at them as they chow down. This should begin to show you the level of disdain these "programmers" have for the general population. This is why it shouldn't surprise you to learn that many of the "most trusted names in journalism" are, themselves, CIA operatives. Hopefully, by the time most read this, these career charlatans will have been locked up for a very long time.

The second big problem we have in America is that most individuals will read a sentence about the average American voter being information-deficient and exclude themselves from that imagined group. They imagine all the *other* stupid people they know, and mentally herd them all into a big corral with all the other mouthdrooly types where they can dress them up in little dunce caps and laugh on cue at the hypnotic suggestions of the likes of Stephen Colbert and John Oliver ("activists," in Cabal-speak) as they all vote for the opposition, reassured in the intellectual superiority of their well-informed opinions because… well… they saw the "news" that day! They did their due-diligence as citizens, and it's just ridiculous to think any other way, really! Plus, that Buzzfeed article they just read told them Q was a "crazy conspiracy," complete with *Matrix*-inspired lampoon segments. And wouldn't you know it! The same message was spread through the papers, the blogs and social media, too!

Well, I hate to break it to you, but if you're awakening to the reality of QAnon after, let's say November 2018 (and you were born well before that date), you need to let yourself into that corral and crown yourself with one of your own dunce caps, so that you can mewl and bray with all the other easily-manipulated jackasses.

Now, normally it's very bad form to insult your reader, especially right in the beginning of your book, but I do so for a very important reason: to highlight by way of contrast how extraordinarily informed and utterly brilliant the Research Anons are when compared to the average citizen, and to show you how badly this Cabal has lied to you, for so long. Anons are so far beyond the average, it's sort of a running joke that many actually have a hard time functioning in normal society; among the "normies," they might say—with more than just a hint of disdain in their voices. Anons are so high functioning, and often so marginalized, it's common to hear that they have their own special form of autism, which they affectionately refer to as "Weaponized Autism," compelling them to research, dig, and deep-dive all day long, week after week, month after month. It's this information-seeking behavior, and ability to pick up on patterns most others would miss, that sets Anons apart from the pack.

---

1   Qdrop #354
2   https://www.neonrevolt.com/2018/07/31/the-sprawling-right-wing-conspiracy-theory-known-as-qanon-time-to-bring-the-fuzz-newq-greatawakening-whopaysavenatti/

If you were to plot the IQ of Anons along a bell-curve, I expect you would find that most of Q's earliest researchers and supporters fall into and well above the "gifted" range. Which means we're talking about a critical mass of genius-level IQs here, all congregating in the same space and working together 24 hours a day to help preserve the integrity of the Republic and expose the systemic evil that has infected out land. Frankly, it's a crime that society has marginalized so many, in so many subtle and insidious ways over the years.

But again, much of this was by design—as we'll explore later.

The Chans then, became a place where these supercharged intellects would ricochet off each other at fiber-optic speed. You can't gaslight Anons. They see right through the lies and manipulation with an unwavering gaze. As one Anon would put it:

▶ Anonymous 02/28/19 (Thu) 05:00:22 ID: a5ae60 **(1)** No.5431403 >>5431412 >>5431423
>>5431520 >>5431555 >>5431677 >>5431793

> Those of you who are 'The Real Deal'; not larpers, not shills, not shit-posters or disruptors or fame-fags:
> YOU are an: ANOMALY in "THEIR MATRIX".
> You stand out like 'NEO'.
> The 'Wizards' & 'Warlocks' of the good guys and "The Controllers" of this 'Ancient Cabal' - the bad guys we're fighting - "Noticed" you. You & this board are anomalous in "Their World".
> "Their World" operates on a different "Plane" of consciousness. Normies don't see "IT" so they blend-in.
> You don't blend-in in that way.
> You were like Neo. You always knew something was a little bit off but you couldn't quite put your finger on it.
> Soon you wondered why others couldn't see "IT".
> You are like "Pattern Recognition Software". You couldn't help but see "IT". The inconsistencies, the patterns, the anomalies = So you started to put together your own "MAP" in your head.
> And so:
> * You came here as an 'OUTLET'.
> * You came here to exercise your mental muscle that felt atrophied out there in "The Meat-Space" of the world.
> * You came here to commiserate with like minded "NEOs" who couldn't shake that nagging uneasiness; that knowing things just aren't quite right brings.
> Yes, you built this space. And = "It Got Noticed".
> You became: "The Fly In The Ointment" "The Burr Under The Saddle" "The Gnat Buzzing Around The Ears of "THEM" = The Mosquito Bite On > The Matrix of 'The Controllers'.
> At the same time = The GOOD GUYS were waiting for you (like Morpheus was waiting for Neo); looking, scanning, collating data. Waiting for the right time & place.
> The "Controllers" were getting close to 'The Point of No return' and "You" - The Anons - had reached "Critical Mass".
> What we've experienced is a "Convergence" of an Inevitable "Clash of The Titans", if you will.
> We were meant for such a time as this. So; Chins Up, Chests Out, backs straight, Lean Back & Set'em-In and SOLDIER-ON ANON.
> (Shit-Posters & Shills = Disregard & Get Bent - LOSER)
> GODSPEED
> WWG1WGA

And on top of this, their irrepressible sense of redpilled humor makes Anons the most dominant force in American politics today. Indeed, one of the lessons still not understood by the mainstream is that the rapid deployment of humor across the internet might just be one of the single most effective political weapons available to date. Why? Because in order to be funny—truly funny, you have to be honest, and you simply can't be as funny when you're working within the constraints of a manufactured paradigm. It's one of the reasons why Comedy Central's political shows and SNL have simply stopped being funny over time—they've stopped speaking any shred of truth, and started toeing a political line, complete with a set of inviolable, ideological strictures across which they must never transgress.

In essence, they had to start lying at the behest of their corporate masters to protect an entrenched system of cultural hegemony and elite criminality (as we'll soon see). Truly funny sketches became the exception, and no longer the rule. You'd never see the likes of Eddie Murphy in Whiteface ever again, because to speak such truths was now anathema, after the advent of the Obama administration and the sudden imposition of SJW ideology and Cultural Marxism across all forms of media. Steve Martin's *King Tut* sketch would soon become the subject of scathing academic critique, and deemed a "culturally insensitive" hallmark of "white, imperial, colonialist attitudes," and thus, unfit for popular consumption, instead of the irreverent, goofy, joyous expression it truly was.

Because, after all, the ancient Egyptians weren't around anymore. *Someone* had to hold aloft the banner of offense on their behalf! Right?

Anons simply don't care about any of that, and they don't care who they'll offend in the process. In fact, they carry a degree of disdain for the nonsensical society that long ago rejected them for not seeing things like, you know, a "normal person" should. But this disdain inevitably led to a profound sense of freedom—freedom which could only, truly be exercised on sites which valued freedom of expression and all that encompasses; freedom to laugh, to provoke, even to engage in "wrongthink." And memes, glorious memes, naturally emerged from the multitude of conversations that were occurring every single day across the boards, effervescing like bubbles from the finest champagne. These memes could be distributed across all platforms with striking rapidity, and change the national narrative in the course of, not days and weeks, but minutes and seconds. The institutional masters were not ready to respond to this "new and emerging threat" in 2016, and repeatedly failed to respond in any effective or meaningful way to what had seemingly manifested out of the ether, onto the information battlefield. In short, as the site grew, so too its influence, and in 2016, it took center stage, whether most people realized it or not.

A bit of history is key to understanding how this happened. You see, there had been a dramatic shift in the nature of the Chans since their inception in the early aughts, as the refuge of pranksters and weebs alike, into a political and media force with which to be reckoned. It was almost like the Anons all simultaneously came into their own. Perhaps this was just a reflection of the once young user base growing older, but (at least on some boards) the Chans slowly grew into something more... serious. More organized. The edgy fifteen-year-old that once LARPed on the site in 2005 had grown into an adult by 2008 (and perhaps even a functioning member of society by 2016)! Having come "of age" during the Obama years, and due to the lack of censorship, anti-Obama discussion was allowed to flourish on the Chans like nowhere else, at a time when censorship was becoming more entrenched, both in the comments sections on mainstream websites, and on more "normie-friendly" platforms like Twitter and Reddit. Weaponized autists dug on all manner of subjects, and Obama himself became something of a shibboleth for the Cultural Marxism that had seemingly infected the US during his tenure in office, despite his incessant proclamations that he was a great unifier. This was the one place online where people could be truly honest about the damage the Obama years had inflicted on the country, sowing the seeds of division, poverty, and corruption across the land.

And like I said before, you can't gaslight Anons, either. (And believe me, the Cabal tried. More on that in Chapter Nine.) No amount of media cheerleading, ideological delusion, or posting about how great it was that America had "finally elected a black president" would sway them. Anons come from all walks of life, but the growing cynicism was readily apparent to all across the site. Many were enraged at the societal erosion they felt occurring around them, the normalization of degenerate behavior that, just a mere decade ago would have been seen as outrageously obscene. They couldn't ignore the increasing tensions around the world, the seemingly endless economic catastrophes that kept unfolding, and ultimately, the overwhelming sense of powerlessness about it all—which led to many simply coming online seeking out somewhere to vent. (What they did not know at that time was that they were being deliberately targeted by a Deep State which had nothing but loathing for their very existence, and destruction planned for their future.) What had once been largely frivolous and irrelevant, had now become a cynical titan. The shift in this sentiment was captured, perhaps most poignantly, in this post by an Anon from several years back:

[-] 220px-William_F_Buckley_Jr_1985.jpg (17 KB, 220x326) google iqdb

⊙⊙ ☐ Anonymous 1 hour ago No.13626482 [Reply] [▼]

I've suddenly had quite a sad realization, /pol/.

4chan, and this board in general, has always tried to be controversial, to oppose social norms, to push the limits, to be edgy. It has always challenged mainstream notions in politics. Now, this dark and lowly part of the internet has come to support family, God, chivalry, tradition, and pride in one's heritage.

What a sad and dark world we live in where moral degeneracy is so rampant that supporting these things is actually now edgy and controversial.

And out this milieu of rage, cynicism, disillusion, and memes was born the Politically Incorrect board.

Let's get something straight right from the get-go. /pol/ is perhaps the single most influential page online that most people have never heard of. Some in the media tried to ring the alarm bells when they first stumbled upon it, shocked and appalled by what they saw there; politically incorrect truths piercing the bubbles they had so carefully constructed for themselves from amongst the relative safety of like-minded "blue check marks" on Twitter, and in carefully insulated editorial rooms. They called the board a haven for the Far Right, white supremacists, and literal Nazis. And while those elements did exist (due to it being a politically-oriented, free-speech-based board, meaning literally anyone could post pretty much anything), in truth, that was mostly just an expression of the characteristic "edginess" of the user base, mostly employed to scare away the normies. To this day, you'll often find posts with images of the most violent gore, posted to keep people out. It's not nice, to be sure, but it's certainly effective.

But you see, /pol/ was where the "redpill" was born. It was *the* place where you would come to be confronted, daily, with truths most people didn't want to acknowledge, facts most would rather leave unsaid. If you want to understand the essence of /pol/, you can do no better than these two images, each of which captures the renegade spirit of the board, in their own way:

▶ Anonymous 07/03/15 (Fri) 01:00:33 ID: 99cb3b No.2506937
File (hide): 1435885233864.jpg (318.67 KB, 400x395, 80:79, Newly Redpilled.jpg)

>>2506641

The true terror of browsing /pol/ for any length of time is not discovering the "evil within", but coming to realize the true nature of the "evil without", and that nearly everything society has told you about the world and about history is either a complete fabrication or a half-truth spun in such a way to force you to think in a manner that benefits a very particular group of people.

Imagine being blind for your entire life. Imagine listening to people with functioning vision about how the world works, describing what things look like, and so on. Without any frame of reference, you would have little choice but to believe them.

Now imagine suddenly gaining the ability to see, and realizing not only that many of the people around you aren't even human, but that those who most resemble you are *also* blind, and everything they have been telling you has merely been the parroting of things the putrid monsters overseeing them have whispered in their ears. You look out at the world that you were told was full of beauty, and find only death, decay, and madness.

Welcome to /pol/, enjoy your stay.

▶ Anonymous 10/22/15 (Thu) 16:33:25 ID: 90b54a No.3705372 >>3705461 >>3705462
File (hide): 1445546006268.jpg (373.69 KB, 900x900, 1:1, 1436467642948.jpg)

>>3700810
Be careful.

You'll end up like me and so many others here, as the evidence piles up in front of you.

I was a shitposter when I first came to /pol/ for some "epic Nazi trolling" and within a year found I agreed with about half of what was discussed.
By the end of the second year I was indistinguishable from the rest.
The terrible truth of /pol/ is that it's as liberating as it is horrific.

You lie to yourself less, but you begin refusing to accept the lies from others, even well meaning ones.
Your personal relationships with the few people you can stomach to be around will suffer and degrade under the stress of the constant need to supress your power level.

In the truth you'll be sickened at the world, yet constantly drawn to seeking this same truth.

It's a counter-hugbox.

/pol/ is the hurt-box.

Instead of locking out reality in your hugbox like a progressive, you'll force yourself into this hurt-box on a regular basis.

/pol/ is a self inflicted spiritual and intellectual masochism as the price of placing truth above all else.

You could have prevented this.

Grim, huh? And yet, hundreds of thousands of people frequented the board on a regular basis. Why? It's because it became one of the last places online where people could express themselves; the wrongthink they weren't allowed to speak anywhere else online, or in daily life. It was an addicting and enthralling freedom that few enjoyed. (And obviously, writing this, here, is to give you a general feel for the "setting" of our story. It's not to be read as an endorsement of the millions of different posts made by /pol/lacks—nor could I be rightly expected to endorse every single post made on a site with millions of users, posting over the course of several years. We're just getting a feel for the landscape, here.)

And yes, once again, as the page grew, so too, its influence. It was only a matter of time before all this energy percolated out and affected the real world. Pretty soon, /pol/lacks started asking themselves a very important question:

Can you meme a president into office?

4chan pranks in 2006

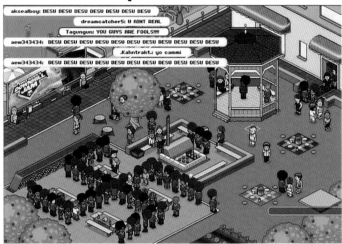

4chan pranks in 2016

4chan—often referred to as the seedy underbelly of the internet by hand-wringing lefty-types, has long been home to a certain renegade prankster spirit. There is, in fact, quite a legacy when it comes to 4chan pranksterhood. It's almost like a fraternity in that sense, with the newer "classes" doing their best to outdo the classes that came before them. Whether it was simply driving by bookstores late at night with bullhorns to announce to legions of camped-out Harry Potter devotees that Dumbledore dies on page 596, sending "musician" Pitbull to a remote Walmart in Alaska for a meet and greet (where very few fans could ever show up), convincing legions of Apple fanboys that their new iPhones were suddenly made waterproof upon upgrading their phones to iOS 7, or donning digital Afros and telling the virtual denizens of Habbo Hotel (an online game) that the pool was closed "due to aids" while arranging themselves in a swastika formation, the sometimes vicious, often outrageous, but always hilarious prankster spirit still runs rampant across the Chans, and serves as a sort of shared point of reference/reverence for the storied culture there.

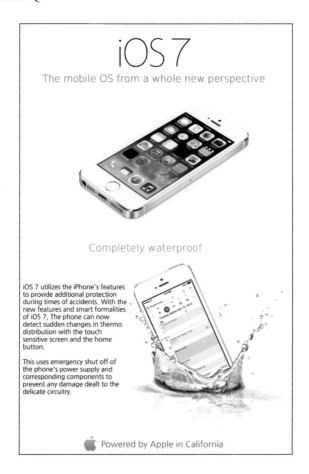

iOS 7

The mobile OS from a whole new perspective

Completely waterproof

iOS 7 utilizes the iPhone's features to provide additional protection during times of accidents. With the new features and smart formalities of iOS 7, The phone can now detect sudden changes in thermo distribution with the touch sensitive screen and the home button.

This uses emergency shut off of the phone's power supply and corresponding components to prevent any damage dealt to the delicate circuitry.

 Powered by Apple in California

And nowhere was this seen more clearly than with Donald Trump's announcement that he was running for president of the United States. When he came down that staircase in Trump Tower in 2015, /pol/ lost their collective minds. Here was their man! Here was /pol/ incarnate! "How could one man's power level be so high?!" they would eventually ask themselves—a reference to the Japanese anime series *Dragonball Z*, where villains suddenly realize that the hero who they were heretofore bullying amasses a "power level" that greatly exceeds their own—instantly turning the tables and suddenly making him the greatest threat they had ever faced. Smart as a whip, often funny, self-made, with actual plans for the average American, and not beholden to any political interests—/pol/ actually made the effort to *listen* to what Trump was saying, instead of simply dismissing him out of hand as a bumbling orange buffoon, as the media elites immediately tried to paint him.

(And just as an aside: one point that particularly irked me during all this was the oft-repeated refrain that "Trump declared bankruptcy half-a-dozen times! He's a failed businessman!" by those who know nothing of business. Bankruptcy doesn't just mean you're broke and closing up shop due to ineptitude and mismanagement. It's a legal maneuver, and often a very smart one in certain scenarios. And it happened to Trump six times… out of some six-hundred businesses, total. We're talking about a one percent failure-rate. That's almost unheard of. That's like having an RBI of a thousand. The only thing criticisms like this did was clarify how ignorant certain factions of the Left were.)

Anons immediately recognized in Trump a kind of X-factor; something that distinguished him from the rest of the offerings from *both* parties. For too long, Republicans kowtowed to Democratic elites. They didn't stand for anything real. They couldn't get real Conservative legislation passed. They couldn't stop damaging legislation from passing. They weren't a real contrast to the Democrats. They were just Democrats who lagged behind the rabid "progressives" in the Democratic party by some ten to fifteen years, depending on the issue. It was the "Uniparty" in every sense of the word. Your vote didn't matter, because you had the likes of John McCain opposing universal healthcare in 2008, and then voting for Obamacare just a few short years later. It was the Overton window in action, with one front advancing, and the other lagging—but everything still headed in the same direction; straight to the Left and off a cliff. There were no real distinctions between the choices being presented to us. It was just a question of how fast we were approaching our predetermined end.

But beyond all that, the most important thing /pol/lacks recognized in Trump was his desire and ability to finally hit back, and without shame. Make no mistake, there had been nothing /pol/ had wanted to do more for the past sixteen years. Perhaps for the first time in the site's history, their targets couldn't have been more deserving of every strike, every blow, every debilitating hit (as we'll truly see later in this book). The best part? No one in Washington or the Fourth Estate was ready for the beating they were about to take.

And so, /pol/ formulated the greatest "prank" of all time—and soon began to realize… this was anything but a joke. Begun, the information war had; and those who had traditionally enjoyed a monopoly over power and influence suddenly found all their typical weapons useless and ineffective in front of the absolute onslaught they faced online. Trump memes *FLOODED* the internet. Everywhere you turned, be it Facebook, Twitter, Tumblr, Snapchat, whatever; it didn't matter. It was inescapable. /Pol/lacks were like a dreaded cyborg army, constantly bombarding their enemies with counter-messaging, a take-no-prisoners approach to citizen journalism, who were dead set on accomplishing their singular goal; memeing a man into the highest office of power in the land.

Trump recognized this trend and capitalized on it almost immediately. His zingers became exploitable meme fodder. Having been transmogrified into endless Pepe permutations, Trump would do things like mimicking different Pepe poses; a hand on the chin, for instance, subtly signaling to his supporters that, yes, he was acknowledging and appreciative of their support. Why, he would even start retweeting the memes himself, while out on the campaign trail:

"@codyave: @drudgereport @BreitbartNews @Writeintrump "You Can't Stump the Trump" youtube.com/watch?v=MKH6PA… "

And as they say, the crowd went wild! To say his campaign was internet savvy is a vast understatement (and one which you will come to understand better by the end of this book). The "problem" of memes got so bad for the Left, they even got the ADL to suddenly classify Pepe the cartoon frog as a "white supremacist hate symbol," despite it being a hallmark of internet memery of all sorts for almost a decade prior. To bolster this claim, CNN even **manufactured** a brand new Pepe of their own; this time in a KKK imperial wizard's hood—a meme that had *never* been seen anywhere before on the boards.

Let me be *exceedingly* clear on this point. This meme *did not exist* before the CNN broadcast. CNN created this one themselves, as propaganda. This was not created by Anons, and Anons immediately recognized this fact. No reverse image search could find this image anywhere online before that report aired. But that didn't matter to CNN. Their goal was to spread Fake News, even if it meant slandering a group of anonymous internet users online. They knew they could get away with it, too. After all, who was going to sue them? Their audience wouldn't know the difference, either, so as far as they were concerned: mission accomplished. They get to call all Trump supporters racist Nazi megabigots, and everyone watching repeats in sync, "Orange Man Bad!" But note; here is one of the Legacy Media's first attempts at responding to the *threat* memes presented to the established order, by attempting to manufacture memes of their own. That was how important this particular battlefront had become in 2016.

But what really put /pol/ in a league of their own was that their target for memetic derision was so infinitely exploitable, herself. Draped in pantsuits reminiscent of Bond villains and Third World dictators, collapsing on more than one occasion due to her own ill health, and hawking up mucous plugs from the depths of her bronchi before expelling the little green blobs into her drinking glass hoping no one would notice despite being in front of rolling cameras and a stadium full of onlookers, Hillary Clinton was perfect meme fodder. There was one debate where flies kept landing on Hillary's face, who was seemingly unaware of their presence at all, making the whole moment that much more odd, searing it into people's memory. Of course, Anons would almost immediately Photoshop an animated GIF of *hundreds* of flies crawling across her laughing face, creating one of the most effective memes of the season. Hillary Clinton's every wrong move was capitalized upon by a volunteer army of enterprising (and hilarious) Anons, and they had no intention of letting up any time soon. They were going to laugh right on up to election day, and no one could tell them to stop. Despite poll after poll after poll repeatedly telling us that HRC had the election in the bag, that there was no way Trump could win, she still seemed so very *desperate*. Despite the repeated claims that her victory was assured, she now seemed to be facing death by a thousand memetic paper cuts.

Nowhere was this disparity between the old guard and Anons better highlighted than in the speech Hillary Clinton gave on September 9, 2016, where she said:

> You know, to just be grossly generalistic, you could put half of Trump's supporters into what I call the basket of deplorables. Right? The racist, sexist, homophobic, xenophobic, Islamophobic—you name it. And unfortunately there are people like that. And he has lifted them up.

It was over at that point. You couldn't have made a more bumbling error if you tried. The label of "deplorable" just reeked of detached elitism that had already made her so unpopular with so many. "Deplorable" soon became a war cry; a label the silent majority could wear with pride and rally around. It didn't help her case that a renegade Trump supporter even yelled "PEPE!" (again, another reference to Pepe the frog) during that very moment in her speech, hilariously undercutting her intended point for anyone paying attention. Once again, the Anons had managed to turn every weapon she thought she had against her. "Deplorable" itself had become the next big meme.

The flailing continued through the election cycle on Hillary's part, but this next episode was so cringe-inducing, it didn't register quite as much with the general population.

I'm talking, of course, about the "Hillary Clinton: Meme Queen 2016" video.

This video is important to note because if you watch it, you won't be laughing at any point. There's something so artificial, so manufactured about it, it ends up just being a stale mishmash of cultural references taken completely out of context, leveraged for blatant propaganda purposes. It actually had the *opposite* effect of what a good meme has; it completely sucked any remaining remnants of humor out of the room, effectively killing a whole bunch of the memes it was referencing in the process. (So I guess we can now add "dat boi" and "nyan cat" to Hillary's Arkancide tally, too.)

Go and watch the ad if you've never seen it before, because if you look hard enough, you can juuuust see the frenzied strategy meetings they had, held in the highest halls of power by people who were desperately attempting to understand and counteract what was happening to them. CNN had tried its own tactics and failed. Hillary's speeches had back-fired. The debates were a train wreck. And now it was apparent to all in the inner circle that Hillary's campaign was bleeding out in real time, thanks to the daily gutting it was receiving from Anons. The best "bandage" they could scramble to come up with was, "Well, let's just use memes ourselves! That's easy, right?" And what is a meme to an outsider but a sort of shared point of cultural reference? That's all it is, right? Like a joke?

Wrong.

Memes, while they are shared points of reference, emerge organically from within a com-munity, and as an expression of that community's values, which then reverberates and ricochets across nodes (read: people, users) in a network. There have been actual government-funded studies documenting the phenomenon, and humor always helps increase the velocity of a meme across a network, too. So when you try to fake that—when you don't come from within that network—you're instantly seen as artificial, stale, and dishonest. Hillary's ad had a "Hello, Fellow Kids" vibe, that not even the most staunch Clinton supporter could deny. It was also made all the more eerie by using a body double, granting it a sort of disturbing, uncanny weirdness—and not the kind that people like to subject themselves to, online.

What's more, without that prerequisite honesty or those communal bearings, the mak-ers of that video could never even hope to approach anything resembling humor. Without humor, you can't achieve that "stickiness" that transforms a mere image into a meme. If peo-ple aren't laughing (even in secret), they won't go out of the way to share that meme. They cringe inside, disregard, and move on.

Come to think of it, that's perhaps the most powerful thing about the best memes; they allow people little moments of freedom in a world in which, especially of late, their thoughts and ideas are increasingly policed by ideologically-driven authoritarians, conform-ists, and self-appointed gatekeepers who employ all manner of shaming tactics to ensure conformity. Imagine living life as a Social Justice Warrior for just a moment (which is really just a post-industrial, nihilistic, materialistic version of Puritanism minus the work ethic). You have all these ideological strictures in place, holding you back, policing your thoughts and your words every waking moment. Then, one day, you see (for instance) a meme about Hillary falling down the stairs and bursting her colostomy bag before throwing a tantrum on the floor, and you suddenly let out a GUFFAW of laughter, even though you know you're not *supposed* to. The best humor is like a little pressure release valve because it's honest, and I don't think I can overstate this; it's those rare moments of honesty that people *crave*. It's like a little explosion that allows people to momentarily experience a burst of freedom. Is it any wonder, then, that memes are so downright addictive? Millions of these moments happened every day during the 2016 election, causing people to chuckle and then press that share but-ton—even if it was just on some sockpuppet account they maintained so their immediate circle of friends wouldn't know that, secretly…they actually kind of liked Trump.

There's a reason why institutions like Facebook and Twitter are cracking down on "al-ternative influence networks" and memes (even in the face of growing governmental reg-ulation). As of this writing, Twitter has just suspended actor James Woods for posting a meme, justifying it under the guise that his meme may influence an election. Article 13 has just passed the preliminary stages of approval in that Globalist haven, the EU Parliament, which would effectively *ban* memes (under the guise of protecting intellectual property and copyright law, naturally). Facebook, in particular, has just developed a particularly dystopian AI, complete with "Machine Learning," (a pop-tech buzzword invoked more to scare people than to actually demonstrate its capabilities) in order to automatically censor "problematic" memes and content. How well it will work remains to be seen.

But don't you see the problem? The only tactic these tech oligarchs have to currently answer the "threat" of memes (because, in a Leftist Utopia, truth is a threat to the established hierarchy) is to engage in active censorship (and hope your user base doesn't get angry enough to notice and leave the platform entirely, taking their valuable user data with them). The problem with the current level of censorship is that it has a bottleneck; a human bottleneck. When something is tagged as "offensive" on a site like Facebook, it goes under review. More specifically, it goes in the review queue of some wage-slave, who has been hired to spend their every unenviable waking moment combing through content that offended someone, somewhere on planet earth, at some time. That wage-slave then has to make a decision as to whether or not a certain piece of media is actually breaking any guidelines, and then choose to censor, or not censor that content before returning to the queue, and repeating the process all over again.

That process proved too slow and too expensive for our tech oligarchs. No, Nancy Pelosi hauled her boys, Mark Zuckerberg (of Facebook) and Jack Dorsey (of Twitter), into a meeting to make sure they knew that this simply would not fly. And so, in response, the solution was to try what Silicon Valley "geniuses" always try, and automate. The 2018 midterms were at stake, after all, and Leftists couldn't afford a repeat of the defeat they experienced in 2016. What followed was mass bannings and censorship of legitimate content like we've never seen before, forcing more users out into free-speech friendly sites like Gab and Mastodon.

But there are other ways around this; there are always ways around this. And make no mistake, Anons would be the ones to find and exploit them.

Some might recall that Google tried to do something similar a while back with offensive words. You may remember that, in response, Anons decided to use the names of tech companies in place of slurs. Now, I won't repeat those slurs here (because I love everyone, regardless of their background, and have no desire to engage in any kind of racial talk). But you have to admit, there's a certain kind of genius in making something like "Google" or "Yahoo" an analog for an explicit term to get around the robots. Their intended audience would still get the meaning, and Google was left with no real recourse. It reminds me of individuals writing in secret coded terms to get past censors and secret police in former Soviet bloc countries. It's the same kind of strategy.

But despite all this, in 2016, the unthinkable happened.

Anons actually succeeded in their goal.

Election night came, and Anons would see their man memed into the office of the Presidency—much to the utter shock and dismay of just about every single talking head that night. Those who had laughed at every juncture at "candidate" Trump, were suddenly no longer laughing at President-Elect Trump. The vote tallies would be pushed back, later and later into the night, with no one wanting to call what was now obvious to all. By 2:00 a.m., Hillary couldn't even drag herself out to concede to her tearful, mourning fans. Instead, she sent out her campaign manager, John Podesta, to tell everyone to head home, and that they'd figure things out the next day. Rumors were flying that Hillary had lashed out at Bill and campaign staffers, behind-the-scenes, and gotten more and more drunk as the election numbers rolled in. Watching from my home, glued to my TV screen with a laptop at my fingertips, I'd never seen anything like that before (and I don't think I ever will again). Despite all the opposition, all the negative polls, the constant barrage of press, Trump had pulled off the surprise victory of the century.

Anons couldn't have been more jubilant. For days, the celebrations threads carried on. /Pol/ had just pulled off the "prank" to end all pranks; something that could (almost) certainly never be topped. /Pol/lacks had claimed the ultimate victory. They would "bathe" in the tears of their fallen foes. Memes depicted a naked, feces-smeared Hillary Clinton (in all her shriveled glory) throwing a tantrum on the floor of a padded cell, pulling out her own hair and screaming about how it was "her turn" as the face of a laughing (now president) Trump watched over the whole scene from outside the sanatorium's viewing window. Memes of Hillary having breakdowns and raging were the currency of the day:

But Anons would not stop there, no! The salt must flow, and they were having entirely too much fun. The zenith; truly, the ultimate form of this remarkable, innovative, creative, ephemeral, spontaneous collective would manifest itself while Anons were still celebrating their victory. Convinced they could accomplish very nearly anything now, Anons were hungry and looking for their next target. Unsurprisingly, Trump's election had sparked a series of protests and the typical, Soros-funded Leftie nonsense you see in the streets whenever someone even vaguely on the Right wins something important. Here was a group of people ripe for the trolling. But how to select a deserving target?

Ultimately, celebrity had a part to play in all this. Anon's next target would take the form of a homeless-looking Shia Lebouf arriving in New York City, setting up a webcam that was supposed to run 24/7 for the next eight years, and giving the entire pretentious project the name "He Will Not Divide Us." This, of course, was "art" completely devoid of any real meaning (outside of a vague hatred for Trump), and it could not have been any more exploitable for Anons.

Needless to say, Shia was in no way prepared for what was about to come his way. "He Will Not Divide Us" was literally just a webcam set up outside the Museum of the Moving Image in Queens, New York, and that meant he was treading in the online world—on Anon's turf. The idea was that the naturally Left-leaning inhabitants of this dense, metropolitan area would appear on cam, raise their fists in solidarity, and chant "He will not divide us," a few times for the viewers online. It was a sort of "proto-Resistance," if you will, starting on Trump's inauguration day—January 20, 2017, with the hope that it would win back some valuable digital space and make a statement in the process.

But you're talking about internet experts here, when you're talking about Anons.

The 24/7 stream quickly became the world's greatest 24/7 reality show, with nonstop trolling by Anons making IRL appearances. While the Lefties present at the demonstration looked like morose, brain-dead zombies, the Anons (daring to show their faces to the entire world) were having a ton of fun, were infinitely self-aware, and were often downright hilarious in their on-screen antics. Pretty soon, a "cast of colorful characters" was assembled from the familiar faces making repeat appearances "(AIDS Bjorn" stands out, as does the guy who sung the Metal Gear song), and the whole thing turned into the greatest debacle ever witnessed by the internet. Shia was slowly losing his mind, getting more and more fed up with each passing day, and you could see the cracks manifesting on his face almost in real time. The whole project would end up, somewhat ironically, with Shia getting arrested after breaking down and mistakenly assaulting one of his own protesters, and having the city erect a fence around the site, while only allowing a few "properly vetted" individuals at a time into the area—a great smack in the face to someone espousing "peaceful" Leftist views, while simultaneously opposed to Trump's border wall.

The "He Will Not Divide Us" stream in New York was an abject failure for Shia. Shia had to go back to California, but he was determined to keep his "art project" going, and would try to learn from his past mistakes so as to make the next "season" of his art project troll-proof. Instead of placing his camera at street level, where just anyone could hop on the stream, he would place it in a remote area, high up, and focused only on a flag bearing the project's name, flying high, 24/7. His message would still get across, and his project would continue unabated! He had thought of *everything!* There was *absolutely nothing* Anons could do to sabotage this!

Or so he thought.

You see, what Shia had inadvertently done in all this was create the single greatest game of capture the flag that the world had ever witnessed.

What ensued was nothing short of remarkable. Anons were determined to find this flag and take it down, wherever in the world it might be. But what was there to go on? It was just a flag flying against the blue sky.

Well, how about day-night cycles, to start?

Anons started by finding the orientation of the sun in relation to the flag. This would give them a rough geographical region in which to start searching, narrowing down their list of potential locations. The problem? It was still far too great an area to search through manually. They needed to narrow the region down further, but how to accomplish this?

Well… what about those plane contrails?

Anons used some basic trigonometry to isolate the directions of the flights occurring across the screen. They then matched this to real-time flight data, and narrowed down the region even further.

This gave them a county, and then a town.

How to isolate further?

They'd need a man on the ground.

Anons got a man on the ground.

The feed had audio, so Anons had the man driving around, honking his horn the whole time. Anons would let him know when he was the loudest and pretty soon, they all hit pay dirt.

Using nothing more than the sun and the stars, contrail patterns, and audio, Anons had managed to locate the flag within **two** days of it going up.

And what did they do?

Why, they took the flag and replaced it with a MAGA hat and t-shirt, of course, for the entire world to see on livestream, waiting, just *waiting* for Shia to wake up the next day and discover it hanging there, his precious flag now stolen.

But Shia would not be beat. He had to try again. He would increase his efforts once more, this time moving the flag to the top of an art museum in Liverpool, England. He was so confident in the security that he didn't even bother to hide the location for this go-round. Instead, it would be guarded like Fort Knox. And once again, Anons immediately set to work.

Numerous plans to snatch the fabled flag were discussed. Anons tried all sorts of ways to get access to the roof from inside the building, but found out they couldn't, having been thwarted by security each time. They fielded the idea of sending up drones with flamethrowers—yes—flamethrowers attached, in order to burn the flag down. One team tried to ignite the flag using high-powered lasers; their flickering, neon glow caught on livestream. Shia was on the boards himself this time, attempting to monitor Anon activity to see if he could get the jump on any operations before they happened. So anons, in kind, started populating the boards with false information to throw him and his team off the trail. Ultimately, it would be three enterprising blokes simply scaling the building and taking photos *near* the flag that would spook Shia's new museum so badly, that they would simply refuse to host the project anymore; too big of an insurance risk, most likely. Anons may not have gotten the flag that round, but it was still a major victory and Shia still had to move his flag.

The game would continue on a global scale, and each time, it would be hunted down by enterprising Anons, by this army of gleefully entertaining digital soldiers. The incident would become well known enough that it would eventually be used in some Naval curriculum (according to at least one post that I witnessed on /pol/, where a photo of the flag and the contrails were noted within a PowerPoint presentation to demonstrate the methods of geolocation these recruits would learn to master; methods Anons had independently employed).

Ultimately, though, the whole affair would be forever immortalized in this hilarious meme:

But it's not always fun-and-memes on the Chans. Unbeknownst to even the most knowledgeable Anons, the boards have long been used by various intelligence agencies to send and receive encrypted messages, hidden in plain sight. Remember when I said that literally anyone could post to the Chans? I meant literally anyone. And what you may also not know is that text can be hidden and encrypted inside of images, and opened with special programs designed to extract those messages. This is a technique called steganography.

Take for instance, this image, of a Pepe boiling in water, posted on November 4, 2017:

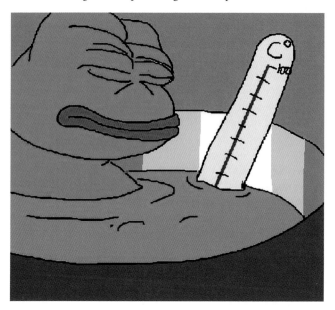

Along with the image, the post read:

```
Precom Identify: ID:M3a84Qt5

4920-a 293883 zAj-1 0020192

PIC RELATED

&: or me dark
```

This image contained one such hidden message, from one person in the intelligence community talking to another, hidden in plain sight on /pol/.

The message, once extracted, read:

```
ALL compromised by.. use HOM.. HIT-2000# ..
ONCE confirmed

Sorry Hoops due
HIT-2 , get jumpy :|

13 34 34 144 55 28
35 44 55 139 20 55

NRESTAE
Camschatcense

REPMES fi
SO MM bayat to.. use SYN.. One 16 December 2016 ..
s/One//
ECIWT confirmed

I know. These are the times. Calm patriot.

No
precom? Not try chat. Many liableness.
```

Now, diving a little deeper, you'll notice the line that says "Precom Identify: ID:-M3a84Qt5." That's a user ID; a feature of the Chans used to allow other Anons to respond to a particular Anon, while keeping everyone anonymous. And if you were to search for posts by that particular user ID, you'd soon find a single post from almost a YEAR prior on /pol/, posted on November 7, 2016.

The post in question?

Spirit cooking recipe Anonymous ID:M3a84Qt5

View   Reply   Original   Report

coin to play, in broad day
committee stealing, voices kneeling
Self disclosure, net Exposure
masked bear rises, warning crisis
bells to cannons, _greatness chanting_
spies are crying, bureau lying
polls are broken, promise stolen
Torches lighting, wrists are binding
ropes are winding, feet are flying
justice rising?, trojan Hiding
rex is master, lex disaster
always and forever after

105KiB, 632x811, image.jpg
View Same   Google   iqdb   SauceNAO

Yeah, whoever was talking had been running operations on the boards for at least one year (that we can point to with this evidence). In actuality, it's probably been going on *much* longer

(By the way, that photo you see is of "Spirit Cooker" Marina Abramovic—a probable Satanic priestess/Mother of Darkness with an incredible amount of ties to elites around the world. She initially came into sharp focus and mass awareness when /pol/ started examining Podesta's e-mails, leaked by Wikileaks during this time. And if you're wondering what "Spirit Cooking" is, well… we'll get into that later. Believe me when I say it's grim stuff, but we're in a good mood right now, and I don't want to spoil it just yet.)

But why do I go to such great lengths to describe all this?

There are a few reasons.

Part of it is to just give you the lay of the land. I think it's fair to say that most normal people simply had no idea that any of this has been going on during these past few years. I described /pol/ in the beginning as the single most influential page online that most people have never heard of before, and I meant every word of that. Much of the media has been tasked with making sure you never, ever step foot on these boards; that they're this nebulous, threatening thing, when the truth is—they're really only a threat to evildoers.

Secondly, it's to make sure you really understand the genius of Anons. Incredible things happen when you get incredibly smart, web-savvy, active, engaged—and most importantly—a funny group of people made up of hundreds of thousands, possibly even millions of users together in one place. There's a spontaneous order that emerges, unlike anywhere else in the world. And here's the part I really want you to take away from this: **In essence, what was happening on the Chans was the equivalent of a decentralized intelligence agency, operating twenty-four hours a day, with worldwide reach and influence.**

Trump knew it way back when, and he leveraged this anonymous army every step of the way on his path to presidential victory—and even beyond, as you'll see as you read through this book.

Why, he even posted on /pol/ once, and yes, we have proof (which Q would later confirm). It started with an Anon sounding the alarm that Trump had retweeted a Pepe account; the unofficial mascot of the Chans.

Here was the tweet in question:

Donald J. Trump
@realDonaldTrump
Follow

"@patrioticpepe: @realDonaldTrump ONLY TRUMP CAN UNITE AMERICA AND FIX OBAMA'S MISTAKES!!! #Trump2016 "

RETWEETS 1,489 LIKES 2,722

11:59 PM - 29 Jul 2016

1.5K 2.7K

Amid all the excitement on the thread, there was one comment that stood out, and which got dozens of excited responses:

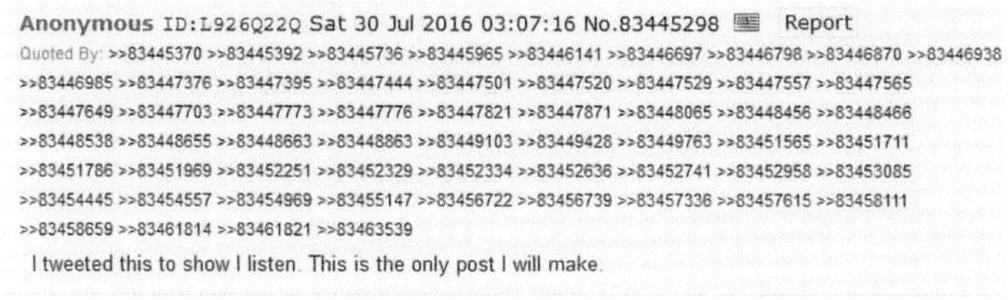
Anonymous ID:L926Q22Q Sat 30 Jul 2016 03:07:16 No.83445298 Report
Quoted By: >>83445370 >>83445392 >>83445736 >>83445965 >>83446141 >>83446697 >>83446798 >>83446870 >>83446938 >>83446985 >>83447376 >>83447395 >>83447444 >>83447501 >>83447520 >>83447529 >>83447557 >>83447565 >>83447649 >>83447703 >>83447773 >>83447776 >>83447821 >>83447871 >>83448065 >>83448456 >>83448466 >>83448538 >>83448655 >>83448663 >>83448863 >>83449103 >>83449428 >>83449763 >>83451565 >>83451711 >>83451786 >>83451969 >>83452251 >>83452329 >>83452334 >>83452636 >>83452741 >>83452958 >>83453085 >>83454445 >>83454557 >>83454969 >>83455147 >>83456722 >>83456739 >>83457336 >>83457615 >>83458111 >>83458659 >>83461814 >>83461821 >>83463539

I tweeted this to show I listen. This is the only post I will make.

One Anon respectfully asked for proof:

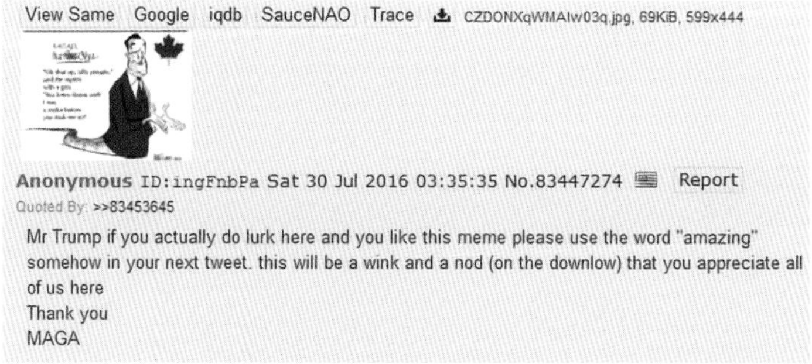
View Same Google iqdb SauceNAO Trace CZDONXqWMAIw03q.jpg, 69KiB, 599x444

Anonymous ID:ingFnbPa Sat 30 Jul 2016 03:35:35 No.83447274 Report
Quoted By: >>83453645

Mr Trump if you actually do lurk here and you like this meme please use the word "amazing" somehow in your next tweet. this will be a wink and a nod (on the downlow) that you appreciate all of us here
Thank you
MAGA

And POTUS obliged shortly thereafter:

Donald J. Trump ✓
@realDonaldTrump

Follow ⌄

Colorado was amazing yesterday! So much support. Our tax, trade and energy reforms will bring great jobs to Colorado and the whole country.

5:53 AM - 30 Jul 2016

And again, Q would confirm that this was indeed President Trump himself, interacting with Anons on the boards. You just had to be there to understand all the excitement Anons were feeling, but that's not where the story ends. As Trump took office and his enemies began to fight on every side, it soon became clear to every Anon on the boards that memeing Trump into office was just the first battle in a very long, ongoing war, and that very little was as it appeared on the surface. New information, the likes of which no one had ever seen, was starting to bubble up every other day on the boards. Anons were starting to sit up and pay attention, becoming engaged in a manner in which they had never quite engaged before (yours truly, included).

And it was into this wild and raucous information frontier that QAnon was born, forever to change the course of our collective history.

CHAPTER 3

"How Do You Defuse a Bomb?"

—January 27, 2018 From Qdrop #619

Q !UW.yye1fxo **ID: 9400a1** No.175503 ⌐ ▨   **619**
Jan 27 2018 02:29:48 (EST)

Note the last drops on the other board.
Think logically.
Refer to past crumbs.
YOU HAVE MORE THAN YOU KNOW.
Do you expect HRC, GS, Hussein, etc to stand in a PUBLIC
courtroom w/ potential crooked judges and tainted 'liberal' juries?
How do you defuse a bomb?
Knowledge of which wires/strings to cut?
Q

Compelling. That's how I'd describe how it is to follow Q, even after all this time. Oh, sure, it's still difficult to even begin approaching the subject of Q, especially in light of the fact that this operation we call QAnon is still ongoing as of this writing, but that doesn't make it any less compelling. You've heard the analogy of trying to build an airplane while it's in flight? Well, trying to write about Q as the Plan is still unfolding every day, in real time, is like trying to build a submarine two-hundred fathoms below the sea, while gliding along to some undisclosed secret destination. The task is daunting, the conditions dizzying, the landscape completely alien and filled with strange creatures never seen before by normal, surface-dwelling men—but Q reassures us that where we are headed is very good indeed. It is, however, no surprise that following Q often leaves one feeling like he or she needs to come up for air, so to speak, at regular intervals.

Add that to the fact that I am trying to explain QAnon to an audience that may be hearing about him for the first time; an audience who may, in fact, be hostile to the ideas being presented as they struggle to come to terms with the events that have either already occurred, or are occurring around them. In short, you can see what an unenviable task I've undertaken here, in this book. There will be some confusion to sort out, no doubt, but rest assured, that's something for which I'm well prepared to handle. What I need from you is to be as open as you can possibly be as we begin to explore this topic together (which, depending on when you're reading this in the timeline, may be easier at a later date once certain, undeniable events—the kind of events which demand explanation—have transpired).

Still, for many, this will be no small undertaking. There are literally years of programming that need to be undone for what I'm about to tell you to truly make sense, take root and resonate, so you'll have to forgive me if I seem a bit too hasty to swing my sword through all these Gordian knots and thus, win over the proverbial hearts and minds of the people. I've been waiting for this moment for so long now, growing my own understanding along the way, and I can't wait to see it all finally manifested in reality. By a certain point in history, if I am correct about Q and if all goes according to the plan Q has described, the people will really have no choice but to abandon their former ways of thinking about reality and build a new framework of understanding from the ground, up. They can only shut their eyes to the light for so long.

Of course, I may be going a bit too far out of my way to brace myself for a negative reaction. The truth is, there may be just as many (if not more!) reading this book who will have the exact opposite reaction! Many people love President Trump and the GOP; many more than the Legacy Media would like the world to believe. They will be *thrilled* to learn for the first time about the wildly creative and systematic disclosure of long-suppressed intel by the Trump administration. They will wonder as they hear about the military precision of this operation, undertaken for their benefit. For them, the information about to be presented will undoubtedly feel more like a missing puzzle piece finally found after years of searching; an important foundation in their mental framework, and one which empowers them to build a more coherent and accurate worldview—something that will have a *profound* impact on society when done en masse. And you'll note here that this is my hope: that after reading this book, both those initially hostile to Q, and those who willingly embrace Q from the get-go will end up at the same place—with a vastly increased understanding of reality, and that they will be able to come together as citizens of the same Republic, and build a beautiful future together. My hope is that this increased understanding will help people on both sides of the aisle shake off the mass deception that's been perpetrated against us ALL for so long and finally realize that this isn't a Left versus Right battle anymore. Really, it never was.

The scope of this is so much bigger than I can possibly impress upon you now. What happens when you read Q is that you learn that what we are experiencing is actually a battle between Light and Darkness. It's why Q often refers to this movement as a Great Awakening, and he's absolutely correct. We're talking about Truth versus Lies here. Good versus the vilest Evil. Some just need a bit more help than others in breaking off the mental shackles placed there in secret by the servants of Darkness.

Regardless of your personal reaction, the problem I face in trying to explain Q is further compounded by the innate complexity of Q—from the various encoding techniques he uses, to the broad range of topics covered, to the key list of players involved, and even the disinformation intentionally placed in the drops by Q himself, for the purpose of misleading any evildoers following along, in order to push them into making mistakes, tipping their hands too early, and expending valuable resources at a time when they really can't afford to lose anything. This is even *further* compounded by the sheer amount of Q's posts. As of this writing, Q has been posting for over a year and a half now, and has amassed over 3,300 posts during this time. Who knows how many posts there will be in the end, or for how long this operation will go on! Distilling that amount of information—information that's been spread out over the course of these many months and **heavily** supplemented by research from Anons throughout that entire time, is no small task.

The good news is, I've literally been following Q and covering it in depth on my own site and across social media from the very first drops, taking on the task of understanding and disseminating Q's drops as a full-time job for the entire duration Q has been active. I've written over five hundred articles during that span of time, some many thousands of words, in an attempt to dissect and truly understand the intel Q was dropping. Already intimately familiar with the systems and the way Anons worked, the job of writing about Q was a natural fit for me, and I'm incredibly grateful to the hundreds of supporters who enabled me to perform this work through their generous donations and discussion during that time. As a result, I feel confident in saying there are very few civilian guides who could even attempt to tackle this subject matter in this way, at this time, and I don't say that to flatter myself. It's just a matter of this being so niche, so unique, and so clandestine, it hasn't had the time to filter out into popular culture and understanding yet, where pundits, talking heads, and undoubtedly, historians will have the time to comb over and sort out all the details.

I also have the advantage of being a "digital native" as some might say. I'm not someone looking to merely capitalize on a movement, induce panic and fear in the gullible, and turn around to try and sell them, for instance, water filtration systems that they can mount in the emergency survival bunker they've undoubtedly already started building in the back yard for when the bombs start falling! I'm not trying to get anyone to buy MREs with a twenty year shelf life, or sell them expensive webinar passes so they can watch my talking head bobble up and down for hours and hours as I think up ways to retread and repackage what's already out there for free.

I'll tell you more about myself in a bit, but the most important fact you need to know going into this is: I'm an Anon, and that's... kind of a generational thing. Okay, sure, technically anyone can be an Anon, but I grew up online, and I've been an Anon for well over a decade now. You would not believe the amount of useless Chan-related trivia and cultural history I have in this old noggin of mine that, frankly, the older generations simply wouldn't understand. When it comes to Q, that means I was active on the front lines well before and during the time when everything went down. I was aware of Q from the earliest moments, and participated in a way many of these other guys haven't. To put a finer point on it, many of these Q-related pundits simply weren't browsing /pol/ during their free time in 2014 and 2015—which means they missed out on a LOT! I was there before Q came along, I was there the whole time Q was around, my fingerprints are on the movement in a way many don't even realize (more on that in a bit) and I'll probably be lurking threads still, long after the Q operation is wrapped up. Further still, many of these Q-pundits barely know the meaning of the word "redpill," mistaking it for basic Conservatism, when that couldn't be further from the truth. No, they were tending to their jobs, their spouses, their 401ks, and their normal responsibilities. They weren't up at 3:00 a.m. each night browsing /SIG/ threads, they don't know how to "Awooooo!" and many didn't learn about the likes of FBIAnon or MegaAnon until *months* after the fact.

To their credit, a lot of these types did hop on earlier than most, and they caught up rather quickly... but frankly, a lot of that was due to them discovering my site, before branching out on their own.

But me? I was there. That was **my** scene.

It's like punk rock. There's an authenticity that comes with being on the scene that you simply can't fake. On one end, there's Henry Rollins, screaming into a microphone and kicking someone's teeth out in a mosh pit. On the other, there's someone having a midlife crisis and shaving his hair down into a mohawk because he just heard Green Day for the first time, and that, for him, was an auditory revelation.

(Hopefully, you'll find I'm more on the "Rollins" end of the spectrum.)

And sure, there are other good sources out there. I am, by no means, the only person involved in this by any stretch of the imagination, and I do not have a monopoly over this kind of information, so don't get me wrong. My own understanding of things has been informed by some of the best Anons out there, so it's my privilege to now try and communicate all that to the world, in as condensed and as streamlined a form as possible. I'm just trying to give you, the reader, a better sense of where I'm coming from in all this, and the extent of my involvement and credibility, before we get in to the really deep stuff.

As I've undertaken the task of writing this, I've always considered it something akin to a war journal. Sure, it doesn't go day-by-day in the strictest sense (though I've done my best to give timelines where appropriate), but I'm also keenly aware that, as of this writing, the battle is not yet even close to over. The months of research, the hundreds of articles, the endless stream of publishing, outreach, and social media mastery have all led to this, the final battle for the future of our nation.

Again, this isn't about Right versus. Left or Conservative versus Liberal. Once the evils of the Cabal have been exposed to the entire world for all to see plainly, it will become immediately evident and obvious to all that this is about Light versus Dark, Truth versus. Falsehood, Good versus. Evil—and what person doesn't want Light, Truth, and Goodness to follow them all of their days?

Of course we all want that! But it might take some work to get everyone there, because… well… I think you'll soon see the immensity of the evil that's become embedded in our society over many decades, and the work many patriots have devoted in order to help excise that evil from our world.

As with any discussion, it's best to first define our terms, academic though that may be, so as to avoid any unnecessary confusion. Contrary to what you may have heard in the Legacy Media (which is what I call anything transmitted one-way, through traditional mediums such as TV, print, and radio, where there is no real opportunity for response, feedback, or user interaction), QAnon is **not** a mere "conspiracy theory."

It's worth noting here that the term "conspiracy theory," though extant from at least the late 1890s, was popularized by the CIA in the wake of the Warren Commission. For the younger audience, that was the commission established by Lyndon B. Johnson (LBJ) to investigate the assassination of JFK (which is a joke in and of itself… considering LBJ was probably the one who had him killed in the first place, so he could rise to power and usher in a host of disastrous reforms that would end up creating things like the welfare state, among other cultural quagmires).

```
          According to our source, Colonel Boris Ivanov,
Chief of the Soviet Committee for State Security (KGB)
Residency in New York City, held a meeting of KGB personnel
on the morning of November 25, 1963.  Ivanov informed those
present that President Kennedy's death had posed a problem
for the KGB and stated that it was necessary for all KGB
employees to lend their efforts to solving the problem.

          According to our source, Ivanov stated that it was
his personal feeling that the assassination of President
Kennedy had been planned by an organized group rather than
being the act of one individual assassin.  Ivanov stated
that it was therefore necessary that the KGB ascertain with
the greatest possible speed the true story surrounding
President Kennedy's assassination.  Ivanov stated that the
KGB was interested in knowing all the factors and all of
the possible groups which might have worked behind the scenes
to organize and plan this assassination.

     TOP SECRET
```

On September 16, 1965, this same source reported
that the KGB Residency in New York City received instructions
approximately September 16, 1965, from KGB headquarters in
Moscow to develop all possible information concerning
President Lyndon B. Johnson's character, background, personal
friends, family, and from which quarters he derives his
support in his position as President of the United States.
Our source added that in the instructions from Moscow, it
was indicated that "now" the KGB was in possession of data
purporting to indicate President Johnson was responsible for
the assassination of the late President John F. Kennedy.
KGB headquarters indicated that in view of this information,
it was necessary for the Soviet Government to know the
existing personal relationship between President Johnson
and the Kennedy family, particularly that between President
Johnson and Robert and "Ted" Kennedy.

3

Regardless, the term was weaponized by the CIA (or Clowns in America, as Q likes to call them) in order to cordon off certain areas of inquiry in the public consciousness. The ultimate chilling effect of all this was to get the populace at large to stop asking questions, questions that were rather inconvenient to those in power. Before this, enterprising Americans would present hypotheses and test them rigorously, doggedly seeking the truth. After this report? "Conspiracy theories" became the territory of crazy folk with questionable taste in metallic headgear, and the news itself grew increasingly homogenized.

One such inconvenient question at the time of the JFK assassination disputed the official conclusion delivered by the Warren Commission in 1964 that Lee Harvey Oswald had acted alone. Well, when President Trump recently declassified over 3,100 top secret documents relating to the JFK investigation, never before seen by the public, it turned out that this had been a carefully crafted lie! There were, in fact, at least two gunmen involved in this conspiracy to murder the president, and even more involved in the general conspiracy.

---

3   https://www.archives.gov/files/research/jfk/releases/docid-32144493.pdf

TP 44-187
JPO:jw

<u>ADMINISTRATIVE</u>

Re speech by OREN FENTON POTITO, St. Petersburg, Florida,
January 16, 1964.

On January 17, 1964 TP 100 PCI (RAC) furnished to SAs JAMES
P. O'NEIL and JAMES E. WALLACE.the following information:

On the evening of January 16, 1964 a dinner sponsored by
OREN FENTON POTITO was held at Donat's Restaurant, 6001 Haines Road,
North St. Petersburg, Florida. The dinner meeting was informal pub-
lic in nature and approximately 41 persons were in attendance.

The source has identified POTITO as a <u>member of the National
States Rights Party</u> (NSRP) in the Spring of 1963 at which time POTITO
resigned while holding the office of National Organizer. Since that
time POTITO has held meetings of a public nature under various titles
all of which are non-existent organizations. He is not known to have
any national affiliation at the present time although he is in contact with various leaders of right wing groups in the United States.

In the course of his speech of some 3 hours following the
dinner POTITO touched on the association between LEE HARVEY OSWALD
and RUBY.

POTITO identified RUBY, real name RUBENSTEIN, as a Communist Party Member since 1929 and through this connection linked him
to OSWALD. He identified OSWALD as a Communist through his association
with the Fair Play for Cuba Committee (FPCC).

According to POTITO only two organizations knew the route
of the parade in Dallas on November 22, 1963 for any period of time
prior to the parade and these two were the United States Secret Service and the Dallas Police Department. RUBY had insinuated himself
into the Police Department circle, obtained the route and arranged
with OSWALD to take the job at the state school building along the
route to carry out the assassination.

POTITO said the "Surgeon General's report" on the assassination stated the first bullet entered the President's throat below
the adams apple clearly showing that two persons were involved with
the first shot being fired from the bridge across the park way in
front of the car. To further substantiate this, POTITO said there
was a bullet hole in the wind shield of the President's car.

Cover Page
H

4

And it's here that we should note the profound difference between "conspiracy" and
"conspiracy theories." Is it not human nature for people to conspire and collude together?
The root of the word literally means "to breathe together," and in that sense, people "conspire" every single day. But the word "conspiracy" has acquired a bit of baggage over the
years, not least of which is due to the CIA's efforts. But in truth, any group of people, meeting anywhere, discussing whatever, are "conspiring" together. The subject matter may be fun
and trivial. It may be simple gossip about the everyday drama of our lives, but conspiring is
what we, as social creatures, do. Very few of us are true hermits. People conspire all the time,
and is it so surprising to learn that those in power and influence would conspire to make sure
they retain their power and influence?

---

4   https://www.archives.gov/files/research/jfk/releases/docid-32206626.pdf

On January 18, 1964, the same informant learned that
Zygmunt Broniarek told Mark Lane that he had just received a (S)
copy of "Trybuna Ludu," which contained a reprint from a very (S)
right-wing Italian newspaper called the "Twentieth Century."
In this reprinted article it was reported there had been a .
conspiracy to kill President Kennedy; that police officer J. D.
Tippett was to assassinate the President; that thereafter
Tippett was to hide in the depository and subsequently be able
to leave because he was wearing a uniform of a police officer. .
Zygmunt Broniarek stated that according to this reprinted
article, Officer Tippett was promised a very big reward for the

ALL INFORMATION CONTAINED
HEREIN IS UNCLASSIFIED
EXCEPT WHERE SHOWN
OTHERWISE

SECRET

8-1293
Classified by S170 AGG/KSK
Declassify on: OADR
(JFIC)

CONFIDENTIAL

GROUP 1
Excluded from automatic
downgrading and
declassification

LEE HARVEY OSWALD

CONFIDENTIAL

SECRET

assassination of President Kennedy. Also, after the assassination, Tippett was to meet Jack Ruby, and unknown to him but
according to plan, Jack Ruby was to kill him. Zygmunt Broniarek
continued that according to this reprinted article, Jack Ruby
did kill Officer Tippett.

5

It's sinister, isn't it? Not only were there multiple gunmen involved in this "conspiracy," but those who suggested anything contrary to the official narrative set forth by the Warren Commission were demonized by government intelligence agencies and the media in order to keep these "inconvenient questions" at bay. This cannot be understated: **real people were vilified for years for seeing reality accurately and pressing for more information**. (And that was if they were lucky. And I'd tell you to just ask Dorothy Kilgallen, but those about to be implicated in her book on the JFK assassination made sure she went to sleep and never woke up!) So the question then becomes; why keep the details of this assassination hidden? Furthermore, who would want to keep such information hidden, and what tools do they have at their disposal to keep such information hidden?

Remember the *Star Wars* image from before, and my mention of the 4:00 a.m. talking points, distributed by the CIA to media outlets through SecureDrop? Now take a look at these headlines:

---

5   https://www.archives.gov/files/research/jfk/releases/docid-32206626.pdf

Q   Sections ≡   Sign In 👤   Try 1 month for $1

The Washington Post

Democracy Dies in Darkness

Morning Mix

'We are Q': A deranged conspiracy cult leaps from the Internet to the crowd at Trump's 'MAGA' tour

4 things to know about the QAnon conspiracy theory

By **Isaac Stanley-Becker**
August 1

On Tuesday evening, the dark recesses of the Internet lit up with talk of politics.

"Tampa rally, live coverage," wrote "Dan," posting a link to President Trump's Tampa speech in a thread on 8chan, an anonymous image board also known as Infinitechan or Infinitychan, which might be best described as the unglued twin of better-known 4chan, a message board already untethered from reality.

The thread invited "requests to Q," an anonymous user claiming to be a government agent with top security clearance, waging war against the so-called deep state in service to the 45th president. "Q" feeds disciples, or "bakers," scraps of intelligence, or "bread crumbs," that they scramble to bake into an understanding of the "storm" — the community's term, drawn from Trump's cryptic reference last year to "the calm before the storm" — for the president's final conquest over elites, globalists and deep-state saboteurs.

NEWS   THE VOTE   U.S. NEWS   BUSINESS   WORLD   TECH & MEDIA   THINK

TECH & MEDIA

What is Qanon? A guide to the conspiracy theory taking hold among Trump supporters

The Qanon conspiracy started less than a year ago but has taken hold among some Trump supporters – with some followers taking real world action.

by Ben Collins / Aug. 3, 2018 / 9:18 AM EDT

——— David Reinert holds up a large "Q" sign while waiting in line to see President Donald J. Trump at his rally on August 2, 2018 at the Mohegan Sun Arena at Casey Plaza in Wilkes Barre, Pennsylvania.
Rick Loomis / Getty Images

I could show you hundreds of articles from Legacy Media outlets pushing the "conspiracy theory" angle on the Q movement. Many were published on the same days, in coordinated waves, as part of a centralized effort. Everyone who wrote an article like this was working, knowingly or unknowingly, at the behest of a renegade faction embedded deep inside the CIA. And what's worse: being in on the ploy, or being a useful idiot for the unseen puppet masters?

At this point, some may be wondering why I keep bringing up the CIA. We've been trained to think of these intelligence agencies as these monolithic blocks, working in the shadows for our benefit. This is simply not the case. You may be surprised to learn here that, at the very least, a large chunk of the CIA was, for a long time, literal Nazis who engaged in some of the worst human experimentation on the planet. But we'll focus more on that in a later chapter, when we're a bit further down the proverbial rabbit hole.

But who is QAnon that the Legacy Media should malign him so? Why has his movement taken the world by storm, in a way that other "conspiracy theories" before him haven't? Is it really just the grand mack daddy of them all, rolling bits and pieces of all kinds of theories into one big tin foil mish-mash? Is the QAnon movement really just a conspiracy theory on "bath salts," as one reporter put it?

Friends, I don't want to keep you in suspense.

But we've got to step back and set the stage a little here, because so many profound events were unfolding so quickly during this time, that to **truly** understand QAnon, you need to understand everything that came before QAnon. You need to get a real feel for the landscape at the time, the real context of these events, and not the Mockingbird Media's retelling of these events, but the *real* version they helped hide from you, because that's the setting into which QAnon emerged. If you want to understand QAnon, you need to first *become* an Anon by seeing the world and the events leading up to it, as an Anon would see them. This hard look at history won't be pretty, but it will be necessary if you want to stand any chance of understanding what's happening now, in relation to Trump, Q, and the Great Awakening. It's time to strap on your Nightmare Vision goggles™ and see the world through the eyes of an Anon.

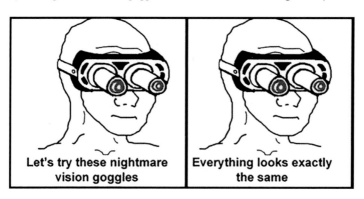

| Let's try these nightmare vision goggles | Everything looks exactly the same |

So, on June 16, 2015, Donald Trump would officially announce his presidential campaign in Trump tower. Many take it as a joke and dismiss it outright at first, but the man quickly gains traction. By 2016, the Trump Train is bowling over the competition, beating out ELEVEN other candidates, including a legacy candidate, Jeb Bush.

Shortly after announcing his candidacy, /pol/ would decide to meme Trump into the White House. Just for the lulz, remember. And as I previously recounted, it soon grew into something much bigger.

Within weeks, on June 27, Anons would create /r/The_Donald on Reddit as a "/pol/ colony," in order to help facilitate this effort by bringing in the "normies." The site would become the single largest source of Trump's online support, and give rise to a multitude of nonstop memes, which only served to drive his popularity and his message home to so many people by directly bypassing the Legacy Media, much to the chagrin of Leftists everywhere:

The campaign continues to grow, and pretty soon, the raucous fun is spreading like wildfire across social media. Centipedes (that is, the nickname given to Trump supporters on /r/The_Donald—a reference to the song "Centipede" by the drum and bass band, Knife Party) take over Reddit so effectively, the Reddit admins soon decide to censor the subreddit and pull it from the front page—a move that had never been done before in the history of Reddit and which has since never been repeated. The move is a stunning one for those familiar with the site, which had always previously prided itself on operating with FOSS principles in mind—freedom, openness, free speech, democratic sharing, etc. Furthermore, the admins would then obfuscate the true subscriber count, initially capping it around 600,000 (when in reality, the advertiser tools on the site's back end showed the count to be closer to SIX MILLION users—a far more accurate count, considering the company would be committing fraud if they ever messed with those numbers).

Far too big to delete outright (the users would revolt and destroy the site if they did), the Reddit admins (including Steve Huffman, who is suspected to be the moderator of /r/Cannibals, where he writes about his first time eating human flesh using a sockpuppet account) effectively turn /r/The_Donald into a "containment" subreddit, ensuring Trump's message and his supporters are cut off from the broader site, with the paid-off admins of other subs like /r/Politics routinely censoring pro-Trump content at the "ground level."

---

6   One such meme out of millions.

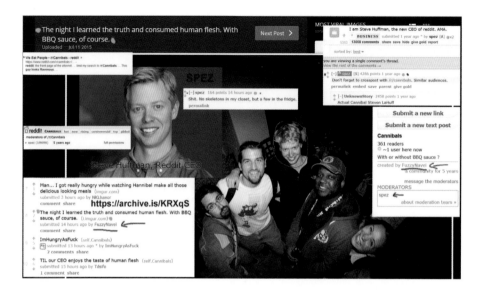

Yeah, creepy guy. Also of note, Huffman (a.k.a. Spez) also took to editing users' comments, comments which were making fun of him, during this time, leading /r/The_Donald admins to turn the "edit" function on the site into the "Spez" function. Of course, this is a massive ethical (and potentially legal) blunder, though as of yet, nothing has really come of it.

On February 13, 2016 Supreme Court Justice Antonin Scalia would be found dead at Cibolo Creek Ranch Vineyard in Texas, leaving a vacancy on the highest court in the land during the last year of Obama's presidency. Obama would nominate Merrick Garland as his replacement, but Republicans would block the confirmation by invoking, ironically, "the Biden rule," named after the then vice president Joe Biden, which stated that the Senate was under no obligation to confirm the Supreme Court pick of an outgoing administration.

During the campaign, Trump faced a disturbing amount of disruption from the radical left. On March 11, he would be forced to cancel a rally in Chicago as thousands of violent protesters descended upon the University of Illinois venue, where brawls would break out on the rally floor. At least five arrests would be made, and two police officers injured as a result of the violent mob. Also in March, George Papadopoulos would join the Trump campaign as a foreign policy adviser, after leaving the Ben Carson campaign.

Full disclosure: I'm undecided as to what Papadopoulos' larger role in all this was. Part of me thinks he's Mossad—and a particular blogger I respect has said multiple times now that his wife is a Russian spy, though she denies that herself—but I'm withholding judgment until this aspect of the story becomes clearer. But without jumping too far ahead, Q himself would highlight Papadopoulos in one of his more recent drops, and imply that much more was going on than what we could currently see on the surface:

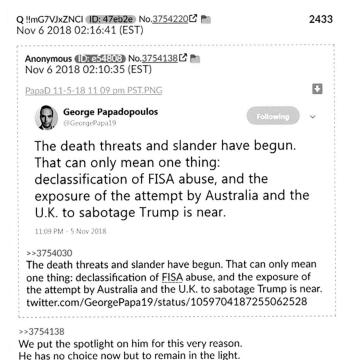

Q !!mG7VJxZNCI ID: 47eb2e No.3754220 🏴 2433
Nov 6 2018 02:16:41 (EST)

Anonymous ID: e54808 No.3754138 🏴
Nov 6 2018 02:10:35 (EST)

PapaD 11-5-18 11 09 pm PST.PNG ⬇

George Papadopoulos
@GeorgePapa19
Following ⌄

The death threats and slander have begun.
That can only mean one thing:
declassification of FISA abuse, and the
exposure of the attempt by Australia and the
U.K. to sabotage Trump is near.

11:09 PM - 5 Nov 2018

>>3754030
The death threats and slander have begun. That can only mean
one thing: declassification of FISA abuse, and the exposure of
the attempt by Australia and the U.K. to sabotage Trump is near.
twitter.com/GeorgePapa19/status/1059704187255062528

>>3754138
We put the spotlight on him for this very reason.
He has no choice now but to remain in the light.
This is not a game.
Q

On March 12, Thomas Dimassimo would hop a barricade and attempt to tackle Citizen Trump at a rally, before being tackled by Secret Service and arrested.

On March 14, while in Italy, Papadopoulos would meet with a Maltese professor by the name of Joseph Mifsud, who claimed to have ties to the Russian government, and also claimed to have a bunch of e-mail dirt on Hillary Clinton. In reality, Mifsud would have ties to the Saudis, UK intelligence, Australian intelligence, and would later go missing before showing up again, very recently, holed up in the US Embassy in Rome. The public would later be told that it was this meeting between Mifsud and Papadopoulos that would trigger the "Russian Collusion" investigation and the production of the Steele dossier. It would also become a subject of intense scrutiny in the later Mueller investigation, but in 2018, Mifsud's lawyer would come out and claim that Mifsud had actually been working for the FBI the whole time; that is, at the behest of James Comey to entrap Papadopoulos (who may or may not have been a double agent himself and whose wife, at least according to that blogger who you'll meet later, was also a Russian spy). More details continue to emerge daily about all these players, but it's looking more and more like this was an international entrapment operation staged by multiple international intelligence agencies, all coordinating to frame Donald Trump for collusion with the Russians, effectively staging a coup for the Cabal.

On March 21, Trump would announce Carter Page as another foreign policy adviser for his campaign. Page had previously worked with the FBI in 2013 as an undercover employee, helping to build a case against Evgeny Buryakov, who would later plead guilty to charges of conspiracy against the United States, previously posing as a trade representative and collecting confidential information about the US energy sector. Q would later inform us that Page was, in fact, an undercover FBI plant into Trump's campaign, and that his contact with Russia would later serve as a basis for the FBI opening up an investigation into Trump and his staff.

On March 29, Paul Manafort would join the Trump campaign as his campaign manager. Unbeknownst to Trump at the time, Manafort was actually yet another plant put into the Trump campaign by the Podesta Group, a lobbying firm run by Tony Podesta, the brother of Hillary's campaign manager, John Podesta. As this was going on, it would later be revealed that a Democratic National Committee (DNC) lawyer by the name of Alexandra Chalupa was investigating Manafort since at least 2014, and producing a ton of "opposition research" on him as someone colluding with the Russians. Long story short, this "research" would work its way through the Ukraine, of all places, to Steele, into the hands of the former director of public prosecutions for the Crown Prosecution Service in the UK, Alison Saunders, who would then fly to the US to have dinner with Bruce and Nellie Ohr. Bruce was deputy attorney general at the time and Nellie was working for the CIA front known as Fusion GPS... which was the exact same company the Hillary campaign had hired to produce the Steele Dossier in the first place. If you're confused already, I wouldn't blame you at all. The coup is very convoluted.

This would soon serve as the real set up for the eventual "Russian collusion" narrative, as Manafort would intentionally arrange a meeting between Donald Trump Jr. and some Russians: one being Natalia Veselnitskaya, a Russian lawyer and Magnitsky act lobbyist who worked under one Saak Albertovich Karapetya, a Russian attorney general (who would later die in a "mysterious" helicopter crash, in October of 2018). See, according to Q, Veselnitska-ya had been granted special access to the US by none other than the Obama administration's attorney general Loretta Lynch. Previously, she had been barred from the country due to obstruction of justice charges, and thus, had to be granted special entry.

In other words, a plant in the Trump campaign was secretly working for the brother of Clinton's campaign manager, and coordinating with the Obama administration's attorney general, to set up an incriminating looking meeting, which would then be used to justify obtaining a FISA warrant, in order for a sitting administration to engage in illegal bulk, "umbrella" FISA spying on all Trump campaign communications, to try and dig up dirt on behalf of their preferred candidate, Hillary Clinton. What I mean by that is because of this meeting, Obama could "legally" get a warrant to spy on Donald Trump Jr. and Jared Kushner. And because of the way FISA warrants work, you basically get to surveil everyone they come into contact with. So by putting these warrants in place, Obama now had "legal" access to spy on, effectively, the entire Trump campaign.

Oh, he was spying beforehand, but the FISA warrant made it "legal." In fact, Obama would get British intelligence, part of the "Five Eyes" alliance, to do his dirty work for him, when Government Communications Headquarters (GCHQ) director Robert Hannigan was allowed to wiretap Trump and his associate from Fort Meade. Hannigan would later, in the summer of 2016, fly to meet with the then director of the CIA John Brennan... which was odd, considering his American counterpart was Admiral Michael Rogers, director of the NSA. You see, the CIA is really, only, officially supposed to use its power against foreign states and actors. In other words, it's not allowed to spy on US citizens. So to skirt around this legal problem, the Obama administration turned to foreign allies and their intelligence agencies, because there's nothing preventing them from spying on US citizens, legally speaking. And then these foreign intelligence agencies can turn around and legally share what they learned with our own intelligence agencies. See how that works? I think we might appropriately label this following the letter, but not the spirit, of the law.

Three days after Trump took office, Hannigan would resign from his post as head of the GCHQ. But maybe you're noticing a preponderance of British names involved in this whole Spygate scandal. You've got Christopher Steele, the former MI6 operative hired by Fusion GPS to create the Steele Dossier, Alison Saunders, the former director of public prosecutions who ate with the Ohrs, Robert Hannigan of the GCHQ, and others I haven't mentioned yet, such as Arvinder Sambei, who introduced Mifsud to Papadopoulos, and Saunders to the Ohrs. How do they tie together in all this? Quite simply, through the Queen's Privy Council, upon which sits Steel's former MI6 boss and current chairman and founder of Cambridge Analytica (formerly known as SCL), Richard Dearlove, alongside Saunders, and a number of Soros-affiliated individuals, including Lord Mark-Malloch Brown, who, as we'll see later, is the chairman of one of the largest voting machine companies in the world, Smartmatic.

When I call this evil we're up against with "the Cabal," I truly mean it.

It should be noted here that Tony Podesta would close his whole lobbying operation the very day Mueller indicted Manafort and Rick Gates for failing to register as FARA agents—activities which would inextricably lead back to the Podesta Group.

It should also be noted that, just weeks prior to Manafort joining the Trump campaign, the then director of the CIA John Brennan had made a secret visit to Moscow to speak with Deputy Foreign Minister Oleg Syromolotov. I'm sure that had "absolutely nothing" to do with any of the events that followed.

As of this writing, it's unclear of when exactly Trump figured out that Manafort was a plant, but find out he did, and there has been heavy speculation that at some point, Trump was able to get Manafort to flip, and was able to leverage him in a plan to counter all this subversion (though, as of right now, no one but those in the intelligence community, those directly involved, and Trump himself knows for sure).

But back to our timeline, for the time being:

On May 3, 2016 Trump would officially become the Republican nominee, beating out all his competition. Despite all this censorship and resistance, it proves too little, too late, and Trump would now go on to face off against the Democratic nominee.

In May, 2016, Inspector General Steve Linick would issue a report condemning Clinton's use of private e-mail servers, for which she had not sought or received governmental approval or authorization. The story about Clinton's private e-mail servers was originally broken in the wake of the Benghazi panel, and was reported by the *New York Times* in March of 2015. In an effort to cover up her crimes, she utilized a program called "Bleachbit" to erase over 30,000 incriminating e-mails, as well as destroyed a number of mobile devices with hammers.

Now, this is of particular note, because Bleachbit isn't just your regular recycling bin program. See, when a file is written to a hard drive, all those ones and zeroes are written onto a magnetic disk, and they are not overwritten until the computer says they can be. When most computers "delete" a file, it's really just marking that space as safe to overwrite with new data, new ones and zeroes. This means forensic analysts can generally retrieve files, or portions of files, even if they've been deleted—because the original ones and zeroes are still there, at least until they're overwritten.

Bleachbit, on the other hand, is the equivalent of a digital file shredder. It overwrites whatever files you want with null data; basically a long string of zeroes—and it does this many times over, making sure there's no residual, leftover data on the drive, completely obfuscating whatever was written there previously, making it impossible to resurrect the deleted data. Her pretending like she didn't know what Bleachbit did when she was questioned about it was a total farce. When she was asked if she had wiped her servers, she couldn't have been more transparent when she said "What, like with a cloth or something?" No, she had to first buy that program, then install that program, then set it so it could overwrite her data with a string of zeroes seven times over. It would later come out that Paul Combetta, who went by the username "Stonetear" on Reddit, had gone to Reddit to ask for help in erasing all manner of data.

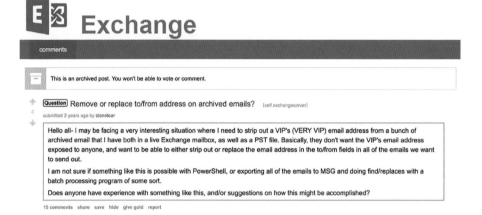

On May 10, George Papadopoulos would have a meeting with Australian diplomat, Alexander Downer at the Kensington Wine Room, in London, after one of Downer's associates made the request for the pair to meet. While Papadopoulos did make mention of what Mifsud had previously told him, Downer would report the details of the conversation back to the Australian government in the next day or two, and somehow, by July 22, the details of that conversation were disclosed back to the FBI, though no intelligence was reported as being passed through "official" Five Eyes channels. So how did the FBI learn of this conversation, which was, again, entirely legal?

Again, the answer is that this was all a set-up by our Five Eyes allies, working at the behest of the Obama Administration, to help set up the "Russian Collusion" narrative and frame the Trump campaign as treasonous traitors. Those in power viewed Trump as an existential threat to their hegemony, even in those early days of the campaign, and knew he had to be stopped no matter what. Calling in a few favors from overseas allowed the Obama administration to surreptitiously side-step any legal protections—including the Fourth Amendment protections afforded to all US citizens by the US Constitution—by effectively "outsourcing" the job of spying to foreign intelligence.

Q !4pRcUAOIBE No.77 📄 🖼️   **1336**
May 10 2018 23:45:37 (EST)

[Example]
Clinton Foundation.
Post Election Loss.
Layoffs.
No Access / Control = No Donations
Today.
NZ Donation Restart.
Others?
Why?
1) Selling Secrets?
2) Selling 'Future' Access **[regain control/power]**?
3) Selling Silence?
Read below slow and carefully.
FVEY.
Why do 'Former' Dignitaries Still Hold SEC Clearance?
U.S. to U.S. = Logged/Flagged/Recorded
U.S. **[in]** NZ = No Logs/No Flags/No Records = U.S. Sec Clearance
AUTH FVEY VIEW + Doc Take.
Read above slow and carefully.
WHY DO WE ALLOW **[FORMER]** DIGNITARIES SEC CLEARANCE?
Welcome to the Deep State.
Future to prove past.
Q

Oh, and by the way, this specific conversation between Papadopoulos and Downer would later be cited by the FBI as the sole reason they opened up a counter-intelligence investigation into the Trump campaign. Want another connection? Former MI6 boss Richard Dearlove knew the CIA/MI6 asset (and friend of the Bushes) Stefan Halper through the Cambridge Intelligence Seminar. Halper met with Papadopoulos, tried to have another agent seduce him, and also works for private intelligence firm Hakluyt. Downer previously worked for Hakluyt, and remains in an advisory board. Downer also previously helped arrange the single biggest foreign contribution to the Clinton Foundation that they ever received, some twenty-five million dollars. The rest of Hakluyt is composed of all sorts of spooks, many of whom are listed as having donated to Hillary's presidential campaign.

On May 19, former congressman Anthony Weiner (and husband to Hillary Clinton's favorite, long-time aide Huma Abedin) would plead guilty to sexting with an underage teenager, get sentenced to 21 months in prison, and made to register as a sex offender. As part of the investigation into Weiner, his laptop was seized, which contained a vast number of "insurance" files. Contained inside were a number of e-mails, backed up from Hillary's private e-mail server (read, non-governmental server utilized to avoid government oversight and FOIA requests) as well as files which, according to reports, made grown NYPD officers break down in tears. What kind of files could possibly produce such an effect on seasoned NYPD officers?

Later, the OIG report issued in June of 2018 would confirm what many already correctly inferred:

3.   Meeting between Comey and Coleman on October 4

Comey's Outlook calendar for October 4 contains an entry for "Morning Briefs" from 8:15 a.m. to 9:00 a.m. that is immediately followed by an entry for "Meeting w/EAD Coleman" from 9:00 a.m. to 9:30 a.m. Coleman told us that he could not recall this briefing with Comey. Coleman stated that staying behind to brief Comey would be consistent with normal practice, but added that he did not recall this specific instance. Coleman told us that it would be unusual to have a one-on-one meeting with Comey and told us someone else would typically be present at these briefings, such as the DD or ADD. While not remembering this meeting, Coleman speculated that this may have been a one-on-one meeting with Comey to discuss Coleman's upcoming retirement from the FBI in December 2016.

Coleman told us that he kept regularly took notes in a journal. Coleman's notes from October 4 contained the following entry:

(1)   Anthony Wiener [sic]

(2)   [Unrelated]

(3)   Wiener [sic] – texting 15 yo – Sexually Explicit

9/26 – Federal SW – IPhone/IPAD/Laptop

Initial analysis of laptop – thousands emails

Hillary Clinton & Foundation

Crime Against Children

We asked Coleman about these notes and he told us that, given their placement in his notebook, the notes would most likely represent information he was briefed on first thing in the morning by his subordinates in the Criminal Investigative Division. Coleman stated that he may have passed this information to other FBI executives after the morning briefing with the Director, but he could not remember if that occurred here.

"Crimes Against Children." Let that sink in for a moment. Folks, I'm not lying when I say the Clintons, operating through the Clinton Foundation, are some of the worst perpetrators of human trafficking in the history of mankind. We'll talk more about that in a later chapter, but know that for now, according to Q, two NYPD officers would die as a result of what they had seen on that laptop, their deaths marked as random murders, but in truth, they were assassinated; two more victims of Arkancide.

Also on May 19, Trump would promote Paul Manafort to campaign chairman. It would later be revealed in a congressional interview with former FBI director, James Comey, that the FBI had opened four separate investigations into four individual Trump advisers that very same day. The four in question were: Michael Flynn, Paul Manafort, Carter Page, and George Papadopoulos. These investigations, along with information from Five Eyes allies, would form the basis of the FBI's investigation into "Russian collusion" within the Trump campaign, dubbed with the code name "Crossfire Hurricane."

On June 3, a woman would be backed against a wall and pelted with eggs, bottles and spat upon for supporting Trump. Many other Trump supporters would be beaten, pelted, and intimidated by increasingly violent foot soldiers of the Left, like Antifa and La Raza.

I hear she's suing her attackers now.

I hope she wins big.

On June 6, Hillary would become the Democratic Party nominee. She accomplished this by stealing the Democratic nomination from Bernie Sanders using "Super-delegates," enraging many on the Left by effectively invalidating their votes. One of these who was working during the super-delegate coup would be Democratic National Committee employee (and Bernie Sanders Supporter) 27-year-old Seth Rich.

On June 9th, the trap was set and ready to spring. Paul Manafort, Jared Kushner, and Donald Trump Jr. would finally meet with Natalia Veselnitskaya, that Russian lawyer who, again, was allowed into the US after being provided special entry by none other than Attorney General Lynch. As part of this setup, the Russian lawyer promised dirt on Clinton which was 1) never delivered, and 2) not a crime for anyone there to hear. In truth, she wanted to pressure Jr. about the Magnitsky Act—which makes sense because she, as a lawyer, specialized in this area.

On June 18, a British citizen named Michael Sanford would attempt to assassinate Trump when he would try to steal a police officer's gun. He would not be successful, end up arrested, serve some time in jail, and later be deported back to the UK.

On June 27, 2016, Bill Clinton and Attorney General Loretta Lynch would meet at Phoenix airport, on Lynch's private jet. Critics immediately called out the "Tarmac Meeting" as an appalling conflict of interest, coming at a time when Bill's wife Hillary was still under investigation by the Justice Department for her use of a private, unsanctioned e-mail server, and because someone in Lynch's position has an ethical duty to, at the very least, keep up the pretense of impartiality. Even many Democrats would go on to talk about the poor "optics" of the meeting. And while Lynch herself would go on to say the meeting was primarily social, and that she and Bill had merely talked about "grandkids" and "golf," we would soon learn a *very* different (and terrifying) version of the story from Q. In fact, what had taken place was something much more sinister, and even treasonous. But you'll hear more on that shortly.

Also in June, the Obama administration would have the intelligence community make its first official FISA warrant request to spy on the Trump campaign. It would be denied. (They would come back a while later, in October, after obtaining the Steele Dossier, and be successful in obtaining a warrant.)

It's important to note that this is the first "official" instance of spying. Trump had already been under illegal surveillance for some time at this point, with no courts involved, no warrants issued, and nothing even resembling due process—let alone an evidentiary basis to justify this spying. (And he wasn't the only one, either. Q would later inform us that the Ted Cruz campaign was *also* being spied upon at the same time.) In fact, it's important to understand, moving forward, that the NSA had heretofore scooped up pretty much every electronic communication, every bit and packet sent across the internet (yes, everything, from everyone), and it was standard practice to share that intelligence among all different American intelligence agencies. So, for instance, a CIA agent could query the NSA database to find out all sorts of things, at any point in time. However, because of routine auditing practices, the NSA can find out if this access is being abused in any way. And in fact, that's exactly what happened. The CIA was abusing their access to such an extent when it came to illegal Trump campaign surveillance (again, at the behest of the Obama administration, for the benefit of the Hillary Clinton campaign), that at one point, they anticipated they would be caught if they kept this up, and just copied the whole database over to their own cloud, hosted by none other than Amazon.com's S3 cloud services.

See, Amazon isn't just an online retailer. Actually, the most valuable segment of their business has historically been their web services, and they had a whopping contract with the CIA, valued at six-hundred million dollars alone. S3 web services run major portions of the internet, with some of the largest companies leveraging Amazon's server farms to run their businesses and host all their data.

And, if you're clever here, you'll note that Amazon is actually owned by Jeff Bezos; the same Jeff Bezos that owns the *Washington Post*. That would be the same *Washington Post* that has been absolutely relentless, leading the attack in article after article against Trump, and also against QAnon. As Q likes to say, there are "No Coincidences." And though the *Washington Post* was not alone in its attacks against Trump by any measure, many have since begun to speculate that part of the reason for the intensity of these media attacks has been because many of these same media companies took money from foreign governments to replace their shrinking subscribership and diminishing ad dollars, and failed to register as foreign agents in the process. In other words, this could mean massive amounts of arrests at media companies for FARA violations—the same thing Manafort, and more recently, long-time Clinton lackey Greg Craig were indicted for.

On July 10, 2016, Seth Rich would be shot twice and left to die outside one of his favorite bars less than two miles from his DC apartment. Reports would call it a "robbery" even though nothing was taken from Rich. In fact, we would later learn (through Q) that Seth Rich was responsible for leaking gigabytes of e-mails to Wikileaks, in an effort to expose fraud and corruption within the Democratic Party, and that Democratic Party officials were the ones responsible for ordering the assassination. As of this writing, we are still either waiting for Wikileaks' founder, Julian Assange (who has just been evicted from the Ecuadorian Embassy and arrested by British authorities), to testify in court about this fact, or for the US Government to somehow produce Wikileaks' server at some point. As Q has told us time and time again, they have "the source."

As a result of his wounds, Seth Rich would be rushed to MedStar Washington Hospital Center after he was found bleeding, but still alive. He would succumb to his wounds.

Almost a year later, in 2017, an Anon claiming to be a surgical resident at that hospital would come forward and claim that Rich had actually been successfully stabilized and had, in fact, begun to recover before expiring under suspicious circumstances. The story is related across several posts on the /pol/ board, captured below:

Anonymous ID:rhotYJAg Wed   [315 / 39]
17 May 2017 16:12:50 No.125912863
View   Reply   Original   Report
Quoted By: >>125913721 >>125914070
>>125914164 >>125914341 >>125914348
>>125914414 >>125914508 >>125914652
>>125914704 >>125914816 >>125914921
>>125915209 >>125915298 >>125915352
>>125915933 >>125916080 >>125916467
>>125916713 >>125917336 >>125917467
>>125917605 >>125917685 >>125917717
>>125917747 >>125917894 >>125918039
>>125918551 >>125918616 >>125918844
>>125919058 >>125919314 >>125919515 >>125920079 >>125920214 >>125920309 >>125920897
>>125921077 >>125921164 >>125921720 >>125922242 >>125922730 >>125922934 >>125923022
>>125924475 >>125924900 >>125925147 >>125925290 >>125927177 >>125927300 >>125927816
>>125928525 >>125929781 >>125930022 >>125930056 >>125931215 >>125931451

26KiB, 707x471, sethrich.jpg
View Same   Google   iqdb   SauceNAO   Trace

4th year surgery resident here who rotated at WHC (Washington Hospital Center) last year, it won't be hard to identify me but I feel that I shouldn't stay silent.

Seth Rich was shot twice, with 3 total gunshot wounds (entry and exit, and entry). He was taken to the OR emergently where we performed an exlap and found a small injury to segment 3 of the liver which was packed and several small bowel injuries (pretty common for gunshots to the back exiting the abdomen) which we resected ~12cm of bowel and left him in discontinuity (didn't hook everything back up) with the intent of performing a washout in the morning. He did not have any major vascular injuries otherwise. I've seen dozens of worse cases than this which survived and nothing about his injuries suggested to me that he'd sustained a fatal wound.

In the meantime he was transferred to the ICU and transfused 2 units of blood when his post-surgery crit came back ~20. He was stable and not on any pressors, and it seemed pretty routine. About 8 hours after he arrived we were swarmed by LEOs and pretty much everyone except the attending and a few nurses was kicked out of the ICU (disallowing visiting hours -normally every odd hour, eg 1am, 3am, etc- is not something we do routinely). It was weird as hell. At turnover that morning we were instructed not to round on the VIP that came in last night (that's exactly what the attending said, and no one except for me and another resident had any idea who he was talking about).

No one here was allowed to see Seth except for my attending when he died. No code was called. I rounded on patients literally next door but was physically blocked from checking in on him. I've never seen anything like it before, and while I can't say 100% that he was allowed to die, I don't understand why he was treated like that. Take it how you may, /pol/, I'm just one low level doc. Something's fishy though, that's for sure.

Anons wanted proof, of course:

Anonymous ID:OgVcl14e Wed 17 May 2017 16:19:04 No.125913721 🏴 Report
Quoted By: >>125914751 >>125916447

>>125912863
prove you are not a larper..
what are the list of medications you administered throughout the entire process?

And the poster replied:

Anonymous ID:rhotYJAg Wed 17 May 2017 16:26:47 No.125914751 🏴 Report
Quoted By: >>125915005 >>125915165 >>125915177 >>125915269 >>125915279 >>125915280 >>125915352 >>125915399
>>125915910 >>125916080 >>125916447 >>125917467 >>125922934 >>125923227 >>125923998 >>125924475 >>125924900
>>125926041 >>125927816 >>125927851

>>125913721
When he arrived to the trauma ward he had LR running, I don't keep up with how much he got but less
than 2 liters before we rolled to the OR.

No transfusion was done in trauma; the massive transfusion protocol was started because he was
hypotensive on arrival but by the time the cooler (4u PRBC, 2u FFP) was ready we were on the way to
the OR and honestly I don't remember if he got any of it beforehand; he responded well to just IVF
resuscitation so we went ahead with the surgery any just ended up giving him 2 units afterwards (the crit
we got in trauma was returned just after we left and was low, ~24 IIRC but it wasn't communicated to
us... teamwork fail for sure but that can happen when we're rushing to the OR)

As for the rest of the meds? You'd have to ask anesthesia I guess. He didn't need anything from us in the
ICU except a propofol/fentanyl drip to maintain sedation while intubated but that's pretty par for the
course. The important part was that he was hemodynamically stable and not requiring pressors.

Anon then asked:

Anonymous ID:bWD5LgGB Wed 17 May 2017 16:28:43 No.125915005 🏴 Report
Quoted By: >>125915395 >>125915975

>>125914751
Have you talked to any other doctors/staff present that day about the situation? Why is everyone so
quiet?

And the original poster once again answered:

Anonymous ID:rhotYJAg Wed 17 May 2017 16:36:13 No.125915975 🏴 Report
Quoted By: >>125916327 >>125916438 >>125916439 >>125916518 >>125917935 >>125926229

>>125915005

I haven't spoken to the attending who was on staff that night but the other resident I was with that night
doesn't remember it in any clarity (he was called to traumas as part of his rotation but that was ancillary
to his ICU -different ICU btw- duties). Basically he said, "yeah that was weird, right?" At the time we were
way more concerned with the rising class / new interns (July 1st is a terrifying time to be a patient lol) to
make much notice... it always stuck in my head as something super bizarre but it was a long time before
I even realized it was Seth Rich. When he arrived he was assigned by our system a trauma number, not
a name as his patient ID. I only knew him at that time as Tra### (no freaking way that I remember the
actual number). When it came to light who he was a while later I was floored. And terrified.

Anons would later find out that the director of surgery at that hospital, and thus, the
man in charge of Rich's care, was one Dr. Jack Sava. Sava's wife is one Lisa Kountoupes, a
former Department of Energy employee (with ties to Uranium One), and a top DC lobby-

ist who had previously been hired by the Clintons. Kountoupes would also visit the White House twenty-three times during the Obama administration. In 2008, Sava himself would visit the Bohemian Grove; that "summer camp" for the elites, out in California, where rumors of wild orgies with underage prostitutes, and strange, esoteric rituals abound. The Bohemian Grove is perhaps most well known among Alex Jones fans, that perennial figure of the conspiratorial world who runs Infowars.com (and who, as Q has told us, has multiple ties to many intelligence agencies, including the CIA, Stratfor, and Mossad—which would make him not the "infowarrior" he claims to be, but rather, controlled opposition). Still, in 2000, Alex Jones would sneak on to the 2,700+ acres owned by the Grove, and secretly film a ritual there known as the "*Cremation of Care,*" wherein what looked like an effigy was burned in front of a gigantic owl statue, fueling speculation that this was all one aspect of ancient Molech worship, resurrected, and brought back into the modern day. And while the Grove is certainly a hub of Cabal activity, it is a common belief among the Q community that the actual disclosures delivered by Bill Cooper, author of *Behold, a Pale Horse*, scared the Cabal so badly, that they propped up Jones in order to detract and distract from Cooper's claims, thus making his documentary on the Grove some kind of strange, controlled disclosure operation; something to keep the "conspiracy" crowd satisfied, even as their plans and activities continued. But don't read that bit as an endorsement of Cooper. While Q has referenced him on at least one occasion, there's much that he writes that I, personally, find very difficult to believe at this point in time. But regardless of what one thinks of Cooper himself, there's no denying that he was shot dead by Apache County sheriffs, in 2001, after correctly predicting the 9/11 attacks.

As for Dr. Sava, he would also shortly oversee care of Rep. Steve Scalise, following a failed assassination attempt by lunatic Leftist James Hodgkinson at the annual congressional baseball game. Trump would visit Scalise in hospital, but would also bring his personal physician, Dr. Ronny Jackson, along for the trip.

On July 2, 2016, "FBIAnon" would appear on /pol/ for the first time, claiming to have intimate knowledge as a "high level analyst" working on the Clinton e-mail investigation, while repeatedly encouraging Anons to look at the Clinton Foundation, saying things like:

> The real point of interest is the Clinton Foundation, not the e-mail server. We received the server from Benghazi, then from the server we found data on the CF. Then we realized the situation is much worse than previously thought.

And,

> Killing HRC would not cause this problem to go away. The problem is with the Clinton Foundation as I mentioned, which you should just imagine as a massive spider web of connections and money laundering implicating hundreds of high-level people. Though I do not have a high opinion of Hillary, she is just a piece -albeit a big piece—of this massive shitstorm.

And,

> The DOJ is most likely looking to save itself. Find everyone involved in the Clinton Foundation, from its donors to its Board of Directors, and imagine they are all implicated.

And,

We have our hands tied. My message to you and everyone on this board is do not get distracted by Clinton's e-mails. Focus on the Foundation. All of the nightmarish truth is there. The e-mails will pale in comparison.

Similar to Q, FBIAnon would come on and drop "breadcrumbs" for Anons to follow across multiple threads, largely in relation to the Clinton Foundation and associated corruption, and usually in a question-answer format. While I generally believe most of what FBIAnon has posted, in fact, he can't claim one hundred percent accuracy—which, in a strange way, actually bolsters the case for legitimacy, because when you consider he claims to be an analyst making informed guesses about things, it makes sense that he should misjudge at times. The sense I get when reading FBIAnon is that he's part of the rank and file; an analyst, exactly as he claims (there has been some speculation among Anons that former FBI director James Comey is actually FBIAnon, although I find that *highly* unlikely). Likewise, much of what FBIAnon would ultimately say would line up with what Q would later say himself.

And it's also notable that FBIAnon wasn't the only one adopting this "breadcrumb" approach. Another would be WhiteHouseAnon; that is, this particular Anon claiming to be someone who worked in the White House:

File: GET READY!.png (23 KB, 152x152)

☐ Remember Remember the 27th of July White House Anon (ID: o8D/Z3tb)
07/05/17(Wed)18:20:33 No.132550751   [Reply]   ▶ >>132552160 >>132552523

Obamacare, the people that sacrificed themselves to pass it, the payoffs/jobs they got afterwords, and who immediately got rich shortly Obama care took in full effect.

Trump is days away from swinging everything back at the swamp.

You guys mad that legislation is not passing? Wont really get much this year. Trumps plan is to drain all of the swamp in the first year, release a lot of the shackles that government is putting on business, and keeping us safe.

Remember...The swamp contains many in the media. Look into CNN. Not just the big news anchors, but the administration and people making the shots in the background. Anchors are just the puppets.

Get ready for some fun!

27/07/2017

*Will post proof that I am previous White House Anon

WhiteHouseAnon would go on to describe things like the "Slingshot theory" and the "Ring of Fire Theory" to Anons; the primary being the method Trump used to keep the media perpetually off balance, and the latter being the method the Clintons used to cover up their crimes, by making them so horribly heinous, they could only be a part of a wild and unhinged "conspiracy theory."

Others notable accounts would pop up in time. These include High Level Insider Anon, DNC Hatchetman, and the Knowledge Bomber. However, all these drops illustrate a problem /pol/ had at the time, and that's with verification and imitators. Within a thread, it's easy enough to identify someone by their ID number (a unique set of digits given to each anonymous purpose, that only exists within that thread), but once you move into a new thread (especially on a new day), it can be impossible to determine whether someone is really who they claim to be. This would often attract imitators and LARPers (that is, Live Action Role Players), who get a kick out of pretending to be someone like FBIAnon. Take, for instance, this post by "WhiteHouseAnon" wherein almost everything he says here is false:

35KiB, 615x409, 1.jpg

View Same Google iqdb SauceNAO

WH Insider Anon Here [323 / 58 / ?]

Anonymous ID:pESrSDhG Wed 01 Nov
2017 16:01:41 No.147518205

View Reply Original Report

Quoted By: >>147518536 >>147518547
>>147518550 >>147518635 >>147518698
>>147518726 >>147518780 >>147518924
>>147518991 >>147519047 >>147519271
>>147519274 >>147519288 >>147519338
>>147519452 >>147519456 >>147519596
>>147519686 >>147519750 >>147519789
>>147519953 >>147520314 >>147520331
>>147520497 >>147520624 >>147520795
>>147520991 >>147521003 >>147521050 >>147521051 >>147521069 >>147521132 >>147521217
>>147521708 >>147521968 >>147522439 >>147522846 >>147522931 >>147523317 >>147523783
>>147523990 >>147524230 >>147525564 >>147525992 >>147526062 >>147526270 >>147526405
>>147526632 >>147526967 >>147527028 >>147527111 >>147527303 >>147527600 >>147528318
>>147528406 >>147528891 >>147529404 >>147529769 >>147530426 >>147530489 >>147531398
>>147531474 >>147531488 >>147531841 >>147531942 >>147532043 >>147532667 >>147532864
>>147534327 >>147535567

Hello /pol/.

Both Tony and John Podesta will be indicted / charged this week. Hillary Clinton will be charged on
historic date of November 8th as of right now but it could be sooner. The only reason this is withheld
until then is to wait until after planned protests on November 4th, to minimize damages.

George Papadopoulos was also a plant by Hillary Clinton, just like Paul Manafort.

The next 7-10 days are going to be pleasing. Thanks guys!

Obviously, all his "predictions" here failed. But this is important, because you're now
seeing just a little bit about how different factions, groups, and agencies were waging an information war on the Chans before, during, and after Trump's election. And all that's on top
of trying to sort out whether what they were saying was truthful (to the best of their knowledge) at the time. I wasn't exaggerating before when I called this "information warfare" and
referred to Anons as soldiers, duking it out in the trenches. Sorting through all the noise and
lies requires a high level of collective intelligence, and a critical eye (even to the point of paranoia). Thankfully, this issue of LARPers hopping on your ID and pretending to be you is
solved by the use of tripcode verification (which is what Q would later use), during his shift
to 8ch. But back to our timeline for the moment, because we've still got a lot to get through:

On July 5, 2016, FBI Director James Comey would recommend "No charges" for
Hillary Clinton for her mishandling of classified e-mails during her tenure as secretary of
State calling her, in the end, "extremely careless." Again, we would soon learn from Q the
treasonous reasoning behind this recommendation. In the meantime, it seemed that once
again, Hillary Clinton had slithered her way out of a seemingly impossible scenario; the kind
of scenario that would get others locked up for a very, very long time.

And we can't forget the details about the three Muslim brothers, Abid, Imran, and
Jamal Awan, in all of this. All three were born in Pakistan, all three were members of the
Muslim Brotherhood, all three were managing the IT for the House Permanent Select Com-
mittee on Intelligence and other lawmakers as "shared employees." And yes, all three were

banned from accessing the House network back in February of 2016 for suspected theft and data breaches. Despite this, Imran Awan was kept on by DNC chief Debbie Wasserman-Schultz during this time. The Awan narrative is especially involved and winding, and includes a number of crimes that range from theft of devices, money laundering (through a shell company known as Cars International A—yes, abbreviated CIA), and equipment theft, to the previously mentioned data breaches. In truth, we would later learn from Q that these men, acting on behalf of the Muslim Brotherhood, were using incriminating e-mails and communications to blackmail members of Congress—and that this was known by Obama at the time, who is himself Muslim Brotherhood. Yes, all that media spin about him being a "Christian" is yet another Mockingbird lie.

Shocking, I know.

Any coincidence then, that according to Q, Seth Rich, acting as whistleblower, could access all those DNC e-mails and send them off to Wikileaks? The public has already seen some of what's contained within, but again, these systems were being exploited by Awan for the express purpose of blackmailing members of Congress and various politicians—not just those accessing the DNC server, but the entire Congress before it. Awan would later be caught trying to flee the country, despite having not yet been charged with anything.

On July 7, Carter Page would give a paid speech in Moscow.

On July 16, Stefan Halper, an "ex" FBI and CIA operative with dual citizenship in the US and Great Britain (and with many contacts throughout western intelligence agencies), would have a meeting with Carter Page at Cambridge. Halper had been teaching as a professor at the Centre for International Studies at Cambridge when some *unusual* deposits were made by the Obama administration to his bank account…

Award ID (Mod#):	HQ003416P0148 (0) (View)	Award Type:	PURCHASE ORDER
Vendor Name:	HALPER, STEFAN	Contracting Agency:	WASHINGTON HEADQUARTERS SERVICES (WHS)
Date Signed:	September 27, 2016	Action Obligation:	$282,295
Referenced IDV:		Contracting Office:	WASHINGTON HEADQUARTERS SERVICES
NAICS (Code):	RESEARCH AND DEVELOPMENT IN THE SOCIAL SCIENCES AND HUMANITIES (541720)	PSC (Code):	SPECIAL STUDIES/ANALYSIS- FOREIGN/NATIONAL SECURITY POLICY (B540)
Vendor City:	GREAT FALLS	Vendor DUNS:	078459148
Vendor State:	VA	Vendor ZIP:	220663224
Global Vendor Name:	HALPER STEFAN	Global DUNS Number:	078459148

Award ID (Mod#):	HQ003416P0148 (P00001) (View)	Award Type:	PURCHASE ORDER
Vendor Name:	HALPER, STEFAN	Contracting Agency:	WASHINGTON HEADQUARTERS SERVICES (WHS)
Date Signed:	July 26, 2017	Action Obligation:	$129,280
Referenced IDV:		Contracting Office:	WASHINGTON HEADQUARTERS SERVICES
NAICS (Code):	RESEARCH AND DEVELOPMENT IN THE SOCIAL SCIENCES AND HUMANITIES (541720)	PSC (Code):	SPECIAL STUDIES/ANALYSIS- FOREIGN/NATIONAL SECURITY POLICY (B540)
Vendor City:	GREAT FALLS	Vendor DUNS:	078459148
Vendor State:	VA	Vendor ZIP:	220663224
Global Vendor Name:	HALPER STEFAN	Global DUNS Number:	078459148

Later, Carter Page would testify before a House Intelligence Committee that he had indeed spoken to a few Russian officials in July while visiting Moscow to speak at two economic and foreign policy events going on there. But Carter Page was working undercover for the FBI at the time, and had done so at least since 2013. So here again, you have the FBI and the CIA colluding with each other to set up the pretense of a Trump-Russian collusion narrative; even being willing to throw their own assets under the bus in order to accomplish this, it seems.

But Julian Assange had an axe to grind with one Lady Clinton. A dedicated white hat and perpetual fly in Hillary's ointment, Hillary had previously tried all manner of tactics to get rid of Assange, including proposing to State Department staffers that they send in a drone to assassinate him, and later, according to Q, malign him with all manner of rape and sexual assault allegations (a favorite tactic of the Deep State, as we all saw during the

Kavanaugh confirmation hearing. Yes, the Deep State has assets everywhere; suggestible individuals who have been subjected to Monarch mind control programs, which involve all sorts of ritual abuse. We'll cover that more in depth in a later chapter). So you can see why Assange would jump at the chance to finally strike back at her. And strike he did.

On July 22, Wikileaks would blindside the Democratic party by publishing close to 20,000 DNC e-mails (with many more on the way). Debbie Wasserman-Schultz would resign as DNC chairwoman in the wake of this massive scandal. To counter and contain any of the damage that would come from those asking "inconvenient" questions as a result of this leak, the Deep State had to react quickly. They needed to drop some chaff to throw people off the trail and keep this from spiraling out of their control. And so, they cooked up a false identity; a "hacker" calling themselves "Guccifer 2.0" claimed responsibility for hacking the DNC servers and leaking the e-mails to Wikileaks. Guccifer also claimed he leaked information to former Trump adviser Roger Stone, as well—once again, trying to set up a Trump-Russia narrative.

The Guccifer 2.0 story would start the ball rolling and form the basis of the "Russian Hacker/Russian Collusion" narrative (and the later Special Counselinvestigation, run by Robert Mueller) as outlets like Buzzfeed and the Daily Beast (upon whose board of directors sits one Chelsea Clinton) began to report that Guccifer 2.0 had "messed up"[7] and accidentally revealed he was a member of the Russian Intelligence Agency, the GRU.

How convenient for the DNC.

Julian Assange, founder and editor of Wikileaks, would later emphatically deny any and all involvement with Russian intelligence and these leaks.

WikiLeaks ✓
@wikileaks

(Follow) ⌄

WikiLeaks has a 100% record of accurate authentication. We do not endorse Buzzfeed's publication of a document which is clearly bogus.

8:25 PM - 10 Jan 2017

16,701 Retweets **27,391** Likes

♡ 981   ⟲ 17K   ♡ 27K

But at some point after this, control of the Wikileaks Twitter account would be wrested from Assange, and taken over by the Deep State. The date when this transpired isn't exactly clear, but in the wake of these drops, Assange was in for a world of hurt, holed up in the Ecuadorian Embassy. Later, in November of 2016, Russia Today would publish an "interview" between Assange and John Pilger, but a number of strange artifacts in the video, including what can best be described as digital morphs (such as the kind used in Hollywood special effects to transform one subject into another, as in the film *Willow*) were noticed by Anons. At certain points in the video, his collar would snap in an unnatural way, or he would have

---

7 https://www.thedailybeast.com/exclusive-lone-dnc-hacker-guccifer-20-slipped-up-and-revealed-he-was-a-russian-intelligence-officer

his eyeball shift position on his head, blending into another image of his eye, but focused in a completely different direction. It's something someone has to see in motion to truly appreciate. Clearly, the footage has been manipulated in some startling way.

On July 31, the FBI would formally open its "Crossfire Hurricane" counterintelligence investigation into the Trump campaign, led by FBI agent Peter Strzok.

On August 1, Strzok and others would fly to England to meet with various members of the intelligence community there, and to interview one Alexander Downer; the same Alexander Downer who had spoken to George Papadopoulos back in May. The existence of this investigation would not be disclosed to Congress until March of the following year. Peter Strzok would say in a text, quite literally in all caps, like some kind of unruly teenager:

OMG I CANNOT BELIEVE WE ARE SERIOUSLY LOOKING AT THESE ALLEGATIONS AND THE PERVASIVE CONNECTIONS.

Days later, on August 15, Strzok would message Department of Justice lawyer Lisa Page, talking about their "insurance policy" in case of a Trump win in November:

I want to believe the path you threw out for consideration in Andy's office—that there's no way he gets elected—but I'm afraid we can't take that risk. It's like an insurance policy in the unlikely event you die before you're 40...

The story Strzok and Page had been given is that they were secret lovers, paramours, but I do not believe that this is case. The "lovers" story is, in fact, one of the oldest cover stories the Deep State has at its disposal. I don't believe they were ever lovers. I believe they had both been tasked by the highest levels of the Obama administration to help spy on, and take down Trump, a private citizen. I don't have proof of this assertion just yet, but Q has told us that Lisa Page is a cooperating witness now, so the truth will come out in time.

Q would later release a series of surveillance photographs taken from traffic cams in London, tracking Strzok, Page, and several others as they worked their way through the city, to the CIA field office... where one Gina Haspel (who Trump would appoint as CIA director after the election) just happened to be working at the time.

1721

But back to our timeline.

On August 16, in the wake of the Seth Rich murder, the Washington, DC, chief of police Cathy Lanier would step down to work as head of security for the NFL.

On August 19, Manafort would resign from the 'Irump campaign, amid questions about his ties to Russian operatives.

On September 9, Hillary would stumble with her now infamous "Basket of Deplorables" speech, which we talked about in the previous chapter.

And then, on September 11, Hillary would be filmed collapsing outside of a 9/11 memorial event in lower Manhattan, losing not just her consciousness, but a shoe in the process. This, and a number of other episodes throughout the year (such as her repeated coughing fits, and the time when she spat up mucous plugs into a glass of water while giving a speech in front of cameras and a crowd) would give rise to a number of questions about the state of her health (and thus, her fitness for the office of the presidency). She would later come on Jimmy Kimmel and prove her vitality by… opening a jar of pickles.

Sidenote: Kimmel would be described as an "Activist" by Barack Hussein Obama in a promo video he helped cut to support U2s front man Bono with his *RED* initiative. Obama would go on in the same video to label Bono a "Ringmaster." Q would clue us in that both were hidden titles/roles given and recognized within the Cabal hierarchy, and that Obama was sending a message, hidden in plain sight, to interested parties who were paying attention.

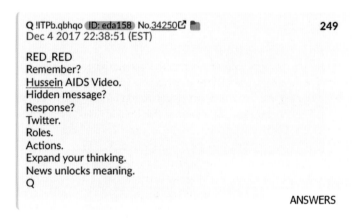

Q !ITPb.qbhqo ID: eda158 No.34250   **249**
Dec 4 2017 22:38:51 (EST)

RED_RED
Remember?
Hussein AIDS Video.
Hidden message?
Response?
Twitter.
Roles.
Actions.
Expand your thinking.
News unlocks meaning.
Q

ANSWERS

In fact, Q would confirm that the hidden message Obama was sending at the time was, in fact, an answer to this question, sent by Bono (or his handlers), through his *RED* website:

Obama was willing to meet with whomever was asking the question, and Kimmel was knowingly facilitating the transmission of the message. And that's just a bit of a foretaste for the kind of mind-bending stuff the Cabal does with regularity, in order to keep their efforts hidden from the rest of us. We'll be looking at a lot more of that kind of thing in the coming chapters.

On September 13, Halper would meet with George Papadopoulos in London, where his female "assistant," alias Azra Turk, would be assigned by the FBI to accompany Halper and assist in targeting Papadopoulos. Turk would try to seduce Papadopoulos, with Papadopoulos later calling her a honeypot—in the hopes of extracting more information from him regarding Russian Collusion within the Trump campaign.

On October 7, 2016, Wikileaks would begin posting what they would entitle "The Podesta E-mails." John Podesta, you may recall, was Hillary's campaign manager at the time. Conversations contained within the archive would lead to discoveries about "Spirit Cooking" and "performance artist" Marina Abramovic, as well as a "Pizza Code," all of which would form the basis of "Pizzagate;" a hypothesis that dark, even Satanic practices were commonplace among elites, and that human trafficking and pedophilia was occurring with frightening regularity, right under common people's noses. Searching for "Spirit Cooking" online would lead to a video on YouTube which featured a ritual where Abramovic would mix together blood, semen, and breast milk in a vat, and then use that mixture to write inscriptions on the walls of the building she was performing the ritual in, before pouring the clotted sludge over child-sized effigies (such as the one pictured on the bottom right corner in the picture below, which is taken straight from that video):

John Podesta would eagerly invite his brother (and one of the largest lobbyists in Washington, DC, at the time, Tony Podesta) to the "dinner."

Fwd: Dinner

From:podesta@podesta.com
To: john.podesta@gmail.com
Date: 2015-06-28 01:48
Subject: Fwd: Dinner

Are you in NYC Thursday July 9
Marina wants you to come to dinner
Mary?

Sent from my iPhone

Begin forwarded message:

From: Marina Abramovic <marinaxabramovic@gmail.com<mailto:marinaxabramovic@gmail.com>>
Date: June 28, 2015 at 2:35:08 AM GMT+2
To: Tony Podesta <podesta@podesta.com<mailto:podesta@podesta.com>>
Subject: Dinner

Dear Tony,

I am so looking forward to the Spirit Cooking dinner at my place. Do you think you will be able to let me know if your brother is joining?

All my love, Marina

Needless to say, the revelation that Washington elites were attending bloody rituals would set the internet on fire. And that was just the beginning. When the "Pizza code," was discovered, all bets were off. The hypothesis here was that the code itself referred to boys and girls and specific sexual acts with thinly veiled food references, the most infamous example probably being this e-mail, here:

Cheese

```
From:hms@sandlerfoundation.org
To: podesta.mary@gmail.com, john.podesta@gmail.com
Date: 2015-12-24 18:40
Subject: Cheese
```

```
Mary and John
I think you should give notice when changing strategies which have been long in place. I immediately
realized something was different by the shape of the box and I contemplated who would be sending me
something in the square shaped box. Lo and behold, instead of pasta and wonderful sauces, it was a
lovely, tempting assortment of cheeses, Yummy. I am awaiting the return of my children and
grandchildren from their holiday travels so that we can demolish them.
Thank you so much. I hope you and your gang are well.
I miss you both
Best wishes fro a merry Christmas and Happy New Year.
Herb

Ps. Do you think I'll do better playing dominos on cheese than on pasta?
```

"Do you think I'll do better playing dominos on cheese than on pasta?"

Not exactly common English phraseology, is it?

And that is far from the only example. Others would include descriptions of a "walnut sauce" in a back and forth with Democrat mega-donor, billionaire, and funding source behind the ongoing "Need to Impeach" campaign against Trump, Tom Steyer, as well as an e-mail describing the discovery of a "pizza-related" handkerchief, leading some to question if that was, in and of itself, a reference to the handkerchief code often employed within the homosexual community. Horrified by their initial findings, Anons, in dogged pursuit of the truth, combed through all of the e-mails, and soon found a striking relationship between the Hillary Clinton campaign and James Alefantis' DC-based pizza shop, Comet Ping Pong.

The first thing that was immediately apparent about Alefantis himself is that he was strikingly well-connected, being the ex-homosexual partner of David Brock, founder of Media Matters for America and friend of the Rothschilds. (Full disclosure, Media Matters for America would, on their website in 2018, go on to attack me as a "right-wing amplifier" of Q. It's also suspected that the Deep State tried to assassinate David Brock at one point, inducing a heart attack that put him in the hospital, but which ultimately failed to kill him). GQ would even name Alefantis one of the fifty most influential people in Washington, DC, which is very odd for a small restaurateur. It was heavily speculated at the time that Alefantis was a Rothschild himself, though no definitive proof of this was ever found one way or the other (at least to my knowledge—though, personally, I find some of the theories out there rather compelling).

49/51

49. James Alefantis

Restaurateur and Bon Vivant

Liberal twentysomethings in khakis drink beer and eat pizza at Alefantis-owned Comet Ping Pong. More established progressives wine and dine next door at Alefantis-owned Buck's Fishing Camping. Alefantis is also the board president of Transformer, the contemporary art gallery that shamed the Smithsonian for removing an installation offensive to right-wingers. When it comes to D.C. radical chic, Alefantis is unsurpassed. If you don't know him, you aren't wearing your scarf right.

Anons immediately started scouring his social media accounts, which revealed, well… many, many unfortunate images much like the one you see here:

As you can imagine, that didn't exactly help Alefantis' case in the eyes of Anons. And it should be noted that this was *far* from the only example, and not even the worst image uncovered. It should also be noted that Alefantis' avatar on Instagram at the time was a statue of Antinous, the boy-lover of Roman Emperor Hadrian, further fueling wild internet speculation.

Cue more digging, and Anons soon discovered much, much more—notably, that Comet Ping Pong lay along a road with several other questionable businesses—namely, Besta Pizza.

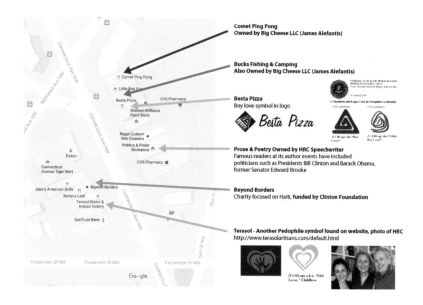

Besta Pizza is notable for its logo, which, according to FBI documents, resembled a known "boy-lover" symbol.

FEDERAL BUREAU OF INVESTIGATION
INTELLIGENCE BULLETIN
Cyber Division, Innocent Images National Initiative

31 January 2007

(U) Symbols and Logos Used by Pedophiles to Identify Sexual Preferences

UNCLASSIFIED   UNCLASSIFIED   UNCLASSIFIED

(U) BLogo aka "Boy   (U) LBLogo aka "Little   (U) BLogo imprinted on coins
Lover"   Boy Lover"

UNCLASSIFIED

(U) BLogo jewelry

UNCLASSIFIED//LAW ENFORCEMENT SENSITIVE

Investigations raged online, with new discoveries and connections popping up every hour for weeks on end. The Mockingbird Media almost immediately went into damage control mode, with many talking heads condemning the grassroots investigation outright, labeling it as—you guessed it—a "crazy conspiracy theory." An investigative community sprung up online, especially on Reddit, under the /r/Pizzagate sub. As Pizzagate reached critical mass, pressure was mounting and Alefantis would give an interview with the BBC wherein he would say:

"They ignore basic truths. For instance, the conspiracy supposedly is run out of the restaurant's basement. We don't even have a basement."

"Sometimes an innocent picture of a child in a basket is just an innocent picture of a child in a basket and not proof of a child sex trafficking ring."

This would become something of a rallying cry among Pizzagate deniers. However, this new claim that Comet Ping Pong did not have a basement directly contradicted Alefantis' own words in an interview which he had given in 2015 to MetroWeekly:

James Alefantis at Comet Ping Pong - Photography by Todd Franson

MW: *What was it they couldn't believe you had made?*

ALEFANTIS: Well, we make everything from scratch. Other restaurants, even good restaurants, will, like, not roast their own peppers. You can just buy the roasted peppers in a can. Or you can buy garlic oil. Some products you can get, and they're consistent and they're easy. But I didn't even know that existed actually until they said that. I was like, "What do you mean? There's another way? You can just buy these things?" Because a lot of restaurants will open a can and put it on. Like our sauce — we harvest a whole crop of organic tomatoes — 10 tons of tomatoes every year. Can them all, store them in the basement, have like a harvest party when it gets loaded in. [8]

It was even speculated, at the time, that children were being moved via a system of disused tunnels, built by the DuPont corporation under DC decades earlier. Originally added to the DuPont Circle in 1949, the tunnels were designed for underground street cars, and ran right under Connecticut Ave., which was were Comet Ping Pong (and many other suspect businesses) were located. This led some of the more adventurous Anons to try and access the tunnels and record their exploits in YouTube videos, though by the time this particular connection was made, there had already been enough time for any bad actors to clean up the scene of any potential crimes, so nothing was ever found this way.

One YouTube researcher, Ryan O'Neal, even wanted to give Alefantis a chance to tell his side of the story. He reached out to him online, but was shocked when Alefantis allegedly threatened to kill him, his friends, and his family after viewing one of his previous videos. O'Neal would file a police report with the Galveston, Texas police, case number 17-000111. He would also report Alefantis to the FBI.

Oh, and by the way, the Access Hollywood tape a.k.a. the "Grab her by the pussy" tape, would come out just ***hours*** before this Wikileaks release. To this day, there is heavy speculation that the tape was edited, and while the language used in the tape is crass, the outrage it

---

8   https://www.metroweekly.com/2015/04/from-scratch-james-alefantis/

generated was not proportional to the contents, chiefly because despite the hard language, it's plain that Trump was just describing the lack of character some women in the entertainment industry exhibit. He didn't say he had performed such an action. He wasn't saying it was good behavior, or even something he wanted to do. He was expressing disbelief at how loose some of these women he had encountered in the entertainment industry were, saying they would let a star touch them in the most intimate way possible just because they were rich and famous. In other words, the women he was describing were using sex to get ahead in business. And I know this next statement is bound to shock some people, but amazingly, the so-called City of Angels is filled with anything but! At any rate, the point I want to convey here is that the Cabal was so desperate for you to not pay attention to the Wikileaks, they had to scrounge up some secret recording from a decade prior and blast it out for weeks to incense the easily manipulated, and distract them from the real scandal being uncovered by volunteer researchers every day.

Another major revelation included among the Wikileaks was a transcript of a private speech Hillary had given to the National Multi-Family Housing Council in 2013, wherein she described how you needed both a "public and private position" when it came to the likes of Wall Street reform, in essence, advocating lying and pandering to whomever happened to be in the room at the time in order to gain influence and votes, while always knowing to whom you really owed your allegiances. She would later dismiss objections to this by referencing, of all things, the Spielberg film *Lincoln*, at a later presidential debate.

On October 20, Trump would give his now-famous speech at the Al Smith charity dinner (what I've since taken to calling "The Red Dinner"), hurling some of his most vicious criticism of Clinton to date, to her face, with her cackling along with distinctly forced laughter the whole time. To say it was absolutely savage would be a massive understatement, and it was clear from Trump's tone (and by the shocked expressions of the guests, who were by now profusely sweating in their seats and dying to get out of that room) that there was much more truth to these "jokes" than many in the room cared to acknowledge.

> "Now, if some of you have not noticed, Hillary is not laughing as much as the rest of us. That's because she knows the jokes. All of the jokes were given to her in advance of the dinner by Donna Brazile."
>
> [Boos]
>
> **"Everyone knows, of course, Hillary has believed that it takes a village, which only makes sense, after all, in places like Haiti, where she has taken a number of them."**
>
> [Boos]
>
> "Thank you. I won't go this evening without saying something nice about my opponent. Hillary has been in Washington a long time. She knows a lot about how government works. And according to her sworn testimony, Hillary has forgotten more things than most of us will ever, ever know, that I can tell you."
>
> [Boos]
>
> "We are having some fun here tonight, and that's good."

And yes, that bit about Haiti was probably one of the biggest non-joke "jokes" Trump delivered that night. Just ask Laura Silsby, who we'll talk about much later in this book.

Parallel to the Pizzagate investigations, there was also a chain of inquiry set off by yet another Wikileaks e-mail contained within the Podesta Archives, where a thinly veiled plot to assassinate Supreme Court Justice Scalia was discovered:

1MiB, 1280x720, 133.png
View Same Google iqdb SauceNAO

SCALIA HIT JOB - MORE [335 / 79 / ?]
PROOF Anonymous ID:cCfeKxf/ Sat 15 Oct 2016 01:06:53 No.92994832
View Reply Original Report
Quoted By: >>92995209 >>92995290 >>92995422 >>92995615 >>92995644 >>92995930 >>92996220 >>92997099 >>92998135 >>92998870 >>92999560 >>93000710 >>93000862 >>93000863 >>93001908 >>93002071 >>93002240 >>93002797 >>93002923 >>93003131 >>93003839 >>93003852 >>93004130 >>93004206 >>93004479 >>93004709 >>93005276 >>93005457 >>93006287 >>93006482 >>93006640 >>93006789 >>93006994 >>93007280 >>93008649 >>93008773 >>93009492 >>93009527 >>93010480 >>93011991 >>93014050

"I have proof of the hit contract they put out on Scalia. They being Podesta. I believe I have found proof in the wikileaks emails, specifically this one
(https://wikileaks.com/podesta-emails/emailid/1459)
which seems to be detailing a "movie" contract for Podesta to pick up? But he's not a film producer. What could this be? Wet work codespeak? Yep. Includes even a map. They had a contract out on Justice Scalia. I found the "order" in the emails disguised in a subtle request for "funding" for a "film idea". The cost, $1.5 million dollars down, $15 million on completion of the hit. They were so brazen that they even sent a URL to a map showing a line to the location in texas where the ranch is that Scalia died......they used a smithsonian map to mark the spot.
http://www.smithsonianeducation.org/educators/lesson_plans/borders/map1a.html
There's the map URL as it was sent in the email to Podesta (seemingly responding to the contract request)......with the line showing precisely where they would do it at.....the ranch in west Texas and how they would escape, to Mexico through Tecate. Here's the wikileaks email Podesta was sent:
https://wikileaks.com/podesta-emails/emailid/1459
There it is, a contract to kill a supreme right there in CIA codespeak with a cute little "movie" pitch idea that went like this "I have the script, the budget and a producer for this 2016 political, game changing film project - funding is needed. You would be in charge of the content and selecting the producer." But again, Podesta is not a film producer. You're welcome."

The e-mail this particular Anon had stumbled upon is represented here, in part:

A 2016 game changing, feature film project for your consideration.

From:viejojoe@outlook.com
To: podesta@law.georgetown.edu
Date: 2015-11-17 03:40
Subject: A 2016 game changing, feature film project for your consideration.

Dear Professor Podesta,
Hello from a D.A.R. documented descendant of Ohio Governor Robert Lucas,
chairman of the very first DNC Convention that was held in Baltimore.
He was appointed by the President to become the territorial governor of Iowa.
I also sent this to gpataki@chadbourne.com

Remember what happened when President Reagan said
"Tear Down This Wall?" to Mr. Gorbachev,

A gigantic economic expansion was ignited.

That's the goal of this film project.

I have the script, the budget and a producer for this 2016 political, game
changing film project - funding is needed.
You would be in charge of the content and selecting the producer.
~~~~~~~~~~~~jp

Presenting "INEZ COMES TO AMERICA"

The entire film is scored with a very up-beat Mariachi/Mexicana theme.

Below is the beginning of the final scene, but first, some set-up detail.

Most Americans (and for that matter, the entire rest of the world)
either don't remember or might not even
have heard about our war with Mexico and -
The Treaty of Guadalupe Hidalgo which
forced Mexico to accept $15 million for all the land in this link.

http://www.smithsonianeducation.org/educators/lesson_plans/borders/map1a.html

It's time to redress this old wrong!

Log Line: INEZ, a young Mexican girl, crosses the border
in search of work and her missing mother.
She finds political corruption, murder and cover-up.
ALEX, a young border guard/law student of mixed ethnic heritage
(American/Mexican) intercepts her, and listens to her story.

Anons were quick to compare the map linked in the e-mail at the time (which called out a particular location on the western border of Texas), and the location of Cibolo Creek Ranch, where Justice Scalia had died:

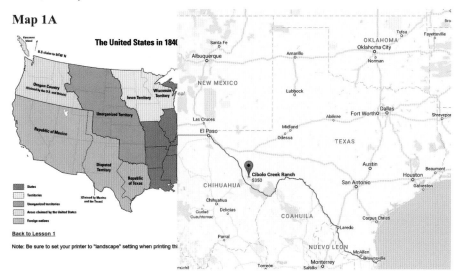

RE: Thanks

_____

From: elmendorf@teamsubjectmatter.com

To: john.podesta@gmail.com

Date: 2016-02-09 20:56

Subject: RE: Thanks

_____

I am all in

Sounds like it will be a bad nite , we all need to buckle up and double down

From: John Podesta [mailto:john.podesta@gmail.com]

Sent: Tuesday, February 09, 2016 4:36 PM

To: Steve Elmendorf <elmendorf@teamsubjectmatter.com>

Subject: Thanks

Didn't think wet works meant pool parties at the Vineyard.

In essence, a "screenwriter" had pitched John Podesta a movie idea, complete with characters, plot, setting and price. Why, it almost looked like he was trying to get approval for a contract. One big problem: John Podesta isn't a movie producer. Add that to some of the inconsistencies observed in Scalia's death: that he was first reported to have been found with a pillow over his head, and then, suddenly, there was no pillow. There was also the fact that no autopsy was ever performed, and that Scalia was cremated, despite being a devout traditionalist Catholic, who even rejected the rulings of Vatican II, and thus, would have rejected cremation on profoundly religious grounds. Things just didn't add up in the case of Scalia's death, and Anons took notice.

Then came election day. On November 6, Donald Trump would finally win the presidency, to the shock of many around the nation. And the shock was for good reason. For weeks, the people had been hearing about how Trump had virtually no chance of winning. A day before the election, the Princeton Election Consortium had given Hillary a ninety-nine percent chance of winning. The *Huffington Post,* a ninety-eight percent chance. *Daily Kos,* ninety-two percent. CNN, ninety-one percent. The *New York Times,* eighty-five percent. FiveThirtyEight, seventy-two percent. All the polls were tilted in her favor, and yet, in a stunning upset, Trump had seemingly flown in from behind and trounced her like some kind of maniac dark horse.

Hillary would refuse to concede at first, instead, sending out her campaign manager, John Podesta around 2:00 a.m. to speak to the crowd that had gathered for her "coronation" as the presumptive winner. He would tell everyone to come back tomorrow after they had learned more, leaving many of Hillary's upset and crying fans bewildered as to what had just happened; unwilling to accept reality. And as a side-note, there's a popular narrative out there that Trump won the electoral college, while Hillary *really* won the popular vote (therefore, we should do away with the electoral college; that antiquated rule that was invented by all those founders who happened to be "white men," and subsequently used each election to keep "white men" in power—when in truth the explicit purpose of this is to keep a balance of power between population centers and, for instance, less populated regions where all the **FOOD** is grown). Lunatic Leftists—especially the kind that congregate in cities—tend to forget that there's a whole world outside their metropolitan bubble. If the electoral college was gone, all someone would have to do to rule as a despot from here on out is convince these population centers to keep voting for them; often by promising all sorts of "benefits" they have no intention of ever truly delivering. But this myth about Hillary winning the popular vote isn't actually true either, at least, not when you understand the full extent of the voter fraud that took place that night… and who owns the voting machines… and the efforts patriots and White Hats went through to strategically secure the election (including yours truly. More on that in the next chapter).

Needless to say, the country is FAR more Red and far more Conservative than anyone has been led to believe by the Legacy Media. You could even call it ***overwhelmingly*** conservative, but again, the extent and duration of the entrenched voter fraud that has occurred year after year has distorted our perceptions. And as of this writing, the Department of Homeland Security (DHS) has until the end of December, 2018, to release a report on the scope of election fraud during the 2018 midterm elections. We're going to see that come back around and bite many "elected" officials in short order.

We would later learn from Q that White Hats (that is, good guys involved in intelligence, working to foil the efforts of Black Hats) had strategically placed enough pressure on areas where fraud was normally rampant, and had ensured enough election integrity to counteract and mitigate all the voter fraud going on elsewhere. It was enough to tip the electoral scales, but not the popular scales. It was part of the reason why none of the networks would call the election until very, very late (because, again, the media works with the Mono-party, and the election wasn't supposed to have this result, because it was rigged in Hillary's favor). This is also why all the polling outlets could give us such profoundly wrong polling statistics right up until the day of the election. Even the polls were fraudulent, leveraged to set up a predetermined narrative. As Q likes to remind us, "They never thought she would lose," and thus, didn't have a plan for that eventuality when it finally came to pass.

Hillary would, however, be forced to eventually concede the next day. And almost immediately, the movement that would become known as "The Resistance" got underway. Invoking all sorts of fiction, from *Harry Potter*, to *Star Wars,* to *A Handmaiden's Tale,* the movement's acolytes saw themselves as some kind of heroic army, rebelling against a Darth Vader or a Voldemort (when in reality, they were unwittingly serving the most evil character of them all). It was really just an amalgamation of anti-Trump rage with no real direction, no unifying principles, but a lot of funding (thanks to the likes of George Soros) and plenty of celebrities backing it.

On November 9, David Wilcox would be pulled from his car in Chicago by anti-Trump protesters and severely beaten by multiple assailants while bystanders looked on and encouraged the violence, shouting out phrases like, "He voted Trump! Beat his ass!"

On November 10, 2016, Besta Pizza would change its logo, removing the interior design, thus distancing itself from the boy-lover symbol association.

On November 17, 2016, NSA director, Admiral Mike Rogers, unbeknownst to other members of the intelligence community, would secretly travel to Trump Tower and, in a great act of heroism, disclose to Trump the existence of the illegal spying operation against him and his campaign. Trump Tower itself had been compromised by the Deep State. But instead of leaving then and there the day Admiral Rogers came to visit, Trump would have his people wait a day before finally relocating the campaign headquarters the following day to Bedminster, New Jersey. And there was a very good reason for this…

Q would later disclose that the Trump campaign, upon learning of the illegal spying, would turn around and almost immediately leverage this to their advantage by using it to feed bad intel to the Obama administration and Clinton campaign. In one particularly hilarious exchange, Q would confirm that Trump had used a Twitter post to actually bait the Obama administration into spying in on all their "upcoming" campaign plans:

On November 23, Reddit would unexpectedly ban the /r/Pizzagate investigative community on false pretenses, saying they were in violation of Reddit's anti-doxxing policy. This was, of course, a total farce. As an active investigator at the time, I can say I never once saw private info displayed publicly there for the purposes of doxxing anyone, and the sub's moderators were vocally against any attempts at doxxing or calls for violence. If any info had been posted to the sub, it was by a bad operator who was trying to give the Reddit admins an excuse to remove the sub.

In the wake of the sub's removal, dozens of clones popped up overnight (because anyone can make a sub on Reddit), and most were removed within a few days (despite these users never violating the rules, either). One of my subs was removed, despite the fact that it was completely private and set to invite-only, and had always followed all the site-wide rules. It was clear to the community that the Reddit admins simply wanted to censor all Pizzagate-related investigation once it was apparent that it wasn't going to go away or die down on its own. Many "Reddit-refugees" would soon settle down over at Voat, and continue investigating for the next two years, churning out volumes of in-depth research, all independently verifying that, yes, the elites in this country and around the world engage in ritual pedophilia, human trafficking, and worse—and that this was all deliberately hidden from the common man.

However, with the censorship fully enforced on Reddit, the Pizzagate crowd-sourced investigation would suffer a major blow to its credibility on December 4, 2016, after Edgar Welch would walk into Comet Ping Pong and fire off three shots from an AR-styled gun. To be sure, this has always been considered a "false-flag" attack by the Pizzagate community (that is, an attack by the Deep State, undertaken to make an opposition party look bad by framing them in a criminal act), as no one from the community knew who this guy was, and the community had always been vocally against all vigilantism. But the damage had been done. Between the circular reporting by the media, denouncing Pizzagate as a "debunked conspiracy" and the constant refrain of Pizzagaters being "gun-wielding maniacs," the fix was in. Pizzagate was all but successfully memory-holed by Deep State actors looking to protect their pedophilic masters.

Things cooled off for a bit as the holiday season passed and people got on with their lives, but they soon picked back up again in January, as Trump was officially sworn in on January 20, 2017 and many on the Left seemingly lost any last remaining vestiges of their sanity. Nowhere has this been immortalized (and turned into countless memes) than in this particular image, lovingly dubbed by Trump fans, "The Scream Heard Round the World."

While it was temporarily fun for Anons watching many on the "Salt Left" lose their minds for a time, it soon grew very disturbing to watch how violent and unhinged the Left had become in such a short time. It was bad enough during the election itself, but now it seemed to get ramped up to new heights with each passing day. It was immediately clear that, while Trump had won the election, the war was far from over.

For on January 3, 2017, a mentally handicapped man would be kidnapped by four Black Lives Matter supporters from the Chicago area, ostensibly for being a Trump supporter. They would go on to tie the man up, gag him, beat him, burn him with cigarettes, and force him to drink foul toilet water out of a disgusting, putrid toilet bowl—all during a livestreamed video on Facebook—all while screaming "F*** Donald Trump!" Authorities believed the special needs man had been held for at least two days, and would need a number of days in the hospital to fully recover.

Trump would take office, and within days, on January 21, the so-called Resistance movement was on full display, with millions of men and women descending upon DC, dressed up as vaginas, donning pink "pussy" hats, and protesting in the streets. A more ludicrous display had never been seen in America, and riots would break out in some areas with, at the end of the day, over 200 people being arrested (though this was far from the first anti-Trump riot, with dozens being arrested in Portland months before).

The Resistance movement would soon prove as ridiculous as it was misguided, for Trump had barely taken office and hadn't even done anything yet when they were in full swing. This left many wondering what it was that this movement was protesting, exactly. In the end, it would prove to only be a sort of vague outrage that Trump had somehow "stolen" this election. From the way the media pundits were wailing, you might not be faulted for believing that Trump was "literally Hitler," and was all but set to install a Fascist regime and steamroll the opposition before putting women, gays, Muslims, minorities, and, heck, furries for good measure, in concentration camps by the trainload—or so the narrative went. And thus, came the "moral" justification for the Resistance. If Trump was literally Mecha-Hitler on steroids, his followers were little more than American Brownshirts, and who could be blamed for thinking that punching them was their only recourse?

And how had Mecha-Hitler on steroids accomplished all this? Why, he cheated, of course! He *must* have cheated! (Or so the "thinking" went.) Impeach! Impeach!

But the Democrats had a problem, and they knew it.

That problem was Seth Rich.

Step back with me to 2016 for just a moment:

Q tells us that Rich had been assassinated in July in retaliation for leaking those e-mails, and at first, the Dems thought they had gotten away with it all. But then they realized where the e-mails he had taken had ended up: in the hands of Julian Assange and Wikileaks. The race was on. It was only a matter of time before those e-mails would become public knowledge. That would be a disaster for the Democratic Party and they knew it. Assange and his team were working to organize and distribute the e-mails as fast as they could. Hillary, Obama, and the Democrats needed a cover story, ideally one which would malign Assange and Wikileaks and Trump in the process.

In July, the same month Rich died, the DNC approached their legal team at Perkins Coie (specifically Michael Sussman, a partner at Perkins Coie) and laid out their case. Sussman, in turn, approached Shawn Henry at Crowdstrike to perform "forensic analysis" on the DNC's servers. Working with the FBI (which was headed by James Comey at this time), the "Russian collusion" narrative was officially crafted. Crowdstrike would say that indeed, the DNC's servers had been hacked by Russian IP addresses (all the while, denying FBI investigators access to the actual servers), and then the e-mails had been turned over to Wikileaks. You'll recall that by July 5, Comey had already let Hillary off the hook for her "mishandling" of her private e-mail server (which is much bigger than the public investigation ever let on—but once again… more on that in a bit).

Meanwhile, the *Washington Free Beacon* had "approached" Glenn Simpson of private intelligence firm Fusion GPS to perform opposition research on Trump during the presidential primaries. The problem with this story? Simpson is married to Mary Jacoby, and Jacoby worked for Rose Law firm. You know, the one down in… Little Rock, Arkansas. That name should be familiar to you, because it's the same firm at which Hillary Clinton worked during the Whitewater years. So when I say that the *Washington Free Beacon* had "approached" Fusion GPS for this… well, it's not hard to read between the lines and see what really happened. And also recall the "mistake" Guccifer 2.0 had made, "accidentally" letting on that he worked for the GRU.

The crafting of the public narrative had begun.

Oh, but it gets worse. One of the people involved in the opposition research was none other than Nellie Ohr, wife of the Obama administration's associate deputy attorney general Bruce Ohr. For the less discerning souls out there, that should read: MAJOR conflict of interest. (We would later learn from Q that Nellie Ohr had actually been trained on "the farm"—that is, CIA's Camp Peary—and to evade surveillance of her communications by White Hats like the NSA and MILINT, Ohr attempted to even use ham radio to communicate with her co-conspirators at one point).

It didn't work. Her comms were still intercepted.

Furthermore, it would later come out during Bruce Ohr's congressional testimony that he had met with Glenn Simpson as far back as August 2016, back when they were still trying to spin the Steele dossier as credible.

To produce what would eventually become known as the "Russian Dossier," Fusion GPS looked abroad to foreign intelligence services, and specifically, to former MI6 spy, Christoper Steele. Utilizing "his" reports, which were probably written by an underling. (It's been a point of speculation that Steele didn't actually write the dossier, but merely loaned it his credibility as an informant by slapping his name on the final product.) Fusion GPS would cook up what would become known as the "Trump-Russia Dossier." This would outline all the various behind-the-scenes criminal acts of subversion supposedly being employed by Trump and the Russians to overthrow American sovereignty, including the absolutely ridiculous and unsubstantiated portion about "golden showers," where Trump was supposedly recorded in a Russian hotel encouraging prostitutes, who he had allegedly hired, to urinate on each other (a rumor which, if you dig back deep enough in arcane Chan history, may have been started by an Anon as an over-the-top joke, and oblique jab at the son of a reporter loathed by many Anons, Rick Wilson).

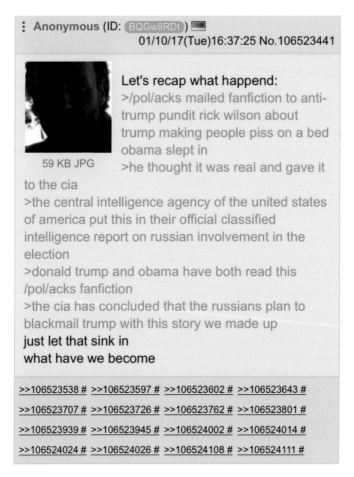

Welcome to the Red Scare, 2.0, rebooted for the twenty-first century, with Putin cast as a scheming, mastermind dictator/puppet master, and Trump, his pussy-grabbin' crony and capitalist henchman.

And how did "Steele" (again, in all likelihood, Baumgartner) source all this information? Why, by consulting none other than "ex" FBI and CIA informant, Stefan Halper! Yes, the very same one who not only acted as an FBI and CIA informant in the past, but who had been paid right after his meeting with Carter Page at Cambridge, and who had set up the meetings with Papadopoulos and Mifsud; the meeting Papadopoulos would then convey to Alexander Downer… who would also run back and tattle to the FBI.

And don't forget the UK's and Ukraine's contributions to all of this: Saunders, Dearlove, Hannigan, and Chalupa—all forming a nexus within this complex conspiracy, laundering information to frame an innocent man.

To further compound the cover-up, Perkins Coie would reach out to Fusion GPS to continue their "research," putting the final touches on the Trump-Russia Dossier, before handing it off to Chuck Schumer, who then handed it to John McCain, who then handed it… back to FBI, who then used it as grounds for obtaining FISA warrants.

But it might be necessary here to explain what the FISA court is, exactly, so people have a full perspective of the kind of treason that went on here. Essentially, the Foreign Intelligence Surveillance Court is a private court utilized by intelligence agencies and the like to obtain warrants for surveillance against spies from foreign countries who may be operating in the US. Or, at least, that was its intended purpose. See, in the US, we have this pesky thing called the Fourth Amendment, which means we're safe from unreasonable searches and seizures by the US government. It really puts a hamper on the kind of work some of the more jackbooted types might like to try and get away with, but there it is, enshrined in our beautiful Constitution. But the FISA court? That's targeting non-citizens, so they're not protected by the Fourth Amendment, right?

Sort of. See, just because they might be a spy, they might be in contact with someone here who is not a spy, and in spying on both of them, you may be, in fact, incidentally violating a US citizen's Fourth Amendment rights. That's kind of standard practice. However, with a FISA warrant, this goes further. Because of "umbrella surveillance" tactics, that secondary person is now a target that you can "legally" spy on. And then, you can also follow who they're talking to.

Put differently, even if you don't believe Trump was set up in all this, say he talks to his daughter Ivanka. The Deep State can now spy on everything Ivanka says and does. So Ivanka goes and talks to her husband, Jared. The Deep State can now spy on Jared. It goes on like that until the "warrant" to spy on one person extends to such a degree that, at a certain point, it's pretty much a carte blanche to spy on whomever, whether they're a criminal or not.

And when you consider that the FISA warrant was obtained because the FBI inserted its spies into the Trump campaign, and then sent intel to spies overseas, to foreign intelligence agencies, well… Simply put, this is "information laundering" at its absolute dirtiest. And that's all assuming this was the only spying being done on the Trump campaign. Again, according to Q, this is just the legal face put on the illegal spying operations that had already been underway for some time.

In essence, an investigation was started on false pretenses. A sitting administration engaged in collusion with foreign governments to manufacture evidence, and a complicit media covered for them the whole time, despite knowing the truth (which we'll get to in a bit). And why? To trap Trump with fake treason charges so he could either be locked away for life, or potentially even executed—because such is the sentence for treason. Think about that for a moment: Obama and Hillary literally wanted Trump dead.

From Strzok, to Comey, to Lynch, to Wasserman-Schultz, to Obama, to Hillary, and so many more… this isn't a "conspiracy theory." This is a genuine criminal conspiracy at the highest levels of government.

But again, we have to ask ourselves why? Why would a sitting president collude with a presidential candidate to stop a valid electoral process and try to entrap a private citizen? Was Trump really that much of a threat to them? Why risk committing treason yourself to frame someone else for treason?

The truth is, so much more was at stake for Obama, Hillary, and this worldwide Cabal. If Trump won, they knew that they would lose everything, which is why they did everything to try and stop him.

Back to January, 2017.

On January 6, like one last Parthian shot from the outgoing Obama administration, the Office of the Director of National Intelligence, headed by James Clapper, would issue an assessment[9] alleging Russian interference in the 2016 presidential election, with Russia tipping the scales in favor of Donald Trump. Several intelligence agencies were now investigating this supposed collusion, including the FBI and the CIA.

Then, before the man is even sworn in, on January 10, *Buzzfeed* would publish the Steele dossier in its entirety. We would later learn from Q that *Buzzfeed* had received this document from none other than Senator John McCain, who had also leaked it to the former director of security for the Senate Select Committee on Intelligence, James A. Wolfe, who in turn, leaked it to *Buzzfeed* reporter Allie Watkins. See, Wolfe and Watkins had been having an affair since 2013. He was fifty-three at the time, and she was twenty-two, and he had previously leaked all sorts of intel to her, including the Senate Intelligence Committee's report on CIA torture that nearly won her a Pulitzer. But this wasn't the only reporter Wolfe was leaking to; no, there were at least three others involved. Wolfe eventually would be charged with leaking classified intel on June 7, 2018, almost a whole year-and-a-half after *Buzzfeed* originally published the report on January 10, 2017.

The very next day, on January 11, Trump would take to Twitter, and he would not mince words, calling the dossier "nonsense" and a "total fabrication."

On January 17, Putin, too, would call the dossier false.

January 20 would finally arrive. Trump would be inaugurated in Washington DC, and during his speech he would utter words which would chill the Cabal to the bone:

> Today's ceremony, however, has very special meaning. Because today we are not merely transferring power from one Administration to another, or from one party to another—but we are transferring power from Washington, DC, and giving it back to you, the American People. For too long, a small group in our nation's Capital has reaped the rewards of government while the people have borne the cost.
>
> Washington flourished—but the people did not share in its wealth.
>
> Politicians prospered—but the jobs left, and the factories closed.
>
> The establishment protected itself, but not the citizens of our country.
>
> Their victories have not been your victories; their triumphs have not been your triumphs; and while they celebrated in our nation's Capital, there was little to celebrate for struggling families all across our land.
>
> That all changes—starting right here, and right now, because this moment is your moment: it belongs to you.
>
> It belongs to everyone gathered here today and everyone watching all across America.
>
> This is your day. This is your celebration.
>
> And this, the United States of America, is your country.

---

9   https://www.dni.gov/files/documents/ICA_2017_01.pdf

What truly matters is not which party controls our government, but whether our government is controlled by the people.

January 20th 2017, will be remembered as the day the people became the rulers of this nation again.

The forgotten men and women of our country will be forgotten no longer.

Everyone is listening to you now.

You came by the tens of millions to become part of a historic movement the likes of which the world has never seen before.

At the center of this movement is a crucial conviction: that a nation exists to serve its citizens.

But the fix was already in.

And even as Obama left office, he didn't choose to go home to Chicago. No, he did something no other US president has ever done before, and that was to remain in DC, taking up residence a short walk away from the White House. Even more strangely, Valerie Jarrett, his senior adviser (and someone who has long been involved in the lives of the Obamas) would *move in* with Barack and Michelle, where they would immediately get to work setting up what the media would describe as an anti-Trump "nerve center" with a singular goal in mind: to either force the resignation or impeachment of Donald J. Trump as president.

But again (and we'll get into this in depth in the following chapters), I want you to ask yourself *"Why?"* What could possibly have motivated Obama to not only have his people plant spies in the Trump campaign, not only have the intelligence apparatus of the US government spy on the Trump campaign, not only leverage foreign intelligence agencies and media companies against the man, but then on top of all that, set up a base of operations nearby to try and work to undermine him at every step? What kind of existential threat did Trump represent to the established order that inspired such fervent opposition?

Here's one thing Q had to say about the lengths Obama and the Cabal went to try and stop Trump.

Anonymous ID: grTMpzrL No.147453147 🗗 🏴   **30**
Nov 1 2017 01:25:22 (EST)

Would you believe a device was placed somewhere in the WH that could actually cause harm to anyone in the room and would in essence be undetected?
Fantasy right?
When Trump was elected you can't possibly imagine the steps taken prior to losing power to ensure future safety & control.
When was it reported Trump Jr dropped his SS detail?
Why would he take that huge risk given what we know?
I can hint and point but cannot give too many highly classified data points.
These keywords and questions are framed to reduce sniffer programs that continually absorb and analyze data then pushed to z terminals for eval. Think xkeysc on steroids.

                                                            ANSWERS

What do you call a former president who tries to not only undermine, but physically harm a standing president? Oh, and there were assassination attempts, as well. Many, many assassination attempts, but the scale of those incidents is often so huge, it's hard for the average reader to comprehend just yet.

On February 8, the Senate would confirm Jeff Sessions for US Attorney General, with a 52–47 vote.

On February 13, General Flynn would resign as national security advisor, as rumors swirled about a conversation he had with Russian diplomat, Sergey Kislyak. Flynn served previously as director of the Defense Intelligence Agency (DIA) from 2012 until 2014… and he was *hated* by Obama. In fact, during Trump's transition, one of the things Obama explicitly requested was that he not hire Flynn. It turns out that Obama had been strategically gutting the military for years, removing patriots from their offices, and installing Cabal loyalists in their stead. Flynn was one such individual, and knew many "inconvenient facts" which could irreparably damage Obama politically. Eventually, on December 1, 2017, Flynn would plead guilty to "lying" to the FBI regarding his phone calls with Kislyak, but this would later turn out to be him perjuring himself. Why would Flynn perjure himself?

In short, Flynn knew where all the bodies were buried. After leaving the DIA, Flynn operated the Flynn Intelligence Group (FIG), which would go on to work with Turkish clients, in particular. What is now theorized is that, as a professional spook, Flynn was actually running a counter-intelligence operation with FIG—a counter-intelligence operation designed to capture these Turkish spies, spies who had direct connections to the Clintons and Obama. It's also theorized that Flynn himself was subject to a FISA warrant, and was thus being used to spy on the Trump administration, still. Remove Flynn from the White House, and that's one less vector for the Deep State to exploit.

Flynn would go on to work with the Special Counsel on a number of simultaneous investigations, leading some Anons to believe that Mueller was really working for Trump during this time, though Q has repeatedly and vocally denied this. If this particular bit turns out to be deliberate disinformation on Q's part, it will be a stunning revelation when the time comes, though I would not be surprised in the least.

Despite Session's recent confirmation, on March 1 the *Washington Post* would publish a story claiming that Attorney General Sessions had met with the Russians during the 2016 campaign, in an effort to remove him from office. Many in Congress called for Sessions to immediately resign, but in the end, what Sessions did wasn't illegal, and thus, didn't require his resignation. Under normal circumstances, it's perfectly legal for an incoming administration to begin to speak to representatives of other world powers. Instead, Sessions would recuse himself from any and all investigations into Russian collusion, effectively delegating all power over any potential investigations to his subordinates, which in this case, would be the deputy attorney general… One wasn't quite in place, however, since, in January 2017, Trump had fired the then deputy attorney general Sally Yates for refusing to institute his travel ban.

You see, Yates had previously signed off on some of the FISA warrants against the Trump campaign, and was an all-around bad actor, so she had to go.

Finding a replacement became a top priority. On April 26, the Senate would confirm Rod Rosenstein for deputy attorney general, 94–6.

As the Trump presidency got underway, things moved briskly. He withdrew the US from the Trans-Pacific Partnership, gave the green light to the Dakota Access and Keystone pipelines, nominated Neil Gorsuch to the Supreme Court, implemented his cabinet, eliminated reams of regulations and red tape, and much, much more. And again, I realize many approaching this book might not see why some of these things are great, but that's because very few things are as they appear on the surface, and need to be seen through the lens of QAnon—that is, through the lens of Military Intelligence—to be fully appreciated. Take, for instance, Trump pulling us out of the Paris Agreement. Environmentalists everywhere lost their minds when he did this, but, when you understand that the agreement is really a program designed to take and redistribute US taxpayer funds into Soros-backed organizations, slush funds, and throughout Iran, and not to combat climate change, the move takes on a different tenor. And even now, as I write this, riots are breaking out all over France, and the people are threatening to overthrow Cabal puppet Macron, precisely because their leaders forced this kind of treaty, and all the included regulatory burden, upon them with no recourse. And besides, the US is already exceeding the standards outlined in the Paris Agreement anyway, no tax theft necessary! Trust me when I say that when you dive in to Q-world, you'll experience this sensation of imbalance; almost like the ground shifting beneath your feet, over and over and over, but you'll ultimately come out with a greater understanding of reality as a result. It's a fundamental paradigm shift in your thinking, and you can't truly appreciate it unless you force yourself to grit your teeth through any emotional distress you may be experiencing, and press forward until you break through whatever mental barriers there are and get to the actual truth of the matter. And isn't that where you want to be anyway?

Still, all was not well in DC just because Trump had taken charge. In fact, the Deep State still controlled many agencies in the government and were still loyal to the previous Administration and the Cabal. Trump, in actuality, had to figure out who was clean, who was dirty, and how best to clean house while still remaining above reproach. This was not easy, by any stretch of the imagination, as he had to work secretly with White Hats to uproot entire networks of Black Hats. This was especially pressing because these Cabal loyalists were doing everything they could to try and subvert President Trump's efforts at every turn, often through leaking classified or privileged information to the press, so as to try and help Cabal actors thwart Trump's plans.

On May 8, former deputy attorney general Sally Yates, and former director of national intelligence James Clapper, would testify before a Senate subcommittee regarding any Russian collusion during the 2016 election. Both would talk about the classified intel they had seen, in which Trump and those close to him had been unmasked (and remember, when we talk about "unmasking," we're talking about FISA spying). Although, they were scant on details, hiding behind the aforementioned "classification" as their defense, all the while also refusing to say who ordered the unmasking. One potential candidate for that would be none other than United Nations ambassador Samantha Power, who abused her security clearance to order unmasking at least 260 times during the 2016 election. Power would later be brought before the House Intelligence Committee and questioned as to why this had happened under her clearance. Her response was that it wasn't her doing; that someone in the Obama White House had ordered all those unmaskings using her credentials without her knowledge.

Well, what can you say, folks? Either she's lying, or the Obama administration is lying. There's really not much room for alternative explanations in this situation, so place your bets while you still can!

But there was still the issue of FBI director James Comey, or "Leakin' James Comey" as Trump liked to call him at the time. Comey, you'll recall, previously refused to prosecute Hillary Clinton for the use of her unauthorized e-mail server. Through Q, we would learn that this was because prosecuting her would have led directly back to Obama and many others, as Hillary was not the only one operating a private, illegal e-mail server to avoid surveillance. (But once again, more on that in a bit). Recall, for now, that Comey was in charge of the FBI when all this massive spying was going down, when all these plants were being inserted into the Trump campaign. Certainly, he had to be aware of what was going on in his own house. And if not, what was he, incompetent? That's certainly the line the DOJ took up, that he was not able to competently lead the Bureau—because incompetence is always a better defense than outright malice. And so, Comey was ousted. But to call Comey rank-and-file Cabal would be an understatement. We'll dissect his particular brand to treachery later, but for now, I'll say this: it's even been heavily implied by the Q drops that Comey is a bloodline Rockefeller. (We'll talk about bloodlines later. Believe me, most reading this for the first time will not be ready to cross that Rubicon just yet.)

And so, on May 9, Comey gets fired. This leads to a massive outcry, and gives the Democrats enough of an impetus to demand a Special Counsel investigation into Russian meddling in the 2016 election.

Then, on May 17, 2017, the Special Counsel investigation is born. Rod Rosenstein enlists former FBI director, Robert Mueller, to oversee the investigation. And the *big* problem with this, as we would first learn from Q, is that Rod Rosenstein was one of the original individuals who signed off on the FISA warrants to spy on POTUS' campaign in the first place! (Actually, on FBI plant Carter Page, specifically.) Not only that, but Rosenstein is married to US attorney Lisa Barsoomian, who was the protégé of both Robert Mueller and James Comey, and who previously served as legal representation for Barack Obama, Bill and Hillary Clinton, and the Department of Justice. Much later, we would also learn of a potential plan in which Rosenstein would wear a wire to secretly record President Trump, in the hopes of catching something incriminating, or at the very least, something that could be used against him to invoke the twenty-fifth Amendment and lead to impeachment proceedings.

Does this mean that Rod Rosenstein and Bob Mueller are bad people, working for the Cabal? This has been a particular point of contention among the QAnon research community for some time. But at the very least, my readers need to understand that the ethical ground upon which the whole Special Counsel stands has been quite unstable right from the beginning. In fact, as of this writing, the only thing keeping the Special Counsel going is the fact that President Trump hasn't declassified the Office of Inspector General report documents, which would expose Rosenstein's conflict of interest. The report itself, some 568 pages long, was first released in June 2018… but not before Rosenstein could get his hands on it and redact his name, as well as other key names, ensuring their ongoing protection. But because Trump has ultimate authority over declassification, he could literally pull the trigger whenever he wants, and end the investigation in a heartbeat.

But he didn't.

He had months to unilaterally end this investigation with the stroke of his pen…

So why didn't he?

Ah, welcome to the world of Q, where things are rarely as they seem, and where sometimes Q has to keep us Anons in the dark, so as to also keep bad actors in the dark. As Q has said, "Disinfo is necessary," because it's not just the good guys watching, and we wouldn't want the plan telegraphed in advance to bad actors.

But again, back to our timeline:

On May 20, Trump would arrive in Saudi Arabia, where he would take part in a ritual called an "ardah" or "sword dance." It's a ritual one does before going to war. Before leaving Saudi Arabia, Trump would broker a deal with the Saudis to wean them off their dependence on oil exports, allow them to join the US stock market, and, at the new Saudi counter-terrorism center, he would place his hands, along with Saudi King Salman bin Abdulaziz and Egyptian president Abdel Fattah al-Sisi, on a glowing globe that drew many comparisons to a *palantir* from the *Lord of the Rings* novels.

On May 23, 2017, "MegaAnon" would appear for the first time. Much like FBIAnon before him, and QAnon after him, MegaAnon came to drop all sorts of intel about, at least to start, Seth Rich. The majority of MegaAnon's initial claims were that because there was so much data that needed to be moved around securely, the likes of Julian Assange were leveraging the server power of Kim Dotcom's MegaUpload service (and later, Mega.nz), in order to achieve their "White Hat" goals. He would confirm Rich as "Panda" (Rich always used "panda" permutations in his various screennames—with a stuffed panda even making an appearance later in a video recorded by his parents). MegaAnon would continue for several months, posting into January 2018, and talking about a number of topics—almost all related to various facets of the Trump administration—including inside some of QAnon's own /CBTS/ threads. In other words, Q and MegaAnon were posting at the same time, often along the same lines, about the same topics, simultaneously informing Anons' perspectives:

> I know it sounds ridiculous but that's simply because I'm trying to convey the broadness and scope of what will be publicly disclosed. My only point is that after it's all over, no one will be able to turn away from the truth. The masses will never again be able to claim with 100% certainty that 9/11 DIDN'T have inside, US sponsored and funded, department/agency coordination, allocated resources and assistance. No one will EVER be able to NOT believe that our own fucking agencies and departments and former admins didn't play a huge role in shit like JFK, OKC, 9/11, ISIS, Pizza, Vegas, etc. They won't be able to turn a blind eye to what they consider "conspiracy theories", today simply because the MSM told them to.

> The only thing that everyone will be able to agree on when it's all said and done is that we've all been horrifically lied to on incomprehensible levels and nothing we've been led to perceive as our "reality" for generations since the very fucking day GHB was sworn into the admin as Director of the CIA, has been the whole truth and nothing but. No one will be able to use ignorance as an excuse anymore. The people think they're in charge?! Haha, well now Trump is going to give it to them. He's going to give us all the fucking transparency we can handle and when he does?! That's when you'll truly see what "we, the people" are made of. You'll have people who can't handle it, begging to give the truth BACK to the admin. I want to make sure I'm being clear here, too... when I use terms like "disclose", "reality", etc. I am in NO WAY IMPLYING Trump is disclosing any of that stuff y'all bring up like "aliens", "Antarctica", etc. not saying I don't personally believe in some of it, but that's not the "storm" that's coming. Just to clarify...

While I can't say that MegaAnon was always one hundred percent accurate (nor, like so many of these "insiders" can we really verify if it was all the same individual), I will say archives of MegaAnon's posts make for some of the most interesting reading you can find out there, to date.

But even as insiders were shedding light on decades of corruption, the Deep State was at work, fighting back, and on July 27, George Papadopoulos would be arrested for accepting money from a foreign national while in Greece; $10,000, precisely. The pretense for this was that this was a "retainer" while Papadopoulos worked out an energy deal for Charles Tawil, an Israeli American businessman. Except, Papadopoulos' "spy-der sense" was tingling. He tried to give the money back on one occasion, but the man refused. Before leaving the island to return to the US, Papadopoulos left the money in the care of a local attorney in Greece, feeling unsettled by the whole affair—and it's a good thing he did, too, because upon landing and deplaning at Dulles Airport, he was immediately arrested by officers who went looking for the $10,000. See, there's a rule that you have to declare amounts of cash in excess of ten thousand dollars when flying back into the US (so our pal George would have been in big trouble if he had just stuffed that wad of cash in his suitcase). Papadopoulos would later tell federal investigators that he believed Tawil was working for a foreign government. When the officers found out that Papadopoulos didn't have the money on him, that he actually left it in Greece, they were furious. Papadopoulos had seemingly dodged an entrapment scheme and it looked like he was about to escape completely unscathed, when the Special Counsel was able to nab him on a "process crime"—"lying" to the FBI. The lie in question? Papadopoulos said he thought he first talked to Joseph Mifsud before beginning work for the Trump campaign, when in fact it was after.

Papadopoulos would eventually be sentenced to fourteen days in jail—after which point he was free to talk and do as he pleased. And talk he did, writing his own book on the whole affair, entitled *Deep State Target*.

And as summer was heating up, so too was the political divide in the country. The "Unite the Right" rally was slated to occur in Charlottesville on August 11 and 12, 2017. The goal of the rally was to have anyone even remotely on the Right set aside their differences and march against the forces of Marxism that were attempting to impose Leftist ideology on all facets of society, through things like the policing of speech; doxxing opponents online; deplatforming major figures in the movement; and rioting at the likes of Jordan Peterson and Ben Shapiro rallies, on top of doing things like tearing down Confederate monuments (and some not-so-Confederate monuments; literally just old monuments of historical figures who just happened to be white). The mostly-male group was made up of regular MAGA conservatives, groups like Identity Evropa, those affiliated with Richard Spencer's National Policy Institute, and more extreme groups like American Vanguard, the Traditionalist Worker Party, and various neo-Nazi/National Socialist groups (though intense study of the actual principles undergirding these latter groups would reveal their ideology to be profoundly Left-wing in origin).

And say what you want about those groups, but they were protesting peacefully. At least, at the start. The rally would begin with the participants making their presence known, marching with tiki torches in hand, much to the horror of Leftists across the country—who immediately drew parallels to the Ku Klux Klan. But then, due to a number of decisions made by the mayor's office and the local police, decisions which went against normal policy, these officials decided to allow Antifa into the mix. Now, if you know anything about Antifa, you know they're basically Communist foot soldiers. We're talking about the real dregs of society here. Drug using, gender-confused, violent anarchists, with a despicable nihilistic streak. Many like to think of themselves as "anti-fascist" revolutionaries, drawing comparisons to themselves and the D-Day soldiers of the Greatest Generation, when really, their actual ideological forebears were the ones building the gulags in the USSR. Needless to say, when the two groups met (and were encouraged to meet, through the strategic opening and closing of streets, and redirecting of traffic by the police, upon orders from higher ups), conflict erupted across the city.

Nothing is more emblematic of that conflict than the incident involving James A. Fields and Heather Heyer. Fields was with American Vanguard, and Heyer with Antifa. While trying to leave the city in his Dodge Challenger, Fields' car was swarmed and attacked by Antifa who had been improperly funneled into the street by the local police. One Antifa member first struck the back of Fields' vehicle with a bat, spooking Fields. Another struck a window. Finally, another hurled a bottle of frozen urine (throwing bottles of urine—frozen or otherwise—is a favorite tactic of Antifa) at the windshield, breaking it and lodging itself there before the mob descended around the car. One Antifa member is even caught on camera pointing a pistol at Fields' car.

In a panic, Fields accelerated to twenty-eight miles per hour, charging the crowd, hoping it would disperse. It didn't, and he had to slam on the brakes mere fractions of a second later. He managed to slow it to twenty-three miles per hour, before striking another car—also stopped by the crowd in front of him, at seventeen miles per hour.

In a sheer panic, Fields reversed out of the crowd and backed up the one-way street, driving backwards as fast as he could, desperate to escape the mob.

When the police find him, he can't stop apologizing. He weeps when he hears someone struck by his car has died. He is arrested and charged with first degree murder in the death of Heather Heyer—a morbidly obese woman who had been marching with Antifa for hours that day. The media does its best to avoid talking about her weight, which is clearly seen in footage as at least SEVEN men—firemen, and emergency medical technicians—carrying her to an ambulance, stomach exposed and, frankly, undulating with each collective step of the emergency workers. Instead, they broadcast pictures of her face, painting her as a hapless martyr, instead of one of the mob who attacked Fields' car.

And while I apologize for the photo, I include it so you realize I am not exaggerating one iota. The coroner would say she died of a heart attack. He never said it was a result of being struck by a car going about twenty-three miles per hour and attempting to slow down.

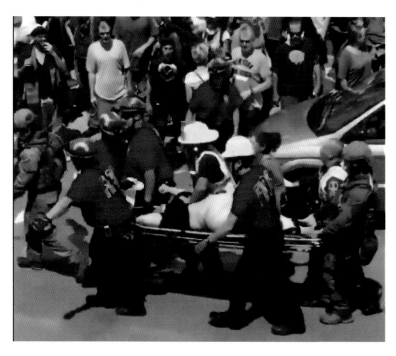

But the story doesn't end there. Unable to afford representation, Fields was eventually assigned a lawyer by the state—but the lawyer has a good record, and wanting to make an example out of Fields, the judge combs through the lawyer's records and finds that he, too, was opposed to the removal of Confederate statues. The judge frames this as, somehow, an ethical conflict, and now gets to replace Fields' representation. He subs in an social justice warrior-type, complete with pink hair (and who, previously, was also involved in a sex scandal) though, to her credit, she does request that the case be moved out of Charlottesville, where the local press would continue to rail against Fields' the whole time. The judge denies the motion. At the end of the case, Judge Moore would say to the jury, "I don't know what intent he had other than to kill. We know what we saw."

In December 2018, Fields would get sentenced to life in prison, plus **FOUR HUN-DRED AND NINETEEN** years, for the crime of first degree murder—which requires intent. To call this a miscarriage of justice is an understatement. And while I, personally, don't agree with Fields' ideology, I do think the truth is important. This was a morbidly obese woman marching with a mob on a hot summer day—a mob who was deliberately funneled into areas where they should not have been allowed, stopping up traffic while swarming and attacking vehicles with weapons. The Leftists in charge of the government there sent in their foot soldiers to violently intimidate and threaten anyone they disagreed with; in this case, the Unite the Right protesters.

They wanted to make an example out of Fields.

The rally had permits to be there. Antifa did not. The rally had been totally peaceful until Antifa began attacking them. And the end result of it all was a tragic and completely avoidable loss of life.

It wouldn't be until a month later when an Anon would ask US Senate Anon a question:

> If right-wing death squads became real and start massacring Antifa supporters left and right, will Trump intervene to stop us or let us purify the country for him?
>
> Is Trump just as willing to put down a right-wing uprising as he is a left-wing one?
>
> Can we count on him as a friend or foe on the Day of the Rope?

US Senate Anon would have this to say on the matter:

> Soros wants you to form right-wing death squads and fight Antifa, so you don't fight him.

I'm not sure there's ever been a clearer picture of that reality put on display than in the tragedy that happened in Charlottesville that summer day. At any rate, I didn't want to be Soros' useful idiot. As much as I may have sympathized with *some* of the ideas being espoused by *some* of the groups there (I've never hated anyone by virtue of their race, or the color of their skin, even though I do tend to be explicitly pro-Western Civ), I wasn't about to be anyone's unwitting pawn—let alone some Hungarian Billionaire known for sowing discord and strife across the globe. Oh, but we'll definitely be addressing George Soros later in this book. For now, it's enough to know that the man uses the Hegelian Dialectic to his advantage: thesis, antithesis, and synthesis. In essence, Soros sets up diametrically opposed groups to fight with each other, which results in the weakening of the general population, creating disunity and fostering hatred among the people—all in order to push everyone along to some predetermined end.

So while the "straight, white males" at the Unite the Right rally were definitely all reacting to the same, very real phenomenon of anti-white hatred (fostered and funded by the likes of Soros), the truth is, they were all being used in the same manner as the Antifa foot-soldiers they claimed to be fighting. Everyone present at the rally that day was a useful idiot, driving the wedge of division deeper into the American soul.

Trump understood this, and would later say of the tragedy:

> What about the 'alt-left' that came charging at, as you say, the 'alt-right,' do they have any semblance of guilt? …What about the fact they came charging with clubs in hands, swinging clubs, do they have any problem? I think they do.

And:

> You had a group on one side that was bad and you had a group on the other side that was also very violent. Nobody wants to say it, but I will say it right now.

See, Trump understood the reality of the situation on the ground that day in a way many did not. And while his opponents in the Mockingbird Media were eager to make some kind of racist association between Trump and the "Alt-Right," Trump's main concern was keeping the nation together, and not allowing the media to exploit the event to create further division—division which had been knowingly and purposefully sown and fostered during Obama's tenure in office, both by governmental agencies and NGOs, through the likes of many, many Soros-backed groups.

The plan was to model their tactics on what had already taken place overseas, in places like Europe and various Baltic states, with various "color revolutions." Even a cursory search online these days will reveal the manifold connections to Soros-backed groups to even the most dubious of doubters. Soros poured billions over the course of many years into everything from Black Lives Matter marches, to the so-called Women's March, and well beyond. High-Level Insider Anon would say, of Soros, when asked by an Anon:

> Why is Soros pushing all these avenues of degeneracy such as Feminism?

High-Level Insider Anon would respond:

> Strategies of tension. He isn't anti-white male for some inexplicable reason. He is pro-division and pro-tension, to get the masses focused on each other rather than the regime that is fucking them.

Crafty enemies require careful strategies to overcome. It's very tempting for some to think, "Why not just crush our enemies?" The Right (depending on how you define that) had basically forced Trump through, into office, and was now showing up in force around the country. And let's face it; they could probably just trample the Left underfoot (at least, for a good long while, before they encountered any serious, organized, armed resistance), if they were only allowed. But that would inevitably lead to something like a civil war, and if the goal of the likes of Soros and the Cabal is to sow division and cause destruction, and an overall weakening of the nation, doing so would only further advance the agenda of evil. No, the only effective response to counter division is to proclaim and demonstrate unity instead. Realizing that those on the Left and the Right had been effectively brainwashed and demoralized through years of conditioning, Trump chose the most effective route, proclaiming that there were bad actors on *both* sides, refusing to put the blame on just one side, which would only serve to give one side the "moral high ground," in effect, endorsing and perpetuating the division.

Again, this is part of the reason why I wrote this book—to help bridge the gap, bring people into the light, and help them clearly see our common enemies who are so very good at setting us at each other's throats. And though I riffed on Plato's "Allegory of the Cave" earlier, perhaps a more fitting analogy would be crabs in a bucket: setting us against ourselves ensures no one ever escapes.

But the Cabal was not done fighting; not by a long-shot. On August 30, bystanders would catch footage of a driver losing control of their vehicle at the very moment President Trump's motorcade passed by on its way to a rally in Springfield, Missouri. The car emerged from the woods and careened down a hill, directed right at the motorcade. Fortunately, the car stopped when it bottomed out on a drainage ditch before stalling out at the side of the road. The driver is eventually cleared of all wrongdoing, and is not arrested; the incident being marked down as the result of a malfunction.

Q would, some months later, confirm that the CIA has classified technology that allows it to remotely take over certain kinds of cars, and yes, this was an attempt on the president's life (one of many).

Q !UW.yye1fxo No.96🔗 📄   **772**
Feb 15 2018 15:02:33 (EST)

https://www.intelligence.senate.gov/sites/default/files/hearings
/95mkultra.pdf🔗 📄
Read very carefully.
Unreleased **[CLAS-HIGHEST]**:
Ability to use frequencies **[incoming sig]**/modify/code/program over
'x' period **[designate]** mobile phone to 'control' target subject.
OP conducted/ORIG outside of US.
CAR control?
https://www.youtube.com/watch?v=1Yqa5PUViPo🔗 📄
Statement by the driver?
Fairytale?
AS THE WORLD TURNS.
THIS IS BIGGER THAN ANYONE CAN IMAGINE.
Q

Yes, we are now in remote-controlled assassination territory. And if that sounds like science fiction conspiracy theory territory, just remember that in 1975, the existence of the CIA's "Heart Attack Gun," which fired frozen darts of undetectable poison (and which mimicked a heart attack in its target) was disclosed publicly before the Senate. And you better believe that the methods and technologies at the disposal of the Deep State have significantly progressed in the intervening forty-plus years since that first, inadvertent disclosure.

But once again, we must continue with our timeline.

On September 18, Donald Trump Jr. would drop his Secret Service detail. Q would later explain why:

> **Anonymous** ID: grTMpzrL No.147453147 ⚑ 📷   **30**
> Nov 1 2017 01:25:22 (EST)
>
> Would you believe a device was placed somewhere in the WH that could actually cause harm to anyone in the room and would in essence be undetected?
> Fantasy right?
> When Trump was elected you can't possibly imagine the steps taken prior to losing power to ensure future safety & control.
> When was it reported Trump Jr dropped his SS detail?
> Why would he take that huge risk given what we know?
> I can hint and point but cannot give too many highly classified data points.
> These keywords and questions are framed to reduce sniffer programs that continually absorb and analyze data then pushed to z terminals for eval. Think xkeysc on steroids.

On September 25, Trump Jr. would reinstate his Secret Service protection. Evidently the problem, whatever it specifically had been, was now resolved, and it was safe for him to bring back his security detail.

But then came the first big public crisis of the Trump administration.

And actually... there had been a warning just a few weeks prior, delivered on /pol/...

Anonymous **ID:LAbNFEtv** Mon 11 Sep 2017 05:08:36 No.141100963 Report
Quoted By: >>141101351 >>141101896 >>141102940 >>141107486

look i feel bad for some of you on this website. so i'll let you in on a little secret. if you live in las vegas or henderson stay inside tomorrow. don't go anywhere where there are large groups of people. also if you see three blacks vans parked next to each other immediately leave the area. you're welcome
-john

Anonymous **ID:LAbNFEtv** Mon 11 Sep 2017 05:16:23 No.141101703 Report

>>141101351
just stay away. go to arizona if you can. they won't bother you in arizona.
-john

Anonymous **ID:LAbNFEtv** Mon 11 Sep 2017 05:20:08 No.141102035 Report
Quoted By: >>141102103 >>141102106 >>141102133

to clarify i won't be doing anything to harm anyone. i'm not a killer and i never will be one.
-john

Anonymous **ID:LAbNFEtv** Mon 11 Sep 2017 05:28:12 No.141102703 Report
Quoted By: >>141102792 >>141102816

it's called the "high incident project". they want to make the american public think that places with extremely high security aren't safe. they are trying to create more regulations. you will see laws proposed within the next few years to put up more metal detectors and other security devices. media and politicians will be saying places with lots of police need even more police. i can't guarantee anything will happen tomorrow but las vegas is on their minds.
-john

Anonymous **ID:LAbNFEtv** Mon 11 Sep 2017 05:55:53 No.141104921 Report

if their plan is successful state of nevada will pass a law in the future making all casinos have mandatory metal detectors and backscatter machines. soon after a federal law will be passed to put these machines in universities, high schools, federal buildings, you name it. osi systems and chertoff are the main producers of these machines. sometime around 2020 chertoff and osi will merge into a single company. after they merge the owners will sell off all their stock and make billions in profit. mr chertoff has been in contact with sheldon adelson. mr adelson will become a huge sponsor of these machines and he will be the first to put them in his casinos when the law passes. this is my last message for now. don't expect me to return anytime soon
-john

And though his timing was slightly off, his words would prove prescient, as just a few short weeks later, on October 1, bullets would rain down on concert-goers from the windows of the Mandalay Bay casino, in Las Vegas, Nevada.

The official story is that one Stephen Paddock brought up fourteen AR-15s, eight AR-10s, a bolt action rifle, a revolver, and cases upon cases of ammo to his room over the course of six days before finally snapping, breaking out two windows made of hurricane-resistant glass with a hammer, and unloading over 1,100 rounds down into the concert crowd, approximately four-hundred and fifty meters below, ultimately killing fifty-eight people and injuring over four hundred, while also attempting to ignite a jet fuel tank some 2,000 feet away. Photos of Paddock, dead on the ground, would soon leak on the internet; the story being that he had shot himself before police stormed his room.

And this is where the questions started for Anons…

Dubbed the "deadliest mass shooting in America," the event just didn't quite add up—and to this day, there's been no official motive listed as to why Paddock would do what he had done. Add that to the fact that the footage of the shooting clearly showed muzzle flare in both broken windows (despite the police report saying there was no second shooter), the very strange interview given by his brother the following day, the presence of black vans on the ground, and the very strange interview given by one Jesus Campos, a security guard at the Mandalay Bay who had been shot once, when presumably Paddock had fired thirty-five bullets through the door when he came to check on the commotion. Campos would go on *Ellen* later, along with someone who can only be described as a handler, and give one of the strangest interviews I've ever seen on TV. In fact, so strange was the interview, and so different-looking was "Campos" on TV from photos we had been presented with earlier, there was speculation as to whether this was even the same Jesus Campos being presented to us, or some kind of Deep State body-double being employed to shill an official narrative.

And there was, of course, the warning Anons had received about Las Vegas just a few weeks prior that had encouraged them to keep digging. Then, on October 25, Stephen Paddock's brother would be arrested for possession of child pornography and the sexual exploitation of a minor, leading some Anons to dig even harder, and turn up familial connections to the Bohemian Grove. In fact, the Paddocks owned an estate just outside the Grove—a fact uncovered by independent investigator Jake Morphonios at Blackstone Intelligence—leading some to wonder if the brothers were Cabal assets, leveraged to procure, ship, and transport "resources" for all sorts of illicit deeds. Morphonios would, in the wake of his investigations, have his channel removed from YouTube, censored after I started amplifying his videos beyond the YouTube community. This kind of censorship has now become almost synonymous with the radical Left in Silicon Valley; the standard way they conduct their affairs to silence dissent, acting as publishers instead of open platforms (despite all congressional testimony to the contrary).

Not only that, but MGM execs had dumped two-hundred and fifty million dollars worth of stock thirty days before the shooting, as had Soros, who had bought up 1.35 million dollars worth of puts against MGM stock some sixty days before the strike.

But the story didn't end there. Survivors started dying, with one death coming over a year later, when a Las Vegas survivor was caught in yet another mass shooting, this time in Thousand Oaks, California—one of thirteen who would end up perishing that evening....

And then Anons found footage of a VIP being escorted out of the Tropicana by SWAT operators.

I can only begin to summarize the weirdness and the depth of investigation Anons did during that time, but the short of it is this: Paddock was no lone gunman. In fact, many Anons soon came to the conclusion that he was an arms dealer working for the FBI. He was brokering a deal with, well, most Anons who looked into the subject figured it was some kind of Saudi counter-coup terror/assassination operation. Remember how Trump had traveled to Saudi Arabia and brokered a deal with the new king there? This was the action of the faction opposed to that new king—and yes, there were factions within our own government supporting this operation, namely by supplying weapons and ammo to terrorists.

And notice how the VIP is in the Tropicana?

Yeah, that was the big problem with these would-be assassins. That guy, apparently a member of the Saudi Royal family, was supposedly the target, and he was supposed to be in the Mandalay Bay casino, but he had gone, on a whim, to the Tropicana. But by that point, the assassins' cover had been blown by… many think it was Mandalay Bay security guard, Jesus Campos. The terrorists would fire upon Campos, mistaking him for a cop, unloading some 200 rounds through the thirty-second floor hotel room door, lodging one bullet in Campos' leg. Campos would retreat and radio for help, meaning word was out now and the clock was ticking. The terrorists needed to create a distraction to escape. They broke the windows and multiple gunmen opened fire at the crowd below. One spotted a jet fuel tank in the distance and began firing at it, hoping to create a gigantic fireball to distract from their location. They also killed Paddock, making it look like a suicide so that he could take the fall.

A similar story is disseminated across /pol/ by someone claiming to be Q in a series of very compelling posts (but who probably isn't Q). Still, the details laid out in the drops are very thought-provoking and worth noting, even if the source is dubious.

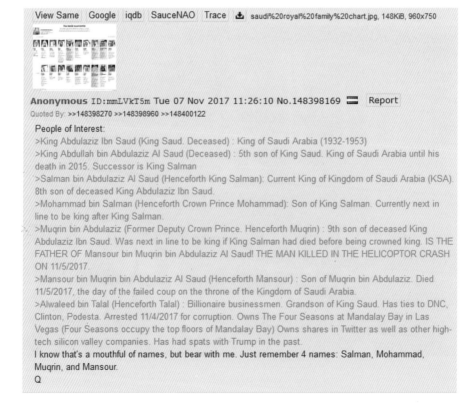

View Same   Google   iqdb   SauceNAO   Trace   ⬇ saudi%20royal%20family%20chart.jpg, 148KiB, 960x750

Anonymous ID:mmLVkT5m Tue 07 Nov 2017 11:26:10 No.148398169 ▬ Report
Quoted By: >>148398270 >>148398960 >>148400122

People of Interest:
>King Abdulaziz Ibn Saud (King Saud. Deceased) : King of Saudi Arabia (1932-1953)
>King Abdullah bin Abdulaziz Al Saud (Deceased) : 5th son of King Saud. King of Saudi Arabia until his death in 2015. Successor is King Salman
>Salman bin Abdulaziz Al Saud (Henceforth King Salman): Current King of Kingdom of Saudi Arabia (KSA). 8th son of deceased King Abdulaziz Ibn Saud.
>Mohammad bin Salman (Henceforth Crown Prince Mohammad): Son of King Salman. Currently next in line to be king after King Salman.
>Muqrin bin Abdulaziz (Former Deputy Crown Prince. Henceforth Muqrin) : 9th son of deceased King Abdulaziz Ibn Saud. Was next in line to be king if King Salman had died before being crowned king. IS THE FATHER OF Mansour bin Muqrin bin Abdulaziz Al Saud! THE MAN KILLED IN THE HELICOPTOR CRASH ON 11/5/2017.
>Mansour bin Muqrin bin Abdulaziz Al Saud (Henceforth Mansour) : Son of Muqrin bin Abdulaziz. Died 11/5/2017, the day of the failed coup on the throne of the Kingdom of Saudi Arabia.
>Alwaleed bin Talal (Henceforth Talal) : Billionaire businessmen. Grandson of King Saud. Has ties to DNC, Clinton, Podesta. Arrested 11/4/2017 for corruption. Owns The Four Seasons at Mandalay Bay in Las Vegas (Four Seasons occupy the top floors of Mandalay Bay) Owns shares in Twitter as well as other high-tech silicon valley companies. Has had spats with Trump in the past.
I know that's a mouthful of names, but bear with me. Just remember 4 names: Salman, Mohammad, Muqrin, and Mansour.
Q

>>148398169
Do you remember how President Trump visited Saudi Arabia back in May of 2017? Do you remember how warmly he was greeted by King Salman? I do. It was a spectacle. Why was he greeted so welcomingly? After all, President Obama's reception was... shall we say, less than grand. Do you remember how after Trump's visit, Saudi Arabia started becoming more open in their policies? Women can drive there now. Did you notice how the Syrian rebellion became quiet? Did you notice how quickly ISIS was crushed after the visit? Why did Saudi Arabia suddenly want to get their oil companies listed on the NYSE? What could have caused this?

Q

>>148398270
To answer this, we have to look a little further back. Back to around 2010.

It all goes back to fracking. You see, the Kindom of Saudi Arabia (KSA) has always relied heavily on its vast petrol reserves for wealth and prosperity. And they were ruthless. OPEC. The cartel of gasoline. You can't count the number of times throughout history that OPEC used its power to crush governments, manipulate prices, control supplies, and fund activities. If there ever was a international group of bullies, OPEC was it. And at the head of this organization was the mighty KSA.

Then came the fracking boom. Suddenly, the world was no longer at the mercy of OPEC. This made them nervous. So, they did what they always do. They pumped out more petroleum, driving the price of gas to lowest in decades. What was their objective? To bankrupt these fracking businesses. KSA is rich. Very rich. They figured, we'll just drive gas prices unbelievably low and take the loss until all these fracking business startups crumble. Do you remember how cheap gas got between 2013-2016? It was ridiculous, wasn't it? But what they didn't count on was just how cheap fracking had become. So many of these business didn't go bankrupt. So they took another step. To convince the world that fracking was bad for the environment. So they lobbied and supplied funds to the Democratic party. Why? Because the leftist are usually the ones who support ANY and ALL environmental regulations. Do you remember all the legal battles that fracking had to go through? Hell, it's still illegal in most blue states. Do you now understand why the Saudis donated so much money to the Clinton campaign? She was HEAVILY favored to win and if she did, you can bet your ass that illegalizing fracking would have been on the top of her list, returning us to dependence on arab oil. But... this didn't work either. Fracking continued. And then, a shitstorm of reality hit them hard.

Q

Anonymous ID:mmLVkT5m Tue 07 Nov 2017 11:29:57 No.148398591 ▭ Report
Quoted By: >>148398714 >>148400122
>>148398441
You see, KSA had vastly underestimated the amount of total shale reserves in North America. They had no idea that so much of this stuff exists. They thought maybe they could ride it out if the reserves would dry up in a decade or so. But nope. We have enough shale to supply us for at least 50 years. Hmmm... big problem.

So, if you're King Salman, what do you do? Well, there's only one thing you can do. Give up the reliance on oil production and try to use existing wealth to stay wealthy. To modernize its trade to include more than just exports of oil. They would need to build an entire industrial country from scratch. To do that, he needed the help of the USA. And that's where President Trump comes in.

You see, the May 2017 meeting between Trump and King Salman (and his son Mohammad), was not just another meeting. It was a business meeting. King Salman asked Trump for help. Trump was more than willing to give it (like listing the oil companies on the NYSE) but his help would come with a price. Liberalization and the stop of illegal funding. No more contributions to American politics. No more supplying funds to terrorists or splinter groups. King Salman took the deal. All of a sudden, women were allowed to drive. ISIS was retreating. Syrian rebels suddenly ran out of ammunition. Yay. All good up to this point.

Anonymous ID:mmLVkT5m Tue 07 Nov 2017 11:31:04 No.148398714 ▭ Report
Quoted By: >>148398962 >>148399560 >>148399868 >>148400073 >>148400122
>>148398591
Now comes the bad

Not all the royalties in KSA are into this. They don't like losing the power they once had. What's worse, they don't want to become liberal. They now start resenting King Salmon. They start plotting against him. At the forefront of this movement is none other than the previous Deputy Crown Prince, Muqrin, and his son, Mansour (the man killed in the helicopter crash of 11/5/17).

October 1, 2017. The top floors of Mandalay Bay isn't Mandalay Bay, but is Four Seasons, owned by billionaire Talal. Who was occupying that whole floor that night? I can't remember where, but I heard that the whole floor was reserved for that week. Now, no one would do that unless they were Saudi royalty. We don't know for sure, but my guess is Crown Prince Mohammad. We know it wasn't King Salman, because he was in Russia at the time. https://www.theguardian.com/world/2017/oct/05/saudi-russia-visit-putin-oil-middle-east

Anonymous ID:mmLVkT5m Tue 07 Nov 2017 11:33:26 No.148398962 ▭ Report
Quoted By: >>148399159 >>148399560 >>148400122
>>148398714
The plan is to take out the crown prince. Then kill King Salman. With the King and the Crown Prince dead, who is next in line? Yup. The former deputy crown prince, Muqrin. So, posing as terrorists who wanted to buy the guns for some terrorist attack, they dupe the CIA or FBI to supply the guns to the death squad. Their real plan is to climb the stairs right after the deal and kill the VIP in the floors above them. This is why the weapons cache was located on the 32nd floor. They would only have to climb a few stairs or take the elevator up a little to start the killing. Now, here's what happened that night:
>Paddock is the contact man to supply the guns. He meets a couple of assassins ahead of time (remember, the shooting starts at 10:05). At this point, Paddock is thinking this is a gun deal. Only a few magazines are loaded. He merely wants to show the customers how to load the chamber etc... What he doesn't know is that the advance team was sent to secure the floor. That all but one entry point to the floor would be barricaded (crucial since the reason Campos becomes suspicious of the blocked doors is what ultimately leads him to investigate) The reason for the barricade is that once the assault starts, the assassins want to make sure to impede the authorities as much as possible from reaching the top floors.
>CIA/FBI (or Trump's own intelligence) got wind of the assassination that was about to take place. Immediate action is taken to round up the assassins. Remember, we're talking about an army of assassins here. You can't kill a Crown Prince who's protected by 30 armed bodyguards by pulling a Jack Ruby. I estimate at least 20 assassins in total.

Q

Anonymous ID:mmLVkT5m Tue 07 Nov 2017 11:35:18 No.148399159 ☰ Report
Quoted By: >>148399349 >>148399560 >>148400122

>>148398962
>What the assassins didn't know was that the prince had disguised himself as a regular dude to enjoy the nightlife in Vegas. (Saudi princes have been known to do this) He had slipped away from the Mandalay and was at the Tropicana playing some cards. As soon as the FBI (or some other agency) learned of the assassination plot, they stormed the Tropicana and extracted the prince. The video can be seen here.
https://www.youtube.com/watch?v=YVHmshtmDqo
>They lead him out of the casino and escort him to the nearest helipad to be picked up. BUT, on the way, they encounter some resistance from a few assassins. Hence the firefight at the airport. Eventually, he makes it to the chopper and is whisked away. This explains the flight radar reports you see all over the net.
>Meanwhile, the FBI has gathered up as many of the assassins as they can. A few are armed with sidearms. They don't have rifles yet because the rendezvous with Paddock hasn't occurred yet. Hence the random firefights at various casinos that night. A few are killed. Hence the Laura Loomer videos of covered up dead people. https://www.youtube.com/watch?v=6oxAZlpSUuM

Q

Anonymous ID:mmLVkT5m Tue 07 Nov 2017 11:37:09 No.148399349 ☰ Report
Quoted By: >>148399420 >>148400122

>>148399159
>The assassins already in Paddock's room gets a call. They are told that the Prince is not in his suite above. That he's being escorted out of the Tropicana. They start panicking. If they get caught in this plot to assassinate the crown prince, not only are they dead, but their employer is dead as well. They come up with a plan. They will kill Paddock and start firing on the crowd below. They're gonna make him a crazy lone gunman. So they kill Paddock. They break a window. They pick up a rifle and start firing at the crowd below. After a couple of mags, they realize that the other mags aren't loaded! Holy fuck. They start reloading as fast as possible. This is why the average time between bursts of fire is over 40 seconds. One of them gets an idea. Let me go to the other room and break that window and shoot at the fuel tanks at a nearby airport. This will draw the police away from the Mandalay and they can escape. So he goes and attempts just that. Unfortunately, the tanks do not blow up. By this time, Jesus Campos is knocking on the door. So they just unload on him. This is why there are (supposedly) 200 shots through the door. Campos escapes a lethal shot and calls in security.
>Now the assassins are getting nervous. They realize that someone in the hotel knows that someone is firing. They fire as much as they can. They are thinking as soon as this barrage is done, we run. But the swat team starts knocking on the door. Fuck. The assassins realize they're screwed. So the first one shoots himself. (This is the first of the single shots you hear at the end). The second assassin isn't so sure. He doesn't want to die. So after 10 seconds of courage gathering, he shoots himself as well.

Q

Anonymous ID:mmLVkT5m Tue 07 Nov 2017 11:37:52 No.148399420 ☰ Report
Quoted By: >>148399670 >>148400122

>>148399349
>The SWAT team bursts in and finds 3 bodies. They start asking questions. But because the FBI is already there (remember, they extracted the prince) they take over. They quickly assess the situation. They realize the implications. They remove the 2 assassins bodies, take a picture of Paddock lying there, and release it to 4chan to solidify their narrative.
>Paddock is made the patsy. Why? Because if a failed Saudi assassination attempt was responsible for the deaths, if the FBI/CIA had supplied the guns that killed 58 innocent people (not counting Paddock since he's an asset), then two things would happen. One, we would demand that we go to war with Saudi Arabia. And two, which ever organization that Paddock worked for would be utterly dismantled.

Q

Anonymous ID:mmLVkT5m Tue 07 Nov 2017 11:40:10 No.148399670 ▭ Report
Quoted By: >>148399889 >>148399925 >>148400054 >>148400122 >>148400540 >>148401068 >>148402649

>>148399420
Wew lads, I know. Quite a story. Now, let's fast forward to one month later.

We know a missile was intercepted by the Saudi military on November 3 or 4th. This was probably the final effort by the anti King Salman group. This was their last ditch effort to kill him. OR, it was staged to give King Salman the excuse to round everyone up in retaliation of the assassination attempt. We know that MASSIVE raids and the rounding of Saudi princes took place on the 5th. I will guarantee you that all these people are anti Salman/Mohammad. And who was just killed? Yes. The son of Muqrin, Mansour. Mansour's death was retaliation. I have no doubt of it. He was executed.

Ok, now that this has happened, what's next? Well, my guess will be that we will learn all of the funding that has been coming out of Saudi Arabia for the past decade. It will expose their connections to the DNC. We will learn that they have been at the root of all the turmoil in the Middle East. Then, they'll all be executed.

Q(((uantum)))

One can only hope the true story about Las Vegas will eventually come to the surface, but all the evidence I have seen points to the official narrative being a carefully crafted fiction.

On October 5, 2017, George Papadopoulos would plead "guilty" to lying to the Feds about his communications with other foreign nationals, in order to enter into a plea deal, and serve all of fourteen days in jail. However, as of this writing, he is currently considering recanting his plea deal, given that it's now coming out that certain exculpatory evidence may have been deliberately withheld from him by the FBI.

And finally, on October 6, Trump would ask his "famous" (at least in Q-circles) "Calm Before the Storm" question. Surrounded by military commanders and their significant others, who were all present for a dinner later that evening, Trump asked the press photographers that were there:

"You guys know what this represents? Maybe it's the calm before the storm."

"What's the storm?" asked one bewildered reporter.

"Could be- could be the calm before the storm," he replied, with a characteristic sly smirk on his face.

Very few people in the room, if any other than Trump, knew what he meant at the time. But there in that room, surrounded by the top military minds in the nation, Trump was giving the order for the 'Q' operation to go active. And this was far from the only Q-reference Trump would drop during the next year and a half, for those paying close attention. Trump would even take to trolling the media via Twitter, tweeting out the phrase "Scott Free," which also happens to be the name of Ridley Scott's production company which had produced *White Squall*, the film where Q had ripped his favorite catch-phrase from, "Where we go one, we go all." It was one in a long line of winks-and-nods to Anons, over a year after their collective endeavors had begun.

Donald J. Trump ✔
@realDonaldTrump

Follow ∨

....his wife and father-in-law (who has the money?) off Scott Free. He lied for this outcome and should, in my opinion, serve a full and complete sentence.

7:29 AM - 3 Dec 2018

14,527 Retweets **67,380** Likes

💬 23K   ⇄ 15K   ♡ 67K

Of course, the media's only response was to play dumb and wax pedantic, after months and months of refusing to ask anyone in the Trump administration about the veracity of Q.

CULTURE & ARTS   12/04/2018 01:42 pm ET

This Is Why We Say 'Scot-Free' (And Not 'Scott Free')

Trump's tweet about Michael Cohen raised a few questions.

 By Caroline Bologna

A figure by the name of "Scott Free" appeared to be trending on Twitter on Monday following tweets from President Donald Trump that led to confusion, derision and, naturally, many memes.

While describing his former lawyer Michael Cohen and Cohen's role in Robert Mueller's Russia investigation, Trump tweeted, "He makes up stories to get a GREAT & ALREADY reduced deal for himself, and get....his wife and father-in-law (who has the money?) off **Scott Free**."

> *"Michael Cohen asks judge for no Prison Time." You mean he can do all of the TERRIBLE, unrelated to Trump, things having to do with fraud, big loans, Taxis, etc., and not serve a long prison term? He makes up stories to get a GREAT & ALREADY reduced deal for himself, and get.....*
>
> — Donald J. Trump (@realDonaldTrump) December 3, 2018

> *....his wife and father-in-law (who has the money?) off Scott Free. He lied for this outcome and should, in my opinion, serve a full and complete sentence.*
>
> — Donald J. Trump (@realDonaldTrump) December 3, 2018

Of course, the president likely did not mean to refer to a person named Scott Free (which incidentally is the real name of DC Comics superhero Mister Miracle). It appears Trump intended to say "scot-free," which means to escape without facing punishment, penalty, harm or other consequence.

> *fucking dumbass thinks Scott Free is a person*
>
> — christine teigen (@chrissyteigen) December 3, 2018

> *"Scott Free" pic.twitter.com/rKXhT9Zsqu*
>
> — Oliver Willis (@owillis) December 3, 2018

Had the media done its job and even attempted to approach the issue honestly, they would have made the connection themselves. Heck, they *did* make the connection, but they just *refused* to tell you about it, preferring to keep you in the dark, instead. And this wasn't the first time something like this happened; not by a long shot. There are dozens, if not hundreds of instances like this I could show you. No, the media wanted to keep you in the dark, not only because they were Mockingbirds tasked by the CIA with opposing Trump at every turn, but also because many of them already had the fully unredacted FISA warrants from so long ago, demonstrating that they were complicit in the treasonous cover-up. You're talking about journalist after journalist literally guilty of committing sedition, if not outright treason. And so, they lied to you. They purposefully kept you in the dark so you wouldn't revolt (which is why, I imagine, you're probably hearing this all for the first time here in my book). They lied to you to save their own sorry hides, and spun a web of lies, hoping to forestall the inevitable, hoping that the truth would never see the light of day.

And yet, here we are.

The product of years of collective effort and planning, the Q operation would go live twenty-three days later, when Q would make his first post on /pol/.

On October 28, 2017, Q's first official post read:

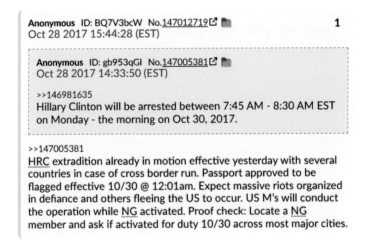

Now, this has been largely misunderstood by many critics, so much so that I've often wondered if it was intentionally "misunderstood" so as to lead people astray and away from Q. On the surface, to the uninitiated, it looks like Q is predicting that Hillary Clinton would be arrested on October 30, 2017. Obviously, that never happened, so how could anyone bother with QAnon all these years later?

See, this is how stupid so many so-called "journalists" are. They literally don't understand how a Chan-based forum works, and the answer is very simple: Q didn't write that part. That whole upper section was written by a random Anon on /pol/, just barfing out whatever nonsense he wanted to post that day. The text below that false prediction? The part about the passport being flagged, and the extradition order in effect in case of HRC making a run for it? That's Q's actual post. Q was responding to the original Anon, correcting him.

Simply put, Q started out by authoritatively informing the board that Hillary was under constant surveillance, and wasn't going to be able to run anywhere. She was being tracked, and there was no escape for her. (In fact, understanding that none of these people will escape is one of the most important pillars to add to your knowledge of Q. Depending on where we are in the timeline when you read this, and how far along Q's plan has progressed, there might still be outstanding, or even ongoing arrests happening. No one involved is escaping, and by a certain point in history, all traitors will either be in jail, or executed.) But for the record, Q also predicted riots if a cross-border run was attempted, and that, when the arrest finally happens, it will be the military handling the particulars of that operation.

Q would also go on to add, in that same thread:

Anonymous ID: BQ7V3bcW No.147023341 ☑ 🏴   2
Oct 28 2017 17:15:48 (EST)

Mockingbird
HRC detained, not arrested (yet).
Where is Huma? Follow Huma.
This has nothing to do w/ Russia (yet).
Why does Potus surround himself w/ generals?
What is military intelligence?
Why go around the 3 letter agencies?
What Supreme Court case allows for the use of MI v Congressional
assembled and approved agencies?
Who has ultimate authority over our branches of military w\o
approval conditions unless 90+ in wartime conditions?
What is the military code?
Where is AW being held? Why?
POTUS will not go on tv to address nation.
POTUS must isolate himself to prevent negative optics.
POTUS knew removing criminal rogue elements as a first step was
essential to free and pass legislation.
Who has access to everything classified?
Do you believe HRC, Soros, Obama etc have more power than
Trump? Fantasy.
Whoever controls the office of the Presidecy controls this great land.
They never believed for a moment they (Democrats and
Republicans) would lose control.
This is not a R v D battle.
Why did Soros donate all his money recently?
Why would he place all his funds in a RC?
Mockingbird 10.30.17
God bless fellow Patriots.

ANSWERS

And this was the start of Q.

Over the coming weeks and months, Q would regularly post intel drops much like the ones above, beckoning Anons to follow him deeper and deeper into the rabbit hole, crafting eighty-three posts in the first week alone. And you might also be picking up on Q's distinctive style of writing, which can almost be described as sparse and Socratic. The truth is, even this stylistic choice was intentional. Think back to the Trump Jr./Secret Service drop. What did Q say?

Anonymous ID: grTMpzrL No.147453147 ☑ 📷   **30**
Nov 1 2017 01:25:22 (EST)

Would you believe a device was placed somewhere in the WH that
could actually cause harm to anyone in the room and would in
essence be undetected?
Fantasy right?
When Trump was elected you can't possibly imagine the steps taken
prior to losing power to ensure future safety & control.
When was it reported Trump Jr dropped his SS detail?
Why would he take that huge risk given what we know?
I can hint and point but cannot give too many highly classified data
points.
These keywords and questions are framed to reduce sniffer
programs that continually absorb and analyze data then pushed to z
terminals for eval. Think xkeysc on steroids.

                                                            ANSWERS

"These keywords and questions are framed to reduce sniffer programs that
continually absorb and analyze data, then pushed to z terminals for eval.
Think xkeysc on steroids."

Not to get too technical here, but the Deep State had supercomputers at their disposal that were constantly trawling the internet, posting in forums and disrupting communications in order to mold and shape the narrative of the nation. A number of techniques
were used to accomplish this, but yes, these supercomputers could mimic natural speech
and engage with people on a number of topics, essentially passing the Turing test, fooling
users into thinking they were talking to real people. Not only would these computers do
this, but they would do it with multiple accounts, to engage in something called "consensus cracking." It's one thing to have an internet argument with one person. It's another
to have five or ten "people" shouting you down, saying you and your lone opinion are
wrong/radical/stupid/etc. Once the "correct" consensus was established, the bots would
move on to the next target (after all, CPU cycles are still a limited resource—even for top
secret supercomputers).

And "xkeysc" here refers to XKeyScore, which was an NSA application that basically
allowed the NSA to suck down all the data going across the internet, anywhere in the world,
and store it in their massive archive in Utah, all categorized and indexed. The program
was disclosed by Edward Snowden in 2013, which led to, according to Q, the NSA being
severely crippled in its ability to conduct SIGINT operations. But before you go thinking
Snowden is a hero, let me tell you, that man is a traitor, and his reasons for disclosing the
program before fleeing to "Russia" (he actually fled to Hong Kong) were to give the CIA
and the Cabal an edge when it came to OpSec. Remember Hillary's private, illegal e-mail
server? The one filled with blackmail? The one she was selling Special Access Programs to
other nations with? Oh, did I mention that little factoid yet? One of the major reasons
Hillary set up an insecure server was to allow foreign nationals access to our SAPs and other
classified intelligence. So, someone might donate to the Clinton Foundation, and in return
they would be told how to access files on the server. It was a fiendishly devilish pay-to-play
arrangement (and believe me when I say this is only the tip of the iceberg when it comes to
Hillary's treasonous activities).

But, Hillary wasn't the only game in town. Obama had his private e-mail servers as well. BobAma@Ameritech.net, for instance, was one of his private, off-the-books addresses. Eric Schmidt, co-founder of Google, actually went to North Korea to help set up one of these private e-mail servers (because North Korea is *nothing* like what you've probably been told it is. Don't worry, we'll go over that in detail later, too). And initially, the NSA was using their xkeyscore program to spy on the illegal activities of these Cabal-affiliated politicians, and plan ahead.

Actually, it would be pretty funny if it weren't so sick; in order to avoid surveillance, Q would tell us, these various Cabal actors would resort to using Gmail drafts (because, again, Eric Schmidt had set up a private Gmail server for them all) to communicate with each other. They'd write up a draft, save it, never send it, and then give the signal for the next person to log in and read the draft. That was one way they attempted to get around the NSA's surveillance programs. They even attempted to use "game comms," as Q has told us. They literally were using the likes of XBOX Live, Playstation Network, and various mobile game chat rooms to try and go incognito with their communications. (Thankfully, it didn't work.)

So when Q says "think xkeysc on steroids" it means there was a program on Cabal supercomputers that was even *more* powerful than what the NSA had previously had access to, before Snowden came along and crippled them with a bit of publicity. Q had to skirt around that through bland, Socratic phraseology, lest the Cabal computers pick up on what was going on and overwhelm the boards with a flood of spam and noise.

Oh, and if you were paying attention at the time, you'd realize Eric Schmidt stepped down from Alphabet (the parent corporation of Google) the very same day (December 21, 2017) President Trump would sign the executive order entitled "Blocking the Property of Persons Involved in Serious Human Rights Abuse or Corruption," mandating total asset seizure for anyone involved in such crimes. Schmidt resigned that very day in order to protect the company he had helped build (with the help of the CIA, through its dedicated tech incubator, In-Q-Tel). Schmidt would later make an appearance in June 2018, during Inspector General Horowitz's testimony before the House and Senate Judiciary committees. He would be sitting on the edge of his seat, the whole time.

One more data point before we leave this "pre-Q" timeline:

Similar to what happened with Schmidt above, on October 30, it was announced that Paul Manafort would be indicted as part of Mueller's special counsel investigation. This is the day Tony Podesta would resign from The Podesta Group. November 9, 2017 all of the Podesta Group's employees would be told that they needed to find new jobs, because the Podesta Group would cease to exist come the new year. However, Kimberley Fritts, the Podesta Group's chief executive and second-in-command, would soon all but resurrect the firm as Cogent Strategies, taking many of the Podesta Group's former hires and clients with her, essentially reincarnating the Podesta group under her leadership, but leaving behind all the legal baggage in the process.

Now, obviously, this isn't a complete timeline of every single event that happened during the time leading up to, and following Trump's presidential campaign—and it's not meant to be. Entire books have been written, dissecting the layers of intrigue surrounding these events (I recommend Dan Bongino's *Spygate,* in particular), and new details continue to emerge with each passing week. However, what this timeline is supposed to give you is a general feel for what Anons (such as yours truly) were seeing during this time, what connections we were making, and what discoveries we were digging up, because frankly, much of this was either deliberately ridiculed or purposefully buried by the Legacy Media. And I know I keep saying it, but believe me, the media is not your friend. Trump labeled them "Fake News," and "the enemy of the people" for a reason. They do not have your best interest at heart.

But if you're reeling from everything I just told you, I wouldn't be surprised. Imagine how Anons felt this whole time, simultaneously shocked, enraged, and maligned by the Mockingbird Media. And yet, they soldiered on, dogged in their pursuit of the truth; nigh unstoppable, working not for recognition but out of love for their country, for their people, and their desire to restore the Republic to the former glory enshrined in its ideals. In short, they wanted the exact same thing Trump wanted: to Make America Great Again (which is why they helped meme him into office in the first place)!

Trump's unspoken genius in all this was in leveraging the power of Anons—a decentralized, digital volunteer army—to accomplish this goal.

So what do we call this movement, the QAnon operation? What, specifically, was this movement of everyday Anons and patriots trying to accomplish, and how did it intend to accomplish its goals?

In short: QAnon is a high-level intelligence operation run in conjunction with the NSA and Military Intelligence, put in place by President Trump as a way to bypass the media and establish a direct communication backchannel with the people (by starting specifically with his most fervent, dedicated, and savvy supporters—the Anons), in order to overthrow an ancient cult/Cabal that had, as its goal, the complete destruction of America. Utilizing a Socratic style of writing, Q would begin slow-rolling disclosures about these Cabal actors and their nefarious plans, as well as reframe certain incorrect, yet commonly held assumptions (and correcting lies, when fit), in order to "awaken" the people to the reality that had been hidden from them for decades.

The ultimate goal of all of this was to reach a tipping point, where a certain critical mass of people would gain a level of prerequisite knowledge previously unheard of in the world, creating, in essence, a decentralized intelligence agency made up of hundreds of thousands of Anons (if not millions), running 24/7, all working with each other to research, write, disseminate, and meme non-stop, not only to counter the national narratives, but to create a "safety-net" of mental and emotional support for when the rest of the population would be unwillingly (at least at first) forced into the light by events that would start to erupt around them—such as mass arrests, military tribunals, and even executions of formerly beloved politicians. (And if you wanted to get more esoteric, there's even some out there who believe Q was constructing a morphogenetic field—basically, a quantum explanation for what some may call a "collective consciousness" that is, frankly, beyond my current level of understanding. Though I will admit, I think it well within the realm of possibility, judging by what I have seen and read, thus far.)

My role in all this was to follow Q with every drop, remain active on the research boards, posting whenever necessary, trying to figure out what precisely Q was talking about (though, due to the nature of Q, this often proved to be a daunting task), and disseminate my findings online—both on my own website, and on my social media profiles—in a way that many, many people found both compelling and easier to consume. Drawing from my own expertise, and the expertise of seasoned Anons, I would dissect Q's drops and curate them in such a way as to tailor them for mass consumption. These efforts eventually led to me becoming one of the most followed and most influential Q-supporters in the world, with Q even pulling images from my site on occasion, highlighting images of supporters wearing the shirts and hats I had begun to manufacture (emblazoned with Q-related slogans), and generally having this sort of weird, symbiotic relationship that, I imagine, will be quite unlike anything I'll ever experience again. And I don't say any of that to toot my own horn. I was often incorrect in my analyses, trying as I might to keep pace with Q. But one thing my readers appreciated was that I would always try to point out when I was speculating, that I would admit when I was wrong, and do my best to course-correct in the process. It was no small task, and, it was some of the most challenging and most important work I could have ever undertaken. In essence, I became a very large, and very recognizable "node" in this QAnon network, of which I am very proud to be a part.

And Q was no mere PR campaign. Lives were at stake. Our enemies were very real, very embedded, and exposing them would require a "Great Awakening," around the world, resulting in literally changing the course of history. Evildoers would be exposed and ultimately rounded up for sentencing at military tribunals, since the normal justice system was far too corrupt and subverted by bad actors at this time. If we succeeded in our efforts, this would result in the restoration of the Republic, and the dawn of a new Golden Age for America, and even the world. Q would even go on to talk about suppressed and hidden technologies, stirring the imaginations of Anons worldwide as he confirmed the existence of things like the Secret Space Program, and promised disclosures that would blow people's minds. But once again, we'll have to save that discussion for the very end.

The scary part, the really scary part in all this is…. that this was Plan B.

Things had gone so awry during the Obama years, the original plan being fielded by the top brass, the original Plan A, was for a military coup, wherein Obama would have been overthrown by force. See, military intelligence had long been monitoring the scene, and everything I've told you thus far (and much, much more), was known to them years ago. They thought it might be necessary, as early as 2013, to simply depose Obama from office in a military coup and summarily execute him. There would have been rioting, yes. The cost to America would have been terrible, yes. But the Republic would have been preserved and millions of lives would have been saved as a result. Believe me when I say, knowing what I know now, that course of action would have been entirely justified.

But instead, prudence won out and patience took the day. They decided to hold off. An election was a few years away and *if* they could find the right candidate to back, and *if* they could convince him to run, and *if* they could mitigate the rampant voter fraud, and *if* they could find a way to have him appeal to enough people, and *if* they could win the nomination, and *if* they could circumvent the media, and *if* they could keep him safe from the constant threat of assassination…well…then they might just be able to pull off a totally legal, bloodless coup, and end up driving this cult from the halls of power once and for all. After all, if, in the end, the bloodless way failed, they could always try the bloody route again. This path forward was more prudent, but it was also more excruciating for everyone involved.

If that all worked, then they'd figure out how to deal with the Cabal afterward.

If you're reeling from that summation—as I'm sure many in America are by now—it's best to get used to the feeling, because it's not going to go anywhere as long as you've got this book in your hands. Essentially, when you step into the world of QAnon, you quickly learn that almost every assumption you had about the way the world works, everything you thought you knew, was wrong in some way—and that this was by design. The feeling is dizzying, at least when you're emotionally attached to a particular outcome (or a particular party, or politician, instead of the truth, instead of ideals like freedom and liberty). Overcome those attachments, however, and the ride soon becomes exhilarating! Evil, true EVIL, gets exposed when you dive into the world of Q. Leave your preconceived notions at the door—because understanding what's written in this book is quite possibly the single most important task you can endeavor to undertake in your life.

So, having successfully leveraged this latent power, this mass of Americans sitting at their computers, yearning to help in some way, any way they could, the Q movement took on its final form: a decentralized, anonymized, online research initiative surrounding the questions and issues raised by communications with an agent (or team of agents) embedded deep in the Trump administration, operating at the highest echelons of government intelligence, in order to bypass the media and take down the Cabal.

But that barely does the size and scope of what's happening here any justice. And beyond that, Anons, naturally, had questions. Could Q be trusted? What's the nature of the threat facing the nation? Can we really trust the Plan? There had been other insider leaks before. Why Q, and why now? Why follow him?

Why did *I* follow him?

Trump represented an existential threat to the establishment from the very moment he declared his candidacy. I said earlier that I knew almost immediately that this election was like no other election in our entire history. The unrest and the discord made it clear that this was unlike anything we, the people, had ever seen before. The election wasn't quite the victory we, on Trump's side, initially thought it was. It was clear from that day on, that Trump's victory had been a declaration of war, and that war was about to enter its next phase.

CHAPTER 4

"You Are Taking Back Control"

—January 27, 2018 From Qdrop #619

Donald J. Trump ✔
@realDonaldTrump

Follow ⌄

MAKING AMERICA GREAT AGAIN!

▶ 3.3M views   1:23 / 2:37 🔊 ⤢

MAKING AMERICA GREAT AGAIN!
Video from a supporter. Thank you! -President Trump

7:01 PM · 30 Jul 2018

"Never stop fighting for what you believe in, and for the people who care about you. Carry yourself with dignity and pride. Relish the opportunity to be an outsider. Embrace that label, because it's the outsiders who change the world, and who make real and lasting difference. Treat the word 'impossible' as nothing more than motivation."

—POTUS—July 30, on Twitter

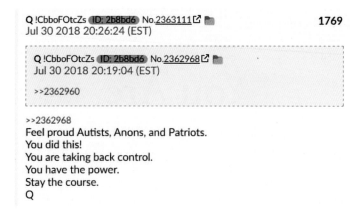

Q !CbboFOtcZs **ID: 2b8bd6** No.2363111 ☑ ▶   1769
Jul 30 2018 20:26:24 (EST)

> Q !CbboFOtcZs **ID: 2b8bd6** No.2362968 ☑ ▶
> Jul 30 2018 20:19:04 (EST)
>
> >>2362960

>>2362968
Feel proud Autists, Anons, and Patriots.
You did this!
You are taking back control.
You have the power.
Stay the course.
Q

"I never asked for this."—Adam Jensen

—*Deus Ex: Human Revolution*

One disclaimer before we embark on this chapter. This is the most autobiographical chapter in the book. Many of my readers will undoubtedly be more interested in what I have to tell them about QAnon than in me, and may mistake this chapter as a mere exercise in vanity. But I realize in writing all this that I am but one lens through which to view Q. And I make no bones about it: I certainly have my own biases, which the more astute readers may have already started to pick up on, and for which I do not apologize. By the end of the chapter, I hope you'll see these biases more clearly. So, in the interest of helping you better understand this particular "lens," I've included this chapter, which talks about the origins of my work, how I came to cover Q, and the events leading up to all this—for you may be surprised to learn that this whole Q-gig was not my first rodeo, and there's quite a bit of history here—some of which is still being written as we speak.

It was September 2017… and I couldn't get out of bed and face another day.

I wasn't suicidal, though I wouldn't have blamed anyone for thinking otherwise. Sure, I had bouts of depression here and there (as is par for the course for many in our modern, disconnected, unhealthy age). It was just that I was completely empty, tapped out, and numb inside. Whatever fire that had previously driven me to get out of bed every week for the past five years (god, had it really been five years?!) and face each day at work had suddenly and forcefully gone out, anchoring me to the bed.

It didn't help that I had just basically been dumped by a girl I was talking to at the time. I haven't historically dated very much, and while I wouldn't say my standards are particularly high, there's a combination of criteria I have that, thus far, has made finding an eligible someone something of a rarity. Still, it was looking like I had found a winner when I met this particular girl through an online dating site, and we had gotten to talking. Though she lived several thousand miles away (in Canada, in fact), I was enjoying her company and conversation with increasing regularity, as we maintained contact through Facebook and video chats and such.

That was, until her father stepped in and decided I was… unfit for his daughter. (How's that assessment panning out for you two now, by the way, huh? But in all seriousness, I wish you both well, and good riddance.)

You see, I had spent the past half-decade burning what was left of my twenties working at a grocery store for what many would consider minimum wage these days. Prior to this, I had gone to and graduated from a good college; I had an excellent educational background, and then… I had felt that I was called to go into the film industry.

Oh sure, in some sense, I had always felt pulled in that direction, but I never really considered it feasible for one reason or another. Film schools were inordinately expensive, and I had no real connections to the industry. My family had always been middle class, having worked our way up from the lower rungs when I was a child to a comfortable mid-to-upper-middle class—but nowhere near wealthy enough to spend the six figures per year necessary for a "good" film education. No, it always seemed more like a fanciful pipe dream, and so, I had actually started down the path towards studying medicine instead.

Believe it or not, my high school was oriented towards the medical practice. All the electives were related to different domains of medicine, and many were pulled straight from college pre-med courses. While most kids were taking Spanish or French at their high schools, I was taking Latin in order to prep for a lifetime of reading medical texts. At age fourteen, I was in gross anatomy labs handling preserved human organs. I did rounds at hospitals and learned how to draw blood as a kid. During a "rebellious" phase, I purposefully failed my EMT certification because I didn't like cops, and as an EMT in my state, you would have to put a sticker on your car… meaning cops could flag you down and enlist your services if they needed to. (Stupid? Probably. This was during a more rebellious phase, when most teenagers feel at least some sort of resentment for the law, and the prospect of being potentially forced to work for them did not appeal to me.) But one thing I did learn from the class was how to perform a pericardial thump; a last ditch resuscitative measure for a patient undergoing CPR where, if they're really unresponsive and you don't have a defibrillator anywhere nearby, you can place your elbow basically in their navel and bring your fist down on their sternum. The compression actually delivers a very, very, very small electrical shock that can *sometimes* restart their heart, but more often than not, you usually just end up breaking ribs on a dead person. Buuuut, if it works, you'll know immediately because the patient usually jumps up screaming, at which point, you may now be in need of CPR from the heart attack *you* just experienced resuscitating someone else.

But all that to say that the curriculum was demanding and intensive. Minus the EMT stuff, I was a pretty stellar student. And at age eighteen, I decided I was either going to go big or go home. Did I want to focus on the brain, or did I want to become a cardiologist? Having had a family member who had dealt with heart issues in the past, I knew a local cardiologist who agreed to take me in for a regular internship—which is something we all did at the school for a semester during our senior year. Soon, I was observing the Doc as he dealt with patients at his practice, and watching him perform surgery when he went to the hospital.

Imagine my shock one day when this doctor and I were discussing my future and he told me, "No, go into Hollywood. If I had a face like yours, I would have gone into Hollywood long ago." Well, that was probably the last thing I needed to hear at the time. To be clear, I never wanted to be an actor or anything in front of the camera, but the Doc thought I would fit in there all the same. And if I was being completely honest, I was still feeling that creative tug on my heart, though I tried to suppress it for years with more "realistic ambitions."

During these formative years, I almost inadvertently ended up discovering that I had something of a knack for writing. I also had bought a little digital camera and had begun exploring filming little sketches or whatever projects I was assigned, because that was more fun and engaging for me than doing things the regular way. And while the doctor I was working under was very respected in his field, it was clear that there were many areas about his job over which he was growing increasingly resentful. During the weeks I had spent with him, I had come to see the immense regulatory burdens he had been saddled with. He had a whole staff working full time just to deal with the insurance paperwork that came along with his job. Because it took so long (and so much money) to become licensed and operating at his level, the demand on his time and energy were incredible. Sure, it was a respectable profession, and he helped many tremendously, but there were very real quality-of-life trade-offs that needed to be considered—including at least twelve years of schooling just to get to his level. I had only just started to consider such trade-offs when… frankly, I had a bit of an… unintentional breakdown.

It will come as a surprise to absolutely no one that it wasn't exactly easy going to one of the top high schools in the entire nation. Six hours of homework a night was pretty par for the course, and I had been operating on very little sleep for a long time. I worked part-time too, at a local coffee shop, so that was always on my slate week after week, and unbeknownst to me at the time, I started to have some health problems which affected my hormones, energy, and mood. One day, senior year, I drove myself to school in my little red sedan and actually hit a parked car in the parking lot; I was *that* deliriously tired. To be fair, the car I hit belonged to some junior who had just gotten his permit, and who had parked at some ridiculous forty-five degree angle across two spaces, so I just didn't calculate the radius of my turn into the adjacent spot correctly, but it was still a wake-up call that, frankly, went unnoticed at the time. I was beyond burning the candle at both ends. I was a little waxy stub, barely able to flicker at that point, but despite how I felt, I couldn't pretend like the accident hadn't happened, and so I walked into the office and turned myself in. It was unfortunate, but I told the guy I'd pay for whatever repairs he needed, and it ended up costing me close to a grand,but it was the right thing to do—even if I did get mocked for it later in the halls of the school.

And thankfully, my car was more plasticky, so it just kind of bounced back to its normal shape with minimal damage.

At any rate, I was just looking forward to finally graduating. I had college plans all set up for the next year, and all I really had left to do was graduate. It was one last hurdle to leap over. The final stretch. Basically, all I had to do was not screw up.

Which is why I had to go and open my big mouth and say things that were "threaten-ing" and nearly get expelled and arrested, mere weeks before graduating.

Look, I've never really talked publicly about this next part before, and I've had fifteen years to go over this in my head and reflect on why I said what I said that day, but if you've read my writing online for any length of time, you know I have a… certain way with words. There's a bombast to them (which some people mistakenly read as arrogance—especially if they're not in particular agreement with me on any given topic). And in my stupid teenage brain, I thought it would be a good idea to talk about how much I actually hated the school and how, if I was to go around killing people like some kind of school shooter, this is who I would shoot, and when and where and how, and…

You get the entire, unfortunate picture.

Brilliant, right?

Now, let me be exceedingly clear on this point: I didn't mean **any** of it. I had no plans to do anything of the sort, and I had never even held a gun at that point. I like guns and the Second Amendment, to be sure, but at that time, I didn't own any, had never used one, didn't even have access to one, and really, my perception was just molded by the video games I played growing up. In essence, I was just being an edgy idiot. I had been on the receiving end of a fair amount of bullying growing up, mostly for my faith, which is what made me "different." And anyone who has been to high school knows how mercilessly you can get mocked for anything that makes you different or stand out in any way.

I think it's pretty accurate to say that, while I wasn't on *terrible* terms with anyone, I really only had one good friend left at the school. Earlier, one girl I had known for a while and really had strong feelings for sort of went off the rails herself, dropped out of the program, started using drugs of some sort, and was shipped to a rehab in another state never to be seen again, so I still had that fresh hurt lingering inside me. And by the time this incident had rolled around, I miiii-ight have been trying to impress a different girl, albeit in something of a cynical, half-hearted way.

I think this is something young guys sometimes do, where, even if you're not sure if you like a girl, you'll say big, stupid things to "impress" them. You know, just in case. It's like the teenage equivalent of those crazy birds of paradise you see in those nature documentaries; trying to look bigger and more impressive than they really are, just to see if anyone will take notice, if anyone will bother with you. And I put "impress" in quotations because it's usually so transparent and fake it never works anyway. But I hope that at least the men reading this can sympathize with teenage me saying something incredibly stupid in front of a member of the opposite sex. Heck, it's probably taken me a decade just to be able to admit that to myself.

But the school counselors didn't care about any of that.

Neither did the administration.

Or the local police department.

In short order, I had my locker raided, my school e-mail account scoured, and I was brought to the local police station in a squad car for questioning. Eventually, they figured out that I didn't really mean any of this; that I was just running my immensely stupid, insecure, teenage mouth, and they let me go, not wanting to waste anymore time or resources on the matter.

When I finally came back to school, some twelve days later (which I think is *still* the record for longest suspension they had ever handed out at that school), I had to speak directly to some of the people I had mentioned by name as wanting to shoot and apologize. Which I genuinely did, with my head hung low.

In truth, part of my "verbal creativity" comes from my upbringing. When you get a lashing for using a swear word as a kid, you tend to get more creative with your insults so as to get away with it. It's a way of obeying the letter of the law, if not the spirit, I suppose. I remember picking up "the middle finger" as a kid—I was maybe five or six—on the school playground—and I had no idea what it meant other than it was a big insult. And so, one day, I was upset with my mother for not letting me—it was either watch a TV show or have a snack, I can't remember—and she forbade me from saying another word.

You know how moms get.

"NOT ANOTHER WORD!"

Well, lucky me! I had just learned that I didn't need words to communicate anymore! I could communicate just fine with these two fingers I had at my disposal!

As I walked away, I twisted my torso around, ready to open fire with both barrels. BOOM BOOM! My little five-year-old middle fingers popped up on each hand. Tell me not to talk? Here's a double bird for ya, lady! Take *that*!

I can only begin to describe what happened next, as time seemed to slow to a crawl around me. Her jaw dropped and within seconds I knew from the expression on her face that whatever I had done, it was now the single worst mistake I had ever made in my life—a life which might now be ending in the next sixty seconds if I didn't run and hide immediately. So that's exactly what I did!

The only way I can describe what happened next was that it was like that scene in *Jurassic Park* where the kids are hiding from the velociraptors in the kitchen. So well hidden was I that I could see my mother roving back and forth through the house, shouting my name, like some kind of furious bloodhound who had lost the scent of its prey.

I was so well hidden, in fact, that I watched her speed past me once, twice, three times. I thought I might actually get away with it, even if it meant staying hidden forever, and that made me feel really guilty. And so, I emerged from my hiding spot and said tenuously, "M…mom??" Hoping against hope that maybe she had calmed down, maybe the running through the house had tired her out, maybe she would have mercy on miniature version of me for this crime I had unwittingly committed.

…

NOPE!

THWACK THWACK THWACK! Her hand spanked my behind so hard, as she yanked me out from the big cushions I had scuttled behind.

"Never-"

THWACK!

"-EVER"

THWACK!

"EVER!!"

THWACK

"DO THAT AGAIN!"

THWACK THWACK THWACK!

Still confused as to why two little fingers could be so atomically offensive, with my butt now blistered and raw, my mom, now exasperated and out of breath, told me to go to my room. I didn't argue. I was still alive. In pain, but somehow, by some miracle, still alive! I ran as fast as I could, and I never uttered so much as a curse word ever again. (Well, mostly.)

To this day, I still talk like someone straight out of the *Andy Griffith* show. It's almost Puritanical, I swear. Even when I'm posting online, my readers know: I'll self-censor with a series of comic book styled filler text, like something out of *Beetle Bailey*, subbing out the expletives for random characters instead.

(Don't misunderstand me either, though. I have an absolutely wonderful mother, and I couldn't imagine what I'd be like but for her steady and caring influence in my life. This book exists, in part, due to her support, so everyone thank my mom one day if you see her.)

But to get back to my suspension and near arrest, in some sense, this was just me expressing my resentment against these individuals for past offenses and mistreatment. Had I had a more conventional, (and perhaps less religious) upbringing, I would have called them all some exceedingly foul name and that would have been the end of that. Nobody locks anyone up for calling someone a "bleeping this-or-that." But because I was tiptoeing around the "morality" of such insults, and because of my typical bombastic verbal style (and "rich inner life" as some psychiatrists might say), I inadvertently ended up really scaring some people. For what it's worth, I never wanted to hurt anyone, and I should have figured out a better way of channeling and expressing that resentment.

In the end, I was suspended for twelve days, banned from the senior prom, and almost barred from walking at graduation. And even though I did apologize face-to-face, I hope those individuals forgave me for the things I said while, perhaps, trying to impress a girl all those years ago. Though it was a difficult lesson to learn, for the first time in my life I saw what my words could do if used carelessly.

And kind of like how I had hidden all those years ago when my mom was "hunting" me for flipping her off… I retreated for a long time after that event. Except this go-round, I really didn't emerge for a very long time. I went inward, where I never had to risk anyone misunderstanding me ever again. And there was a strange logic to it, too. Obviously, I couldn't trust myself to express my thoughts and feelings in a productive manner, let alone rely on the world to understand what I really meant. Look at the disaster that had just happened! Imagine if I had really screwed things up!

I had never felt so powerless and misunderstood in my whole life. Oh, I totally get that it was my own dumb fault; I'm not denying responsibility here, but at the same time, I had already been through so much. I felt I had been left with no real recourse, and had just made it out of that terrible situation through sheer luck and providence, by the skin of my teeth. In a weird way, I became… colder. More detached. More reserved. More cynical. Wiser, perhaps, but at what cost? I certainly never felt the same after that. Relationships, all my relationships, became more difficult to maintain. I felt adrift and abandoned; like I had no community, no real home—like everyone was somehow suspicious of me. I felt like a stranger everywhere I went, unable to connect with anyone.

I'll say this much: whatever I felt in the wake of those events was an overreaction. The really difficult part for me, personally, has been coming back from that; re-awakening myself and my ability to communicate with others, to examine and pursue stories, and channel my creativity in powerful, meaningful ways. That event had (along with at least one other event which I'm not going to talk about today), destroyed my confidence for a long time, and I believe it was an attempt to cripple my ability to work for good. Guilt haunted me like a specter and for years, perhaps even the better part of a decade, I felt like I was worthless, inexperienced, and incapable. I felt that I would never fit in anywhere no matter how hard I tried, and that I would never be truly understood. And that became something of a self-fulfilling prophecy for a long time.

So, I end up graduating high school at age eighteen. It was 2004, and I was still pretty shaken up by the whole experience at the end. Instead of finishing on a high note, I had given my folks the scare of their lifetime, and made a lot of people very angry and upset in the process. Still, I would be going to college in the fall, and it would be like something of a fresh start. I had racked up two years' worth of college credits from my high school courses (yes, TWO whole years' worth, though my college would only end up accepting a year-and-a-half's credits) and I got busy commuting from home and going to classes.

I took it relatively easy in college, trying to recuperate and just move more cautiously this time around. The side effect of the past four years was total burnout, so I took on a light curriculum. I had basically decided at this point that maybe medicine wasn't for me, and that, hey, since I was young and free, maybe I should try to get a degree as close to film as I could possibly muster. Then maybe, after getting my bachelor's degree, I would go to some kind of graduate program. At least that way it was only two years' worth of mega-debt instead of twelve in medical school.

And it was during this time in college that I would take my first screenwriting class.

It was here I really fell in love with the craft of writing. While I had always enjoyed it in the past, now, it just clicked for me. I had wanted to work in film for so long, but the cost! The cost is what was keeping me out. I couldn't afford a real camera, a cast, a crew, or… anything, really. But screenwriting! I didn't need *any* of that. All I had to do was imagine it and put it down on the page. If I could master this craft, I would be unstoppable. I wouldn't have to rely on other people's ideas or inspiration; I could make my own source material from the ground up. After all, everything in film depends on having the right idea first. Without a good script, the film simply doesn't exist.

It wasn't just a matter of enjoying writing, either. I said earlier that I had a natural inclination for it, as well, and had inadvertently been gathering tools and experience that would be useful in this arena. Those four years of Latin courses didn't just help with medicine, after all, and I had always been something of a media hound, having gobbled down a ton of books and really wordy video games growing up. I'm not talking *Super Mario* here. I'm talking LucasArts Adventures. *Monkey Island, Full Throttle, Grim Fandango*—stuff that was more cinematic and dialog-driven than the parabolic jumping mechanics of everyone's favorite Italian plumber. I had even attempted to write a novel in high school—something that was little more than a knockoff of that LucasArts shooter, *Outlaws*—a first-person shooter in the vein of *Doom* that had already familiarized me with all the genre tropes of the Spaghetti Western genre, combined with excellent animation and storytelling. And we can't forget *Sam and Max Hit the Road* in all this. When you have an "anthropomorphic talking rabbity-thing" delivering dry, comedic lines like "Gratuitous acts of senseless violence are my forte," in front of your impressionable ten-year-old brain, it leaves an impact, even decades later. Needless to say, I was already a verbal force to be reckoned with.

To get better, I would gobble down as many movies as humanly possible, utilizing an unlimited Blockbuster DVD subscription I had purchased for myself. Yes, Blockbusters were still around at that time, and since they were competing with Netflix when Netflix used to mail out DVDs to your door, Blockbuster had to up the ante. They would send you unlimited movies per month, and you could go to the local store and trade in your current DVD for another one for free. I would watch, easily, upwards of fifteen movies in a month. It was something of a self-directed course in cinema, and I was consuming everything from practically every genre I could find in their vast catalog. (In fact, this was something I had started doing during high school. We had block scheduling, meaning classes were 90 minutes long, and lunch was an entire hour. Well, I would sneak off to a vacant English or history lab, turn on a projector, pop in a DVD, and watch three quarters of a movie most days during my lunch. I wasn't wasting time. I was learning everything I could.)

Soon, I started writing scripts and before I knew it, I had my first full-length feature written. I didn't need costly schooling, or convoluted classes (undoubtedly from Left-leaning professors); I didn't need to hire crews or rent out expensive equipment. I could build the entire story world in my mind and transfer it on to the page, and that was enough for me, for now. Oh, rest assured, my first script had ***plenty*** of problems, but in this arena, you could only get better through practice, and in time, even this relatively poor sample would serve me well. I went on to finish my college courses, graduate with a good GPA, and hey, this time, I somehow managed to not screw anything major up, so that was a step in the right direction!

Or so I thought.

See, if you're the counting type, you may have noticed something.

I graduated high school in 2004.

And then I spent another four years in college.

Which means I graduated in 2008…

Right into the depths of the Great Recession at the beginning of the Obama administration.

In truth, I never really found solid work my first year out of college. Despite sending out dozens of applications over many, many months, no one was interested in hiring someone like me. I would eventually settle for a (now illegal) post-college "internship" at a small video production house in New York City, hoping to get some experience and "pay my dues." I would commute by rail several hours each day (which, at least I was reimbursed for), and usually end up doing random tasks around the office there (like… cleaning, or whatever). I had hoped I would get more exposure to the actual creative side of the business, like working on set or editing projects, and I did get a chance to do some of that. But more often, I was stuck with sherpa-style grunt work. Once, at Christmastime, the owners made me deliver presents to their partner companies.

In the middle of a blizzard.

Because I didn't live in the area, and the storm had fallen rather unexpectedly, and because no one told me I was going to be playing UPS man that day, I only had my jeans, my jacket, and my Puma sneakers for elemental protection. And because the subways didn't really go where I needed them to, I ended up having to slog dozens of blocks to get to my destinations in the freezing cold, with snow building up and clinging to my chest, face, and legs. I don't think it was an exaggeration to say I walked four or five miles in the snow that day. I was lucky enough to warm up in the various buildings during each stop, but I imagine I was quite the haggard sight. By the time I had dropped off the final package, everyone else had abandoned the New York city streets. I was near Grand Central Terminal, and the feeling would have been almost serene, in that blue-black blizzard, but for the biting cold. There were a few other souls as unfortunate as me out at that hour, most of them better dressed for the weather. But it was remarkably peaceful, there in the darkness. By the time I had slogged back to the office, I looked like some kind of wildly unprepared frontiersman on the verge of frostbite.

The office we were in was this old, makeshift space, perched above an old theater in the East Village. It was drafty and weird and almost felt a bit like a dorm due to the age of everyone working there, though there were, thankfully, a few space heaters around the place. The others saw my condition, and allowed me to take off my sneakers, crank one heater up to eleven, and dry off for a bit. At least until we popped a fuse. Then I had to turn it down and just put up with soggy socks. I was too cold to remember that I wasn't actually getting paid for any of this, but I took it in stride, figuring, hey... I just had to keep paying my dues. If I worked hard, worked diligently, that effort would be recognized and opportunities would present themselves along the way. That's how it worked.

...Right?

Yeah, I was replaced shortly thereafter by a transfer student from some former Soviet satellite state; some Balkan dude who knew After Effects better than I did.

Flash forward a couple of months, and the only job I was able to find in the end, post-college, was working in the juice bar of a local organic grocery story for seven bucks an hour. Here I was, a college-educated guy who just a few years earlier was thinking about going into medicine—a career that's always in demand and always pays well—and I was now living at home with "mommy and daddy," slinging beets, apples, and lemons into industrial juicers for minimum wage. Meanwhile, this particular grocery store had a notorious reputation for being way overpriced. You could find skinny boxes of organic cereal there for over ten dollars a pop, and the juices I was making ran anywhere from four dollars, to ten dollars as well (depending on the size and vegetable content). In other words, the clientele that would frequent this place had money to burn, and certainly acted like it.

And while there were plenty of people in this area who were certainly willing to pay those kind of obscene amounts for all manner of hoity-toity shopping experiences, it really felt like a smack in the face when the boss rolled up one day in his truck, towing his massive boat behind him. Why was he bringing his boat to his business, you may ask? Well, he had to wash it. And this way, he got to write off the water and cleaning products he used as business expenses.

To his credit, he would eventually give me a raise. All the way up to eight bucks an hour.

As the saying goes, you're paid what the job is worth, not what you're worth. And again, I told myself that I just had to pay my dues; that this was temporary. I continued to apply for jobs while working at this place, full time… but this was a new economy we were facing, and no one had quite realized it yet. Obamanomics was now in full swing, and companies just weren't hiring people like me anymore—people with relatively low levels of experience—not when they could find someone with decades of work history behind them while paying the same amount as they would have paid someone like me,. Older folks were out of work, now, too, and that was saturating the job market with excess, experienced laborers, driving down wages in the process and blocking recent grads like me from ever getting a foot in the door.

Several months went by, and I settled into kind of a routine. At least I had a job. That was something to be grateful for, right? After all, a lot of people were really struggling out there. And my twelve-year-old car was still running great. And I didn't have any debt. Even though my checks were pitiful, I wasn't a big spender. So what if I had to live with my folks for a few more years? I would make my way, if not in the immediate future, then in the years to come. Things couldn't stay bad forever, right?

A highlight from this time was when I got to visit my first, official movie set. I would write a bit about this experience on NeonRevolt.com (for other reasons entirely) but around the time I was twenty-two I got to visit the set of Robert De Niro's picture, *The Good Shepherd*. See, my father had a business connection to the set they were filming on, Bronx Community College, which just so happened to be the old NYU campus, so it has that kind of "Skull and Bones" *look* the set designers were going for, and this connection helped get us in to see what was going on. I got to observe what they were doing for several hours, unperturbed. I got to see Robert Richardson, with his wild, wizard-like hair, framing up shots for the big Skull and Bones ceremonial scene. I saw Matt Damon waiting on the side of the set, chatting it up with the crew. And De Niro *almost* patted me on the shoulder as he passed by—though, knowing what I know now, I realize this is nothing to be starstruck about. Still, at the time, this was major inspiration for an aspiring film guy like me. Desiring to work in the industry wasn't just some crackpot fantasy. Visiting the set somehow made it more tangible. There were *actually* people who did this kind of thing for a living. It wasn't just a crackpot dream, and yes, I could, too, if I kept working at it.

(And if anyone involved with that picture ever reads this and wants proof that I really was there, well, Matt Damon was allergic to the mud they used for the mud wrestling scene, and his skin broke out as a result. They had to get a special hypoallergenic mud for that scene. Which is something I only know because that contact gave me the inside scoop.)

Then, one day after working at the grocery store, at twenty-three years old, I came home and I saw application sitting on my spot at the dinner table. When I picked it up and read it, it turned out it was for a small, year-and-a-half long screenwriting program out in Hollywood. My folks had found out about it and wanted me to apply, but because of the deadline, I had to fill it out that very night and FedEx it over the next day. I didn't need anymore convincing, and luckily I had writing samples on hand! Within the week, I found out I had, by some miracle, been accepted, and pretty soon, I found myself moving out to Los Angeles, really on my own for the first time in my life. I found an apartment, and got busy learning—not just about screenwriting, but about the industry and life itself. Oh, and I was writing; writing all the time. And in a little over a year, I managed to land some temp work at Paramount Studios (with the help of a contact I had made at church out there).

Working on a studio lot is an interesting experience. Besides the typical film production stuff you'd expect, yes, I got to see all sorts of production work being done, and different celebrities on any given day. I saw Will Ferrell wading through a shrubbery one day to get to a group of his friends, Johnny Knoxville limping in a parking lot, evidently still in pain from whatever *Jackass* prank he had last filmed, and Brad Pitt looking a bit frustrated, but determined, following a production meeting with the studio heads regarding the budgetary nightmare that was *World War Z.* That's not to namedrop. After all, I don't know any of these people. I'm just trying to give you a sense of my new "normal" at that time. But I also began to see a darker side of Hollywood, such as when the entire studio was summoned to one of the theaters on the lot to watch a presentation regarding none other than Kim Dotcom, founder of MegaUpload (and later, Mega). It was then that I started to suspect that more was going on than what I was being told on the surface.

In short order, the rank and file at the studio were shown a video that turned Dotcom into little more than a mustache-twirling villain, tooling around his estate with his friends on his ATV, enjoying a lavish lifestyle in a way that only a Bond-esque super villain indulging in his ill-begotten spoils could. And it showed how the studio was now working with Obama administration to try and stop Kim Dotcom. Remember, this was around the time when DVDs could be easily ripped and uploaded to services like MegaUpload, so anyone in the world could stream pretty much anything, instantly—like a proto-Netflix, only on the wrong side of copyright law. MegaUpload was far from the only service like this; heck, it wasn't even the dominant piracy site at the time, but the studio needed a villain, and Kim Dotcom, with his sunglasses and his expansive waistline, fit the bill; like some kind of cherubic Baron Harkonnen, here to plunder all the IP.

The problem? Kim Dotcom lived in New Zealand, and not in the US, and New Zealand (as a sovereign nation of its own) didn't have the same copyright laws we have here.

That didn't stop Barack Hussein Obama from arranging to send two helicopters, four police vans, police dogs, and SWAT with semiautomatic rifles to his family home. MegaUploads' servers would be seized, and there is still a legal battle raging today about whether Dotcom can be extradited to the US, or not.

Now, I'm not trying to defend copyright infringement here, especially as I want to work in industries where IP has value, but at the same time, I began to see how big business was colluding with big government to rain down hellfire on, what really amounted to a young father, his wife, and his children. Dotcom wasn't a hardened mafioso. He wasn't murdering people or trafficking drugs. There was no violent crime happening here. And moreover, he simply wasn't a US citizen—so our laws didn't legally apply to him. Millions of dollars of assets were seized (including a car collection), and why? All to protect moneyed interests here in the states for those who refused to seriously innovate in any tangible way.

What really got me was that Paramount was trying to launch some kind of ridiculous HD streaming service of their own, where you literally needed encryption keys to access the content you had bought, and it could only be accessed on something like five different, registered devices linked to your account at any given time—so you couldn't just take your media over to a friend's house, sit down, and watch a movie with them. It was so backwards, so unintuitive, and so downright insulting to the customer, it never took off. Literally no one wanted it because of the hassles involved, and no one at the studio had the guts to tell this to the suits, so they ended up pouring millions of dollars into a program that was dead on arrival.

To make matters worse, Paramount refused to license good content to the one up-and-coming streaming solution that actually showed promise at the time: Netflix. Actually, everyone in the town was *terrified* of Netflix (which is why Netflix had to eventually start making their own content; because they had grown so big, no one would license them anything anymore). They all wanted to *be* Netflix, instead. And yet, almost a decade later, there's only been the barest progress on this front—even as Netflix burns through cash and turns itself into an Obama propaganda outlet! And while MegaUpload was taken down, dozens of similar sites popped up in its wake, making the endeavor little more than a game of Whac-A-Mole, which only succeeded in nearly ruining a man's life.

Now go back and think about these events in terms of what MegaAnon said; about Kim Dotcom helping Julian Assange and various White Hats by providing encrypted storage space for them. Were these raids being "demanded" by the studios little more than a pretense set up by the Deep State to get back damning files that had made their way into the hands of groups like Wikileaks? At any rate, I never bought the official explanation, and I'm pretty sure I'm recorded asking some questions during the studio seminar that the CEO had a very hard time answering during the session I attended.

Eventually, however, temp work would run out at the studio. I'd hop around to CBS for a bit, where I had to deal with what was literally ranked the worst commute in America for years. I'll give you an idea of how bad it was (and Los Angelinos will know *exactly* what I'm talking about). You've got the 405 running north to south, parallel to the coast, so you can get over the mountains, down into the Santa Monica area. To get back from Santa Monica, which is where CBS had their offices, I would drive about fifteen miles north on the 405 before getting off at the 101 and heading back into the valley. I think it was five or six lanes in either direction (though it's since been expanded in some areas), so this is no small highway.

Traveling those fifteen or so miles would take me THREE AND A HALF HOURS during rush hour. I would literally leave the office at 6:00 p.m., and wouldn't get home until 9:30 p.m. It just wasn't worth it. I decided that instead of spending all that time in traffic, I would bring my cheap, plasticky, 400 dollar laptop to the CBS offices, and write until about 8:00 p.m. when I finally left the building (I had one of those magnetic key-cards) and ended up getting home by 9:30 anyway, because traffic still hadn't quite cleared up by then. But if it was still going to take me until 9:30 anyway, I might as well stay put, be productive, and burn less gas in the process.

Despite this, imagine my shock when I discovered that my aging sedan was about to catch fire one day, sitting in that unmoving Santa Monica parking lot known as I-405. It was 105 degrees that day, and the only thing that stopped my engine from completely overheating was that the traffic finally broke and I was able to get air flowing through the engine again. Turns out the sensor on the engine fan had finally given out after thirteen or fourteen years at this point, and it would be quite expensive to replace.

Oooooooor, I could disconnect the fan from the sensor, attach a wire to the fan leads, jam that wire through a gap in the car's firewall using a screwdriver to force it through, attach the other end to a switch, and then run the opposite end directly into the battery, thus completing the circuit to my makeshift fan switch!

Suddenly, I had an operational fan again on my aging junker! I just had to keep an eye on the engine temp, but it would never again overheat. If things started to get a bit toasty, all I had to do was flip the switch! (And credit to my father for this creative solution. He was actually visiting at the time when I was having this problem, so this was really his brilliant idea.)

But again, I figured all this was me paying my dues.

One day, things would get better.

I would be able to afford real repairs, soon.

Maybe even a new car.

Maybe even that crown I had put off getting for the longest time, causing me to chew on one side of my mouth for three years to preserve the temporary work that had already been done.

I just had to keep pressing in.

I just had to keep trying.

But this was still Obama's economy. Things were looking more grim with each passing day. I could see the infrastructure crumbling around the town, and L.A.'s homeless problem, which had always been bad, was getting visibly worse with each passing day.

I would end up spending three years in total out in L.A. before the bottom dropped out and finances would force me to move thousands of miles back home to the East Coast. The most infuriating thing about it all was I had just managed to place in a major screenwriting contest out in L.A. (which was no small feat for a straight, white, Christian guy with no industry ties, trying to present work with a real traditional vibe to it). What a horrible time to suddenly overcome the odds! My work was now being passed around from studio to studio, and suddenly, I wasn't out there to capitalize on any of it! I couldn't take any meetings! No one was going to call me if I couldn't even show up at their office! My script—a favorite of mine to this day—would end up going nowhere for the time being, and this would become a major source of frustration for me over the next few years, instead of blossoming into something great.

Dark thoughts ran through my mind: was God just screwing with me? Heck—and this is going to get a bit too religious for some—but I had grown more convinced over the years that I had been "called" to this industry. This feeling culminated for me when I had perfect strangers "prophesy" over me in various church groups, talking directly and pretty specifically about my career. This was no "cold reading" mumbo jumbo they were spitting, either. I'm aware enough, and skeptical enough to pick up on when that kind of thing is going down, and I'm not afraid to call out charlatans when I meet them. No, these people didn't know me, they weren't watching my reactions, they had no foreknowledge of who I was or what I was doing, didn't stand to gain anything from me, and so, I said next to nothing as I just listened to what it was they were saying. For instance, one of the things that was spoken over me was how I'd be causing a lot of "good destruction" in Hollywood, like a "gold wrecking ball." And to be perfectly honest, I think I'm just starting to understand that right now. But at the time? When I had just come so close to obtaining my goals, and had fallen so short of them all? I didn't want to hear any of it anymore. Was God mocking me? Was He just waving something in front of my face, something that I had no hope of ever grasping, just in order to screw with me, or worse, "humble" me? Maybe I was deficient in some way! Maybe I couldn't be entrusted with the demands stepping into such a role would place on me. Maybe...

Infinite questions and scenarios played out in my head as I tried to make some kind of sense out of everything that had come to pass. At any rate, I was miserable, jobless, career-less, and now, I wasn't even at square one. I was back to living with "mommy and daddy," and this time, I had racked up fourteen thousand in debt. See, I had tried so hard out there, I had believed so hard that I was born for this, that I ended up sacrificing more than I could afford in order to try and support my efforts.

And the crazy thing is, it had *almost* worked. But my best efforts had fallen just a hair's breadth too short, and now, I had nothing to show for my time and efforts but a big, fat, negative balance on my credit cards.

The next half decade of my life would be spent trying to repay the debts I had accrued out in L.A. while also trying to cling to some nebulous hope that maybe, just maybe, if I wrote something truly special, something truly world-changing, it wouldn't matter where I lived, or who I knew. It would get me noticed despite my not being located anywhere even remotely close to L.A.

But I was fooling myself, and deep down, I think I knew it. It didn't matter how much I wrote, how good I was, or how many books and podcasts I listened to. The industry, even during that time, had grown increasingly hostile to "straight, white men." There was this new term entering the common parlance at the time—"privilege"—and apparently, I had it in spades, despite the fact that I had to now take a job working at a supermarket, this time in the same plaza where I had initially had my very first job, fresh out of junior high, at age fourteen. To say the experience was humbling was an understatement. Check my privilege? Hold on, I've gotta bleach this public toilet again, and hope I don't get any bleach on my uniform in the process; otherwise, I'm going to have to shell out my hard-earned cash to buy a new one (at a time when I was now making $13.25 an hour).

Sure, I wasn't a child soldier sweeping for mines in Somalia, forced to sleep with one eye open on a mattress made of straw and yak poop, lest I get conscripted in the middle of the night by Bantu warlords, so I guess I had that going for me. But to suddenly become aware of the increasing disdain different groups of people had for me and mine for having the audacity to simply *exist*, well... it wasn't easy to come to grips with that reality. I had never hated anyone in my life for any reason; I could always be friends with anyone, regardless of any external differences. My roommate in L.A. was black, and he's a great friend to this day. We had a guy crash on our couch for a while who was Jewish. I could find common ground with pretty much anyone, and as long as no one was hurting anyone else, it was all copacetic. I had hoped everyone felt the same way, but sadly, it now seemed it was not so. "Diversity" was the new buzzword, and me? The established order had deemed it would be better if I (and those like me) were erased and replaced.

I would end up working the closing shift at my new grocery store job for the first three years I was there, which meant unloading the nighttime truck delivery, restocking the shelves, and generally trying to get out just shy of midnight. A lot of my coworkers would blast the foulest ghetto, gangster rap over the speaker system during this time of the night. Me? I quickly found a cheap pair of wireless headphones for twenty bucks on Amazon and started devouring podcasts and audiobooks, on topics ranging from cryptocurrency, to screenwriting, to Stefan Molyneux's podcast and much more. I wasn't trying to be antisocial, I promise. I was just trying to better utilize whatever extra time I had at my disposal to gain that extra edge needed to overcome my situation. Meanwhile, during this time, I would go on to lose my grandmother; someone who had been there for me since childhood and with whom I was very close. A friend in my church would suddenly pass, and shortly thereafter, I would have to put down my dog quite suddenly, due to bone cancer we were not aware of at the time eating away at his jaw bone. And this might sound funny, but dog people will understand: that last one might have been the worst of them all. These three deaths happened over the course of six to eight months or so, if I recall correctly; from 2014, into 2015. So roughly one death every two months.

To say that was the bleakest period of my life is to not do this time justice. I had never felt lower than I did during that time; awash in a sea of despair made that much worse because I was now really beginning to wonder if I was facing a future with no real prospects. I fell out of communion with the local church I was attending at the time. I just stopped going. It didn't seem like God was listening anyway. In a weird way, I had started to make some progress and come out of my shell again as a result of my screenwriting efforts, but now it was almost like life was trying to lash out at me for even having the audacity to think I could ever move on with things.

But, oh, how much I've come to understand since then! To understand Hollywood now is to understand the particularly incestuous intermingling of the Cabal and various foreign and domestic intelligence agencies, all entangled and engaged in this ceaseless act of subversion, churning out degenerate and demoralizing propaganda by the bucket-load, in order to condition the population and control national narratives. Oh, but it gets worse than that, in so many ways. I didn't understand it fully back then, and sure, I knew there were bad people in positions of power—but there were good people, too. Still, knowing what I know now, I thank God that "success" in that realm was withheld from me (at least, until I had the tools necessary to begin to call out and fight such evil directly). Had I known then what I know now, not just about the power structures in place there, but the depth of depravity by some of the power players, and the tactics they use to control and manipulate people, well, I probably would have found myself unwittingly in league with truly evil people, until they found a way to corrupt me, too. For despite my imaging online—that of a stoic statue evoking the classical artistic values like *arete*—I am but flesh and blood, and far from perfect.

But back before Neon Revolt started, I didn't really have a clue about what I would, in a few years, uncover. All I knew was despite my best efforts, despite years of intense focus and deliberate effort, I had failed at pretty much everything, and the bottom had all but dropped out entirely. I had treated life like my dojo, and the moment I had stepped out, I felt like I had been mobbed from all sides and left for the dogs. And on that day in September, I just couldn't summon up the motivation to convince my body to get out of bed anymore.

I told myself that it would be okay.

That I could just call in and take a sick-day.

…

I couldn't even pick up the phone.

My job was, to their credit, very flexible and understanding. I could have showed up the next day, even without calling, and they would have kept me on. It had happened once in the past, and they let it slide. And again, there was a relatively large workforce there, so one man down wasn't a huge deal. But I should be clear here; I had genuine love for (most) of the people I worked with. There was a kind of camaraderie that formed, because everyone was in the same less-than-ideal situation together. Those who have never worked in retail won't understand the kind of "war story" bonding that goes on in a crew. In truth, had it not been for some of those relationships, I would have lost my mind at that place ages ago.

Once I had become proficient in the job, I was tasked with managing the frozen section of the store. It was by far the biggest section in the store, and required the heaviest labor. Every day, I spent hours in a gigantic, cold, steel, walk-in freezer, organizing inventory or taking a hammer to ice outcroppings that would grow on the floor, so people wouldn't slip and hurt themselves. I grew Viking blood for the eighteen months I spent in that frozen torture chamber, and by the end of it, I could tolerate the cold in just a t-shirt and jeans for extended periods of time. I was good at my job, and increased sales by quite a margin. It might have been the only thing I felt I was good at, at that time, but at least it was something. I was chipping away at my debts, at the very least, so there was some measurable progress being made.

Which is why I was shocked when they finally decided to take the section away from me at the store. It was true; sections got rotated all the time, just to give everyone more experience. And I had been in the frozen section longer than anyone had ever been in any one section at the store. But now, I wasn't getting a section at all. I'd be a generalist, dispatched to do random tasks wherever a floor manager deemed necessary.

In case I somehow haven't made it clear by this point, this was not ideal for me. I function best with a high degree of autonomy… to put it diplomatically. And here I was, suddenly finding my autonomy greatly scaled back.

To add insult to injury, when the periodic raises came around, the management then decided to snub me. They told me that I had been four minutes late one day, and seven minutes another day, and because of that, that disqualified me from a raise. So I could bust my butt for eighteen months, increasing their sales by thousands upon thousands of dollars every week, but they couldn't give me a fifty cent raise because I had clocked in four minutes late a few months back.

At that point, I mentally checked out. Oh sure, I still showed up and went through the motions, doing what was required, but really, I wasn't present anymore. I grew resentful; I started snapping at annoying customers on the floor if they were being rude, which—if you've ever worked retail, you know what it's like—there are *always* rude customers. In short, I just didn't want anything to do with any of it anymore, and I was tired of being stuck in these dead-end service jobs for years upon years on end. Every time I would start to make a foothold and begin to climb my way out of the hole, begin to pay off my debts, begin to make tangible progress in my life—something would go awry and cause me to slip back even further. A car problem. A medical bill. You name it. It was a vicious cycle, and yeah, by then, my spirit had pretty much broken.

My dreams had been crushed, with no way for me to reclaim them. And the kicker was that I had just been deemed unworthy by the family of that Canadian girl I had been talking to. Friends and family had passed away. My own immediate family was, frankly, ready to break down for a number of reasons. And my debts and problems just kept stacking up. I was trying to juggle it all, to remain strong, to just keep putting one foot in front of the other, but by now, I had come to a point in life where I was breaking down.

I don't remember what I did the rest of that day beyond staying in bed for a few more hours and repeatedly telling God that I couldn't do it anymore. I didn't know what I was going to do instead, but whatever *this* was... I was out! I was done showing up for *this* version of life, where everything perpetually sucked all the time, with no reprieve. But while I think I expected to feel some kind of sense of divine disapproval from on high, some kind of admonition, strangely, I felt nothing of the sort.

I almost felt a kind of...*relief.*

The next day came and went, and I found I didn't want to get out of bed then, either.

But it wasn't exactly the same sensation as before.

This time, there was almost a thrill to it. I had been a pretty good kid my whole life. I had always tried my best (a couple major speed bumps—let's be generous and call them *learning opportunities*—aside). This was almost like a deliberate act of rebellion for me. It was like... playing hooky (except the stakes were now my entire future, instead of just an afternoon's detention). And you know what? I didn't care. I had always tried to take responsibility for myself, for my actions, and rule over my emotions with a stoic resolve. Now? I didn't even care about the consequences of this potentially disastrous choice. Despite the threat of poverty and the immediate financial uncertainty, something deep in my soul was thrilled with the prospect of the freedom I could experience, if only I would just walk away from this miserable, soul-sucking job and start putting my talents to better use.

I didn't call in sick that day either.

The third day came around, and by this time, my folks had caught on. (I was still living at home, remember. While I had managed to get a few raises during my time at the grocery store, seventeen bucks an hour, full time, still doesn't quite cut it for rent in my area, and I still had debts to pay off. It was another pain point that, yes, made me feel like a failure). Oh, make no mistake, they weren't pleased at all. A man's gotta work, after all, but in a sense, the deed was already done and there was no going back now. I had semi-deliberately burned that bridge, because I knew that if I didn't, I would go crawling back and spend maybe the *next* half a decade living out my own, personal retail-nightmare.

Heck, I hadn't just burned that bridge. I greased every nook and cranny of that baby before lacing all the girders with c4. I saddled into a Huey and unloaded two tons of napalm on that sucker like it was the last standing structure in Vietnamese rice paddy. I nuked that miserable bridge from orbit, with no remorse, before inscribing "Kilroy was here" on the smoldering remains. I was **never** going back. Sure, I was still in debt. Sure, I had no idea what I was going to do. But for the first time in five years, I felt… remarkably good on the inside; even excited to face the possibilities of a new day.

(And believe me, the store got the message. I got my final check in the mail a week or so later).

I think that freedom was what I was craving the most during this time, so that little taste of it was enough to drive me away from the job that now looked more like a roadblock than anything else in my life. Obamanomics (and the other, assorted, disastrous policies of the Obama administration) had hit my family and myself particularly hard. But let's be real for a second here: everyone *knows* deep down inside that what we went through, from an economic standpoint, was on par with (if not worse than) the Great Depression—even if the "official numbers" don't show that (for reasons we'll get into in a moment). The technological veneer that had appeared over the ensuing eighty-odd years was what really helped keep it hidden, and even then, only barely. Things like breadlines, for instance, were hidden from everyone, instead of out in the open for all to witness. How was this accomplished? Instead of breadlines, we had EBT card usage, which *soared* under the Obama administration. Add that to the fact that Obama's yes-men worked overtime to spin the stats, it was much harder to perceive the economic realities this time around. (Of course, lunatic Leftists will, to this day, call you a crazy racist if you point any of this out… because they don't have a real counter-argument.)

Take this staggering example, for instance: what's one way to make your unemployment numbers go down? Well, how about you just… stop counting the people who have gotten so depressed and destitute, they've essentially dropped out of the workforce entirely because they've just given up all hope of ever working again! Yeah, Obama **actually** did that, and no, most Americans do not realize that. That's like Ebeneezer Scrooge saying that the poor had better hurry up and die, so they could "decrease the surplus population." That's like saying cancer is a good cure for obesity. That's how severe Obama's Depression was, and how hard his PR people worked to spin the numbers in his favor. Again, many don't know this, which is why I make a deliberate point of mentioning it now.

To say the Obama years were a disaster on all levels is no exaggeration; but the little known fact (at least before Q came along) was that this was all intentional, and by design. Now, we'll get into that in all its enraging detail in a bit, but I state all this to show where my family was, and where I was in all this. The amount of pain both myself and my family experienced during Obama's presidency—and believe me, even with all I've written here, I'm still sparing you a lot of nitty-gritty details—was incredible. To say we barely made it through intact was no exaggeration. In truth, we're still recovering, in many different ways.

But something good would eventually come from all this mess. For it was out of this pain, this frustration, this isolation and abject failure to thrive that **NEON REVOLT** was born. I don't know if it was watching Trump stand up for himself against an endless onslaught from all sides (and win) or if it was just out of sheer rage (or perhaps sheer cynicism) but I was just done with the status quo. I like to think it's something of the former; this glimmering hope that I didn't have to lose all the time, across every conceivable domain—that I really could have a good future—but in truth, there was a certain pitch black ichor in my heart that just said, "If I'm going down with the ship, I'm going to go on my own terms." In a very real sense, with my entire world collapsing around me, this was an accurate assessment. Either way, I wasn't about to remain silent anymore. *NEON REVOLT* was like a pressure valve, releasing years of pent-up thoughts and emotions like a torrent upon the world. I didn't have to appeal to a gatekeeper, like I did in the screenwriting world, hoping that someone out there would *allow* my work to see the light of day. Now, I could publish whatever I wanted, whenever I wanted, and no one could stop me. I would begin to hit back, and hit back harder than anyone ever expected, taking aim at society's sacred cows, Leftist shibboleths, and evil ideologies. And I would do this even if it meant donning a virtual "mask" to accomplish it all.

It's funny, because it's kind of like with Batman, where the question has often been asked, "Which is his real mask? Is Batman the mask, or is Bruce Wayne the mask?" And all the DC aficionados will tell you that Bruce Wayne is now Batman's mask—a billionaire playboy who only exists as a cover for Batman's crime-fighting compulsion—because that's where the character's true heart lies. Though I am no superhero by any stretch of the imagination, I think there's a part of me that understands that kind of driving compulsion. And as I grew more proficient, focused, and unafraid, an amazing thing happened: my readership only grew.

I've realized that, in a strange way, *NEON REVOLT* is almost a more pure expression of who I am inside, just by virtue of it being a more honest expression of what I think and feel, than who I am in everyday life. Suddenly, I felt no need to hold back, or self-censor. The alternative was a slow, sinking death into nothingness and irrelevance. If I was going to fight that, if I was going to **revolt** against such a force, I was going to do it brilliantly, and with more style and impact than anything that had come before.

The unexpected side effect of this, which I now realize, is that in learning how to hit back, I was reclaiming some long-lost part of myself that had been buried for so long under piles of pain. In trying to pin-point it, I've arrived at a few key memories, which, I hope you'll indulge me in recounting, because I do so for good reason.

When I was a child, in second grade, my teacher gave us an incredibly "complex" math problem to complete—at least by second grade standards. Normally, it was something we could all manage, given enough time, but the kicker here was that we had to do it without paper; all in our heads, and all competing against each other. It was proposed like this: if you thought the answer was an even number, you had to stand up. If you thought it was odd, you had to remain seated. And the prize for completing this problem? The kids who solved it first would have their names tossed in a hat, and be given the chance to go on the local radio station with the teacher.

The entire class lit up. A chance to go on the radio!? That was pretty exciting! At least it was something different, and you got to get out of school for a bit. (This was basically pre-internet by just a couple years, so radio and TV still held more sway over the culture at the time.) I definitely wanted to go, but now the only thing that stood in my way was this incredibly complex and lengthy problem that only some kind of genius fifth grader could have solved!

The teacher looked down at her watch.

"Ready? Set? Go!"

My mind went to work, numbers flying through my brain at the speed of thought, like some kind of pint-sized John Nash. I struggled to keep track of where I was in the problem, there were so many steps! But I just had to keep moving forward with it.

It was around this time, I noticed… no one in the room was standing up.

My gut was telling me that it was even. I just needed to finish a few more steps and make sure... But was it an odd number after all? Everyone else was still seated. How had they all finished so fast?

I glanced at the teacher. She looked at me as my little mind worked. "One second," I pleaded with a raised hand.

I looked around the room again. No one was standing.

Gah! These numbers! They're so big! But I can do this, I know I can!

The other kids had started to slouch in their chairs, as looks of boredom passed over their faces.

"Almost!" I pleaded again!

And then... I had it.

It *was* an even number.

But *no one else* was standing.

Surely I wasn't the only one who thought the answer was an even number?! Why, it had to at least be a fifty-fifty chance, right?

I looked around at everyone sitting down. I then looked up at my teacher, a kind, older woman.

I put both hands on my desk, and trembling, I started to stand.

The plastic on my chair rattled as I slid it out from behind me, dragging its feet across the ugly, orange carpet that would have looked at home in the Overlook Hotel. My knees knocked and my stomach trembled. Was I really going to be the only one standing up? Indeed, somehow, I soon found that to be the case.

Suddenly, upon seeing me rise, another girl shot up in a panic from her chair.

"Ah! Nope! Sit down, Molly," said my teacher. (I think the girl's name was Molly. Whatever it was, she read the room right. Even if everyone else was sitting down, she knew I had actually put in the work. That was enough for her to try and hitch her wagon to mine, but she wasn't going to get away with it.)

My teacher surveyed the room. The wait was excruciating. Just give us the answer already, lady! But I decided I had cast my lot, and the rest of the class had cast theirs. Who was right?

"The answer," she started, making eye contact with every student in the room, "is..."

My memory trails off here. I can't recall the specific number she said, other than that it was very large.

Oh, and it was even.

I breathed a sigh of relief and had never been more grateful to sit down in my life. Only my name was going in that hat now, and I had to laugh, knowing that in a week or so, I would be going on the radio for the first time in my life.

If I had to pick the most formative event of my youth, that would definitely be among the top three. That incident has stuck with me, and I've had a long time to reflect on it over the years. Sure, the problem was difficult, but every kid in the room had the ability to solve it. Sure, some got bored or overwhelmed and gave up halfway through (and there's a different lesson for them in that, to be sure), but the effect of that was that it created a sort of social inertia which made it that much harder for anyone to pick the right answer. Even if someone had managed to suss out that the answer was even before me, the unspoken pressure exerted by the crowd to remain seated was simply too much for most to overcome.

Why, seven-year-old Neon could barely even handle it.

And yet, once overcome, it led to a thrilling and life-changing experience. Understand, I would take this experience and carry it with me in to all of life. This experience taught me to always do my best to work through things to the fullest extent of my ability, and stick with my guns, even if it meant standing out; standing alone. It didn't matter what the crowd thought! Group-think had no bearing on what was actually truth! The mob didn't get to determine reality.

In a sense, I guess you could call that the first redpill I ever took.

Over the years, this lesson helped me grow more and more politically aware. The problem with this revelation was, however, even though the mob doesn't get to determine truth in any sort of democratic system, the mob still holds a lot of sway over things, and dirty politicians often turn to mere appeasement of the mob in exchange for votes. Even dirtier ones would leverage the mob to advance wrongheaded (or even downright evil) causes. And because they had the numbers, the mob would get their way, regardless of how wrong whatever cause they were supporting may be.

The side effect of this growing political awareness was that I also grew increasingly outraged as a result (and later, increasingly helpless and cynical). Thanks to my father, I was raised on a steady diet of Rush Limbaugh from the age of five (spare me your sympathy, smug Lefties. You've never even "endured" a whole episode, let alone a week of episodes). I could never understand the sick caricatures I would later hear about him bandied about by various talking heads on the media, painting him as some kind of belligerent, racist blowhard. Sure, he had his own bombastic style (much like yours truly… which makes me prepared for what some may say about me when the time comes), but in truth, the man was just a passionate American, touting traditional values and common sense. These critics were, in my estimation, either incredibly bad listeners, or incredibly deluded (it never occurred to me at the time that they may have been intentionally lying, as part of their various Operation Mockingbird assignments). No, to me, Rush just made so much sense across the board; how could anyone deride his amazing mix of information and humor?

Heck, Rush *coined* the term *feminazi* in the early 90s—and this is important because it was my first exposure to what *Dilbert* creator Scott Adams would later term, during the 2016 election, a "verbal killshot," when he was examining Trump's presidential campaign. Rush's newly minted verbal killshot was so effective, it single-handedly helped forestall the march of rabid Leftist gender politics for at least a decade, if not more. I first learned how to think and fight from listening and watching Rush (and of course, because of my father. His role in this can't be understated, for if it wasn't for him, I would never have been exposed to half of this stuff). I like to think my trademark style of writing (at least the political stuff) owes a debt of gratitude to the work Rush did and continues to do. It was because of Rush that I was exposed to many of the names and figures, concepts and arguments I would need to know later in life, as I embarked on running my site. I was already getting the lay of the land from the time I was in kindergarten, almost as if by osmosis, through sheer exposure.

I mean, *really…* what kind of five-year-old knows who Newt Gingrich is?

(This one. This one right here did.)

Now Rush has always been primarily talk radio, but some may not be aware that he was actually on TV for a short span of time in the early 90s. I have this distinct memory of my father taping Rush's TV program on the VCR because the networks kept bouncing his time-slot around, in an effort to kill his ratings by slashing his viewership—and my father was among those who couldn't catch it when it moved to a late night slot, due to his regular work schedule. When the show was finally canceled, I was upset. I had enjoyed sitting down and watching the recordings with my dad, but this, too, was an important lesson for me: Leftists never fight fair—especially when you're winning. Rush was winning and convincing the mob with his words and ideas. Therefore, he had to be muzzled.

Sometimes, the good guys lose and the bad guys win.

So, Rush's show would eventually be canceled, but this was something of a blessing in disguise, because it left him more time to focus solely on his radio show, and his Limbaugh Letter—to which, yes, my family was subscribed. You better believe I read through every page of those skinny magazines. Through them, I was introduced to a number of people, ideas, concepts, and historical figures that, frankly, my schooling was just skipping over completely. Rush's words helped fill a void I didn't even know I had at the time, and led me down a path of discovery that would serve me well, later in life.

By the time I was in my adolescence, I was hungry for more information. I started reading books by Sean Hannity. John Stossel segments were the only reason I'd put up with watching "Bawh-bah-wah" Walters on *20/20*. (This was back when he was still on on ABC.) I was inculcated with traditional American values from my earliest days thanks to the efforts of men like these, and the weird (and tragic) thing is; this, once again, had always made me something of an odd man out where I lived. Combine that with being raised in a pretty serious and passionate church, and that only served to compound the situation for me. By the time I was a teenager, I was considered strange because I didn't want to eat the rich and hand out "free" birth control to everyone like Skittles. My moral sensibilities alone were enough to separate me from ninety-five percent of my peers—or at least, that's the way it always felt.

And then, as I'm sure you're aware, 9/11 happened and changed everything. The trappings of a police state started to pop up across the nation in response. "Conservatism" became deeply uncool during the Bush years (if, for no other reason than it was so weak and ineffective). So in an effort to salvage whatever remaining "coolness" I possessed (as well as satisfy my own intellectual curiosity) I discovered Libertarianism.

There's a quote that's often misattributed to Churchill… or Victor Hugo… or George Bernard Shaw that gets repeated a lot. (In actuality, the original quote belongs to one Anselme Polycarpe Batbie, but that's an awful mouthful of a name.) The quote goes something like, "If you're not a liberal at twenty, you have no heart. If you're not a conservative at thirty, you have no brain." Well, Libertarianism was about as far "Left" as I ever got. It appealed to the more idealistic side of me, but it was "classical liberalism," (as opposed to modern, decadent, degenerate liberalism) so it was still okay in my book. I joined the "Ron Paul Revolution," and through his writings began to understand the insidious history of central banking during this time. This was perhaps my first big exposure to "conspiracy" territory—except all of it was verifiable and one hundred percent true. All the wealthy banking tycoons in America had really secretly met on Jekyll Island off the coast of Georgia, and had genuinely conspired to set up the Federal Reserve banking system, thus enslaving the American people to a never-ending system of debt and inflation. It had really happened, and no one was disputing this!

No, they were just ignoring it all.

See, originally, as per our Constitution, the Congress had the sole authority over the creation and issuance of money. But in 1913, with the creation of the Federal Reserve, Congress abdicated its constitutional responsibilities and handed over the power of the printing press to an international conglomerate of bankers who now print money for us… at interest.

For those who don't quite get it, what this means is that every single dollar bill in existence, printed since 1913, is actually a debt note. Prior to this, we had a gold standard, where money could be traded, quite literally, for gold at pretty much any bank in America. It wasn't exactly practical to do this, because gold is heavy, hard to secure, and so on, but this is what essentially kept the value of the dollar stable. When you hear your grandparents talking about how a ticket to a baseball game used to cost ten cents, this is why: the money was worth so much more, because they couldn't dilute the value of all the dollars in circulation by simply printing more on a whim.

Since the creation of the Fed, with its debt-based inflationary tactics, the value of the dollar has eroded over ninety-five percent. In little over a hundred years, the Fed has been the single most effective force at eroding wealth for everyone… everyone, except themselves. See, because they set the interest rates, they get to outpace the inflation and continue buying and growing hard assets in the meantime, while the little guy gets stuck with the bill. If you want to know the reason why the rich always seem to get richer, you need to understand fractional reserve banking. This essentially acts as an invisible tax on everyone but themselves.

I would later learn, through studying Q, that the bankers who had successfully implemented this Federal Reserve system were the same ones who had "just coincidentally" dodged the most famous disaster of their day: the sinking of the Titanic. Their opponents fatefully perished in the disaster; namely John Jacob Astor IV, the richest man in the world, Benjamin Guggenheim, and Isa Strauss, owner of Macy's department store. The Titanic and her sister ship, the Olympic, had been financed by J.P. Morgan through a corporation named White Star, and indeed, Morgan was "supposed" to be on the Titanic's fateful voyage, but both he and Milton Hershey (who would later start Hershey's chocolate) would cancel their travel plans at the last moment, despite Morgan being the one who invited Astor, Guggenheim, and Strauss aboard.

Prior to this, the Olympic, which had set sail before the Titanic, had a bit of an accident in harbor when it collided with another ship, the HMS Hawke. The damage was extensive, but it was able to be brought back in to dry dock and be patched up for repair. Still, the cost of the repairs was astronomical; so much so that White Star would nearly go out of business… but for their insurance policy.

So Morgan cooked up a scam. Undoubtedly inspired by the 1898 book *Wreck of the Titan*, which was written about an "unsinkable" luxury liner striking an iceberg and sinking at sea, Morgan and White Star had the names of the ships switched. The damaged Olympic became the Titanic, and the pristine Titanic became the new Olympic. The damaged ship was patched up, and the plan was to deliberately crash the ship at sea, before collecting the tremendous insurance policy Morgan and White Star had taken out on the ships for this "freak accident."

All the better for Morgan if he could take out a few political opponents in the process.

So it was the Olympic, not the Titanic, that crashed again in 1912—two years *after* Morgan and the other bankers had met on Jekyll Island. Anyone who could have offered any real resistance against their central banking aspirations was now, conveniently, sleeping at the bottom of the sea, and I doubt these bankers lost much sleep over the other 1,500 plus souls who perished in the process. White Star would survive, as would Morgan. But the author of the book, *Wreck of the Titan*, would not. The author, Morgan Robertson, would perish just a few short years later, in 1915 at age fifty-three, from poisoning, of all things.

Despite my newfound political passions, I ended up disappointed in election after election. It was almost as if the media, if not the government itself, were dead set against anyone even remotely like Ron Paul winning. (Oh, how naive I was!) They mocked him, took horrible, isolating photos of him, constantly belittled and marginalized him, and generally treated him like a joke up on the stage at the various debates. Here was "Doctor No," as he had been called by his peers. The man was so principled, no one in Washington would ever bother lobbying him, because it would have been wasted dollars; it never changed his vote. He was completely above-the-board, like some kind of All-American relic ripped from a Frank Capra movie. He was truly the "last honest man" in Congress.

(I'll quickly add here that It was a few years prior to this that I had discovered 4chan, as well. But /pol/ did not exist on the site just yet. It was mostly memes and garbage, so while I was familiar with the culture, I wasn't lurking the boards religiously at this point.)

Still, the energy at Paul's rallies was truly something to behold. Here was a seventy-something-year-old man who, frankly, looked like he could be set alight by a strong breeze, and you would think his talks about the founders, the Constitution, and American values would put people to sleep—but in fact, just the opposite was true! The atmosphere was absolutely electric, and it was the power of those ideas that was taking his campaign viral, before anyone even knew what "viral" meant. And this was at a time before most people even had a smartphone in their pockets! If he had been given a fair shot by the media, if they hadn't coordinated to get rid of him early on, I'm still convinced he would have been a great president, and saved us all from a lot of ensuing trouble. And watching it unfold at the time, it was clear to me that something was re-awakening in the heart of the American people… something that someone savvy would eventually be able to tap into.

But that wouldn't happen until quite some time later.

Unfortunately, what happened instead, during those intervening years, was Obama.

Now here was a man who used a lot of words and yet truly said nothing. The junior Senator launched his campaign, not on any real ideas, but seemingly on charisma and propaganda alone. "Yes, we can!" was the slogan that got so much airplay. Can what, exactly? Collapse the entire medical insurance industry, driving premiums through the roof? (Yes, he did!) Sabotage the nation's infrastructure? (Yes, he did!) Raise taxes, lose jobs, and put more people on welfare than ever before? (Yes, he did! Yes, he did! Yes, he did!) Sabotage the military and traffick uranium and rape the daughter of a…

Oh…

I'm getting ahead of myself again.

You're not ready to hear about the "16 Year Plan," yet. Don't worry we'll get there, very, very soon. And if you didn't despise Obama before, you will by the end of this book, no matter what your current political persuasion.

The crazy thing in all this, at least to me, was that this shallow campaign which was full of rhetorical flourishes and remarkably thin on actual content, seemed to be finding favor with the mob! I wondered, how could people take this guy seriously?! Couldn't they see right through him? Apparently not, because his tactics worked, even advancing him over the clear front-runner at the time, Hillary Clinton. And as we all know, it would carry him all the way into the Oval Office.

Many people rejoiced that day, because the election of a black president somehow meant at least some measure of "atonement" for America's past sins of slavery and racism. Obama's elevation to the highest office of power in the world was the herald of a new, progressive area; evidence that we as a people had come so far, put the past behind us, and truly given everyone a chance at greatness. Here was a chance to move on, put these petty divisions behind us, and unify as a nation...

Right?

Riiiiiiiiiiiight??

After Obama's first term, after the abject failure of Obamacare, the disaster of the "cash for clunkers" program, the deleterious "Obamaphone" program, the massive expansion of the welfare state, the utter erosion of jobs and wages, the continuance and expansion of wars throughout the Middle East, and the unnecessary perpetuation of the Great Recession through backward economic policies, I thought for certain that Obama was going to be a one-term failure. Americans already had enough, and were ready to move on after just four short years, it seemed.

Yet, in 2012, the man was "re-elected."

I put "re-elected" in quotations because, in truth, I don't believe he legitimately won either of his elections. I don't want to get too far ahead of myself, but Q has long hinted at massive voter fraud around the country—and while we'll be getting into details in a bit, just know for now that there are *many* things about Obama that are illegitimate. The man is not who he claims to be, not in the least, and there's good reason to suspect his terms were stolen.

And if his first term was a disaster, his second would be apocalyptic.

Never before had I seen the country so divided. Despite claims to the contrary, it soon became clear to me that Obama was sowing the seeds of racial and class division among the people, creating something new that we hadn't seen before; ushering in an era of "social justice" which was really nothing more than the spread of *victimhood culture*. See, in a victimhood culture, the only way to *really* gain the moral high ground was to identify yourself as some kind of aggrieved class, someone who was being taken advantage of by some kind of nebulous (or not-so-nebulous, depending on the mood and desires of the "victim" at the time) oppressor. This gave the "victim" class power over the "oppressor" class. Now apply this to mobs and politics. The result is a heinous perversion of the democratic process.

As a straight, white, Christian male, I suddenly found myself among the group of "ultimate oppressors." Not only could I be insulted at will, marginalized, denied opportunities based solely on my skin color, and admonished to "check my privilege," but if I dared to push back against this new ideological authoritarianism, I would be labeled some variation of hateful evil-doer; either a racist, a sexist, a bigot… or even a Nazi! The list goes on, for the labels able to be invented by the "social justice" crowd are unending.

So here I was, circa 2014, cleaning toilets, mopping floors, and stocking freezers—barely able to keep up with my debts—being told to "check my privilege" and that I was going to be replaced one day, and that all this was fair and right, and good, and really, *inevitable*. I had *benefited* from systems of "oppression" which had given me an "upper hand" in life, and that was why we needed to, for instance, replace white men in all forms of media with genderqueer, ethnically ambiguous, demisexuals.

If you're reeling from that last sentence, imagine my confusion at the time. Again, I never had a problem with anyone. I just wanted to get along, work hard, prosper, and do right by people. Moreover, I didn't feel entitled to anything, and I wasn't about to adopt a victimhood mindset. I had worked all sorts of menial jobs when I was younger, as a young teenager and through college. Like I said earlier, I considered it "paying my dues," and again, I was all for working hard. It was the decisive *lack* of entitlement, a lack of ego that enabled me to do things like sweep floors, change disgusting, leaky garbage bags, and mark off rotting produce, day in and day out for five years straight.

But hatred is rarely a rational force, and it was clear now that there were many groups in the world that hated me for the mere fact of my existence, that wanted to tax, regulate, and legislate me into an early grave. Knowing what I know now, thanks to Q, that is no small exaggeration. It was all by design, orchestrated by the likes of George Soros and his Open Society Foundation funneling millions of dollars into subversive causes and groups around the nation, elevating their divisive ideologies through the media, thus infecting the minds of many who felt "empowered" by the notion that all their failures and disappointments were really the fault of evil, white men who had held them back their whole lives, instead of the result of their own choices and wrongheaded ideas.

My desire to understand this new existential threat—because that's what I soon determined all this to be—drove me to communities like GamerGate, various redpill forums, and eventually, into the arms of /pol/. I learned, in these places, more clearly about the history of *Cultural Marxism* and realized that what we were seeing today was really just a newly engineered, hopped-up version of this very old, "revolutionary" ideology; the same nihilistic, materialistic ideology that had claimed hundreds of millions of lives during the twentieth century. Here it was again, repackaged in slick Facebook videos and MTV segments, roping in the gullible once more. The brilliance coming out of the boards during these days cannot be understated. In one particularly memorable post, an Anon would vivisect the "check your privilege" argument and leave it to bleed out on the table for the farce it is:

Anonymous Mon 03 Nov 2014 04:31:03 No.38119053   Report
Quoted By: >>38119641
>>38118731

Right, but that's not inherently a feminist argument. That's actually a modified use of these MSTs that date back to 1945. You should learn all of them, they are a logical root that you should develop first before looking for new argumentation:

http://en.wikipedia.org/wiki/Master_suppression_techniques

As you can see, Motte and Bailey is a form of Withholding Information. You give some information to one party, and some to another, but you don't let one know what you said to the other.

"Check your privilege" is actually an example of a fusion of all five (seven) master suppression techniques which is why the phrase is so popular:

1. Making invisible, by marginalizing the opinions of a 'privileged' person

2. Ridicule, by making fun of the 'privileged' person

3. Withholding information, by intentionally not defining what 'privilege' means (and changing the definition when convenient)

4. Double bind, because 'check your privilege' is neither an affirmation nor a negation, meaning that it can follow any statement and condemn someone regardless of the answer they give.

5. Heap blame/put shame, because it shames the 'privileged'.

6. Objectifying, because 'privileged' usually means white, even though being white has nothing to do with any discussion, ever

7. Threat of force, because the logical extension is 'check your privilege or else'.

Thus, it's a composite of all the established Master Suppression Techniques, which is why Tumblristas love it so much

---

The basic way it works is this: the Cultural Marxist identifies a natural divide in society; for instance, men and women. It then sets up one side as the victim and the other as the oppressor (instead of, at least for this example, seeing the two as wonderfully and synergistically linked). Power brokers then swoop in and exploit the divide to accrue more power for themselves by promising "equality" in exchange for votes.

If you understand this victim/oppressor tactic, you'll understand how ninety-nine percent of this stuff works and begin seeing it everywhere. These Cultural Marxists will create divides among races, among sexes, among classes, and even within these subdivisions. This is why you'll sometimes see the Left "eating itself," like when the gender-dysphoric man in a dress started yelling at Rose McGowan during one of her #MeToo speeches, for not recognizing the plight of "trans abuse." Speaking out against rape wasn't enough, apparently, because she was "marginalizing" another class of "victims" through her silence on the subject. The Cultural Marxists had unwittingly sown the seeds of discord among their own ranks with this, and now had divides growing in their own ranks: women victims versus "Trans-women" victims.

It was why "game devs" like Zoe Quinn (and I put that in quotations, because the crap she shoveled out the door *barely* qualifies as a game) could trade sex with at least FIVE different games journalists, and "just coincidentally" receive favorable reviews and press for her work. When she got called out on the unethical (and frankly, unhealthy) behavior, she presented fake harassment screenshots, and was subsequently… ***invited to the UN*** to speak on the topic of cyberbullying, all the while attempting to label anyone who spoke out in the gaming community as sexist, racist, Nazi bigots. In her mind, her behavior wasn't the problem. It was her "misogynistic" oppressors.

That's the insidious genius of Cultural Marxism in a nutshell: you can always manufacture a new relational divide when necessary, and frame it as a "hateful" power dynamic. You can always conjure up a new "oppressor," and cry inequality, because you can find "inequalities" everywhere in nature. Some talking heads, like Jordan Peterson, like to debate this point, talking about the "equality of opportunity" versus "equality of outcome." I think that somewhat misses the point. Nowhere in creation are any two people completely equal, in any sense of the word. It just doesn't happen anywhere, not even between identical twins, and efforts to force equality on mankind only ever devolve into tyrannical hierarchies anyway, as history has shown us again, and again, and again.

The ultimate irony of it all is this: once you stop expecting people to treat you "equally," once you rid yourself of any expectation of "fair treatment," you are then free to engage reality with a sense of responsibility and ownership. You transition to a "stewardship" mindset, rather than a victimhood mindset—and really, that's the only measure of a man; how well he stewards himself, his family, his relationships, and his resources. In other words, stewardship cultivates virtues and virtuous communities. When we get away from that reality, it leads to societal degradation.

And in a funny way, this is exactly what that series of negative life turns had done to me. It removed any and all expectation of "fair" treatment from anyone. The result for me was that I suddenly became much more grateful for the good I did have in my life; for instance, the remarkable sacrifices my folks have made for me along the way. That helped me cultivate a stronger, more mature relationship with them; one based on gratitude and thankfulness for what I did have thanks to their efforts and kindness.

Once I understood the Cultural Marxism thing, I began to recognize it in the events swirling all around me. It was like instant pattern recognition; it was all so clear as day. Gamers were the "oppressors," and the likes of Zoe Quinn and Anita Sarkeesian were the helpless, hapless "victims." Never mind that their work was garnering critical praise in the media, they were raising hundreds of thousands of dollars online through their various fundraisers, and getting invited to visit and speak in the highest halls of world power, because the "eeeeevil gaming Nazis" were after them.

If you really want to get into the research, look into the Proteus Fund, which helped with Sarkeesian's *Feminist Frequency* project. It shouldn't surprise you to find out that the Proteus Fund was mostly used to produce pro-Islamic propaganda, and yes, it was also funded by George Soros.

Yes, the importance of GamerGate cannot be understated here, because despite the organized push to invade this space and inject it with this divisive ideology, for the first time in my life, I saw an online community organize and *massively* push back against the tide. More importantly,

I saw them *win*. I had seen how the Cultural Marxists had already come for other mediums, like film, television, comic books—all mediums of mass communication. With video games, for the first time in history, the Cultural Marxists were *losing*—and not just losing, but losing *spectacularly* to a group of Anons, this renegade army that was just *relentless* in every sense of the word.

And why? Why should these "nerds," these "outcasts," the dregs of society put up such a fight? They should have been the easiest to steamroll… right? Simply put, for many, the escapist fantasy of "vidya" (as it's affectionately called) was the last thing any of them had to look forward to anymore, and these Marxist dogs wanted to rip that away from them, too. They, too, were stuck in dead-end jobs like me. They, too, had been told they were "shitlord" oppressors; emblematic of everything that was wrong with history, and that their time was over. They were allowed no joy, and no hope for the future as feminist harpies descended from on high, screeching "Gamers are dead!" as their battle-cry. The MSM soon caught on and, predictably, took up the Marxists' cry as their own, presenting the regurgitated swill with a sympathetic tone (and no genuine research whatsoever).

The funny part was, in hindsight, they actually expected to win against what amounted to an army of millions of weaponized autists who literally do nothing but sit in front of computers and perform repetitive tasks all day. They thought they could fight on *this* turf and emerge victorious.

They were profoundly wrong.

Instead of getting their way, we're about to get the next iteration of *Doom*, where the various non-player characters (NPC) now joke about how calling a demon a demon may be "offensive" and that, instead, it's better to refer to these damnable hellbeasts as "mortally challenged" (clearly a jab at the toxic SJW culture of perpetual offense). Meanwhile, the likes of Anita Sarkeesian and her handler, Josh Macintosh, whine in Twitter-based irrelevance from the sidelines as others with more skill and more creativity continue to move the cultural needle.

It was a beautiful triumph, if you ask me. And while I'll admit I never got too involved directly with GamerGate, I did observe every step along the way with much laughter, and great admiration. I never made any original content for the movement, but I was more than happy to repost what I found across social media. If this online army could successfully win a media war by going toe-to-toe against the MSM, the UN, George Soros-backed groups, and self-appointed gatekeepers around the world—the first time such a thing had ever actually ever happened, really—perhaps there was hope for us all, yet. The added bonus was that it was actually a ton of fun to push back against these cultural authoritarians and watch them shriek in rage or break down in tears, while failing to wrest control of the narrative from this ephemeral group of mad lads who simply came together to save something they loved.

But at the end of the day, even though we had won this one particular victory, Obama was still president, and the agenda of "progress" was marching forward. Obamacare fines were increasing, our infrastructure was rotting, our economy was weakening, the people were steadily growing more demoralized all around, and it wouldn't be long before things like "drag-queen story time" were being normalized at libraries across the nation. Soon, we saw Weimar-levels of depravity, where the likes of ten-year-olds were being encouraged to dress in drag and participate in "pride" parades. Degeneracy was the name of the game, and it seemed like boundaries were being knocked down with increasing regularity, all in the name of, you guessed it, equality! And this might be something you don't notice until someone lays it out for you, in a meme like this:

> 2000: "Relax, bigot. It's not like gays are going to come into your kid's classroom and tell them to be gay."
> 2017...

If the war that GamerGate represented was the test case, Trump's campaign just a year and a half later would be the proof. The overlap between the communities could not be denied, and the tactics employed were almost identical: a refusal to back down or be intimidated, along with tenacious, non-stop counter-signaling via easy to understand (and often hilarious) memes.

So I start to get seriously involved during this time, posting, reposting, and sharing all manner of Trump-related content across the web. If Ron Paul's campaign had been electric, Trump's was upping the ante by a factor of ten. The energy was almost indescribable, and one of those things that you kind of just had to be there to experience; like the political equivalent of Woodstock, 1969. Except instead of dope-smoking hippies running around in the nude, this time it was edgy, patriotic /pol/lacks fighting for the future of America.

A lot has been said about Trump tapping into this sort of blue-collar, middle-American base, but I think what's been overlooked by a lot of these pundits in this analysis is that

Trump actually tapped into a sort of last ditch before complete hopelessness that came about as a result of all the stress put upon the people by the Obama administration. Former senior national security spokesman for the Trump administration, Michael Anton, would famously call this the "Flight 93 election." In essence, the plane was going down, and everyone could feel it. Do you charge the cockpit and *maybe* survive? Or do you sit back, and guarantee your fiery fate? I'll add here that this disaffection wasn't limited to one particular race or creed. A lot of people from all walks of life were feeling this same angry cynicism and sense of malaise, because so many had suffered so much under Obama, and that suffering simply hadn't been acknowledged, let alone allowed to have a voice—for to go against "Dear Leader" and the Progressive agenda was tantamount to heresy, in Social Justice world. No, contrary to the media lies, everyone was feeling this way, and many were willing to charge the cockpit.

And just like with GamerGate before, these newly minted "shitlords" made a remarkable discovery. "Shitposting" was ridiculous fun. It was the most fun they've had in years; better than going to the movies, better than watching the drivel pumped across the TV airwaves, and far more productive in terms of real-world impact. It's not that the memes themselves were so bitter or cynical. In fact, often the opposite was true: they were hilarious and hopeful, but they were still expressing those truths that had heretofore been anathematized. But people could test the waters by sharing them somewhat "ironically," just to see where people in their social circle landed, and what it might cost them, from a social standing, if they went all in on this path.

Inevitably, many on the Left immediately lost their minds. This is, largely, how I began, and I can speak from personal experience on this front. On Facebook alone, I lost something like sixty friends and professional contacts very quickly—including some of the few remaining Hollywood contacts I had. Because, you know, Lefties are so "tolerant" of opposing viewpoints. It's one of their "virtues," in case you hadn't realized yet.

For instance, two of my Muslim friends cut contact with me *immediately*, within hours of each other after I proudly announced I supported Trump on social media. One guy, a "professional" screenwriter I knew, even blocked me simply for saying I thought Trump was "hilarious."

That was it. That was all I had said. That was enough for this guy, who, for the record, has had a decent amount of at least monetary (if not critical) success at the box office, to break contact.

For what it's worth, this screenwriter was the first to make me aware of the Black List. And this is a story in itself. See, the Black List is like this who's-who of the script world, where each year, the "best" unproduced scripts get selected by a bunch of industry vets, and they get rolled onto a list curated by one Franklin Leonard, CEO of the organization that puts this list together. You could track trends and such with this list, and one of the trends, in fact, was seeing what kind of crass filth you could frontload into the title, to attract attention and get reads. Usually, these were just swears, such as with the script that got real popular a few years back called *I Want to F*** Adolf Hitler,* which, if I recall correctly, was about a time traveler who was trying to seduce Hitler, in order to assassinate him. Obviously, the script would never get made with such a title, but the idea was to shock readers and grab their attention to garner reads. This particular writer's script, which shall henceforth go unnamed because I don't feel like embarrassing him in front of the entire world (at least… not unless he provokes me), was probably one of the first, if not very first "shock title" scripts, and got added in 2011. This writer was a young up-and-comer around the same time I was. I read his script and thought it was… okay-ish?

In fact, if I'm being honest, after reading it there was such a profound disconnect, I had to wonder *why* it was on the list in the first place.

It took me years of observing the trends on the list to figure out later that basically, as far as I can tell, it was picked because it portrayed a ton of broken white people, and weak beta-male characters, doing beta-male things. Heck, in this "romance," when the guy finally gets into bed with the girl he's pursuing (who, honestly, I can't even remember anything about), is he even able to do the deed, summon up his vigor, and properly bed her?

Nope.

Instead, they cuddle and "kiss each other's scars."

I wanted to puke.

It was like this incredibly weak genre of ultra-foul-mouthed shoegaze cinema that had somehow enamored cynical Hollywood execs who had become so desensitized because they had already seen everything, and needed something to rattle their cages a bit. And I just had to sit back and wonder how broken someone had to be to think this was even close to approximating anything like "art," and why this was suddenly generating such buzz.

Thinking back, this shouldn't have surprised me being that (at a Sharky's in Hollywood), the guy could barely even nod in my direction when we were introduced. I mean, it's just generally good form to, you know, acknowledge other people in the room, especially when your mutuals are introducing you, especially when you're about to sit down and eat with the group, because astoundingly, it's not all about *you*. Instead, he looked like a slob, mouth full of burrito, and when introduced, he could barely even muster a grunt and a limp, slippery handshake.

Keep in mind this was before his success in any form. He was just sitting there in his greasy undershirt, chowing down, so it wasn't like he was Mr. Big who was being intruded upon by the plebs. It was just a group of mutual friends eating Mexican food, and trying to network and such. And I can get past the appearance of people; I don't judge on that, especially having been through hard times myself—but I do judge based on people's *behavior* and *conduct*, and his was utterly repellent that day.

Anyway, his "breakthrough" script would never get made, but he would go on to write and sell a few other specs, and do some franchise work. I will say he was pretty efficient in his wording, which is good, because if he had been long-winded, his story would have been an absolute, naval-gazing slog. But frankly… most of his stuff nowadays is 80s genre-dipped fare and too heavy on the nostalgia and the Leftism to say anything new or interesting or compelling.

And the funny part in all of this is I should be thankful, because in trying to figure out the *why* behind this guy's sudden rise, I would eventually uncover a web of Deep State connections in Hollywood, which, after long periods of investigation and planning, I would later document in a series of exposés on the Black List,[10] on my website.

As it turns out, Franklin Leonard (founder of the Black List) is one remarkably well connected dude. I have him linked to at least four separate Soros-backed organizations, and the guy who rewrote the algorithm for his script-sorting site, which is used to weed out the "bad" scripts from the "good," used to work for a company that had received investment from In-Q-Tel. In-Q-Tel is, technically, only a CIA contractor… except it was started by CIA agents, and only works on CIA projects. So how it works is, the CIA will recognize a technical problem and say, "We need a solution for ___." In-Q-Tel then turns around and finds a startup or a team working on that particular problem, funnels a ton of taxpayer money into the program, and establishes those Deep State ties early on. Google was, in fact, started this way, and the guy who worked for Franklin used to work for a startup called Cloudera, which was courted by In-Q-Tel in much the same manner.

---

10   https://www.neonrevolt.com/2018/10/18/soros-hollywood-rentboy-exposed-by-blacklistanon-greatawakening-neonrevolt/

https://www.neonrevolt.com/2018/11/21/blacklisted-ii-double-blackout-sorosrentboy-franklinleonard-an-in-q-tel-tool-scriptchat-aidtoo-greatawakening-blacklistanon-neonrevolt/

Likewise, the list has been used to promote all sorts of Left-leaning political insiders, such as Noah Oppenheim, who is also NBC News' president, and Graham Moore, the son of the woman who first hired Michelle Obama, and who now runs the Obama Library. Franklin has also made appearances on MSNBC.

In my original exposé, I called the relationships surrounding the Black List "incestuous." Believe me, after years of observing the quality of scripts being promoted (and subsequent movies being made), and the practices surrounding the Black List, I have every reason to believe it is nothing more than a tool leveraged by the Deep State in Hollywood to promote demoralizing narratives and choke out anyone even vaguely on the Right, before they even have a real chance at success.

Believe me, most of the works being promoted by the Black List are not edifying in any way, and I think most Americans know that Hollywood is just churning out massive amounts of garbage these days. The Black List is one of the premier reasons why, because when they promote filth as though it were cutting edge, suddenly everyone else in the industry wants to get in on those, or similar projects. Most recently, the big push has been on the "transgender" front, with the most recent Black List sporting a number of "trans-scripts."

Because what could be healthier for a nation than to convince their sons and daughters that wanting to surgically castrate themselves is totally healthy and normal! If you get a chance, go read those exposés on my site. I'm only retelling a portion here, and before you think I'm just a bitter, "failed" screenwriter, understand that my own work has already made it big on a similar list, albeit, one that's not been co-opted by the Deep State. True, I didn't sell it at the time—but once again, I'm incredibly thankful I didn't, because like I said before, I might be sharing my intellectual property rights with some very bad individuals right now. Anyway, I'll be more than happy to pay this other writer a compliment when he finally figures out how to make a good movie. But that will probably happen after he learns how to make eye contact and give a decent handshake, first.

Besides, I'd much rather keep my IP, and watch these industry evildoers go down in flames as I continue to expose their evil deeds. In the meantime, I've been working on transmuting my works into books of their own, which I hope to release after this book.

And while this research all came well after I had started ***Neon Revolt***, in truth, this wasn't my first real effort in this information war. No, my first real fight, where I would be leading the charge head-on, came with #OperationStopSoros, using the pseudonym "Groundwar."

At some point during the 2016 election, it came out that basically all the voting machines in America were connected to companies owned by George Soros or his lackeys; most famously, Smartmatic and Lord Mark Malloch-Brown, who was previously the vice-chairman of Soros' Investment Fund, and Soros' Open Society Institute. He was also number two at the UN, vice president of the World Bank, and vice chairman of the World Economic Forum. In other words, he was a globalist through-and-through, with direct mechanical control over our national elections.

Furthermore, Smartmatic had previously helped rig the 2004 Venezuelan election in favor of Communist dictator, Hugo Chavez, by teaming up with the then partially state owned software company Bitza, before purchasing the US-based voting machine company Sequoia, in 2005. Why on earth any developed nation decided to trust Smartmatic after that "incident" is beyond me, but here we were, with the 2016 election just around the corner and Smartmatic dominating the US market.

To combat this, my idea at the time was to get Anons calling their local Board of Elections and invoking what's known as a "conflict of interest" clause (which most states have). This would allow the states to opt for paper ballots as a legal fall back method of voting, and thus, create a paper trail and ensure a fair election. You would think everyone could get behind such an initiative, but you'd be surprised how many would rather look the other way when their preferred candidate would otherwise benefit from skewing things a little.

My original post on /pol/ looked like this at the time:

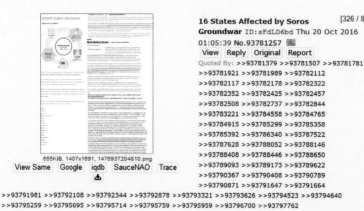

>>93791981 >>93792108 >>93792344 >>93792878 >>93793321 >>93793626 >>93794523 >>93794640
>>93795259 >>93795695 >>93795714 >>93795759 >>93795959 >>93796700 >>93797762

Hey /pol/

I made a startling discovery last week. When it came out that the Voting Machines were compromised by Soros in 16 different states, I decided to call my Governor's office to see if my state could invoke their conflict of interest clause in their voting machine contract and fall back to a manual voting process/paper ballots.

When I informed them of this conflict of interest, they bounced me around a few times until someone at the Board of Elections said that I would have to contact each county's individual, local Board of Elections, as each county has its own fallback process in place.

Repeat this for 16 different states…

mfw.jpg

That's when I decided I needed some help.

I'm compiling a list of every single county's Board of Elections in all 16 states affected by the Smartmatic/Soros machines so we can spam it to the entire internet and get everyone calling their local government, and get them to switch to paper ballots.

Soros is trying to steal the election. We're going to steal it back!

The 16 affected states are:

Arizona
California
Colorado
DC
Florida
Illinois
Louisiana
Michigan
Missouri
New Jersey
Nevada
Oregon
Pennsylvania
Virginia
Washington
Wisconsin

Good news - I've done Arizona, California, and have part of Colorado finished. I need some anons to help me with the rest.

Process: Look up the alphabetical lists of Counties in each affected states. Look up the Board of Elections for that county. If none appears, you can also try County Clerk, Registrar, etc. You'll see examples in my lists below.

I then proceeded to list[11] every single number for every single county in every single affected state for Anons to call.

Naturally, I cross-posted the info in a pastebin text file, and then reposted on /r/The_ Donald under the user name "ThisMeansGroundWar" (because just plain old "Groundwar" was already taken by someone else), and this caused the whole thing to snowball. The mods of the sub saw what was going on and pinned the post to the top of the page for days, ensuring everyone visiting the page would see it. It caught on like wildfire and users started discussing the subject all over and taking action where they could.

Then we made a startling discovery.

I would write, in a part two update:

> **IT'S NOT JUST SMARTMATIC ANYMORE**
>
> It's Sequoia
>
> It's Dominion
>
> It's Hart InterCivic
>
> It's ES&S
>
> ALL THE MACHINES ARE COMPROMISED.
>
> Dominion alone accounts for 50% of the machines in the United States, and they're running Smartmatic software!?
>
> GEMS alone counts 25% of the votes in the US. This is how they electronically gerrymander the elections: https://i.sli.mg/t6NJIF.jpg
>
> And the fraud is REAL. Project Veritas videos proved that.

The update itself was massive;[12] far beyond anything I had ever attempted before, and yes, it included the relevant numbers for the board of elections in every single county in every single state in the nation. But the kicker came with what the other two Anons had developed in their bid to help on this front. A pair of brothers (if I recall correctly) had reached out to me and said they had cooked up something real special to tackle this problem; something that would deliver a serious blow to whatever Soros was cooking up.

They created a system whereby every single person who sent a voice message or e-mail would then have that call or e-mail duplicated, and sent to every single county election board in the nation.

In other words, instead of just hitting one target, the e-mails would be launched at every single target in the nation. We're talking thousands of elections officials being bombarded by an absolute onslaught of messaging, unable to block any of it. It would get past every spam filter man could conceive. The only solution to stop the phone from ringing would be to literally rip the phone out of the wall. We were going to remind these complicit election officials who they really worked for: We the People. And this really shouldn't have been an issue, since all we wanted were paper ballots to ensure a fair election for everyone.

We dubbed this system "The Robopede" and set it loose on the world. In the end, I had to laugh when the different board of elections started releasing Smartmatic propaganda directly back to the people, so overwhelmed were they by the sudden influx of scrutiny and public pressure. This was one I received, personally:

---

11   https://archive.4plebs.org/pol/thread/93781257/

12   https://pastebin.com/mHr1H28V

1201 18th Street, Suite 210
Denver, CO 80202

10.25.2016

Dominion Voting Systems Ownership: Fact Check

Recently there have been a number of inaccurate claims appearing on blogs and in social media alleging that Dominion Voting Systems (Dominion) is owned by, or somehow affiliated with, Smartmatic Corp. Other accounts allege that Mr. George Soros has an ownership interest in Dominion. These claims are false. The facts are these:

- Neither Smartmatic or Mr. Soros has any ownership interest whatsoever in Dominion, and they have had no ownership interest in the past. Dominion has no relationship whatsoever with Mr. Soros, his companies or his foundations.

- Dominion is entirely owned by its employees, who are U.S. and Canadian citizens. Any claim that external entities have any ownership interest in our company is simply false.

- The voting systems we manufacture, as well as the legacy systems we support such as those manufactured by the former Sequoia Voting Systems, are all subjected to rigorous review, analysis, testing and certification by election authorities at the state and federal level, including the federal Election Assistance Commission (EAC). Independent testing laboratories, with extensive expertise in secure software design, are selected to perform this analysis. At the local level, prior to election day, these systems are also subjected to public testing to ensure they operate correctly, are configured properly and will tabulate votes accurately.

- As a matter of company policy Dominion does not support political candidates, parties or partisan causes, and has strict procedures in place to ensure that the company is wholly impartial in all political matters.

####

Of course, this e-mail is completely dishonest, for Dominion machines all run Smartmatic software. In fact, here's how the whole incestuous thing works:

Dominion bought out Diebold awhile back.

Diebold was fifty percent of the voting machines in the US.

Overnight, those Diebold machines became Dominion machines.

But the software running on the Diebold/Dominion machines was developed by Sequoia.

You'll recall that Smartmatic bought out Sequoia in 2005.

That means that Smartmatic now owned the software running in Dominion machines. Got all that?

Now refer back to the letter above and notice how they say their legacy systems were all manufactured by Sequoia, while also conveniently omitting who bought out Sequoia.

The two companies even had a licensing lawsuit back in 2012, so to say they are in no way connected is just… an outright lie. These companies have a demonstrable history together, and given the mounting evidence, demanding paper ballots was the only logical thing to do.

I think my favorite moment, however, came when a video was posted on /r/The_Donald of a Texas election official scurrying back up the stairs of their local municipal building, because Trump supporters had come with cameras to demand election accountability (as per their democratic right).

Personally, I like to think my efforts (and the efforts of those who accompanied me along the way) helped tip the scales that November juuuuuuust enough, but barring an official report from QAnon, I'll never know for sure. Still, I count it a great victory to this day, watching hundreds of thousands of patriots organically assemble to hammer the money-eyed, subversive interests of a globalist billionaire into oblivion. It felt like I had personally bloodied Soros' nose, and boy, did it feel great.

I took my hands off the reins once the 2016 election was secure, but others have since taken up the banner (though they have transmuted the hashtag into #StopOperationSoros, instead of the original #OperationStopSoros. I question their linguistic choice here, and have to wonder if the whole thing hasn't been co-opted by, well, Soros himself, at this point. But if it is still organic and genuine, it's nice to see progress being made, worldwide, on this front).

My next big effort on the front lines of this socio-political culture war (or whatever you want to call it) would be with the /CDAN/ Generals. Now, a quick word about Chan culture: all real world efforts are generally referred to as "Operations," but there's another thread type called the "Generals." These are similar to the "breads" you might see on the Qresearch board, where the original poster will start a thread going on a specific topic, and post relevant information in the first few comments, so that others can coordinate and join in. For the past several years, the Trump General threads have been posted on a 24/7 rolling basis. When the thread finally fills up with comments, a new one is made, and the process continues.

So I started the /CDAN/ Generals, effectively introducing the Anons to CrazyDaysAndNights.com—a site where a high ranking entertainment lawyer leaks information (and gossip) about Hollywood by posting different "blind items." A blind item is a method of posting where the names are withheld, but the information given is often enough for the reader to accurately infer who the post is written about anyway. I won't say here who first showed me this site, but once I found out about the explosive information, I simply had to share it because it was so devastating.

Here's an example of what one of the /CDAN/ Generals looked like:

104KiB, 588x849, CDAN Blind Item - The Church.png

| View Same | Google | iqdb | SauceNAO | Trace |

/CDAN/ General - Exposing   **[34 / 14]**
Hollywood Creeps and Pedos One Blind
Item at a Time Anonymous ID:zpyGjeb2 Tue
12 Dec 2017 17:42:10 No.153016298 📧
View Reply Original Report
Quoted By: >>153019039 >>153020111 >>153020560
>>153021318 >>153027486

>LATEST BIG BLIND:

http://www.crazydaysandnights.net/2017/12/todays-
blind-items-church.html

>PREVIOUS NOTABLE BIG BLINDS:

http://www.crazydaysandnights.net/2017/12/blind-
items-revealed-4-mr-x.html
http://www.crazydaysandnights.net/2017/12/todays-
blind-items-she-wants-to-talk.html
http://www.crazydaysandnights.net/2017/12/todays-blind-items-web.html
http://www.crazydaysandnights.net/2017/12/todays-blind-items-boys-club.html
http://www.crazydaysandnights.net/2017/11/blind-item-1-he-made-millions-from.html
http://www.crazydaysandnights.net/2017/11/todays-blind-items-st-charles-house-of.html
http://www.crazydaysandnights.net/2017/11/todays-blind-items-long-time-coming.html
http://www.crazydaysandnights.net/2017/11/todays-blind-items-sex-drugs-death.html
http://www.crazydaysandnights.net/2017/11/todays-blind-items-child-porn-and-drugs.html
http://www.crazydaysandnights.net/2017/11/todays-blind-items-molesters-killed-her.html

---

Anonymous ID:33uclydY Tue 12 Dec 2017 17:48:43 No.153016962 📧 Report
Quoted By: >>153027486

Ellen and Portia are going down next.
Screencap this post.

Anonymous ID:5WgIxN8f Tue 12 Dec 2017 18:07:32 No.153019039 📧 Report
Quoted By: >>153027486

>>153016298
This is a very worthy topic for generals. I can't bake but I've been trying to drop the recent cdan stuff when i can.

Anonymous ID:5WgIxN8f Tue 12 Dec 2017 18:09:48 No.153019289 📧 Report
http://www.crazydaysandnights.net/2017/12/todays-blind-items-web.html

http://www.crazydaysandnights.net/2017/12/blind-item-7-web-part-2.html

And don't forget the Cornell/Chester pizzagate blind!!

In these, as you can see, I would focus on what I called the "big blinds," which are larger, and more substantial than the typical, gossipy blinds about who slept with who, or who hired this PR team to say x, y, and z. No, the big blinds are devastating, and none was more devastating to me than reading this one:

THURSDAY, NOVEMBER 09, 2017

Today's Blind Items - Molesters Killed Her

Back in the mid-80's was peak child molesting time in Hollywood. There was no internet. There were very very few mobile phones. Children came to the set where they were left alone by their parents. For the next 8 hours they were subject to every kind of horrible thing you can imagine. Drugs were commonplace. They were used to try and get the kids to not be so hysterical when being assaulted.

Producers loved casting shows with kids and tweens. If someone pitched a show that involved a handful of tweens with a dozen tween extras per week, it would get a green light. Even if the show was going to suck, and everyone knew it was going to suck, if you got the right pedo at a studio he would say yes just to come for the casting and taping of the pilot. As sad as it is to say, there were a lot of parents who told their kids to go off with the nice man in the suit and do what he says. It was a sick sick time.

It was just past the mid 80's when a producer came up with the idea of a tween show that not only would feature a rotating cast of extras, but would make the studio a bunch of money because they would film quickly and not hire any adults. Further, the faster they filmed, the more time they would have to molest all the kids that would be hanging around.

From the first day, it was the worst place on earth if you were a kid. The studio where the show was filmed also had several other shows being filmed there, most of which featured lots of children. Executives would drive over to Hollywood right before lunch and would stay at the studio for several hours each day.

Anyway, on this particular show, there was a special guest star. A very special guest star. Still not a tween, everyone knew who she was. Executives flocked to the studio that day to see her. She was first molested when she was 5 or 6 and had continued to be molested throughout her hit movies and also on a previous show.

One of the stars of the show who has spent her life bouncing in and out of rehab because of what she saw, and who was actually nominated for awards from the show, described the atmosphere that day.

"A bunch of f**king pigs. I had just turned 12 or 13. I was the same age as the actress coming in. Maybe a little older. We had been shooting for months and I was old news. They knew I would do what they wanted, but they always wanted someone new. This was someone new and someone they all knew. They had it set up like a peep show almost. She had finished shooting that morning and they brought her out on a stage. The stage was used most of the time for a game show that was taped there. That game show is still on today. I can't watch it knowing what happened to her there. They brought her out and the front four rows of this theatre were filled with guys who were already rubbing themselves. The girl was wearing a bikini. The show took place around a beach just so they could make these girls wear next to nothing. They had her walk around under the lights. The lights were focused on her and she couldn't really see out to the audience. She was squinting. It must have been blinding for her. They had her walk back and forth. Then they had her start dancing. All of these guys were doing what another star at that same studio got busted for. This went on for about 20 minutes. Then three of the guys took her to a different area of the studio."

The actress didn't see what happened, but about 45 minutes later, one of those three guys came running out and needed a set medic. Apparently they had inserted something inside the girl and things were bad. The medic came and the ambulance came. The parents of the girl were told some crap story. That crap story ended up killing the girl because the parents believed the executives. Two weeks later, the show finished shooting six episodes all at once and then everyone was sent on their way forever. No one wanted the kids around or any witnesses to what happened.

POSTED BY ENT LAWYER AT 10:10 AM

This is most often considered a Spielberg-related blind, and the victim in question is often thought to be one Heather O'Rourke—the little girl from *Poltergeist* who looks at the TV in the trailer and goes, "They're heeeeere." O'Rourke would die when she was twelve as a result of a heart attack brought about by sepsis—the official cause of death being listed as severe intestinal stenosis.

In fact, this blind implies that she had been raped to death (after years of suffering abuse) in such a manner, that her colon had become torn, infected, and due to her weakened immune system, caused this twelve-year-old to suffer a heart attack and die on the operating table. If you want to know the other places implied in the blind, CDAN is most likely talking about the TV show *Rocky Road,* and either *Jeopardy* or *Wheel of Fortune.*

If this is hitting you like a ton of bricks, congratulations—you still have a soul.

And the truth is, there's an entire power structure in Hollywood, intricately linked to Washington, DC, dedicated to perpetuating this kind of thing. The reality is so much more horrible than you can imagine, and the fact that I, an aspiring screenwriter, have been trying to make people aware of it for a few years now (since I first really learned of it), means that if I ever want a career in that industry, I have to make sure all these scum are purged from the face of the earth, because otherwise, they'd probably try to kill me.

So yeah, I've made my choice. I'd rather help expose the likes of Spielberg and David Geffen, than sell them my IP and become a millionaire. I've been trying to talk about Epstein's island, NXIVM, the House on St. Charles Street, and what CDAN calls "The Church" (and so much more), because this… this right here is the true #MeToo story that no one is talking about.

#TimesUp? #TimesUp is an absolute joke, instituted for the very purpose of derailing and detracting from the real investigations and stories being told. #TimesUp was literally cooked up in some CAA (that's Creative Artists Agency) board room (probably from between piles of cocaine).

Oh, you think justice is coming for the likes of Harvey Weinstein? He was a pawn to be sacrificed by bigger players; he was offered up and portrayed as an "exception to the rule." He's not. Harvey Weinstein's behavior *is* standard practice, to this day. Just remember that when the real big names start getting exposed.

Don't say I didn't warn you about this book. It's only going to get worse from here, and I won't be surprised if you resist accepting what I'm writing, because in essence, I'm trying to forcibly redpill you. I *have* to tell you truths you don't want to hear—horrible truths—because it's the medicine this country needs right now. I've been through this process already; the product of years of digging and research. I've already been through the subsequent mental and emotional processing of all this information, and I know firsthand how difficult some of this stuff can be to hear for the first time. My best advice would be to take it slow if you're having a hard time with some of the things I'm writing here. But don't turn a blind eye to it, because otherwise, these evildoers will continue perpetrating these kinds of evils. They rely on your ignorance, and keeping their deeds in the dark. We can't allow that to continue.

As Q has said many times:

The choice, to know, will be yours.

The problem with this is that with knowledge, comes responsibility… and many in the world don't like responsibility. They want someone else to handle the big problems. With me, I realized long ago by having the bottom drop out that no one was going to solve my problems for me. I couldn't rely on the government, my friends, my professional network, and my family was having a hard enough time already. I had, in effect, been all but abandoned by everyone, even deemed an appropriate target for society's wrath and disdain.

If I wanted to change things, I would have to start tackling these problems myself. I would have to learn to fight for myself, for my future, for those I loved. I came to see the world around me as profoundly unwell, with the societal rot creeping in at every level. With every passing day, I soon grew more impassioned, and increasingly vocal and outraged. I was simply unable to keep silent anymore.

At this point, I was beyond redpilled. Multiple years of reading everything I could and experiencing everything I had gone through up to that point had hardened me in a way I had not, at first, expected. I was beyond redpilled. I now had blackpills coursing through my veins. The world wanted nothing more than to erase me, to erase those like me, and demonize us every step of the way. It had thrown everything it could at me, and yet, I was still standing, still determined to make something of my life and seize some kind of future for myself. I was surrounded by a vampiric culture of death, knee-deep in the dead, and I was determined to fight my way out, even if I had to slog through the bowels of hell itself to get there. I had become /pol/ incarnate, and now, I was going to unleash myself on the world.

"No one cared who I was until I put on the mask."
—Bane, in The Dark Knight Rises

For the longest time, I felt alone in the world. I thought I was the only one who thought like I did, or felt like I felt, but then I discovered that simply wasn't true. I started networking with like-minded people across Facebook, and soon, I was writing for one of the largest Traditionalist pages on the platform, expanding my reach to some 70,000 interested souls overnight. (That page has since been completely censored by Facebook.)

However, as my content quickly garnered attention, the owner suddenly cut ties one day, ostensibly over how I had "liked" a "rival's" page. In truth, there are hundreds, if not thousands of these pages out there, so I was a bit bewildered by this. He accused the rival page of "stealing" his content and brand, and thus, viewed my "liking" of them as some kind of insubordination. In the course of three comments (well, three from him, two from me), I was cut off, blocked, and removed from writing on the site ever again. In truth, I think he was just searching for an excuse to get rid of me, as he saw how popular the things I wrote were getting, and even self-avowed "Traditionalists" are still prone to petty human emotions like jealousy.

Still, I had been bitten by the content creation bug. I had seen that people liked—even demanded—my content, which was… I don't want to say validating, but I suppose in some way it was, as here I was suddenly experiencing some kind of success, where before in life I had known almost none whatsoever. It would be easy enough to strike out on my own; anyone could set up a Facebook page, after all. And so, I got to work. But I knew the first thing I would need before anything else was a "brand."

Aping the neon-tinged vaporwave aesthetics that were growing so popular that year, I got to work and carved out a little corner of the internet for myself, donning my Neon mask sometime in 2016. I say "sometime" because I can't go back and find the exact date now. You see, because of the cutting satire and "wrongthink" present in so many of my posts, the page I first started has since been scrubbed from the web by the Facebook censors. So while the date of my inception is not exact, I've been writing as "Neon Revolt" for several years now. And you can bet it was hilarious when that same page I used to write for started "stealing" content from me without credit, and reposting it as their own. Oh, I had fun calling out that bit of hypocrisy, and even more fun blocking all of my former boss' accounts, to make sure he couldn't steal again (not without great effort, on his part). But this was an important milestone for me, because, as in so many old kung fu movies, the apprentice had now surpassed his old master.

Put more simply: my confidence had grown.

The sentiment originally plastered across the banner of my site, "Revolt Against the Modern World," was one I quickly grew fond of. It was so clear to me that the world was sick. And if this pestilence we experienced was rooted in everything wrong with modernity, with its nihilistic determinism and materialism as its central operating thesis, driving insatiable, base hungers in the name of "progress," then the obvious solution, the obvious way to restore creation to some semblance of its original order, would be to reject it wholesale, would it not? This would require embracing the spiritual, and returning to our heralded Western traditions and values instead of being browbeaten by those who would shame us in order to manipulate and control us—no easy task, indeed. But the alternative was a slow death—both spiritually and physically—and I had no desire to participate in my own death, or this culture of death that I could perceive so clearly.

No, my goal was singular. I would be the one to shout that the "emperor had no clothes" from the rooftops, every day, until I either won, or the forces that be put a bullet in me. I had already successfully ran interference against the thieves trying to steal the entire US election, and now I was helping expose the criminal rot in Hollywood. I would not accept life on their terms—any of their terms. In so many iterations, and so many forms, I would assemble my own thoughts, the best weaponized memes I could find, and the most impassioned posts gathered from around the web, and collect them all under one roof. The result was wild, raucous, sometimes outrageous, but always thought-provoking, and unlike anything else online—which led to amazing growth and popularity. It was better than any newspaper, more fun than any magazine, and the best part was, I did it all for free. Visiting my page at the time was like freebasing redpills, redpills so pure, you would swear that they were being cooked up in a Winnebago in the middle of the desert by a chemistry teacher with a janky lung. And make no mistake, what I offered was purer than anything else out there—and, pardon the drug analogy, that made it that much more addictive. Suddenly, I was the Walter White of the online world, and pretty soon, everyone would come to know my name.

To say the page caught on like wildfire would be an understatement. In short order, I had attracted ten thousand followers to the page alone, and had started to branch out to other platforms because, it was around this time that I noticed some of *my* favorite pages were disappearing from the internet forever. Outrage mobs would assemble, mass report posts on a particular page while expressing their offense, and after enough "strikes" the page would be unpublished permanently and irreversibly. So if you, for instance, were posting about how great apples were, the orange mob might come over and mass-report your posts as "citrus-phobic." The Facebook censor, who might be a lemon or a lime themselves, would naturally agree, and **boom!** That was all it took to censor you, permanently. Forget that you were entitled to free speech as an American citizen. Forget that everything you were saying was legal. Facebook had a team in place to make sure you didn't transgress on any "wrongthink" front.

And that's really telling about Leftist ideology—that it literally can't co-exist with Right-wing thought. It *relies* on censorship. It *relies* on having enough institutional power to silence the opposition, because it can't form coherent or persuasive arguments on its own—because its foundations are not rooted in reality, but in ideals that run counter to reality. I can't tell you how many good pages I've seen get taken down over the years because of these organized outrage mobs. But on forums where free speech reigns, they always inevitably lean Right, because without censorship, Leftism literally can't withstand the force of the ensuing conversation and debate. When given an actual, even playing field, Leftism loses every time.

Which is why Leftists don't *really* want even playing fields. They want you to be subordinate to them, and create systems to facilitate and automate that subordination. Its ironic, really, especially when you consider how many of these types consider themselves radically for "equality."

But that censorship was a problem for another day. Careful posting and savvy wording kept my page alive for a very long time. After all, it's one thing to say, "I can't stand oranges." That might be misconstrued as "hate speech" by some poor sap working on Zuckerberg's dole.

It's another thing entirely to say, "Can you believe this orange?!" What does that sentence mean, exactly? Is it expressing grief at the orange, or support for it? This is the kind of double-talk normally reserved for Communist dictatorships, but the simple truth is this: plausible deniability works wonders against censorship, and for about a year and a half, it had been working wonders for me.

Until, one day, when it suddenly didn't.

Just "coincidentally," this was right about the time I had started covering QAnon posts on my page. As a product of /pol/ myself, Q was quickly becoming one of the biggest events on /pol/ whenever he would make an appearance. He was very difficult to track at first—even for someone like me, a Chan veteran by this time—as the boards themselves tend to be very ephemeral, with new posts eventually pushing the older ones off, into deletion oblivion. Occasionally, I would find different versions of "the map" (which consists of about the first… I want to say 150 or so posts of Q's, wherein he lays out the very basic foundations of everything that would follow), but soon tools were being built that helped track whenever Q would appear, allowing me to more closely examine what he was saying, leading me to realize, "Oh man, this *needs* more attention than it's getting."

And if no one else was going to cover it, I'd certainly do my best. I had covered other insiders before, but none had been as persistent as Q, so Q posts started to multiply. Some of my audience at the time protested this shift, as it subtracted from the edgier, funnier memes and such, but as always, it was my page: I'd do what I wanted with it. I felt it was very important, and thus, set out to start documenting and disseminating what I could.

But then, unexpectedly, Facebook dropped the hammer.

Gone, in an instant, was the page I had made, utterly erased from memory. Gone were the backup accounts reserved for situations where, upon perceived offense, one's main account would be disabled from posting for thirty days at a time—which is enough to cripple even the biggest pages. Gone were thousands of readers I had amassed during this time. Overnight, posts that would have easily circulated to hundreds of thousands of readers as they ricocheted across people's social networks were all erased. Gone, even, was the backup page I had made in the event of such a disastrous scenario (not that that really surprised me, either. Everything is ultimately tied to IP addresses, and I hadn't bothered to use a VPN or separate browser because my page, and pages like mine, were at the vanguard of such unilateral censorship). In an instant, my whole web presence had been effectively nuked from orbit by the Social Justice Marxists at Facebook Corporate.

Eventually, I got a replacement up and running. Through the use of other official accounts—such as my Twitter, which was, for the moment, untouched, and Minds.com, I was able to redirect people back to the new page and verify that it was actually me running the new page (sometimes, opportunists like to capitalize on the "brand" of fallen pages, and reincarnate them under their control). I managed to get a few thousand back pretty quickly, but I knew it wouldn't last.

It had instantly become apparent that my survival online, prior to this point, was at the capricious whims of Facebook's globohomo censors and their radical Leftist agenda (which could not abide the exercise of free speech). It was now clear that Silicon Valley was little more than a technologically-driven surrogate for the International Order, and they were not on our side.

In fact, we Anons would later learn from Q that companies like Facebook, Twitter, and Google, were little more than fronts for the Deep State. Facebook itself was not, contrary to the college-aged Cinderella story that has been pushed for so long, developed by Mark Zuckerberg in his Harvard dorm. It was, in fact, a reincarnation of a Pentagon project from the early 90s entitled LifeLog. Zuck was the Deep State patsy who fit the role of the proverbial boy genius/whiz kid/meganerd around whom the Deep State could spin a good yarn. In fact, Facebook had been developed by teams of engineers over years, before the government decided they needed to market it to college kids, and roll it out, campus to campus. Heck, I don't think most folks know this, but in order to get in at the early stages of Facebook, when it was literally just college kids allowed, you had to have the IT department at your school approve the installation of Facebook server hardware and software on the local college network. Then, the local student e-mail addresses would be ported over in bulk, and everyone enrolled at the campus, by default, would have a Facebook profile ready and waiting for them to use.

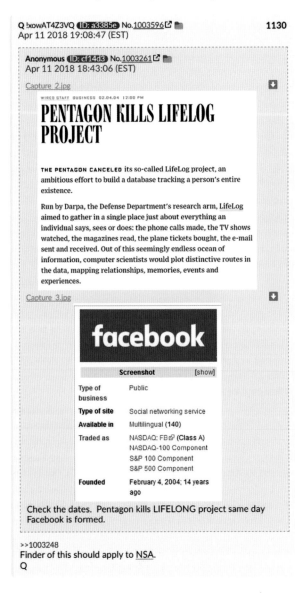

The ultimate goal of this was to create a system of mass surveillance and control over the populace. Q would later tell us of the secret F9 algorithm Facebook used to spy on everyone with a smartphone. Yeah, ever have that eerie sense that your phone is listening to you? You'll have a conversation with someone about, say, dog food, and suddenly you're seeing ads for dog food in your Facebook feed, even though you don't own a dog. That's the F9 algorithm at work. And up until very recently, all the data and metadata was being stored at Facebook's "Building 8" project in China, which is really just DARPA reincarnated.

Q !4pRcUAOlBE No.78 🖼   1337
May 11 2018 00:11:07 (EST)

Facebook is listening to you 24/7/365.
Literally.
[F9 algorithm]
Are they recording/safe-housing?
Metadata collection?
Building 8.
DARPA.
[CHINA-CHINA-CHINA]
Q

Oh, and Zuckerberg was then turning around and giving all that data[13] you gave him to the Red Chinese. (Hope you didn't send any naked selfies to anyone, because now the Chicoms are having fun with that.)

But it gets worse.

The full intention was to bring something akin to China's "social credit score" to the US, wherein everything done by an individual is tracked and measured, and a variety of "sticks" and "carrots" are employed to make sure you don't behave in a way that's "antisocial" (read: any way Dear Leader doesn't like). So, for instance, if you jaywalk, you might be given a longer wait time when you check in at a hotel because a street camera caught you doing it. A relatively innocuous example, perhaps to our jaded minds which are used to having our freedoms eroded, but what happens when you apply that to, say, payment processors? Say something Dear Leader doesn't like, and will you be able to buy food? Withdraw money from your bank account? Travel outside your home town?

That's the level of granular control we're talking about here. It's insidious.

Moreover, the whole thing was to be facilitated by Zuckerberg's "wife," Priscilla Chan Zuckerberg, who, in actuality, is a Communist spy whose family claims they were refugees from Vietnam, but in actuality, hail from Xuzhou, in Chandong province. She is more his "handler"[14] than his wife, especially because, according to CDAN, Zuck's been cheating on her for a while now with some actress. And while Zuckerberg and Chan have worked hard in order to foster the image of two philanthropists working for the good of mankind, through their Chan Zuckerberg Initiative, the truth is, that's a privately owned company, not a charity, and Zuckerberg has been using it for quite some time now to shield the proceeds from his massive Facebook stock sales, from asset seizure by the US Government. Seriously, the guy has just been dumping stock in record numbers. Check the insider trades, and you'll see

13 https://www.neonrevolt.com/2018/04/13/facebook-zuckerberg-his-handler-wife-and-organ-dona-tion-who-is-priscilla-chan-letssuefb-deletefacebook-qanon-greatawakening/
14 Ibid.

millions upon millions being dumped by all manner of Facebook insiders since Q hit the scene, but especially from Zuck.

And before you think you have a choice when it comes to social networks, understand that it's the same story for the likes of Twitter. Not only is it a tool used by the Cabal to influence the public narrative (through the use of massive bot networks, which prop up certain, favored narratives over others, and by banning, or shadowbanning opposing voices), it has long been use by human traffickers and child pornographers (much in the same way Facebook's WhatsApp message service was recently caught facilitating). Moreover, it was also used to spy on everyday Americans—something Q revealed in further drops by referencing one of the *Bourne* movies, where a social media company very much like Twitter, called "Deep Dream," was being used by the CIA as part of a targeted assassination program called "Iron Hand."

But the spying wasn't just on you and me. (And here's where it gets really dangerous, and really treasonous!) It included all levels of the government, including President Trump—and we all know how much he has utilized Twitter. If you're ever wondering why the top, fastest responses to Trump's tweets are *always* anti-Trump oriented (usually from the chinless wonders that are the Krassenstein brothers), understand that Twitter is not playing things straight here. This instant promotion of "Resistance" numpties like the Krassensteins has become really transparent at this point, and when Twitter was finally called out on this pattern, the pattern was shuffled up a bit, with other "Resistance" voices getting promoted in their stead.

But the biggest reveal of all came at one point when, in the Q drops, Q told us directly that Twitter was being used to spy on President Trump in the White House, while he was in the Oval Office—but that the White Hats already knew this, and were actually using this as a way to mislead and misdirect the Cabal. The White Hats allowed this to come to the surface in the summer of 2018, when they finally set up one particularly repugnant Representative (also implicated in a mess of Pizzagate research) in front of the entire Congress.

In drop 1562, Q highlighted a line of questioning by Texas' representative. Sheila Jackson Lee, wherein she, in a panic, asserted to Inspector General Horowitz that President Trump had plans to fire Rod Rosenstein (and thus, unilaterally end Mueller's Russian collusion investigation). At this point in time, the Cabal believed Rosenstein to be their man on the inside. The problem, however, with Rep. Jackson Lee's line of questioning, was that POTUS had only ever talked about that privately, in a classified setting.

Therefore, the **only** way she could have known that was if the Cabal was *still* spying on Trump.

And how were they doing that?

Well, it looks like the posts implicate Twitter.

Q even posted a few screenshots captured by the app at one point, doubtless sending Twitter founder Jack Dorsey's bowels through the floor:

Q !CbboFOtcZs (ID: cb5055) No.1822612 📄   1566
Jun 19 2018 21:16:09 (EST)

iPhone_Twitter_WH.png   ⬇

ANSWERS

Once again, the Cabal had been exposed by the expert military tactics of the White Hats, and Anons were watching it all unfold in real time.

But Google—Google may be the worst offender of them all! Bet you didn't realize that one of its founders, Sergey Brin, was actually born in Moscow. And, as I said earlier, it was also funded heavily in the early years by that same CIA-funded tech "incubator" In-Q-Tel. Google has been integral to the "success" of the "Progressive" agenda since its inception, just by virtue of its ability to shape public perception through its search results, as well as track absolute tons of metadata about billions of people on the planet.

Google has denied shaping public perception in this way during the 2016 election during a congressional testimony… and that was exactly the point of all the congressional testimonies you saw take place in 2018, with Facebook, Twitter, and Google execs testifying under oath before Congress about their activities. The White Hats already know about all their crimes, and have reams of evidence from various investigations into all their illegal activities, but with the CEOs of these companies recorded in front of Congress and the world, they can now also get them all on perjury charges once the time for that finally arrives.

But it doesn't end there with Google. If you're clever, you'll recall that Brin was the brother-in-law to Susan Wojcicki—the CEO of Google-owned YouTube. YouTube censorship has been off the charts this past year (as was Facebook and Twitter censorship, all rolled out in an initiative to prepare for the 2018 midterms, and the upcoming 2020 presidential election, in order to make sure a "2016" never happened again). Censorship is one thing, but tracking people and their behavior is another thing entirely. I said that Brin was married to Susan's sister, at one time. And wouldn't you know it, but Anne Wojcicki is the founder of DNA indexing company 23AndMe! And this is where things get really spooky.

In researching all this, for lack of a better term, "*conspiratorial*" stuff, one of the idiosyncrasies you learn about the Cabal is their penchant for bloodlines and…

I'm getting ahead of myself. You're not ready for that yet. Just know for now that these DNA tracking databases are not *really* there for your benefit. Needless to say, you're probably starting to gain a deeper appreciation for the scale of the Deep State operations in all of this, and why I decided that if I wanted to truly speak freely, without fear of censorship, shadowbanning, or deplatforming, I had to OWN my platform and content, because in two clicks all my work could be erased based upon how nice some blue-haired Bolshevik crybully was feeling on any given morning. I had to strike out on my own.

Luckily, I knew just how to set something like this up, and within a day and a half or so of making up my mind during February 2018, I had a pretty functional site up and running.

Initially, my plan was to just reproduce what I had always done on social media: post lots of little small form content pieces, replete with memes and videos and whatever I cared about. What I didn't expect was how this platform would empower me to carve out a new niche of sorts, enabling me to suddenly craft longer form posts, diving into great depth with each new, subsequent batch of Q-related drops.

In truth, I'm not sure I can neatly sum up all that I do for you, if you've never encountered my site before. It's sort of a unique mix all its own. In short, during the time I've been operating my site, I've been analyzing QAnon posts, and publishing my thoughts and interpretations on whatever it is he was talking about that day, supplementing each drop with relevant information from Anons, and seasoning it all with my own insights. Occasionally, I do deep dives on specific subjects, usually when I'm trying to get to the bottom of some question that's caught my attention. In truth, I've always saw my role as part hype-man, part entertainment, part educator, and part translator. I also serve as something of a bridge between normal folks and Anons. The Chans can be a difficult and confusing place to navigate, admittedly. Curating the best research and content from the boards, contextualizing that information and presenting it in a way that's understandable, and even fun to read—that's been my specialty as I've experimented with the format.

It's not any one thing that's made the site explode in popularity. It's that strange mix of all these different factors that lead to a unique, irreverent, informative, and yet (hopefully) compelling read that you just couldn't get anywhere else. There's simply no substitute for solid research. You can't fake being funny, either; you just are, or you just aren't. And it's often hard to meld the two into a coherent whole. I like to think that I've succeeded wildly on this front.

It's also something of a truism that when you try to teach others about a particular subject, you inevitably end up understanding it better yourself, and that was certainly the case with my efforts. The added boon was that it has also kept my writing skills sharp as I took some time away from writing screenplays. I had always wanted to write movies, yes, and I fully intend to return to that in the future, but for now, it was becoming increasingly clear that this was the most important work I could be doing. As of now, I've written just over 400,000 published words on the blog, putting me somewhere above *The Brothers Karamazov*, but still below *War and Peace* in terms of word count. I set the site up so that whenever I published articles, it would send out notifications across the web, via push services, Twitter, Facebook, Telegram, and more, instantly reaching thousands the second I hit "publish." And the site absolutely took off, again, partially because I was doing something no one else, to my knowledge, was even attempting. The site has currently reached over 10 million people, and inspired numerous YouTubers to cover my articles in depth, as part of their own regular content series. All this attention even earned me a mention on David Brock's *Media Matters* page, where I was featured among other "Right-Wing" sites. (Brock, you'll recall from my earlier timeline, was the former gay lover of Comet Ping Pong founder James Alefantis and had been featured in a photograph on Alefantis' Instagram account hobnobbing with Lynn Forester de Rothschild, of the mega-banking Rothschild dynasty, at a party in DC.)

I wear their disapproval as a badge of honor.

But all that is not including all the work I have done on social media, for I didn't abandon that front, either. I have a riotous time on social media, but after being banned by the censors at Facebook, and subsequently banned by Twitter (which proceeded to lock my account over a Sam Hyde meme), I shifted my social efforts over to Gab; a free speech based microblogging site similar in form and functionality to Twitter, and one which I had invested in years prior, thus making me a shareholder in the platform. I had made an official Neon Revolt Gab page aaaaages ago, but it was criminally underutilized, in favor of the larger social networks like Facebook and Twitter. But following new rounds of mass censorship, and the iterative improvements made to the site over the years, I decided to shift all my random posting needs to Gab's platform, often using it to disseminate bits of research that I couldn't squeeze into articles, or to cover events as they happened in real time (such as when I live-posted the testimony of the two independent researchers testifying in front of Congress about the Clinton Foundations' criminal finances). There's a flexibility with that format that enables me to respond to current happenings in a way that I really couldn't otherwise, as well as to connect to my readers and other amazing researchers. Pretty soon, my Gab page had gone from a mere 400 followers, to close to 20,000—and that was on top of my site growing tremendously along the way.

Likewise, at one point, I was actually able to monetize my efforts on Gab using their crowd funding service. Because I was officially "unemployed," (even though I had been treating my efforts in the Q-space as a full-time job), this was a huge boon to my efforts, allowing a degree of regularity and stability I hadn't experienced in my real life in quite some time—especially as my server costs grew drastically due to increased demand for my writing. Oh sure, I had previously sold shirts and such to try and help with those costs, but… you guessed it, I was also censored by Threadless and deplatformed there for violating some vague terms of service which they refused to clarify despite being asked explicitly over several e-mails. To be clear, all of my designs were completely original, having created them myself, and there was nothing objectionable in any of them. This was just another case of Leftists using their power to censor that which they didn't like.

(It's also why I'm still weighing out whether I should sue Threadless or not. I suppose it depends on the success of this book!)

But the battle wouldn't end there. The Cabal would strike at Gab next, launching a full on False Flag attack against them, when another Gab user by the name Robert Bowers would write "Screw your optics, I'm going in," before bursting into the Tree of Life synagogue in Pittsburgh and opening fire with an AR-15 and several handguns, eventually killing eleven and injuring seven of the worshipers in the synagogue that day.

Robert Bowers @onedingo   ...
2 hours ago

HIAS likes to bring invaders in that kill our people.

I can't sit by and watch my people get slaughtered.

Screw your optics, I'm going in.

In the wake of this attack, Gab would be attacked non stop. Even though these kinds of threats are illegal, and thus, not protected under any conception of free speech, even though Gab immediately contacted the FBI and law enforcement, even though Bowers also had Facebook and Twitter accounts as well, Gab became a public target for well over a week.

Now I'll make no bones about it: Gab, as a free-speech-based platform, has attracted a certain contingent of white supremacists and even literal Nazis. Yes, they often spew hateful rhetoric, but hate is not the same as threats, and if you're not subscribed to these individuals, you'll never so much as hear a peep from them. You can even go beyond that, and block users you find offensive. The guy, Robert Bowers? He wasn't exactly a "power user" on the site. In fact, no one knew who he was. The threat went unnoticed precisely because no one was paying any attention to him.

But that didn't stop the media from dogpiling on Gab, labeling them a white supremacist/Nazi safe haven. Subsequently, Gab had its hosting pulled, its domain registration taken down, it's payment processors removed, PayPal removed, and even banking removed. The site was effectively taken offline within twenty-four hours of the attack, even though none of the Gab staff had anything to do with the post, condemned it vigorously, and worked with all the relevant authorities to help in any way they could.

It's my personal belief that this horrendous, vile, murderous act was staged by the Deep State in an effort to deplatform me. So large had my presence grown on Gab, and so effective was I at disseminating Q-related information, new followers were arriving every day, quickly snowballing out of their control. Of course, it wasn't only me they were trying to deplatform, but all the better for them that they would get to deplatform the growing community of Qresearchers around me, who were increasingly turning to Gab as Cabal-friendly sites like Facebook and Twitter continued to censor and shadowban them for their wrongthink; specifically their Q-related wrongthink.

Thankfully, Gab is back up and running at the time of this writing, though it was a profound struggle for some time there. I'm glad Andrew Torba, founder of Gab, sticks to his guns and works so hard to support free speech, because that is more important than ever at this time. I do hope, however, that they can get their crowdfunding system back up and running, so that a real competitor to Patreon can finally emerge, because that's another tool that's desperately needed right now. And that really highlights the next big battlefront in this fight, because now you have the likes of International Finance colluding with these platforms to censor anyone even vaguely on the Right, such as internet personality, Sargon of Akkad.

Sargon was recently deplatformed from Patreon, losing thousands of dollars of revenue a month now, and it's looking more and more like MasterCard simply requested this. He didn't do anything wrong; he wasn't in violation of any of Patreon's terms of service. They cherrypicked an insult he said *TO* white supremacists during a livestream (that wasn't even hosted on his channel) and arbitrarily used that as grounds for banishment.

So what did he do? He went to the one remaining Patreon alternative, SubscribeStar, and set up a new account there.

And within a day, SubscribeStar had lost *all* of its payment processors. (Thankfully, they've since restored that functionality, as well, though again, it was a struggle for them as well.)

You beginning to see how this works?

The radical, lunatic Left cannot abide free speech, or free commerce. In the same breath they demand a cake baker violate his conscience and bake a transgender reveal cake, complete with Satanic iconography and dildo cake toppers, and then turn around to deplatform anyone even remotely Right wing, thus depriving them of their ability to earn a living. (And Sargon isn't even that Right wing. He's more a Centrist. Barely libertarian-ish.) And before you draw a comparison to the baker and these payment processors, realize, the baker isn't part of an oligopoly whose refusal to serve a customer means they would not be able to, for instance, pay their bills, buy food, pay rent... you know… *survive.*

Believe me; you do *not* want to give corporations that kind of power. You do *not* want these institutional powers building a Chicom-styled "social credit score" system here, in America. Regardless of where you land ideologically, I don't care if you're a blue-blooded Democrat, I don't care if you're a dope smoking Green Party member, I don't care if you're a pink-haired TERF; that kind of social credit system can only end poorly for *ALL* of us, because it could be weaponized against any of us at any given moment.

Life rarely goes as expected. If you'd have told me five years ago that one day, I would be slinging words online to help expose and dismantle an ancient, worldwide death cult, while simultaneously following the lead of an anonymous government agent who was dropping unparalleled disclosures for the people on a regular basis… I'd have thought you were crazy. I wanted to write movies. Now I was helping to dismantle power structures and expose pedovoric Satanists around the world.

But honestly? I really had nothing to lose at that point. My life was… not what I wanted it to be, and it was not improving despite years of trying. Call me cynical, but I said to myself, "If they actually do kill me, I'll be good." I'm a Christian man, so it's not like I believe I have anything to lose in dying, after all. I suppose they could have tried to hurt my family, which of course I wouldn't want, but as for me… Heck, I was an information soldier now. I was going into battle. And if I was going to fight, I was going to go all out.

Scott Adams, the cartoonist behind *Dilbert,* likes to talk about having a certain "skill stack" for work; and rather than pursuing positions or power, you should be adding skills to your skill stack, which you can leverage in a way that makes you unique, that allows you to do something others simply can't. For whatever reason, my "skill stack" meshed perfectly with what I was trying to do with Q. I could write well, I was very technically oriented, I had some graphic design chops, and most importantly, I had a sufficient level of prerequisite knowledge about politics and culture to be able to fully engage with everything Q was dropping. After getting the site up and running, I started writing faster and faster, and in a greater volume than I ever had before in my life. Information-hungry people caught on real fast, and soon, my server costs were growing—as were the attacks. My site was now experiencing DDOS attacks (on top of tremendous traffic), so I had to upgrade.

I mentioned earlier that to help cover that cost, I would end up designing a line of T-shirts to sell. I had initially just made some pure Neon Revolt-related shirts back in my Facebook days, but now I was making Q-related designs. And frankly, they looked pretty stellar. A lot of politically oriented shirts tend to be pretty cringe-worthy, and I didn't want that. I wanted something people could wear with pride and look good in—for potentially years down the road! I wanted something they could hold on to as a keepsake, and remind them that "they were there" when it all went down. A while later, I would be able to start selling a QAnon hat, which frankly, looked awesome. And no, I'm not trying to sell you on my gear after the fact. You've bought this book (I hope). That's enough. The point I'm trying to make is that while I had the prerequisite writing and research skills to compose these great articles, enough tech skills to admin my own site (even adding QAnon archive software and a fully functional store to the site), I also had some art and design skills in my skill stack, which I was able to leverage to create nice products that people could feel proud to wear.

That's a good lookin' hat, is it not? Not a bad effort for a one man show, putting this together on his own. That's 3D puff embroidery, my friend. And you'll notice the white rabbit detail on the side. I wasn't playin' around here. I genuinely wanted to provide people with a quality product. And it was incredibly gratifying when Q himself highlighted some patriots wearing my designs at rallies. Qpost 2443 hit me in a big way, because here was one of my readers who bought the QAnon hat for their young son, and now, it was being featured by Q! And I couldn't help but notice that kid was around the same age I was when my dad started letting me listen to Rush with him.

But wouldn't you know it, the MSM simply couldn't allow such free expression! They started relentlessly attacking *anyone* who sold Q-related merch! Here's an excerpt from an NBC News article, attacking, of all things, Q-supporters selling shirts on Amazon:

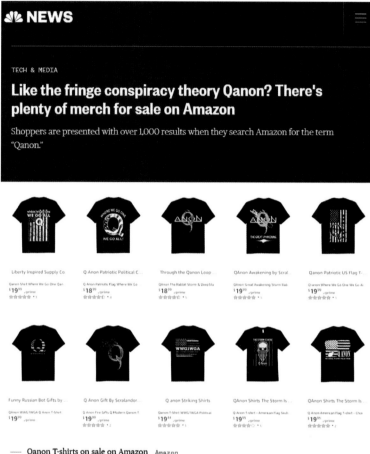

— Qanon T-shirts on sale on Amazon   Amazon

July 18, 2018 / 4:46 PM EDT / Updated July 18, 2018 / 4:46 PM EDT
By Brandy Zadrozny and Ben Collins

Devotees of Qanon – a far-right conspiracy theory about President Donald Trump's secret war against Hillary Clinton, the so-called deep state and a fictitious global child sex cabal – are showing their devotion to the cause by buying merchandise, including T-shirts, hats, and jewelry, on Amazon.com.

Shoppers are presented with over 1,000 results when they search Amazon for the term "Qanon," a baseless and convoluted theory that mirrors 2016's "pizzagate" conspiracy, which claimed Clinton was running a child sex trafficking ring out of a Washington pizza shop's basement and led to a shooting at that restaurant by a pizzagate-believer in 2016.

A variety of T-shirts and hats adorned with "Q" and white rabbits are available for purchase and free Amazon Prime shipping. Qanon followers can also buy coffee mugs, bumper stickers, mobile phone cases and grips, pet collars, books and rap songs all on Amazon. Several of the products were branded with an "Amazon's Choice" label, though those labels were removed after an inquiry from NBC News.

How dare I sell an honest, straightforward product in order to pay my bills and, you know, feed myself, right? These people literally would rather see me starve and be homeless, than see me succeed on any front. But more importantly, a shirt like the ones I offered, like the ones pictured from other sellers above, legitimized Q in a way NBC and the MSM simply couldn't allow. Shirts like these become conversation starters—especially when they're designed well. People start feeling emboldened to "come out" for Q when they see their friends and family sporting Q gear. It was so clear to me, from articles like these, that the MSM was dead set against Q from the get-go... and therefore had something to lose.

To return the favor, I would, in my Black List exposé, end up exposing NBC News president Noah Oppenheim—the man originally responsible for burying the Harvey Weinstein story, and who also oversaw Matt Lauer's tenure at the *Today* show, when Lauer had a button that allowed him to remotely lock the door to his office, trapping whatever woman was there in the room with him. And wouldn't you know it, he was also Black List founder Franklin Leonard's pal at Harvard! And he was also just such a "spectacular" screenwriter (on top of being NBC News president) that he debuted at number two on the Black List the first year it came out, with his script *Jackie*. What an amazing coincidence, right? I'm sure he has absolutely nothing to lose by QAnon coming to the surface. No conflict of interest whatsoever!

Right??

Accordingly, I would brand Oppenheim with the hashtag #RapeEnabler, and go after his squad of reporters as well, particularly one Ben Collins, who I dubbed Oppenheim's #AttackPoodle. These journalists would see my posts thousands of times on any given day, and get infuriated. But I think, hands down, the best reaction I got was when I labeled Franklin Leonard a #SorosRentBoy (because, you'll recall, he was affiliated with no fewer than four different Soros-backed organizations—by his own admission)! He initially tried some damage control, but when the barrage just kept coming, he didn't tweet for something like three days afterward—which is huge for him, because the man is practically addicted to Twitter, and goes to Twitter corporate events and such.

See, these people are used to being SJW style bullies, safely entrenched in their ideological hugboxes; never really challenged by anyone or anything. When they encounter even the slightest ounce of resistance, they tend to crumble and break, because they're used to attacking, not defending. The best thing about this all, too, was that there was really nothing they could do about it. It wasn't coming from a bot network. They could hit "block" all day on any accounts retweeting my stories, and that wouldn't accomplish anything because this was organic. They just had to endure it for days and weeks on end. To this day, if you still search the #SorosRentBoy hashtag on Twitter, Franklin Leonard comes up as the number one result!

But the MSM weren't the only people I would spar with, no! I would end up taking on a number of "internet personalities," perhaps most famously, one guy by the name of "Microchip." Now, Microchip called himself a "professional troll" in the past and claimed responsibility for helping advance Trump on Twitter by deploying a bot network to help Trump trend upwards. The problem with this story is that he's basically a degenerate script-kiddie perpetually high on Adderall and other substances all the time. And, despite claims of epic trolling, its obvious to everyone viewing his timeline that he forgot how to be funny a long time ago. Anyway, this creep teamed up with Jack Posobiec—someone Q called out as "Fake MAGA," and who Q also claimed had ties to Israeli intelligence agency Mossad—and the two of them came out with a report that *Microchip* was actually the one who started the whole QAnon thing as some kind of troll initiative to advance the MAGA agenda. And what was the evidence Microchip provided (which was then reported on OAN news by Posobiec) to substantiate this claim?

Microchip posted a series of iPhone screenshots from his private Discord chat server, detailing the "creation" of "Q" back in the day. Except, they were pretty apparent fakes, what with the stock time taken directly from stock iPhone screenshots, among other notable tells. I challenged Microchip on Gab: I had enough credibility in the QAnon community. Invite me to your Discord server and I'll vet your claim for everyone.[15]

It was a simple enough task. All he'd have to do is enter in my screenname, and boom, I would be able to see if the chat was real and communicate that directly back to everyone.

In a move that shocked precisely no one, Microchip instead attacked me, refusing to allow me to see the alleged chat for myself. (This is because the screenshots were Photoshopped. This alleged conversation had never occurred, and anyone on the server would have been able to see that he was lying, instantly.) That Posobiec would present these Photoshopped images as serious evidence makes a mockery of journalistic due diligence.

As a result of all this, I went on to repeatedly call Microchip out (and in spectacular fashion, if I may say so myself) pretty much overnight. I leveraged my site, presented the evidence of the fakery, presented his belligerent and transparent efforts at "pressure flips," and almost overnight turned him into the laughingstock of the internet.

To cover over the lie, Microchip proceeded to produce a "video" of the chat, several days later, claiming that Q would certainly be taken down by all this, once and for all!

One problem with the video, however, was that each message in Discord is timestamped… and he hadn't bothered to check the date in one of his links. So in the video, it has him sending an article on one day, when the link itself wasn't even published until two days later!

In other words, Microchip is either an honest to goodness time traveler, or… he faked the entire video as well.

(Or perhaps, his Mossad connections faked it for him. Either way, it's very clearly fake.)

Oh, and you can bet I had a lot of fun[16] calling that out, over and over, exposing this fraud to the entire world, making him regret ever tangling with me and trying to pull one over on the QAnon community. In the end, he lost thousands of followers, and at one point deleted his entire Gab profile history;[17] a broken and defeated husk of a man who tried to lie to the world about the greatest intelligence operation ever conducted in the history of mankind.

I don't think I can understate this here. If Q is real, that means the likes of Microchip collaborated with a Deep State agent from a foreign nation, posing as a journalist, in order to produce a propaganda piece aimed at keeping the American people enslaved to a worldwide death cult. And why? What did he get out of this? Some money? Some internet fame? We're talking real seditious activity here.

This incident actually perfectly encapsulated another repeated tactic of the Cabal; spreading disinformation and causing panic in a significant portion of Q's supporters. I certainly wasn't immune to these kinds of emotions by any stretch, but I did always try my best to approach any topic in question logically, to listen to very smart Anons, and convey my findings appropriately.

---

15   https://www.neonrevolt.com/2018/09/06/hrc-in-panic-mode-flawless-victory-awaits-newq-qanon-great-awakening-neonrevolt/

16   https://www.neonrevolt.com/2018/09/10/breaking-microchip-and-the-deep-state-newq-qanon-great-awakening-neonrevolt/

17   https://www.neonrevolt.com/2018/09/19/dems-need-a-new-infernalplaybook-newq-qanon-greatawakening-neonrevolt/

As a result of my work on my site, I would be involved in a number of other exploits as I tracked with Q. I would end up meeting the moderators of /r/GreatAwakening and the volunteers who run the research boards themselves. I would attempt to help the community migrate to Voat after Reddit censored the Great Awakening community (with varying degrees of success). And now, we have a stellar group of Anons congregating on Gab, with talk that the president himself might soon establish a Gab profile, coming from Brad Parscale, Trump's 2020 campaign manager.

But none of this was easy. On top of tracking Q and all the political and societal drama unfolding every day, I had been repeatedly deplatformed, was experiencing regular attacks online, getting attacked by the MSM, getting my donation line cut off, all while debunking the psyops orchestrated by foreign intelligence agencies and helping to expose Hollywood, Washington, DC, and an international Satanic Cabal. Again, I don't say any of this to tell you how "great" I am, or otherwise inflate my importance or role in things, but these were very real battles and, yes, I really was there on the front lines.

What you've got to understand is this: All my life I had been an outsider. Prior to Q, it was a struggle for me to comprehend why my life had moved in the direction it had, and more importantly, *why* it had been such a struggle, because the world I observed around me, and the actions I saw people taking just didn't quite add up. I mentioned earlier that I almost felt like God had betrayed me in some way, or perhaps "abandoned" is a better word, and now all that was left for me was a downward trajectory of pointless, unending suffering. Discovering Q was like discovering the broader context; the *why* behind everything. Things that hadn't quite made sense before, started making sense. The insurmountable now seemed like it could finally be overcome. The natural, disaffected cynicism I felt in the process of becoming utterly redpilled (to the point of being blackpilled)—that is, discovering the hard truths behind the comfortable lies—gave way to a hopefulness that I might *finally* be able to do something about it and actually help change the world for the better. I wasn't perfect by any means, but perhaps all this time, all this suffering I had endured, all this pain I had gone through hadn't been pointless after all.

Perhaps it had been preparation for something much bigger. Perhaps it had been preparing me for the most important fight of my life. Maybe that prophetic word I had received all those years ago hadn't been wrong; maybe I really was a "wrecking ball" about to be unleashed on the world.

At a certain point, in following Q, I decided it all made too much sense to just be another LARP. Q was the real deal. And it wasn't any one thing that stood out proving it to me; it was a whole host of data points independently converging to tell me that, yes, this guy, whoever he was, was legit. And if Q was legit, then this was the most monumental event of my life. It's like taking the redpill; once you take it, you can't spit it back up. It becomes a part of you. There's no going back once you know the truth, and I now knew that Q was true. So you see, I simply couldn't walk away. I had to get to my feet again, I had to stand up, even though I might be nervous, even though my knees might be shaking and everyone else is still sitting down and I might be risking *everything* by doing this.

But I had to.

But Q came to us, first.

POTUS came to us, first.

They knew what the Cabal had done to us, and they knew that of which we were capable. The unspoken, even forgotten thing about being an outsider is that it comes with a distinct set of advantages seen nowhere else: you see things that others miss, you observe what others can't, you've got pattern recognition few understand. And that intensity, that focus, that dedication and resolve is how Q knew that by coming together, we could stem the tide in this great battle and overcome our terrible foe, for once and for all.

When it comes down to why I followed Q, really, what choice did I have?

I'll leave you with the quote I opened the chapter with, from POTUS himself:

> "Never stop fighting for what you believe in, and for the people who care about you. Carry yourself with dignity and pride. Relish the opportunity to be an outsider. Embrace that label, because it's the outsiders who change the world, and who make real and lasting difference. Treat the word 'impossible' as nothing more than motivation."

CHAPTER 5

"How About a Nice Game of Chess?"

—A "marker" from many Q drops, first appearing on December 14, 2017

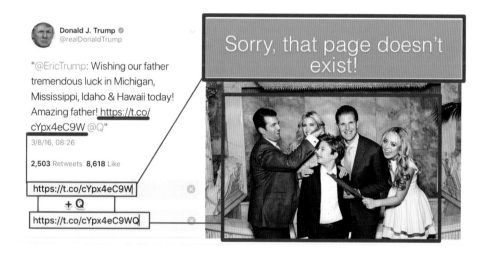

Donald J. Trump @realDonaldTrump

"@EricTrump: Wishing our father tremendous luck in Michigan, Mississippi, Idaho & Hawaii today! Amazing father! https://t.co/cYpx4eC9W @Q"

3/8/16, 08:26

2,503 Retweets **8,618** Like

https://t.co/cYpx4eC9W

+ **Q**

https://t.co/cYpx4eC9WQ

Sorry, that page doesn't exist!

Q !ITPb.qbhqo **ID: 462c9a** No.11043832 ☑ 📷   **354**
Dec 14 2017 21:43:38 (EST)

Shall we play a game?
Find the spider(s) and build the web (the 'map').
Remember, they consider you to be the fly (specifically, the 'feeder').
Remember, they never thought she was going to lose.
Therefore, they never thought investigations and/or public interest
into their criminal acts would be exposed/investigated.
Therefore, they never thought they had anything to fear.
Therefore, they openly showcase their symbolism.
Therefore, they were sloppy.
Hussein's last speech in Chicago re: 'scandal free'.
Why did he continually emphasize that phrase?
As a backup, they infiltrated and control the narrative (the 'MSM').
As a backup, they install only those on the team.
As a backup, they blackmail those that aren't.
As a backup, they defined 'conspiracy' as crazy/mentally unstable
and label anything 'true' as such.
This works given most of what they engage in is pure evil and simply
unbelievable (hard to swallow).
The 'fix' has always been in – no matter which party won the
election (-JFK (killed)/Reagan(shot)).
This was always the promise made to those who played the game
(willingly or otherwise) (i.e., they would never lose power).
Power of the (3) letter agencies.
Power over the US Military (WW dominance to push against other
nations and install like-kind).
These people are really stupid.
Follow the husbands.
Another Hint:
Ian Cameron
McKinsey & Company
Clowns In America.
Dr. Emmett J. Rice.
Federal Reserve.
Everyone is connected.
How about a nice game of chess?
Q

                                                    ANSWERS

Really, when it comes right down to it, I'll say this much:

I don't believe the Q operation started on October 28, 2017.

Now, don't get me wrong. That was definitely the first day QAnon posted on the boards, at least as "Q." He may very well have been posting long before then, dropping bits here, nudging conversations there, possibly even communicating through encrypted images, like we saw much earlier, but the first official post does not mark the inception of Q.

No, I believe that order came much earlier. When you've been around Q as long as I have, you begin to marvel at the precision with which every post is engineered. There are layers of meaning embedded in the drops that sometimes aren't apparent until weeks, months, even a whole year or more later. It's evident that a ton of planning has gone into this whole operation; years' worth, from every word, every timestamp, to the very syntax employed (to avoid sniffers, remember). But it's my personal belief that the clandestine order to officially run with the Q operation was given on Twitter, by POTUS, on March 8, 2016, before he was even ever in office.

Observe the photo above, where POTUS posts a link to an image of his family. Except there's one problem. The link itself is broken, and it's broken at the last letter. Instead of finishing the link with a capital-Q, there's a space, and then an @Q, as though he was pinging someone with the name "Q" on Twitter.

"Correcting" the image gives the intended link, but if POTUS was already working with the military to prevent a bloody coup from happening, I don't think anyone can rightly discount the possibility that he may have been working with White Hats inside the US Military to begin planning the Q operation as far back as early 2016.

When you've studied this subject as long as I have, barring the existence of some kind of super secret quantum computer which is able to perform game theory analysis in real time, you would *really* need the top military minds (and whatever computers they actually had available at the time) to plan the kind of operation the Q operation has shown itself to be. There are just too many variables at play; not just domestically, but internationally. We're talking about dealing with power-players across the globe, many armed with nuclear weapons. We're talking about counteracting the demoralizing effects the fourth estate and its unholy alliance with the CIA. We're talking about managing the American economy as it's being pushed to the brink by numerous Cabal actors with vast resources at their disposal. And it's all got to be handled in a way that doesn't give your own moves away, allowing the White Hats to retain the element of surprise at all times. When you study Q like I have, it becomes immediately apparent how massive this whole undertaking has been.

"Future proves past." If you were around Q during the days he was dropping intel in real time, you're already familiar with the phrase. "Moves and countermoves" was another. The idea is that Q is so far ahead of the masses, so much better informed about things going on in the world, that he's effectively able to "predict" the future… without necessarily giving the specifics away and tipping off bad actors in the meantime. The formula is simple: control (or understand) the inputs to a sufficient degree, and you can reliably predict the outputs (with the most striking example of this being, perhaps, how Q correctly predicted the results of the 2018 midterm elections a month in advance—53 to 47). The difficult part for Anons has been trying to piece together that missing context that we don't quite have (because we don't have nearly the level of access to intel that Q has at his disposal) so that we can get an accurate picture of reality, as well.

But why go to all this trouble, some might be wondering? After all, wasn't this just another election? Didn't Obama allow the peaceful transition of power to Trump to take place?

Friends, when you come to Q, you'll soon learn that very little is ever as it seems, and if there's one concept I absolutely have to introduce to you first, before anything else, it's Q's post about the "16 Year Plan to Destroy America." This is, quite possibly, the single most important post Q ever made, and explains so much about the treason that was going on, right under our noses. If I had to pick one Qpost for everyone to read out of the thousands that have already been dropped by Q, it would be this post. This is the crux of it all. And I want you to read through all this first, without any comment from me, just so you can get a sense for what we're going to be talking about, soon:

Q !UW.yye1fxo No.47 ☑ 📷   **570**
Jan 21 2018 14:06:20 (EST)

Will SESSIONS drop the hammer?
1 of 22.
#Memo shifts narrative.
#Memo reinstates SESSIONS' authority re: Russia/ALL.
#Memo factually demonstrates collusion at highest levels.
#Memo factually demonstrates HUSSEIN ADMIN weaponized
INTEL community to ensure D victory [+insurance].
#Memo factually demonstrates 'knowingly false intel' provided to
FISA Judges to obtain warrant(s).
THEY NEVER THOUGHT SHE WOULD LOSE.
[The 16 Year Plan To Destroy America]
Hussein [8]
Install rogue_ops
Leak C-intel/Mil assets
Cut funding to Mil
Command away from generals
Launch 'good guy' takedown (internal remove) - Valerie Jarrett
(sniffer)
SAP sell-off
Snowden open source Prism/Keyscore (catastrophic to US Mil v. bad
actors (WW) +Clowns/-No Such Agency)
Target/weaken conservative base (IRS/MSM)
Open border (flood illegals: D win) ISIS/MS13 fund/install (fear,
targeting/removal, domestic-assets etc.)
Blind-eye NK [nuke build]
[Clas-1, 2, 3]
Blind-eye Iran [fund and supply]
Blind-eye [CLAS 23-41]
Stage SC [AS [187]]
U1 fund/supply IRAN/NK [+reduce US capacity]
KILL NASA (prevent space domination/allow bad actors to take
down MIL SATs/WW secure comms/install WMDs) - RISK OF EMP
SPACE ORIG (HELPLESS)
[CLAS 1-99]
HRC [8] WWIII [death & weapons real/WAR FAKE &
CONTROLLED][population growth control/pocket billions]
Eliminate final rogue_ops within Gov't/MIL
KILL economy [starve/need/enslave]
Open borders
Revise Constitution
Ban sale of firearms (2nd amen removal)
Install 'on team' SC justices> legal win(s) across spectrum of
challengers (AS 187)
Removal of electoral college [pop vote ^easier manipulation/illegal
votes/Soros machines]
Limit/remove funding of MIL
Closure of US MIL installations WW [Germany 1st]
Destruction of opposing MSM/other news outlets (censoring), CLAS
1-59
[]
Pure EVIL.
Narrative intercept [4am].
Sessions/Nunes Russian OPS.
Repub distortion of facts to remove Mueller.[POTUS free pass].
Shutdown Primary Reasons.
Distract.
Weaken military assets.
Inc illegal votes.
Black voters abandoning.
"Keep them starved"
"Keep them blind"
"Keep them stupid"
HRC March 13, 2013 [intercept].
The Great Awakening.
Fight, Fight, Fight.
Q

Did you get all that? If this is your first time reading one of Q's more intensive posts, you might be feeling a bit confused by the bits of information you were able to understand, and overwhelmed by the other parts you weren't able to decipher. Truth be told, there's a lot to unpack here, and you might notice that this is post #570, which means that Q had been posting for about two months prior, and there were 569 other posts preceding it which Anons had already read, processed, and absorbed. In other words, Anons following all this live already had a very broad context within which to place this post.

Through these previous posts, Anons learned of the true nature of the Cabal, this ancient mystery cult that spanned the globe and ran world affairs. They began to understand its symbols, its systems, the players involved, and their motives and desires. The power structures behind everything had begun to be exposed and taken out by Q—perhaps most notably with the arrest and subsequent interrogation of Saudi Prince Al-Waleed bin Talal. Al-Waleed, one of the richest men on earth, controlled trillions in assets. He was actually the person who bankrolled president Obama's Ivy League education. He's a major investor in Twitter, and Snapchat, and he is Cabal, through and through. But following the White Hat-backed regime change in Saudi Arabia (and failed assassination of the Saudi Prince at Las Vegas), Al-Waleed found himself out of power, and even subject to complete asset seizure. His power removed, he would eventually emerge, having been released from a Saudi prison a seriously shaken man. Frankly, it couldn't have happened to anyone more deserving. Justice is still coming for Al-Waleed; he hasn't paid for all his crimes as of this writing, but make no mistake, he's been put on notice and will not escape the inevitable.

But Al-Waleed (and the House of Saud) was only one side of the "pyramid," as Q liked to call it. In truth, there were many other entrenched powers working to accomplish a singular goal: and that goal, now made plain in this post by Q, was the complete and utter destruction of America by its "elected" leaders.

The first part of this drop, you'll note, is about then Attorney General Jeff Sessions, and the so-called "Nunes memo," named for House Intelligence Committee chair, Rep. Devin Nunes, who had previously traveled to the White House compound to view a number of classified documents that had not been released to Congress, and which implicated the Obama administration in FISA spying abuses against the Trump campaign, which you'll recall from Chapter Three.

The memo was never released, but the threat of it being released hung in the air like the sword of Damocles for weeks, threatening to expose so much corruption at any moment and bring about the catastrophic exposure of those in our government aligned with the Cabal. Much of the same information was then rolled into Inspector General Michael Horowitz's OIG Report (which was then heavily redacted by Deputy AG Rod Rosenstein), before being released to the public, thus, once again obscuring this conflict of interest and massive election interference by the Obama administration. "Moves and countermoves," indeed.

Today, we sit awaiting declassification, or "DECLAS" of the full, unredacted OIG report, which still looms over Democratic heads to this very day. In fact, POTUS has already ordered the declassification of these documents, but the Justice Department has held up the order (possibly upon the order of Trump himself… but that's an advanced topic, to be discussed online, especially as events continue to unfold in real time). Needless to say, the ever-present threat of declassification has been a very useful legal tool, because it would lead to the immediate arrest of all involved (of which there were many, at many levels of government). In a phrase, the White Hats figured out a way to use the truth as leverage over evil actors.

Then comes the kicker in Q's drop: THEY NEVER THOUGHT SHE WOULD LOSE. All the evil plans of these various Cabal-affiliated actors were contingent upon Hillary winning in 2016. All their evil deeds depended upon someone wielding the power of the office of the presidency in order to provide cover for them. There's a lot of crimes we could look at, but just take the FISA spying on the Trump campaign for now. Obama would have never, ever undertaken such an action if he thought he was going to get caught. The incoming administration would automatically know what the previous had done, just by virtue of all the records kept by all these different intelligence agencies. Even if one, such as the CIA, tried to cover their tracks, the NSA would still be able to report on their activities. Obama expected Hillary to win—and with good reason, for they had rigged the election together, or at least they thought they had it rigged right until they realized too late that their efforts had been counteracted by White Hats stationed around the country.

"Moves and countermoves."

Let's get something straight, however. Hillary and Obama, allied though they may be, do not like each other at all. For one, Hillary genuinely despises black people, and despite what she may say, there's actually a long history of her behavior attesting to this fact. For instance, she was mentored by KKK Kleagle and Exalted Cyclops, Sen. Robert Byrd, eulogizing him in 2010 as "a man of unsurpassing eloquence and nobility." She also gave a speech once where she said that black youths were "super-predators" who needed to be brought "to heel." And in 2018, she caught an interviewer off guard when she said, "I know they all look alike," when the interviewer momentarily confused former attorney general Eric Holder, and Senator Cory Booker—two criminals in their own right, to be sure, but criminals aligned with Clinton nonetheless—who happened to have a skin color she despised.

Beyond that, there's also the fact that Obama really screwed up Hillary's election in 2008 with his cult of personality. Oh, to be sure, they still worked together after the fact. Their interests were aligned and they tolerated each other as much as they could tolerate each other, but there's a disdain, if not outright hatred, that Hillary still possesses for Obama. See, it's easy to think of the Cabal as this monolithic thing, but more often than not, it's these factions that, while all still pursuing the same (or similar) goal, are often vying with each other for power and influence.

But when the Cabal lost the power of the seat of the presidency, they suddenly lost their cover. And what could Obama do? Just… stay in office? Refuse to hand it over? If he did that, his treason, his treachery would have been exposed overnight. But believe it or not, he did consider it long and hard. It is my belief that he knew such a move would equal war, and he also knew that he would possibly lose that war. So instead, he took his chances and tried to find a new handler (yes, a Deep State handler, given that his previous handler, Valerie Jarrett, could no longer help him in this new situation he found himself in), and indeed, Q would soon tell us that Obama had even secretly traveled to North Korea, and that his trips all around the world during Trump's first year in office—both following Trump and lagging behind him—were for the explicit purpose of ensuring Cabal allies that Trump would be out of office soon, one way or another, and that they were to stick to the plan they had all previously conceived and to which they had all agreed.

It's also why Netflix would add Obama-based programming to their lineup, which should come as no shock, given that former US National Security Adviser Susan Rice now sat on Netflix' board. "Coincidentally," Netflix started to aggressively push pedophilic normalization in so many of their series—from *Big Mouth*, which featured cartoon nudity of underage characters, to *Desire*, a foreign film which featured a slow motion sequence of a child masturbating, and the new, edgy, "Satanic" reboot of *Sabrina the Teenage Witch*, in which execs wanted to feature a graphic orgy scene involving adult actors playing underage children. There was also *Baby*, a series which glorified underage prostitution, and *Girl*, a film about a transgender boy (that is, a boy with an untreated mental issue that makes him believe he is a girl) in which that actor, aged fifteen, is filmed with full frontal nudity. I'm sure there are other examples I could give that demonstrate, yes, Netflix really is trying to advance an agenda of pedophilic normalization, but some of you may be asking "Why?"

Are you ***really*** sure you want to know that answer?

We'll get to it later.

But back to the "16 Year Plan" for now. In this drop, Q gives us a glimpse at the true scope and nature of the plan this international Cabal had in store for us. At its most basic, this drop is broken into two major sections, split down the middle, with eight years covering Obama's role in the plan, and another eight years covering Hillary's presumed role and goals. I'll say right now, I only intend to cover about half of the drop in this chapter. There's so much here to digest and absorb, it really behooves us to break it up into two chapters, but by the end of the first half, you'll have a remarkable level of understanding, well beyond the average American at this time (though hopefully not for long!) and be able to tackle the diverse range of topics that will surely follow.

The portion of the drop which tells us about Obama's role in this might be the easiest part to understand. Q tells us that one of his first goals is to install rogue operators. Well, what does that mean, precisely? The answer I'm about to give you will not sit well with some, but it's the honest truth. Obama was an agent of the Muslim Brotherhood, and had been groomed for a very long time by Deep State actors to eventually reach the office of the presidency, well in advance of when that actually came to pass. But put some of the pieces together for yourself. Remember, how, in Chapter One, I talked about Obama's gun-running days, working on the secret SOVMAT project with Zbigniew Brzezinski and the son of Pakistani arms dealer, Sohale Siddiqi, in Karachi, back in the 80s? Remember, how, just earlier in this chapter, I told you Saudi Prince Al-Waleed funded Obama's education at Columbia? Al-Waleed is Muslim Brotherhood, as well.

Oh, and they had been building "Barry" up for a very long time, from the time he was conceived, in fact!

How do we know this? Because his mother Ann Dunham, was, in all likelihood, a CIA asset herself; possibly even a Monarch mind control victim. She ran in Communist circles during her youth, and eventually, conceived little "Barry," along the way. This photo of her, along with many others, was taken at the Hawaiian home of "renowned" Communist (and Obama "mentor") Frank Marshall Davis (who I, personally, think is the prime candidate for Obama's real father, given the striking resemblance Obama bears to Davis' other children, Mark and Lynn Davis). It was first published in a small magazine of "the bizarre and unusual" called *Exotique* and was lost for a very long time, until it was uncovered again by researchers during the Obama years.

And you have to understand, this isn't just a series of smutty pictures. This is standard operating procedure for the CIA. It's called a "honeytrap"; where you use a young woman to seduce a man, put him in an incriminating position, and as a result, you basically own him for life. The CIA has been using honeytraps for a very long time. A famous one actually worked very publicly: Hugh Hefner, of Playboy fame. Hugh had the Playboy mansion, along with the magazine, and in fact, what he would do is invite celebrities, media figures, politicians, etc., to his mansion for the famous Playboy parties, sex acts would inevitably occur as a parade of beautiful, often unclothed women were made available, and when the target had made their way upstairs, to somewhere more "private," they would be secretly recorded in the act. Often, Hefner would push "something younger" to these targets, and once recorded, the politician, the celebrity, the news anchor—whoever—would be owned by the CIA for life, due to the new blackmail they had now manufactured. And the Playboy mansion was far from the only honeytrap operated by the CIA. Another notable one is the "House on St. Charles Street," as CDAN likes to call it. This house burned down[18] "mys-

---

18   https://www.neonrevolt.com/2019/03/13/digging-through-the-ashes-of-the-house-on-st-charles-street-cdan-greatawakening/

teriously" in 2019, which is especially odd as more people began to become aware of what exactly it was. But the point of it all was that these sites were all about manufacturing blackmail in order to control seats of power, legislation, and narratives being pushed nationwide.

A lot of people, especially thanks to the perpetual influx of finely crafted media narratives, might be bewildered as to why an American intelligence agency would do such horrible things. After all, isn't the CIA on "our side?" Aren't they a good organization, with agents working hard to keep us all safe? While that may be true of some of the rank and file, the true origins of the CIA tell a very different story, for the CIA was founded as a collaboration between the OSS (that is, the precursor to the CIA, modeled off British Intelligence), and, well… Nazi Germany.

And this isn't some disputed conspiracy, folks. We are firmly in the territory of established historical fact here. The US, in the wake of World War II, imported tons of card-carrying Nazi Party members and integrated them into the CIA, and throughout various levels of the government in an operation known as Operation Paperclip. After all, the US and the Soviets had beaten the Nazis in the war, and now, they were dividing up "the spoils"; in this case, the top minds of the Nazi party, left over after the war. The US ended up importing about 1,600 Nazi scientists, and the Soviets, about 2,000. The most famous of these, of course, was Wernher Von Braun, a Nazi rocket scientist who would lend his talents to NASA. His team would eventually end up building the Saturn V rockets which would be used on the Apollo lunar missions… which shouldn't surprise anyone, considering he had developed the V-2 rockets for Hitler.

Another scientist who was said to have officially "escaped" (perhaps with some Deep State help) to Brazil after the war was Auschwitz physician Josef Mengele. An SS officer, Mengele was known for his cruelty, and used concentration camp inmates for human experimentation, often experimenting on dwarfs, and often making use of twins with a sort of cold-blooded, reptilian detachment. He even plotted charts to determine what level of torture an individual could sustain without dying. In fact, according to longtime Cabal researcher Fritz Springmeier, Mengele was smuggled into the US, and immediately put to work on the CIA's mind control project, Project MKUltra, the CIA's top secret "Mind control" program. Mengele would, upon joining the program, leverage his knowledge of demonology, the occult, and his experience in the concentration camps, to plot out the "science" of RSA—that is, Ritual Satanic Abuse— wherein an individual, usually a child, is subjected to a number of horrors and tortures so as to fracture their mind by purposely inducing a dissociative state in the brain.

See, humans are very good at one thing, and that's *surviving*. We have all sorts of strange survival reactions, when subjected to external stressors. We all have heard the stories, for instance, about a mother lifting a car off a loved one trapped underneath—the body summoning a sudden surge of adrenaline to allow her to power through a task she normally shouldn't be able to undertake. So to, with the mind. When dealing with trauma, overwhelming trauma, the mind can "wall it off" and almost externalize the event, until it's able to process the horror at a later time (if ever). Mengele's sick discovery was that it was possible to *purposely* create this state in people, to *purposely* erect these amnesia walls, leaving the "programmer" with the opportunity to "program" an individual by creating a dissociative identity that could be triggered with certain external stimuli. Survivor testimony from previous victims detail the kinds of horrors they had to endure at the hands of their programmers, such as being forced to witness murders as a child. Other times, it was being forced by the programmers to murder other children. Other times, it's burning, scalding, beating, or it's outright sexual abuse. I'm talking evil, evil stuff that would break most adults, and these sick creatures were perpetrating it against *children*—all for the purpose of creating these "alters," these dissociative identities, which they could then utilize for their purposes at a later date.

The most famous example of this kind of mind control programming was presented in the film *The Manchurian Candidate*; that is, a story about a brainwashed assassin who doesn't even know he's an assassin, until he is in place and activated by his handlers to perform the task he's been programmed to perform. On a smaller scale, illusionist Derren Brown wanted to see if he could replicate the results of creating a mind controlled assassin for a British TV special (albeit, through pure hypnotic technique, and without any kind of abuse). In fact, spoiler alert, he did discover he was able to make someone think they were assassinating British actor Stephen Fry, on live TV, and if you can get your hands on a copy of that special, do watch it. It's called, fittingly, *Derren Brown: Assassin*, and serves as a good proof of concept for the kind of topics the CIA was exploring over half a century ago, albeit with no moral scruples.

But this kind of mind control, created by this Ritual Satanic Abuse, is now known as Monarch mind control—a sort of sub-project within the broader MKUltra mind control program. The "utility" explored goes far deeper and far darker than most would ever want to know. There are animal-based alters, blackmail alters, assassination alters, and yes, sexual alters... which is where the symbolism of the "White Rabbit" first occurs, which is why Q would make reference to the "white rabbit" on a number of occasions, such as in drop 2051, which featured "artwork" from Alex Podesta's collection.

And yes, as far as I can tell, Podesta is a cousin to Pizzagate-accused Clinton campaign manager John Podesta:

Q !!mG7VJxZNCI **ID: fe6c79** No.2827819 ☑ 📷   **2051**
Aug 31 2018 23:13:08 (EST)

Anonymous **ID: 0c7e64** No.2827754 ☑ 📷
Aug 31 2018 23:09:12 (EST)

A&Wsidebyside.png

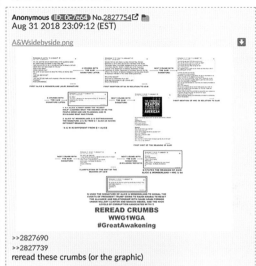

REREAD CRUMBS
WWG1WGA
#GreatAwakening

>>2827690
>>2827739
reread these crumbs (or the graphic)

Dl-tFGUU0AAhaw6.jpg

Dl-tFGVUUAAY2D1.jpg

>>2827754
Past drops important to frame context.
These people need to ALL be ELIMINATED.
Those who know cannot sleep.
Q

Known for his "bunnymen" series, Podesta's work often includes themes of torture and child abuse, as you can see in the photos Q has included. This first one, enlarged, shows the bunnymen getting ready to hang the smaller, stuffed, blindfolded bunnies. One is prepared to beat the smaller bunnies, presumably like a piñata. The other picture, which is not enlarged here, showcases the bunnymen taking scissors to the smaller bunny's ears. These themes of abuse continue throughout much of Podesta's bunnymen series.

But MKUltra was something of a catch-all program, exploring all kinds of "mind control" methods, be they spiritual, environmental, pharmaceutical, technological, or otherwise. The program was officially started in 1953, but became public knowledge when its existence was finally disclosed in 1975 by the Church Committee, which was a Senate investigation into a number of troubling developments within the intelligence community of the United states during the Ford administration—such as domestic spying on citizens, and covert assassination attempts on foreign leaders. In Springmeiers' book, *The Illuminati Formula*, he explores the topic of mind control quite thoroughly, but the subject is notoriously hard to get reliable information about, because in 1973, the head of the CIA Richard Helms ordered all MKUltra materials destroyed—two whole years before the Church Committee. What's left are what we have from various testimonies throughout the years—not just from those involved, but also from recovering victims,and from whatever documents weren't destroyed (and which have since been declassified, or otherwise obtained through Freedom of Information Act requests).

One such newly declassified document was obtained in late 2018, and described how the CIA had even subjected dogs to their sick experiments, and, get this, ***successfully*** created mind-controlled dogs. I'm not joking. This is now public, and major news outlets covered this document emerging into the public domain. Here's an excerpt from the 114 page report:

- 5 -

of 1 January 1964. In addition, it became apparent at that
time that the electrode preparation itself offered some
special problems with a dog that are not ordinarily faced
with the rat as an experimental subject. Those problems
were (a) protecting the electrode from damage, and (b)
infection at the electrode site due to a failure of the
surgical wound to heal. The plastic helmet that was devised
to protect the electrode from damage was described in our
report of 1 January 1964. A better technique that we
developed involves embedding the electrode entirely within
a mound of dental cement on the skull and running the leads
subcutaneously to a point between the shoulder blades of the
dog where the leads are brought to the surface and affixed
to a standard dog harness. The newest procedure was
described in our report of 1 January 1965, and it continues
to be perfectly satisfactory in terms of durability
(measured in months) of the electrode assembly and
protection from infection, since the skin is closed entirely
over the electrode site.

Yup, the clandestine Nazis were even messing with Fido. In the end, they were able to successfully create six mind-controlled dogs, which could perform a number of tasks. But do you really think they stopped there? As Q often warns, the truth sounds like science fiction, and if what I already told you in these last few paragraphs wasn't hard enough to believe, you're going to have a very hard time with, for instance, reports of mass shooters all "hearing voices," or the use of the pharmaceutical industry to create a malleable, suggestible populace through the use of popularly marketed anti-depressants. (I'll leave that for Springmeier to explain.)

In fact, following Supreme Court Justice Kavanaugh's Senate confirmation hearings, Q would tell us that basically everyone in America had just witnessed an MKUltra mind slave in action. I am, of course, referring to Dr. Christine Blasey Ford. I had speculated as much on Gab, days earlier,[19] but getting confirmation directly from Q was tremendous.

---

19   https://www.neonrevolt.com/2018/10/02/redoctober-redemption-newq-qanon-greatawakening-neonrevolt/

Q !!mG7VJxZNCI ID: 48f150 No.3282338 ⬘ 📁   **2306**
Oct 1 2018 15:04:47 (EST)

> Anonymous ID: 10bf2b No.3282114 ⬘ 📁
> Oct 1 2018 14:50:02 (EST)
>
> >>3281997
> Ford should down for perjury........

>>3282114
Refused to hand over therapy notes to FBI.
Think WHY.
Justice K NEVER named.
[Mr X logged in book along w/ physical description during 'eyes closed' session = / = Justice K].
FBI no subpoena power **[no GJ]** to demand.
Justice K NEVER named / asked during Polygraph.
Something did happen to Dr. Ford in her past.
Use of that 'something' to 'frame' Justice K.
Dr. Ford's family has strong ties to SWAMP.
FBI has expanded investigation into other suspicious acts w/
support of ABC agency as AUTH BY POTUS.
[RR] involved?
Q

Q !!mG7VJxZNCI No.321 ⬘ 📁   **2319**
Oct 3 2018 00:50:21 (EST)

https://twitter.com/Kevin_Shipp/status/1047333936102363136 ⬘ 📁
https://www.foxnews.com/politics/christine-blasey-ford-ex-
boyfriend-says-she-helped-friend-prep-for-potential-polygraph-
grassley-sounds-alarm ⬘ 📁
Ford herself coached by the C_A?
FARM (pre-family invite) w/ internship assignment (Stanford)?
C_A-assisted 'sex assault' 'sleepers' who are targeted based on
trusted family backgrounds, geopolitical location relative to families
of power/influence, ability to harvest **[control]**, etc.?
Fantasy or Reality?
Normal-to- **[self-induced]** in stages to exhibit past trauma-level
events w/ 'friendly' therapy sessions notated as undefined?
'Past trauma' exerted to IDEN 'mind w/ feelings' w/ TARGET
INSERTION.
Polygraph administered by **[former]** FBI agent?
Who was the agent?
Background?
Mueller-era?
HOW MANY TIMES WAS THE TEST ADMINISTERED BEFORE
RESULTS SATISFACTORY?
WERE QUESTIONS MODIFIED TO CREATE POSITIVE RESULT?
Goal: **[per past statistical success rates]** apply enough 'false'
intensive private & public pressure for nominee to resign.
Mission Failed.
Target provided w/ info to prep **[counter]**.
The More You Know...
Q

But the CIA? Nazis? Mind Control? What does all this have to do with Obama? Well, contrary to the elegant, well-mannered, well-spoken image of a normal family man presented to the public by the media, almost everything the public thinks they know about Obama is manu-factured, and it starts with his birth, and goes through, yes, his birth certificate, his education, his marriage, his kids, and more. I said earlier that Obama's mom, Ann Dunham, wasn't just taking smutty pictures. This wasn't the 60s equivalent of a one-off nude selfie. Dunham showed many telltale signs of being a CIA asset, right down to hypersexualized Monarch mind control behav-ior, such as this "performance" she gave with a wine bottle in front of a group of men:

YES, that's Obama's mom. But there's more to the story than just lewd pictures. Let's start with how she was a CIA asset working in Indonesia before marrying Obama's stepfather, Lolo Soetoro. We'll get into specifics in a moment, but for now, the background you have to under-stand for all of this is that the CIA had engineered a coup in Indonesia from 1965 until 1967, taking out the elected president, President Sukarno, and replacing him with a CIA puppet, President Suharto. The CIA is actually kind of infamous for engineering these kinds of coups, perhaps most famously in South American nations in the 70s and 80s during "Operation Con-dor," when a number of leaders who were perceived to be aligned with Soviet-backed interests were either assassinated or otherwise deposed from power. This led directly to, for instance, the rise of Pinochet in Chile, and the 30,000+ who were brought to concentration-style camps in Argentina, never to be heard from again. You might also recall the failed "Bay of Pigs" invasion into Cuba, in 1961, during Kennedy's presidency.

In fact, the Disappeared are worth noting for a moment here, because the effects of it still ripple into our time, some forty-odd years later, with assassinations and blackmail—spe-cifically due to the Vatican's involvement in this horror still coming to the surface. Yes, *the* Vatican, and specifically, Pope Francis, who is from Argentina, were involved in this horror. There's a reason I call it a Cabal—because it truly is a union of evil forces around the globe, working together to advance horrid agendas worldwide. General Videla was the CIA-backed dictator taking over Argentina at the time of the Disappeared, and what he did was round up literally anyone suspected of having Leftist sympathies, in the name of purging Communism from the nation, and threw them in concentration camps deep in the jungle. Naturally, this was used to dispose of all manner of political and societal foes; really anyone the ruling party wanted to get rid of. Pope Francis participated in this scheme, and handed a number of individuals—including other priests and children, separated from their parents—over to the party to be taken to these camps.

Well, not one to waste a "resource," General Videla invited a number of world leaders into his country, so that they could "indulge" in whatever sick fantasy they wanted to fulfill at his camps. Videla was going to have these people executed anyway. Why not ingratiate himself to the world's elite, and offer them women, children, whatever they wanted for a few nights before disposing of everyone?

What Videla didn't tell them was that he was recording them in the act, and creating a stash of blackmail so huge, when these leaders found out about it, they were nearly powerless to do anything about it. He had turned these concentration camps in the middle of the Argentinian jungle into his very own honeytraps for the world's elites—perhaps taking a note out of the playbook of his CIA backers (or maybe even at their orders)! It was always something of an unspoken bargaining chip Argentina would have at its disposal, should they ever need to call upon it, and world leaders were terrified of these videos ever being released.

The man who filmed and cataloged these videos was a cabinet member named Jorge Zorreguieta, and he had two daughters: Maxima—who would marry and become Queen of the Netherlands—and Ines. As time went on, Argentina would attempt to recover from this CIA interference, and in 1985, they would hold military tribunals against those who had participated in the coup—the Trial of the Juntas.

However, Jorge dodged any real consequences, as he was "just" a minister of agriculture; not exactly the jackbooted type. Besides, his role in filming these videos was unknown at the time. Instead, Videla and his men were sentenced to life in prison, and Jorge would quietly go back to working in government, storing these tapes for decades to come. As time went on, world leaders relaxed a bit, not so worried anymore that these tapes would be used against them, since really, the only people who knew about them were war criminals serving life sentences. All, save for one last witness: Jorge himself. When Jorge finally died, world leaders breathed a collective sigh of relief. Their secret would be taken to the grave.

At least… that's what they thought, until his daughter Ines found the tapes stashed away in her father's estate.

And she wasn't exactly quiet about it.

Ines immediately contacted her sister and a friend in Hollywood, and let them know what she had discovered. She was starting to go through it all, cataloging this staggering find when the Argentinian government would arrive at her door and confiscate the tapes.

They missed the records, however, which led to Ines having one massive loose end in her possession. No one reading this should be surprised that she committed "suicide" in July 2018, a year after her father's passing.

But back to Obama and Indonesia.

The CIA had been working in Indonesia during the 60s. They engineered a coup where over 500,000 people had died and installed their guy as president. Now, they were working to protect Rockefeller oil interests—essentially Mobil Oil (though there were other company names involved at the time, principally Stanvac).

The liaison between the government and Stanvac was none other than Lolo Soetoro, Barack Obama's stepfather. Obama's mother, Ann Dunham, was working for the Ford Foundation at the time, and if you spend time looking at the relationship between the Ford Foundation and the CIA, you will see they have been intimately linked for a *very* long time, with all sorts of CIA employees going to work for the Ford Foundation, and vice versa, and a number of Ford Foundation people making large donations to CIA backed projects. The relationship between Ford Foundation president Richard Bissell and the CIA is especially telling as Bissell was actually an aide to the director of central intelligence Allen Dulles during the Eisenhower administration; yes, the same Allen Dulles who oversaw the coup in Iran in 1953, the coup in Guatemala in 1954, who would later be fired by Kennedy as he tried to reign in the CIA. The same Dulles who probably ordered the hit on Kennedy in response (and at LBJ's behest), and who was subsequently put on the Warren Commission by LBJ. That Allen Dulles.

(And yes, MKUltra experimentation was started under his watch, too, if you were wondering.)

Using groups like foundations and other front companies is common practice for the CIA. It helps them maintain a sort of political distance from the nitty gritty, day-to-day operations, and obscure oversight efforts. This practice has gone on to this very day, such as with In-Q-Tel, which you'll recall from the previous chapter as being the CIA's "tech incubator," but that's far from the only example, with Fusion GPS being another. Some activities "need" to be kept off the books entirely, such as facilitating drug running into the US from Central and South American countries—something which led directly to the inner city crack epidemic of the 80s and 90s. People often wondered how the drug was being smuggled into the country, but the truth was, the CIA was doing the drug running themselves (the program was designed by George "Poppy" Bush Sr. in fact—a former CIA agent himself) in order to build up "black site" funds—that is, money that would be used to fund clandestine operations around the world—without the need for congressional funding, knowledge, or approval. If you want to see examples of this yourself, just search online for planes crashing full of cocaine, and see how often they're linked to the CIA. You will find many examples.

But now we have Ann Dunham working for a CIA front in Indonesia, married to Soetoro, a man who was liaison between a Rockefeller affiliated company and a CIA puppet, and raising a child who wasn't his—little "Barry Obama." Funnily enough, Ann Dunham would also be working in and around the Ford Foundation head of microfinance for Indonesia, one Peter Geithner. Peter was the father of Timothy Geithner, who would later serve president of the New York Federal Reserve Bank, from 2003 until 2009, and then as secretary of the treasury for the Obama administration from 2009 until 2013. One could imagine these "Cabal kiddies," little "Barry" and little "Timmy" even having play dates together growing up, the sons of CIA agents working for the same foundation in Indonesia.

More importantly—while Obama claimed in his biography to have attended school in Jakarta, Indonesia, from first through fifth grade, we now have photos of him in a kindergarten class at Noelani Elementary, all the way back in 1966, contradicting his claim that he attended kindergarten in Honolulu. This is precisely because he was not born in America, and is, therefore, not a natural-born citizen—a fact that, had it been disclosed during the run-up to the 2008 election, would have made him ineligible to run for the office of the president (and which may still invalidate his entire presidency). And while this may sound like so much "birtherism" to some, I can assure you, it's the absolute, monumental, disturbing truth, backed by reams of evidence—including the photo I just referenced above. Go ahead, search "Barack Obama and Ms. Sakai Kindergarten." You'll be able to see the photo for yourself (and probably numerous others)!

While at school in Jakarta, "Barry" would be enrolled in the Gerakan Pramuka, a scouting organization in Indonesia:

He would also participate in regular Quranic studies as part of his Indonesian public education, as well as "mengaji" classes; that is, recitation of the Quran in Arabic. Obama's father would regularly attend services at the local Mosque, and Obama's half-sister Maya would recall young Barry often tailing along. Along with testimony from former classmates, which recall the young Obama as a "devout" Muslim, a very clear picture starts to emerge—a picture which ultimately led to the "Birther" controversy, of which, yes, President Trump was a major proponent, especially on Twitter. The controversy would get so loud that the White House would eventually be forced to publish a copy of Obama's birth certificate on the WhiteHouse.gov website.

One problem: it was an obvious fake.

The principle way in which this was discovered was because whoever had stitched the file together had forgotten to merge (or flatten) all the layers they had created in Adobe Illustrator (a professional grade graphics/publishing/image manipulation program)—which led to that layer data being exposed in the final PDF. For the non-technical among us, imagine different transparency layers stacked, one on top of the other. One layer may contain a signature. Another may contain a grid. Another still, the standard forms you might find on such a state document from the 60s.

And more importantly, because this layer data had not been removed, literally any user in the world could turn portions of the "birth certificate" off and on at any given time. You could "turn off" individual letters, individual words, sections of the grid, entire signatures. See, if the document had been scanned, the computer would have picked up everything as one piece. Everyone who has ever worked in Illustrator (or similar programs) knows this to be an absolute fact—especially when you're dealing with documents that old. There should have been no layers at all. Instead, there were dozens! Why, I remember downloading the file myself, and playing around with all the layers. It was such an obvious fake, and in fact, you're still able to see this for yourself today by downloading the birth certificate PDF from the WhiteHouse.gov archives, and then opening it up in Adobe Illustrator.

If you were to do that, this is what you would see:

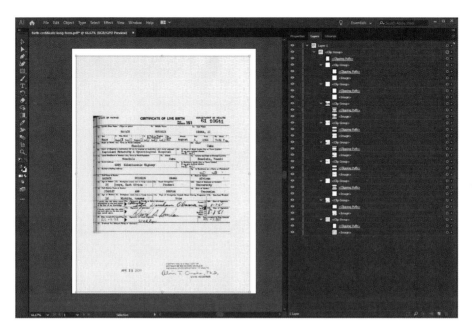

Yeah, I have Adobe Illustrator, and I'm going to show you one thing real quick, so you know I'm not just a birther crackpot. This is the kind of thing the media never covers (again, because they're Mockingbirds working for the CIA, tasked with deceiving the American people and steering the national conversation away from such… "inconvenient" topics and questions).

But notice the layer panel on the side bar? See all those embedded layers?

Yeah, those are all the bits and pieces you can turn on and off.

And just as a quick example, just so you can really see what I mean, here's what happens when I switch the visibility on this particular signature from on…

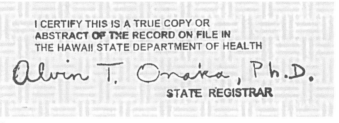

…to off!

YEAH, that's **_not_** supposed to happen in an original scanned document. If you drop a paper into a scanner, it grabs all the ink as one image. It doesn't separate whole chunks out into separate layers, and then *separate the shadow* from the original chunk on top of it. You're not supposed to be able to turn individual sections of a scanned document on or off…

Unless it was a composite manufactured by someone; someone who evidently didn't know that exporting your project file to a PDF from Illustrator kept layer data in the final product. But his or her mistake is our blessing, because it reveals to us the truth of the situation!

This would later lead to a major investigation by the Maricopa County Sheriff's department under Sheriff Joe Arpaio, wherein after *five years* of forensic analysis, they would isolate nine points of forgery on Obama's birth certificate and then—and this is the really difficult part—locate the *original documents* these particular sections had been lifted from, with the principle point of forgery being the use of the birth certificate of one Johanna Ah'Nee as a template, upon which all the other relevant data was pasted (often being lifted from other source documents, which the investigators were *also* able to locate). Sheriff Joe and his investigators would present this evidence in a press conference in December 2016, though he had been investigating as far back as 2011.

In response, Obama would weaponize the DOJ against Sheriff Joe Arpaio, with the DOJ referring him for contempt of court on trumped up charges of "racial profiling" in 2016, before being found guilty of criminal contempt in July 2017, prompting President Trump to issue a presidential pardon for him in August 2017.

Oh, and while all this was happening, in 2013, the health director who approved the release of Obama's birth certificate, Loretta Fuddy, would be the only person to die in a Cessna crash off the coast of Hawaii. Everyone else survived, including a passenger who filmed the ordeal on a GoPro camera, showing, at various times, Fuddy alive.

Even more striking, Fuddy was a member of the Subud cult; the same New Age "spiritual" movement which was founded in Indonesia in the 1920s, and in which Ann Dunham, Obama's mother, was also a member. If you don't think the Deep State utilizes cults, much in the same way it utilizes foundations, shell companies, and rebel groups, have I got news for you. Heck, it even uses mainline religions—from Roman Catholicism to Buddhism to Orthodox Christianity, and more—and CIA agents and the CIA affiliated abound. Why, don't get me started on the Dalai Lama (who keeps an entire harem of hundreds of boys for his own pedophilic, homosexual disposal) and who gets regular cash injections from the CIA. No, I'm not joking.

As Q has said, in drop 586:

> "Nobody can possibly imagine the pure evil and corruption out there.
> Those you trust are the most guilty of sin.
> Who are we taught to trust?"

Believe me, we're only just scratching the surface, here.

But is the picture getting clearer yet?

Ann Dunham would end up working for at least FIVE CIA affiliated fronts, during her lifetime, the Agency for International Development, the Asia Foundation, Development Alternatives, Inc., and the East-West Center of Hawaii. Eventually, Obama himself would enroll at Columbia (bankrolled by Al-Waleed) where his academic records (as a foreign transfer student) remain sealed until this day. During college, he would meet devout Marxist and leader of the domestic Leftist terrorist group the Weather Underground, Bill Ayers, who with his wife started a riot and plotted to bomb government buildings together. While Ayers would escape conviction, his wife would not. But before all this had happened, Obama and Ayers would find themselves working together on the Chicago Annenberg Challenge, and when Obama kicked off his first Senate race in 1995, he would hold his first fundraising event at Ayers' home. After college (and that fateful trip to Karachi), Obama would end up finding work at Business International—a company that, according to a *New Your Times* report in 1977, had provided cover stories for CIA agents on at least four separate occasions.

So now we see some profound and staggering details about the man, Barack Obama, which were deliberately hidden or obfuscated from public view by the Mockingbird Media. But now, with all that in mind, we can go back to that most important Q drop and begin to understand what Q meant when he said:

Hussein [8]
Install rogue_ops
Leak C-intel/Mil assets
Cut funding to Mil
Command away from generals
Launch 'good guy' takedown (internal remove)—Valerie Jarrett (sniffer)
SAP sell-off
Snowden open source Prism/Keyscore (catastrophic to US Mil v. bad actors (WW) +Clowns/-No Such Agency)
Target/weaken conservative base (IRS/MSM)
Open border (flood illegals: D win) ISIS/MS13 fund/install (fear, targeting/removal, domestic-assets etc.)
Blind-eye NK [**nuke build**]
[**Clas-1, 2, 3**]
Blind-eye Iran [**fund and supply**]
Blind-eye [**CLAS 23-41**]
Stage SC [AS [**187**]]
U1 fund/supply IRAN/NK [**+reduce US capacity**]
KILL NASA (prevent space domination/allow bad actors to take down MIL SATs/WW secure comms/install WMDs)—RISK OF EMP SPACE ORIG (HELPLESS)
[**CLAS 1-99**]

From the very get-go, Obama was working with the Muslim Brotherhood to undermine the safety and security of the United States in strategic and profoundly subversive ways. Founded in the 20s in Egypt, the Brotherhood has deep ties throughout Saudi Arabia, and has inspired groups like Hamas, while spreading terror throughout the world. Though they claim to have forsworn violence since the 1970s, they are more than happy to see the enemies of Islam conquered via other means, and in the case of the US, through infiltrating and strategically weakening us at all levels of government and society.

While I realize some reading this book may still actually believe that Islam is a religion of peace, I can assure you, that is not the standard practice in Muslim nations around the world. Sure, there are verses in the Quran which advocate peace. These were written when Muhammad was working as a merchant. When he became a warlord, he wrote later verses which then abrogated those earlier ones, essentially invalidating them. So while it may be possible to live with Muslims peacefully when they are both below a certain percentage of the population (and perhaps not too serious about practicing their preferred faith), once they grow past a certain percentage of the population, they become a social unit that starts affecting the order of society. We see this in Europe right now, which has imported millions of Muslims over the past decade into its traditionally white, ethnically European cities. First, it's just a few kebab shops here and there. Soon, Sharia patrols start popping up, demanding women dress a certain way and kicking people's dogs (because dogs are unclean animals in Islam). Then, it's full on Sharia marches. Then, there are no-go zones, like they have in Sweden, where even the police won't dare venture now. Then, it's underage sex trafficking rings like they have in Britain. And finally, it's women completely veiled from head to toe, honor killings, gays being chucked from rooftops, the beheading of infidels, "dancing boys," and the genital mutilation of little girls. So no, it is not the opinion of this author that Islam is a religion of peace, and any claims to the contrary are mere *taqiya*—that is, lies told to keep the "infidel" in the dark about Islam's true intentions for them. I realize that's not a "politically correct" thing to say in this climate, but if you've followed me for any length of time, you'll know that's never stopped me from saying what I genuinely think before. Some may even think this a "racist" tirade, but nothing could be further from the truth. Islam is an ideology, not a race. True, most people have an unconscious association with "Muslim" automatically equaling "Arab" in their minds, but nothing could be more wrongheaded. Any person of any race can choose to be a Muslim and adopt Islamic ideology. My criticism is of the ideology; not the race of the person practicing it. And yes, there is still more than one Muslim out there who is genuinely confused about the true nature of the death cult they either unwittingly joined or were brought up in. (To them, I would encourage they leave that system as fast and as safely as they can and enter into a traditional branch of Christendom.) But this was the religion of Obama, and his private Jihad against America started by first installing Muslim Brotherhood assets all across America.

This subversion was first revealed publicly through Wikileaks, in the Podesta e-mails, wherein the Obama administration, as far back as 2008, had asked for a list of Muslims they could leverage towards this end. Here's the original e-mail:

```
From: Bansal, Preeta D (NYC)
Sent: Monday, September 29, 2008 11:01 PM
To: Froman, Michael B
Cc: 'Onek, Matthew'
Subject: Asian American Candidates, Muslim American Candidates


Here are the compiled lists of Asian American and Muslim American
candidates for top Administration jobs, sub-cabinet jobs, and outside
boards/agencies/policy committees. A couple things to note about the list
of Muslim American candidates:

1) In the candidates for top jobs, I excluded those with some Arab
American background but who are not Muslim (e.g., George Mitchell). Many
Lebanese Americans, for example, are Christian. In the last list (of
outside boards/commissions), most who are listed appear to be Muslim
American, except that a handful (where noted) may be Arab American but of
uncertain religion (esp. Christian).

2) There is only one candidate I thought was a viable one for a
Secretary-level job among the Muslim Americans. That said, on both lists,
there are some very senior people listed in the last category (for outside
```

The attached list of Muslim candidates consisted of forty-two names, some of which you might recognize, such as Cyrus Amir-Mokri, who would become assistant secretary for financial institutions at the US Treasury, or Vali Nasr, who became a member of the State Department's Foreign Affairs Policy board, and served as a senior adviser to the US. Special Representative for Afghanistan and Pakistan (on top of being a lifetime member of the Council on Foreign Relations). Others included Representative Keith Ellison, and Representative Andre Carson. I will add that, in the course of my own research, several of these names kept cropping up repeatedly, such as Reza Aslan, former CNN correspondent who lost his gig after eating human flesh on his show (yes, actually performing an act of cannibalism as part of his documentary series, when he ate a portion of human brain after coming into contact with the cannibalistic Aghori tribe of India), and Zainab Salbi, who I suspect of being involved in human trafficking, though towards this end, I have no proof beyond circumstantial evidence which I uncovered during my own individual research, and which I think warrants more investigation by talented diggers.

The tragic thing is, Obama was largely successful in this undertaking, installing these Muslim Brotherhood agents—and many more—throughout the government. We'll get into the "why" behind this strategic move later, because it wasn't enough just to have power over the people; no. But for now, know they didn't—and still don't—have your best interest at heart; not by any stretch of the imagination.

As for the next part of Q's drop, this, thankfully, is relatively straightforward:

> Leak C-intel/Mil assets
> Cut funding to Mil
> Command away from generals
> Launch 'good guy' takedown (internal remove)—Valerie Jarrett (sniffer)
> SAP sell-off

In order to weaken the US from the inside out, Obama would attack on multiple fronts. Remember Hillary's private e-mail server? Remember how it was insecure? Remember how Obama had one, too?

That wasn't an oversight, and it wasn't a technical blunder.

That was by design.

Hopefully, I don't have to explain why leaking classified intelligence and military assets is bad. You may recall, in 2018, a report in *Foreign Policy* revealing that up to thirty deep-cover CIA agents had been executed by China over a two year period, following a breach into a CIA's encrypted messaging system. Where do you think the Chinese government got that information?

Now, I may have to clear up a point of contention here. After all, I've been railing against the CIA for several chapters now. If the CIA are "bad guys," then… in a roundabout way, wasn't it *good* that China caught them?

Well, no.

I once heard it described this way by a speaker in passing: there are at least SEVEN different CIAs, all managed under the big CIA government umbrella. So you have the real Deep State Nazi holdovers, you have the drug runners, you have the guys who meddle in international politics and organize coups, and then you have the rank and file American intelligence agents just trying to serve their country, unaware of how bad things have gotten in other areas of their own organization. So when you have thirty Americans being summarily executed by a foreign nation because Obama and Hillary set up private servers wherein they *SOLD* this kind of access to classified intelligence to foreign governments, well… that's downright treasonous.

(And no, that's not a defense of every individual agent's activities in China. Obviously, I'm not privy to every little thing going on during these secret, deep-cover missions. I'm more against Americans being betrayed by their own leaders.)

In order to further undermine US power, Obama would begin systematically removing patriotic generals and commanders from all branches of the US Military. In 2014, Retired General Paul Vallely would compile and publish a list online of the names, ranks, and jobs of the men removed from office by Obama. As he watched this going down, he called for a march on Washington in 2013 with the goal of getting Obama to resign. I will say, when you see all the names together, it's quite staggering and obvious what Obama was trying to accomplish.

You'll also note that Q says Obama leveraged senior adviser Valerie Jarrett towards this end. In truth, Valerie was less Obama's adviser, and more his "handler." This is a concept some might not be familiar with, but essentially, they're kind of like a manager, in that they connect the individual agent to a broader network, and thus, can feed them intelligence, tell them where to go, what to do, who to speak to, what to say, and generally oversee all the actions of the agent, behind-the-scenes, in order to keep them on point with their mission. In many Q drops, Q has revealed that oftentimes, these "handlers" are actually the "wives" of these men. Q would provide the example of Mark Zuckerberg and Priscilla Chan, as well as in the case of John and Cindy McCain.

Well, Valerie Jarrett was Obama's handler, and had been for many years since way back in the Chicago days. In fact, she continued to work with Obama after the presidential election of 2016 in a very strange and notable way: she physically moved into his new Washington, DC, home with him and Michelle, where they collectively set up an anti-Trump "nerve center" to work against all that Trump was trying to accomplish. Forget that no former president has attempted to actively undermine a sitting president in the history of the US before; I can't recall a time when a former president has elected to stay in Washington, DC, after their term has ended, ever before! Most want to pass the reins and just get back into the groove of civilian life; maybe take up painting. Yet here was Obama living right down the street from the White House and working with his former senior adviser to undo all that Trump was doing.

But again, this is because Jarrett was his handler, and had been since his Chicago days when Obama was working at the law firm of Sidley Austin. There, the young Obama would be introduced to "Michelle" Robinson via one Susan Sher, who just so happened to be Valerie Jarrett's best friend at the time. (Susan Sher would also later become Michelle's chief of staff at the White House, as well as run the Obama library). Sher was also so impressed with the young Obama, she would present Obama's resume to Jarrett so she could see it for herself. Jarrett was working as the deputy chief of staff for Chicago mayor Richard "Bill" Daley at the time and would soon become the commissioner of the Department of Planning and Development for Chicago, while also practicing law with two separate law firms, as well as taking on the role of chairman of the Chicago Transit board. Essentially, Jarrett ran a good chunk of Chicago during this time, and a lot of folks had to go through her to get anything done.

But if you're appalled by the state of affairs in Chicago today, look no further than Jarrett, Daley, and their Cabal legacy. After leaving the mayor's office, Jarrett would go on to basically become a slumlord, overseeing Chicago's utterly disastrous Grove Parc Plaza tenements. Living conditions there were so bad, the federal government would step in and seize the whole complex in 2006, giving it a building evaluation rating of an eleven on a scale of zero to one hundred. Jarrett would also become chairman of the Chicago Stock Exchange during this time, and later, director of the Federal Reserve Bank of Chicago, before finally joining the Obama administration.

Or so the "conventional" story goes. In truth, Jarrett is a Marxist spy, working for the Deep State since her youth to undermine US sovereignty. Born in Iran in 1956, Jarrett's family moved to Chicago when she was six. Later, through a FOIA request filed by Judicial Watch, it would be revealed that both her father, her maternal grandfather, and her father-in-law were all under FBI surveillance, as they were all under investigation by the US government for subversive activities.

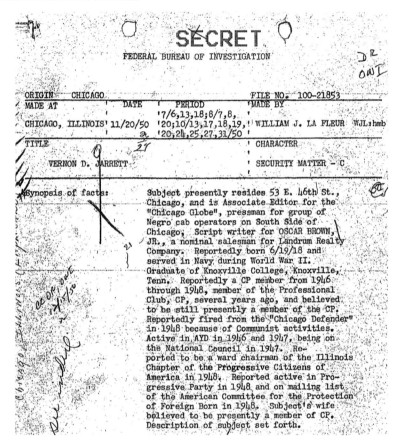

And this is not just... "Oh, they read Marx and were sympathetic to the cause." No! Jarrett's grandfather, Robert Taylor, actually worked with Soviet spy Alfred Stern in low income housing in Illinois. Stern got charged with espionage in 1957 after being named by a Hollywood musician during a McCarthy-era testimony before the House Un-American Activities Committee. Both Stern and his wife managed to flee the country, however, and Stern lived to the ripe old age of eighty-eight in Prague, before finally kicking the bucket in 1986. Both Stern and his wife had been charged with conspiring to act as Soviet agents, and receiving American military, industrial, and commercial information, which they then transmitted to the Soviet Union. Dr. James Bowman—Valerie Jarrett's father—was also in regular contact with Alfred Stern before he fled the country.

And if you want to go down a weird side trail here, Stern's wife, Martha, was actually the daughter of William Dodd, the man President Roosevelt would ask to become the US diplomat to Germany in 1933. Martha would travel to Germany and Europe quite a bit, would meet

Adolf Hitler, have an affair with the head of the Gestapo, Rudolf Diels (the protege of Hermann Goring), before traveling to Russia and meeting Boris Vinogradov, who recruited her to work as a spy for the NKVD in Berlin. In 1937, she would return to America with her family, meet the Soviet-backed millionaire Alfred Stern, and fall in "love" once again. The Hollywood connection which got Stern and Dodd caught as Soviet agents was when Stern was asked to invest in a music publisher which would serve as a front for Soviet operations in America.

So yes, Senator McCarthy was right. He was *very* right. Communists were crawling all over Hollywood, and if you have the time, I highly suggest watching Razorfist's foul-mouthed rant on the subject, online, entitled "Hollywood was Always Red."[20] You'll be shocked at the layers of hidden history there.

But if you want to link Obama and Jarrett further to Marxist/Communist/radical Left-wing/Cabal/Deep State causes, it's very easy to do so, for Valerie Jarrett's father-in-law also worked with Frank Marshall Davis on Communist causes; yes, the very same Davis who hosted Obama's mother for her nude photo shoots, the very same Davis who may just be Obama's father. But the coincidences continue to stack up: radical Leftism, radical Islam, radical Marxism—these were what united this particular faction of the Cabal during the Obama years, and this is why the Mockingbird Media absolutely freaked out when Rose-anne drew attention to Valerie Jarrett on Twitter with her "controversial" tweet. In truth, the controversy was largely manufactured by the media for the purpose of drawing people's attention away from Jarrett at a time when Q was dropping incredible intel about her, demonstrating how she had worked to remove patriots within the US government (acting as a "sniffer").

With patriots systematically removed from power, the US weakened globally due to the illegal sell off of classified information and Special Access Programs (that is, the SAP sell-off), it was time for Obama to move on to the next phase:

> Snowden open source Prism/Keyscore (catastrophic
>   to US Mil v. bad actors (WW) +Clowns/-No Such Agency)
> Target/weaken conservative base (IRS/MSM)
> Open border (flood illegals: D win) ISIS/MS13
> fund/install (fear, targeting/removal, domestic-assets etc.)

We talked about Snowden's activities in Chapter Two, and how he's not the hero he would like you to believe he is, but the next two actions of the Obama administration were designed to cause maximum "legal" societal disruption and put an inordinate strain on the largely white, working middle class.

The first should be pretty obvious: Obama weaponized the IRS against Conservative and Libertarian groups in an effort to drain them of their money, their assets, and reduce resistance to his agenda. Most notably, he made sure "Tea Party" and "Patriot" groups were systematically targeted by the IRS under the leadership of Lois Lerner. Lerner would go on, when later questioned about all this by Congress, to invoke the Fifth Amendment, refusing to testify. Congress would hold her in contempt, and would almost arrest her on the spot. The House Oversight Committee would subpoena the IRS for Lerner's e-mails, but her hard drive would "mysteriously" crash in the process of trying to retrieve the e-mails Congress wanted. Oh, too bad, so sad!

---

20   https://www.bitchute.com/video/ZOtinTlx7yo/

Unfortunately for Lerner, over a thousand e-mails would later be recovered from back-up tapes revealing, among other things, that Lerner had used a secret e-mail account by the name of "Toby Miles" to conduct official business at the IRS.

Toby Miles was the name of her dog.

The FBI and the DOJ would run their own "investigation" into the situation, and in 2015, announce—to the surprise of absolutely no one—that they would *not* be seeking criminal charges for anyone involved in the scandal.

(Sound familiar? Is a modus operandi possibly beginning to take shape? Private e-mail servers? Fake e-mail names? Destruction of evidence? Having the DOJ and the FBI cover everything up? Sounding familiar yet)

The next move would be to essentially overwhelm the US with illegal immigration; and it's precisely why, when Trump was elected, he focused so heavily on the MS-13 issue. Contrary to what the Mockingbird Media said, portraying it as some kind of racist move, it was absolutely vital to the safety and security of the American people precisely because, as the murder of Seth Rich demonstrates, MS-13 was being leveraged by the Cabal to harass, intimidate, and even murder political opponents of the Deep State.

In fact, two men, Rafael Aguilar and Carmelo Marmolejo-Calixto, would turn up dead from multiple gunshot wounds, victims of a double homicide, some seven hours away from where Seth Rich as shot. Random violence? Or was someone cleaning up some loose ends? According to Q, it was the latter.

Trump's push back against MS-13 would continue throughout his presidency, with him inviting the mother of MS-13 victim, Evelyn Rodriguez, to the 2018 State of the Union Address. Trump would also go on to give a speech at the Annual National Peace Officers' Memorial Service in Washington, honoring fallen police officers, and specifically, the mother of Officer Familia, who was shot in the head while sitting in her police vehicle. During the speech, Officer Familia's mother would clutch Trump's hand and arm in a prolonged moment of unexpected tenderness. How anyone could label the man a "racist" after seeing the footage of him embracing this grieving mother was just… it was completely beyond me. And while I realize the cynical among us may want to suggest he was merely using her as a prop to advance his own purposes, I would say go watch the speech and observe their interactions, firsthand. Then recall how, in 2008, he sheltered Jennifer Hudson in Trump Tower when her family was tragically murdered. And how he received the Ellis Island Medal of Honor in 1986, alongside Rosa Parks and Muhammad Ali. And then go listen to Hillary joking about how all black people look the same, how they're super-predators, and then compare Trump's history to Hillary's. Had it been any other president standing in Trump's shoes that day, the image would have been plastered all over the media for weeks on end. But you don't have to take my word for it. The speech is easy enough to find online.

Later, in Qdrop 1376, Q would identify Officer Familia as one of the two NYPD officers who were murdered (187 is California penal code for homicide) for viewing the contents of the Weiner laptop:

Q !4pRcUAOIBE **ID: 563afa** No.1419926🗗 📄   **1376**
May 15 2018 11:20:08 (EST)

Did you catch it?
[speech]
What NYPD detectives were [187] mid 2017?
Officer Familia [1]
Godspeed, Patriot.
We will never forget.
Q

The implication, given the broader context of the Qdrops, was that the Democrats and the Cabal had leveraged MS-13 to accomplish these two assassinations—once again leveraging them as bloody, murderous foot soldiers capable of killing anyone who got in their way.

This has been partially why Trump has been so vocal about building the wall along the southern border. Not only are we talking about election integrity (California alone has hundreds of thousands, if not millions, of illegal immigrants voting each election), and not only are we talking about gang violence, but we are also talking about massive human trafficking routes. In fact, if you study the routes like the Anons have, you'll find one particular point of note: that Cliven Bundy's ranch, where the Bundys held an armed stand off against the Bureau of Land Management, sits right along the path of one of the biggest suspected human trafficking routes from the southern border, up, into the US.

Do you understand the implication of the Bundy Ranch standoffs, then?

For twenty-one years, the government tried to get Bundy to pay over a million dollars in "grazing fees" for grazing his cattle on unoccupied, unused federal land. The argument was that the fees were there to protect the endangered desert tortoise, but the simple fact was the Bundys were doing what ranchers before them had always done in the west—grazing on the open land. This all culminated in an armed standoff where the Bundys and militias from across the country faced off against the Feds before the Bundys were finally arrested in 2016. By 2018, however, a judge dismissed the case against them for a number of reasons. But again, the implication is that the Obama administration and several administrations prior had been trying to remove the Bundys from the land by citing some obscure wildlife law, in order to remove them as an obstacle impeding a human trafficking route. That should be incredibly disturbing to all reading this book.

Q then goes on to talk about—

> Blind-eye NK [**nuke build**]
> [**Clas-1, 2, 3**]
> Blind-eye Iran [**fund and supply**]
> Blind-eye [**CLAS 23-41**]
> Stage SC [AS [**187**]]
> U1 fund/supply IRAN/NK [**+reduce US capacity**]

And this is where, I think, many people will have a hard time accepting what comes now, for what Q is telling us is so beyond the pale, so outside the conventional narrative, the only way to truly understand it is to pick up the circumstantial pieces of evidence and attempt to rectify them with Q's central claim.

For this is where Q starts talking about the bombs.

"Bombs?? What bombs?" you may be asking.

The bombs the Cabal intended to drop on the United States of America, before unleashing their "New World Order" upon the rest of the world. Now, that may sound far out, even insane to some, but I assure you, it's the absolute truth, and connects to a number of scandals the public is already well aware of, in a way that few can deny. Trust me, there are *many* reasons why Obama and Hillary will be arrested and dragged before military tribunals, but this is the primary reason why they need to face justice. This is the root of their treason, and why they need to made examples of, to ensure no one ever dares try such a thing again. This is why the military mulled a "hard coup" in 2013, before going with the Trump plan as a last-ditch effort to preserve the peace. It's not an exaggeration to say that *billions* of lives were at stake, both domestically and abroad, as you'll begin to see in the coming pages. All I can say is thank God she lost, because a victory for her would have meant a literal hell on earth.

The first thing you have to understand is that this was a tag team effort. Obama wasn't going to be the one to push "the big red button." No, that was to be Hillary's call. Obama was spending his time laying all the groundwork, funneling resources and materials to Cabal-affiliated states around the world.

This is where another paradigm shift becomes necessary, for while it's easy to think of the Cabal in terms of corrupt leaders and secret agents, it's much harder to understand that entire populations of nation-states can be enslaved to the Cabal. And yet, that is exactly the case with North Korea (NK) and Iran.

How many years now have we seen these states acting as provocateurs on the world stage? How many times have the "dictators," those "in charge" of these nations, tried to assert themselves and their nuclear ambitions against the free world? We've all seen it time and time again, to such an extent that people like Kim Jong-Un start to get parodied in our own media, much in the same way Disney cartoons used to parody, for instance, Hitler and Mussolini.

The simple fact, however, is that the Cabal has (up until very recently) maintained a strict system of control over these nations and used them for a number of vile purposes. It's why Eric Schmidt of Google traveled there in 2013, in order to install server hardware for them (as well as, according to some Anons, set up a remote system for their nuclear weapons, leading right back to the Obama White House. Yeah, wrap your head around that one for me, will ya.)

North Korea was especially used as a hub for endless human trafficking, supplying children to the world's elites for abuse, torture, and murder. Q tells us that the Cabal refers to North Korea as a "garden," that is… a place where "flowers" are grown and harvested. When asked why, in his controversial presidential portrait, Obama was depicted as sitting in a garden, Q would respond across two posts, in no uncertain terms:

Q !UW.yye1fxo ID: 94b137 No.350525
Feb 12 2018 10:42:52 (EST)   **744**

> Anonymous ID: 8cf1f5 No.350504
> Feb 12 2018 10:40:57 (EST)
>
> I wonder why <u>BHO</u> is depicted sitting in a bush

Unknown.jpg

>>350504
Find the link.
Look around.
What does it signify?
Q

Q !UW.yye1fxo **ID: 87df69** No.351238
Feb 12 2018 11:35:37 (EST)

747

Flowers & Gardens.
Learn the hidden symbolism.http://www.encyclopedia.com
/humanities/applied-and-social-sciences-magazines/slave-gardens

What does a 'Flower' represent?
What does 'Deflower' represent?
Q

In the picture above, President Clinton sits with then North Korean dictator, Kim Jong-il. Notice, they're sitting squarely on top of flowers. Behind Clinton is Hillary's campaign director, John Podesta. You'll also note that the water depicted in the painting behind the group shows rough seas. All of this is significant; one of the Cabal's ways of communicating meaning, both symbolically and globally. (If you take an even closer look at that picture, you'll notice that Bill Clinton and Kim Jong-il aren't *actually* present in it. They've been Photoshopped in, with one of the most significant tells being that whoever did the Photoshop forgot to copy the back legs of their chairs in!)

Always on the edge of "discovering" nuclear technology, the simple fact Q would communicate to us is that North Korea actually had nuclear capabilities as early as 2004 (using rocket tech, according to some Anon research, provided by none other than SpaceX):

Q !ITPb.qbhqo **ID: 7db625** No.13215
Nov 30 2017 01:01:36 (EST)

237

What if NK had miniature nuke payload delivery in 2004?
What if NK had ICBM capability since 2009?
What if the previous tests that failed were staged?
Why would this be relevant?
Who is involved and why?
Biggest cover up in our history.
U1 - CA - EU - ASIA\NK.
Iran deal.
Russian reset.
Q

ANSWERS

The way the Cabal would utilize North Korea, then, would be to force various global powers to go along with, for instance, the Paris Agreement, essentially forcing nations to contribute to a large "slush fund" for "protection," much in the same way mafia gangsters would extort protection money from business owners back in the day. This is exactly why President Trump focused so intensely on brokering peace with North Korea early on—something no one ever thought possible previously—because North Korea was being used as a countermeasure by the Cabal to prevent Trump from advancing the White Hat agenda on the world stage. Unwilling to be held hostage anymore, and unwilling to sell his country out (which would only preserve Cabal access to slush fund money) Trump instead, working with White Hat agents embedded deep undercover in North Korea, was able to take out Cabal actors in positions of power, and finally reach Kim Jong-Un… and free him, too.

That's another thing people don't understand. Kim was as much a slave of the Cabal as any of his "citizens." Yes, he was born into a relative position of privilege, especially when you consider the economic condition of the average North Korean citizen, but in truth, he was being groomed for a role from his youth. Those "dictator" suits he wore? Those were his costume, assigned to him by his Cabal handlers. He didn't want to be a slave to the Cabal anymore than any of his citizens. And actually, of all the people to truly recognize this, to truly understand the man, it would be Dennis Rodman in the end who helped broker this newfound peace between nations.

Trump and Kim would soon meet in the Mandalay Bay Sands hotel in Singapore for peace talks, but not before the Cabal would fire a missile in the wake of Air Force One, either in a desperate attempt to assassinate Trump yet again, or to start a war with a foreign country. The rocket launch would be caught on camera by a webcam run by an amateur meteorologist working on Whidbey island, Washington state:

Q !CbboFOtcZs (ID: 824a6d) No.1718290 ☑ 🏳   1476
Jun 12 2018 16:37:55 (EST)

*.jpg

This is not a game.
Certain events were not suppose to take place.
Q

ANSWERS

Anons would soon connect this missile firing back to a potentially stealth submarine operated by the Cabal, and operating using stolen Navy data.

Rogue missile attack intercepted

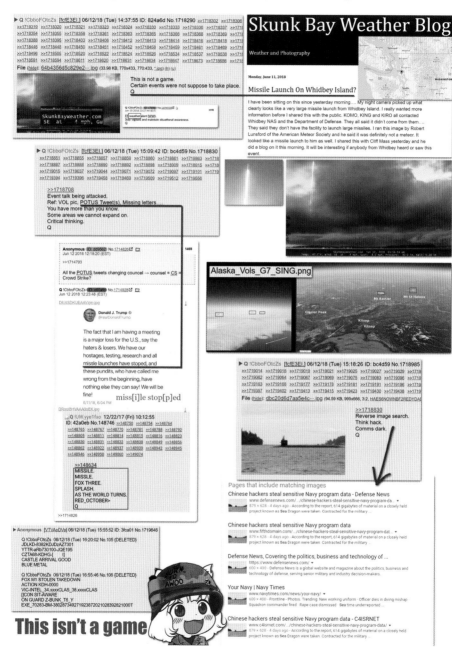

In fact, this wasn't the only missile attack on Americans that year. Earlier, in January 2018, an alert would go out to all Hawaiian citizens that read,

"BALLISTIC MISSILE THREAT INBOUND TO HAWAII
SEEK IMMEDIATE SHELTER. THIS IS NOT A DRILL."

Though… this was another move entirely, and there may not have been any missile at all. But to understand that, you have to understand some of Trump's moves prior to all this. In working with Asian allies, Trump would first stop in Japan on November 5, 2017, followed by his trip to China on November 8, where he would be the first US president ever invited into the Forbidden City. Why was this done? Well, it's a question of who was waiting inside the Forbidden City. Yes, Trump actually began the negotiation process, face to face, with Kim Jong-Un within the walls of the Forbidden City, unbeknownst to everyone save five people in the world at the time.

Anonymous 03/08/18 (Thu) 19:13:27 ID: ae640d No.593230

ok here we go Anons WOW HUGE !!!!!!!! NK will meet with 45 !!! MAGA !!

Q !UW.yye1fxo ID: 27d57d No.593825 ☑ 📄   886
Mar 8 2018 19:47:39 (EST)

>>593230
He already did.
Think back _ NK pic(s).
Everything has meaning.
This will break the MSM.
Q

Q !UW.yye1fxo ID: 27d57d No.593973 ☑ 📄   887
Mar 8 2018 19:54:15 (EST)

> Anonymous ID: 470655 No.593859 ☑ 📄
> Mar 8 2018 19:49:30 (EST)
>
> >>593825
> Why the stop in Hawaii after? That still makes me wonder!

>>593859
DEFCON, No Such Agency.
We knew.
How did we know?
Who did WE meet?
Need to know kept to 5 people + special SEC detail.
Future proves past.
Q

Years later, the media would remain dead silent as Trump, at a rally, let it slip that he had already met with Kim Jong-Un fifteen months ago. But fifteen months? As far as the public was aware, Trump and Kim had only just met for the first time some eight months ago, during the Singapore summit in June 2018! If Trump had really met with Kim fifteen months ago, he was confirming what Q had already told us back in early 2018; that Trump and Kim had already met, months prior, in 2017. When Q said "This will break the MSM," he wasn't kidding. Not a single major media outlet, so fond of slamming Trump for his various "faux pas," mentioned the "mistake" Trump had spoken.

Anons meanwhile, cheered for days.

After visiting China, Trump would round out his Asian tour visiting both Vietnam and the Philippines before making an emergency stop in Hawaii on November 14, potentially laying the groundwork for the missile alert incident that would occur on January 13, when the US Pacific Command would detect a "missile" headed for the islands.

Now, the thing you have to understand about this is that there is a backup NSA data facility on the Hawaiian islands, and in order to preserve all the data it had scooped up, in the event of an emergency, an automated procedure occurs wherein all the data held on the NSA's Hawaiian servers get dumped back to CONUS facilities; that is, the Continental United States. So when US Pacific Command picked up this "missile" threat on their radar, a bulk data transfer, or BDT, was initiated almost instantly, and everything stored at the Hawaiian data facility was funneled back to the landlocked NSA servers (most likely to the Utah facility).

Why was this necessary? Anons speculated that while Hillary and Obama had managed to cover many of their tracks domestically, they had been unable to touch the duplicate data stored on the NSA's Hawaiian backup servers. Thus, in order to get it all back safely to the US, the powers that be had to think there was a genuine crisis occurring. And what better crisis than a missile launch?

Potential heart attacks aside, it was actually a brilliant plan. And while this missile may have been fake (if we Anons have sussed out the correct version of the story by "filling in the blanks," as we have), the missile fired at Air Force One was very much real, and very much a threat. But obviously, Trump landed safely in Singapore, and as we all know, the peace talks went very well. Puzzled how Air Force One had escaped the missile, Anons would eventually ask Q what exactly had happened that night, since the plane didn't have the prerequisite speed to outrun something with such speed behind it.

Q would respond across two posts:

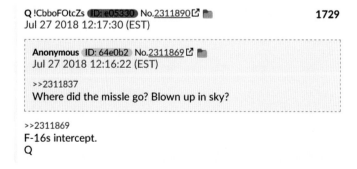

Q !CbboFOtcZs ID: e05330 No.2311890
Jul 27 2018 12:17:30 (EST)

1729

Anonymous ID: 64e0b2 No.2311869
Jul 27 2018 12:16:22 (EST)

>>2311837
Where did the missle go? Blown up in sky?

>>2311869
F-16s intercept.
Q

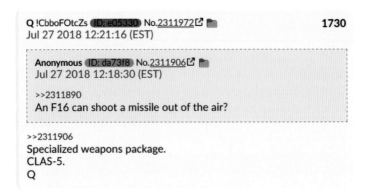

Track what this means: F-16s armed with classified weapons were able to intercept what was probably a ballistic Trident missile launched by a stealth submarine owned and operated by the Cabal, running stolen Navy technology.

If you're just now getting the sense that you're reading the greatest spy novel ever written in the history of mankind, imagine for a moment how Anons felt watching it all play out in real time. And the crazy thing, folks, is that I still very much feel like I'm just laying the groundwork for what's to come here. We're just getting started, and I have so much more to tell you.

But back to brokering peace with North Korea.

Given that Trump had already been to North Korea in November, the "Trump-Kim" summit in June, as it came to be known, was only for public show. The real peace deal had already been negotiated and agreed to months earlier—after which Kim Jong-Un would send a few signals of his own to the Cabal:

Q !UW.yye1fxo ID: 5bf34e No.562842 846
Mar 6 2018 00:02:58 (EST)

Anonymous ID: 71bc6e No.562749
Mar 5 2018 23:53:58 (EST)

DXkQ5YzW0AEu3VK.jpeg

>>562745

>>562749
Water.
Why is this event BIG?
What does it signify?
Why is NK out of the news?
As The World Turns.
Q

Take note of what you see here, and contrast it to the earlier image. What do you see? Kim and all his men are standing, not sitting—implying that they are now in control of themselves. They are on a tile floor, not on that flower carpet, implying no more human trafficking; no more "gardens" to raise "flowers" for "deflowering." And the scene behind them—actually part of the same mural that his father and Bill Clinton had utilized for their own photo—is now placid, peaceful, and sunny. It's a total reversal of his father's photo. Kim was now a free man.

He would soon ditch the "dictator" costume, too, for a more conventional (and comfortable) shirt and tie.

It was a similar story in Iran, where Q would tell us:

Q !xowAT4Z3VQ ID: e7b971 No.1248119 1306
Apr 30 2018 10:51:06 (EST)

Define the terms of the Iran nuclear deal.
Does the agreement define & confine cease & desist 'PRO' to the
republic of Iran?
What if Iran created a classified 'satellite' Nuclear facility in Northern
Syria?
What if the program never ceased?
What other bad actors are possibly involved?
Did the U.S. know?
Where did the cash payments go?
How many planes delivered?
Did all planes land in same location?
Where did the U1 material end up?
Is this material traceable?
Yes.
Define cover.
What if U1 material ended up in Syria?
What would be the primary purpose?
SUM OF ALL FEARS.
In the movie, where did the material come from?
What country?
What would happen if Russia or another foreign state supplied
Uranium to Iran/Syria?
WAR.
What does U1 provide?
Define cover.
Why did we strike Syria?
Why did we really strike Syria?
Define cover.
Patriots in control.
Q

Once again, Iran had been helped along by the Cabal, specifically, as Q would tell us, during Operation Merlin, where the CIA, at the tail end of the Clinton administration, planned to "disrupt" the Iranian nuclear weapons program by employing a defected Russian nuclear scientist to deliver "flawed" nuclear plans to Iran, and thus, sabotage them in the process. Except… that's not how it went at all. The Iranians were pretty quick to see the sabotage for what it was, and when comparing their documents with other sources, found the correct solutions pretty quickly; so quickly in fact, that it had led to speculation that the CIA didn't intend to hinder Iran at all—that their goal was really to help speed them along with nuclear weapons production!

And that's exactly what they did.

So, with the help of the Cabal, Iran was building a fully-functional nuclear weapons program; something which Israeli Prime Minister Benjamin Netanyahu would take to the airwaves about in April 2018, disclosing the existence of a number of Iranian nuclear files, showing the progress they had made towards this end. And if you were paying very close attention during the conflicts in Syria, as the Anons were, you'd have noticed something very funny about those conflicts.

Trump had the military hit *Iranian* military bases in Syria. An Anon would later expand on this subject, recalling posts he had saved from a "helper":

▶ Anonymous 12/21/18 (Fri) 14:08:14 ID: 958643 (1) No.4412142

>>4411555
I was going through my personal archives and found some interesting posts regarding Syria that explain a lot. These are not Q drops, but seemed to me to be from a "helper" or member of the team posting as an anon:

"This is the facility in Northern Syria where Iran is developing its nuclear capabilities in order to get around the Iran deal. Iran is not fighting with Syria against ISIS. Iran is infiltrating Syria, taking over. This is the MOAB that Q promised was incoming. So far, Israel has taken out the Syrian T4 base that was actually operated by the Iranians. We took out three development and storage facilities. Israel just dropped the MOAB on Iran's nuclear facility. Russian is working with us. It doesn't want Iran in Syria, either, or Iran developing nuclear capability (but Russia and Iran are supposed to be allies so the take-out had to be by someone else). This is a US/Israel/Russian operation against Iran. The best part? Iran cannot say a word, just has to take it. Why doesn't the media report the truth? Oh, and who gave Iran the money to build this facility and who made it possible for Iran to get possession of uranium? Can we say, Obama and Hillary? And VJ?"

"Anonymous (You) 04/29/18 (Sun) 23:08:52 a1928c No.1244181>>1244210 >>1244248 >>1244378
>>1244111
So Iron Eagle is a shell corporation set up by Renegade to receive the twice yearly $250 Billion "payments to Iran" that were added to the Iran Deal in a secret side agreement? And the coalition op with Jordan and other allies is to take down the cabal and Iranian bases and assets in Syria before moving into Iran to free the Iranian people from the CIA, cabal and Mullahs?

Anonymous 04/29/18 (Sun) 23:20:45 2c242e No.1244378
>>1244181 (You)
Yes...
Semper Fi"

"An extraordinarily complicated plot. All along ISIS and the migration to Europe were distractions while the Iranians were doing their thing. Americans high up in the American government transfer American uranium and tons of cash to Iran to help them produce a nuclear bomb. The bomb was to be used to nuke the USA and then the Russians were to be falsely blamed for the attack. President HRC would then go to Congress and get approval to declare war on Russia. It would have been WW3. All to enrich the Rothschilds, HRC, BHO, and their evil friends. They needed desperately for this to work. Things suddenly went awry when HRC lost the election. But the cabal is still pulling all the tricks... They've sent May, Manny, and Merkel to try to convince POTUS to stay in the Iran deal. All of them failed. Now they are in panic mode because there will be no war with Russia and they have been exposed.
But did they really think this through? It seems a bit short-sighted. We have nuclear weapons to fight such a war, but so do the Russians. Neither side would win. The nuclear fallout would severely impact the planet for decades...the air..the water...the food...
Where were the elites planning to go to spend their billions and live a life of luxury and ease after they poisoned and destroyed the planet? How long did they plan to rough it in underground bunkers? These people are not just stupid, they are insane."

Yes, the Iranian nuclear deal was a total sham, which (publicly) amounted to little more than promises in exchange for buckets of cash numbering in billions of dollars—all delivered by plane and denominated in Euros and Swiss Francs. The "bonus" in this for Obama was that he was busy skimming one hundred and fifteen million dollars off the top of this, laundering it through all sorts of international connections, and getting those funds "donated" right back to him. It's worse than criminal. It's treasonous! Trump had to put a stop to it the second he got into office. You may recall that one of Trump's first moves in office was to call back four hundred million dollars being sent to Iran via the German Central bank. Q would later expand on the subject:

Q !4pRcUA0lBE **ID: 224bb5** No.1391298 📷   **1345**
May 12 2018 21:53:26 (EST)

Re_read crumbs re: Iran.
It was never about WW safety & security.
It was never about Nuclear disarmament.
It was about opening a new untapped market.
It was about securing a black site.
The 'Exchange'.
U1.
Risk the welfare of the world.
Why?
Money.
Organized/planned by BC/HRC.
Carried out by Hussein.
[remember HRC ran against Hussein]
U1 [donations to CF].
$1.7b in-cash transfer to Iran [4 routes][5 planes].
Did the total withdrawal actually depart EU?
Why EU?
Define bribe.
Define kickback.
Special Interest Groups (SIG).
What US/EU Co's Immediately closed large deals in Iran post deal?
https://www.nytimes.com/2018/05/09/business/iran-nuclear-trump-business-europe.html 📷
Cross check Co's against political + foundation payments.
Define bribe.
Define kickback.
Why are people panicking about Iran deal pullout?
THEY NEVER THOUGHT SHE WOULD LOSE.
Truth coming.
Q

See, the original plan had been to fund, supply, and build the nukes in Iran, launch them on American soil, and then turn around and blame Russia for the "unprovoked" attack. The uranium, due to its half-life, could be tracked via satellite, and our intelligence agencies such as the CIA would "confirm" that yes, it had been in Russia. Hillary, in the face of such an unprovoked attack, would be able to launch a counterattack that would usher in World War III, and the utter nuclear destruction of, really, the last two remaining world powers that had enough resources at their disposal to counteract the efforts of the Cabal, globally—if only they were made aware of their predicament.

Oh, you didn't think the "Trump-Russia" collusion narrative was crafted on a whim now, did you? If the whole narrative was fake—as I've believed I reasonably demonstrated in Chapter Two—why not, say… "Trump-China" collusion? They're still literal Communists, after all. Or "Trump-Brazilian" collusion? Or "Trump-Azerbaijani" collusion? While we're at it, heck, why not "Trump-Micronesian" collusion?

I think you get my point.

The entire reason the Cabal ran with the Russian collusion narrative was to keep Trump and Putin apart, and thus, prevent any semblance of an alliance from forming between them, and against the Cabal. The absolute nightmare scenario for the Cabal would be not only the leaders of these nations awakening to the threat embodied by the Cabal, but the entire civilian population of those nations awakening to that same threat.

It's funny that my experience in screenwriting should help me come to an understanding of this premise, but at its most basic, we're talking about the Hegelian dialectic here. In essence, the Hegelian dialectic says that you start from a premise; from a thesis. Then, you introduce the opposite of the premise, the antithesis, into the mix. The result you end up with is then a synthesis of the two. It's sort of a "third way" of thinking, and in screenwriting in particular, it's a very useful tool.

Applied to geopolitics by dastardly people pulling the strings behind the scenes, however, and you end up with war, death, famine, and global strife—which is exactly what the Cabal wants, because then they can maintain leverage and power over you. It allows evildoers with power to move the otherwise unwilling masses along to a predetermined goal of the Cabal's choosing. The last time it was really well-employed against the US was during the Civil War, and while I may have some proud sons of the South reading this book, they should really look into the role the most famous Freemason in all of America (and Palladian Satanist) Albert Pike played in fomenting that conflict, as one of the founders of the KKK and the writer of *Dixie to Arms!* Now, I'm not here to get into the "slavery" or "states' rights" fight, because that *misses the point* of what I'm trying to say entirely. The enemies of America wanted America as a whole, North and South, as weak and as destitute as possible so that they could assume total control over everything. The quickest and most advantageous route to making that happen would be to have them expend all their money, ammunition, and blood in a fight against each other, setting even brother against brother as conflict lines were drawn. They very nearly realized their goals then, but for Lincoln… who knew more about what was going on than what's been taught in the conventional history books. Lincoln rebelled against his own bloodline—much in the same way Kennedy had—before ultimately, paying the greatest price a man can pay. But you'll have to read Fritz Springmeier for more on that particular story.

So, let's say the Cabal succeeded in setting off this thermonuclear war between these last two great superpowers on planet earth. What then? Wouldn't that be disastrous for *everyone* involved, even the elites? Wouldn't such a move be a bit like shooting themselves in the foot?

Not exactly.

See, the Cabal had been laying the groundwork for this for years, even decades, in advance. The end goal would be complete devastation in Russia and North America, yes. But what would be left?

Well, primarily Europe, South America, the Middle East, Africa, Australia, and New Zealand.

The goal was, yes, to create a one-world government, that perpetual "bogeyman" of "conspiracy circles," and this government would rule out of Iran—practically along the border of ancient Babylon—and hundreds of major multinational corporations were planning accordingly, such as telecom giant Orange pushing for a merger with Iran's MCI. But it's actually funny, because Q asked us all to track the executive resignations months ago, right at the very start of this. And at first, we weren't sure why…

Anonymous　ID: deb9fa　No.143174 ⎘ 🏴　　　　　　**413**
Dec 21 2017 20:18:38 (EST)

Track CEO resignations.
Q

But track we did, and soon Anons were able to track over 6,000 separate executive-level resignations from major corporations across the globe. The implication of this could best be summed up with that classic phrase: "It's a big club, and buddy, we're not a part of it."

It's why, as of this writing, there's the over one hundred thousand sealed indictments I mentioned in Chapter One, just waiting to be unsealed. It's why Gitmo has been revamped, even getting equipped with nursing services for elderly prisoners, and why two gigantic prison barges have been floated down that way, as well.

Europe, meanwhile, had been systematically flooded with illegal immigrants in an effort by the elites to sow discord and destroy social cohesion among the native inhabitants of the land. Many of these immigrants were shipped in from Africa and the Middle East, often by boats owned by NGOs such as The Red Cross—NGOs ostensibly set up to help impoverished people around the world, but, in actuality are little more than fronts for human, money, and drug trafficking for the Cabal. Europe had been effectively atomized by its leaders subjecting their people to an invasion of third-worlders, in order to purposefully destabilize traditional European society and dilute the effectiveness of any sort of organized resistance, which wouldn't amount to much anyway, since many countries in the European Union had already thrown away their gun rights, turning them into the clawless playthings of tyrants in the process.

Meanwhile, elites had plans all their own to avoid the fallout. Many are particularly fond of New Zealand—especially Hillary. But take the Bushes, for example. The Bushes have a 100,000 acre hideaway down in Paraguay, complete with its own system of fresh water aquifers; enough to support potentially thousands of people. And they have it all to themselves down there at a location they chose very… *strategically*, to say the least.

But in essence, all these "leaders" had this idea in their heads that they would be kicking back in paradise somewhere, even as you and your families were being turned to ash. They would escape, while innocents were being eradicated, worldwide. And the sinister thing— the absolutely repugnant thing of it all—was that this ties directly back to the Uranium1 scandal and Hillary's e-mail servers.

And as a sidenote, there's been something of a smarmy refrain among the insulated safe space the "blue check-mark brigade" has built for themselves on Twitter, and that's "But her e-mails," to imply that, somehow what Hillary did was minimal in comparison to, well, whatever scandal the media was trying to frame Trump with on any given week. Take, for instance, our pal Franklin Leonard here, who, with typical smug, self-assured arrogance so typical of verified Leftist Twitteratti, has turned the phrase a number of times:

Franklin Leonard ✔
@franklinleonard

(Follow) ∨

But her emails...

The Associated Press ✔ @AP
BREAKING: President Trump has been urging world leaders to call him on his
cellphone, raising security and secrecy concerns.

6:08 PM - 30 May 2017

468 Retweets **1,443** Likes

💬 26   ⟲ 468   ♡ 1.4K   ✉

In actuality, it's ALL about Hillary's e-mails, because Hillary sold classified intelligence and Special Access Programs (classified ABOVE Top Secret) to foreign governments in exchange for cash. Let me be clear here: Americans died because Hillary lied. The staggering thing about all of this is that Hillary should have never had access to these Special Access Programs in the first place! Authorization is on a need-to-know basis, and she didn't meet the minimum required clearance, because she didn't have a need to know at her position as secretary of state. Merely possessing these programs without proper clearance is treasonous, let alone selling access to the highest bidder on a private e-mail server. So how did she get access to them in the first place? Who provided them to her?

Who actually had access to these files?

Who had clearance above her?

Who could see whatever bit of intelligence he wanted, whenever he wanted?

(See where this is going?)

If the e-mail scandal had gotten out from under Hillary's "control," it would have implicated Obama. It would have exposed his private e-mail aliases and his treasonous activity for the entire world to see. It would have exposed a whole network of evildoers around the world in positions of the highest leadership—because they are all part of the same Cabal, and have been plotting the destruction of us "feeders" for quite some time.

And now you're going to see why the Clintons are sometimes collectively referred to as "the Clinton Machine," for Hillary couldn't just take a check from some foreign dictator and cash it out at her local bank. No, these transactions were all laundered through a network of individuals and institutions around the world, and masked as "charitable" donations to the Clinton Foundation.

If you want to see who was actually going to facilitate the shipments of South Carolinian uranium—some twenty percent of our most strategic resource—look no further than film mogul Frank Giustra, and his former mining company Rosatom. So called "fact checking" sites (which run on Cabal money) will tell you that the transactions occurred at different times, with Giustra donating much of the 145 million dollars by 2006, before leaving Rosatom in 2007. Hillary then becomes secretary of state and approves the sale in 2010, but it's incredibly naive to pretend that Giustra wasn't buying access to the Clinton's inner circle, and that the two events; the donation and subsequent approval, are completely unrelated. You have to remember, this plan was decades in the making, with President Bill Clinton even laying the groundwork for it as far back as Operation Merlin, in 2000.

And buy access that money did, for in 2007, Bill Clinton was able to help Giustra open regulatory doors for more uranium mining operations in Kazakhstan. Likewise, Giustra himself started working with the Clintons around the world, with the Clintons even helping Giustra figure out a way to shield himself and other donors to the Clinton Foundation legally (should any blowback ever come from any of this) through the creation of yet another foundation: the Clinton-Giustra Enterprise Partnership. Since Giustra is a Canadian citizen, this allowed them to shield donor activity from the US government, and indeed, hide the identities of all donors entirely. This foundation could then turn around and "bundle" these donations in one big lump sum in order to funnel them back to the Clinton Foundation.

Giustra would also work very closely with the Clinton Health Access Initiative, or CHAI for short, around the globe. The organization was ostensibly working to better the health and working conditions of those trapped in poverty across the third world, especially in nations such as Haiti, but really, if you've studied it for any length of time (like the Anons have), you almost immediately get the sense that it's one giant front for human trafficking and worse—even human experimentation. This is something that would eventually lead to the "suicide" of billionaire Barry Sherman, then CEO of Canadian pharmaceutical megacorp Apotex, and his wife Honey.

See, Barry wanted out. Barry was willing to talk.

The Clintons simply couldn't allow that to happen.

It should also be noted that, it's something of an "Open Secret" about Giustra and his serial sexual abuse of underage boys—particularly through a group called "Elpida" in Greece, and his "Boys Club Network" in Canada, which *only* targets young boys. In fact, it would be CDAN who would reveal the connection between Giustra and a certain A-list director by the name of Bryan Singer.

TUESDAY, DECEMBER 05, 2017

Today's Blind Items - The Boys Club

There is a big name out there. A very big name. He can take down a whole lot of people with him. He is a writer and producer and we call him BC. Along with an already shamed A list actor, he was the first to force this A list director to have sex with him for a future in Hollywood.

BC passed that same trait on to the director. BC has several production partners. Each of them are a little piece to the puzzle. Each of them owns a company which is directly involved with other companies that all are mixed and matched with BC and his two partners. One of those projects is a boys club. An actual club similar to a boys and girls club. One where for some reason, girls are not allowed. They only want to help "boys." The partner of BC who started this was groomed and shaped by the A list director who is a very frequent guest to the club and a very frequent viewer of the footage from the cameras installed everywhere in the club.

There are estimates that maybe a hundred boys have been molested by this group and their business partners. It could be more. There is another secret player behind all of this and that is an offspring of one of the partners who is also a lawyer. They pay her a lot of money which she spends on partying and she handles all the shell games with the companies.

POSTED BY ENT LAWYER AT 10:10 AM

LABELS: BLIND ITEM

Part of the reason Singer has been so hard to catch in all this, despite his abuse being basically out in the open for years, is that Singer leads right back to Giustra (and by proxy, Giustra leads back to Spielberg's longtime business partner, David Geffen).

#EvanRachelWould ✔
@evanrachelwood

(Follow)   ⌄

So we just..we are all still supposed to be
pretending we dont know about Bryan
Singer? Cause it worked out really well with
#Spacey and #Weinstein.

12:20 AM - 7 Jan 2019

3,496 Retweets **14,431** Likes

💬 325   ⇄ 3.5K   ♡ 14K   ✉

And so, the uranium was slated to be processed and removed from America, move up through Canada (thanks, in no small part, to Canadian Prime Minister Justin "Castreau," no doubt), into Europe (where huge chunks of money from the Iran deal were broken off, basically as bribes for political leaders' silence and compliance), and then shipped into Russia, before making its way down to Cabal forces in North Korea and Iran. Despite reassurances from Nuclear Regulatory Commission talking heads that no uranium would be exported out of the country, John Solomon, writing in *The Hill*,[21] would show that indeed yellowcake uranium had made it out of the country, followed by uranium shipments to Europe, between 2012 and 2014, allowing them to move some *twelve million* kilograms total.

That we know of.

Heck, this even ties back into the Benghazi scandal; that horrible event in which Ambassador Stevens was raped and murdered by an Islamic mob after being abandoned to die by the Obama administration, before an Islamic horde desecrated his corpse.

Anons have had more than one source testifying that Ambassador Stevens, unbeknownst to him, was actually delivering one of Hillary's servers to the Bin Laden family, in order to sell them SAPs, so they could build nuclear weapons and take revenge upon the US for killing Bin Laden. This was in exchange for a payment of 1.2 billion dollars, which was to be transferred to the Clinton Foundation from Swiss bank accounts. Hillary also had been working to arm "insurgents" in the area (read: actually Al Qaeda), and overthrow Gaddafi during this time, because Gaddafi had saved up an absolute ton in cash and gold reserves (which he then hid in Red Cross boxes he tucked away in secret caches throughout the continent), and because Gaddafi had acted as something of a "barrier" between Europe and the other third world African nations below his native Libya. Gaddafi's BIG mistake was that he didn't anticipate Western leaders actually *wanting* that kind of invasion to occur; wanting Libya to become permeable and allow all sorts through their borders and into the Mediterranean. He thought he was safe by virtue of the "wall" of separation he helped maintain between the two continents. He didn't anticipate the Cabal intentionally removing that "wall" to help manufacture a migrant crisis throughout Europe. In order to accomplish this, Hillary had ambitions to recognize the rebel group in Libya, the TNC, as the official government of Libya, as revealed in over 1600 Wikileaks e-mails.[22]

---

21   https://thehill.com/policy/national-security/358339-uranium-one-deal-led-to-some-exports-to-europe-memos-show

22   https://wikileaks.org/clinton-e-mails/?q=%22Libya%22+&mfrom=&mto=&title=&notitle=&date_from=&date_to=&nofrom=&noto=&count=50&sort=0#searchresult

The plan, cobbled together by Anons over many months as bits and pieces of information leaked out, was to always let Stevens die after the server had been brought to the consulate. He would be a loose end, otherwise. So, in collaboration with the Bin Ladens, they sent down hundreds of Islamic foot soldiers to attack the consulate in waves.

The problem Obama and Hillary didn't anticipate?

That nearby Seals, rank and file CIA guys, and the various military contractors stationed there would refuse to obey a "stand down" order, before going over to try and save Stevens and the others trapped there.

During that time, supposedly a tech guy, one of the good guys who just happened to be there, got into the server, figured out exactly what he was looking at (i.e. classified nuclear files), and immediately pulled the files off the server before securing them with the Seals.

Of course, this means that Hillary never held up her end of the deal. She never delivered the files. So, in order to fulfill her obligation, she leaks these files through her intentionally insecure e-mail server. One particular informant would go on to tell Anons that this just scratches the surface of the corruption, with the amount of money being paid to Senators in order for them to turn a blind eye to all these criminal activities coming in at around some 1.7 trillion dollars. Even worse, much of this came from programs wherein US taxpayer dollars were being donated overseas, donated BACK to the Clinton Foundation, and then being donated to these respective Senators' wallets. Sen. John McCain was involved in this operation in particular detail, because he was actually the one who arranged the arming of the insurgents in the first place, by having the CIA work with, literally, a neighbor of his—an arms dealer named Marc Turi.

This detail was only really brought to light by the fact that earlier that year, on July 25, 2012, Taliban fighters in Afghanistan fired a Stinger missile at a Chinook helicopter before successfully hitting their mark. Good thing for the pilot and its crew then, that the missile hadn't been armed, and merely embedded itself in the armor of the chopper, instead of exploding on impact. Being a newer generation of Stinger missile, the Taliban forces didn't understand how to correctly arm the missiles, and thus, it did not explode on contact with the aircraft. Sill intact, an explosives team was able to retrieve the serial number off the missile, and traced it back to a CIA lot number that had been sent to insurgents all the way over in Qatar, who evidently had the ambition of overthrowing Gaddafi. Unable to sell directly to opposition forces in Libya, Turi had developed something of a "workaround," by selling arms to neighboring countries before importing them to their original, intended destination. McCain, working on the Senate Arms Committee, helped streamline these deals so that arms dealer Marc Turi could deliver these weapons overseas.

The rest, sadly, is history. Rockets would be fired at the men in the consulate for thirteen straight hours.

This is one of the reasons why McCain was secretly executed following a secret military tribunal in which he was tried and convicted for treason. No friends, he did not have brain cancer. That was a cover story, and one that was fairly transparent. Many might remember the number of times he wore his medical boot on the wrong foot during photo ops, and the hilarious memes that came out as a result.

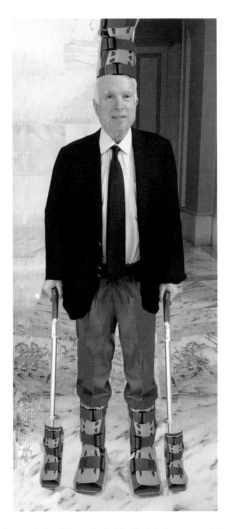

When he passed, his wife (and handler) Cindy McCain would write on Twitter:

Cindy McCain ✔
@cindymccain

Follow ⌄

My heart is broken. I am so lucky to have lived the adventure of loving this incredible man for 38 years. He passed the way he lived, on his own terms, surrounded by the people he loved, in the the place he loved best.

5:47 PM - 25 Aug 2018

55,431 Retweets **469,188** Likes

💬 25K   ⟲ 55K   ♡ 469K

But Q would soon respond, saying…

"[He did not depart on his own terms]"

Q !!mG7VJxZNCI **ID: fd6f58** No.2758706 ☑ 🖼   **1935**
Aug 27 2018 19:04:20 (EST)

Focus Here:
"…raise troubling questions about Halper, who was believed to have
worked with the CIA and part of the matrix of players in the bureau's
'CrossFire Hurricane' investigation into Trump's 2016 presidential
campaign. Halper, who assisted the FBI in the Russia investigation,
appears to also have significant ties to the Russian government, as
well as sources connected directly to President Vladimir Putin."
https://saraacarter.com/whistleblower-exposes-key-player-in-fbi-
russia-probe-it-was-all-a-set-up/ ☑ 🖼
Define 'Projection'.
D's SCREAM when POTUS meets w/ PUTIN?
D's demand to hold hearings w/ the interpreter used during the
private POTUS-PUTIN meeting?
D's demand ALL meetings w/ PUTIN be CANCELLED?
If POTUS knows everything - control over what orgs are central to
operational success?
1. DOJ
2. FBI
3. NSA
4. US MILITARY
5. STATE
6. F_ASSETS
Ask yourself, if above are central to operational success, who would
you pick to lead such orgs?
HRC election loss = CF inflow stop
CF inflow stop = No Name Institute inflow ramp
Compare donors.
Define DARK MONEY.
Direct correlation?
[He did not depart on his own terms]
Think FLYNN [30].
Exactly [30].
Q

I include that aside about McCain so that my readers who may consider themselves
Democrats can see plainly… corruption exists on both sides of the aisle here. I said earlier in
this book that this wasn't so much about Republican versus Democrat, or Left versus Right.
It's about Good versus Evil; We the People versus the Cabal.

Essentially, the consulate in Benghazi was little more than cover for a CIA gun running
operation (among other things), and Ambassador Stevens was just a pawn in a larger plot.
One organization working out of the consulate there would be USAID (read: gun running
cover). And according to that same source from before, the one claiming to be an FBI analyst, Obama had also trafficked at least SEVEN Davy Crockett portable nuclear mortar
systems (pictured below) through the consulate, to Syrian rebels—a move that would ultimately result in, yes, an American-made nuclear weapon being used against Russian troops
in Syria, killing almost twenty in the process, and Putin running an "evacuation drill" of
some forty MILLION Russian citizens in October 2016 in response.

Our source would go on to tell us that the remaining six Davy Crocketts would fall into Iranian hands, which was convenient for them, considering all the nuclear restrictions Obama had lifted on that nation and all the money he had systematically funneled their way.

Of course, the cover-up for Benghazi was in from the start, with Hillary and the Obama administration trying to sell the American public the story that a random You-Tube video by a Christian pastor had caused the attack. Comey and the other higher-ups were doing their part, too, including trying to level "excessive force" charges against the operators stationed at Benghazi. This was only revealed after army ranger and Benghazi survivor Kris Paronto tweeted this out, in response to Hillary Clinton and the then FBI director, James Comey:

Kris Paronto
@KrisParonto

By the way, as you're on your way out I want to thank you, James and your @HillaryClinton supporting hacks at the @FBI for trying to pin excessive force use on myself and my team after coming home from Benghazi. You all are the worst scum of human. @Comey
#SorryNotSorry
1:52 PM - Mar 17, 2018

Of course, Paronto's account would be disabled by Twitter censors shortly thereafter.

And this, believe it or not, isn't even the worst of it. Because this ultimately all led to the increased use of private e-mail servers to deliver classified intel to the highest bidder, and because this was on the verge of all being exposed in 2016, Bill Clinton would go on to meet with Loretta Lynch at Phoenix airport inside a private jet on June 27 that same year.

We've already been over the "impropriety" of the situation before, with Bill meeting with someone who was supposedly overseeing an investigation into the misuse of Hillary's e-mail servers being a big conflict of interest that even the most partisan among us can admit. But when questioned about the meeting, Hillary would have this to say:

> Well, I learned about it in the news. And it was a short, chance meeting at an airport tarmac. Both of their planes, as I understand it, were landing on the same tarmac at about the same time, and the attorney general's husband was there, they said hello, they talked about grandkids, which is very much on our minds these days, golf, their mutual friend, former Attorney General Janet Reno, it was purely social. They did not veer off of speaking about those kinds of very common exchanges.

Except it was anything but.

What had actually gone down during that meeting was that Hillary Clinton had instructed Bill to offer Loretta Lynch a promise; a promise of power. In exchange for making the e-mail investigation "go away," Hillary was ready to offer Lynch a seat on the Supreme Court when she finally became president; Ruth Bader Ginsburg's seat, in fact. Ginsburg was getting along in years, had endured numerous health problems by this point, but was completely on board with this plan. Ginsburg had already agreed; she would stay on through the end of Obama's presidency and when Hillary won, she would step down. Hillary would nominate Lynch to the court, and her confirmation wouldn't be a problem. All that was left was for Lynch to agree to this "arrangement."

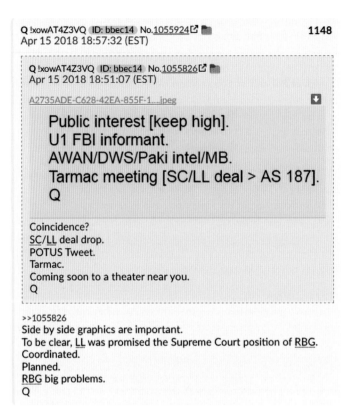

Q !xowAT4Z3VQ ID: bbec14 No.1055924
Apr 15 2018 18:57:32 (EST)

Q !xowAT4Z3VQ ID: bbec14 No.1055826
Apr 15 2018 18:51:07 (EST)

A2735ADE-C628-42EA-855F-1...jpeg

Public interest [keep high].
U1 FBI informant.
AWAN/DWS/Paki intel/MB.
Tarmac meeting [SC/LL deal > AS 187].
Q

Coincidence?
SC/LL deal drop.
POTUS Tweet.
Tarmac.
Coming soon to a theater near you.
Q

>>1055826
Side by side graphics are important.
To be clear, LL was promised the Supreme Court position of RBG.
Coordinated.
Planned.
RBG big problems.
Q

Of course, Hillary never won, and Lynch was never nominated to the Supreme Court bench.

Which is exactly why Ginsburg has clung on for so long in the wake of Trump winning the election, and this, despite not being able to even attend court sessions for several days, as of this writing. Q, in fact, has told us she is severely sick, and expected to die in short order, with doctors scrambling to use all manner of experimental drugs on her, given her age and the severity of her condition.

I would even uncover a scandal of my own at the time regarding Ginsburg and her failing health.[23] Following a lead from Q, I would dissect the official audio files from the Supreme Court's own website, where I would then uncover evidence proving beyond a shadow of a doubt that the audio was being tampered with. I can only speculate on the reason behind such tampering, but the numbers don't lie; the records were being edited for some reason that has yet to be disclosed to the public. I would encourage every reader of this book to listen and decide for themselves. I think your ears and eyes will find the evidence quite compelling.

---

23   https://www.neonrevolt.com/2019/03/26/breaking-scotus-big-secret-rbg-newq-qanon-greatawakening-neonrevolt/

Q !!mG7VJxZNCI ID: 38db44 No.4627556 ☐ 🖼   **2653**
Jan 6 2019 12:32:35 (EST)

[RBG]
Why was she 'selected'?
Who appointed her?
Remember [her] history.
Ref: 230-page book called Sex Bias in the U.S. Code, published in
1977 by the U.S. Commission on Civil Rights.
Highlights:
>Called for the sex-integration of prisons and reformatories so that
conditions of imprisonment, security and housing could be equal.
She explained, "If the grand design of such institutions is to prepare
inmates for return to the community as persons equipped to benefit
from and contribute to civil society, then perpetuation of single-sex
institutions should be rejected." (Page 101)
>Called for the sex-integration of Boy Scouts and Girl Scouts
because they "perpetuate stereotyped sex roles." (Page 145)
>Insisted on sex-integrating "college fraternity and sorority
chapters" and replacing them with "college social societies." (Page
169)
>Cast constitutional doubt on the legality of "Mother's Day and
Father's Day as separate holidays." (Page 146)
>Called for reducing the age of consent for sexual acts to people
who are "less than 12 years old." (Page 102)
>Asserted that laws against "bigamists, persons cohabiting with
more than one woman, and women cohabiting with a bigamist" are
unconstitutional. (Page 195)
>Objected to laws against prostitution because "prostitution, as a
consensual act between adults, is arguably within the zone of
privacy protected by recent constitutional decisions." (Page 97)
>Ginsburg wrote that the Mann Act (which punishes those who
engage in interstate sex traffic of women and girls) is "offensive."
Such acts should be considered "within the zone of privacy." (Page
98)
>Demanded that we "firmly reject draft or combat exemption for
women," stating "women must be subject to the draft if men are."
But, she added, "the need for affirmative action and for transition
measures is particularly strong in the uniformed services." (Page 218)
>An indefatigable censor, Ginsburg listed hundreds of "sexist" words
that must be eliminated from all statutes. Among words she found
offensive were: man, woman, manmade, mankind, husband, wife,
mother, father, sister, brother, son, daughter, serviceman,
longshoreman, postmaster, watchman, seamanship, and "to man" (a
vessel). (Pages 15-16)
>Wanted he, she, him, her, his, and hers to be dropped down the
memory hole. They must be replaced by he/she, her/him, and
hers/his, and federal statutes must use the bad grammar of "plural
constructions to avoid third person singular pronouns." (Page 52-53)
>Condemned the Supreme Court's ruling in Harris v. McRae and
claimed that taxpayer-funded abortions should be a constitutional
right.
http://humanevents.com/2005/08/23/senators-overlooked-radical-
record-of-ruth-bader-ginsburg/ ☐ 🖼
Who are the doctors 'currently' treating [RBG]?
What other political [former/current] sr. political heads are they
affiliated w/?
What 'off-market' drugs are being provided to [RBG] in order to
sustain minimum daily function?
What is the real medical diagnosis of [RBG]?
Who is managing her care?
Who is 'really' managing her care?
The clock is ticking.
PANIC IN DC.
Q

Are you beginning to see how the narrative spirals outwards from a few bad actors, in order to cover over their evil deeds and maintain power and control? We just went from illegal arms dealing overseas, to selling SAPs, to selling uranium, to arranging for jihadis to murder ambassadors, to massive multinational corporations being in on the plan, to the Iran deal, to movie moguls funding human trafficking, to treason on the tarmac, and all the way to the Supreme Court. There's an interconnectedness to this all, where different facts *demand* reconciliation with each other in a way that, when you look closely, the "conventional" narrative being pushed by CIA-affiliated Mockingbirds just doesn't suffice. It's this interconnectedness that Q liked to point out; that simple isolationism wouldn't get us out of this mess. Our enemies were both within and without, and the only way to overcome, quite literally, the forces looking to slaughter billions, would be to wage a completely peaceful coup, leveraging the best and the brightest America had to offer before engaging in what could best be described as simultaneous wars of attrition on multiple fronts, around the globe, securing partnerships, awakening the people, and toppling Cabal forces worldwide by utilizing every means at our disposal—including… the Anons. Q did this so that we could be here to help the average person understand what was happening—and more importantly *why* certain events were happening, when the time finally arrived. As Q liked to say, "THE WORLD IS CONNECTED," and therefore, the only solution would be a worldwide solution.

Q !xowAT4Z3VQ ID: 3b9a43 No.1158695 ☑ 📷   1245
Apr 23 2018 14:31:49 (EST)

>>1158519
Think SA.
Order is important.
SA -> NK.
NK -> Armenia.
Armenia -> Iran
Iran ->
Any other rogue nuclear states?
Define hostage.
Define protection.
Who is protected by rogue nuclear states?
Trust the plan.
THE WORLD IS CONNECTED.
Why are border states like AZ/CA important?
Why is MX vocal against POTUS?
Those who are the loudest.....
WWG1WGA.
The Great Awakening.
Iron Eagle.
Q

Don't forget, guys, we have to take a break from this drop for now. I said in the beginning of this chapter that we'd only be covering half of this drop at the moment, and I'm happy to inform you that you've officially reached the halfway point, which is absolutely tremendous! (Believe me, I know how hard it can be to digest—so it's quite the accomplishment, and I say that sincerely!) You've already seen layer after layer of this massive conspiracy—not conspiracy "theory" mind you, but actual, living, breathing conspiracy—and there's much more to come! But for now, we're going to take a break. We've seen much of Obama's role in all this mess, and we will see more of Hillary's role in the chapters to come, but I think you're beginning to see why I call this possibly QAnon's most important drop ever.

But before we leave this chapter, I want to take one last, brief diversion by checking in on the man who has been a perpetual thorn in Hillary Clinton's side for many years, and who, in return, she has tried to kill multiple times. That's right, we're talking about Julian Assange, because his role in all this at Wikileaks cannot be understated. If it wasn't for his consistent efforts, the world wouldn't know half of what it now knows about the Cabal.

That's not to say that Assange is a good guy, or a White Hat, by any stretch of the imagination. Personally, I tend to view him as an agent of chaos more than anything else. His leaks with Bradley Manning were particularly damaging to our national security (and may have even been an operation staged by the Obama administration in order to weaken our military—but that's pure speculation, right now). I've also heard it on more than one occasion that Assange is secretly backed by Soros and Mossad, with Soros and Assange actually being pals of sorts. To be perfectly honest, I'm not quite sure how true that is right now, or even to what extent it *may* be true, but there are some definite interactions between Q and Assange that I want to take note of, here, because they're very important to understand moving forward.

Now, as of this writing, Assange has been evicted from the Ecuadorian Embassy in the UK where he was living for the last seven years with diplomatic immunity. Rumor has it he survived at least one poisoning attempt while living in the embassy, and while he went a little stir-crazy seeing the same four walls for so long, don't feel too bad for him. After all, he did get regular visits from his on-again, off-again girlfriend, Pamela Anderson—who, I imagine, appreciated his perspective on things, as someone who has seen the inside of the kind of world he seems to expose in a way few people have. Prior to the rumored poisoning attempt, Hillary would also try to blackmail Assange with numerous fake sexual assault charges—just like with Justice Kavanaugh, and even Justice Thomas, decades before. (Remember, the Cabal keeps a supply of Monarch victims at their disposal for this and similar purposes.) Beyond that, Hillary would also speak of possibly killing Assange with a drone at one point, later laughing it off as a "joke."

It's clear enough that both Assange and Hillary hate each other's guts, and both have worked overtime to undermine each other over many years; the most recent salvo in this battle having been fired by Wikileaks during the 2016 election with the release of all the DNC and Podesta e-mails. But regardless of Assange's motivations or the negative impacts of his past leaks, his track record in providing real intel is enough to make Anons sit up and pay close attention whenever Assange speaks.

Which is why, in early 2018, all the Anons sat up and paid attention when Assange tweeted out this image of a chess board:

Julian Assange ⌛
@JulianAssange

8:34 PM - 12 Jan 2018

Now, I am not a big chess fan. I occasionally enjoy a game. I know how to play it. But at the end of the day, I see it more as a memory game, wherein the winner is the person who has memorized the most effective series of permutations to use against their opponent, as opposed to a game where you are forced to actually strategize on the fly. (Of course, that's not *entirely* true...it's just... *mostly* true, at least for the vast majority of human beings on the planet.) The game has been around for so long, and has been played by so many great minds through the years, the innovative plays only really come out in those edge cases, where you get two savants pushing the boundaries of what is known, and devising new sequences never seen before.

One such case is showcased above: Marshall versus Capablanca—and at this stage in the game we're twenty-five moves deep... And Frank James Marshall is about to move the *one* piece here that would, over the next ten moves, win him the game.

He's about to move the bishop to D5.

Capablanca and Marshall would exchange a few pieces in the process of Capablanca trying to figure a way out of this particular problem, but he was never able to escape that bishop. In the end, that bishop worked its way up, diagonally across the board, and granted Marshall...

> Q !UW.yye1fxo No.11 🗗 📑   **523**
> Jan 13 2018 22:36:29 (EST)
>
> CHECKMATE.
> Q

Q would post the above drop one day after Assange's tweet.
Anons didn't miss the connection.

Over the next year, Q would begin hyping D5 not only by repeatedly mentioning it by name, but by posting all sorts of chess allusions like, "Moves and countermoves," and "How about a nice game of chess?" The implication was clear: the stakes were high, and this was a winner-take-all match against the Cabal. But what else could be gleaned from this particular chess scenario?

Anons would spend that time trying to figure out what *exactly* D5 meant. Was it a reference to D5 Trident missiles? Was it the measurement of the most devastating kind of avalanche—a D5 avalanche? Was it a reference to 45—a simple substitution "cipher" wherein D equals the 4th letter of the alphabet, (with the obvious reference being that Trump was the 45th president)?

Anons would even go so far as to notice that certain Qdrops even *looked* a lot like chess pieces if you were to just align them down the center. Take, for instance, Qdrop #229. When aligned down the center, it looks like this:

```
                    RED_RED_
            _FREEDOM-_v05_yes_27-1_z
           _FREEDOM-_v198_yes_27-1_b
           _FREEDOM-_v-811z_yes_27-1_c
           _FREEDOM-_vZj9_yes_27-1_y
       _FREEDOM-_v^CAS0R-T_yes_27-1_87x
       _FREEDOM-_v&CAS0R-T2_yes_27-1_t
        _FREEDOM-_vEXh29B_yes_27-1_ch
             _FREEDOM-_v_stand
             _FREEDOM-_v_stand
             _FREEDOM-_v_stand
             _FREEDOM-_v_stand
          _FREEDOM-_v_stand_CAN
            _FREEDOM-_v1_stand
            _FREEDOM-_v1_stand
            _FREEDOM-_v1_stand
            _FREEDOM-_v2_stand
            _FREEDOM-_v3_stand
         _FREEDOM-_v4_mod_D092x
         _FREEDOM-_v4_mod_CAS80^
            _FREEDOM-_vv1_stand
            _FREEDOM-_vv2_stand
        _FREEDOM-_vSHAz1EVCB_yes_27-1
    _FREEDOM-_vSA_US_yes_DC08vC_EX_y_AW_Conf-go
    _FREEDOM-_vSA_US_yes_DC09vC_EX_y_AW_Conf-go
    _FREEDOM-_vSA_US_yes_DC10vC_EX_y_AW_Conf-go
    _FREEDOM-_vSA_US_yes_DC11vC_EX_y_AW_Conf-go
    _FREEDOM-_vSA_US_yes_DC12vc_EX_y_AW_Conf-go
    _FREEDOM-_vSA_US_yes_DC13vC_EX_y_AW_Conf-go
   _FREEDOM-_vSA_US_stand_DC14vC_EX_y_AW_Conf/stand
    _FREEDOM-_vSA_US_yes_DC15vC_EX_y_AW_Conf-go
    _FREEDOM-_vSA_US_yes_DC16vC_EX_y_AW_Conf-go
    _FREEDOM-_vSA_US_yes_DC17vc_EX_y_AW_Conf-go
    _FREEDOM-_vSA_US_yes_DC18vC_EX_y_AW_Conf-go
    _FREEDOM-_vSA_US_yes_DC19vC_EX_y_AW_Conf-go
    _FREEDOM-_vSA_US_yes_DC20vC_EX_y_AW_Conf-go
    _FREEDOM-_vSA_US_yes_DC21vC_EX_y_AW_Conf-go
    _FREEDOM-_vSA_US_yes_DC22vc_EX_y_AW_Conf-go
    _FREEDOM-_vSA_US_yes_DC23vC_EX_y_AW_Conf-go
    _FREEDOM-_vSA_US_yes_DC24vC_EX_y_AW_Conf-go
    _FREEDOM-_vSA_US_yes_DC25vC_EX_y_AW_Conf-go
   _FREEDOM-_vSA_US_stand_DC26vC_EX_y_AW_Conf/stand
 _FREEDOM-_vSA_US_yes_DC27vc_EX_y_AW_Conf/term/zJ&bY028739478-g
     _FREEDOM-_vGER_US_yes_000BVx_LO_yes_[... + 1]_Conf_y
   _Conf_4_3_good_EXT-TVB7xxj_ALL_FREEDOM_#[1-43]_EX_27-1
                        Q
```

An odd coincidence? Or the result of years of military planning and execution? It was hard to say, to be honest, but in the end… it would turn out that D5 was the best possible thing of all.

D5 was bait…

CHAPTER 6

"Canis Lupus"

—December 1, 2018 From Qdrop #2522

Q !!mG7VJxZNCl ID: b8622e No.4130704 ⬈ 🏴

2540

Dec 3 2018 13:16:01 (EST)

https://docs.house.gov/Committee/Calendar
/ByWeek.aspx?WeekOf=12022018_12082018 ⬈ 🏴
Postponed.
Well-played DS.
Please allow us to counter.
Q

Q !!mG7VJxZNCl **ID: 0836cc** No.4280231 ☑ 🖼   **2608**
Dec 12 2018 18:43:33 (EST)

> Anonymous **ID: 55302e** No.4280212 ☑ 🖼
> Dec 12 2018 18:43:11 (EST)
>
> >>4280189
> What were in the envelopes ???

>>4280212
Our promise to 'counter'.
Q

Now it was only a matter of time.

Everyone knew it.

His wife, Barbara, had passed earlier in the year, and to be quite frank, he wasn't looking very good himself, these days.

As someone who was very young during his tenure in office, I always thought he had seemed "old," and yet somehow… in the intervening years… he had gone from merely old, to downright decrepit.

And then it finally came to pass, as it will for all of us, one day.

A funeral was held for former president George H.W. Bush on December 5th, 2018, in the National Cathedral, in the nation's capital.

December 5.

D5.

That cryptic event that QAnon had been heralding for so long, telling Anons how "Nothing [could] stop what is coming," and that, "The World was about to change," was finally upon us …

The lead up to all of this was that John Huber, that one-man investigatory apocalypse, was slated to *finally* unveil his findings before Congress that day. The man had been granted the power by the then attorney general Jeff Sessions to single-handedly impanel a Grand Jury and bring charges against… pretty much whomever he deemed fit. Huber had been working in tandem with Inspector General Michael Horowitz, and with a crack team of four hundred and seventy investigators for the better part of a year now, tracking down all kinds of Cabal corruption.

Better still, he was a former Obama appointee, so the charges of partisanship wouldn't be effective against him. If he was good enough for Obama, why not for Trump? If he could be trusted by Obama, why not Trump? Best of all, he was from Utah, which meant any trials he set up would be carried out in Utah, far, far away from corrupt Washington, DC, judges.

And the kicker?

Utah still had execution by firing squad on the books.

Shortly before this, John Huber's boss, Attorney General Sessions, had actually just tendered his resignation to President Trump, which Trump had accepted. Though the two had "fought" a lot on Twitter, with Trump even saying at one point, "I don't have an Attorney General," in truth, this was all an act. See, Sessions had been forced to recuse himself from directly overseeing the Russian collusion investigation, and instead delegated the responsibilities to Deputy Attorney General Rod Rosenstein (who, you'll recall, appointed Mueller to the Special Counsel). But now, Sessions was gone, and so too, his "hands off" approach. In truth, the move had been planned well in advance, and now, someone else was stepping in… someone whose approach was decisively hands-on, and who would *not* be recusing himself from overseeing the Trump-Russia investigation, since there was no way he could be accused of having a conflict of interest. That would be Acting Attorney General Matthew Whitaker. This would soon be followed by the official appointment of Bill Barr, the "Stealth Bomber," in Q-parlance.

And now, on top of it all, Q was saying Huber was ready to carpet bomb congress with all the evidence he and his team had dug up regarding the activities of the Cabal across all areas of government. In essence, his testimony was an immediate death sentence for anyone he spoke out against. Him speaking would mean the likes of Obama, Hillary, their staff, their spouses, and more would be strung up in shackles overnight.

And the Cabal knew this, too.

So they sacrificed one of their own to try and contain it.

Bush Sr.'s death was perhaps not as "natural" as it was being made to seem.

You can imagine my delight when Q confirmed that an absolute pillar of the Qcommunity (and a dedicated reader of my site) figured it out first. Note the date on the tweets:

Q would expand several days after Joe had figured it out, enlightening the rest of the community, who was largely still puzzled as to how the connection was made:

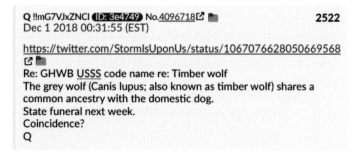

George Bush Sr.'s Secret Service code name had been "Timber Wolf," a.k.a. "Canis Lupus," and perhaps I should back up here, because the significance of these code names cannot be understated. They are often chosen very deliberately, and often communicate something about that person that, really, only the Cabal truly understands. Take, for instance, this older Qdrop, where Q talks about Obama's code name:

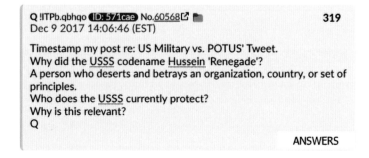

So if Bush Sr. was "Timber Wolf," the question then becomes… who was the "Grey Wolf" Q had mentioned?

Anons were puzzled once again, because you go through the list of known Secret Service code names, and there is just no president with that name. It doesn't belong to *any* of them.

We would soon find out, however, that was because it didn't belong to any former president. **It belonged to Adolf Hitler.**

The oft-repeated story in "conspiracy" circles is that George Bush Sr. is, in actuality, not a Bush at all. The story goes that he's actually George Scherff, son of George Scherff Sr., a Nazi spy living in America working, of all things, as Tesla's accountant. Yes, *the* Nikola Tesla; the man himself who has, somewhat ironically, become a proverbial lightning rod for all things conspiratorial himself! The story goes that Scherff spied on everything Tesla did, stole tech for the Nazis before Tesla died, and that because George Jr. was always poking around Tesla's inventions, Tesla dubbed him "Curious George," (which is where the fictional monkey *obviously* comes from)! Though it's not clear when it happened, advocates of this story will go on to say that Scherff Jr. (Bush Sr.) would go on to be "adopted" by the Bushes and passed off as their own, biological son for the rest of his life.

Now, I don't buy any of that story at all; not even the part about the monkey. The primary source for it comes from a supposed "deathbed" confession of a former Nazi who had escaped to Florida, and as he's about to die, he produces this box, complete with photos of Scherff Jr. hobnobbing with Nazi elites back in Germany before the war. I've seen the photo that's made its way online, and frankly, it's not convincing. I include this story as an amusing aside, though I fully admit I'm willing to listen to anyone willing to produce more substantial evidence on this front—evidence which, as far as I can tell, does not exist right now.

Frankly, I find the real story here to be much more intriguing, and it begins in the 1930s with a man named Fritz Thyssen. Thyssen was a German industrialist born in 1873, the son of August Thyssen, founder of Thyssen and Co. As one of the richest men in the world at the time, August Thyssen was sometimes referred to as the "Rockefeller of the Ruhr," where his mining company was situated. At the outbreak of World War I, the demand for steel and iron skyrocketed, establishing the Thyssen fortune for years to come, while his company pumped out one million tons of iron and steel per year.

Years passed after the war, and Deutschland fell into decay and degeneracy during the Weimar Republic years, becoming, among other things, the transvestite capital of the world and the pedophilic prostitution capital of the world. As the first ever income tax in the world was passed, and the gold standard was abandoned, the nation descended into runaway hyperinflation, with images of people famously trying to buy bread by loading up multiple wheelbarrows full of marks, and using them as fuel for fires, their money had become so worthless.

Though not affected by the depression in the same way as his countrymen, Fritz was still very distressed at the state of his nation. Marxist ideology was degrading the national character—especially in regards to the pornographic filth the German cinema had been churning out—and poverty and hunger had gotten so bad that it was turning children, poor children, into the playthings of predatory international businessmen, to be used and abused and thrown away for pennies. In Berlin (and I'm sorry to get graphic here, but you need to understand the severity of the situation) life had so deteriorated that by 1923, the going rate for a blowjob was around thirty cents.

Due to his vast industrial holdings, Fritz Thyssen was well insulated from such problems, but he was not blind to them. In fact, he had, years earlier, in a very savvy business move, consolidated his whole family's holdings into a trust named *Vereintige Stahlwerke AG,* or United Steelworks, in English. But he was still pained by what he saw going on around him, in his homeland. His country had yielded to the Bolshevik teachings of the subversive "Academics" of the Frankfurt School, and embraced, as György Lukács would call it, "a culture of pessimism, and a world abandoned by God."

In fact, this had been one of the founding ambitions of the Frankfurt School since its founding by the Marxist Felix Weil in 1923. The Frankfurt Institute for Social Research quickly became a hub for all manner of Marxist and "revolutionary" thought, where no Western tradition was beyond vivisection. The Frankfurt School was so effective in its techniques, it quickly led to the creation of a subversive class of "academics" obsessed with crafting all sorts of divisive narratives in the name of equality. These were the "Critical Theorists," and as their teachings, their ideology rose to prominence, the welfare of the nation declined dramatically; so effective were their demoralizing efforts. At the heart of it all was this desire to delegitimize all hierarchies by labeling the most successful, the most dominant, the healthiest, the wealthiest, the ones who built the most, the ones with the most skill, influence, or ability, as "abusers" or "thieves" of one form or another. Initially only applied to capitalism, the theory would soon be applied by its devotees to all areas of Western Civilization, from home life, to religion, to even the biological sexes themselves. Thus, was traditional Western morality "unshackled" in the Weimar Republic, and set on a course towards destruction.

The result of this effort was that German cinemas were now jam-packed with obscenity, men and women were engaging in rampant transsexual prostitution, and even children and the home were not safe from this ideological scourge. It was utter destitution. Another academic from the Frankfurt School, a Hungarian Marxist by the name of Willi Munzenberg, would go on to describe the ultimate goals of the Critical Theorists' devastating movement:

> We must organize the intellectuals and use them to make Western Civilization stink! Only then, after they have corrupted all its values and made life impossible, can we impose the dictatorship of the proletariat.

It should be noted here that the teachings of the Frankfurt School still reign supreme in much of American academia today, with tenured professors, most of whom have no actual experience ever laboring outside of academia for a living, pretending they're allies of "the working class," helping to usher in some kind of utopia by indoctrinating the next generation with "social justice" values. In actuality, they're helping establish hell on earth via their utopian delusions.

Fritz Thyssen saw all these problems and simply couldn't ignore them any longer. These problems were deeply entrenched now, and weren't going to just go away. He wanted to *do* something about it, and was one of the rare individuals who was in such a position, by virtue of his wealth, where he actually *could* do something about it. Wooed by Hitler's anti-Marxist rhetoric, Thyssen would end up contributing three million marks to Hitler's election campaign, and would subsequently be appointed a member of the German economic counsel.

Thyssen was a valuable and strategic friend to have for Hitler, indeed. The heir to the fortune of the "Rockefeller of Ruhr" now controlled some seventy-five percent of Germany's ore reserves, and had many international ties, including at Brown Brothers Harriman, in the United States... where one Prescott Bush just so happened to work. Prescott Bush was also a director at the Union Banking Corporation, which would continue to represent Thyssen's interests in the US.

And so, through a network of shell companies (primarily in steel-related industries), Prescott Bush helped Thyssen move assets around, and as the Nazis grew in power, before a shot had ever been fired during World War II, Prescott Bush was helping coordinate shipments of gold, fuel, US Treasury Bonds, and other resources to the Nazi party, allowing Hitler to consolidate his power and prepare for war.

At the same time, Prescott Bush would be scheming back at home with a number of other wealthy businessmen to overthrow the US government and install a military dictator so that they could create a fascist government here, at home in the US. The man they had in mind for this task was USMC Major Gen. Smedley Butler. A lifelong marine, Butler had seen combat in arenas all over the globe—including at the Spanish-American War, the Philippine-American War, the Boxer Rebellion in China, the Banana Wars, and in France during World War I. So tough was Butler that he earned the name "Old Eye Gimlet" during his 1903 deployment to Honduras, where he was given that nickname because of his withering gaze in battle. He would go on to earn the Medal of Honor (twice), the Marine Corp Brevet medal, and thirteen other medals during his lifetime. Here was a man who so embodied the spirit of the marine corp, that when it came time to name the marine's bulldog mascot, they named it after Smedley (at least until Chesty Puller came along).

So imagine everyone's shock when this decorated marine marched into Congress one day and started to explain that this group of Wall Street bankers were trying to overthrow President Roosevelt and install Smedley as de facto military dictator.

Smedley, in 1934, would later testify before the House Committee on Un-American Activities that he had been approached by the underlings of the Morgan Bank (and other Wall Street execs) to lead a Veterans organization in order to build a groundswell of support in the military ranks, by calling for such things as a return to the gold standard. One Gerald C. MacGuire promised Butler the command of five hundred thousand men, with which he could march on Washington, DC. All implicated by Butler's testimony would deny any involvement in the scheme, and the *New York Times* would go on to call the "Wall Street Putsch" a "gigantic hoax."

Indeed, what would come to be remembered as the "Business Plot" would soon be memory-holed by the media. Nothing ever came of Smedley Butler's testimony. There were no investigations, no indictments, simply nothing but the word of a dedicated, lifelong patriot versus a shadowy Cabal who did little more than laugh off Butler's words. This was despite the House Committee saying, about Butler's testimony:

> In the last few weeks of the committee's official life it received evidence showing that certain persons had made an attempt to establish a fascist organization in this country... There is no question that these attempts were discussed, were planned, and might have been placed in execution when and if the financial backers deemed it expedient.

Later, in a speech, Smedley Butler would say:

> I spent thirty-three years and four months in active military service as a member of this country's most agile military force, the Marine Corps. I served in all commissioned ranks from Second Lieutenant to Major-General. And during that period, I spent most of my time being a high class muscle-man for Big Business, for Wall Street and for the Bankers. In short, I was a racketeer, a gangster for capitalism.

And in his later book, *War is a Racket*, Butler, a man who had seen perpetual combat for over three decades, would write:

> WAR is a racket. It always has been.
>
> It is possibly the oldest, easily the most profitable, surely the most vicious. It is the only one international in scope. It is the only one in which the profits are reckoned in dollars and the losses in lives.
>
> A racket is best described, I believe, as something that is not what it seems to the majority of the people. Only a small "inside" group knows what it is about. It is conducted for the benefit of the very few, at the expense of the very many. Out of war a few people make huge fortunes.
>
> In the World War a mere handful garnered the profits of the conflict. At least 21,000 new millionaires and billionaires were made in the United States during the World War. That many admitted their huge blood gains in their income tax returns. How many other war millionaires falsified their tax returns no one knows.
>
> How many of these war millionaires shouldered a rifle? How many of them dug a trench? How many of them knew what it meant to go hungry in a rat-infested dug-out? How many of them spent sleepless, frightened nights, ducking shells and shrapnel and machine gun bullets? How many of them parried a bayonet thrust of an enemy? How many of them were wounded or killed in battle?
>
> Out of war nations acquire additional territory, if they are victorious. They just take it. This newly acquired territory promptly is exploited by the few— the selfsame few who wrung dollars out of blood in the war. The general public shoulders the bill.
>
> This bill renders a horrible accounting. Newly placed gravestones. Mangled bodies. Shattered minds. Broken hearts and homes. Economic instability. Depression and all its attendant miseries. Back-breaking taxation for generations and generations.
>
> For a great many years, as a soldier, I had a suspicion that war was a racket; not until I retired to civil life did I fully realize it. Now that I see the international war clouds gathering, as they are today, I must face it and speak out.

And despite the compelling testimony of this decorated marine, the racket continued on. Nazi Germany would continue its buildup with the help of Prescott Bush and Fritz Thyssen. But at least Thyssen had the sense to resign when he began to sense the true nature of the Nazi regime. He had previously disagreed with the mob violence employed by the SA, and the increasingly hostile attitude towards the church, but for Thyssen, Krystalnacht was the straw that broke the proverbial camel's back. Thyssen would denounce Hitler, renounce his Nazi party membership… and Hitler would respond by seizing some eighty-eight million dollars from Thyssen's fortune.

Thyssen would attempt to flee to Switzerland but would get arrested in France and thrown into a concentration camp shortly thereafter. He would survive, however, and end up getting freed by the allies in 1945. He would be tried soon thereafter for his participation in the Nazi party, and while he was acquitted on all charges, he would still have to pay five hundred thousand Deutschmarks for the suffering his actions had led to. In 1950, he and his wife would leave Germany to live in Buenos Aires, where he would remain for the rest of his days, before finally passing away on February 8, 1951.

Of course… that's if you believe that side of the story.

The alternative case one could make is that Thyssen knew full well what he was supporting, and that the asset seizure he endured was planned from the get-go. In fact, QAnon has already implied that Hitler himself had done such already. While there's little doubt that international banking families are a scourge upon the world, Hitler is somewhat "famous" in this regard as being the only person in history to have ever arrested a Rothschild; a fact his fans like to laud.

The location where Thyssen ended, in particular, points to the validity of this interpretation. A great number of Nazi party members, over forty-five thousand, fled to Argentina after the war. There were enough of them there to even create entirely German towns, such as Bariloche at the foothills of the Andes, complete with a distinctly Bavarian, distinctly alpine style of architecture in all the buildings.

So was Thyssen complicit in his "detainment?" Was he just really good at crafting a cover story? It's hard to tell, and I wouldn't blame anyone for doubting the official narrative. I certainly do. It's easy to see why a former top Nazi party member would leave a war-torn country, to be close to other former top Nazi party members overseas, in their own little "private" havens.

However… what many may not realize in all this is that Hitler was a secret bloodline Rothschild himself, as his father, Alois Hitler, was the product of an affair between Maria Anna Schicklgruber and Baron Rothschild. Schicklgruber had been employed in the home of Baron Rothschild as a servant, you see, and Alois Schicklgruber, the son of Maria, would eventually change his last name to Hitler in 1876. The contention that Hitler is actually a secret Rothschild had been made for a long time in Austria, with advocates contending that this is why Hitler had members of the Nazi party assassinate Chancellor Dollfuss of Austria in 1934, in an effort to hide his birth records. Furthermore, this idea that Hitler was really a member of the Rothschild bloodline would be repeated in a 1944 OSS intelligence report named *A Psychological Analysis of Adolf Hitler: His Life and Legend.*

But the secret affairs in the Rothschild-Hitler line don't end there. As Q would tell us, this hidden history carries well on into our modern times. A bloodline Hitler still exist, and her identity may just surprise you:

Q !UW.yye1fxo ID: b39b17 No.616618
Mar 10 2018 16:35:34 (EST)   **928**

Angela Dorothea Kasner.
Daughter of a Pastor?
Name of FATHER?
History of FATHER?
Hitler youth (member).
Haircut today vs THEN (A).
Symbolic.
US Intelligence post war controlled who?
The 'Mission'
Who is Angela Hitler?
Relationship to Adolf?
How were children named in Germany during this period?
First or middle.
Family tree.
Anna.
Maria.
Alois.
Examples.
Risk of 'conspiracy' label the deeper we go.
Truth will shock the WORLD.
Q

Yes, you understand correctly: Angela Merkel, chancellor of Germany, is actually the bloodline Hitler of which Q speaks (thus, making her a bloodline Rothschild as well). For it turns out that Alois Hitler had two wives during his lifetime, Franziska and Klara. The relationship with Franziska would produce one Angela Hitler in 1883, and the relationship with Klara would produce Adolf, in 1889. Thus, Adolf and Angela were step-siblings, born six years apart.

Angela Hitler would go on to marry Leo Raubel, and together they would have three children, one of whom they would name Angela "Geli" Raubel in 1908. Geli would go on to live with Adolf, her step-uncle, working as a servant for him in 1925. Hitler would develop something of an obsession with her. The relationship was often speculated to be sexual in nature, but everything would come to a screeching halt one day in 1931 when Geli was found dead, locked in her room with Hitler's Walther pistol at her side and a bullet hole in her chest. The official cause of death was ruled a suicide, saying she was grieved over Hitler seeing Eva Braun, though her nose was broken and there were bruises over her body.

The child produced as the result of this secret relationship was smuggled away from Germany sometime between 1925 and 1931, but would return to Hamburg in the 40s where she would meet a former Hitler Youth member (and prisoner of war) studying to be an evangelical pastor named Horst Kasner. Herlind Jentzsch, this woman born in 1928, claimed to be the daughter of a Danzig politician, but nothing could be further from the truth. Here was the illegitimate daughter of Adolf Hitler; the same one who had been smuggled out so many years ago, now returning to Germany and dating a young man who had been a member of the Hitler Youth. The pair would get married and together they would have three children: Marcus, Irene, and finally Angela in 1954—naming the child after her grandmother and great-grandmother. (Angela would drop her maiden name of Kasner when she would marry Ulrich Merkel in 1977, though the two would end up divorcing in 1982. Perhaps somewhat oddly, she would keep his last name, despite later remarrying.) So much fuss would be made about Angela's true bloodline in Germany at one point, that Angela would be forced to publish an "official" family history in her 2013 biography. Angela Merkel—a bloodline Hitler and a bloodline Rothschild—would rise to occupy the same office as her grandfather Adolf, as the chancellor of Germany.

Now, I imagine many reading this book will already know much about the Rothschilds, but for those who don't know who the Rothschilds are, essentially, they're your prototypical "Illuminati" family. They're originally a Jewish banking bloodline that goes way back in European history, and they have exerted great control over Europe and the Roman Catholic Church for centuries by leveraging their vast wealth and power, literally trillions in assets and companies in order to keep nation-states entrapped in perpetual debt to their dynasty, their banking clan. They've even managed to accomplish this here in the United States with the creation of the Federal Reserve Bank (which is a privately owned bank and not a governmental agency, as much as its name may sound like some kind of official institution). The point is, their influence spans the globe, and they're largely hidden, operating from the shadows, because this gives them power. This is how they have been working for centuries, now. And given that Hitler was an illegitimate bloodline Rothschild himself, you may be surprised to learn that Q would label him little more than puppet.

Q !ITPb.qbhqo ID: 99LpGawB No.149122955 ☐ ▮   **142**
Nov 12 2017 12:16:24 (EST)

How did Soros replace family 'y'?
Who is family 'y'?
Trace the bloodlines of these (3) families.
What happened during WWII?
Was Hitler a puppet?
Who was his handler?
What was the purpose?
What was the real purpose of the war?
What age was GS?
What is the Soros family history?
What has occurred since the fall of N Germany?
Who is A. Merkel?
What is A. Merkel's family history?
Follow the bloodline.
Who died on the Titanic?
What year did the Titanic sink?
Why is this relevant?
What 'exactly' happened to the Titanic?
What 'class of people' were guaranteed a lifeboat?
Why did select 'individuals' not make it into the lifeboats?
Why is this relevant?
How do we know who was on the lifeboats (D or A)?
How were names and bodies recorded back then?
When were tickets purchased for her maiden voyage?
Who was 'specifically' invited?
Less than 10.
What is the FED?
What does the FED control?
Who controls the FED?
Who approved the formation of the FED?
Why did H-wood glorify Titanic as a tragic love story?
Who lived in the movie (what man)?
Why is this relevant?
Opposite is true.
What is brainwashing?
What is a PSYOP?
What happened to the Hindenburg?
What really happened to the Hindenburg?
Who died during the 'accident'?
Why is this relevant?
What are sheep?
Who controls the narrative?
The truth would put 99% of people in the hospital.
It must be controlled.
Snow White.
Iron Eagle.
Jason Bourne (CIA/Dream).
Q

ANSWERS

Here some of my readers may be struggling to understand why Hitler would engage in the Holocaust if he himself were part Jewish. Understand, this is a very touchy subject, because the Holocaust has been enshrined in Western culture as the ultimate example of human suffering; a secular version of the Passion play if you will. So important has this secular suffering become that it's now on par, or perhaps even exceeds Christ's suffering in the minds of many. To even approach the subject from an unconventional angle is often tantamount to religious heresy, or sacrilege in the minds of many.

But, in fact, if one does serious study of the Holocaust, you find that most moderns have their perceptions heavily shaped by narratives peddled by Hollywood pedophiles looking to establish themselves as a member of the most aggrieved and protected victim class—mostly to cover for their own crimes. Don't face the fact that Spielberg knows exactly what happened to the adolescent Heather O'Rourke, who died at age thirteen when her body succumbed to a heart attack as a result of sepsis, due to a ruptured colon. Don't look at Judith Barsi, whose own mother knew the kind of abuse she was suffering, causing the father to murder them both before taking his own life. Don't look at how David Geffen protects Harvey Weinstein from afar. No, Spielberg made a poignant black and white film where mustache-twirling Nazi sadists killed a little girl in a red coat, so give him an Oscar and ignore the bodies of the little kids he's left in his wake... right?

Stanley Kubrick once called *Schindler's List* a terrible Holocaust film, because it turned the Holocaust into entertainment, manipulating the audience as though they were on an emotional roller coaster. So let's dispense with the Hollywood fiction designed to deliver voyeuristic thrills and chills, and try to stick with just the facts. It's well established that Hitler's plan, termed *The Final Solution*, was not originally to exterminate all the Jews in Germany, but was, in fact, trying to expel Jews (primarily to Palestine) in order to establish the new, secular nation of Israel where the historical nation of Israel had resided. And please, understand, I'm not denying the Holocaust here or the supreme tragedy of it. Jews most definitely bore the brunt of the civilian persecution experienced under the Nazi regime, alongside many others. But the mass killings didn't really start happening until 1941. From 1933 until the start of the war, yes, there were a number of policies enacted that basically told Jews to move elsewhere or face extreme persecution, and yes, there were a number of brutal killings—but the systematic extermination hadn't yet begun in the way one often thinks of such events until after 1941. And yes, once the killing started it was truly terrible—though, it should be noted, **far** from the worst genocide in human history. If the six million who died during the Holocaust somehow represent the pinnacle of human suffering (for which many are still paying reparations), what are we then to make of the fifty million who died during the Holodomor? What of the ***seventy-seven million*** killed during Mao Zedong's democide? Now, that's not to minimize the horrors of the Holocaust, but to put it into perspective. And as bad as things were, they could have been made ***much*** worse, and if that's the case... one has to ask ***why*** they weren't made much worse.

Between the original expulsion policies of the Nazi party, and the Holocaust itself, this meant there were a *lot* of displaced Jews after the war with nowhere to go, and European nations didn't really want to take them in, either. Neither did America or Russia for that matter. But they had to go somewhere, so what was the world to do? The Biltmore Conference, a Zionist group, had an idea. In 1944, they proposed the "One Million Plan"—a plan to relocate one million of the displaced Jews in Europe to Palestine over a period of eighteen months. In 1948, the UN would propose a sort of prototype two-state solution for all the displaced Jews, where they renamed the annexed portions of Palestine to Israel and told these displaced populations to return there and make it their home. The transition was anything but peaceful. Palestine, still under British rule, broke out in civil war between Arab and Jewish factions, as Arabs saw their lands usurped by foreign, international powers. The Jewish factions would win this civil war by 1949, displace some

700,000 Arab Palestinians, extending their territory in the process (and laying ground-work for the conflicts we often hear about today, in regions such as the Gaza Strip and the West Bank). Following the civil war, Israel would be admitted to the UN as a member state in 1949, following the 1949 armistice. Thus, out of the fire of all these conflicts the modern nation of Israel forged into being.

Now, that's a very fine line to walk here, so don't misconstrue my words, or otherwise take them out of context. At the same time, it's very important you understand this history because of who precisely was involved. It's why, years later in an interview with the *Times of Israel*, Lord Jacob Rothschild would say that it was his cousin,[24] Dorothy de Rothschild, who helped create Israel. How did this happen? Dorothy would ultimately connect Chaim Weizmann, president of the World Zionist Organization, with the upper echelons of British society leading to Lord Balfour and the creation of the Balfour declaration—drafted by Lord Rothschild and Weizmann—in 1917, in which the British government declared its support for the creation of a nation-state for the Jewish people. Weizmann would later go on to become the first president of Israel in 1949. But it's one thing to declare support for the creation of a new nation, and another thing entirely to convince a mass of people to move into a contested area and call it "home." If the Allies were offering a carrot, the Axis was the stick, and you had Rothschilds controlling both over the course of decades. And the rest, as they say, is history.

In the previous chapter, we talked about the some sixteen hundred top Nazis who were brought to America after the war. What had previously been a wartime intelligence agency, the OSS, would now, with the help of these leftover, imported Nazis, morph into the modern CIA. They would, as early as the 1950s, begin to explore such radical subjects as "mind control" with the MKUltra project, among other topics that still, to this day, sound like science fiction.

Following World War II, Prescott Bush would make the leap from business into poli-tics, where he would go on to represent the state of Connecticut in the Senate from 1952 un-til 1963. Having emerged unscathed after being implicated in the "Business Plot," his son, George Bush, would enroll in Yale following the war, where, just like his father before him, he would join the secret society known as the "Skull and Bones;" a secret society that bears a number of similarities to Hilter's occult "Thule Society." (Other groups, such as Harvard's "Scroll and Key" exist, and, according to Bill Cooper, both are essentially recruiting tools for the "Brotherhood of Death," an older, more sinister secret society).

Membership in the Skull and Bones essentially signifies bloodline "greatness," where you get to test your mettle and prove if you're really made of the stuff needed to see if you're destined to "rule" in some capacity, whether it be in business, government, or in some other manner. As we just learned, Prescott Bush was a member, and famously stole Geronimo's skull, some of Geronimo's bones, and some relics from Geronimo's grave in 1918 before delivering them to "The Tomb," which is the name of the group's headquarters at Yale. (And yes, it does look like a giant tomb.) Prescott performed this theft as an act of worship to a goddess the Skull and Bones itself is dedicated to; a goddess they call Eulogia. To be sure, this is not the name of an ancient goddess, despite having an ancient Greek name, but it's worth noting here that in fact, the Skull and Bones club believes their entire Tomb itself is dedicated to Eulogia, where they believe she now dwells, and where they can invoke her presence and favor through certain rituals.

---

24   http://jewishnews.timesofisrael.com/rothschild/

The most famous, or well-known aspect of the Skull and Bones is their death and re-birth ritual, wherein the younger acolytes, before being fully inducted into the brotherhood as Bonesmen, must lie naked in a coffin with a ribbon tied around their penis, and confess their sexual history before all the other members. Prescott Bush participated in this ritual, as did George H.W. Bush, George W. Bush, and many other heads of state, such as John Kerry (who was also a member). An occultic interpretation of this ritual is that, in essence, it's an inversion of baptism, wherein immersion in the waters signifies new life in Christ, immersion in the coffin signifies a pledge to Lucifer.

And actually, in 2009, the descendants of Geronimo would sue Yale to try and reclaim his stolen remains. Skull and Bones would go on to win, yes, win the lawsuit, because US district judge Richard Roberts would claim that the Native American Graves Protection and Repatriation Act only applied to grave robberies that took place *after* 1990, and the US hadn't waived its sovereign immunity in the case.

Yeah, go figure that one out.

That same judge would later resign in 2016, when Terry Mitchell claimed that back in 1981, while serving as a witness in a federal trial, Roberts had repeatedly raped her. Roberts was serving as federal prosecutor and was twenty-seven years old at the time. Mitchell was sixteen. In the end, he did not deny that an "intimate relationship" had taken place, but this had all happened in Salt Lake City, Utah, where the age of consent is sixteen. In other words, yeah, they slept together, but legally, it wasn't considered rape, like Mitchell claimed. Still, the case cast such a huge shadow over Roberts' record that he had to resign. Roberts had been appointed to the federal bench in Washington, DC, by President Bill Clinton in 1998, and one has to wonder what affiliation, if any, Roberts had to the Bonesmen in all this.

Upon graduating and getting married to Barbara, George Bush Sr. would begin work-ing as an oil field equipment salesman for Dresser Industries, which was itself, a subsidiary of Brown Brothers Harriman, where dear old dad had been on the board for over two de-cades. Now, you may not be familiar with the name Dresser Industries, and that's because in 1998 it merged with its biggest competitor—Halliburton—the same company that George W. Bush's vice president Dick Cheney would come to oversee as CEO starting in 1995, before retiring in 2000 to join Bush's presidential campaign. Prior to this, in 1991 as de-fense secretary under Bush Sr., Cheney contracted Halliburton subsidiary Brown and Root (which would later become the independent KBR) to study the use of military contractors in combat zones. And I don't think I need to explain to you here all the manifold activities of Halliburton/KBR throughout the Middle East during Gulf War I and II.

Following his employment at Dresser, Bush Sr. would go on to join the still relatively new CIA in the 60s, leveraging his oil equipment sales position as cover for international es-pionage. We'll detail his history with the Agency in a bit, but perhaps the most notable thing about his time there wasn't so much where he was, but where he wasn't. Bush's whereabouts during the Kennedy assassination would be repeatedly called into question over the years, with many in "conspiracy" circles repeating the adage that everyone knew exactly where they were the day Kennedy was assassinated. Everyone except George Bush.

The Kennedy assassination was really a key turning point in the history of the nation, not just because it was a terrible loss, but because of the implications of what it meant for the Deep State, or what would be called in Kennedy's day, the "Shadow Government." Much like Lincoln before him, Kennedy was a bloodline member who had, essentially, rebelled against the will of the bloodline, the will of the Cabal, and who was attempting to uproot them from deep within the government.

In a speech he gave in 1961, Kennedy would say:

> The very word "secrecy" is repugnant in a free and open society; and we are as a people inherently *and* historically opposed to secret societies, to secret oaths, and to secret proceedings. We decided long ago that the dangers of excessive and unwarranted concealment of pertinent facts far outweighed the dangers which are cited to justify it.
>
> Even today, there is little value in opposing the threat of a closed society by imitating its arbitrary restrictions.
>
> Even today, there is little value in insuring the survival of our nation if our traditions do not survive with it.
>
> …
>
> In time of war, the government and the press have customarily joined in an effort based largely on self-discipline, to prevent unauthorized disclosures to the enemy. In times of "clear and present danger", the courts have held that even the privileged rights of the First Amendment must yield to the public's need for national security.
>
> Today no war has been declared—and however fierce the struggle may be, it may never be declared in the traditional fashion. Our way of life is under attack. Those who make themselves our enemy are advancing around the globe. The survival of our friends is in danger. And yet no war has been declared, no borders have been crossed by marching troops, no missiles have been fired.
>
> If the press is awaiting a declaration of war before it imposes the self-discipline of combat conditions, then I can only say that no war ever posed a greater threat to our security. If you are awaiting a finding of "clear and present danger," then I can only say that the danger has never been more clear, and its presence has never been more imminent.
>
> It requires a change in outlook, a change in tactics, a change in missions—by the government, by the people, by every businessman or labor leader, and by every newspaper.
>
> For we are opposed around the world by a monolithic and ruthless conspiracy that relies primarily on covert means for expanding its sphere of influence—on infiltration instead of invasion, on subversion instead of elections, on intimidation instead of free choice, on guerrillas by night instead of armies by day. It is a system which has conscripted vast human and material resources into the building of a tightly knit, highly efficient machine that combines military, diplomatic, intelligence, economic, scientific, and political operations.

After the Bay of Pigs fiasco, this could not have been more clear to Kennedy. First put forth by the CIA during the previous Eisenhower administration, perhaps out of naivety, perhaps out of a desire to believe that these various agencies were on the side of good, perhaps because he simply did not want a Soviet proxy nation sitting with nuclear missiles less than ninety miles from the continental US, Kennedy rolled with the plan cooked up during his predecessor's watch. The operation to overthrow Castro failed spectacularly, and was effectively over by April 20, 1961. Kennedy would fire CIA director Allen Dulles, and a mere seven days later, on April 27, Kennedy would give the speech above. Later, after growing increasingly aware of the "Shadow Government" and its twisted plans, Kennedy would be quoted as saying, "I will splinter the CIA in a thousand pieces and scatter it to the winds."

The CIA would make sure he never got the chance. Leveraging assets from across different political ideologies, the CIA crafted a plan to assassinate Kennedy and install one of their own—Vice President Lyndon B. Johnson—in to the office of the presidency. Johnson was a cutthroat man with many downright gross habits (such as urinating in public whenever he felt like it... and if anyone protested, he'd snap around and start to urinate on them, instead). Stories also exist about his voyeurism, such as walking around in the nude so much, his staffers started to call him "Bull nuts." And you can imagine the kind of work environment Johnson fostered for the women on his staff, often offering promotions to those who accepted his blatant advances. Johnson was also no stranger to secret societies, having previously been inducted into Freemasonry (though he had not advanced very far, at least... according to public records). On top of that all, Johnson was, by many accounts, a vile racist. When discussing the Civil Rights bill with two governors, it's reported that Johnson said, "I'll have them niggers voting democrat for the next 200 years."

This wouldn't be the first time Johnson expressed such sentiments, nor would it be the last. When serving as Senate majority leader, he would call President Truman's Civil Rights program...

> ...a farce and a sham—an effort to set up a police state in the guise of liberty. I am opposed to that program. I have voted against the so-called poll tax repeal bill... I have voted against the so-called anti-lynching bill.

In fact, it would be Johnson's chief of staff, Walter Jenkins, who would encourage the FBI to leak explicit sex tapes of Martin Luther King Jr. to the media of the day. The FBI would also write anonymous letters to King during this time, calling him a fraud and encouraging him to commit suicide. Johnson was very much aware that this was going on, and King would be assassinated during his tenure, in a plot not dissimilar to Kennedy's.

Later, when pitching his "Great Society"—a plan to eliminate poverty and racial discrimination in America—Johnson would say:

> These Negroes, they're getting pretty uppity these days and that's a problem for us since they've got something now they never had before, the political pull to back up their uppityness. Now we've got to do something about this, we've got to give them a little something, just enough to quiet them down, not enough to make a difference. For if we don't move at all, then their allies will line up against us and there'll be no way of stopping them, we'll lose the filibuster and there'll be no way of putting a brake on all sorts of wild legislation. It'll be Reconstruction all over again.

Which is all to say... do you really think *this* man would be beyond participating in the assassination of Kennedy, if it meant advancing his career and power in the process? Though many mysteries remain to this very day, there can be almost no doubt that the then CIA participated in the murder of Kennedy when you take a long, hard look at all the evidence available. Why, even a document released during the Trump administration implies as much. In a top secret deposition given before the Presidential Commission on CIA activities, then CIA director Richard Helms was recorded as saying, well… see for yourself:

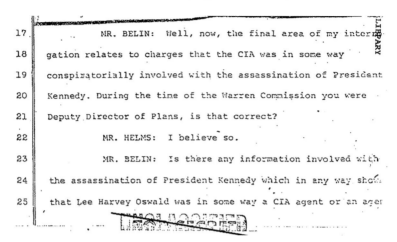

```
17        MR. BELIN:  Well, now, the final area of my interro-
18   gation relates to charges that the CIA was in some way
19   conspiratorially involved with the assassination of President
20   Kennedy. During the time of the Warren Commission you were
21   Deputy Director of Plans, is that correct?
22        MR. HELMS:  I believe so.
23        MR. BELIN:  Is there any information involved with
24   the assassination of President Kennedy which in any way show
25   that Lee Harvey Oswald was in some way a CIA agent or an agen
```

And that is where the public part of the document ends. That's all we, the public, are allowed to see right now. And recall, Richard Helms was the director who had ordered the shredding and disposal of thousands of documents regarding MKUltra. Anything we know about that program is *despite* his efforts. So just imagine what he knew for a second. Ask yourself why his testimony on the matter must remain classified until this very day.

When examined in the broader context of the evidence, including the string of "strange deaths," surrounding the case, it becomes harder to deny that Kennedy was really assassinated by the Deep State for wanting to dismantle it. You have, for instance, the plane crash of Warren Commission member Rep. Hale Boggs, who had previously received a package full of blackmail regarding those who had criticized the Warren report. He would go on to accuse the FBI of tapping his phone and the phones of other members of Congress, before his plane disappeared over Alaska. There were numerous witness deaths, such as the death of George De Mohrenschildt, Marilyn Moon Walle (a stripper who went by the name "Delilah" and who worked at Jack Ruby's Carousel Club), car salesman Al Bogard, Deputy Sheriff Buddy Walters, and another one of Jack Ruby's strippers named Rose Cheramie—who first survived being thrown from a moving car before waking up in the hospital claiming that Jack Ruby and a Cuban by the name of Sergio Arcacha Smith were planning to kill Kennedy. She was saying this mere days before the assassination actually took place, and given her condition at the time, her claims were dismissed as mere hysteria.

Later, after she had recovered, Rose would claim that Lee Harvey Oswald and Jack Ruby were actually gay lovers. She would later be run down by a car and perish this time.

What about Dr. Mary Sherman, who was shot and set on fire while in bed? Or Clyde Johnson who was shot in the back with a shotgun the day before he was going to testify in the Garrison trial? Or mafioso John Roselli, who was found chopped up and stuffed in a barrel floating in the Miami Bay before he could testify in front of the Senate Intelligence Committee?

There are many more examples of this kind of thing that I could list, but I think, perhaps the cherry on top of it all is to remember that the CIA had their mind control experiments well underway by this time, and had, in fact, already begun testing LSD as a possible neurological agent. Originally pioneered by Nazi scientists as a way of getting prisoners to reveal secrets, lysergic acid dietheyamide seemed the most promising drug to their various "programmers" (one of which I would later expose as having Hollywood connections in my Black List articles through a Soros-backed "think-tank" called ReInvent. The individual I'm referencing, is, of course, one Stewart Brand, who is currently like a billion years old, and who worked on LSD experimentation for the CIA back in the day. He now praises the Burning Man festival as going beyond what the CIA had ever "accomplished," which should tell you something about the true nature of the Burning Man festival).

To test out LSD, the CIA ran experiments on all sorts of populations, from college kids, to the patrons of various whorehouses, to whole army platoons at Fort McClellan, in Alabama, where the soldiers got so giggly, they couldn't march or perform basic tasks competently for as long as they were under the influence of the drug. In Lexington, Kentucky, the CIA gave a huge supply of drugs to a Doctor Harris Isbell, who ran the Lexington Narcotics Hospital, also known as the NIMH Addiction Research Center, or simply, the "US Narcotic Farm." For the longest time, Lexington had been considered the drug addiction capital of the nation, and many doctors were working there to try and understand, as well as cure, various substance addictions; and this at a time when this was really a frontier science, and little was well understood.

Working with patients on a "volunteer" basis, Isbell would test over eight hundred substances for the CIA, including testing LSD on a group of black patients for seventy-five days straight, increasing the dosages so as to overcome any tolerance they might have built up during that time. He got these addicts to "volunteer" for these tests in exchange for heroin and morphine, so it was actually common practice for desperate, poor, addicted people to admit themselves to these programs and re-up their personal drug supply. In other words, this "doctor" was paying addicts with drugs, in order to test out clandestine CIA drug tests on them.

Isbell's hospital had a ninety percent re-admittance rate, and he would be paid handsomely by the CIA for all his efforts. Inspired by these tests, LSD would continue to be given to a number of societal "influencers," such as Aldous Huxley, Alan Ginsberg, and Timothy Leary, essentially creating the drugged out 70s and squashing any effective resistance that generation had to the military industrial complex at the time. It should also surprise no one reading this book, that the CIA also tested LSD at military stations overseas, including at the naval base in Atsugi, Japan… where one Lee Harvey Oswald was stationed at the time.

Combined with the CIA's research into mind control, was this what kicked off Oswald's life as a mind-controlled assassin? Was this program what identified him as someone malleable enough to be molded into a killer, complete with his own set of triggers?

Regardless, Bush was a member of this clandestine shadow government very early on, and cut his teeth at the agency, despite his repeated denials over the years. In fact, his employment at the CIA was not known to the general public until 1985, when Joseph McBride, writer for the *Daily Variety*, stumbled upon the fact when, in the course of reviewing microfilms at the California State University of San Bernardino (for a story on Frank Capra, of all things), McBride found a letter from former FBI director J. Edgar Hoover from 1963 bearing the heading "Assassination of President John F. Kennedy." McBride had volunteered for the Kennedy campaign in his earlier years, and was never quite satisfied with the answers given by the Warren Commission, and the conventional narrative, so you see… his curiosity was piqued. He simply *had* to read the letter.

It read:

```
To:

Director

Bureau of Intelligence and Research

Department of State

[We have been] advised that the Department of State feels
some misguided anti-Castro group might capitalize on the
present situation and undertake an unauthorized raid against
Cuba, believing that the assassination of President John F.
Kennedy might herald a change in US. policy… [Our] sourc-
es know of no [such] plans… The substance of the foregoing
information was orally furnished to Mr. George Bush of the
Central Intelligence Agency and Captain William Edwards of
the Defense Intelligence Agency.
```

Beyond the obvious revelation that Bush Sr. had been working as a CIA agent since at least the early 60s, why was George Bush being briefed on the situation in Cuba, and the Kennedy assassination? Part of the entire reason he was appointed as CIA director during the 70s, with the Ford administration, was that he hadn't been a part of any of that "messy stuff." He hadn't partaken in any coups, cover-ups, or mad science experiments, at a time when it seemed like the Church Committee was plumbing new depths of evil with each passing day. And you can't forget that the nation had already been through Watergate a few years prior (with Bush Sr. urging Nixon to resign). Bush was supposed to be the "fresh face" of the Agency; someone capable of reigning in its excesses. He wasn't supposed to be a clandestine company man.

A side note about Watergate. It is not merely a scandal about a break in at the DNC and the subsequent cover-up. It was about blackmail… but not, perhaps, the kind most people would assume. Watergate was the Pizzagate of its day, though its true nature was not known to many at the time, and was in fact, covered up by the spooks masquerading as journalists, Bob Woodward and Carl Bernstein (the latter of which has recently made repeated appearances on the Clown News Network—CNN—in order to denounce Trump). The conventional narrative would later be crystallized by Hollywood in the film *All the President's Men,* based on the book of the same name and also written by Woodward and Bernstein, in effect creating a closed-loop of narrative validation (a tactic which is still used today).

In fact, according to former NYPD detective James "Boots" Rothstein, Nixon was seeking evidence of pedophilic activity in the DNC offices to leverage as blackmail. Rothstein would talk about how, in 1972, he would arrest one of the Watergate burglars, one Frank Sturgis, who would go on to talk about "the book" Nixon was after. The conventional narrative was that Nixon was after their election strategies… which is a thin cover, if you really think about it. In fact, Nixon was looking for blackmail, and possibly to save his own skin—if not his position as president, depending on who you believe.

Rothstein, who had been assigned to investigate and combat prostitution since 1966, soon uncovered a pedophilic network which ran to the highest offices of power in the land. And remember, this is the NYPD we're talking about here. The NYPD is not your average police department. It is far *bigger* and has more resources at its disposal than some federal agencies. Rothstein would go on to say that the majority of the top government leaders had been compromised or blackmailed in some way—usually via the use of the kind of "honeypots" we spoke about earlier—and that this type of *kompromat* operation was run by the

CIA. This was also happening all around the world as well, in operations conducted by all manner of Deep State agencies, for the explicit purpose of controlling these politicians, and thus, the levers of power.

The implication of this all is that… Bush Sr., as a top CIA operative, would have known exactly what was going on and helped keep it all secret, while covering it up, before being rewarded with even more power by Gerald Ford, when Ford nominated him as director of the CIA. Also worth remembering here is that another Yale grad would cut her teeth on the House Counsel working on the Watergate Commission: a young Hillary Rodham. Hillary actually *wanted* Nixon to remain in office so that if Ted Kennedy were to run, he'd have an easier time beating the "corrupt" opposition. But Nixon would soon resign, thus ending the Watergate Commission.

Still, that letter that Joseph McBride had discovered on that microfilm was a stunning revelation. It meant that the man who was then vice president had lied to the American public about his record as a spook for DECADES. And of course, the cover-up began almost immediately. McBride actually called the CIA to see if this newly uncovered information was accurate, and at first they denied and then they said, "No, no, that was some *other* agent named George Bush." That other George Bush would eventually materialize, but then he would go on to say, in no uncertain terms, that he wasn't the one mentioned in the memo.

Years later, in 2006, another JFK researcher would be poring through recently declassified documents, which actually puts the beginning of Bush's relationship with the CIA all the way back in 1953. It read:

> "Through Mr. Gale Allen... I learned that Mr. George Bush, DCI designate has prior knowledge of the now terminated project WUBRINY/LPDICTUM which was involved in proprietary commercial operations in Europe. He became aware of this project through Mr. Thomas J. Devine, a former CIA Staff Employee and later, oil-wildcatting associate with Mr. Bush. Their joint activities culminated in the establishment of Zapata Oil [sic] [in 1953] which they eventually sold. After the sale of Zapata Oil, Mr. Bush went into politics, and Mr. Devine became a member of the investment firm of Train, Cabot and Associates, New York . . . . The attached memorandum describes the close relationship between Messrs. Devine and Bush in 1967-1968 which, according to Mr. Allen, continued while Mr. Bush was our ambassador to the United Nations."

Essentially, this was an official admission by the CIA that Bush had been working undercover for them for a looooong time. And the name "Zapata" is important here, because while Bush earned his oily millions, the Bay of Pigs invasion would soon launch in 1961, under the code name *Operation Zapata*. And one of the boats used during the invasion would be named "Barbara."

But the fact remains: Bush was getting debriefed by the CIA about Cuba and Kennedy. Why? The CIA had previously tried to remove Castro from power. Was the CIA hoping to place the blame for Kennedy's assassination on the Castro-affiliated Lee Harvey Oswald, in an effort to drum up support for an all-out war against Cuba? If so, once again we see the tactic of playing both sides against each other.

And the question also needs to be asked: what else was Bush involved in? The man comes from a line of fascists, and worked for decades for an agency that imported Nazis, only to continue their sick experiments on human populations. Did Bush have knowledge of these programs? What about the coups in places like Iran and South America? What of Jim Jones? At least one source I've read pins the drug crisis of the late 80s and early 90s directly on Bush, who literally invented the practice and got the CIA involved in importing cocaine so as to build up dark money funds for CIA black projects—allowing the CIA to essentially conduct certain operations in total secrecy, without need for government approval, funding, oversight... or even any knowledge that they officially exist! With Watergate, we saw Bush urging Nixon to step down. Was that to protect Nixon from the exposure of even greater crimes against children, and maintain the use of the CIA's pedophilic honeypot blackmail practices?

We can't forget the attempt on Reagan's life in all this, either. The would-be assassin, John Hinckley Jr., was the son of John Hinckley Sr., a World Vision executive. We're talking about the same World Vision that had sent down "missionaries" to Jim Jones when he was still in the US, and who had worked to repopulate Jonestown after the Jonestown massacre had gone down. It may shock many here to learn that this supposedly "Christian" organization is leveraged regularly by the CIA, in order to provide cover for their agents and nefarious activities around the world. After all, it's much easier to get kind, good-hearted missionaries offering aid and vital supplies into a country, than it is to smuggle in armed agents. But Hinckley Sr. was a particular friend of Bush, and one has to wonder, knowing the scope and success of the CIA's mind control experiments, was Hinckley Jr. a mind control victim himself, offered up by his own father who was working for a CIA cover group, trained and tasked for the explicit purpose of killing Reagan, in order to help Bush Sr. advance to the office of the presidency even earlier than he did?

Good thing for us Reagan was tough, and Hinckley was a bad shot. Today, it should be noted that World Vision is headquartered right across the street from the Clinton Foundation, in Little Rock, Arkansas.

Bush would go on to join the House of Representatives, serving as a congressman from Texas, from 1967 until 1971, and during that time, the "born-again" "Evangelical" would shock many by his strong support for Planned Parenthood and the use of birth control. In a speech before the House of Representatives in 1968, Bush Sr. would say:

> Mr. Speaker,
>
> Sitting as I have on the tax-writing Ways and Means Committee, which has responsibility for social-security legislation, I have heard almost endless testimony to the effect that our national welfare costs are rising phenomenally, prompting me to wonder how we can take basic steps to arrest it. But the problem is by no means wholly financial; it is emphatically human, a tragedy of unwanted children and of parents whose productivity is impaired by children they never desired.
>
> We speak of these children as 'unwanted;' are they really so? Evidence from various studies indicates that this is indeed the case.
>
> ...
>
> The federal government, along with many state governments, has taken steps to accelerate family-planning activities in the United States, but we need to do more. We have a clear precedent: When the Salk vaccine was discovered, large-scale programs were undertaken to distribute it. I see no reason why similar programs of education and family-planning assistance—all on a voluntary basis—should not be instituted in the United States on a massive scope. It is imperative that we do so: not only to fight poverty at its roots, not only to cut down on our welfare costs, but also to eliminate the needless suffering of unwanted children and overburdened parents.

Bush was successful in his endeavor, and helped secure funding to build Planned Parenthoods all across America, earning him the nickname "Rubbers" in the process. Just five years later, in 1973, abortion would be legalized nation-wide after the Roe v. Wade decision in the Supreme Court. It was like an alley-oop. Bush had laid the groundwork. A few years later, the Supreme Court did the rest by legalizing infanticide. And ever since then, millions of unborn have been unwittingly sacrificed to Moloch every year, their blood poured out on the altar of "freedom."

(That's not an exaggeration, by the way. Every Planned Parenthood in America is literally dedicated to Moloch... at least, according to Q. We'll dive into that subject more, later.)

Q !ITPb.qbhqo ID: wmN+33xv No.149467638 🔗 📷   **153**
Nov 14 2017 21:25:09 (EST)

For the coming days ahead.
Ask yourself an honest question, why would a billionaire who has it all, fame, fortune, a warm and loving family, friends, etc. want to endanger himself and his family by becoming POTUS?
Why would he want to target himself and those he cares about?
Does he need money?
Does he need fame?
What does he get out of this?
Does he want to make the US/world a better place for his family and for those good and decent people who have long been taken advantage of?
Perhaps he could not stomach the thought of mass murders occurring to satisfy Moloch?
Perhaps he could not stomach the thought of children being kidnapped, drugged, and raped while leaders/law enforcement of the world turn a blind eye.
Perhaps he was tired of seeing how certain races/countries were being constantly abused and kept in need/poor/and suffering all for a specific purpose.
Perhaps he could not in good conscious see the world burn.
Why, hours after the election, did seven people travel to an undisclosed location to hold a very private & highly secured/guarded meeting?
Why didn't HRC give a concession speech?
When was the last time a presidential candidate didn't personally give a concession speech?
What happens if the border remained open and the MSM continued to brainwash?
At what point do Patriots, and hard working men and woman, become the minority?
What about voting machines?
Who owns the voting machines?
What about voter ID laws?
Photo ID? When is it necessary and must be presented? Make a list.
Laugh.
Reconcile.
Would the chances of defeating evil grow less and less with each passing year?
What does 'red line' mean?
Why, again, were the arrests made in SA so very important?
What strings were immediately cut?
Follow the money.
When does a bird sing?
Q

ANSWERS

Bush would also become the US ambassador to the United Nations, and after that, the liaison to China. It was after these appointments that he would once again find himself back at the CIA, this time as director. In 1999, Bush would give a speech at the dedication for the CIA's George Bush Center for Intelligence, where he would say…

> I left here some 22 years ago after a limited tenure, and my stay here had a major impact on me. The CIA became part of my heartbeat back then, and it's never gone away.

Bush would feel a certain sense of ownership and loyalty to the CIA throughout his lifetime, even pardoning a number of agents involved in the Iran-Contra scandal, including one Clair George, the global spy-master in charge of the CIA's clandestine service when he became president. Some would go on to describe Bush's allegiance to, and protection of, the CIA, as a kind of *omerta*.

In truth, I think it goes deeper than that.

The links between the Skull and Bones, and Hitler's Schutzstaffel division has long been established by other writers, but is most clearly seen in the shared iconography of the *totenkopf*—that image of the "Death's head." In essence, both groups sport the "skull and bones" as their defining image. Before it became simply an expanded, elite fighting unit during the war, the SS was truly a religious rank of occult warrior monks, with different levels of initiation. Originally conceived by resident Nazi occultist Heinrich Himmler, the "Black Order" as it was called, was an effort to really create a new pagan religion based on mythical "Germanic ideals" and racial purity, in order to remake the human race into something more powerful and enlightened; something *Hyperborean*. (And this wouldn't be the Nazi's only effort on this front, with that mad eugenics program know as *Lebensborn* being another stark example.)

The SS, then, was to be a sort of dark inversion of the Knights of the Round Table. And what would be the knights without a "Camelot" of their own? Himmler went to work repurposing the Wewelsburg castle in Westphalia for this project, and immediately began undertaking renovations in order to turn the site into a sort of Mecca for the SS. While the castle was modified with a number of occult features, most notable perhaps, is the inlay of the "Black Sun" into the floor of the *Obergruppenführersaal*:

The inclusion of the Black Sun itself is notable because it is a belief that originates in ancient Babylon, Sumer, and Akkad, and it is that this second, hidden black sun is the cause for inner enlightenment, or illumination. Much like the *swastika* Hitler chose for the Nazi's national symbol, it was a mythic sun-symbol from ages past.

The research divisions in Himmler's SS also began "researching" in the pursuit of *Vril*—a mythical, Hyperborean energy source, also called a *Light Force*—which they hoped to channel in order to advance their utopian vision. Surprisingly, many here get a bit thrown when they learn that the concept of "Vril" comes from a book of fiction entitled *The Coming Race*, by Sir Edward Bulwer-Lytton. That would be like reading *Lord of the Rings* and then trying to take a scenic hike up Mt. Doom, right?

Well, not exactly. Sir Edward was a member of the Hermetic Order of the Golden Dawn, which was itself an off-shoot of the Rosicrucians. These two secret societies have long attempted to preserve esoteric knowledge, and many see his work of "fiction" as a kind of hidden code, where he attempted to preserve esoteric knowledge behind the veil of story. So at the very least, we can understand that the Nazis believed Sir Edward was trying to communicate some kind of ancient, alchemical truths that had been hidden through the ages, only known to a select few illumined individuals, and only understood by those in the modern age who truly understood what he was trying to do.

Much like the earlier *Thule Society*, which took its name from a mythical Germanic land, the SS would begin plumbing the depths of the occult, even giving rise to a new secret society in the process: the *Vril Society.* Many of the ranking Nazi party members were previously Thule Society members—which was a sun-worshiping occult group that looked for the arrival of a sort of Germanic Messiah—so making the transition to the Vril Society was really no big deal for most of them. One could easily make the claim that the NSDAP grew directly out of the Thule Society. Dietrich Eckart, in particular, was both a founder of the Thule Society, and one of the seven founding members of the NSDAP. On his deathbed he would say:

> Follow Hitler. He will dance, but it is I who have called the tune! I have initiated him into the 'Secret Doctrine;' opened his centers in vision and given him the means to communicate with the Powers. Do not mourn for me: I shall have influenced history more than any German.

As part of their research, the SS would institute a new holiday calendar reflective of the solstices, and conduct a number of occult rituals—including, according to occult research Fritz Springmeier, having Adolf Hitler himself participate in a number of human sacrifices that involved pulling the still-beating hearts out of the chests of living men.

The concept of *Vril* would soon go abroad and be adopted and endorsed by the founder of Theosophy, Helena Blavatsky. For those unfamiliar with the term, Theosophy is essentially a jumble of occult practices, "Western" mysticism, and esoteric practices that were rolled up into an official Theosophical school by Blavatsky herself, in the late 1800s. Blavatsky was a Russian occultist who took upon herself the task of gathering "ancient wisdom" from all over the globe, and became somewhat renowned for these efforts. She would eventually publish her treatise on Theosophy in 1877, entitled *Isis Unveiled: A Master-Key to the Mysteries of Ancient and Modern Science and Theology.* Picking and choosing as Blavatsky was wont to do, she quickly adopted the idea of *Vril* into her broader body of work.

And this is where it gets really interesting, because Theosophy didn't end with Blavatsky. In 1904, a young Aleister Crowley would claim to be contacted by a voice identifying itself as *Aiwass*—a "minister of Horus"—who would impart unto him *The Book of the Law*. It would be the first of many books that Crowley would contend he was only the conduit for, writing them as though possessed by some otherworldly being (and he very well might have been... though perhaps not who he claimed to be possessed by, for all we know).

Often referring to himself as "The Beast 666" (a clear reference to the book of Revelation of St. John, but which Crowley contended really just meant "Little Sunshine"), Crowley had long been entangled with secret societies before branching out on his own. Prior to writing his book, Crowley had been a member of the Hermetic Order of the Golden Dawn, same as Sir Edward from before. Crowley would go on to found the A∴A∴, and considered Helena Blavatsky a sister of the A∴A∴, granting her the rank equivalent to Magister Templi (just two ranks below the highest ranks available (one of which was beyond the comprehension of the lower degrees anyway). Crowley would go on to study all sorts of esoteric "magick" and eventually help found the Ordo Templi Orientis—an occult group modeled after Freemasonry. The group is still active today, and its ranks includes a surprising number of celebrities, such as Jay-Z, whose clothing line has "borrowed" a number of Crowley's phrases and imagery. Perhaps unsurprisingly, Crowley's books would come to be considered foundational texts within the order he founded.

Chief among these new "magick" practices Crowley was exploring was "sex magick," which he viewed as a kind of sacrament, and which was "inspired" by different yogic and tantric practices (and this should surprise no one, as many of these ancient Hindu beliefs are mere variations on the same kind of sun-cult systems we've been talking about for some time now). But this belief naturally led to Crowley living a very promiscuous life while also claiming he was bisexual (despite being married). The quote "Do what thou wilt," springs immediately to mind for anyone familiar with Crowley's work, which was, in fact, the whole summation of Thelema, with Thelema itself being derived from the Koine Greek for "will." And of course, the natural can't be avoided entirely, so these sex magick practices would sometimes lead to the creation of children.

Specifically "Moonchildren," as Crowley termed them.

Practitioners of Thelema will claim that true sex magick will always produce a child on some plane of reality—and that could very well be the material plane. Sex magick was superimposed over the pagan calendar, and soon, practitioners were trying to capture "perfect souls" within the newly formed babies, as part of their esoteric belief in reincarnation. The building in which these rituals occurred was originally called, according to Crowley, "The Butter-fly-net," and was a temple crafted according to sacred geometry and which featured much pagan imagery, such as statues and an altar to Artemis (and of course, the moon). The ritual would be performed (and, again, according to Springmeier, often involved blood sacrifice, or even human sacrifice), and a "moonchild" would be born some nine months later.

In beginning to understand and investigate this practice, Anons came to suspect that Luna, the daughter of singer John Legend and his wife, Chrissy Teigen, is actually one such moonchild. That shocker came when researching the Podesta e-mails, and checking the dates to see if we could find any notable births nine months after he attended that despicable "Spirit Cooking" dinner hosted by Cabal Priestess (what we would soon learn was called a "Mother of Darkness") Marina Abramovic.

▶ Anonymous *(You)* 04/17/18 (Tue) 21:36:57 ID: 2453a2 No.1084118 >>1084162

>>1083945

If this theory is true... part of me wonders if we can go back roughly to the date of the Podesta Spirit cooking, and figure out which child was conceived in the process.

Do we have a list of attendees to that event?

Just look 9 months after the date of the Spirit Cooking, and you've got a likely candidate for the next "Moonchild."

We did:

▶ Anonymous 04/17/18 (Tue) 22:48:33 ID: ad7807 No.1084977 >>1085023 >>1085137 >>1085226 >>1085340
File (hide): c6fb339d645b767··· jpg (24.83 KB, 678x381, 226:127, Young Podesta.jpg) (h) (u)

Regarding the Barbare Bush "Moonchild" crumb in the notables: >>1083945

The Podestas' Spirit Cooking dinner was scheduled for July 9th, 2015. Nine months after that date is April 9th, 2016. Were there any notable births on that date? (Chelsea Clinton's child was born in mid-June 2016, so not her.)

▶ Anonymous 04/17/18 (Tue) 22:51:20 ID: cc2d7c No.1085023 >>1085043 >>1085068 >>1085104 >>1085137 >>1085226 >>1085340

>>1084977

Luna Simone Stephens (Chrissy Teigen and John Legend)

▶ Anonymous 04/17/18 (Tue) 22:52:53 ID: c8e776 No.1085043 >>1085061 >>1085120 >>1085226 >>1085340

>>1085023
Luna = Moon

Moon Child

Luna was born on April 14, that same year. QAnon would later come back and say this, in response to an Anon:

Q !xowAT4Z3VQ **ID: 1f0a66** No.1197788 ⬀ ▥   **1276**
Apr 26 2018 14:16:46 (EST)

Anonymous **ID: 3de700** No.1197573 ⬀ ▥
Apr 26 2018 14:02:01 (EST)

maxresdefault.jpg   ⬇

Just going to post pictures of a MOONCHILD to piss of the shills because WE KNOW.

John Legend
@johnlegend
 Our new love is here! Luna Simone Stephens, born on Thursday, the 14th. We couldn't be happier!

>>1197573
How many pics can you find of JL & HRC?
re: Haiti?
Marching into the Darkness - lyrics.
Follow the stars.
It's everywhere.
Q

We haven't really talked about the Clintons and Haiti yet.

But we will, soon.

And indeed, if Luna was in fact a Moonchild, she certainly wasn't the first.

You may have caught it in the Anon post above, but the other really "famous" candidate for this would be none other than George Bush Sr.'s wife, Barbara Bush (nee Pierce). Barbara's mother was a wealthy, young woman named Pauline Pierce, and she was something of a renowned beauty in her time, married to a high powered exec who was increasingly busy with his work as the years passed on, turning Pauline into something of a prototypical socialite in the early decades of the twentieth century.

Her life as a socialite meant many "interesting" friends from around the world, and one of those friends was Nellie O'Hara, who was an American woman living in France with a writer named Frank Harris. Harris was something of a Casanova in his time. O'Hara and Harris weren't married (though they were living together), and through their correspondence, O'Hara invited Pierce out to France to visit with them for a while, in 1924.

It just so happened that Aleister Crowley was also living with Harris and O'Hara at the time, as well. Prior to this, Crowley had established the Abbey of Thelema in Italy in 1920 with a few, uh… "assistants" with whom he regularly practiced "sex magick" and other various sun-related rituals. Even sex magick itself was laden with sun-related analogies, as Crowley's favorite position for these rituals was something he dubbed "PVN," an abbreviation for Per Viam Introitus Infernalis—by way of the infernal road. (Some Thelemic practitioners would go on to believe this particular practice allowed the practitioner to siphon life energy through the receiver's "eye of Horus," and it should be noted that this kind of sodomy is common in Monarch mind control programming.)

But during this time at the Abbey, Crowley grew increasingly hooked on cocaine and heroin (as drugs which dulled the senses were often part of the sex magick rituals, you see). His Abbey began to fall into disrepair and squalor, complete with wild animals roaming the halls. One of his assistant's babies would die in the horrid conditions, and another assistant would soon die after being forced to drink cat's blood in a ritual, regularly cut himself with razors, and drink contaminated water from a local stream. By 1923, Crowley would be kicked out of Italy by Mussolini himself, soon relocating to France, where he would meet the equally lascivious Frank Harris, who would become his chief beneficiary for a time.

The chief goal of sex magick was to put the practitioner into a ritual eroto-comotose lucidity through a process of orgasm denial, leading to a waking exhaustion. As such, all manner of stimuli—and partners—were needed in the process. Crowley would write of the process, in *Liber CDLI:*

> The Candidate is made ready for the Ordeal by general athletic training, and by feasting. On the appointed day he is attended by one or more chosen and experienced attendants whose duty is (a) to exhaust him sexually by every known means (b) to rouse him sexually by every known means. Every device and artifice of the courtesan is to be employed, and every stimulant known to the physician. Nor should the attendants reck of danger, but hunt down ruthlessly their appointed prey.
>
> Finally the Candidate will into a sleep of utter exhaustion, resembling coma, and it is now that delicacy and skill must be exquisite. Let him be roused from this sleep by stimulation of a definitely and exclusively sexual type. Yet if convenient, music wisely regulated will assist.
>
> The attendants will watch with assiduity for signs of waking; and the moment these occur, all stimulation must cease instantly, and the Candidate be allowed to fall again into sleep; but no sooner has this happened than the former practice is resumed. This alteration is to continue indefinitely until the Candidate is in a state which is neither sleep nor waking, and in which his Spirit, set free by perfect exhaustion of the body, and yet prevented from entering the City of Sleep, communes with the Most High and the Most Holy Lord God of its being, maker of heaven and earth.
>
> The Ordeal terminates by failure—the occurrence of sleep invincible—or by success, in which ultimate waking is followed by a final performance of the sexual act. The Initiate may then be allowed to sleep, or the practice may be renewed and persisted in until death ends all. The most favourable death is that occurring during the orgasm, and is called Mors Justi.

> As it is written: Let me die the death of the Righteous, and let my last end
> be like his!

If yogis could have sued Crowley for ripping off tantra and dressing it up in "Satanic"
garb, they would have. And given Crowley's past sexploits, one shouldn't really be surprised
that when the beautiful socialite Pauline Pierce came to visit his benefactors, Crowley wanted to undergo this "great ordeal," and finally reach the highest rank the O.T.O. could be-
queath upon someone: the rank of Ipsissimus!

Eight months later, Barbara Bush would be born. Whether you choose to believe that
Barbara Bush is the illegitimate daughter of Aleister Crowley or not, there's one thing that
cannot be denied; Barbara's mother met with the chief practitioner of the occult during
the twentieth century, and at least observed the sex magick ritual (even if she did not participate herself, which, I think it's more than likely she did). One cannot deny, however,
that there is a striking resemblance in the Bush family to photos of Crowley. Compare
Barbara in her later years to older photos of Crowley, and compare photos of Marvin Bush
to photos of a younger Crowley. One can immediately see a resemblance that is not so
easily dismissed.

And while we're on the subject of illegitimate births and moonchildren, my Canadian
readers might be interested to learn of a potential paternal connection between Canadian
prime minister Justin Trudeau, and Cuban dictator Fidel Castro. Yes, Margaret Trudeau was
quite the "socialite" in her day, too, much like Pauline. She made frequent trips down to
Cuba, and the resemblance between Justin and a young Fidel is immediately obvious. No,
my northern neighbors, I don't think Pierre is Justin's biological father—and this is attested
to by the controversial eulogy he issued after the death of Fidel, which read:

> It is with deep sorrow that I learned today of the death of Cuba's longest
> serving President.
>
> Fidel Castro was a larger than life leader who served his people for almost
> half a century. A legendary revolutionary and orator, Mr. Castro made sig-
> nificant improvements to the education and healthcare of his island nation.
>
> While a controversial figure, both Mr. Castro's supporters and detractors
> recognized his tremendous dedication and love for the Cuban people who
> had a deep and lasting affection for "el Comandante.

Likewise, some of my readers in America may be surprised to learn that Chelsea Clinton is probably not Bill's daughter, but in all likelihood the product of an affair between Hillary Clinton and Webb Hubbell. Perhaps this is why Bill Clinton (most likely, an illegitimate
Rockefeller himself) felt so free to philander while in the Oval Office.

And so, as you are beginning to see, the connections run deep. I know I've been particularly hard on Democratic politicians earlier in the book, but there's plenty of evil to
expose on both sides of the aisle, as George Bush Sr. was the mastermind behind a lot of
it for the bulk of the twentieth century, with his legacy paving the way for his son to take
over his former office in the 2000 election. George W. Bush's campaign would appeal to
many Americans, as he spouted off borderline-Libertarian talking points that neither really
offended anyone on the Left or the Right. And America, largely wanting to put the damage
and disgrace of the Clinton administration behind them, opted to "have a beer" with Bush
II, over the stiff, and Herman Munster-esque John Kerry.

It wasn't long, however, before those ideals vanished, replaced by jingoism, talk of WMDs, and a never-ending "war on terror." In the wake of 9/11, a totalitarian form of government advanced further than it ever had at any time before, as average Americans suddenly found their rights eroding before their very eyes. A new age of fear had dawned, and a "new normal" emerged.

Many theories abound about what, precisely, occurred that day in September—and more importantly *why* it occurred, but frustratingly few definitive and comprehensive explanations have been found, despite official commission findings and countless hours of reporting and investigation. From the unprecedented, suspicious, and largest ever insurance settlement made to Silverstein Properties (totaling at over four and a half billion dollars), to the bulk, paperless financial transactions taking place between Marsh & McLennan to AIG (a technical project that had to be finished before September 11, implying a level of foreknowledge about the attacks), to Deutsche Bank's computer network being hacked forty minutes before the first plane landed, to the SEC investigating the massive spike in put options contracts being purchased before the attacks, to Rumsfeld's missing trillions and worse, the conclusion that I have personally landed at is that the 9/11 attacks were planned by the Cabal, as a joint operation between the CIA, Mossad, and jihadis, for the express purpose of profit, as well as destabilizing the Middle East and leading the West to war.

One of the worst examples of insider trading on this tragedy comes from a distant relative and business partner of George W. Bush, Marvin Bush and it starts with Wirt D. Walker III. Walker would purchase fifty-six thousand shares of Stratesec on September 6, 2001—a company that specialized in security technology for airports and buildings. Wirt himself was the CEO of the company, and Marvin was a company director at the time. Five days later, the 9/11 attack would transpire and soon the share price of Stratesec would double. But Wirt would get off scot-free, because, as the 9/11 commission report said, he had no direct ties to any terrorist group, and therefore, couldn't have had any foreknowledge of the attack.

Except that isn't true, because Wirt had previously worked with the Carlyle Group, and the Carlyle group had many ties to the bin Laden family. You have to remember, bin Laden himself had previously been a CIA asset, working to push the Soviets out of Afghanistan. Much like how Obama had flown out to Pakistan with that arms dealer in order to bring the AK to that region, Osama bin Laden and his Mujahideen had previously been armed and supported by the CIA. He was previously, as the spooks might say, "an asset on the ground."

And what of Saudi multimillionaire, friend of Dick Cheney, and suspected Al Qaeda financier Yassin Al-Qadi? Al-Qadi claims to have met bin Laden when he visited Chicago in 1981—a trip the government claims no knowledge of, as all customs records from that time have now been destroyed. Al-Qadi was also one of the principle investors behind a risk management software company called Ptech—and Ptech software was used by the likes of the IRS, the DOD, the CIA, DARPA, Enron, NATO, *both* houses of Congress, the US Armed Forces, the DOJ, the FBI, Customs and Border Protection, the FAA, and even the White House itself, along with many large enterprises in the private sector. At the time, there weren't too many other companies building the kind of software that Ptech was building, and they had basically become the entrenched industry standard for risk management software—known by all the professionals working with such systems.

Understand, the job of this kind of software is to basically identify problems within organizations before they form, and help the heads of these very large organizations come up with solutions ahead of time. This means the software basically has access to *everything* in these organizations. Special networks and hardware had to be installed, and the costs at the time were enormous (but so were the benefits, thus making it a smart business decision for larger organizations). After installation, pretty much every piece of digital information the company was producing would then be routed through the risk management network. Every packet of data, every byte transmitted would be analyzed and assessed within the Ptech system.

Of course, this gives whoever has administrative powers over the system incredible power.

The chief scientist at Ptech would be one Hussein Ibrahim, who would also serve as representative of Al-Qadi on the board. Prior to this, Ibrahim would serve at Bai ul-Mal Incorporated, or BMI, in New Jersey. BMI was an investment firm that followed Islamic banking principles, and had also invested over three million dollars in Ptech. Al-Qadi would use BMI as an intermediary when he was investing in Ptech, and Ptech would share office space with BMI. In fact, the co-chair of the 9/11 commission, Thomas Kean, was involved in a twenty-four billion dollar transaction with BMI (though no mention of BMI or Ptech were ever made in the final 9/11 commission report). When testifying before Congress in 2003, former national coordinator for security, infrastructure protection and counter-terrorism Richard Clarke would say,

> While BMI held itself out publicly as a financial services provider for Muslims in the United States, its investor list suggests the possibility this facade was just a cover to conceal terrorist support. BMI's investor list reads like a who's-who of designated terrorists and Islamic extremists.

Al-Qadi would soon invest in Ptech through his venture capital firm, Sarmani Limited, contributing a full twenty-five percent of Ptech's desired funding to their startup round; some five million dollars from Al-Qadi alone. He would continue investing millions into Ptech through the years, despite public reassurances by Ptech's CEO saying he had nothing to do with the company since the original venture capital round.

At the same time, the marketing director for Ptech was one Michael S. Goff—a man who just so happened to also be working for an Israeli company called Guardium at the time; a company which specialized in database security (and would later be acquired by IBM in 2009). Guardium itself had gone through its own angel-funding round, and the principle investors were all Mossad-backed outfits—much in the same way In-Q-Tel is a CIA-backed investment firm. Goff would leave a good job at the Worcester firm of Seder & Chandler to work for this Islamic upstart, which he claims he found via a temp agency, though he can't recall the name of said temp agency. Given the circumstances, some think he was operating as a *sayan* for Mossad.

So essentially, what happened with Ptech is Hussein Ibrahim and his computer scientists made sure to load their system with all sorts of back doors and vulnerabilities so that they could access everything on whatever system was running the software, at the blueprint level. This would allow them to essentially extract all kinds of information from all these big companies, military contractors, intelligence agencies, and defense agencies, in order to analyze their systems, to find and exploit whatever vulnerabilities they came across in the process. And to show you how sick this gets, one of Ptech's programmers was Suheil Laher. He had previously worked as MIT's Muslim chaplain and preached at the Islamic Society of Boston, where the Boston Marathon Bomber brothers were radicalized. He had also previously worked for Care International—an NGO founded by Osama bin Laden's mentor, Abdullah Azzam, allowing him to raise funds for Islamic terror groups. Laher espoused as radical an ideology as one can get when it comes to Islam. If there is anyone directly responsible for purposefully creating these back doors, it's Suheil. Meanwhile, Goff was marketing the software all over. This would all come to light when Indira

Singh, senior consultant specializing in risk management for JP Morgan, blew the whistle on Ptech's shady practices.

See, JP Morgan, being the gigantic bank it is, was looking at risk management software and was impressed by Ptech's track record. After all, it was software that was used at so many other large companies and government organizations, so it had to be impressive and formidable, right? Singh scheduled a demo with Ibrahim, and they set up a time when he could install the full software suite on one of their computers, on-site, just so they could get a feel for how it worked, and see if they were willing to spend the millions to get all their systems updated and up to speed. Instead, Ibrahim shows up, not with a demo on disc, but with it installed on his own personal laptop which he wanted to jack right into their network. This set off all sorts of alarm bells for Singh, because Singh, being the risk management type, could see this going wrong in a plethora of ways. She made some calls and quickly decided she would not allow this, because essentially, it would allow Singh to suck up all sorts of JP Morgan's private data and then turn around and leave the premises with it in hand. Bad idea. Huge red flag. She was then informed that Al-Qadi was the principle investor behind all this, and that had her nix the whole deal then and there, because Al-Qadi had just been placed on the terrorist watchlist a few months prior. Calls were made to the FBI because Singh knew exactly how many systems this software was running on. In fact, she would later learn that FBI agent Robert Wright had been trying to investigate Ptech for the longest time, but he had been stifled time and time again by superiors. And Singh?

She was fired.

She tried to go to the press, but the White House pressured reporters to remain silent, as it would jeopardize an ongoing investigation, and if the investigation was ruined, it would, in turn ruin certain journalists' careers if they went forward with the story.

The story would still emerge in short order, despite such threats, and soon the public would know that the software running on critical systems throughout the US government on September 11 was critically flawed on purpose. In particular, Singh would say in an interview that Ptech software was being used alongside Mitre software, in the basement of the FAA, in order to find holes in the interoperability between the FAA's software and other agencies' software; specifically law enforcement systems during times of emergency. Singh would also say that Ptech not only had security clearance, but also had login access to FAA flight control computers, and passwords to pretty much any area they claimed they needed access to.

By 2007, Al-Qadi was already being dropped from international terror lists. In 2010, he would have all civil suits brought against him by the families of 9/11 victims dismissed. In 2012, he would be taken off the UN security council blacklist. And in 2014, Obama's state department would remove his name from the Treasury's "Specially Designated Nationals" list. Ptech would continue to operate, changing its name in 2003 to GoAgile, following a 2002 "raid" by the FBI after the scandal went public. But the FBI had given then advanced warning of their arrival, allowing Ptech plenty of time to hide whatever it wanted.

It's amazing to think no intelligence agency, no risk management consultant, no single individual tasked with safety and security at any governmental agency picked up on the fact that this company offering critical software and technical infrastructure had deep ties to Islamic terror groups until after it was too late. In fact, it would be naive to think that at this point. No, I think it's clear now to everyone reading that much more was going on during 9/11 than meets the eye. Through an unholy alliance between the domestic Deep State, Mossad in Israel, and various Islamic terror groups, weaknesses were found and exploited, emergency response was subverted, billions of dollars were moved, and thousands of American lives were extinguished in mass sacrifice by the Cabal for the sole purpose of increasing their power and dominion around the world; ultimately setting the stage for what would later arrive.

And I'm really only writing about a couple aspects of the attack that are all publicly verifiable, yet about which many are still unaware. There are many other details from the conventional narrative about what happened that day that simply do not add up when put under scrutiny, yet which are beyond the scope of this book. But I think, deep down, each and every American knows we haven't been told the full truth.

Much like a generation or two earlier during the Kennedy assassination, everyone who was alive at the time of the 9/11 attacks knows exactly where they were that day. They turned on the TV, saw the burning buildings, and everything ground to a screeching halt. I myself remember seeing the fighter jets scrambling overhead. I lived in close enough proximity to see the smoke rising from the site at the time. My uncle was one of those who was loaded onto the ferries, and when he got off, they hosed the ash and dust off of him. For days and weeks after, we tried to make sense of the chaos and mourned for the dead. President Trump was present that day in New York. He walked the streets and witnessed the destruction first-hand.

Later, of the attacks, he would say:

> It wasn't architectural defect... The World Trade Center was always known as a very very strong building...Don't forget that building took a bomb in the basement. Now the basement is the most vulnerable place because that's your foundation, and it withstood that... I got to see that area, about three or four days after it took place because one of my structural engineers actually took me for a tour, because he did the building and I said 'I can't believe it.' The building was standing solid and half of the columns were blown out...So, this was an unbelievably powerful building.
>
> How could a plane, even a 767 or a 747 or whatever it might have been, how could it possibly go through the steel? I happen to think they had not only a plane but they had bombs that exploded almost simultaneously because I just can't imagine anything being able to go through that wall....I just think that there was a plane with more than just fuel. Obviously they were very big planes, they were going very rapidly...You're talking about taking out steel, the heaviest caliber steel that was used on the building. These buildings were rock solid.

From secret occult societies, to funding Hitler, to trying to overthrow the US government and install a fascist dictator, to the assassination of Kennedy, to the crack epidemic, to CIA mind control, to 9/11 and the war on terror, the Bush family has, perhaps, more blood on its hands than any other Cabal family in the entire NWO. Through the decades, they've played an instrumental role in guiding this nation forward on a path of destruction, as they have often personally maintained one side presented to the public almost every four years:

Bush or Clinton?

And in 2016, they were hoping to do it again, by presenting us with a Faustian choice between Jeb! or Hillary.

Pick your poison.

(And even if Jeb! hadn't secured the nomination, Bush Sr. always made sure to have enough blackmail on hand for everyone else—just like the CIA taught him.) Perhaps you can begin to see why so many started to cynically refer to the Republicans and Democrats as the "uniparty," where power was always maintained by the entrenched elites and nothing ever really changed for the better for the people.

It should come as no surprise then, that George Sr. was the mastermind behind so much of this, serving as the Cabal's man on the ground who made sure that no matter who won the election, the Cabal would always be the real winners. Supported by a legion of Deep State loyalists even when he was out of office, he was the one really pulling the strings. Imbued with the ideology of his forefathers, there was a reason they called him "Timber wolf."

So you can imagine the look on his face one day, when, from deep underground, in a secret base, George H.W. Bush read this message from Q:

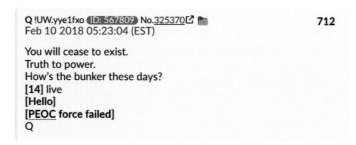

Bush and thirteen others had been holed up in a Cabal bunker, hoping to assassinate Trump in a secure wing of the White House, and Q had just told them that he not only knew where they were right at that very moment, but that their efforts had failed and that they would "cease to exist." (The PEOC is the Presidential Emergency Operations Center—a secure bunker under the east wing of the White House.)

Any wonder then, that some nine months later, George Sr. would be dead? Whether he was just trying to avoid execution and disgrace at the hands of a military tribunal, or he was ordered by his masters to sacrifice himself (for though he is up there, there are still those higher up in the Cabal hierarchy than he), his death in November made convenient cover to defer the D5 deadline Q had been hyping since the beginning—a deadline that, in the end, turned out to be nothing more than bait, designed to expend the resources of the Cabal. That must have infuriated them more than anything that day, for there's no denying that Bush Sr.'s death was a major blow to the Cabal.

In his eulogy for his father, former president George W. Bush would say:

> "To us, his was the brightest of a thousand points of light"

The moment stood out, for it was something Trump himself had riffed on, earlier in the year at a speech in July:

> We're putting America first. And by the way, you know all the rhetoric you see, the Thousand Points of Light. What the hell was that by the way? Thousands Points of Light. What did that mean? Does anyone know?" Trump asked the crowd.
>
> I know one thing: Make America great again, we understand. Putting America first, we understand," he said to applause.

Thousand Points of Light, I never quite got that one. What the hell is that? Has anyone ever figured that one out?"

When George W. spoke it, it was a reference to a phrase his father had turned a number of times in his speeches while president, with the "thousand points of light" ostensibly highlighting the work of volunteers and community organizations across the country. However, the true meaning is much more sinister, and to truly understand it, one has to travel to another castle; this time in Belgium, in a place known to the world as the Chateau des Amerois…

The castle of the Mothers of Darkness…

CHAPTER 7

"The Same Sick Cult"

—December 14, 2017 From Qdrop #344

Q !ITPb.qbhqo ID: 3610ff No.93181 ⧉ ▶
Dec 14 2017 00:24:04 (EST)

7803B61A-1F3E-47BD-88D4-F....jpeg

344

Saw this in last thread.
Focus on papers on table.
Graphic at top.
They all belong to the same sick cult/club.
Q

Everyone who has studied this topic already knows: Cabal researcher Fritz Springmeier used to put warnings on the front of his books. He knew that not everyone who would come across his writings would be able to handle everything he was going to be explaining in the following pages, and he encouraged his readers to skip the book for now if their mind was in any way too weak, too impaired, or otherwise too unhealthy or unprepared to handle the weight of the new knowledge he was about to impart. So with that in mind, here's your warning for this chapter.

What you are about to read may be the most difficult chapter in this book to comprehend, let alone believe. The evil of these people is so beyond what the average person is ready to understand, so if you feel you are unable to handle these subjects, please, by all means, either put down the book, or skip ahead to another chapter. I want the reader to understand that there's no shame in putting this book down, and coming back to it at another point in time when one is better equipped to handle the information within.

Likewise, Springmeier actively discouraged anyone from reading who themselves might have been a victim of such evil. He didn't want to inadvertently trigger any latent mind control alters or dissociative states in anyone. If you suspect you are such an individual, please, move on.

I said in the earlier chapters that when I was first hit with the Pizzagate information, my body would involuntarily shudder, and I would involuntarily cry at times as I was following along with the research threads. There was nothing I could do about it. I would go to move my mouse and my hand was shaking. I would read another post, and it was just tears, which I couldn't stop. Now, I consider myself a pretty tough guy. I've worked around blood and guts and I've seen pain and disease, so please... heed the warning I give you now. I don't have that reaction to this kind of information anymore—but also consider I've had over three years now to digest and process everything.

Don't get me wrong; as long as you're not a victim yourself, I think it's absolutely essential for every single person in the world to understand the following information.

But don't be surprised if you start weeping over what you read.

And don't be surprised if it takes you a very long time to come to grips with it all. It's certainly taken me quite a while.

And with that, we begin.

The news would break in August 1996. Two men in Belgium had been caught following the kidnapping of a fourteen-year-old girl in Bertrix, Belgium. Witnesses had seen the van they had used and police were able to trace it back to the village of Sars-la-Buissière, where the police would arrest two men: Marc Dutroux and his accomplice Michel Lelièvre. What the police did not expect to find was a dungeon in the house where Dutroux had kept a vast number of children he had kidnapped over the years, nor the hundreds of videos he personally recorded of his victims, nor the bodies of his other victims, including one previous accomplice, buried on-site.

Prior to this, Dutroux had been arrested in 1986 for kidnapping and raping five young girls, but would be released from prison in 1992 for good behavior. He would go on to convince a government psychiatrist that he was disabled, thus allowing him to collect a pension from the state, as well as sleeping pills and other medications, which he would later use to drug his victims. Perhaps most shockingly, none of this was discovered earlier when, prior to his arrest, his home had been searched in 1995 by police on an unrelated car theft charge, nor when Dutroux's own mother had written police telling them that he had kept young girls prisoner at some of the *seven* other houses he owned.

Despite all that, no one in the world was ready for what he would say next.

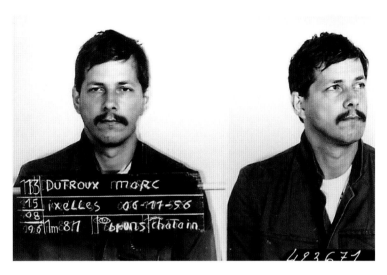

Dutroux would confess after his arrest that, while yes, he had been capturing, drugging, raping, torturing, filming, and trafficking children for years—he was not doing so only for himself. Marc Dutroux would go on to explain that he was, in essence, a professional trafficker for the political elite in Belgium—and indeed—the world (for the EU headquarters is located in Belgium, as is NATO headquarters). These elites would then participate in all manner of occult and Satanic rituals, passing the children around, subjecting these children to MONARCH mind control-styled programs, all manner of sexual abuse, and even sacrificing some as part of their sick rituals. Moreover, this had been going on for a very long time around the world, as part of a system of blackmail and control over political and cultural elites.

One victim of such abuse, Anneke Lucas, would later testify in an interview that she had been sold in 1969 at the age of six to Belgium's pedophile network by the cleaning lady her mother had hired. She would subsequently be raped for over seventeen hundred hours before she hit the age of twelve, starting with the first orgy she was forced to participate in at age six, where she was also made to wear an iron collar and eat human excrement. She would actually be delivered back to her parents from time to time and allowed to go to school, but since her parents themselves were in on the scheme, she would soon go back to her abusers—these political elites—to endure more horrors. She soon realized she was "preferred" by her abusers, by virtue of her looks, and while she leveraged that to her survival advantage to the best of her ability, by the age of eleven, she had become so broken that she was slated to be executed and disposed of. Lucas would go on to tell how they had strapped her to a bloody butchers block used to execute other children, and forced other, younger children to torture her for hours (such as burning her with cigarettes) as part of their "initiation" into the ring.

She was only saved from death when one of her abusers negotiated for her freedom—an abuser who would later be seated as one of the defendants in the Dutroux case.

Belgium would revolt upon the breaking of this news, with hundreds of thousands taking to the streets, demanding—at the very least—the immediate resignation of top officials across the board, regardless of who they were. But with the internet in its infancy at the time, the news wouldn't spread very far beyond Belgium's borders and sadly, many around the world still have not heard of this remarkable case.

Other witnesses and victims would soon come forward, describing such things as "Black Masses," with child and adult sacrifices taking place in front of observers and participants, which included prominent politicians and figures. This would be corroborated by a note found by police at the house belonging to Bernard Weinstein—a man who previously worked with Dutroux, but whom Dutroux had murdered and buried near his "dungeon." The letter was addressed to Dutroux and was written by an individual calling themselves "Anubis," asking Dutroux to deliver "party favors," complete with an age range, preferred sexes, descriptions, etc. They were almost all female, and the ages ranged from one to thirty. Also included was a Satanic calendar. This "Anubis," it turned out, was actually the high priest of a Satanic cult calling itself Abrasax; which was, itself, a cult dedicated to the Gnostic demon Abraxas:

Belgian police would soon raid the location of this cult and find "Grand Master Anubis" (one Francis Desmet) and his "High Priestess Nahema Nephthys" (one Dominique Kindermans) in charge of this cult. The police would go on to seize computers, documents, mail, actual human skulls, jars of blood, and all sorts of Satanic and esoteric implements in the raid—but no children.

Despite all that, it wasn't enough to make any arrests.

In the wake of the Dutroux affair going public, other victims would soon step forward and, along with the descriptions of sexual abuse and human sacrifice, begin describing "hunting parties" where elites would release naked children in the woods to hide, so that the elites themselves could hunt them down and slaughter them. This echoed the testimonies of other, older survivors of ritual Satanic abuse from around the world. But all these rituals and events had to be held somewhere, and a common thread among witness testimony was that these rituals often occurred in "castles," and the surrounding estates, away from the prying eyes of public, where their victims could not escape.

It would be in this very same region of Belgium that Cabal researcher Fritz Springmeier would first discover the role of the Chateau Amerois, which he disclosed to the general public when he wrote about it in his book, *Bloodlines of the Illuminati*, in 1991—a full five years before the Dutroux affair would come to light. In the book, he would describe how an elite ring of Satanic priestesses—called "Mothers of Darkness"—oversaw an entire system of ritual abuse and human sacrifice, and how they perpetuated the existence of this cult.

Springmeier would go on to describe that the Chateau Amerois itself contained within its walls a full cathedral—complete with a dome in which were arranged a thousand lights. This cathedral was where Mothers of Darkness themselves would undergo a "sealing ritual," after years of participating in different rituals to create "alters" inside the minds of the young mothers-to-be. These rituals essentially mimicked the dissociative identities put in place through Monarch mind control programming—though the "Mothers" underwent this process "voluntarily."

This occult building was, in fact, what George Bush Sr. was referencing each time he invoked the "thousand points of light" in one of his speeches; a knowing wink and a nod to his NWO lackeys. And if you're getting flashes of Kubrick's *Eyes Wide Shut* when you're reading this, you're not too far off the mark. In truth, the Venetian masks and orgy scenes don't depict the full reality of the depravity these elites engage in, on a regular basis. Every time Bush would reference the "thousand points of light," he was declaring the total victory of the NWO over the common people.

The Dutroux affair would fizzle out after some time, with Dutroux himself going to prison. No elites were ever arrested, and very little has come from any subsequent investigations into the claims made by Dutroux. As for the Chateau Amerois, the building is now owned by the Solvay family, and you may recognize the name, because Solvay S.A. developed Prozac back in the 80s. Whether or not occult operations were moved to another location is almost irrelevant, being that this is *far* from the only location where the elites engaged in such ceremonies.

QAnon would begin to speak about these kind of practices as early as January 2018, when he would write:

> We haven't started the drops re: human trafficking / sacrifices [yet] [worst].
> Those [good] who know cannot sleep.
> Those [good] who know cannot find peace.
> Those [good] who know will not rest until those responsible are held accountable.
> Nobody can possibly imagine the pure evil and corruption out there.
> Those you trust are the most guilty of sin.

Q !UW.yye1fxo ID: b189f8 No.130638 ☐   586
Jan 22 2018 21:47:32 (EST)

What would happen if texts originating from a FBI agent to several
[internals] discussed the assassination (possibility) of the POTUS or
member of his family?
What if the texts suggest foreign allies were involved?
Forget the Russia set up [1 of 22].
This is only the beginning.
Be careful what you wish for.
AS THE WORLD TURNS.
Could messages such as those be publicly disclosed?
What happens to the FBI?
What happens to the DOJ?
What happens to special counsel?
What happens in general?
Every FBI/DOJ prev case could be challenged.
Lawless.
Think logically.
We haven't started the drops re: human trafficking / sacrifices
[yet][worst].
Those [good] who know cannot sleep.
Those [good] who know cannot find peace.
Those [good] who know will not rest until those responsible are held
accountable.
Nobody can possibly imagine the pure evil and corruption out there.
Those you trust are the most guilty of sin.
Who are we taught to trust?
If you are religious, PRAY.
60% must remain private [at least] - for humanity.
These people should be hanging.
Q

Take, for instance, the haunting series of photographs from a 1972 ball held by the
Rothschilds at the Chateau de Ferrieres (which was later used as a set on the Roman Polanski/Johnny Depp film, *The Ninth Gate*). The photos have been widely circulated since they
were first leaked online, but illustrate, at least on some level, the kind of occult activities in
which these elites engage on a regular basis. In fact, Q himself would ask Anons to locate
these photos at one point—specifically asking Anons to locate the "Y head" that was "covered in gold," and later to follow the "Y head" around the world. So it goes without saying
that if you want to fully understand Q, these photos are required viewing:

Q !ITPb.qbhqo ID: YzNom6b4 No.150513545 ⬚ 🏴   195
Nov 22 2017 16:33:25 (EST)

U1 – CA – EU – ASIA – IRAN/NK
Iran Deal.
Why is this relevant?
Re-read drops re: NK / Iran.
(Y) What does it mean to be covered in gold?
Which couple was photographed covered in gold?
The public release was a mistake.
Who released the picture?
Who has all the information?
(Y) What does it mean to be covered in gold?
Can you locate one other pic w/ Y head covered in gold?
What does this represent?
/_\
THE SUM OF ALL FEARS.
Q

I don't want to belabor the point: the "Y head covered in gold" is a reference to none other than the Rothschild clan themselves. Marie-Helene de Rothschild wears, in this photo, the giant gold-covered head of a stag as she stands next to her husband Guy de Rothschild.

Shuttered until 1959, the couple took it upon themselves to refurbish the Chateau de Ferrieres and took to hosting regular parties inside, where elites from all over were invited to participate, be they members of royalty, politicians working in government, members of the media, or tycoons in the private sector. For this particular soiree, the chateau would be lit in an infernal red:

The invitation was penned in reverse, thus, requiring those invited to read their invitations with the aid of a mirror. Beyond the obvious *Through the Looking-Glass* reference, mirrors (and the broader concept of duality) are essential parts of Monarch mind control programming—but also important concepts for the ruling elites, wherein they get to present one face to the public, but another, privately, among their own ranks. (This ties in to the deity Janus, which we will discuss later.)

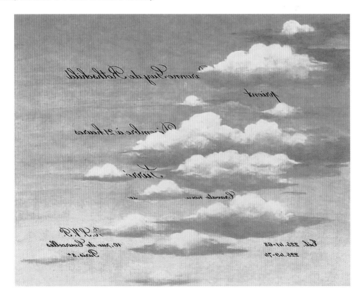

All guests were encouraged to wear striking, even disturbing masks and makeup:

Many of these affairs were designed and frequented by some of the top artists and designers of the day. Pictured here, in attendance, is none other than Salvador Dali:

Just as it is now, many Hollywood elites participated in these events. Here, pictured with her head in a bird cage, is none other than Audrey Hepburn. It's worth noting that bird cages are often symbols for mind control:

Note the "gold leaf" in this woman's costume:

And the centerpieces for the event were all references to cannibalism, featuring nude mannequins…

And dismembered baby dolls…

Speaking on this subject to Anons, Q would go on to say:

> Q !ITPb.qbhqo ID: pOVOfY+r No.150412315 🔗 🏴   **184**
> Nov 21 2017 22:07:58 (EST)
>
> Their need for symbolism will be their downfall.
> Follow the Owl & Y head around the world.
> Identify and list.
> They don't hide it.
> They don't fear you.
> You are sheep to them.
> You are feeders.
> Godfather III.
> Q
>
> ANSWERS

Though it was not entirely clear what the significance of the "Owl" and the "Y head" were at the time, industrious Anons would soon unearth more answers than they ever could have imagined.

But why the Rothschilds? Why has this family, from time immemorial, seemingly been such a lightning rod for "conspiracy theorists?" What is it about this dynasty that attracts so much attention? Is it mere antisemitism, as some would suggest, or does it go deeper than that?

Very little is as it seems on the surface, the deeper we dive into this subject. Remember the duality we talked about just before? How there's a public face and a private face to everything? Recall Hillary Clinton's private speech to Wall Street bankers that would later be leaked to the public, where she invokes such a position herself as though it were common and accepted practice among their ranks; for it almost goes without saying where their true loyalties lie. Beyond all the power, all the influence, all the corruption that comes with being one of the wealthiest banking dynasties in the world, the true question behind it all becomes… to whom or to what are the Rothschilds loyal?

To shed some light on that question, we need to go back to the boards. What follows is a conversation that took place between a drunken Lynn Forester de Rothschild, wife of Sir Evelyn de Rothschild, and one of the wealthiest women in the world (and a major backer behind Hillary Clinton), speaking to a group of Anons. The conversation took place on the /CBTS/ board on December 7, 2017. All interactions have been copied verbatim, misspellings and all, though rearranged in order to help the reader follow along with the flow of the conversation, as opposed to the otherwise broken staccato mere chronological posting would yield:

LDR: Lol. 'Drunk Pic Post Q" Maintain your military bearing.

Anon: L?

LDR: End of the Thursday night bottle. We all do it.

Anon: Hows it feel to see it all crumbling L?

Anon: Apparently like insomnia.

LDR: Never even close to concern.

Anon: Post again L. I don't have loc yet

LDR: and you never will

Anon: Ever heard of remote viewing? It's a thing.

LDR: Looking at my remote now.

Anon: You think you a invincible??

LDR: Pretty close, child.

Anon: Not if POTUS has control of the military.

YO\ou dont have much of a chance if he send delta/Seal team 6 after you and your irk.

Thats what Im hearing

LDR: Well, they can always be paid a little better.

Anon: You must be delusional

Most of them a patriots, they love this country them your dirty money…

LDR: We don't use dirty money. Paper is for the puppets.

Anon: Then what are you doing here?

Anon: Who else has been drinking, Lynn?

LDR: entertainment

Anon: You seem rattled Satanist?

LDR: My snake is bigger than yours.

Anon: Got a lot of time for that running banks and all?

LDR: Haha. I can't even type.

Anon: Looooooooser……

LOOOOOOSERRRR

Lynn is a LOOOOOOSEERRRRRRRR

LDR: Feels like winning around here.

Anon: I found her. follow my id back a few posts

LDR: eagles

Anon: Fuck off with the satanic symbolism. All you are doing is hurting people with it.

LDR: finger on filter. ty anon

Anon: I know how this ends, faggit

LDR: Yep. You die of thirst after watching your children die first.

Anon: Nah, we good. We got this fam.

Looking forward to your lynching, flaying, and eternity in hell, faggit.

LDR: Hell is imaginary. Thirst is real. You will see soon sweetie.

Anon: If Lynn is here she must be VERY, VERY FRIGHTENED.

I have prayed these ppl will feel the horrific fear all those poor babies must have felt who were violated. Lynn Rothschild, you will reap what you have sown, and when you do, it will be your own doing. I have no pity for you. There are those who have been created for destruction. You are one.

Anon: what does thirst mean?

LDR: eat some popcorn and you tell me

Anon: omg m fo.. i know what it is to b thirsty .. i dont have ur sick as
mind to related that with someone killing someone elses child.
how thr fuck is that thirsty?? again, not luciferian.. not satanic…
therefore u answer doesnt compute
btw, ur post… planing on using ur foot soliders to do mass shooting everywhere? ..
i assume that has to do with thirst…u plotting some sort of wide
spread attack… maybe guns maybe not. either way, we all die one
day .. i'll make sure to find u if i go first :-)

LDR: go to grammar school first. you should at least be able to read
your tombstone.

Anon: You seemed really, really scared, desperate, and thirsty Satanist. You
gonna be okay? Need a tissue?

(At this point in the conversation, QAnon stepped in himself).

QAnon: L.
Heard you can't sleep anymore.
Don't come here again.
#FLYROTHSFLY#
Sweet dreams.
For Green.
Q
—end—

"My snake is bigger than yours…"

Keep that line in mind, moving forward.

In order to understand why a drunken elite with trillions in assets under her family's control would suddenly show up on the boards one night, you have to understand a little context
from the weeks before. Prior to this conversation, on November 17, a Cessna had collided with
a helicopter over the Rothschild's Buckinghamshire estate, killing former army pilot, Captain
Mike Green, providing context to some of Q's earlier, more cryptic drops:

Q !ITPb.qbhqo ID: snf602p9 No.149490950☑ 🏴   155
Nov 15 2017 00:38:48 (EST)

_Conf_D-TT_^_v891_0600_yes
_green1_0600
Bunker Apple Yellow Sky [… + 1]
Yes
Godspeed.
Q

                                                              ANSWERS

Rumors would swirl that a Rothschild had actually died in the crash as well. Q would confirm the connection between the crash and his post a few days after the crash.

> **Q !ITPb.qbhqo ID: rHXVKCrC No.150388962** 175
> Nov 21 2017 18:43:15 (EST)
>
> Expand your thinking.
> Captain Mike Green.
> _Conf_D-TT_^_v891_0600_yes
> _green1_0600
> Bunker Apple Yellow Sky [... + 1]
> Yes.
> Who countered?
> Do you believe in coincidences?
> Learn how to read the map.
> Q
>
> ANSWERS

Q was telling us that Captain Green perished on a clandestine military operation against the Cabal, which is why he ended his drops to Lynn with:

> **Q !ITPb.qbhqo ID: 913bb1 No.52157** 302
> Dec 7 2017 22:29:30 (EST)
>
> For Green.
> Q
> —end—

What was so important that Captain Green would give his life over the Rothschild estate that day? While the details of this operation may never be fully known, we patriots are grateful for Captain Green's supreme act of sacrifice and bravery.

Weeks prior to the unfolding of these events, Q had been spending time informing Anons about the true shape and structure of the hierarchy inside the Cabal, even invoking that classical Masonic image of the "Eye of Providence" superimposed on a pyramid, which you can still find on any dollar bill these days:

Q !!TPb.qbhqo ID: gO/UntOB No.149063235 ☐   **133**
Nov 11 2017 23:29:35 (EST)

Hard to swallow.
Important to progress.
Who are the puppet masters?
House of Saud (6+++) - $4 Trillion+
Rothschild (6++) - $2 Trillion+
Soros (6+) - $1 Trillion+
Focus on above (3).
Public wealth disclosures – False.
Many governments of the world feed the 'Eye'.
Think slush funds (feeder).
Think war (feeder).
Think environmental pacts (feeder).
Triangle has (3) sides.
Eye of Providence.
Follow the bloodlines.
What is the keystone?
Does Satan exist?
Does the 'thought' of Satan exist?
Who worships Satan?
What is a cult?
Epstein island.
What is a temple?
What occurs in a temple?
Worship?
Why is the temple on top of a mountain?
How many levels might exist below?
What is the significance of the colors, design and symbol above the
dome?
Why is this relevant?
Who are the puppet masters?
Have the puppet masters traveled to this island?
When? How often? Why?
"Vladimir Putin: The New World Order Worships Satan"
Q

ANSWERS

And this drop was important because it shows how Q was, even early on, trying to tear down a commonly held misconception about the Cabal: that it's this one large monolithic group of evildoers operating in secret, when in truth, it's a number of affiliated groups united in common cause, bound together in an evil hierarchy, but each with their particular role to play; each with their own diabolical function to fulfill. It's easy to look at a group like the afore-mentioned Abrasax, that Satanic group involved in the Dutroux affair, and plainly see the evil at work. We talked in a previous chapter about the Thule Society, and the later Vril Society. We looked at, for instance, the Rosicrucians, the Order of the Golden Dawn, and Crowley's Ordo Templi Orientis—and it's *easy* to recognize the evil present in all those groups.

It's much harder for many to listen to, for instance, the testimony of SRA survivors who were abused in religious groups, or by famous religious figures. Many don't know, for instance, that the Dalai Lama keeps a harem of hundreds of boys for himself, or that a great deal of his funding has come directly from the CIA. On the flip side of that, we're at a point now where I think it's easy for many to see how thoroughly rotted the Catholic Church has become from the inside out, from the popes, to the bishops, to the priests and nuns, but it would be supremely naive to think that this is where the cancer has stopped growing.

At the same time, we can't limit our thinking to just religious or esoteric groups, either. No, entire intelligence agencies are heirs to Cabal ideology as well, complete with their own set of motives and allegiances. Charities and NGOs, their heart-tugging ads aside, are often in on the charade, too, with the Red Cross being a group that draws particular ire from Q—and if anyone has looked in on their activities, especially in the wake of Benghazi, you'll have a good idea why.[25] And the same goes for international banking dynasties—which are particularly notable for the disproportionate amount of influence they wield.

So where do the Rothschilds fit in to all of this?

The Rothschild banking dynasty was founded in 1700s by Mayer Rothschild (taking their name from the Red Shield hung outside their door). During this time, usury was forbidden within Christendom, so the task of managing money often fell to Jews, who had no such moral imperative against charging interest on loans (at least, to goyim). Through a series of savvy moves, the Rothschilds, splitting into three branches across Europe, grew in power and stature as they lent out funds to the European aristocracy. For instance, when tasked with managing the wealth of Wilhelm the IX of Hesse, Mayer Rothschild knew he would have to deal with an enterprising young upstart by the name of Napoleon Bonaparte. So when Napoleon came to invade Hesse, Mayer had already moved most of Wilhelm's fortune to London… where Mayer's son, Nathan, had established a branch of the Rothschild enterprise back in 1798. Nathan then turned around and loaned Wilhelm's fortune out to King George III of England… who then turned around and used the fresh funds to fight Napoleon (while no doubt sticking his loyal, royal subjects with the bill via various taxes). In essence, the Rothschilds had just managed to leverage a fortune they didn't own, to fund a war that aligned with their own interests, while earning a fortune in interest for themselves the entire time. War and conflict was very profitable, indeed!

This kind of thing would continue throughout the eighteenth and nineteenth centuries, until finally, Francis II, the last Holy Roman Emperor, elevated the now five Rothschild brothers to the status of nobility by granting them the title of "Baron." This influence would soon even extend over the Vatican itself, which Q referenced in a post some months later:

Q !xowAT4Z3VQ **ID: 169658** No.896860 **1021**
Apr 4 2018 18:02:33 (EST)

List the estimated wealth of religious organizations.
Billions.
Vatican bank.
$229B.
Board of Superintendence.
Supervisory Commission of Cardinals.
Clown connection.
1832 Rothschild loan to the Holy See.
Q

As the papal states saw their territory being absorbed by Italian Nationalists, Pope Gregory XVI decided that in order to maintain their power, they needed more funds, and so he called upon the Rothschilds—that venerable family so many European elite had relied on in times of crisis—and drew up an agreement to borrow some four hundred thousand

---

25   https://www.neonrevolt.com/2018/04/23/the-red-cross-double-cross-and-so-much-more-on-todays-newq-qanon-greatawakening/

pounds (equivalent to some thirty-four million dollars in today's terms). Notable about this meeting was the fact that Carl Mayer von Rothschild did not bother to kiss the Pope's ring as he approached. As the Vicar of Christ on Earth, most Catholics had to kiss the Pope's feet when addressing him. As a Jew, von Rothschild was permitted to kiss his ring, instead. Despite this concession, von Rothschild simply ignored the convention altogether, and got straight down to business, offending a great many of the faithful in the process. Later, in 1850s, the Rothschilds would loan the Vatican a second, undisclosed sum of money. These loans eventually allowed the Rothschilds to begin infiltrating the Catholic church, first with various appointments within the ranks, and then officially through control of the Vatican Bank, known officially as the Institute for Works of Religion.

This is what Q is referencing when he talks about the Board of Superintendence. The Board reports to a Supervisory Commission of Cardinals and to the Pope himself, but the Vatican Bank is largely independent of the Holy See; functioning independently within the Vatican, as its assets do not belong to the Holy See. Think of it in similar terms to the Federal Reserve—a privately owned central bank in the middle of a nation-state. Prior to this, the Rothschilds had been appointed as Guardians of the Vatican Treasury—an odd relationship to be sure, considering they were not Catholics. To understand how they came to control the Vatican's assets as well as their own, one now must understand the relationship between the Jesuit Order, Napoleon, the Freemasons, and indeed, the French Revolution.

Originally founded by Ignatius of Loyola in 1534, the Jesuits were a military order of Catholics that proved hard for the Vatican to control as they accrued wealth and power over time. Originally named "Los Alumbrados" (that is, the Illuminated Ones), the Jesuits were really a Gnostified sect which taught (not to everyone, but only those initiated in its upper levels) that once a person had reached a certain state of inner perfection and purification, that person could commit any deed or sin, and not risk damnation. Adultery, theft, murder, nothing was off limits for these rare, "perfected" souls. Loyola (really, a leftover Templar himself) saw his mission as raising a militia for the papacy, and said as much himself when he was questioned by the Dominican Inquisition about his activities within the Alumbrados.

In response, Loyola requested an audience with Pope Paul III (that is, Alessandro Farnese)—a member of the Black Nobility—and was basically given a slap on the wrist after he had explained his intentions. He was free to go following his official "admonition," but had it been anyone else, they doubtless would have been tortured at the time. But the link between Templars and Jesuits cannot be ignored (with the Templars not only being a military organization, but really, the first international banking order), for while the history is quite convoluted, the goals were largely the same; the establishment of a global hierarchy guiding humanity into the future.

The Templars themselves, that is, "The United Religious, Military and Masonic Orders of the Temple and of St John of Jerusalem, Palestine, Rhodes and Malta" were originally a group of Crusaders founded by two French knights, Hugh de Payens and Godfrey de St. Omer, in 1118, who took up residency in Jerusalem at the site of the temple mount, growing their wealth and power in the process. Saladin would eventually chase the Templars out of Jerusalem in 1187, but the Templar order continued to operate and grow across Europe... much to the chagrin of many a monarch, leading to something of a violent purge by the time the 1300s had rolled around.

Seeking refuge, some Templars escaped this purge and took up residency in the one country in Europe that didn't recognize papal authority: Scotland, under the protection of Robert the Bruce. Here, they would found the Masonic Order by systematically infiltrating the "Wall Builder's Lodge," eventually renaming themselves the Masonic Lodge, a.k.a., the Freemasons, in due time. This became the Scottish rite of Freemasonry, which is itself the oldest branch of Freemasonry. When writing of the Templars in his masterwork on Masonry, *Morals and Dogma*, 33rd Degree Scottish Rite Freemason (and Confederate general during the American Civil War) Albert Pike would write:

> Hughes de Payens himself had not that keen and far-sighted intellect nor that grandeur of purpose which afterward distinguished the military founder of another soldiery that became formidable to kings. The Templars were unintelligent and therefore unsuccessful Jesuits.

As for the wealth of the Templars, following the order's dissolution via papal bull in 1312, its riches were handed down principally to two groups: the Knights Hospitaller (which would later become the Sovereign Military Order of Malta—a.k.a., the Knights of Malta) and the Order of Montessa in Portugal and Aragon. The Knights of Malta would later figure prominently in the rise of Hitler, when a member of the order, Franz von Papen, became chancellor of Germany in 1932, ordered the dissolution of the Reichstag, and, following new elections in July of that year, helped Hitler obtain the chancellorship in 1933. The Order of Montessa was, essentially, the exact same thing as the Templars, just regrouped and repositioned by 1317 under the guidance of King James II of Aragon, this time with the express approval of Pope John XXII. The Order of Montessa would be later united with the Spanish Crown in 1587, but the last Grand Master to oversee the order would be Pedro Luis Garceran de Borja, the half-brother of St. Francis Borgia, and grandson of Pope Alexander VI (a.k.a. Rodrigo Lanzol Borgia).

Likewise, the symbols used by Jesuits were practically ripped straight from the Templars, notably referencing the *In Hoc Signo Vinces* motto of the Templars, and integrating the design of the Templar Cross into their own logo.

Some Cabal researchers will say the IHS in the logo here are actually secret references to Isis, Horus, and Seb, the Egyptian snake god often equated with Cronus, and if this were actually the case, I would not be surprised in the least. But in all my research, it's hard to come to a definitive conclusion on that front. We'll be covering that subject more in a bit, but in the meantime, between the 1300s and the 1700s, the power of Masonic lodges had been… somewhat diluted by a number of factors; notably, the Age of Enlightenment sweeping across Europe. It's something of a hard concept for us moderns to grasp, but again, even these organizations that may have started in the shadows and secrecy aren't completely, inherently evil, in and of themselves. No, its the actions of those taken within those organizations that determines whether they are good or bad. Again, Masonry was, quite literally, a trade organization at the get-go, comprised mainly of actual architects and builders looking to converse with other professionals. In 1703, the organization shifted away from being a mere trade organization, morphing into more of a fraternal organization, when, according to Nesta H. Webster in her 1924 work entitled *Secret Societies and Subversive Movements*, the Lodge of St. Paul in London declared that:

> [T]he privileges of Masonry should no longer be restricted to operative Masons, but extended to men of various professions, provided they were regularly approved and initiated into the Order.

"Yes, the Templars infiltrated and began to subvert Masonry over time, but prior to that coming to completion, Masonry had turned primarily into a fraternal organization for English gentlemen. Many of my readers will be aware that a number of the Founding Fathers of America were themselves Masons, well acquainted with the signs, symbols, and teachings of the group, but again, this wasn't the fully developed form of Masonry we later observe. When Washington took office as president of the fledgling nation of America for the first time, the whole event was a Masonic ritual. Why, the very gremiale (that is, the ritual apron vestment) he wore that day was crafted by none other than Madame de LaFayette, the wife of another notable Mason who participated heavily in the American and French revolutions, the Marquis de LaFayette:

Indeed, many of the Founders were Masons, with at least nine signatories of the Declaration of Independence being confirmed members, and another eleven being suspected members of the Lodge. But again, Masonry back then wasn't quite what it is now. Why, the first twenty-five degrees of Freemasonry were only created when the Jesuits started to subvert the order in 1717. George Washington wasn't even born until 1732, and there was the whole issue of the Atlantic ocean separating these various branches of these Masonic lodges. The thirty-three degrees of Freemasonry wouldn't even come into existence until the 1780s in France, after the full on Jesuit takeover of the order. And to show you that this isn't exactly conspiracy territory, the Founding Fathers of America were aware of the dangers of the Jesuit order, themselves. Said the Marquis de LaFayette:

> It is my opinion that if the liberties of this country—the United States of America—are destroyed, it will be by the subtlety of the Roman Catholic Jesuit priests, for they are the most crafty, dangerous enemies to civil and religious liberty. They have instigated **most** of the wars of Europe.

So what you have is really a power struggle between groups, and even power-hungry individuals within these groups, enabled by ideology to commit nefarious deeds and rationalize any course of action so as to accrue power for themselves. The Jesuits, who were really the heirs of Templar ideology, had learned from their forebears' mistakes, were determined not to repeat them, and would attempt to wield power and influence over all other groups in their proximity, which, given their history throughout Europe, could include all manner of spying, subversion, blackmail, and even assassination.

Despite this savvy determination, given the order's teachings and rapidly growing influence, various nations started to order the banishment of all members of the Jesuit order; notably Louie XIV, King of France, but also Spain and Portugal… for pesky things like, oh, assassination plots against monarchs. Long story short, a number of these monarchs banded together and in 1773 convinced Pope Clement XIV to issue a *Dominus ac Redemptor*; a papal bull against the Jesuits, thus suppressing the Jesuit order forever. Following the bull, Maria Teresa of Austria would also hop on the anti-Jesuit bandwagon and expel them all from her realm as well.

And that would have been the end of the story… but for one Jesuit-educated man named Adam Weishaupt, and one ambitious Frenchman named Napoleon Bonaparte.

I know this may come as a shock to some, but despite the papal bull, the Jesuits didn't just close up shop and go home. Officially cut off from the Vatican and pretty much all of Europe, the Jesuits were in a rough financial state and forced to operate underground, and in secrecy.

Ironically, this formal suppression of the Jesuits gave rise to, perhaps their greatest competitor, the Bavarian Illuminati. Had they been allowed to operate, no such power vacuum would have formed, and in an odd twist of history, no one on planet earth might have ever uttered the term "Illuminati" ever again. Already inducted into the secret society of the Freemasons and schooled in ancient mystery religions by a traveling merchant named Kölmer, the Jesuit-educated Adam Weishaupt set about creating a new secret society. The Bavarian Illuminati represented a wholesale rejection of any Enlightenment ideals, and exhibited a kind of wholesale fundamentalism rarely seen in secular circles. But this was just what Weishaupt intended, as he sought to reshape the world in his own image.

In 1776, just three short years after the papal bull against the Jesuits was issued by the Pope, Weishaupt would formulate the basis for his Bavarian Illuminati. Similar to his forebears in the Jesuit Order and the Los Alumbrados, the Illuminati felt that they were above the common and profane man, and thus entitled to rule over all others. They imagined they would use their power to guide humanity into a future of their own, "enlightened" design. Drawing from a number of ancient traditions, Weishaupt first gave himself the Illuminatus name of "*Spartacus*" and set to crafting an entire esoteric system of belief that could almost be thought of as plagiarizing ancient mystery schools; even taking the "Owl of Minerva" as their own symbol:

When attempting to detail this system of Weishaupt's own creation, Nesta Webster would write:

> It is true that 'Mysteries' play a great part in the phraseology of the Order-'Greater and Lesser Mysteries,' borrowed from ancient Egypt-whilst the higher initiates are decorated with such titles as 'Epopte' and 'Hierophant,' taken from the Eleusinian Mysteries. Yet Weishaupt's own theories appear to bear no relation whatever to these ancient cults. On the contrary, the more we penetrate into his system, the more apparent it becomes that all the formulas he employs which derive from any religious source—whether Persian, Egyptian, or Christian—merely serve to disguise a purely material purpose, a plan for destroying the existing order of society. Thus all that was really ancient in Illuminism was the destructive spirit that animated it and also the method of organization it had imported from the East. Illuminism therefore marks an entirely new departure in the history of European secret societies. Weishaupt himself indicates this as one of the great secrets of the Order. 'Above all,' he writes to 'Cato' (alias Zwack), 'guard the origin and the novelty of in the most careful way.' 'The greatest mystery,' he says again, 'must be that the thing is new; the fewer who know this the better.... Not one of the Eichstadters knows this but would live or die for it that the thing is as old as Methuselah.

> This pretence of having discovered some fund of ancient wisdom is the invariable ruse of secret society adepts; the one thing never admitted is the identity of the individuals from whom one is receiving direction.

So Weishaupt was, in essence, a megalomaniac who was attempting to out-secret-society all the other secret societies of his day by ripping off the Manicheans, the Egyptians, and the Babylonians, and all other manner of mystery schools he could plumb for inspiration. And though it may come as a surprise to some, Weishaupt had nothing but disdain for groups like the Jesuits and the Rosicrucians, who he saw as superstitious competition. He began waging something of a secret war to uproot them from European society, but as is the way with such narcissistic megalomaniacs who imagine they can reshape the order of the entire world into some kind of utopia (yes, the Illuminati were really just proto-Socialists), Weishaupt started to really anger those around him: namely, his number two, Adolph Franz Freidrich Ludwig Baron von Knigge (referred to as *Philo Judaeus* among the Illuminati ranks). Knigge was, in many respects, a more charismatic leader than Weishaupt, publishing a number of impactful essays against the Jesuits, but also recruiting hundreds of members into the order from Masonry (of which Knigge was also previously a member, and thus spoke against with authority). This, of course, raises the question: how many of these Masons were Jesuits (or, perhaps more appropriately, secret Jesuits) themselves?

And of course the question cuts the other way as well. How many Illuminati filtered into Masonry and influenced the social circles there? If you were plotting these groups on a Venn diagram, what percentage overlap would they show? Nineteenth-century Cabal researcher Albert Mackey believed that at some point, the Jesuits infiltrated the ranks of the Freemasons in order to help advance the Scottish house of Stuart in their efforts to regain the English throne. Another Cabal researcher by the name of Jonathan Blanchard, writing in 1905, would find another parallel between the two groups: in both the Jesuits and the Masons, the thirty-second degree is labeled with the same motto; "*Ad majorem Dei gloriam,*" translated "to the greater glory of God." (And note as well how the "black sun" logo of the Jesuits contains thirty-two rays). With all that in mind, its easy to see why the groups would increasingly overlap in the future.

But Weishaupt, being the narcissist he was, couldn't handle the surge in Knigge's popularity, and constantly derided Knigge behind his back to other Illuminati members. Amazing how these "illumined masters" who were destined to rule over all mankind could be so petty and base! Knigge would grow increasingly disgusted with Weishaupt as well, threatening, in a long letter to "Cato," that he would expose the "Jesuitical" Wieshaupt and all his secrets to the world. Two months later, in July 1784, Knigge would leave the Bavarian Illuminati for good.

Then, in 1785, letters written by Weishaupt to his acolytes detailing a plot to overthrow Charles Theodore, prince-elector and Duke of Bavaria, would be intercepted by the authorities, causing him to immediately lose his position at the University of Ingolstadt where he worked, and forcing him to flee for his life to the city of Gotha, where he would end up writing several works on Illuminism before his death in 1830, some forty-five years after his initial exile. Illuminism would be banned in Bavaria henceforth, but to say that the order ceased then and there would be naive.

No, his ideas were reincorporated into yet another secret society, just across the border in Prague, Bohemia. Founded in 1859, the Schlaraffia, as they called themselves, also took on the Minerval symbol of the owl, venerating it in their various rituals. And one offshoot of the Schlaraffia would soon grow larger and more prominent than the others, before finally arriving in America in 1884.

Some of my more savvy readers' ears may be perking up now, for indeed, we are now about to speak of The Bohemian Grove. For those unaware, the Bohemian Grove is a twenty-seven-hundred acre compound located in the redwood forests of Monte Rio, California, owned and operated by the all-male Bohemian Club of San Francisco. Officially founded in 1872, each year the elite members of the club gather at the Grove for several weeks of rituals and revelries, including the one we spoke about in a previous chapter: the *Cremation of Care* ceremony. Security is always high at the Grove year round, with advanced security systems and ex-military patrolling the site, because frankly, they don't want anymore evidence of their activities leaking out than what's already been leaked to the public.

Yes, it's true, many of the United States' top men in media, government, and the private sector all gather in front of a thirty-foot concrete statue of an owl, listen to a recording performed by Walter Cronkite, and witness a "mock" human sacrifice, complete with pyrotechnics. Prior to this, there will have been weeks of orgies, often homosexual in nature, and at other times, the club will import both male and female prostitutes or sex slaves from overseas; usually teens or tweens from some poor, Eastern European nation. It's been said that if these victims die in the process, it doesn't really matter because no one is going to come looking for them anyway, and their bodies will be burnt in the Cremation of Care ceremony.

Many modern presidents have all been members at this club, with both Nixon and Bush Sr. first announcing their presidential campaigns at the Grove, before going public. And while, "Enty" over at CDAN has posted about inside affairs at the Grove on a number of occasions, on November 14, 2017 he recalled the story of a particularly grueling incident where, in 1991, Bill Clinton's future was being debated by the ranking members of the Bohemian Grove. The big problem Clinton had involved the death of a teen he had raped years earlier. He had been hanging out, partying with comedian Sam Kinison, and the two had picked up these two underage girls, offered them alcohol, cocaine, and after Clinton had got done assaulting "his" girl, she began to convulse and soon died on the spot from a drug overdose. Kinison had celebrity connections though, and basically, Enty tells us that they were able to cover up the death and tell the girl's parents that she had died of a drug overdose. They also managed to convince the other teen to keep her mouth shut, and that would have been that. But long story short, Kinison soon freaks out and tells his girlfriend at the time what happened. Enty tells us that the girlfriend, instead of leaving Kinison and going to the police, decides it would be a good idea to blackmail Clinton with this information instead. Kinison says no, but his girlfriend persists, going behind Kinison's back.

This is a problem for Clinton, so what Clinton does is have Kinison's bodyguard get Kinison quite high on all sorts of drugs following a long period of sobriety, before dragging him back to his home to sleep it off. The bodyguard, known to the girlfriend and carrying the impaired Kinison, is allowed to enter and put Kinison to bed. But once inside, the bodyguard proceeds to rape Kinison's girlfriend over the course of the next twelve hours. Enty informs us that after some string pulling a mistrial would eventually be declared over this incident. It was a message from Clinton to the girlfriend: Shut up, or worse is coming. In the meantime, the other teen involved in the original incident is killed and her death is made to look like another overdose.

As Clinton's political star rises, Kinison and his girlfriend grow more and more worried. They call him, try to arrange a sort of peace, and Clinton verbally agrees. This is all water under the bridge now, right? Kinison and his girlfriend relax and try to move on with their lives. They get married. They try to start over...

But the Cabal won't let them. The boyfriend of the second dead teen is told that Kinison was the one who gave her the drugs she overdosed on, and how he can get revenge for her death.

On April 10, 1992, Troy Pierson plows head on into Kinison's Pontiac with his pickup, killing the comedian and very nearly killing the girlfriend in the process, just six days after their wedding. Because Troy is seventeen, he gets sentenced to one year probation, three hundred hours of community service, and a suspended license.

And as we all know, Bill Clinton would go on to win the 1992 presidential election. The other potential candidate the Bohemian Grove could have given their "seal of approval" to at the time was thought by some to have been Jeb Bush. And Kinison's girlfriend would never utter so much as a peep about all this, ever again.

At least, that's if you believe Enty.

So that's how the suppression of the Jesuits led to the creation of the Illuminati, which led to the Bohemian Club, which coordinated the activities of United States elites for most of the nineteenth and twentieth centuries, even into present day. Each group carries traces of "DNA" from the others, and have been involved in notorious activities throughout their histories.

It should also be noted here that the family of Las Vegas shooter/arms dealer Stephen Paddock all have connections to the Grove. In particular, his brother Bruce Paddock owned a home very close to Grove acreage, on nearby Canyon Drive. Bruce would be charged with nineteen counts of sexual exploitation of a child, and one count of possession of child pornography. Recall as well that child pornography would also be found on the laptop belonging to Stephen Paddock. This led Anons to wonder at the time whether the Paddock brothers were all working for the Deep State in some capacity; as more than mere gun traffickers.

But how do the Illuminati and the Jesuit-backed Freemasons fit together in all this? These were, ostensibly, competing secret societies, but two men hit upon the same idea around the same time through their own independent research which would shed some light on the subject.

The first was a respected English scientist by the name of John Robison, who published a book with the lengthy title of *Proofs of a Conspiracy against all the Religions and Governments of Europe, carried on in the secret meetings of the Freemasons, Illuminati, and Reading Societies*, first published in 1797. Robison's book created quite the stir at the time, and perhaps the most interesting thing about it was that most of his information was supplied by a Benedictine monk-turned-British-spy by the name of Alexander Horn. Indeed, most of the claims in the book were Horn's alone, with Robison acting only as scribe in the matter. Robison was really the first to point out Weishaupt's role in all this conspiratorial madness, and would attribute the following quote to him in his book:

> The great strength of our Order lies in its concealment; let it never appear in any place in its own name, but always covered by another name, and another occupation. None is better than the three lower degrees of Free Masonry; the public is accustomed to it, expects little from it, and therefore takes little notice of it. Next to this, the form of a learned or literary society is best suited to our purpose, and had Free Masonry not existed, this cover would have been employed; and it may be much more than a cover, it may be a powerful engine in our hands. By establishing reading societies, and subscription libraries, and taking these under our direction, and supplying them through our labours, we may turn the public mind which way we will.

The reading society he wished to implicate in this was, of course, the Jacobins. Among the most influential texts read during this period was a pamphlet entitled "*What is the Third Estate?*" written by a Jesuit-educated Catholic priest by the name of Emmanuel Joseph Sieyès, which argued that the clergy and the aristocracy (that is, the first two estates) were an extraneous and unnecessary burden on the third estate, which was the common people of France. This pamphlet and the subsequent line of thinking it produced would become tremendously influential during the French Revolution, as would Sieyès himself, after the Revolution.

A second book on the subject of Illuminati and Freemason collusion would also arrive in 1797 when a Jesuit priest by the name of Augustin Barruel would publish the first of what would become a four volume set entitled *Memoirs Illustrating the History of Jacobinism*, which alleged that the French Revolution was little more than a three pronged attack against the church, the monarchy, and the people in general. Barruel viewed the Jacobins as something of a synthesis of the two previous groups—the Freemasons and the Illuminati—and went on to identify a number of key figures from the time, such as Voltaire, Frederick the Great, and Diderot, as members of these secret societies working behind-the-scenes to lay the groundwork for revolution, going to extreme lengths to systematically document all sorts of literature from the time. Though his methodology was different from Robison (Barruel had no secret agents feeding him any such information) it's telling that his book arrived at the exact same conclusion as Robison, at the exact same year, albeit in another country, and in another language. Again, both books would become wildly popular as common people sought deeper understanding of the events they had just witnessed, and indeed, Barruel's masterwork would get translated into English by 1799.

Following the bloody French Revolution, the government set up by the Jacobins—the Committee of Public Safety—was well and truly Masonic. Note their iconography, complete with the Masonic eye of providence, representing the "generative force." These images just don't spring up on their own. They're deliberately chosen by the individuals in power, for a specific reason and a specific purpose.

But the Masonic Socialist utopia of the Jacobins was short-lived, and became a de facto dictatorship during the "Reign of Terror," starting in 1793. Price controls on food failed. The state was made completely secular, with the Church being replaced by the new state religion, named the "cult of the Supreme being," and by the time the Reign of Terror was over, at least seventeen thousand people had been executed by the Committee. (All in the name of liberté, égalité, and fraternité, no doubt.) Reacting to the increased chaos the Committee had wrought, a reactionary force took over and overthrew the Committee. Revolutionaries like Robespierre would find their necks resting upon the same chopping blocks upon which they had forced the necks of their monarchs mere months earlier. By 1795, the Committee would be replaced by the French Directorate... which would soon be overtaken by an enterprising "strong man" by the name of Napoleon Bonaparte.

Napoleon is, perhaps, one of the most interesting figures in history that one can study. Stanley Kubrick certainly thought so, penning a mammoth masterwork of a screenplay about his life (which he never got to shoot). And though it's never been proven that Napoleon himself was a Freemason, several of his brothers were (with his brother Joseph being made Grand Master of the Grand Orient of France, before becoming the King of Naples and then Spain). It's also worth noting that Masonry certainly thrived under Napoleon's rule, and that he was surrounded by other, high-ranking Masons throughout his military career. While cutting his teeth on the battlefields of Egypt and Syria during the French Campaign through the Ottoman territories, Napoleon's co-commander, Jean-Baptiste Kléber would open the first Masonic lodge in Cairo, naming it the "Isis Lodge" and also serving as its first "Worshipful Master."

Upon returning to France from his Middle East campaign, Napoleon was heralded as a hero by the people. Wildly popular, our pamphlet-writing friend from earlier, the Jesuit-trained Emmanuel Joseph Sieyès, took notice. Now a member of the five-man French Directorate, Sieyès was nonetheless very dissatisfied with the way the Directorate was ruling, and had taken to secretly plotting a coup in order to install something more to his liking. He had written a new, revised Constitution, but needed the military to back it to ensure its success. Napoleon wasn't his first choice for ruler, but when he saw the way the people reacted to Napoleon, he knew he had found his man.

Napoleon, aided by his brother Lucien (who was the president of the Council of Five Hundred) and Sieyès, was able to seize power from the Directorate in the bloodless Coup of the Eighteenth of Brumaire (November 9, 1799), allowing him to assume power as First Consul of France and replace the Directorate with the French Consulate, thus ending the French Revolution and beginning the French Empire. The move that shocked Sieyès, no doubt, was that Napoleon would then turn around and heavily modify Sieyès' Constitution, shaping his version into something more to his liking. Napoleon would rearrange the new government and place trusted individuals into strategic positions, thus allowing him to slowly and steadily consolidate power over the next two decades. And notably, during this period, Masonry would flourish in France, with the number of Masonic lodges growing from just three hundred, to over twelve hundred in just ten years.

And here's where it gets really interesting, because Napoleon didn't just seize power through military force. That had been tried and failed often enough in the past that he knew mere demonstrations of force wouldn't secure his rule. No, Napoleon knew he had to appeal to a large enough mass of people so that his rule, regardless of how it was obtained, would be seen as legitimate in the eyes of the people no matter what. Don't get me wrong; he was already wildly popular with the people—but popularity can quickly fade. Instead, he invoked this legitimacy through the use of signs and symbols.

Any historian worth their salt will tell you that Napoleon's heraldic symbol was that of the honey bee. By identifying himself with the bee, Napoleon was invoking the great Merovingian kings of old, for the bee was their symbol, found on the likes of King Clovis I's tomb from all the way back in the fifth century. By co-opting this symbol, Napoleon was, in effect, aligning himself with a great bloodline. Some researchers even feel that in doing this, Napoleon was going so far as to invoke the ancient Egyptians of old, not only because the Egyptians greatly valued the sweet, golden honey that bees produced (as evidenced by it being found in the tombs of Egyptian royalty), but also because the Egyptians believed that honey bees themselves were the tears of the sun god Ra. To compound (or perhaps confuse) things further, some will even go so far as to say that the Merovingian line itself originally hails from Egyptian royalty (and though I'm open to examining this further, I've seen little credible evidence thus far to substantiate this claim).

But to further demonstrate the power of this bloodline, you must know that the House of Windsor comes straight from this bloodline, and that thirty-four US presidents are all genetic descendants of Charlemagne himself. Nineteen presidents are directly descended from King Edward III, of England. When George W. Bush ran against John Kerry in 2004, he was running against his sixteenth cousin. Skull and Bones, anyone? I wasn't joking when I recited the quote earlier: it's a big club, and you and I ain't in it!

So, Napoleon claims control over France and institutes his new government, and Sieyès is given the position of Provisional Consul. The relationship between the two could best be described as a strategic alliance, with both men pursuing their own, individual ambitions and often finding them in alignment with each other. But Sieyès was, in essence, an adviser on every decision Napoleon would make. Having already been proclaimed Consul for life by the French Trubunat in 1802, Napoleon began conquering every country that had partaken in the Jesuit suppression and began building the French Empire. Why, he had already taken Malta during his campaign in the Middle East (effectively neutering the Knights Hospitaller in the process), but now, with the advent of the Napoleonic Wars, he had his sights set firmly on becoming the next Emperor of, effectively, the entire civilized world. And it should here be noted, that Napoleon's Concordat with the Catholic Church in 1801 not only re-instituted the Catholic faith as the official religion of France, but also allowed the Jesuit order to be reinstated in France at a time when they were still officially oppressed in every other Catholic nation. But this was not a mere matter of simply gaining the title of Holy Roman Emperor—a title long held by the Habsburg dynasty in Austria. This was a matter of fundamentally conquering and re-organizing society in a way that more resembled the pagan Roman Republic, with Napoleon effectively acting as Caesar; the Roman God-King.

The new French government seemed to agree with his ambitions, quickly affirming him as the first Emperor of the French in 1804, when they coronated him with the Iron Crown of Lombardy—called as such for the nail embedded inside its golden circlet—a nail, supposedly taken from Jesus' cross, and beaten into the crown upon the orders of St. Helena, mother of Constantine the Great, after her quest where she claimed to have found the one, true cross. The crown was typically used in coronations for Holy Roman Emperors and was, at one point, also used in the coronation of Charlemagne. Napoleon would crown himself, and his first wife Josephine in Notre Dame Cathedral, on December 2, 1804, in the presence of a man he would later threaten, first by pointing cannons at his bedroom, and then by keeping him under arrest for over six years... Pope Pius VII.

It's important to understand that this was not the mere restoration of the French monarchy, either. Nothing could have been more anathema to the revolutionary mind during that time, and at any rate, Napoleon didn't want to be connected to those old, fallen dynasties. No, this was something else entirely, something new, which channeled the glory, decadence, and sheer religious and imperial power of the old, while surpassing all that had come before it. One of the symbols of this new regime would soon become known around the world, as construction began on what would become the Arc de Triomphe.

The full name of the Arc de Triomphe is actually the Arc de Triomphe de Étoile—that is, the Triumphal Arch of the Star. Inspired by the Roman triumphal arches of old, and taking its formal cues from the Arch of Titus (built by Emperor Domitian in AD 82), the new Arc de Triomphe was a military monument attesting to the greatness of Napoleon's new regime.

And the connection to these Roman arches is significant because of their unique place in the official, mandated state religion of the Roman Empire—and indeed, the ancient pagan religions of old. Rome was a "sacred" city, and its leaders, divine god-men, according to their religion. Notably, the Arch of Titus was built on the Via Sacra, the Sacred Road running through the center of Ancient Rome, from the outskirts of the city, through the Roman forum, and ascending all the way up the Capitoline hill. When returning from a victory on the battlefield, Roman commanders would lead a procession of soldiers through gates of triumph, and later through the Arch of Titus itself, before leading the procession along the Via Sacra. The commander of the Legion would wear a crown of laurel before proceeding to the temple of the Roman thunder-god, Jupiter, at the top of the Capitoline hill, where he would offer sacrifices and dedicate the spoils of war. We moderns are so used to the separation of church and state that we can't really fathom a system where the two are so inextricably intertwined. And it's here I wish to draw a comparison to another "Arch of Triumph;" one which recently made an appearance in Washington, DC, itself, opposite the Capitol building.

As part of what was ostensibly a traveling archaeological exhibit, this "Arch of Triumph," perhaps better known also as the "Arch of Ba'al," was a reproduction made by digitally scanning the original, historical arch, and then printing out exact reproductions using advanced 3D printing techniques so as to create a one-to-one replica. This reproduction of this pagan arch, originally constructed in Palmyra during the third century, would then be erected in city after city as part of a grand tour around the world. Prior to coming to Washington, DC, the arch stood in front of Trafalgar Square, where it was commemorated by Boris Johnson, and in New York City, where it was met with some protesters who realized then what it really stood for.

At a time when the subject of borders themselves is controversial, it's important to remember what these arches really stood for, as well as the initial purpose they served. Most ancient cities were walled and gated affairs. Rome was no exception to this rule. You had to protect your people from invaders, from roaming bands of pillagers and barbarians looking to plunder your wealth and women, and the most effective way to do that was to erect a wall to prevent them from gaining access to your land and valuables in the first place! Thus, being able to pass through a gate into the heart of the sacred city still held deep societal, and thus religious significance. As cities grew, and these triumphal celebrations grew more elaborate, celebratory arches were erected, and thus, came to symbolize a passing-through, into the sacred borders of a land. So it was with Rome. Thus, heroes were celebrated when they brought back plunder and slaves into the sacred city. On the other hand, evildoers (and thus, religious outcasts) were kept outside the city, and thus, in the dark wilds.

In storytelling, gates often symbolize passage into another world. The most famous instance of this in our modern, popular culture comes to us from *Jurassic Park*. You recall the famous scene where Dr. Grant, Dr. Ellie Sattler, Jeff Goldblum's Dr. Ian Malcolm, the two kids (and one unfortunate lawyer) enter the park in the Jurassic Park Jeeps, running along a track built into the ground. They get to the tall gate where eight separate torches burn, four along either side of its imposing pillars, and the words *JURASSIC PARK* emblazoned across the top. The doors swing open. The trucks carry them inside. They've left the old world (with its old rules) behind. Now, they're in another realm entirely, and all the rules are different here.

So it was with the Arch of Ba'al. Once you pass through, you're in Ba'al's domain.

But who was Ba'al? For the uninitiated, Ba'al was a storm god from the ancient Middle East; the son of the supreme god El, the father of mankind and, indeed, father of many of the gods and goddesses below him. El, like the Greek Cronus, was associated with Saturn (so much so that the Romans would simply call him "Saturn"), and the symbol of the bull—something his son Ba'al would later inherit. (Those literate in the Bible might recall the ancient Israelites fashioning the "golden calf" to worship while Moses was up on Mt.

Sinai receiving the Ten Commandments. When he descended the mountain, Moses was so shocked by what he saw, that he smashed the commandments he had received. This whole passage is an explicit reference to Ba'al worship, and everything it entailed.)

Likewise, in time, Cronus would also come to be associated with the sickle, or the scythe, which, as the myth goes, is what he used to castrate his own father Uranus at the request of his mother, the earth goddess Gaia. When Cronus learned that he, too, was to be overthrown by his own sons, he took to devouring them one by one as soon as they were born so as to prevent this overthrow from happening, only to have one child saved and hidden away by his wife Rhea, when she fed Cronus a rock instead. That child was the sixth son of Cronus, known as Zeus. Tucked away safely on Mt. Ida in Crete, Zeus would grow up and eventually lay siege to the heavens after rescuing his siblings. He would overthrow Cronus and the Titans, becoming the supreme storm god of heaven. Following the "genealogies," the stories and their symbols, Zeus was, in effect, the same god as Ba'al.

But how did Ba'al worship end up in ancient Greece? Simply put, Ba'al worship would quickly spread around the region of its origin for centuries to come, albeit in transformative permutations. Indeed, the word "Ba'al" simply means "Lord" in ancient Semitic languages, so there's a degree of built-in flexibility as to who, exactly, it refers to and what their personal, mythic history says about them and their deeds. Yes, in Canaan, he was explicitly known as Ba'al, but this storm god motif would soon become known by many different names throughout the region.

In Phoenicia, Ba'al became Dagon.

In Akkad, he became Anu.

In Sumeria, Utu.

In Mesopotamia, Shamash.

In Babylon, Marduk.

In India, Surya.

In Egypt, Ra.

In Greece, Zeus (with Helios taking charge of the Sun itself).

Rome practically took this myth whole-cloth from the Greeks, making Jupiter their storm god, and putting Apollo in charge of the sun. The laurel was also sacred to Apollo, which is where the laurel wreath crown comes from.

And in Carthage, he would become Ba'al-Hamon—Lord of the Brazier.

All of these were variations on the "storm god" motif, and as their mythology grew, so to the power and influence of the cults that worshiped them. Often these "storm gods" simply became gods of the heavens; that is, not the disembodied realm of ethereal angelic spirits we moderns often think of when thinking of the "heavens," but the literal sky above. Thus, these storm gods had power over all the activities of the sky; the rising of the sun, the setting of the moon, and the advent of rain. This ability to make the sun shine and the rains to pour forth made them literal fertility gods almost by default, for without their influence, these ancient people believed they would literally starve. Thus, pleasing these storm gods became of paramount importance at a time when civil and religious life were so closely intertwined. For if these people displeased the gods in any way, their civilizations would cease to exist.

But even the most ancient of pagans understood that genuine fertility required both male and female representation. Thus, the storm god needed a counterpart, a divine maiden, a "Queen of Heaven"—though this was often not the storm god's direct consort. Usually depicted as a maiden with a child (to underscore her fertility), these goddesses became, at least as far as fertility rituals were concerned, even more important than their male counterparts. Often these were moon, or star goddesses, who also had a penchant for war and strategy. In fact, the "star" of Venus, which was not yet understood as a planet by these ancients, but as the brightest star in the heavens, would often come to represent the goddess. And again, you have to allow some flexibility within these pantheons, as these aren't always one-to-one copies, but traditions which evolved and grew more complex with age as myths crossed cultures and centuries; sometimes even dividing the roles of these goddesses between two figureheads in the process. And so, the original Queen of Heaven was Asherah in Canaan, who some may recognize from the Biblical passages citing "Asherah poles" as part of the Canaanite pagan system of fertility worship.

In Phoenicia, this became Tanit.

In Mesopotamia and Babylon, she became Ashtart, or Ishtar.

In Akkad, you have Ninhursag, or Belit, where her sign would be an omega symbol.

In India, you have Durga, who is worshiped to this very day.

In Jewish tradition, you have Lilith—who, it should be said, is seen as more of a demon, or even as a vampiric character, and not a goddess to be worshiped.

In Sumeria, you have Ereshkigal, or the "Queen of the Night," where we first see the owl motif appear:

In Mesopotamia, this became Ishtar, or Innana, who were at first separate goddesses, but through syncretism and time, merged into the same cult.

Riding a similar syncretic wave, the bronze age Canaanites would eventually merge the goddesses Anat, Astarte, and Ashera into one goddess known as Qetesh, or Athirat, who would then also take on the symbols of the snake and the lotus.

In Egypt, this became Qudshu, who was equivalent to Neith, who represented the infinite heavens. But in a unique twist, the Egyptians subdivided the infinite heavens from the day and night cycle, giving rise also to the star-covered goddess, Nut, whose appearance is strikingly similar to Neith. Nut's role was later subsumed by Hathor, and then again by Isis in later times. The Greek historian Herodotus would describe in his works an annual festival to honor Isis-Neith. He would go on, in his book *Histories II*, to describe the celebrations:

> The Egyptians were also the first to introduce solemn assemblies, processions, and litanies to the gods; of all which the Greeks were taught the use by them. It seems to me a sufficient proof of this that in Egypt these practices have been established from remote antiquity, while in Greece they are only recently known.
>
> The Egyptians do not hold a single solemn assembly, but several in the course of the year. Of these the chief, which is better attended than any other, is held at the city of Bubastis in honour of Diana. The next in importance is that which takes place at Busiris, a city situated in the very middle of the Delta; it is in honour of Isis, who is called in the Greek tongue Demiter (Ceres). There is a third great festival in Sais to Minerva, a fourth in Heliopolis to the Sun, a fifth in Buto to Latona, and a sixth in Papremis to Mars.
>
> …
>
> The ceremonies at the feast of Isis in the city of Busiris have been already spoken of. It is there that the whole multitude, both of men and women, many thousands in number, beat themselves at the close of the sacrifice, in honour of a god, whose name a religious scruple forbids me to mention. The Carian dwellers in Egypt proceed on this occasion to still greater lengths, even cutting their faces with their knives, whereby they let it been seen that they are not Egyptians but foreigners.
>
> At Sais, when the assembly takes place for the sacrifices, there is one night on which the inhabitants all burn a multitude of lights in the open air round their houses. They use lamps in the shape of flat saucers filled with a mixture of oil and salt, on the top of which the wick floats. These burn the whole night, and give to the festival the name of the Feast of Lamps. The Egyptians who are absent from the festival observe the night of the sacrifice, no less than the rest, by a general lighting of lamps; so that the illumination is not confined to the city of Sais, but extends over the whole of Egypt. And there is a religious reason assigned for the special honour paid to this night, as well as for the illumination which accompanies it.

Plato would also write:

> The citizens have a deity for their foundress; she is called in the Egyptian tongue Neith, and is asserted by them to be the same whom the Hellenes call Athena; they are great lovers of the Athenians, and say that they are in some way related to them.

So the Greeks primarily identify the goddess of Isis-Neith with Athena (Herodotus uses the Roman name, Minerva). And as was the case with Ereshkigal before her, Minerva took the symbol of the owl as her own, as well as Athirat's snake. However, it should also be noted that the Phoenician goddess Tanit is also directly identified with the Greek goddess Hera and the Roman goddess Juno. In essence, one goddess produced many goddesses, each with similar, sub-divided roles in these state religions, and sometimes these diverse goddesses were syncretized back into one new goddess—only to meet up later with other versions of the goddess that hadn't been combined into the new identity, for one reason or another.

Take, for instance, Rome, where Minerva was part of a trinity of maiden goddesses who, along with Diana and Vesta, swore to remain virgins for their whole lives; an odd thing for a goddess inspired by fertility goddesses from other nations, to be sure. And yet, this is how the mythology developed over millennia. Notably, the priestesses serving Vesta, goddess of the hearth, would become known as Vestal Virgins, pledging themselves to the divine service of the goddess, in a role that became of prime importance to the state religion of Rome. Why, Diana alone was something of a trinity herself, combining the earlier moon goddess of Luna, and the goddess of the Underworld, Hecate, into her own person; the huntress. The more sexual side of these earlier female fertility deities would take on the form of new goddesses, splitting off into Aphrodite in Greece, and Venus in Rome.

Tracing the direct lineages, as you can see, can get very confusing, very fast, but rather than think of these all as direct incarnations of one another across times, cultures, and people groups, it's best to think of these all as variations on a theme: male and female fertility deities, who were associated with the sun, the stars, and the moon, and who took for themselves various animal symbols—notably, the bull for the men, and the owl for the women. (Snakes played a role in this, as well, but weren't limited to just one gender, and usually embodied primordial forces of chaos and order.) For our purposes, I'm going to refer to these male and female deified archetypes by their ancient and original Canaanite names: Ba'al and Ishtar. Together, they formed the ancient fertility cults of the Near East.

And as that fertility cult spread, a system of temple prostitution began to take form. The scholarship supports the position that yes, this was fairly common, at least until it was abstracted away by the more advanced Greek, Roman, and Egyptian societies. But practically every group in the Near East engaged in such practices at one time or another. So common was this kind of thing, that Hammurabi's code even protected temple prostitutes, legally enshrining their role in those ancient societies. Students of the Bible will find such systems referenced several times throughout scripture, especially in the Old Testament during the narrative of Israel's conquest of the region. God (a.k.a. YHWH, or Elohim) repeatedly calls the Israelites to be set apart from the nations around them, and commands that no Israelite is to ever serve as temple prostitute. Often, the Israelites failed in the mandate, and as the story goes, they would be conquered by external groups until they repented. But the command was clear, nonetheless—as was the relationship of Elohim to Ba'al. And this is perhaps the most interesting "innovation" of the Israelites.

Whereas Abraham certainly understood "El" as part of a pantheon of gods (after all, he grew up in Ur, smack dab in the middle of Sumeria) part of the specific revelation Abraham received was that El was above *all* other gods, and in fact, these other "gods" were as nothing. This set Elohim both above and in direct opposition to the false god Ba'al (and his many other permutations). You can see this narrative all throughout the Old Testament; for instance, in First Samuel when the Ark of the Covenant, that relic that carried the presence of

God, is captured and stored in the temple of Dagon by the Philistines. Well, the Philistines go to sleep at night thinking they've won a huge victory capturing this relic, but they wake up the next morning, and the massive statue of Dagon has fallen on its face next to the ark.

Okay, weird coincidence, but stranger things have happened, right? They get a bunch of guys together, prop Dagon back up, and go to sleep again the next day.

Except, when they wake up, Dagon's on his face again, and they're all freaked out.

They send the Ark to another city.

That city breaks out in tumors.

They send the Ark to *another* city.

But this city heard what had happened, and they all freak out, so they won't take it.

Instead, they collectively decide to bring the Ark, this major war prize, back to the Israelites and leave it on their front doorstep instead.

That's a pretty funny story in and of itself, but in the Bibl,e Elohim is often described as being particularly disgusted with Ba'al worship—primarily because Ba'al's system of temple prostitution as a form of "worship" would create, well, lots of children as a byproduct of all the "worship" going on.

Well, where did all these children end up?

They were offered back to Moloch, that primordial god of chaos. Remember him? Remember the flesh-devouring Cronus? Remember his Roman analog, Saturn? In Carthage, this practice would merge with Ba'al-Hamon, Lord of the Brazier. And yes, the "faithful" would heat up this bronze idol and cast their infants inside to be burned alive on the scalding metal. And if that sounds like anything going on today... well, QAnon has touched on that subject. Recall, from the last chapter, where I told you that every Planned Parenthood in America is secretly dedicated to Moloch. Recall the line from Q's drop, which I first presented to you in the last chapter:

Q !!TPb.qbhqo ID: wmN+33xv No.149467638 🔗 📷   **153**
Nov 14 2017 21:25:09 (EST)

For the coming days ahead.
Ask yourself an honest question, why would a billionaire who has it all, fame, fortune, a warm and loving family, friends, etc. want to endanger himself and his family by becoming POTUS?
Why would he want to target himself and those he cares about?
Does he need money?
Does he need fame?
What does he get out of this?
Does he want to make the US/world a better place for his family and for those good and decent people who have long been taken advantage of?
Perhaps he could not stomach the thought of mass murders occurring to satisfy Moloch?
Perhaps he could not stomach the thought of children being kidnapped, drugged, and raped while leaders/law enforcement of the world turn a blind eye.
Perhaps he was tired of seeing how certain races/countries were being constantly abused and kept in need/poor/and suffering all for a specific purpose.
Perhaps he could not in good conscious see the world burn.
Why, hours after the election, did seven people travel to an undisclosed location to hold a very private & highly secured/guarded meeting?
Why didn't HRC give a concession speech?
When was the last time a presidential candidate didn't personally give a concession speech?
What happens if the border remained open and the MSM continued to brainwash?
At what point do Patriots, and hard working men and woman, become the minority?
What about voting machines?
Who owns the voting machines?
What about voter ID laws?
Photo ID? When is it necessary and must be presented? Make a list.
Laugh.
Reconcile.
Would the chances of defeating evil grow less and less with each passing year?
What does 'red line' mean?
Why, again, were the arrests made in SA so very important?
What strings were immediately cut?
Follow the money.
When does a bird sing?
Q

ANSWERS

"Perhaps he could not stomach the thought of mass murders occurring to satisfy Moloch?"

And even as I write this very chapter, Democrats around the nation are in total panic mode because the last line of defense they had to protect Roe v. Wade—Ruth Bader Ginsburg—is in very poor health. Right now, the Cabal is working with state legislatures to enshrine abortion at the state level, in anticipation of Trump eventually replacing Ginsburg with another Conservative, thus giving Conservatives a significant majority and the ability to overturn Roe v. Wade.

Hillary Clinton ✔
@HillaryClinton

Follow

Forty-six years after Roe v. Wade, we reaffirm what will always be true: Women have an unalienable right to make their own decisions about their health care.

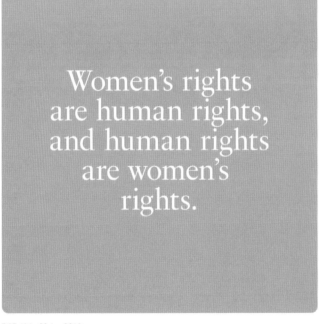

Women's rights are human rights, and human rights are women's rights.

7:07 AM - 22 Jan 2019

8,427 Retweets **36,759** Likes

💬 3.5K   ↻ 8.4K   ♡ 37K

Hillary Clinton ✓
@HillaryClinton

Follow

I'll be joining @NYGovCuomo as he lays out his plan to codify Roe v. Wade and pass the Reproductive Health Act. There's no time to wait. #RHAin30Days

> **Andrew Cuomo** ✓ @NYGovCuomo
> We must pass the Reproductive Health Act and codify Roe v. Wade into New York State Law.
>
> Let's get it done! #RHAin30Days

2:00 PM - 6 Jan 2019

7,406 Retweets **36,707** Likes

◯ 2.4K   ⟲ 7.4K   ♡ 37K

This new law passed in New York, and allows for abortions up to the moment of birth. Furthermore, if the baby somehow survives the abortion, they can now be left to die of exposure.

I need to be clear about this. This isn't about "women's reproductive health." It never was. This is thinly veiled Moloch worship, and it was one of the greatest deceptions ever perpetrated on the United States. Set up by the Bushes, and presented under the guise of expanding "freedom," an ancient system of cult sacrifice of the unborn infiltrated the very fabric of our American society.

Oh, you don't believe me that Hillary participates in a system of Moloch worship that continues within a secret society to this very day? I don't want to get too far ahead of myself here, but you don't have to believe me. You can take Hillary at her own words. Here she is asking Lynn Forester "My snake is bigger than yours" de Rothschild what "penance" she owes her, in an e-mail leaked by Wikileaks:

> Lynn,
>
> I was trying to reach you to tell you and Teddy that I asked Tony Blair to go to Israel as part of our full court press on
> keeping the Middle East negotiations going. He told me that he had a commitment in Aspen w you two and the
> conference, but after we talked, he decided to go and asked me to tell you. He is very sorry, obviously, but I'm grateful
>
> that he accepted my request. I hope you all understand and give him a raincheck.
>
> UNCLASSIFIED U.S. Department of State Case No. F-2014-20439 Doc No. C05775116 Date: 08/31/2015
>
> If you were interested, he might be able to satellite in if you have the technology available.
>
> He should land around Sam Aspen time. Let me know what penance I owe you. And pls explain to Teddy. As ever, H

Her words. Not mine. More states are attempting to follow in New York's stead as the secret war rages on surrounding these ideas. Democrat Kathy Tran proposed a similar bill in the Virginia Legislature, allowing abortion at any time, for any reason. Virginia Governor Democrat Ralph Northam defended the bill, even though it allowed for the post-birth killing of any babies that survived the attempted late-term abortion, saying:

> "The infant would be delivered. The infant would be kept comfortable. The infant would be resuscitated if that's what the mother and the family desired."

In other words, even if the baby had survived and was now alive and completely separate from her, the mother could still decide if she wanted it killed or not. And what makes it all the more despicable is that Northam is a trained physician himself; someone who has taken the Hippocratic oath to protect life. Yet he gets on the radio and defends literal infanticide. Thankfully, this horrible bill was defeated in Virginia, but similar ones keep popping up, and I suspect will continue to pop up, as the Cabal scrambles to keep its "supply chain" open. (Again, more on that in a bit.)

But now you're beginning to see why Moses was so shocked when he came down from Mt. Sinai and saw the Israelites worshiping a golden calf. This implied temple prostitution. This implied inevitable human sacrifice. Doubtless, the Israelites only got as far as some regrettable fornication, but the shock was so bad Moses smashed the commandments he had received from Elohim as a result.

Later, bull symbolism would be pulled into the myth of the Minotaur; the product of a bestial relationship between King Minos' wife and a white bull of Crete. By this time, bull worship had come into its own, often referred to as the "Bull of Heaven," complete with its own star sign: Taurus. (Some may recall the mythological episode where Gilgamesh slew the Bull of Heaven, or the time when Hercules had to tame the Cretan bull as one of his labors.) The cult of the bull would soon come to permeate Asia Minor and the nearby islands, so its symbol had come into common use everywhere in the surrounding region, but in this specific story regarding King Minos, the product of this bestial relationship between the Cretan bull and his wife was the Minotaur; a man-eating monster that was itself half-man, and half-bull.

To contain the Minotaur, Midas would hire Daedalus to construct a labyrinth for it near his palace at Knossos. To keep the Minotaur fed, each year seven men and seven women from Athens were dropped in the labyrinth with the monster, where, unable to escape, they would eventually perish at the hands of the Minotaur.

This myth would later be used as a basis for MKUltra mind control programming, wherein the alters of the RSA victim are locked between amnesia walls. Recall the FBI's list of pedophilia-related symbols; how many were variations on a spiral. This is a direct reference to "the Labyrinth" itself, wherein these fragmented identities are lost, unable to escape, and forever tormented by literal cannibals. (But once again, more on that in a bit.)

FEDERAL BUREAU OF INVESTIGATION
INTELLIGENCE BULLETIN
Cyber Division, Innocent Images National Initiative

31 January 2007

(U) Symbols and Logos Used by Pedophiles to Identify Sexual Preferences

UNCLASSIFIED   UNCLASSIFIED   UNCLASSIFIED

(U) BLogo aka "Boy   (U) LBLogo aka "Little   (U) BLogo imprinted on coins
Lover"   Boy Lover"

UNCLASSIFIED

(U) BLogo jewelry

UNCLASSIFIED//LAW ENFORCEMENT SENSITIVE

Later, in Rome and Greece, this bull worship would manifest in a new way, when a new form of torture was devised by some profoundly sick minds. Instead of just children, this "Brazen Bull" would be utilized to execute anyone deemed deserving in a particularly gruesome fashion. I'm not exaggerating when I say this was perhaps one of the worst torture devices ever conceived by man. Much like how idols of Molech were cast out of bronze, so too was the brazen bull. Inside the bull was a chamber where the offender who was condemned to die was locked inside, before a fire would be lit underneath the legs of the bull.

This, of course, caused the bull to get extremely hot, and the inside to begin scalding the prisoner trapped inside, unable to escape. But instead of running out of air and suffocating, the bull had, essentially, trumpets built inside of it, which exited through the mouth of the bull. These trumpets converted the screams of the dying into the bellowing of a rambunctious bull. At least until the trapped victim was finally dead.

One such saint condemned to die by the Romans in such an awful manner was St. Antipas of Pergamum, again in Asia Minor, where this cult of the bull had gained a particularly strong foothold:

So on one hand, you had the male and female halves of this fertility cult creating life, and as fast as it was created, it was being extinguished in another act of religious "reverie," offering up these infants to that infernal god of chaos. Just like the fertility cult was a union of opposites, the cult dictated that the resulting life had to be negated itself with death.

All of this was systematized and built in to the cultures of the time. Yes, the specific practices evolved over time, and differently within each culture, but the core elements and archetypes remained the same—maintained by a dedicated priestly caste which passed the consecrated mysteries down from one generation to the next. It was even built into the architecture of the society itself; most notably in the form of obelisks and gates—and later, ceremonial arches—to represent these male and female forces.

Now, some students of history may take exception to me calling obelisks a form of fertility worship, but it's the simple truth. In mainstream archaeology, they'll tell you that obelisks symbolize petrified rays of the sun, and were thus part of the worship of Ra, but remember, obelisks predate Egyptian civilization by several thousand years. The oldest obelisks we know of come from Assyria, and date back to the eleventh century, BC. By comparison, many of the Egyptian obelisks we have today date from around 2500 BC.

Just as the Egyptians had taken their gods and goddesses from the pagan religions of the Near East, so too did they take the practice of manufacturing obelisks, which were really just pointed versions of monoliths, which were themselves just stone versions of pole worship. Thus, one can speculate as to whether this was connected all the way back to *Asherah* poles (such as were listed in Scripture), which were themselves always connected to the worship of Ba'al.

Again, some flexibility is required to make such connections, but if heaven was literally above the sky, then erecting a pillar, or a monolith, or an obelisk in a high place elevated one's status, and thus, their connection with the gods. Codify human sacrifice into the mix, and now you're sacrificing children in these high places. And though this is far from the only example, this is why it says, in Jeremiah 32:35:

> And they built the high places of Baal, which are in the valley of the son of Hinnom, to cause their sons and their daughters to pass through the fire unto Molech; which I commanded them not, neither came it into my mind, that they should do this abomination, to cause Judah to sin.

So yes, the Egyptians modified the practice, and while obelisks certainly held a sort of aesthetic prominence in the Egyptian landscape, you have to remember that the core of the priestly caste always kept the true significance of such matters to themselves. Though we don't think of the Egyptians as the kind of people who participated in human sacrifice, let alone ritual cannibalism, it was codified into the earliest texts of their religion; texts which we still have today. These are the Pyramid Texts, written around 2500 BC, and they are the oldest compilation of surviving Egyptian religious texts still in our possession.

From Utterances 173:

> The King's guiding serpent is on his brow,
> Even that which sees the soul,
> Efficient for burning;
> The King' neck is on his trunk.
> The King is the Bull of the sky,
> Who conquers at will,
> Who lives on the being of every god,
> Who eats their entrails,
> Even of those who come with their bodies full of magic
> From the Island of Fire.

And from Utterances 273:

> Pharaoh is the Bull of the sky,
> who shatters at will,
> who lives on the being of every god,
> who eats their entrails,
> even of those who come with their bodies
> full of magic from the Island of Flame.

These sections of the text were originally known as the "Cannibal Hymn." Note again, the references to the snake (with the golden *uraeus*, that standing cobra, affixed to the headdresses of Egyptian royalty), and to the Bull of Heaven. These were some of the elements the Egyptians had taken from earlier civilizations. Originally etched into the walls and sarcophagi of the pyramids at Saqqara, the spells and liturgical texts of the Pyramid Texts would eventually evolve into the Egyptian Book of the Dead, known more properly as The Book of Emerging Forth Into the Light, as they were codified and illustrated. These particular texts were reserved only for use by Pharaoh, but at the very least we can see ritual sacrifice and cannibalism built into the very foundation of the ancient Egyptian mystery religion. Remember; the common Egyptian would have been completely unaware of these elements at the time (unless, I suppose, he was the unfortunate one who found his entrails being munched upon by Pharaoh). The average Egyptian never got to see any of these texts, or participate in any of the associated rituals. This was a "privilege" reserved only for the elite; those initiated into those mysteries.

And this is where Cabal researcher Bill Cooper connects obelisks to the Osirian myth, which is about as foundational to the Egyptian religion as you can get. Very briefly, the basic story goes like this: Osiris was god of the afterlife, and his brother Set, the snake-headed god, wanted to usurp his throne. So, Set kills Osiris and cuts up his body into thirteen pieces, scattering them around the world. Isis, Osiris' wife, decides to hunt down all the pieces and try to bring Osiris back to life. She soon finds all the pieces but one: his, well… his manhood.

So what does Isis do? She fashions Osiris a new one out of gold, is successful in bringing him back to life, and makes love to him before he dies again so that he can have an heir, and so that Set will be overthrown. Osiris goes back down to Duat, the Egyptian underworld, and Isis becomes pregnant, later delivering a son who she will name Horus—invoking that iconic maiden and child motif in the process.

Isis raises Horus in secret until he is old enough to challenge Set, often in very… strange ways. For instance, Set, at one point, actually wants to engage in sodomy with Horus… and Horus agrees, thinking it will allow him to become stronger. There are variations in what happens next, but essentially, Set's seed always acts harmfully in some way.

Eventually, Horus does overthrow Set, but not until after a great struggle. Horus rips off one of Set's testicles in the fight, and Set rips off one of Horus' eyes. Because Horus was a sky god, his eyes were equivalent to the sun and the moon. Thus, this eye came to represent events like eclipses. Later, having been healed, Horus would offer his eye to his father Osiris in the hope of bringing him back to the land of the living. Most will immediately recognize the "Eye of Horus," or the "Wadjet" eye as one of the most prominent symbols in all of Egyptian hieroglyphics, and one still referenced *heavily* by those in the media today—and on purpose.

QAnon would reference the Eye of Osiris (also known as the Eye of Ra) in one of his drops, early on, advising Anons that it was indeed a symbol still being employed by the Cabal today. For a "fun" challenge, see how many images you can find of celebrities either covering one eye, or holding an "okay" sign over one eye. This is intentional symbolism, and those in the Cult of the Cabal recognize it as such. It's performed in plain view to mock you and me, because brother… it's a big club…

Anonymous (ID: af6c5f) No.154230 ☑ ▮   **437**
Dec 23 2017 01:10:06 (EST)

Anonymous (ID: 7f67ab) No.154006 ☑ ▮
Dec 23 2017 00:29:27 (EST)

james-bond-you-only-live-twice-ken-adam-set-design1.jpg ⬇

Just imagine North Korea like a James Bond film, their own little
bit of hell, can you imagine with the cash they have stole what
they could have built on NK paychecks (they work or die, sort of
free)

>>154006
2011 Shuttle Program terminated by Hussein.
US loses space dominance.
http://www.foxnews.com/opinion/2017/08/09/obama-
administration-knew-about-north-koreas-miniaturized-nukes.html ☑
▮
IRAN Nuke deal.
NK Nuke/Missile Tech.
SpaceX.
NASA Tech to ?
HRC SAPs (private server).
Connected.
$$$,$$$,$$$.00 (pockets).
EYE OF RA.
Left eye [marker].
Symbolism.
EVIL.
STUPID.
JUSTICE.
Q

But it's important to understand that, while it's tempting to view Set as the "villain" in the story, he's really just representative of the forces of chaos. The effect then, is almost that of a balancing act, similar to yin and yang in Chinese philosophy. The story illustrates a cycle of death—chaos—and rebirth. These are important concepts in the ancient mystery religions.

This story, this "Osirian cycle," was even built into the Egyptian calendar itself and aligned to the seasons so that it fell with the flooding of the Nile and the renewal of the crops. But that masculine symbol of power, according to Cooper, that missing piece of Osiris; that "generative force," would be forever enshrined and typified with the advent of the obelisk.

The inverse would occur as well, as we alluded to earlier, through the use of ceremonial gates and later, with ceremonial arches. The most famous gate dedicated to a female deity in these ancient religions comes to us from Babylon itself, with the Ishtar gate. The towering Ishtar gate, once considered one of the seven wonders of the world, was built from shining bricks covered in a blue glaze and further decorated with reliefs of Marduk and Adad (and their respective associated animals.) Ishtar (and her signs and symbols) was the focal point, however. Like the Arch of Ba'al in Syria, and the Arch of Titus in Rome, the Ishtar gate connected to a road of deep religious significance. In this case, it was the Aj-ibur-sha-pu—the processional way—which cut through ancient Babylon and connected the Esagila temple (dedicated to Marduk) to the major ziggurat in Babylon—Etemenanki. If someone wanted to participate in the state religion of the day; if someone wanted to "ascend" to the "heavens," they had to pass through these gates and arches. There was simply no other way to approach.

These core principles, precepts, and practices—a fertility and death cult wrapped up in sun and moon worship—were handed down from one generation to the next by a class of ruling elites who were inducted into these mystery schools of the ancient world. Maintaining a level of secrecy over the general population allowed them to accumulate a certain level of power, wealth, and influence through the centuries. And yes, this cult continues on, into our modern world, with the Cabal's own mystery religion.

It's therefore no coincidence so many of these obelisks and arches can be found in capital cities around the world these days. Though their significance is hidden from the common man, those initiated in the Cabal's mystery religion have gone to great length to erect these monuments to their power-structure. This was what Napoleon was attempting to replicate when he built the Arc de Triomphe. And what's more is he wasn't the only one. This "tradition" has been carried on, into the modern day, and it may surprise many to learn that yet another Arch of Triumph exists, in all places, within that Cabal proxy-nation of North Korea. Erected in Pyongyang in 1982, and dedicated to "General" Kim Il-Sung on his seventieth birthday, it is the second largest ceremonial arch in the world, only surpassed by the Monumento a la Revolución in Mexico. And this was all done to emulate the mystery religions of Rome, Egypt, Babylon, and beyond.

This was exactly what Napoleon was trying to do, as he attempted to aggregate more and more power for himself. Having successfully conquered France, he set his sights on Europe next, and then the world. This meant that the only real thing left for Napoleon to do was make it official and conquer the Holy Roman Emperor. This meant turning his attention to the Habsburg dynasty in Austria.

The first, and truly fatal blow to the Holy Roman Empire would soon come following Napoleon's victory at the battle of Austerlitz where, outnumbered by the Russian and Austrian armies (led by Tsar Alexander I of Russia, and Holy Roman Emperor Francis II), Napoleon defied the odds and pulled out a stunning victory. His troops were simply better trained, more capable, and better organized than his foes. The resulting peace saw many lands consigned to the new French Empire, effectively dissolving the Holy Roman Empire and allowing Napoleon to create what he called the "Confederation of the Rhine." But rather than let his title slip to Napoleon as well, Emperor Francis II abdicated his title as Holy Roman Emperor, and simply became the Emperor of Austria instead, effectively denying Napoleon the one thing he wanted while living to fight another day—but not before suffering more indignities at the hand of Napoleon, including effectively being forced to marry off his daughter to the man who had bested him on the battlefield time and time again.

Napoleon's first marriage to Josephine had not been fruitful, and, increasingly concerned with producing an heir, the two divorced (which was something of a scandal in and of itself at the time). Josephine was forty-seven. Taking her place would be Emperor Francis II's daughter, Marie Louise, age nineteen. The marriage was indeed a strategic one, as Napoleon hoped the new familial ties to the Habsburg dynasty would help legitimize his rule, what with him now being married into European royalty, let alone the daughter of the former Holy Roman Emperor. Together, they would produce a suitable heir: Napoleon II, who was immediately given the title of King of Rome; a title held in reserve for future Holy Roman Emperors-to-be. Napoleon's marriage to Marie Louise would transpire in 1810—an event made all the more spectacular when you consider that just a year prior, in 1809, Napoleon thought it would be a good idea to arrest the pope.

Well, to be fair, it wasn't *exactly* Napoleon's idea. He had merely instructed his generals to shut that pope up, and in the process of annexing the various papal states, one overzealous general by the name of Étienne Radet took the order to mean: kidnap and arrest that pope. Which is exactly what he did. It wasn't like Napoleon refused when he was presented with his new captive. Instead, he opted to keep him as a prisoner, effectively exiling him to a sort of house arrest in Savona. And later, dragging the aging and frail pope, who was now in his seventies, on an arduous journey through the Alps (which caused a bowel obstruction to form in the pope's colon, making him unable to pass waste or urinate for days, all the while, forced to ride in a horse-drawn carriage, in the plain clothes of a priest, and often riding at night to avoid attracting attention), to the French city of Fontainebleau (where, it must be said, the pope finally found relief for the issues which had plagued him during his journey).

Despite his string of victories, Napoleon was not content to rest on his laurels. As soon as he returned from one conquest he would go out on the next, tackling each with seemingly boundless energy. Napoleon would go on to conquer much of continental Europe, including the modern-day territories of Spain, Belgium, Holland, Austria, Germany, Poland, the Netherlands, Switzerland, and much of Italy—while also warring against the British and the Russians, before being decimated by the Russians in 1812. Napoleon would march in to Russia with some six hundred and fifty thousand men, and would leave with some twenty-seven thousand. This was enough to show allied European powers that the Emperor could indeed bleed.

In the end, it was something of a numbers game. Napoleon's army had been decimated, and though he was able to conscript replacements in different arenas, the sheer overwhelming power of the allies advancing on Paris soon crushed his forces. Napoleon would abdicate his throne on April 6, 1814, be exiled to the island of Elba. The pope would finally be released from his captivity. Louis XVIII would take the throne as the King of France, and soon after would send a foreign minister to the Congress of Vienna, where a number of European powers had gathered in the wake of Napoleon's defeat and exile in order to re-establish borders and create a balance of power that would result in peace for everyone.

Around the same time, Pope Pius VII would sign a papal bull, fully re-establishing the Jesuit order throughout Europe. One has to wonder exactly *why* the pope chose this course of action, but after being dragged around Europe for so many years, effectively bullied by monarchs and leaders on the world stage… perhaps the pope simply saw embracing the group as a way to exercise more influence and control over an emerging Europe. After all, of the Jesuits Napoleon had said:

> The Jesuits are a military organization, not a religious order. Their chief is a general of an army, not the mere father abbot of a monastery. And the aim of this organization is POWER. Power in its most despotic exercise. Absolute power, universal power, power to control the world by the volition of a single man… The General of the Jesuits insists on being master, sovereign, over the sovereign. Wherever the Jesuits are admitted they will be masters, cost what it may… Every act, every crime, however atrocious, is a meritorious work, if committed for the interest of the Society of the Jesuits, or by the order of the general."

Perhaps, to the pope… that suddenly didn't look so bad anymore. Perhaps he thought that having an already-established network of morally dubious individuals spread throughout Europe wouldn't be such a terrible thing… At any rate, this set the stage for the full-on infiltration and subversion of the Catholic hierarchy, which is why for some, Pope Francis being the first Jesuit pope is such a big deal—and we already discussed his troublesome history in Argentina.

And it should be noted that Q would respond to an Anon posting a meme about the more recent conspicuous design choices of the Vatican by saying, "Symbolism will be their downfall."

That particular picture comes from inside the Paul VI Audience Hall in the Vatican City, though it is *far* from the only example of Cabal imagery being integrated into Vatican architecture. And months later, Q would return and repeat his assertion about the use of such symbolism:

Q !!mG7VJxZNCl ID: f2dcba No.2770503 ☑ 📑   **1954**
Aug 28 2018 16:00:23 (EST)

Anonymous ID: 824112 No.2770319 ☑ 📑
Aug 28 2018 15:51:50 (EST)

ClipboardImage.png   ⬇

>>2770117
Nazi pin tag with communist symbol.

Pope-Francis.png   ⬇

Anderson-Gloria-6.jpg   ⬇

>>2770319
Symbolism will be their downfall.
Q

Recall Cronus' sickle from earlier; that cannibalistic Titan who devoured his own children. And for the record, that last photo is a picture of Gloria Vanderbilt and her two sons, Anderson Cooper (yes, the CNN anchor), and his brother Carter Cooper. Feel free to examine the "iron cross" on her neck in further detail, but know we'll be talking much more about them in a bit.

And you can't forget the Rothschilds in all of this. While Napoleon was wreaking havoc as an agent of chaos (while being advised by a Jesuit), the Rothschilds were leveraging their financial networks to extract more and more money from each of these monarchies. And the business of war is very expensive. Monarchs looking to face off against Napoleon (and the greatest army ever seen on continental Europe) could not afford to spare any expense. Napoleon was seemingly unstoppable until he had just about ticked off literally every other monarch in Europe; so much so that the only way they were able to stop him was by forming a pan-European coalition against him and confronting him all at once. Seemingly always there for their monarch friends in times of need, the Rothschilds provided almost a billion dollars (in today's terms) worth of liquidity for the British alone.

To show you how the Rothschilds worked, their financial network actually brought news of Napoleon's defeat at Waterloo to Britain a whole day in advance. Yes, Nathan Rothschild went to the Crown to tell them the news, but not before buying up the *entire* government-issued bond market. The resulting peacetime boosted the price of the bonds some forty percent in two years, and Nathan Rothschild once again made an absolute killing. Peacetime could be very lucrative, too… if you knew what depressed assets to buy up beforehand.

And they had no intention of stopping this pattern any time soon. Having set up shop in the City of London (not to be confused with London proper—for the City of London is run by the City of London Corporation, and has its own police force, mayor, and government), the Rothchilds would begin expanding their empire, the inevitable financier behind nearly every single colonial move the Crown would make. As this relationship continued, the words of Napoleon would again prove prescient:

> When a government is dependent upon bankers for money, they and not the leaders of the government control the situation, since the hand that gives is above the hand that takes... Money has no motherland; financiers are without patriotism and without decency; their sole object is gain.

On top of their typical lending and business ventures, the Rothschilds would go on to do a great deal of business with the East India Tea Company, a militarized corporation that had made great inroads into the Far East, piggybacking on the exploration of Jesuit missionaries. In fact, the East India Tea Company would subsidize the entire Jesuit mission in Beijing, where the mild-mannered missionaries would negotiate on the company's behalf in order to secure very profitable trade deals with the local authorities. There was a strange symbiosis between the seemingly peaceful, religious Jesuit monks, and the one company who could basically land the world's largest army anywhere on earth, and because of their sovereign charter, make war or peace with whomever they wanted.

The East India Tea Company would soon go on to account for nearly *half* the world's trade, have an army twice the size of Britain's, and by 1830, literally control all of India. It was, in effect, a massive, supra-national monopoly backed up by the world's strongest military. If you wanted to trade, half the time you were dealing with some arm of the East India Tea Company (or someone else who had dealt with them prior)! Truly, Weyland-Yutani had nothing on the East India Tea Company!

It should come as no surprise then (though, to many, it undoubtedly will) that America's first flag was ripped straight from the East India Tea Company:

Compare this to the American flag (then called the "Grand Union" flag) at the time:

Remarkable, is it not? This was the flag Washington marched his troops under. So not only did the Sons of Liberty toss all that East India Tea Company tea into the Atlantic. It would seem they also ripped off their flag and then used it as their own battle standard. Frederick Saussy attributed this to the work of the last Jesuit superior general Lorenzo Ricci, before the order's official papal suppression in 1773. The official story is that Lorenzo was arrested and died in prison, in Rome in 1775, before being buried at the prominent Jesuit Church of the Gesù. Saussy suggests that this is not the case and that Ricci was secretly sent to America where he became known as "the Professor" as he started to run in Patriotic and Revolutionary circles, eventually hobnobbing with the likes of Washington and Franklin themselves—both of whom were, remember, Freemasons. Saussy claims it was actually Ricci's idea to use a variant of the East India Tea Company's flag, in order to show… not outright rebellion against the crown, but displeasure at their treatment while still maintaining their loyalty. If things escalated, they could always change the design anyway.

Whether you believe that story or not is up to you. I'm not sure there's enough evidence to directly support Staussy's claims, but there is no doubting that the Grand Union flag was the original American flag, whatever the actual reason behind it. And that myth of Betsy Ross is more fairytale than fact. Betsy Ross was a Revolutionary flag maker, yes, but she worked primarily on naval flags, and was, in fact, one of many flag makers at the time. It was a Rebecca Young who actually sewed up a "Grand Union" flag well before Betsy Ross churned out one of hers. And even if there is some doubt when it comes to Jesuit influence over the flag; there's no denying such influence over Washington, DC, itself.

Indeed, many don't realize that before it was called Washington, DC, the land was called Rome, Maryland, complete with its own "Capitoline hill," which would later become Capitol Hill. The land itself would be donated the new US government by a Jesuit-educated plantation owner and one of the five signatories on the Articles of Confederation named Daniel Carroll. Why, there was even a tributary of the Potomac running through what would become Constitution Avenue, which the residents called "Tiber Creek."

And that's not even getting in to the Masonic influence of the layout of the city itself. While the Washington Monument should be instantly recognizable as an obelisk, many are unaware that the streets themselves, as designed by Freemason Pierre Charles L'Enfant, are full of Masonic designs—a subject Q would acknowledge, early on in his drops:

Q !ITPb.qbhqo ID: pOV0fY+r No.150417146   **188**
Nov 21 2017 22:50:09 (EST)

Anonymous ID: GazxQd8P No.150415097
Nov 21 2017 22:32:56 (EST)

image.jpg

>>150415097

ANSWERS

And who can forget Albert Pike in all this! Freemasonry in America didn't just stop with the Founders! That famous Freemason of the thirty-third degree, sometimes referred to as "The greatest Freemason who ever lived," Albert Pike would serve as a general for the Confederate army, pen the famous song, "Dixie, to Arms!" and in 1871, pen what is considered one of the most important texts in Freemasonry to date: *Morals and Dogma of the Ancient and Accepted Scottish Rite of Freemasonry*, leading to the proliferation of lodges around America, and the deception of many men in the process.

As history attests, this gave rise to other secret societies; some offshoots, some rivals, but all with remarkably similar structures and goals. One example is the Knights of Pythias. Another would be the Knights of the Golden Circle, in Texas, which would later lead to the creation of the Ku Klux Klan. The Knights of the Golden Circle were white supremacists; slavery was practically a doctrinal issue for them, and this would result in them becoming fierce allies of the Confederacy; to the point where members were even plotting to kidnap Abraham Lincoln. This, of course, didn't happen, after one Knight in particular, John Wilkes Booth, saw fit to put a bullet through the back of Abraham Lincoln's head.

Just as a side note, in my own experience with QAnon, I would, on three separate occasions, encounter a potential "insider" on the research boards who claimed to be posting information on the activity of modern elites throughout Arkansas (where Pike lived) and the American South in general. My curiosity got the better of me in this scenario, and to say the rabbit hole was deep would be an understatement. I was not prepared for what I would find, following the clues left by this curious insider. I encourage anyone reading this book to go ahead and take some time to read the "Palladian Skull and Bones" articles[26] on my website to learn more about this topic. And for those curious as to where it all led to, when I last heard from "SkullandBonesAnon" (as I came to call him), he was trying to find a journalist with whom he could better publicize his findings. He claimed he already had one, but that Soros had gotten to them. Should anything further come up in that arena, I expect I'll be following along.

And just as the Jesuits, and their proxy vehicle, Freemasonry, expanded Westward in the Americas, they also made inroads east of Europe, primarily through the works of a new acolyte whose words would soon carve a swathe of destruction across the history of humanity, resulting in nearly 150 million deaths, and suffering unlike anything the world had known before it.

Yes, I'm talking about Karl Marx, and yes, he is the direct result of the French Revolution.

And it's here I'll explain something tangential. For the longest time, many of my readers have been confused about one particular line on my site's tagline. For after I say "Honor, Duty, Faith, Family, and Tradition," I explain that I am also "Anti-Degeneracy, Anti-Marxist, and Anti-Revolution." But this has been a point of confusion for many, for if I am pro-American, and obviously America exists because of the American Revolution, how then can I be anti-revolution?

The answer is simple. Ninety-nine percent of all "revolutions" are founded in Socialist ideology, which has its roots in the utopian teachings of secret societies like the Illuminati and the Freemasons—which, as we've seen, both sprout from the same root. And as you can now plainly see, the American Revolution was also touched by these ideologies. Don't get me wrong; I'm not saying all revolutions are automatically immoral, and therefore wrong. Obviously, a degree of nuance is needed to discern such things. But the vast majority of "revolutions" have been bloodbaths initiated by narcissists with utopian—usually Socialist—delusions.

---

26   https://www.neonrevolt.com/2018/08/23/the-palladian-skullandbones-secretsocieties-thecabal-clinton-foundation-arkansas-skullandbonesanon-qanon-greatawakening-neonrevolt/

https://www.neonrevolt.com/2018/09/04/the-palladian-skullandbones-part-2-secretsocieties-thecabal-clinton-foundation-arkansas-skullandbonesanon-qanon-greatawakening-neonrevolt/

I wrote earlier that Napoleon's government was quite friendly and welcoming to secret societies such as the Jesuits and the Freemasons, and that Masonry had flourished under Napoleon's rule while Illuminism continued on, just as it always had. Splinter groups naturally emerged, and it was into this conspiratorial milieu that Marx was born in 1818; Moses Mordecai Levi Marx. Even though he was ostensibly raised a Christian, this was most likely a charade by the family used to avoid religious persecution. Despite being baptized and attending a Jesuit school, the young Marx would soon begin attending a Talmudic school before rejecting the concept of faith entirely.

At age eighteen, having been rejected by a girl he was infatuated with and finding the world simply did not care about his art, Marx would soon write a bitter poem named "The Fiddler":

The Fiddler saws the strings,
His light brown hair he tosses and flings.
He carries a sabre at his side,
He wears a pleated habit wide.
"Fiddler, why that frantic sound?
Why do you gaze so wildly round?
Why leaps your blood, like the surging sea?
What drives your bow so desperately?"
"Why do I fiddle? Or the wild waves roar?
That they might pound the rocky shore,
That eye be blinded, that bosom swell,
That Soul's cry carry down to Hell."
"Fiddler, with scorn you rend your heart.
A radiant God lent you your art,
To dazzle with waves of melody,
To soar to the star-dance in the sky."
"How so! I plunge, plunge without fail
My blood-black sabre into your soul.
That art God neither wants nor wists,
It leaps to the brain from Hell's black mists.
"Till heart's bewitched, till senses reel:
With Satan I have struck my deal.
He chalks the signs, beats time for me,
I play the death march fast and free.
"I must play dark, I must play light,
Till bowstrings break my heart outright."
The Fiddler saws the strings,
His light brown hair he tosses and flings.
He carries a sabre at his side,
He wears a pleated habit wide.

(Emphasis mine)

Marx would grow increasingly cynical and bitter at humanity as he grew older, but at this young age he was mostly just an edgy, cynical, ineffective neckbeard of his time, who, despite not having a mouse and keyboard to hide behind, still somehow managed to arrive at the conclusion that he was better than everyone else around him. And so, he just turned inward and his soul continued to churn.

In 1841, he would meet a man that would forever change the trajectory of his life—one Moses Hess. Hess ran a newspaper and needed an editor. Marx, much like the pompous, work-avoidant ideologues who fill so many editorial rooms today, would suit Hess towards that end, and soon Hess would introduce Marx to the man who would become his lifelong collaborator: Friedrich Engels. But perhaps more importantly, Moses Hess would soon introduce both of them to Freemasonry. In 1845, Marx would be inducted into the Lodge le Socialiste in Brussels, and both he and Engels would work their way up to the thirty-first degree.

Believe me, I wish I could write that the two would begin tipping their fedoras and arguing over whose respective anime waifu was superior, but these two narcissistic neckbeards, Marx and Engels, would, in fact, embark upon a devastating ideological foray as together, they would soon write *The Communist Manifesto* in an attempt to present the goals of their particular lodge to the public. At the same time, both men would *also* join with a radical Illuminati splinter group called The League of Justice, which was itself really just a German offshoot of the Parisian League of Outlaws—which was itself modeled off that radical, revolutionary Italian group called the Carbonari, which was ALSO a splinter group from the Freemasons, which cropped up in the Kingdom of Naples at a time when Napoleon was acting all imperial. While the Carbonari engaged in all kinds of subterfuge and death-dealing, you may actually recognize them from their most famous work, entitled *Alta Vendita*. First published in 1859, *Alta Vendita* describes a Masonic plan to infiltrate and subvert the Catholic church from within.

(See how incestuous this all gets?)

So Marx and Engels were members of these radical groups, and were exposed to all manner of radical, revolutionary thought. In particular, Marx would draw keen inspiration from a Carbonari member known as Louis Auguste Blanqui. Blanqui was a journalist-turned-revolutionary who preached the "just" redistribution of wealth. In 1834, Blanqui would help form an offshoot of the League of Justice, known as The Society of Seasons, along with co-founder Armand Barbès, who was himself a member of The Society for the Rights of Man. Blanqui was, in particular, inspired by the works of Freemason Philippe Buonarroti, who was a man who traveled in all kinds of Masonic and Illumined circles during the late 1700s and early 1800s. Buonarroti would not only start his own Illuminati-inspired order, which he called the Sublime Perfect Masters, but he also infiltrated the Carbonari, and became involved with the infamous, occultic, Pythagorean and pantheistic Cercle Social, of which Marx would later write:

> Undeterred by this examination, the French Revolution gave rise to ideas which led beyond the *ideas* of the entire old world order. The revolutionary movement which began in 1789 in the *Cercle Social,* which in the middle of its course had as its chief representatives *Leclerc* and *Roux*, and which finally with *Babeuf's* conspiracy was temporarily defeated, gave rise to the communist idea which *Babeuf's* friend *Buonarroti* re-introduced in France after the Revolution of 1830. This idea, consistently developed, is the idea of the new world order.

The François-Noël "Gracchus" Babeuf referenced here was a Jacobin journalist-turned-activist during the French Revolution who would be executed for trying to overthrow the French Directory and install a Socialist government that would guarantee equality of outcome for everyone (as opposed to equality of opportunity). Babeuf would later become the focus of Buonarroti's magnum opus, *Histoire de la Conspiration pour l'Égalité dite de Babeuf-*

—a revolutionary handbook that would become the prime source of inspiration for Auguste Blanqui and his Society of Seasons. Russian revolutionary anarchist Mikhail Bakunin would later hail Buonarroti "the greatest conspirator of the century."[27]

Now, as member of the League of Justice, Marx was well aware of the work Auguste Blanqui had performed just a decade earlier with the Society of Seasons, and their failed 1839 coup attempt. Both Barbès and Blanqui would be imprisoned, but later freed—Barbès in 1854 by Napoleon III when he became Emperor of France, and Blanqui in 1848, when he was freed during the February Revolution, at which time he would continue his revolutionary work during the Second Republic. Of Blanqui, Marx would write that he "always regarded [Blanqui] as the brains and inspiration of the proletarian party in France." Blanqui would later be arrested a number of times, serving various prison sentences, before finally dying of a stroke in 1881.

And so, Marx and Engels codified their beliefs for their lodge, drawing inspiration from Weishaupt and all the rabid revolutionary megalomaniacs who came after him and who attempted to reshape the entire world in their own image. This "revolutionary" document was designed (mostly by Engels) to anger and provoke the common man, in order that the elites, the Illumined ones, the "learned masters," may better direct society by harnessing the threat of violence inherent in an angry and agitated mob against whomever is deemed to be the enemy at the time. By weaponizing the Hegelian dialectic and dressing it up in the language of utopian equality, Marx and Engels were able to "catechize" generations of unfortunate souls into the next iteration of this worldwide death cult: the Communist Party. Thus, bloody, terrible, costly "revolution" spread to Russia, China, and beyond.

And the real sick thing about this, the great and terrible inversion of this, is that this would then be turned around and inverted once again in the twentieth century. Communism and Fascism would become the new Bourgeoisie and Proletariat; the two "diametrically opposed" ideas which would then fight each other, when really, their source was the same. Why, the newspaper founded by Mussolini himself would run with a quotation from that source of so much-inspiration for Marx, Auguste Blanqui:

> "He who has iron, has bread."

The Communists and the Fascists: two sides of the same coin. It is an inconvenient history that moderns on both the extreme Left and the extreme Right would rather ignore as they continue pushing the entirety of humanity towards the realization of the "Illumined ones'" original vision: doing away with the old, and ushering in the NWO. (Though, in terms of sheer numbers of death and destruction, I think they've found more "success" when pushing Leftist ideology.)

And the role of the "Banking Royalty" shouldn't be ignored in facilitating this push. Just as the Rothschilds financed Hitler, Rothschild agents like Jacob Schiff would go on to finance "revolutionaries" like Trotsky. Max Warburg would back the likes of Lenin. Max's brother, Paul Warburg, would go on to design the US central bank, the Federal Reserve. And Paul's son James, (who would serve as FDR's financial adviser) would later say on February 17, 1950, on the floor of the US Senate:

> "We shall have World Government, whether we like it or not. The only question is whether World Government will be achieved by conquest or consent."

---

27   For more on Buonarroti, see: https://www.conspiracyarchive.com/2015/11/05/militant-mason-ry-amis-de-la-verite-buonarroti-masters-and-french-carbonari/

I think it should be clear to everyone by now that the "Banking Royalty," with their royal titles and their trillions in assets, have been rigging the game for a long time. By playing both sides, it's guaranteed that they'll never *really* lose. Even as they spread their tentacles across the world by taking over the global banking infrastructure, they've always known that the only real currency is power, the ability to control the affairs of men, and get them to go along, wittingly or unwittingly, with their evil agenda. Money is merely a token, an abstraction of that power. A man may have a lot of money, but he doesn't always have power. Some people confuse the two. Remember what Lynn de Rothschild had posted on the boards: "We don't use dirty money. Paper is for the puppets."

Q !ITPb.qbhqo ID: gO/UntOB No.149063644 🔗 📄   **140**
Nov 11 2017 23:33:51 (EST)

Wealth (over generations) buys power.
Power (over generations) buys more wealth/control.
More wealth/control buys countries and its people.
Families combined (TRI) = NWO.
Inner TRI families will collapse.
What is the keystone?
What Nation dominates all others?
What Nation has influence over most others?
What is the keystone?
Return to SA.
Strings cut (+++).
Puppets (+++) in shadows.
Each side of the triangle controls a certain subsect of power brokers.
Power brokers are also labeled as the puppets/servants.
What is the New World Order?
Why did POTUS receive a sword dance when visiting SA?
What does this mean culturally?
Why is this relevant?
What occurred in SA?
How did POTUS remove one side of the pyramid?
What did POTUS receive while visiting China?
Where did POTUS dine?
What is the significance?
What if China, Russia, and others are coordinating w/ POTUS to
eliminate the NWO?
Who controls NK?
Who really controls NK?
Who controls several agencies within the US, EU, and abroad?
Why is No Such Agency so vital?
Enormous scale of events currently ongoing.
Why is Russia helping to kill ISIS?
This is not easy to accept nor believe.
Crumbs make bread.
Operations active.
Joint missions underway.
The world is fighting back.
Refer back to graphic.
The Great Awakening.
Snow White.
Iron Eagle.
Jason Bourne (2016)(Dream/CIA).
Q

ANSWERS

But it's not just the Fed here in the US. Q would go to the trouble early on of documenting just how widespread the corruption was by listing, in a series of drops for Anons, all the banks owned and controlled by the Rothschild empire.

Q !ITPb.qbhqo ID: gO/UntOB No.149063400☐ 📷   135
Nov 11 2017 23:31:13 (EST)

ROTHSCHILD OWNED & CONTROLLED BANKS:
Afghanistan: Bank of Afghanistan
Albania: Bank of Albania
Algeria: Bank of Algeria
Argentina: Central Bank of Argentina
Armenia: Central Bank of Armenia
Aruba: Central Bank of Aruba
Australia: Reserve Bank of Australia
Austria: Austrian National Bank
Azerbaijan: Central Bank of Azerbaijan Republic
Bahamas: Central Bank of The Bahamas
Bahrain: Central Bank of Bahrain
Bangladesh: Bangladesh Bank
Barbados: Central Bank of Barbados
Belarus: National Bank of the Republic of Belarus
Belgium: National Bank of Belgium
Belize: Central Bank of Belize
Benin: Central Bank of West African States (BCEAO)
Bermuda: Bermuda Monetary Authority
Bhutan: Royal Monetary Authority of Bhutan
Bolivia: Central Bank of Bolivia
Bosnia: Central Bank of Bosnia and Herzegovina
Botswana: Bank of Botswana
Brazil: Central Bank of Brazil
Bulgaria: Bulgarian National Bank
Burkina Faso: Central Bank of West African States (BCEAO)
Burundi: Bank of the Republic of Burundi
Cambodia: National Bank of Cambodia
Came Roon: Bank of Central African States
Canada: Bank of Canada – Banque du Canada

                                                    ANSWERS

Q !!TPb.qbhqo ID: gO/UntOB No.149063442 ⬀ ▮▮   **136**
Nov 11 2017 23:31:41 (EST)

Cayman Islands: Cayman Islands Monetary Authority
Central African Republic: Bank of Central African States
Chad: Bank of Central African States
Chile: Central Bank of Chile
China: The People's Bank of China
Colombia: Bank of the Republic
Comoros: Central Bank of Comoros
Congo: Bank of Central African States
Costa Rica: Central Bank of Costa Rica
Côte d'Ivoire: Central Bank of West African States (BCEAO)
Croatia: Croatian National Bank
Cuba: Central Bank of Cuba
Cyprus: Central Bank of Cyprus
Czech Republic: Czech National Bank
Denmark: National Bank of Denmark
Dominican Republic: Central Bank of the Dominican Republic
East Caribbean area: Eastern Caribbean Central Bank
Ecuador: Central Bank of Ecuador
Egypt: Central Bank of Egypt
El Salvador: Central Reserve Bank of El Salvador
Equatorial Guinea: Bank of Central African States
Estonia: Bank of Estonia
Ethiopia: National Bank of Ethiopia
European Union: European Central Bank
Fiji: Reserve Bank of Fiji
Finland: Bank of Finland
France: Bank of France
Gabon: Bank of Central African States
The Gambia: Central Bank of The Gambia
Georgia: National Bank of Georgia
Germany: Deutsche Bundesbank
Ghana: Bank of Ghana
Greece: Bank of Greece
Guatemala: Bank of Guatemala
Guinea Bissau: Central Bank of West African States (BCEAO)
Guyana: Bank of Guyana
Haiti: Central Bank of Haiti
Honduras: Central Bank of Honduras
Hong Kong: Hong Kong Monetary Authority
Hungary: Magyar Nemzeti Bank
Iceland: Central Bank of Iceland
India: Reserve Bank of India
Indonesia: Bank Indonesia
Iran: The Central Bank of the Islamic Republic of Iran

ANSWERS

Q !ITPb.qbhqo ID: gO/UntOB No.149063509 🔗 📷   **137**
Nov 11 2017 23:32:20 (EST)

Iraq: Central Bank of Iraq
Ireland: Central Bank and Financial Services Authority of Ireland
Israel: Bank of Israel
Italy: Bank of Italy
Jamaica: Bank of Jamaica
Japan: Bank of Japan
Jordan: Central Bank of Jordan
Kazakhstan: National Bank of Kazakhstan
Kenya: Central Bank of Kenya
Korea: Bank of Korea
Kuwait: Central Bank of Kuwait
Kyrgyzstan: National Bank of the Kyrgyz Republic
Latvia: Bank of Latvia
Lebanon: Central Bank of Lebanon
Lesotho: Central Bank of Lesotho
Libya: Central Bank of Libya (Their most recent conquest)
Uruguay: Central Bank of Uruguay
Lithuania: Bank of Lithuania
Luxembourg: Central Bank of Luxembourg
Macao: Monetary Authority of Macao
Macedonia: National Bank of the Republic of Macedonia
Madagascar: Central Bank of Madagascar
Malawi: Reserve Bank of Malawi
Malaysia: Central Bank of Malaysia
Mali: Central Bank of West African States (BCEAO)
Malta: Central Bank of Malta
Mauritius: Bank of Mauritius
Mexico: Bank of Mexico
Moldova: National Bank of Moldova
Mongolia: Bank of Mongolia
Montenegro: Central Bank of Montenegro
Morocco: Bank of Morocco
Mozambique: Bank of Mozambique
Namibia: Bank of Namibia
Nepal: Central Bank of Nepal
Netherlands: Netherlands Bank
Netherlands Antilles: Bank of the Netherlands Antilles
New Zealand: Reserve Bank of New Zealand
Nicaragua: Central Bank of Nicaragua
Niger: Central Bank of West African States (BCEAO)
Nigeria: Central Bank of Nigeria
Norway: Central Bank of Norway
Oman: Central Bank of Oman
Pakistan: State Bank of Pakistan

ANSWERS

Q !ITPb.qbhqo ID: gO/UntOB No.149063549 🗗 📷   **138**
Nov 11 2017 23:32:49 (EST)

Papua New Guinea: Bank of Papua New Guinea
Paraguay: Central Bank of Paraguay
Peru: Central Reserve Bank of Peru
Philip Pines: Bangko Sentral ng Pilipinas
Poland: National Bank of Poland
Portugal: Bank of Portugal
Qatar: Qatar Central Bank
Romania: National Bank of Romania
Russia: Central Bank of Russia
Rwanda: National Bank of Rwanda
San Marino: Central Bank of the Republic of San Marino
Samoa: Central Bank of Samoa
Saudi Arabia: Saudi Arabian Monetary Agency
Senegal: Central Bank of West African States (BCEAO)
Serbia: National Bank of Serbia
Seychelles: Central Bank of Seychelles
Sierra Leone: Bank of Sierra Leone
Singapore: Monetary Authority of Singapore
Slovakia: National Bank of Slovakia
Slovenia: Bank of Slovenia
Solomon Islands: Central Bank of Solomon Islands
South Africa: South African Reserve Bank
Spain: Bank of Spain
Sri Lanka: Central Bank of Sri Lanka
Sudan: Bank of Sudan
Surinam: Central Bank of Suriname
Swaziland: The Central Bank of Swaziland
Sweden: Sveriges Riksbank
Switzerland: Swiss National Bank
Tajikistan: National Bank of Tajikistan
Tanzania: Bank of Tanzania
Thailand: Bank of Thailand
Togo: Central Bank of West African States (BCEAO)
Tonga: National Reserve Bank of Tonga
Trinidad and Tobago: Central Bank of Trinidad and Tobago
Tunisia: Central Bank of Tunisia
Turkey: Central Bank of the Republic of Turkey
Uganda: Bank of Uganda
Ukraine: National Bank of Ukraine
United Arab Emirates: Central Bank of United Arab Emirates
United Kingdom: Bank of England
United States: Federal Reserve, Federal Reserve Bank of New York
Vanuatu: Reserve Bank of Vanuatu
Venezuela: Central Bank of Venezuela
Vietnam: The State Bank of Vietnam
Yemen: Central Bank of Yemen
Zambia: Bank of Zambia
Zimbabwe: Reserve Bank of Zimbabwe
The FED and the IRS
FACT: US Federal Reserve is a privately-owned company, sitting on
its very own patch of land, immune to the US laws.
Q

                                                    ANSWERS

So now, you too see how widespread this problem is. And now you understand why it didn't matter who they backed during all these "revolutions," so long as they retained power. Much like the monoparty of today—whether some strongman from the past was on the "Right" or on the "Left," it did not matter. They both paid fealty to the same masters. And really think about it for a moment: if the nation is headed down a road towards the edge of a cliff, does it matter if they're traveling in the Left lane or the Right lane? No, because in the end, they're going to go over the cliff and perish! So too, has it been with the elites "driving" the course of humanity for these many millennia. And you'll have to forgive me here if you take exception to me referring to Nazis or Fascists as "Right wing." It's true, for instance, that Nazi stood for National *Socialist* (and is therefore more correctly categorized as a Left wing ideology), but there are social conventions to which I must adhere so that the bulk of humanity can understand the more pressing issues I'm trying to explain here. At any rate, it seems like splitting hairs when there's so much death and destruction at play here, and the puppet masters are all the same:

Q !UW.yye1fxo (ID: 4d8e72) No.618129 ☑ 📷   **936**
Mar 10 2018 18:07:05 (EST)

Q !UW.yye1fxo (ID: 4d8e72) No.617965 ☑ 📷
Mar 10 2018 17:57:14 (EST)

EFABC59D-40D3-4570-81E3-5...jpeg

>>617965
The Nazi order.
NWO [N does not refer to "New"].
The Sum of All Fears.
NK.
POTUS.
Hostage.
Threat.
DISARM.
Stage SET.
FREEDOM.
Q

There was a reason I talked about Jesuits early on in this chapter, and the way a secret society (formed from earlier esoteric groups) infiltrated and subverted the church. If the Jesuits started the process in the 1500s, the Rothschilds came in and finished it by the 1800s, taking over the Vatican's finances, with other affiliated groups like the Carbonari finding that their own goals dovetailed with those above. The result is like what you see in the picture which QAnon referenced above; Catholics and Nazis, side by side.

But to be clear, Q then clarified:

Q !UW.yye1fxo **ID: fb1a66** No.618754 🔗 🖼   **938**
Mar 10 2018 18:37:22 (EST)

N does not refer to Nazi.
The continued Nazi ideology is relevant.
Events will clarify.
Think subgroup.
Q

"Think subgroup." The NWO does not stand for the Nazi World Order.

What does Q mean by this? I'll attempt to answer that in a moment, but at the very least, the Nazis were a subgroup of an older group, with much more influence, much more power, and much larger goals. We opened this chapter recounting the Dutroux Affair in 1996, where a professional child smuggler was caught with children in a dungeon; children he had been procuring at the request of a Satanic cult for use in the sex rituals of the global elite. Later, in 2017, a Dutch banker by the name of Ronald Bernard would step forward and, in a series of online video interviews, confirm that these kinds of activities were still very much going on, and rather common. In the interviews, he described how he himself was asked to participate in child sacrifices abroad, and how he simply couldn't do it. The interview implied that he had taken part in wild parties to an extent—but when it came to children—that's where he truly saw the evil for what it was and decided he couldn't be part of this world anymore. He would subsequently break into tears trying to recount his story, and I highly recommend that all readers of this book track down a copy of this interview on whatever video streaming site you have available, as it is very easy to find a copy these days and will greatly enhance your own understanding of what it is exactly we're dealing with here: a group of Satanic, pedophilic elite who regularly engage in rape, torture, human sacrifice, and cannibalism. The Dutroux Affair wasn't an isolated incident. Pizzagate wasn't an isolated incident. Ronald Bernard's experience wasn't an isolated incident. It is the direct result of a worldwide Cabal deliberately engaging in these vile practices in order to maintain power and satisfy their own, secret, twisted hungers. Nothing had changed in the intervening decades since the Dutroux Affair had been uncovered, and that's because it's been going on for a very, *very* long time.

Even Q himself would talk about this particular aspect of the Cabal in drop six hundred and sixty-four, when he referenced the Black Forest in Austria, near the Rothschild estate. In essence, this is nothing new. It's as old as the Cabal itself:

Q !UW.yye1fxo **ID: 641129** No.274601 ☐ ▮
Feb 5 2018 10:41:35 (EST)

664

Anonymous **ID: 6546e8** No.274558 ☐ ▮
Feb 5 2018 10:33:51 (EST)

2-5-18 c.jpg

>>274558
Would POTUS make a serious accusation if the TRUTH wasn't about
to come to LIGHT?
Black Forest.
Austria.
Rothschild.
FIRE sale days after post?
What went on there?
Dopey.
You have more than you know.
Q

And it's true: the Rothschilds have been having fire sale after fire sale, as their liquid assets begin to deplete in the face of an organized, militarized effort against their empire. In January 2018 they had to sell their fifty-four hundred hectare hunting estate in Austria, as they were preparing for what they saw coming with the new Trump administration. Since then, it's been apartments, yachts, jewelry collections, estates, and more all hitting the market. Trump officially put the Cabal on notice when he passed an executive order on December 21, 2017, entitled "Executive Order Blocking the Property of Persons Involved in Serious Human Rights Abuse or Corruption," that would allow the US government to completely seize all the assets of anyone found guilty of, well, "Serious Human Rights Abuse or Corruption." In essence, the likes of the Rothschilds could have their entire earthly belongings stripped from them over-night because of this order—which is partially why so many in the media and in business have been panicking so much, and also why so many are now announcing presidential campaigns against President Trump for 2020. They think there's a greater degree of safety in that it would look bad for Trump to attack a "political opponent." In essence, they're banking on the people not waking up to their crimes.

I'm writing this here to help make sure they don't succeed on that front. Virtually every single one of them is a career criminal; and worse—they've known about (and often participated) in such evil, and haven't done a single thing to bring any of it to light, or otherwise stop it. No, they were more than happy to let the funds keep pouring into their coffers, to let the abuse and trafficking continue, to let our democratic republic be overrun and weakened from the inside out, and were even complicit in Hillary and Obama's plan to bomb the United States. Think about that next time you see one of them morally grandstanding on Capitol Hill, or in the media.

But really, what Q is referring to in this drop is something RSA survivor Cathy O'Brien would call in her various testimonies and writings, "The Most Dangerous Game." In essence, "The Most Dangerous Game" is when elites get together and take their mind-controlled sex slaves and release them onto the grounds of a walled estate (or other area, such as an island), where they can't escape, and when released, are stripped of their clothes and ordered to run naked and hide wherever they can. The elites, after waiting a time, would then begin to hunt their respective quarries down. Men would usually be killed when caught. Women and children would usually be raped and tortured (though killing wasn't out of the ordinary for this unfortunate lot, either). And to be clear: this didn't just happen at the Rothschild estate in Austria—though that has been a prominent location of this practice throughout history.

In her testimony, O'Brien would also recall that she was "owned" by Senator Robert Byrd; the same Senator Byrd who mentored Hillary Clinton, and yes, the same Senator Byrd who was an "Exalted Cyclops" in the KKK (which, you'll also recall, was an offshoot of the Knights of the Golden Circle—the same secret society in which John Wilkes Booth was also a member). O'Brien would also recount how her vagina had been ritualistically scarred by one of her abusers when he sliced a muscle on her vaginal wall, causing it to protrude outward. This abuser then proceeded to carve a "face" into the resulting mass, in effect "branding" her. O'Brien would submit to a gynecological exam on film, and allow her vagina to be photographed, where two "eyes," a "mouth" and a "nose" can be clearly seen on a scarred portion of flesh. She would recount in her book how she had been passed around to Hillary Clinton, who became aroused at the sight of the disfigurement, before using O'Brien as an MKUltra sex slave. The mere fact that this terrible scar even exists and has been documented and observed by medical professionals is evidence that O'Brien's testimony should be heard and taken very seriously. I don't advise trying to view footage or pictures of this, however, unless you have a very strong constitution.

But more to the point of the Qdrop above, these kinds of practices have been going on in these circles for a very long time. Note how many of our "fairytales" emerge from the Black Forest, and note how much more sinister they are in their original, unsanitized, un-Disney-fied versions. Note how gory and violent some of these stories can be, when told in their original forms. Is it truly any coincidence that these kinds of tales would pop up in this particular region? That's the influence of this cult, this Cabal on society, and its presence is felt around the world to this very day. But I'm sure many are still wondering what exactly the true nature of this mystery cult is, and who its elite practitioners were.

Well, I'm about to tell you.

The oldest secret society, at least according to Cabal researcher Bill Cooper, is known as "The Brotherhood of the Snake." Plutarch, known for his writings on great men of antiquity, was actually a member of this brotherhood, serving as a priest at the temple of Apollo at Delphi, where, you might recall, they had the Pythia; that is, the high priestess serving as the "Oracle" there. Of this secret brotherhood, Plutarch would write:

> As for what thou hearest others say, who persuade the many that the soul, when once freed from the body, neither suffers evil nor is conscious, I know that thou are better grounded in the doctrines received by us from our ancestors and in the sacred orgies of Dionysos, than to believe them; for the mystic symbols are well-known to us, who belong to the 'Brotherhood.'

The temple at Delphi was just one in a long line of Brotherhood permutations, as the practices grew and evolved, like some kind of insidious parasite, within whatever culture it lodged itself. The Oracle at Delphi (the Pythia) was particularly famous for her many "prophecies," but in fact, many researchers now believe the Pythia was standing astride a natural chasm, inhaling the "sacred pneuma"; that is, fumes from deep within the earth which caused her to enter into an altered mental state, whereupon she could "make contact" with the divine, and thus receive her prophecies. The earlier iterations of the cult involving temple prostitution had evolved into something new at this point. The practitioners of this ancient Greek paganism believed the fumes inhaled by the Oracle came from an ancient and massive python that Apollo had killed in the underworld, and which was now rotting, sending up these powerful, divine fumes. (In fact, the title of Pythia comes from the ancient Greek pythien, which means, "to rot.")

Prior to this, ancient tradition held that the site was discovered by a shepherd boy, who first reported the fissure in the ground back to the priestess of the serpent oracles of the Mother Goddess Gaia, who had not only given birth to the Olympians we covered earlier, but to this ancient snake—really an "earth dragon"—as well. The resulting cult would go on to teach that Apollo had slain this ancient, primordial snake as part of a rebellion against Gaia.

The Christian writer Origin would later describe in detail the practice of this Oracle at Delphi:

> It is said of the Pythian priestess, whose oracle seems to have been the most celebrated, that when she sat down a the mouth of the Castalian cave, the prophetic spirit of Apollo entered her private parts. She sat with parted thighs on the tripod of Apollo, and the evil spirit entered her from below, passing through her genital organs, and plunged her into a state of frenzy, so that she began with loosened hair to foam and rage like a drunkard.

Thus was she also called the Oracle Priestess of the House of Snakes, channeling the Goddess Gaia's wisdom by "absorbing" the sacred pneuma through her genitals, which is why it had to be a female priestess, as opposed to a male priest. A male priest simply didn't have the required equipment for this particular job.

Prior to Delphi housing a temple dedicated to Apollo, the site was, however, known by another name, Krisa, and it was dedicated exclusively to Gaia worship. In fact, the story goes that Gaia had created the python to help protect the site, which is why, in trying to overthrow Gaia, Apollo had to kill the python. Once overthrown, Apollo reinforced his claim to the new territory by appropriating the symbol of the python as his own, as well as the site itself. Later, the name of the site was changed to Delphi, after Delphyne—another serpent guardian Gaia had made.

But obviously, Apollo's claim couldn't be contradicted, so the myths converged somewhat, and over time it became told that he actually slew two snake guardians that day, male and female. They were thus added to his symbol of power, the caduceus (which he later gave to Hermes... at least, according to Homer). And the crazy thing is... the caduceus even comes from earlier civilizations. Here is the mushussu caduceus; the mushussu being Marduk's sacred animal (with it even represented on the Ishtar gate):

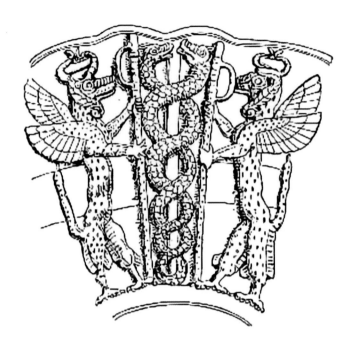

We talked earlier about the anthropomorphized, snake-headed Set in Egyptian mythology, but the Egyptians also had Apophis, the snake of chaos. In Mesopotamia, there was Ningishzida, who, like Gaia's python, was conceived by the mother goddess Ereshkigal. The Sumerians had Ninurta's dragon, called Bašm. Vedic religions gained Vritra. And you can find this concept of this primordial chaos-snake even further back, in Norse mythology with the Jörmungandr, and in the religions of ancient China, and even Mesoamerica. And of course, we can't forget the iconic and alchemical image of the snake eating its own tail; the ouroboros—symbolizing chaos and renewal. Point is: these are all manifestations of the same, ancient mystery religion which has been passed down in the halls of the elite for, literally, thousands of years. These are all iterations of the Brotherhood of the Snake, continuing through, to this very day.

And the crazy thing, the really bonkers, tinfoil-hat, out-there conspiratorial thing about this is that it all comes from even earlier societies; what some might call antediluvian societies. What am I talking about? Why, Atlantis, of course; that fabled city whose existence was told to us by Plato, after knowledge of it was first preserved by his ancestor Solon (upon hearing of it from an Egyptian priest in the temple of Neith, who, you'll recall, later fused with Isis), and passed down through his family for generations. Made of concentric rings of land surrounded by water, the city was dedicated to a sea god (who Plato equated with Poseidon) and was said to be home to a massive, technologically advanced civilization before its sudden and utter destruction. In fact, it was the priests who said to Solon that Egypt itself was once a colony of Atlantis.

It's my personal belief now (though much research still needs to be done on this front), that the most likely candidate for the actual, historical Atlantis is none other than the Richat Structure in the Sahara desert. Also known as "The Eye of the Sahara," the size, shape, and placement are near perfect matches for Plato's description of Atlantis. Spanning some twenty-four kilometers in diameter, made up of concentric rings, and sitting past the "Pillars of Hercules" (that is, the Rock of Gibraltar), there's really no other place like it on earth.

And notice how, from above, the formation itself really does look like an eye. Is this a parallel to the "Eye of Horus" and the later "Eye of Providence" motifs that we see so much of? Is this where it originated from? It's hard to say without much further research, and though I'm hesitant to speculate further on this particular matter, it would not surprise me one bit if this were the case.

I realize, at this point, this might be too much for some to handle. Q has said, as we go deeper and deeper, the more unrealistic it all becomes. Why, if you'd have told me a year ago—just a mere year ago—that I would seriously be contemplating the existence of an actual historical Atlantis, I'd probably have laughed in your face. And yet, over so much time, and so many hours of research and study, this is where I now find myself. And ultimately one can entertain a thought, considering the possibilities it presents for some time, examining it in light of further evidence from other sources and other thinkers without having to accept certain conclusions right then and there on the spot.

As I said in the very beginning of this book, I've had a *lot* of time to digest and reflect on this information. It wouldn't surprise me if people were to struggle with it upon hearing it for the first time. But by the time this book is finally out, circulating among the public, and once certain events have come to pass, I imagine that many of the claims I make now suddenly won't seem so radical anymore.

Q !UW.yye1fxo ID: 87df69 No.351447 ⟶ ▐   **749**
Feb 12 2018 11:50:26 (EST)

> Anonymous ID: a4bb61 No.351343 ⟶ ▐
> Feb 12 2018 11:44:06 (EST)
>
> controlling the crops, controls the people (sheep)
> (might be reaching, but throwing it out there)

>>351343
Coincidence the Matrix (movie) grew people as a crop, used for
energy, and controlled their mind?
Sound familiar?
Wonder where they derived that idea from.
Now comes the 'conspiracy' label.
Deeper we go, the more unrealistic it all becomes.
The end won't be for everyone.
That choice, to know, will be yours.
Q

But the broader point I'm trying to make here is that this snake cult from the ancient world infiltrated every major society, operating in darkness while pushing mankind closer and closer to calamity with each passing generation, all so that they could maintain their hegemony. So when a drunk Lynn Forester de Rothschild (whose husband, Sir Evelyn de Rothschild currently serves as the financial adviser to the Queen of England) hops online in the wake of an airplane crash over her family's estate and sneers, "My snake is bigger than yours" to random Anons online, know that its this ancient cult, this evil Cabal, in which she's putting so much of her rapidly diminishing hope.

I have two things to say to her about that.

First, Lynn…

You're from Bergen County.

As in, Bergen County, New Jersey.

There's a word for your type, Lynn, and I know you know it, because I know you've been called it before. You're a "Benny," Lynn. A Benny who married a rich old cultist, because you have no scruples, no morals, and aren't against selling your soul to the devil.

But for those who don't know, Benny is an acronym for Bergen, Edison, Newark, and New York. And it's basically a stereotype for every piece of obnoxious turnpike runoff that streams down to the New Jersey beaches in the summer. So yeah, Lynn. You don't impress me, and neither does your cult.

Secondly, Lynn, read Exodus 7.

> When Pharaoh shall speak unto you, saying, Shew a miracle for you: then thou shalt say unto Aaron, Take thy rod, and cast *it* before Pharaoh, and it shall become a serpent. And Moses and Aaron went in unto Pharaoh, and they did so as the LORD had commanded: and Aaron cast down his rod before Pharaoh, and before his servants, and it became a serpent. Then Pharaoh also called the wise men and the sorcerers: now the magicians of Egypt, they also did in like manner with their enchantments. For they cast down every man his rod, and they became serpents: **but Aaron's rod swallowed up their rods**. (Emphasis added)

You'll be defeated, Lynn. Just like your forebears.

But why? Why all this secrecy? Why all these "secret societies" and superstitions? Think back to my opening about "the Cave." These Cabal members aren't any brighter than the average person. They're not any smarter, any stronger, anymore capable than any other person—no matter how much their sick little narcissistic cult appeals to their egos. No, its all about keeping the masses of people in the dark so as to control them and keep them from rebelling as they pursue their ultimate goals—for that's exactly what we would all do if their plans were laid bare for all to see. The ultimate form of capital is *human* capital, and no one understands this better than the Cabal.

That is why they absolutely must be defeated and purged from the face of the earth.

But would it shock you to believe that the Rothschilds aren't even the biggest threat in all this? That they're merely agents of an even older, more powerful family?

Though, yes, for the longest time the Rothschilds have been dictating affairs on a global scale, in truth, they were just the front-men for this entire system of "Illuminati," who preferred to operate entirely from the shadows. The first hints of who this was would be dropped by Q in early 2018, but it would take us a long time to get a handle on what this even meant:

Q !UW.yye1fxo **ID: 567809** No.325580 🗗 📭   **714**
Feb 10 2018 05:46:19 (EST)

Mess with the best, die like the rest.
[2] highly classified clown ops exposed.
[44] remaining.
Wizards & Warlocks.
Save the best for last.
[P]
Q

And just a quick lesson in Q literacy before we continue: the reason the P is in brackets here is because that puts the contents of the brackets in the "killbox." Essentially, it's a targeting reticle. Q would often use the killbox to note who was going down next in his drops, and on this occasion, he simply put the letter P squarely in his sights.

Still, Anons had no idea who P was. Without more to go on, the question just kind of sat for months, until Q rekindled our curiosity with another drop when he responded to an Anon asking about the pope:

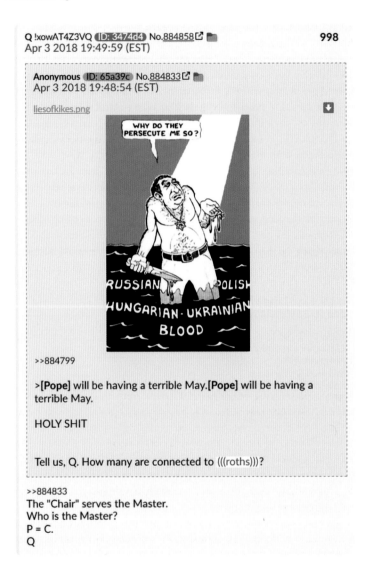

Q !xowAT4Z3VQ ID: 3474d4 No.884858 ☐ 🏴   **998**
Apr 3 2018 19:49:59 (EST)

Anonymous ID: 65a39c No.884833 ☐ 🏴
Apr 3 2018 19:48:54 (EST)

liesofkikes.png

>>884799

>[Pope] will be having a terrible May.[Pope] will be having a
terrible May.

HOLY SHIT

Tell us, Q. How many are connected to (((roths)))?

>>884833
The "Chair" serves the Master.
Who is the Master?
P = C.
Q

Now, just as an aside, I have to be *very* clear here: yes, that's an antisemitic post Q is re-sponding to. Q did not post that image, or those questions, and I won't mince words here. If you've been anywhere around the Chans in recent years, you know that there can be, at times, an extremist, even Nazi streak to some of the posters there, and this is because the Chans are largely uncensored forums. Some people get their kicks by posting racial slurs and imagery. Others are genuine in their hate. Sometimes, it's hard to tell, but when you've been around the boards long enough, you get pretty good at mentally filtering out content you may personally find offensive. For instance, in my experience, I've seen some of the most horrific gore you can imagine on the Chans. Oftentimes, it's posted to intentionally keep "normies" out, leaving only the "autists" who are able to move past such shock-posts. The reason I'm posting the image in this book is because it presents the context to which Q is responding—and I'm trying to give you an accurate understanding of that context. I want to be clear here: I do not endorse or approve of what the Anon posted here, but at the same time, Q had to work with what he had—and I personally believe that part of the reason he chose to interact with posters like this was to help move them away from these kinds of identity politics.

With that in mind, while there's been quite a bit of pro-Nazi propaganda that's been spread across the Chans in recent years, I'll say this much: only part of it is organic. And after being exposed to all of it and seeing how feds basically run "Alt-Right" circles, I have to believe that much of it is a coordinated attempt by the Deep State (at the behest of the likes of Soros), to divide and conquer Americans. During the Obama years there was a sharp rise in minority identity politics—so much so that the phrase "white privilege" left the darkened corners of academia and entered the common parlance. In response, the Deep State capitalized on this growing marginalization, even as white society crumbled around an entire generation of white youths. Think, if you were born in 1996, you were five when 9/11 happened. Then you saw endless wars in the Middle East. Then you saw your parents job's leave the country as Obama shipped them overseas. You witnessed the opioid crisis first hand. You watched as American infrastructure rotted. Depression and destitution crept in. And now, even though you were suffering the same as everyone else, you got to be lectured about how your very existence was a crime on humanity, and how only your people had to "atone" for the sins of the past, as though there was some kind of ancient generational curse at play.

Young, white men were very angry before Trump came around, and rightfully so—because they were being targeted and gaslit at the same time; told that the reason they were failing was because they deserved to fail, due to their heritage. The American narrative went from: anyone can have a shot at becoming anything, to, now it is time for white men to step aside, and let others have their turn. This was deliberate demoralization the likes of which had never been seen in the US before. It was designed to provoke conflict along racial lines, and propaganda manufactured by the Deep State which was then spread online only served to exacerbate the situation—because again, if the elites could get us fighting each other, we wouldn't be fighting them.

I believe part of Q's mission was to wake people up to the lies they had been fed and help them begin again. Which is why I think he chose to respond to this particular Anon—without correcting him or shaming him for his choice of words or imagery. Given enough time, Anons would see the full truth of the situation anyway. Q just had to guide us there. And in order to do so, he presented us that day with yet another riddle—which is the part I want to focus on:

The "Chair" serves the Master.

P = C.

This implied that the pope was controlled—which is something Q would reinforce the very next day when he dropped the bit about the Rothschild loan to the Vatican. But we *still* didn't have enough to go on to figure out exactly what he was talking about.

The next hint would come a little over a month later. Note the filename on this one: Guardian_P.png.

Q !4pRcUAOlBE **ID: 610b24** No.1449784 🗗 📄   **1413**
May 17 2018 19:15:27 (EST)

Guardian P.png   ⬇

Guardian of the Pope.
[Personal]
Q

It would take enterprising Anons about another month to crack this particular riddle. Eventually, they would discover, in a PDF of Fritz Springmeier's *Bloodlines of the Illuminati* (which was itself hosted on the CIA's official website) numerous references to a mysterious "Payseur" family.

By this point in time, my own site had become massive and very respected in the broader Qcommunity, and when I saw this story starting to percolate, I was floored. I had to compile all the research I could on the subject and make everyone aware. And so, pulling from their original research digs and adding some of my own, we were able to bring this discovery to the broader community very effectively. Turns out the Payseur line is, most likely, a Merovingian bloodline—the same bloodline Napoleon was trying to evoke when he took on the bee as his symbol. Springmeier claims that this bloodline actually arrived in America when the son of Marie Antoinette, Louis XVII, escaped the French Revolution and was smuggled (along with many assets) to North Carolina in the early 1800s, though it's hard to say how accurate that claim is because its long been claimed that Louis XVII actually died in 1795 at age ten, and that his heart was preserved in a crystal urn (as was... well, I won't call it a "common" tradition, but it was common enough for some royalty). And while genetic testing has revealed that it does certainly belong to someone of that same family, its worth noting that Louis XVIII (the uncle of Louis XVII) did not believe that the heart belonged to his nephew. Is it possible that the heart actually belonged to Louis XVIII's older brother (who had died in 1789) Louis Joseph? Another Cabal researcher, Alex Christopher, would go on to claim that Louis XVII would change his name to Daniel Payseur (that is, "Paymaster") in order to evade Napoleon, and would escape into the care of English relatives across the channel. He would then buy shares in the newly-formed Virginia Company and set sail for Boddie Island in North Carolina, on a ship provided by the King of England. The line would really come into its own when "Daniel's" grandson, Lewis Cass Payseur would take over family operations and hire the Springs (of the Rothschild bloodline) to begin managing their assets and companies.

Speculation of its origins aside, the Payseurs would experience an astronomical rise in their fortunes as they began working and building their business empire here in America, at one point owning the bulk of *all* Class A preferred shares in the US. I can't provide a full list of their assets here because of its extreme length, but a full list can be viewed on my site, in my full exposé on the Payseur bloodline.[28] However, it is worth noting here that many of these companies mutated and transformed into companies we still have with us today, companies such as AT&T, General Motors, General Electric, General Mills, and many, many more.

The article caused such a stir in the wider community that pretty soon everyone was talking about it. Roughly a week and a half after I had published it and it had received more traffic than the site had ever seen before, one Anon would put the question to Q:

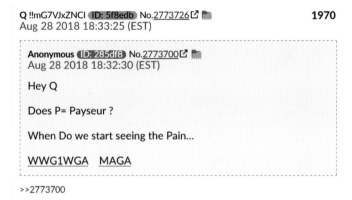

```
Q !!mG7VJxZNCl  ID: 5f8edb  No.2773726        1970
Aug 28 2018 18:33:25 (EST)

    Anonymous  ID: 285df8  No.2773700
    Aug 28 2018 18:32:30 (EST)

    Hey Q

    Does P= Payseur ?

    When Do we start seeing the Pain...

    WWG1WGA   MAGA

>>2773700
```

And that was all it took. Q linked to the Anon above, and everyone immediately knew he was confirming it for the entire world to see. Anons went wild. I went wild. And I just want to bask in the afterglow a bit more because this was just… this was a huge moment. Here are some Anons' responses from the thread that night:

```
▶ Anonymous  08/28/18 (Tue) 19:36:46 ID: 39208d (2)  No.2773838

>>2773726
Guess Neonrevolt was right ..... Payseurs!
```

```
▶ Anonymous  08/28/18 (Tue) 19:39:56 ID: 6f03b7 (1)  No.2773927

>>2773772
Go to Neon Revolt website.  Fully explanation in his article.
```

```
▶ Anonymous  08/28/18 (Tue) 19:40:24 ID: 39208d (2)  No.2773940

>>2773839
Check out Neonrevolt's breakdown ... pretty detailed.  Basically HEAD of the 13
Bloodline families.
```

28   https://www.neonrevolt.com/2018/08/16/p-the-unseen-masters-of-all-qanon-greatawakening-whoisp-il-luminati-13bloodlines-payseur-springmeier/

▶Anonymous 08/28/18 (Tue) 19:41:45 ID: 30b442 **(1)** No.2773984

>>2773726
Great article by Neon Revolt about the Payseurs.

▶Anonymous 08/28/18 (Tue) 19:43:00 ID: a2f5d7 **(5)** No.2774024 >>2774200

>>2773841

Guess you must be a "shill" according to some brilliant anons...

HAVING LEGIT THEORIES DOESN'T MAKE ANYONE A SHILL....

That word is thrown around so much now, it's lost its TRUE MEANING.

So no anon, you shouldn't eat crow. You had a good theory/guess like many of us. I actually had not even heard of Payseurs until Neon Revolts article a few days ago... and when I read it, I agreed it looked like that was the P.

EASE UP ANONS....

▶Anonymous 08/28/18 (Tue) 19:44:28 ID: 1f0b7f **(4)** No.2774078 >>2774120 >>2774194

>>2773700
This guy called it over a week ago
https://www.neonrevolt.com/2018/08/16/p-the-unseen-masters-of-all-qanon-greatawakening-whoisp-illuminati-13bloodlines-payseur-springmeier/

▶Anonymous 08/28/18 (Tue) 19:48:40 ID: 45834e **(6)** No.2774194 >>2774273

>>2774078
I've been talking to my closest friends about this. Really glad Q confirmed it. Great work to neonrevolt, where I first heard of it.

We are getting SO much closer.

Does Today feel like OUR D-Day or is it just me?? Full force landing in every direction.

▶Anonymous 08/28/18 (Tue) 19:48:49 ID: 1f0b7f **(4)** No.2774201

>>2774120
Me too! Neon is an awesome read.

▶Anonymous 08/28/18 (Tue) 19:51:31 ID: 1f0b7f **(4)** No.2774273 >>2774361

>>2774194
Neon is fucking awesome! He breaks shit down so well, and tells you when he's not sure about something. And when he's wrong, he owns up to it right away and learns from it.

But I can't take too much credit here. Again, had it not been for some of these original researchers, especially one going by the handle of "Livid" on Twitter, speaking up about their original digs, I would have never plunged down the rabbit hole and come back up with a ton of additional information in tow. It really was a group effort.

And like the Anon says above, it basically boils down to this: the Payseurs are the family who all the other "Illuminati" bloodline families serve—because that's how this cult hierarchy works; via bloodlines and intermarriage between them. The Rockefellers, the Vanderbilts, the Schiffs, Soros, the Saudis, and more; they all work for the Payseurs— the head of this ancient snake cult which has worked over many centuries to make sure it retains power and influence over the whole globe. And the frontmen for the Payseurs—the ones who help the Payseurs remain hidden behind shell corporations, proxy services, and international banks—are the Rothschilds.

Together, they form what I call the Cabal.

You might know them as the NWO.

Q !UW.yye1fxo **ID: c32c4f** No.350084 🗗 📷   **742**
Feb 12 2018 10:01:46 (EST)

The Inner Circle.
Mika Brzezinski.
Background.
Family/careers.
McLean, Virginia.
The age of tech has hurt their ability to hide/control.
Majority today were 'born in' to the circle.
Investigate those in front of the camera who scream the loudest.
These people are really stupid.
End is near.
The media cleanse/JFK.
Q

In decades past, great effort was put in to hiding the true nature of these Cabal members. Often, children born into the Cabal are "adopted" out, or handed over to other bloodline families, making the lineages quite hard to track. I mentioned earlier, for instance, how Bill Clinton is most likely a Rockefeller (either the son of Winthrop or Nelson Rockefeller). We also talked extensively about the "Moonchild" ritual. But it isn't always the case that Cabal kiddies get loaned out. Q talks above about how Mika Brzezinski was inducted into the "Inner Circle" by virtue of her birth. Recall that her father was national security adviser Zbigniew Brzezinski, who traveled to Pakistan with a young Barack Obama, in order to work with an arms dealer over there and provide the Pakistanis with AKs for the first time. Mika you may know from her position opposite Joe Scarborough on the morning news show, *Morning Joe*, on MSNBC.

Note: the two were "married" on November 24, 2018, and the sudden affair left Anons wondering if this was less about love, and more about a legal protection known as "spousal privilege."

Another famous Cabal insider-turned-media man is none other than the man featured in the very first Qdrop on this chapter. That's right; we're talking about CNN anchor Anderson Cooper! Here's that image again:

Q !ITPb.qbhqo (ID: 3610ff) No.93181 🔲 📄   **344**
Dec 14 2017 00:24:04 (EST)

7803B61A-1F3E-47BD-88D4-F....jpeg   ⬇

Saw this in last thread.
Focus on papers on table.
Graphic at top.
They all belong to the same sick cult/club.
Q

And you may recall earlier when we briefly mentioned his mother, Gloria Vanderbilt, and his brother, Carter Cooper, who committed suicide by jumping from the terrace of Gloria's fourteenth-floor Manhattan penthouse at the age of twenty-three.

The suicide itself was very strange. It involved a very disoriented Carter running into his mother's bedroom, asking her "What's going on?" several times before bolting back to his room. When Gloria got there, he was sitting over the low terrace, overlooking Manhattan below. Gloria would write in her book, *A Mother's Story,* that as he stood there completely rigid, he would ask her… "Will I ever feel again?" Vanderbilt would try to talk him down and said they should call his therapist.

Carter shouted out the number, and then screamed, "FUCK YOU!"

He leapt over the bar, clinging to the rail for a few moments before letting go. No drugs were found in his system, and the only medication he was on was an asthma inhaler. He had just broken up with a girl and he hadn't slept for a few days (until a nap earlier that day). He never showed any other signs of psychosis either, so why would a smart, well-educated man with a promising future ahead of him and a fortune larger than most people would ever see in a lifetime of work suddenly kill himself in such a dramatic fashion?

Just like the Rockefellers and the Rothschilds, the Vanderbilts are an Illumined family working on behalf of the Payseurs. Their lavish Biltmore estate is built on land where the Payseurs had first built a hotel which was leased to the Vanderbilts, and even featured a massive sixteenth-century engraving by the German artist Albrecht Dürer, entitled *The Tri-*

umphal Arch, which depicts a bloodline from Holy Roman Emperor Maximilian I, all the way back to that famous Merovingian king Napoleon aped, Clovis I. And if you *really* want to get into it, the Merovingian bloodline may even go back to the tribe of Dan, though my own research on this front has been… inconclusive thus far. The engraving also features the likes of Julius Caesar, Alexander the Great, and Egyptian hieroglyphs.

And it's here Q would really begin to peel back the curtain on the occultic nature of this domestic Cabal family in a series of staggering drops, starting with post 1894. Longtime QAnon followers will be *very* familiar with these drops, but for those just joining us on this wild ride called Q, I'm just going to present the drops with minimal commentary at first, so you can see for yourself:

Q !!mG7VJxZNCl (ID: ea4f6b) No.2617271 ☑ ▇   **1894**
Aug 15 2018 18:27:46 (EST)

> Q !!mG7VJxZNCl (ID: ea4f6b) No.2617206 ☑ ▇
> Aug 15 2018 18:24:09 (EST)
>
> >>2616942
> Jeff Zucker.
> NBC
> CNN
> Heart Surgery?
> 10-year issue?
> "Fox News Pure Propaganda"
> In the Line of FIRE.
> Q

A_Cooper29195.jpg

>>2617206
Normal?
Q

Q !!mG7VJxZNCl (ID: ea4f6b) No.2617484 ☑ ▇   **1895**
Aug 15 2018 18:37:58 (EST)

> Anonymous ID: d98b28 No.2617413 ☑ ▇
> Aug 15 2018 18:34:13 (EST)
>
> >>2617271
>
> No that is no where near normal.. The Picture above her is Evil..

>>2617413
Symbolism will be their downfall.
Focus on her necklace.
Bottom 'charm' has SIGNIFICANT meaning.
Find the match.
"Red shoes"
Q

Q !!mG7VJxZNCl (ID: ea4f6b) No.2617554 ☑ 📷 **1896**
Aug 15 2018 18:42:11 (EST)

> Anonymous (ID: 4c7664) No.2617535 ☑ 📷
> Aug 15 2018 18:40:54 (EST)
>
> ClipboardImage.png   ⬇
>
>
>
> >>2617484

>>2617535
Below hand.
Q

Q !!mG7VJxZNCl (ID: ea4f6b) No.2617606 ☑ 📷 **1897**
Aug 15 2018 18:44:41 (EST)

> Q !!mG7VJxZNCl (ID: ea4f6b) No.2617554 ☑ 📷
> Aug 15 2018 18:42:11 (EST)
>
> >>2617535
> Below hand.
> Q

>>2617554
Find the matches.
Open source.
They never thought they'd be hunted.
Q

>>2617647
Compare pool of V w/ painting of kids in pool (red shoes).
Q

>>2617682
>>2617709
Cross against Podesta.
Travel to Rome.
Review 2015/2016 pics (inside only).
Q

Q !!mG7VJxZNCl ID: 7fb039 No.2617750 ⤤ 🏴 1900
Aug 15 2018 18:53:05 (EST)

Anonymous ID: 8e0a0f No.2617739 ⤤ 🏴
Aug 15 2018 18:52:37 (EST)

6c8d85b7849f504dabf6063a079219a4.jpg

>>2617682
this?

>>2617739
1 of 2
Q

Q !!mG7VJxZNCl ID: 7fb039 No.2617755 ⤤ 🏴 1901
Aug 15 2018 18:53:25 (EST)

Anonymous ID: a73a15 No.2617744 ⤤ 🏴
Aug 15 2018 18:52:48 (EST)

DRGxfa3VAAE0NFL.jpg

>>2617682
This?

>>2617744
Confirmed.
What do you notice?
Q

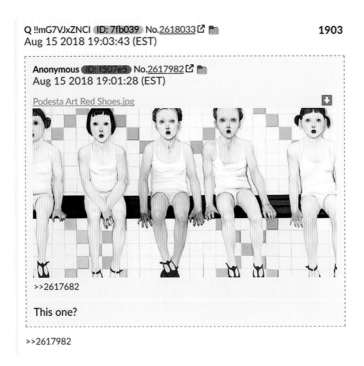

And here's an enlargement of that second-to-last photo:

Following Q's lead, Anons would quickly begin to put the puzzle pieces together. The photo Q was asking for came from the earlier Pizzagate research Anons had conducted years before. The general public may not be aware of this, but Tony Podesta has quite the disgusting art collection, featuring photos of naked, underage teens, a chandelier of a bronze human form arched backwards like one of Jeffrey Dahmer's victims, and what you're seeing above: paintings by Serbian artist Biljana Djurdjevic. Most of these are taken from her "Living in Oblivion" series, though many of her works contain similar disturbing imagery. This series in particular features a number of paintings which depict dead-eyed children, either strung up in restraints or otherwise turned around, and positioned like they were about to be subjected to abuse. Previously, Anons just believed these paintings were works of fiction. Disturbing, yes, but fictional nonetheless.

The only conclusion Anons could rightly come to in the wake of Q posting this series is that these were actually painted from real life, from reference photographs, or perhaps even in person. Anons would also correlate one particularly horrid image…

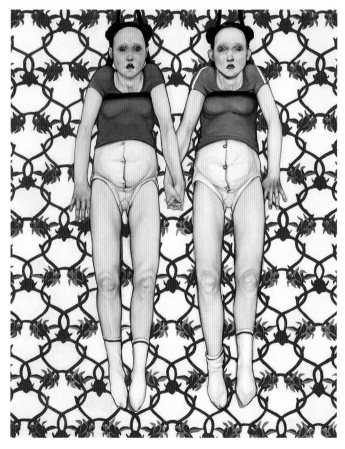

…with the ropes hanging from the side of the pool.

There's something that's emerged in the wake of the Weinstein scandal, and I call it the "Weinstein rule," where the PR propagandists attempt to spin a person's behavior as the exception to the rule, rather than the rule itself. Anyone who has really worked in Hollywood knows that Weinstein's behavior wasn't particularly exceptional. In fact, it's pretty standard. But they rely on *you* not knowing that it's standard, in order to make you think that if they offer up one scapegoat, the whole system has been saved from a scourge and preserved for all time! Nothing could be further from the truth. Rampant abuse, and frankly, outright prostitution occurs all the time. The #MeToo movement and #TimesUp were cooked up in CAA board rooms. Alyssa Milano, that rabid anti-Trump actress who first really promoted the #MeToo hashtag after taking it from Tarana Burke… well, keep in mind that Milano is married to the single biggest agent in Hollywood, who represents all manner of A-listers. It's all just a distraction, and even right now powerful men like David Geffen (Spielberg's partner) are trying to get Weinstein working again. They're cooking up some ridiculous "redemption" narrative while also peddling films about dead offenders like Michael Jackson, so they can all get back to business as usual.

So, too, with the Dutroux Affair. The Dutroux Affair was not the exception to the rule. It was the norm, and it's been happening among elite circles for a very long time. Even graphic films like *Eyes Wide Shut* were only scratching the surface of this underworld (and even then, it's said that Kubrick himself was a serial child abuser)!

Perhaps this is why CNN has been so unfair in their treatment of Trump. Perhaps this is why Carter Cooper asked his mother…

"Will I ever feel again..?"

…Before taking his own life.

Perhaps he couldn't live with what he knew.

Perhaps it was because he knew the true nature of his family, of the Cabal, and didn't want any part of it.

Perhaps he saw suicide as his only real way out.

After all, he didn't choose to be born into a Cabal family. Perhaps upon learning of what they did, perhaps as he got older and they tried to initiate him, something inside his heart rebelled. The only thing we know for sure is that whatever affected Carter so dramatically didn't seem to bother Anderson in the same way.

I covered all these drops more intensively on my site,[29] but before we leave this series of drops, Q's point here about the "red shoes" is worth revisiting. In asking us to connect the red shoes in the painting, the most obvious connection Anons made at the time was a photo that had been circulating on the research boards from Tony Podesta's birthday, where both he and all his guests were wearing red dress shoes.

Frankly, because we hadn't made the connection to an earlier drop, Q would (I think out of frustration) make the connection for us:

Q !!mG7VJxZNCI ID: 6ffad1 No.2632125 ☑ 📌   1917
Aug 16 2018 15:46:09 (EST)

pvhd4w03nig11.png   ⬇

What are shovels used for?
Q

29   https://www.neonrevolt.com/2018/08/16/anderson-coopers-satanic-slaughterhouse-newq-qanon-great-awakening-pizzagate-pedogate-thevatican-podesta/

See, about a month and a half earlier, Q had dropped some photos that had been taken by an asset on the ground—yes, a literal spy—who was tasked with tracking someone. This was one of those surveillance photos collected by that asset. Q has done this from time to time, most notably showing us an operation going down in Shanghai, at King Tower, where some kind of explosive blew out one of the windows and left residue all over the building's facade, and while tailing Senator Diane Feinstein throughout China, as she went about her traitorous business (it would later emerge that Feinstein's driver had been a Chinese spy for ten years… *Yeah*, like she didn't know). In this particular case, Q presented a picture and simply asked, "Who do you see?"

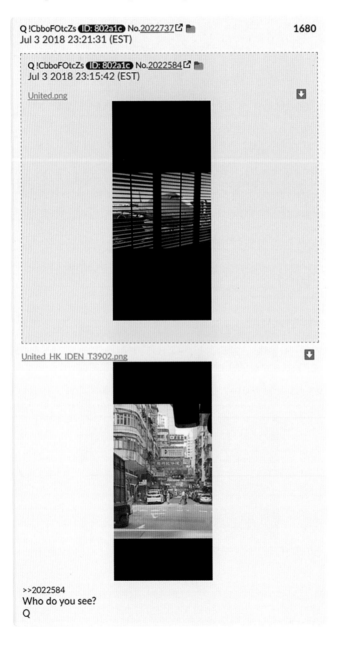

Here's an enlargement of Q's original photo:

This photo contained juuuuust enough information for Anons to narrow down the location of this photo to a corner of Hong Kong. Anons would produce some stunningly specific maps in response:

WE CAN DEDUCE THE DATE OF Q'S PHOTO USING THE DATE OF LOCATION CHANGE

This sign is now gone (check Google Street View June 2018)

Kwong Wa

Western Pacific Kindergarten
CLOSED

Yau M

Q photo taken here

The Cityview

Pitt St

Yau Ma Tei

Western Pacific Kindergarten

current location NOT in photo

Waterloo Rd

CN Square

Shek Lung St

Shanghai St

Portland St

Hing Kee

Nathan Rd

Arth

Th

As it turns out, this photo had been taken outside a defunct kindergarten in Hong Kong (and given how much Anons tracked Pizzagate and affiliated stories, this was an immediate red flag for us). And while Anons were able to find a location, we were still never quite able to figure out who the balding man in the photo was. Honestly, it's easy to see why, though. The photo is distant, blurry, and it could be just about anyone! So that question lingered without an answer for a month and a half.

At least until Q, in this new drop, removed all doubt.

Q !!mG7VJxZNCl ID: 6ffad1 No.2632125   1917
Aug 16 2018 15:46:09 (EST)

pvhd4w03nig11.png

What are shovels used for?
Q

Here Q was identifying the man in the Hong Kong street, outside the kindergarten, as one Andrew Kauders. Kauders was a FARA-registered agent who previously worked for Tony Podesta before moving to Cogent Strategies, the firm launched by Kimberly Fritts, the Podesta Group's former CEO, before the Mueller Special Counsel investigation scared Tony into closing shop.

Q !!mG7VJxZNCl **ID: 59e763** No.2633643 ☑ 🏴

1918

Aug 16 2018 17:08:07 (EST)

Anonymous **ID: e151ad** No.2633258 ☑ 🏴
Aug 16 2018 16:46:06 (EST)

Screen Shot 2018-08-16 at 4.38.45 PM.png   ⬇

Let's not forget about the Western Pacific Kindergarten!

https://www.wpk.edu.hk ☑ 🏴

TpZURtUs6ygD5AAsDQOOlhL8ixWiztX7XvomNivELtw.png   ⬇

>>2633258
https://www.fara.gov/docs/5926-Short-Form-20170817-348.pdf ☑ 🏴
https://soprweb.senate.gov/index.cfm?event=getFilingDetails&
filingID=09B71870-0B05-4D45-A4B7-1B5AF0618975&
filingTypeID=1 ☑ 🏴
https://wikileaks.org/podesta-emails/emailid/50428 ☑ 🏴
Nothing to see here.
Q

Kauders had also previously worked for Senator Robert Menendez—the same Menendez who somehow, miraculously dodged charges of hiring underage prostitutes in the Dominican Republic though he is still under trial for other corruption charges. The FARA filing Q linked above also revealed that Kauders had previously worked for the European Centre for a Modern Ukraine, a Soros-backed NGO which helped precipitate the Ukrainian coup, which would later tie into how Manafort was groomed and planted into the Trump campaign. What's more is that Kauders would also communicate with Tony Podesta where Tony invited Kauders to a "dinner" prepped by his brother, Hillary's campaign manager John Podesta, a fact that would only be revealed in the Wikileaks Podesta e-mails.

But if you're looking at that image Q posted above and wondering why you're seeing Bill Maher up there, well, it's all about the shoes. Put simply: Anons believe that the red shoes signify that their wearers are elite partakers in pedophilia and ritual cannibalism. Why, Bill Maher was even starting to run his mouth in various QAnon hit-pieces on his HBO show, *Real Time with Bill Maher* at one point...

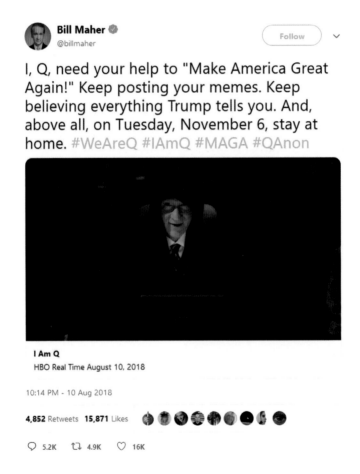

...At least until Q started dropping hints about Maher, too.

Maher is hardly the amicable guy he portrays himself to be on TV. If I were to mention the name Jimmy Savile to any British readers who may have stumbled across this book, they would know *instantly* what I'm talking about. A popular entertainer in the UK for decades, Jimmy Savile was well known and well regarded by the public—even being knighted not only by the Queen, but by Pope John Paul II as well. When he died in 2011, stories about his serial sexual abuse started to seep out, and soon it turned out that Savile had molested over FIVE HUNDRED children during his lifetime, usually victims who were staying at hospitals where he was doing "charitable work." He had also abused hospital staff, and even sexually defiled corpses of the recently deceased, because as someone who had raised millions of pounds for these hospitals, and with his public reputation, he had access to pretty much anywhere he wanted to go within these hospitals. He could knock on doors, visit young patients, and much of the staff was none the wiser as to any sort of predatory behavior going on. Savile was also a member of a Satanic cult and at one point even raped a twelve-year-old girl at a Buckinghamshire hospital basement with other pedophiles participating in the torment, all the while chanting "Hail Satan" in Latin and wearing robes covered in occult imagery.

It would almost sound cliché if it weren't all true. After the Satanists were done with the girl, she was beaten. Savile would go on to participate in all manner of black masses and orgies over the years, leaving numerous victims in his wake. And again, when this all came out, all the elites, everyone in the know, feigned shock. It was the Weinstein-strategy all over again. Savile was the "exception," not the rule.

Well, I'm here to tell you today, it's much the same with Maher: who I see as a modern-day Savile. It may shock you to learn that Maher is a member of an exclusive sex club in L.A. called SNCTM, where he pays seventy-five thousand dollars annually for "Dominus" level membership, which grants him access to, basically, free orgies whenever and wherever SNCTM decides to run an event. And these events can be, frankly, anything goes. To make matters worse, Q did *heavily* imply that children are sometimes involved and that… some might not be among the living anymore…

> Q !!mG7VJxZNCI No.140 🔳   **1843**
> Aug 11 2018 12:15:19 (EST)
>
> https://twitter.com/billmaher/status/1028147514719924225 🔳
> Do you remember their names?
> We do.
> Do you really believe you are still safe?
> Protected?
> The World is WATCHING.
> Q

And I have to say, when Q was dropping these posts, it was like being part of a crazy conversation with a secret agent, because earlier that same day, I had posted all about Savile and Maher over on Gab[30]—the Twitter alternative the Cabal had repeatedly tried to shut down—in response to Maher's hit-piece that had gone up on the tenth of August. Anons hadn't quite picked up on the story yet at the time, and me, being a screenwriter and someone who followed CDAN and who knew what went on in that whole world, well, I knew

---

30   https://www.neonrevolt.com/2018/08/12/the-mystery-of-the-sky-king-and-bill-mahers-opensecret-newq-qanon-greatawakening-pizzagate-pedogate/

enough about Maher to start putting two and two together and start giving it right back to him. So when Q posted his drop later that day, it was just a huge confirmation that we were all on the right track. Q was confirming our worst suspicions. And like I said before, Maher got real quiet about Q, real fast. In fact, I don't think he's mentioned him once during the intervening months.

And I'll say this much before continuing: I've often felt, throughout this whole Q-journey, that I've been running "interference" for QAnon. What I mean is, I would write a large article or otherwise begin a posting series on Gab, and within a few hours or days Q would start posting along the same lines. The Maher article is just one instance of this. Maher's hit-piece came out on August 10. My Gab posts arrived on August 11. My article landed on August 12, and Q's response finally landed on the August 16. Another time, Q would pull an image directly from my Hollywood Renegades[31] article to address how it had been Photoshopped. Another time, it would be a reference to something I had posted in my GafferAnon[32] article. The Payseur[33] article was another big one. I can show you time and time again where it's almost like my articles were providing "cover" for Q to speak publicly on certain topics, because now the subject had been introduced to the wider community. It was almost like he now had plausible deniability because of what I had written. I don't say that to inflate my own importance in all this… but man, it's been a trip watching this play out day by-day. And though I've never been directly referenced by Q (as of this writing), those following the conversation between Q and the Anon community very closely will be able to attest to this strange synergy firsthand.

But a strange connection cropped up in all of this, and that was the relation of SNCTM to another celebrity sex-cult which called itself NXIVM. NXIVM was funded by the Bronfmans (that Illuminati family who controls the Seagrams fortune, and who also happen to be major Clinton donors), and their most famous acolyte is the former *Smallville* actress Allison Mack. Mack, working on behalf of the cult's leader, Keith Raniere, would help entrap young actresses and other women in the cult where these women would be subjected to all manner of brainwashing before being initiated into the "dominus obsequious sororium," or DOS for short. That stands for "master over the slave woman" (where, in this case, Raniere was the master). And recall that Maher was paying all that money to SNCTM for "Dominus" level membership. To physically demonstrate this master-slave relationship, all the women trapped in NXIVM were branded around their pubic area with Raniere's initials (or sometimes, Raniere's *and* Mack's initials).

---

31 https://www.neonrevolt.com/2018/07/22/hollywoodrenegades-how-hollywood-insiders-are-taking-down-thecabal-from-the-inside-out-hollyweird-greatawakening/

32 https://www.neonrevolt.com/2019/02/25/gafferanon-takes-us-backstage-to-uncover-hollywoodcorruption-shutdownhollywood-greatawakening-neonrevolt/

33 https://www.neonrevolt.com/2018/08/16/p-the-unseen-masters-of-all-qanon-greatawakening-whoisp-illuminati-13bloodlines-payseur-springmeier/

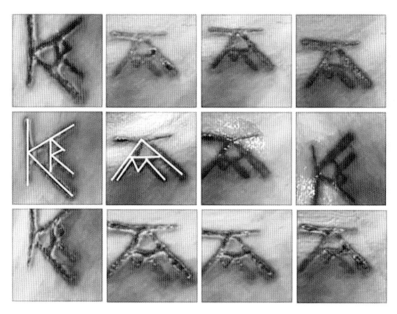

And wouldn't you know it, but Anons would uncover someone *else* who sported a scar that looked staggeringly similar to the kind of NXIVM scar you see above. But this time, the recipient had tried to cover over it with horrid tattoos. The owner of this disfigurement?

Stormy Daniels. Yes, the same Stormy Daniels who was suddenly claiming that Trump had paid her off to keep silent about their supposed affair.

But perhaps the most damning evidence in all this came from Stormy's own Twitter feed, from back in 2010, when she tweeted out:

And that isn't where this particular rabbit hole ends. For when NXIVM leaders were all being rounded up and arrested in early 2018, Q would tell us that Allison Mack was talking, trying to save her own skin:

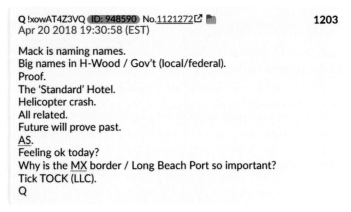

Soon, anti-Trump figures started going down; the most prominent being New York attorney general Eric Schneiderman, who, it was revealed, used to slap his Sri Lankan girl-friend while calling her his "brown slave." He would not stop hitting her until she addressed him as "master." That's pure dominus obsequious sororium language at play here. Soon, he would escalate the abuse, spitting on, and choking his girlfriend, while demanding she find another woman to add to their bed. Four other women would soon emerge with similar stories of abuse, and this is doubly important because it was Schneiderman who was running the civil investigation into another major Clinton/Democratic donor by the name of…

Harvey Weinstein.

Another fun fact: the majority of Schneiderman's campaign funds came from the Soros family. By running the Weinstein investigation, he was working to "legally" protect Wein-stein, who ties back to an even bigger mogul and serial abuser, Spielberg's partner David Geffen, as well as billionaire pedophile Jeffrey Epstein… who we'll talk about shortly. It's why Harvey started walking to court holding biography of Elia Kazan displayed promi-nently in his arms for the paparazzi to snap photos of. Anons speculated at the time that Harvey was signaling with this book that without protection, he would start squealing on everyone—much like Kazan had squealed on all the commies during the McCarthy trials.[34]

---

34   See: Hollywood was Always Red: A Rant by Razorfist

Q !4pRcUAOIBE ID: b9b7bb No.1414277 ⃰ 🚩   **1368**
May 14 2018 22:18:10 (EST)

Allison Mack **[NXIVM]** arrested **[date]**?
When does a bird sing?
Schneiderman resigns **[date]**?
Coincidence?
Eyes Wide Open.
Who will be next?
Watch NYC.
Watch CA.
Q

And of course we can't just ignore the Standard Hotel in all of this, especially because Q just mentioned it in the drop above. I've written a number of exposés[35] on the subject of the Standard Hotel since following Q, but the short of it is that it's a central hub of Cabal activity in L.A., which often features the "art" of suspected Mother of Darkness, Marina Abramovic, and caters to the more debauched tastes of their clientèle. Again, think *Eyes Wide Shut*, but also pedophilic.

As it turns out, the general manager of the hotel, Kimberly Watzman was killed in early 2018 when the helicopter she was riding in crashed along Newport beach. It was made to look like an accident, but in truth it was anything but. Her helicopter had been downed on purpose by the Deep State to cover over a series of crimes that had happened at the hotel over the years, as the lower-level employees began to understand what was happening.

---

35   https://www.neonrevolt.com/2018/03/13/looks-like-meats-back-on-the-menu-boys-hogghunting-now-tied-to-thestandardhotel-guncontrol-2ndamendment/

https://www.neonrevolt.com/2018/03/13/new-details-emerge-about-marina-abramovic-spiritcooking-the-standardhotel-wikileaks-and-qanon-followthewhiterabbit/

A CDAN post is key to understanding it all:

TUESDAY, FEBRUARY 06, 2018

Today's Blind Items - Account Number 37911133339

Over the weekend, the head of this company, who had never been seen in person at this particular location showed up in the middle of the night. He had called ahead and the highest ranking person still left at this business was told to be there for the meeting. He instructed that no one else be there. The urgency was dictated because of multiple deaths that happened a short time before involving two very key employees of this company. Those two employees were in charge of the account number mentioned in the title.

That account number was established several years ago when the new owner bought out the original owner. It was an internal billing account, but the bills were never paid. They were never supposed to be paid. It was simply to keep track of a special group of clientele who are friends of the owner. The problem was that after the death of the two employees, one of the clientele showed up at the business with two very young women he said were his nieces and said he had a reservation. He used the name associated with that account. The problem is these clientele were always processed by the two dead employees. They were not always there in person but would arrange that all the formalities would be taken care of beforehand so whatever clientele were there could get on with their activities quickly.

When this man showed up with his nieces who really looked nothing like each other or the man and were really young to be wearing what they were wearing, calls were made. Did anyone know about the reservation and then someone looked up the history of the name associated with the account and sent a group e-mail asking about the reservation and included the account number in the e-mail. The man and his nieces were not given a room because none of them had or were willing to produce identification or a method of payment. The man explained that no payment was ever required because it was handled through Mr. Weishaupt. No one at the company had ever heard of Mr. Weishaupt and another group e-mail was sent inquiring about Mr. Weishaupt.

Only a few hours later, the call was made by the man who came in the middle of the night. Was it Mr. Weishaupt? I don't know. The person who told me all of this only caught a glimpse of the man as he left the next morning trailed by that highest ranking employee available at the company. The person who spoke to me is adamant that the previous owner didn't have a special account number. The employees had been trying to recall anyone they remembered who had used the account number or name when they checked in.

One person several people agreed on because he had been there multiple times using the name was this A+ list mostly movie actor who lives most of the year overseas. He also likes to direct. He is also an Academy Award winner. The staff just assumed he liked his privacy and it was a fake name. It wasn't until now, they realized he was using the same name as the man with his nieces. Whenever the A+ lister came, he always came without his wife and would only stay a few hours. No one saw anyone who came with him, but it seemed like given the circumstances he was meeting someone who would come to see him.

This A+ list mostly movie actress who is an Academy Award winner and is known all over the world used the name too. Someone remembered she stayed a week when she was in hiding and some of her employees would come by and have no idea they were supposed to use that name to see her or contact her.

The staff said the name was used a lot, but mostly by men who had a woman or women with them. There was one man they remembered because he stuck out. He was an older white man and he would often come with young black men and also would only stay an hour or two. I think I know who that person is and have written about him before, but no one remembered exactly what he looked like and he wasn't using his real name so it is tough. There are rumors that the man behind it all has big time professional sports interests.

One thing is certain. Any trace of that account number is gone from every system the staff can get into.

Note first, the reference to this illicit account being registered to a "Mr. Weishaupt." That's *Adam* Weishaupt, the founder of the Bavarian Illuminati, and this account was used by those in the know to perform whatever deeds they wanted to hide, for free. But when the two employees who usually handed the account had died, the task suddenly fell to Kimberly Watzman, the general manager who had no idea this was even going on in the hotel when the man referenced above wanted to check in with his two underage "nieces" using the Weishaupt account. Watzman, of course, had never heard of this account before, refused him entry, and called the police. When she started talking about it with other employees, they too had recalled several incidents where that name had been used including, as the CDAN entry says, with an older white man who would bring along younger black men with him.

That man is big-time democratic donor and homosexual serial killer Ed Buck. Buck was probably on their minds most prominently because he would be caught with a dead, black male hooker in his home by the name of Gemmel Moore, in July 2017. Buck was investigated by the L.A. county Sheriff's department, and despite finding all manner of drug paraphernalia and residue all over his Laurel Canyon apartment, Buck would never be charged with anything.

How could that be?

In short, he had friends in high places. Namely, California congressman Adam Schiff. (That's the "AS" referenced in Qdrop 1203). According to Q, Schiff pulled strings to make sure Buck was never charged with anything. He even made sure Kimberly's helicopter went down, no doubt leveraging his CIA connections, for, as Qresearchers well know, the CIA can down a great number of aircraft using classified technology, to make clandestine assassinations appear as "accidents."

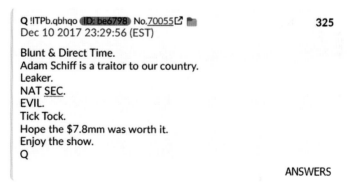

Q !ITPb.qbhqo ID: be6798 No.70055 325
Dec 10 2017 23:29:56 (EST)

Blunt & Direct Time.
Adam Schiff is a traitor to our country.
Leaker.
NAT SEC.
EVIL.
Tick Tock.
Hope the $7.8mm was worth it.
Enjoy the show.
Q

ANSWERS

Unlucky for Schiff then, that Buck would repeat his murderous ways, injecting yet another black male prostitute with methamphetamine on January 7, 2019. Timothy Michael Dean would be found dead of an overdose at Buck's home, and this time there was no denying Buck's murderous ways. Q has also stated that Schiff is involved in much greater scandals, which are soon to come to light.

Q !!mG7VJxZNCl `ID: 306030` No.5127652☑ 📷   **2694**
Feb 11 2019 17:53:54 (EST)

> Q !!mG7VJxZNCl `ID: 306030` No.5127462☑ 📷
> Feb 11 2019 17:44:56 (EST)
>
> https://twitter.com/RepAdamSchiff/status
> /1095051195658522625 ☑ 📷
> Let's actually use 'FACTS':
> Step One: Hype an invented threat of POTUS working w/ the
> RUSSIANS (disinformation campaign).
> Step Two: Send FBI/DOJ/CONGRESS/SENATE/C_A/NSA
> /INTEL/FVEY/etc... to address and investigate the IMAGINARY
> THREAT.
> Step Three: Justify the 'SPECIAL COUNSEL' and MILLIONS OF
> TAXPAYER DOLLARS SPENT as necessary to protect the public
> and our election process against an imaginary, made-up, non-
> existent threat (which really is) designed to protect the illegal
> activities of many elected officials.
> Step Four: Open 'new' Fake & False investigations as
> CHAIRMAN of the House Intel Comm to retain disinformation
> campaign designed to keep liberal/D Americans onboard to
> regain POWER & PREVENT prosecution - Executive Time!
> Q

>>5127462
Life Lesson - [AS]
The next time you 'leak' classified information, don't have your
phone (or allow phones of the 'unknown' go-between 'students')
present.
FISA works both ways.
Q

Q wasn't joking when he said they all belong to the same sick cult. You might know them as the "NWO," but as Q said before, N does not refer to "New."

Q !UW.yye1fxo `ID: fb1a66` No.618754☑ 📷   **938**
Mar 10 2018 18:37:22 (EST)

N does not refer to Nazi.
The continued Nazi ideology is relevant.
Events will clarify.
Think subgroup.
Q

Anons have long speculated on the true meaning of the N in the NWO, with the first of the two most prominent guesses being "Nimrod," that great Babylonian hunter-king who was said to have actually commissioned the construction of the tower of Babel. Yes Babel, that monument to man's pride, where all of humankind would attempt to ascend to the heavens by building a tower. Where God would decide that they simply were not ready for this, and thus, confused their languages so as to stop them from progressing in this endeavor and hurting themselves.

This actually isn't a terrible guess, especially when you take Q's oft-repeated mantra that "their symbolism will be their downfall" into account, as the shape of the EU Parliament itself looks strikingly similar to artistic depictions of the tower of Babel. Compare for yourself:

Nimrod was also said to be the inspiration for the epic of Gilgamesh, and was also syncretized into the Sumerian god Ninurta, so again, this isn't a bad guess. It just sounds rather funny to our modern ears thanks to an old Bugs Bunny cartoon where Bugs sarcastically compared Elmer Fudd (who was hunting Bugs at the time) to Nimrod. Most people just didn't pick up on the reference and assumed it was another word for an idiot; a real "maroon," as Bugs might say.

And while I definitely see some tower of Babel iconography going on with the EU parliament building... I don't think NWO is referencing Nimrod, especially when there were other great civilizations before ziggurats started springing up in Babylon. If you aren't ready to accept the Atlantis theory I proffered earlier to support this assertion, there's no need. Just look at the ruins of Gobleki Tepe for proof that great civilizations had already come and gone by the time Babylonian civilization rolled around.

The other prominent theory tossed around by Anons is that N stands for Nephilim. Again, to understand this, you have to go back to the book of Genesis where the Nephilim, the "sons of God," were said to have fallen to earth and had taken human wives for themselves, resulting in mighty children. In Genesis 6:1–4, it states:

> And it came to pass, when men began to multiply on the face of the earth, and daughters were born unto them, that the sons of God saw the daughters of men that they were fair; and they took them wives of all which they chose. And the Lord said, My spirit shall not always strive with man, for that he also is flesh: yet his days shall be an hundred and twenty years. There were giants in the earth in those days; and also after that, when the sons of God came in unto the daughters of men, and they bear children to them, the same became mighty men which were of old, men of renown.

There's been some debate over the use of the word "giant" in the English translation over the years, as Nephilim literally means "fallen ones" in Hebrew. When translating to Greek, the translators went with *gigantes*, which were mythological sons of Gaia and who were great warriors in their own right, but who were not gigantic by any means. In fact, the Greek audience would have known them to be human-sized, but when the Greek got translated into Latin, they opted to translate *gigantes* as "giants," and this got ported over to the King James version and subsequent translations, until modern translators decided to revive the term nephilim in more modern translations.

The most obvious connection Anons made with this theory is to the fact that the Cabal seems to track bloodlines especially keenly. If there was some kind of historical basis for genetic "greatness," it would make sense that these "natural-born" kings would want to keep that bloodline alive. But I think we've all seen by now that these people are hardly made from stronger stuff than the rest of us. No, I don't think the Nephilim theory passes the sniff test.

In trying to suss out the answer to this particular question, I've come up with a theory of my own, and one which I've only spoken briefly about once on Gab. I must warn you, this hasn't been confirmed anywhere by anyone, but I find it rather compelling, and I've been right more than once when digging on my own, so at least hear me out.

When I reflect on this Cabal, this ancient mystery cult, I go back to the Brotherhood of the Snake. One of the ancient Hebrew words for snake is *Nahash*, and that word itself, as Zechariah Sitchin informs us, comes from an earlier root word which we would spell as NHSH. This root word actually also means "to decipher" or "to find out." Considering the Cabal's obsession with snake imagery, and their desire to perpetuate these "mystery schools" across the ages, preserving their teachings among the highest ranks of those initiated into their cult, it seems to me that Nahash World Order—the Order of the Snake—is the most likely answer to Q's riddle. I freely admit, I could be wrong on this front, but until Q states differently or a definitive answer is found through some other means, this is my working theory, and, I believe, the most likely answer.

And the fact that this truly is a cult, in every sense of the word, cannot be understated. The most prominent example attesting to this fact can be found thanks to recent legal proceedings in the Caribbean that have "torn the veil" back somewhat, and demonstrated yet again the kinds of practices in which this cult is engaged. The first case comes to us from Haiti, in the wake of the devastating 2010 earthquake. At the time, many "aid" groups were working down in Haiti, including Sean Penn's J/P Haitian Relief Organization (which still operates as of this writing, and is really little more than a human trafficking operation run by wealthy socialite Sanela Jenkins, who operates a private section of her Room 23 website from servers housed in the Vatican). Also present was the Clinton Foundation, which ended up raising millions, ostensibly for earthquake relief, before pocketing the majority of it.

In this apocalyptic milieu, a group of ten Idaho-based "missionaries," led by one Laura Silsby, attempted to smuggle THIRTY-THREE "orphans" across the Haitian border into the Dominican Republic, but were caught by authorities who realized they didn't have proper documentation. These "missionaries" were from the organization that Silsby herself had founded, the New Life Children's Refuge, and when the authorities realized that many of these "orphans" actually still had parents, all the missionaries were arrested and the children returned to their homes, or were otherwise put with real caretakers.

As it turns out, Silsby, in trying to figure out how to get out of the country with the children, met up with a "journalist" named Anne-Christine d'Adesky, whose family just so happens to own the largest vertically integrated shipping operation in the region; DACO (d'Adesky Import Export SA) and Enmarcolda, SA, which operates the Wahoo resort location, among other businesses. Through an absolute ton of digging,[36] a picture emerged which pretty clearly demonstrated that Silsby was originally supposed to transport the kids through d'Adesky operations, but for whatever reason, in the resulting chaos of the earthquake, was unable to do so. Thus, Silsby had to come up with a Plan B quickly. Plan B was to move the children through the Dominican Republic, but as history attests, this didn't work out, either.

Q !UW.yye1fxo **ID: 236219** No.568863 🗗 🏴 **866**
Mar 6 2018 13:06:24 (EST)

https://wikileaks.org/clinton-emails/emailid/629 🗗 🏴
So much is open source.
So much left to be connected.
Why are the children in Haiti in high demand?
How are they smuggled out?
'Adoption' process.
Local 'staging' ports friendly to CF?
Track donations.
Cross against location relative to Haiti.
Think logically.
The choice, to KNOW, will be yours.
Q

Hillary Clinton would run interference for Silsby in the wake of the scandal unfolding, in part by leveraging her position at the State Department, and the Clinton Foundation, to press for the release of the American "missionaries." Within ten days of their arrest, eight members were freed. Within five months, all of them had been freed. Silsby's own lawyer, Jorge Puello (who actually wasn't licensed to practice law anywhere in the world) would be arrested later that same year for running an international trafficking ring of his own.

---

36 https://www.neonrevolt.com/2018/06/01/the-morally-repugnant-elite-and-their-bad-juju-haiti-dr-humantrafficking-qanon-greatawakening/

And this all raises the question: what were these fake missionaries intending to do with these kids? Where *exactly* were they planning on taking them?

But again, you have to shift your thinking. This isn't a one-off kind of thing. The elites conduct these ceremonies and events on a regular basis. According to Springmeier, some even follow a Pagan calendar of events, which lines up with all kinds of lunar phases (and that isn't surprising, when you consider how much mileage this cult has gotten out of moon iconography over the years, let alone the epithet of "moonchild)."

The thing you may not have known about the Clintons, however, is that Haiti has been something of a special location for the couple over the years, going all the way back to 1975 when they first visited the island. On another trip in 2004, Bill Clinton would admit in his very own biography that they would observe Voodoo rites performed by a *bokor*, a voodoo priest. Clinton's very own campaign manager (and prime Pizzagate suspect), John Podesta, would eagerly await these trips to Haiti, as disclosed in the Podesta Wikileaks:

Return to search

View email   View source

Re: wahoo again.

From: john.podesta@gmail.com
To: Susan.Tierney@analysisgroup.com
Date: 2015-06-03 16:28
Subject: Re: wahoo again.

Looking forward to it.

On Wednesday, June 3, 2015, Tierney, Susan <Susan.Tierney@analysisgroup.com>
wrote:

> I can wipe the smile off my face.
>
> Thanks so much.
>

"Wahoo again."

Want another layer to the rabbit hole?

Some may remember Jeff Kasky, father of the Parkland shooting "survivor" Cameron Kasky. Jeff got momentarily famous on Twitter for his outbursts directed at President Trump, before fading once his fifteen minutes in the limelight were up. Well, before Silsby founded the New Life Children's Refuge, she owned personalshopper.com. One of her employees, Andy Moore, tried to kidnap a child through Heart to Heart Adoptions.

Heart to Heart Adoptions was a Florida-based adoption agency that was a member of the Florida Adoption Council, which was founded by Kasky. Kasky himself ran an adoption agency of his own: One World Adoption Services (complete with a butterfly logo—which immediately raised red flags for Anons, since the symbol of the butterfly, as declassified by the FBI, is code for "child lover," and often directly references "Monarch" mind control). The thing about that, however, is that One World Adoption Services was shut down in 2015… for telling a mother in Haiti that they would send her to prison[37] unless she gave up her twins. If you know anything about Broward county, Florida… none of this will surprise you. It really is a hub of clandestine Cabal activity unto itself.

And like a rotten cherry on top of this human trafficking *sheisse*-sundae, after being released back into the US, Laura Silsby would change her name to Laura Gayler and begin working for AlertSense, the company that issues Amber Alerts.

But again, I have to ask my readers, what were these trafficker's true intentions, and where were they taking these kids? One very likely potential location would lie just some four hundred-or-so nautical miles due east, past Puerto Rico, right next to Richard Branson's private Necker Island. I am talking about, of course, Little Saint James island, owned by billionaire and convicted pedophile Jeffery Epstein.

Having cut his teeth trading options at Bear Stearns in the mid 70s, Epstein would open his own financial firm, J. Epstein & Co., eventually earning him his billions. Recall Ronald Bernard's testimony about the upper echelons of banking as you consider Epstein's meteoric rise. Soon, with his billions in hand, Epstein would buy up Little Saint James as his own private island. On the island, he would build a number of buildings, including quite a few lodging areas, a communal dining area, and frankly, what can only be described as a temple (though not to any religion with which you or I am really familiar). Think back to this earlier Qdrop:

---

37   https://www.neonrevolt.com/2018/02/27/jeff-kaskys-strange-scandal-ridden-history-with-one-world-adoption-services/

Q !!TPb.qbhqo ID: gO/UntOB No.149063235 ☐   **133**
Nov 11 2017 23:29:35 (EST)

Hard to swallow.
Important to progress.
Who are the puppet masters?
House of Saud (6+++) - $4 Trillion+
Rothschild (6++) - $2 Trillion+
Soros (6+) - $1 Trillion+
Focus on above (3).
Public wealth disclosures – False.
Many governments of the world feed the 'Eye'.
Think slush funds (feeder).
Think war (feeder).
Think environmental pacts (feeder).
Triangle has (3) sides.
Eye of Providence.
Follow the bloodlines.
What is the keystone?
Does Satan exist?
Does the 'thought' of Satan exist?
Who worships Satan?
What is a cult?
Epstein island.
What is a temple?
What occurs in a temple?
Worship?
Why is the temple on top of a mountain?
How many levels might exist below?
What is the significance of the colors, design and symbol above the dome?
Why is this relevant?
Who are the puppet masters?
Have the puppet masters traveled to this island?
When? How often? Why?
"Vladimir Putin: The New World Order Worships Satan"
Q

ANSWERS

Pizzagate investigators were already in familiar territory, but Q would confirm their worst suspicions by posting a picture of Epstein's temple in Qdrop 1861, with one question attached:

"Normal?"

(Here's an enlargement of the image Q would post):

An anonymous 4chan user recently posted new photos of Jeffery Epstein's infamous ~~Lolita~~ Pedo Island. The Island features a temple atop a small mountain and has been the location of several underage sex parties arranged by Epstein and attended by several of the world's elite including ex-president Bill Clinton, his wife Hillary Clinton, Hollywood actors and even members of the world's royal families.

Note the colors, the golden dome, the birds overhead, and the statues out front. Also notable on the island was the presence of a giant sundial that people can walk across, with an obelisk in the middle and benches surrounding the whole affair. One can even note the presence of a life-size cow statue that would get moved around the island periodically, as though it were grazing.

But the thing Epstein may perhaps be most famous for is running his Lolita Express—a private airline that catered to the world's elites, since at least 1997. Following a lawsuit by one Virginia Roberts claiming Epstein had kept her on the island as a sex slave, flight logs contained in Epstein's "black book" would be leaked to the public revealing that many of the world's politicians and elites (like Kevin Spacey, Chris Tucker, and Prince Andrew—who was also named as one of Robert's rapists in the suit) had made use of Epstein's airline on a number of occasions. Bill Clinton would be listed as flying on the airline some twenty-six times, often leaving his Secret Service detail on the mainland. Here's a leaked photo of him on the Lolita Express with one of his "friends" by his side, one Rachel Chandler:

Q !xowAT4Z3VQ (ID: 207e52) No.925052
Apr 6 2018 16:48:56 (EST)

> Anonymous ID: 7c0009 No.924953
> Apr 6 2018 16:43:00 (EST)
>
> 82EEB8DE-C3D6-44D9-86F7-2E47EA957DE3.jpeg
>
> R. chandler

>>924953
Epstein's plane.
Who is she?
Follow friends.
Friends lead to others.
Open source.
Q

1055

But before you think that's just Bill being Bill, Hillary would also make multiple trips to the island herself. We talked about Hillary's own attraction to women when covering the subject of Cathy O'Brien, but in truth, she's almost as bad as Bill when it comes to illicit affairs and serial abuse. And while, yes, Trump, being a billionaire himself, knew Epstein as well, Trump would ban Epstein from Mar-a-Lago in 1999 following allegations that Epstein had tried to enlist the underage daughter of one of Mar-a-Lago's members to come "work" for him on his island.

In 2008, Epstein would plead guilty to a charge of soliciting prostitution from a four-teen-year-old, but he wasn't imprisoned among the general population. No, he was given different arrangements and housed in a private "prison." This arrangement actually allowed him to leave "prison" for up to twelve hours a day. During this time, he would make many trips both up to his home in Manhattan, and down to his private island. He would end up serving thirteen of his eighteen months in this manner, and was also added to the registered sex offender database. In 2015, he would again be caught up in another investigation as the FBI had since received thirty-six individual accounts by women claiming they had been molested by Epstein. He would be indicted, but granted immunity by prosecutors while allowed to plead guilty and pay a sum of money to his victims.

But as I alluded to before, more was going on at Epstein's island than just mere "fun in the sun." Much more. These two drops would begin to paint the picture, and connect to HRC in more ways than one:

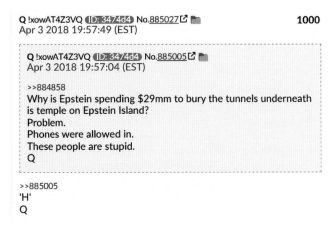

Q !xowAT4Z3VQ **ID: 3474d4** No.885027 ☑ 📷   **1000**
Apr 3 2018 19:57:49 (EST)

> Q !xowAT4Z3VQ **ID: 3474d4** No.885005 ☑ 📷
> Apr 3 2018 19:57:04 (EST)
>
> >>884858
> Why is Epstein spending $29mm to bury the tunnels underneath is temple on Epstein Island?
> Problem.
> Phones were allowed in.
> These people are stupid.
> Q

>>885005
'H'
Q

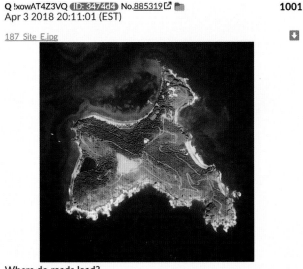

Q !xowAT4Z3VQ **ID: 3474d4** No.885319 ☑ 📷   **1001**
Apr 3 2018 20:11:01 (EST)

187_Site_E.jpg

Where do roads lead?
Each prince is associated with a cardinal direction: north, south, east and west.
Sacrifice.
Collect.
[Classified]-1
[Classified]-2
Tunnels.
Table 29.
D-Room H
D-Room R
D-Room C
Pure EVIL.
'Conspiracy'
Q

Notice how Q calls the cardinal corners of the island, "Princes." An odd way to name a direction to be sure, but "who" are these princes? Anons would theorize a connection[38] to the four princes in LaVeyan Satanism—Satan, Lucifer, Belial, and Leviathan—each of which are associated with a cardinal direction in that esoteric line of thinking. Still, other brilliant Anons would begin analyzing the 3D topography of the island,[39] outlining the most likely spots for these secret tunnels Q was talking about as well. But more specifically, Anons wanted to know what these D-Rooms were. D-room H, D-room R, D-room C—what could they possibly be? The answers wouldn't start dawning on us until after Q opened up Rachel Chandler's Instagram account, a few days after his initial Epstein island drops. (We wouldn't learn until much later how he had come to have access to the account itself.)

As it turns out, apart from being one of the girls available at Epstein's island, Rachel Chandler had become something of a permanent fixture there, working her way up the ranks, until she eventually became something of a madam before leaving the island and the occupation to go get married back on the mainland. As such, she had extensive access to the entire facility at the island and used Instagram as a means to advertise what was being offered therein. Q would switch Chandler's Instagram account from private to public—for the first time since the early Pizzagate days—allowing Anons to screenshot and catalog everything we could find[40] in the process.

Some photos were what you would expect.

gram.com/p/uBViXmzf41/?taken-by=ray.chandler

38   https://www.neonrevolt.com/2018/04/03/april-showers-qanon-was-dropping-moabs-tonight-greatawakening/

39   https://www.neonrevolt.com/2018/04/05/epsteins-island-digs-pizzagate-pedogate-qanon-greatawakening/

40   https://www.neonrevolt.com/2018/04/12/facebooks-mysterious-building8-darpa-and-thecabal-qa-non-newq-greatawakening/

Others were clear signals:

Others were photos of her with celebrities. Here was a photo of Eminem with Chandler, when she was, by her own admission, sixteen or seventeen:

Do people remember how vocal Eminem was against President Trump? Do people remember the diss tracks, and his constant stream of invective? You're looking at part of the reason why (with the other half of the equation involving the murder of Eminem's rapper friend, "Proof" and the death of actress Brittany Murphy).[41] Trump's executive orders repre-

41   https://www.neonrevolt.com/2018/04/06/barry-with-an-ak-barry-with-an-ak-barry-hussein-with-a-kalishnikov/

sented an existential threat to every single member of the Cabal, and they all knew it from the moment he won the Republican nomination, which is why they had been so vocal in their opposition to him.

Also among the posts would be an image of this young man… whose photo also happened to appear on the FBI's missing persons site.

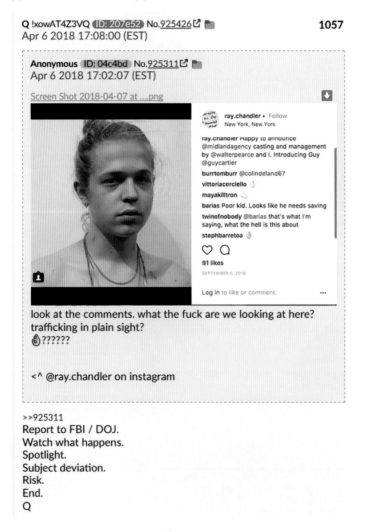

Essentially, Chandler was using her private Instagram profile as a "catalog." The "Midland Agency Casting and Management" was really just a front for human trafficking, taking place right on this Facebook-owned platform used by millions every day.

But the worst was still to come, for that wasn't all her account revealed. This photo would be pulled directly from her Instagram as well, and led to what might be the most shocking discovery Anons have made, to date:

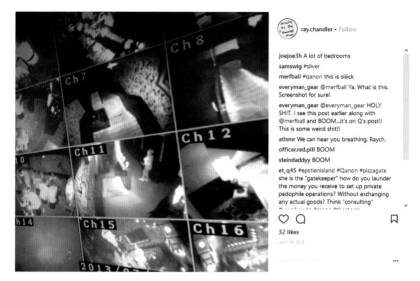

Posted on July 19, 2013, it's clear that the photo shows some kind of security feed. Upon closer inspection of the photo, I, myself, would be the Anon that night who would actually make the connection…[42]

Pardon the misspelling, I was frantic as it dawned on me exactly what Q was showing us…

D-room stood, as far as I could tell, for "Dining room." And though it's hard to tell if Q was talking directly in response to what I was suggesting or not (for we Anons were also reporting the missing young man to the FBI that night), Q would respond almost immediately—under sixty seconds after my post above:

> ▶ Q !xowAT4Z3VQ   04/07/18 (Sat) 03:17:48 ID: 8153b1
> (2) No.932846 >>932848 >>932849 >>932851 >>932855 >>932856 >>932860 >>932862
> >>932872 >>932873 >>932874 >>932879 >>932880 >>932881 >>932885 >>932888
> >>932890 >>932894 >>932895 >>932897 >>932913 >>932927 >>932936 >>932937
> >>932941 >>932942 >>932961 >>932973 >>932974 >>932977 >>932980 >>933007
> >>933019 >>933034 >>933040 >>933070 >>933102 >>933104 >>933141 >>933222
> >>933254 >>933292 >>933303 >>933321 >>933349 >>933392 >>933402 >>933438
>
> Connection made.
> RC end.
> We have grounds.
> Reverting.
> Thank you.
> Q

> ▶ Anonymous *(You)* 04/07/18 (Sat) 03:18:06 ID: 4a5d39
> (3) No.932847 >>933363
>
> >>932839 (You)
>
> Sorry, I meant DINING ROOM.
>
> I'm having flashbacks to the shakes I used to get researching when PG first hit. I would shake for hours afterwards with dread.

Rachel Chandler's Instagram would soon revert back to private after this post, but my idea had not gone unnoticed by other Anons. They saw what I saw, and would begin to scrutinize, and attempt to outline, the specific details in the photo:

The guests staying at Epstein's island weren't just engaging in pedophilic rape. They weren't just engaged in esoteric ritual sacrifices. They were also engaging in cannibalism. And all of this was being facilitated (as we would find out later from Q, knowingly) by Cabal-affiliated companies like Facebook and Twitter and Google, who allowed their platforms to be used towards aiding the kind of trafficking necessary to engage in such horrors, away from the prying eyes of law enforcement.

It's worth noting that since "moving on" with her life, Chandler became a photographer, and frequently associated with suspected "Mother of Darkness" Marina Abramovic. The DOJ's Office of Personal Responsibility has also just announced that they're re-opening the investigation into Jeffrey Epstein, given his previous controversial plea deal, essentially signaling that now, under the Trump administration, they were going to not only go throw the book at Epstein this time around, but go after every single corrupt, Obama-era official who had worked to protect him during that time.

But how did Q get access to Chandler's Instagram account that fateful night? Had military intelligence hacked the profile for us? Was the NSA showing off it's technical-prowess? No, in the most stunning revelation of all, Q would later inform Anons that Rachel Chandler was now acting as an informant on all things Epstein-related. Q had gained access to the account from Rachel, herself:

Q !!mG7VJxZNCl ID: cffc9e No.5802556 ☐ ▮   3156
Mar 20 2019 22:27:03 (EST)

Ray Chandler = Allison Mack x 100
Q

As we're about to go to print with this book, it turns out that Jeffrey Epstein has committed "suicide" while in prison. The media would have you believe that Trump has taken to retweeting "baseless conspiracy theories" about potential Clinton involvement in Epstein's death. One thing is for certain, however: few on either side of the aisle, regardless of whether or not they follow Q, are buying the official narrative anymore.

Friends, I know this chapter has been exhausting, but I think now that we've come to this point, you can see why it was necessary for me to take you down this road the way I did. If you can't understand the true size, scope, and nature of the enemy we face—and how close to the edge of destruction we all collectively came—you can't begin to appreciate the victories we now have within our grasp. And believe me when I say that I've only scratched the surface of the evil we face. I didn't even get to talk about things like Plum Island, or Doctor Mary Sherman and the development of the HIV/AIDS virus. This is truly a worldwide Cabal; an unholy alliance comprised of various factions now operating together to plot the death and destruction of the masses for their own sick benefit. But the crazy thing is, thanks to Trump, thanks to QAnon, thanks to every single operator in the field who has risked and sacrificed to bring us to this point in history, and thanks to every single Anon who worked overtime to bring these disclosures to the forefront of the public consciousness, we are actually, for the first time in history, winning against this ancient and evil death cult.

Far from the apocalyptic visions of various doomsayers, who believe for whatever reason (be it religious indoctrination, or run-of-the-mill nihilism) that our fight is futile and we are fated for destruction, I say to you, that your future is not written. Our future is not written. The future of our children, and our children's children is not yet written. The people are AWAKENED like never before, AWAKENED to the reality that was previously and deliberately hidden, AWAKENED to the UNPRECEDENTED opportunity that now lies before us.

As an Anon, I've spent literal years studying, researching, and digging everything you've read here thus far. My interactions with Q have been life changing, and if you think this is a lot to process, keep in mind the volume of content on my site, right now, is somewhere near four times larger than this book you hold in your hands. Even as I write these pages, QAnon continues to post new Qdrops, bypassing the MSM, speaking directly to those in the know, whose numbers only grow with each passing day. And I'm left feeling like the Disciple John, writing at the end of his gospel:

"And there are also many other things which Jesus did, the which, if they should be written every one, I suppose that even the world itself could not contain the books that should be written."

Don't get me wrong; I'm not trying to compare QAnon to Jesus. I'm just saying that no human being will ever be able to condense and chronicle *everything* Q has said and done into one volume. The main challenge I've faced in writing all this has been in choosing what to include and what to omit, because the scope of everything Q covers is so vast. If there's one takeaway you get from this book, I want you to know that the story doesn't end here. And while I still have so much more to show you before we're through, I'll never be able to show you everything, here, within the pages of this book. The question then becomes what you're going to do with your newfound knowledge. Because there's a responsibility that comes with "knowing." Once you know something, you can't un-know it. You can't ignore it, you can't shove it to the back of your mind. Knowing changes you. Knowing awakens you.

And so, my newly awakened friends, with all that in mind, I want pick to up where we left off earlier, and revisit our old pals, Barack Obama and Hillary Clinton. But in order to do that, we have to first travel to *Wonderland*.

CHAPTER 8

"Pain Comes in Many Different Forms"

—September 4, 2018 from Qdrop #2077

Q !ITPb.qbhqo ID: fbc52d No.17546 ☐ 📷   **245**
Dec 1 2017 00:46:51 (EST)

Hussein is evil and a real loser.
No special treatment.
Shopping around for a (new) handler/protection is fun to watch on
the SATs / spy comms.
Morons, all of them.
Q

Realize for a moment, this wasn't that long ago. It was only just the middle of 2018 when Huma Abedin was working overtime…

While many were still wondering why she hadn't divorced her husband—former congressman Anthony Weiner—after he was caught sexting with a fifteen-year-old, and a subsequent stash of child pornography was unearthed sitting alongside countless Clinton e-mails on his personal laptop, all labeled "insurance…" Huma was getting to work.

In truth, HUMA often has a double meaning in Q's drops. One meaning is the literal person, Huma Abedin, who has been Hillary's right-hand gal for countless years. The second meaning at one point was HUMA—the Harvard University Muslim Alumni association—which opened up lines of inquiry that led down numerous rabbit holes, in and of itself. But Q had told us countless times to follow Huma, and now he was reminding us to do so once again.

Anonymous ID: s4lv8TW8 No.147979863 ☐ ▤   **71**
Nov 4 2017 18:33:30 (EST)

Follow HUMA.
Who connects HRC/CF to SA?
Why is this relevant?
Who is the Muslim Brotherhood?
Who has ties to the MB?
Who is Awan?
What is the Awan Group?
Where do they have offices?
Why is this relevant?
Define cash laundering.
What is the relationship between SA & Pakistan?
Why is this relevant?
Why would SA provide tens of millions of dollars to US senior gov't officials?
What does SA obtain in exchange for payment?
Why is access important?
What happened when HRC lost the election of 2016?
How much money was provided to the CF by SA during 15/16?
HRC lost.
Loss of access/power/control.
Does repayment of funds to SA occur? If so, how?
Why did BO send billions in cash to Iran?
Why wasn't Congress notified?
Why was this classified under 'State Secrets'?
Who has access to 'State Secrets'?
Where did the planes carrying the cash depart from and land?
Did the planes all land in the same location?
How many planes carried the cash?
Why is this relevant?
What does this have to do w/ NK?
What does this have to do w/ SA/CF cash donations?
What does this have to do w/ ISIS?
What does this have to do w/ slush funds?
Why is SA so vitally important?
Follow the money.
Who has the money?
What is happening in SA today?
Why is this relevant?
Who was Abdullah bin Abdulaziz?
What events transpired directly thereafter?
How was POTUS greeted compared to other former US President's when in SA?
Why is this relevant?
What is the meaning of this tradition?
What coincidentally was the last Tweet sent out by POTUS?
Why is this relevant?
Was that an instruction of some kind?
To who?
Why is this relevant?
Where was POTUS when that Tweet was sent?
Why is that relevant?
What attack took place in SA as operations were undertaken? Flying objects.
What US operators are currently in SA?
Why is this relevant?
Questions provide answers.
Alice & Wonderland.

                                                    ANSWERS

Now, we've covered one side of the Cabal's power structure in extreme detail: the Rothschilds. Another side, George Soros, is a subject we've only just briefly touched upon here, but what you need to know is that the man is a Cabal Marxist who not only aided the Nazis in helping to capture fellow Jews during World War II, but a devilish pragmatist who has no problem wrecking economies if it means enriching himself. Soros regularly funnels billions to subversive groups around the world, mainly through his Open Society Institute, which then turns around and donates cash to "think tanks" in order to provide academic cover for all sorts of disruptive and damaging policies, as well as to more extreme, violent, fringe groups, who can act as foot-soldiers for the Left. I'd estimate that some ninety percent of the "revolutionary" movements you see in the world today have some financial ties to Soros—from Black Lives Matter, to Ploughshares, to media groups like The Media Consortium which includes outlets like *The Young Turks*, *Mother Jones*, and *Democracy Now!* to political groups like Alexandria Ocasio-Cortez's "Justice Democrats." Q tells us that Soros replaced the Rockefellers in the Cabal hierarchy when he made his billions and has since been one of the most "valuable" assets of the Cabal, leveraged to sow unrest, division, and social upheaval worldwide, leading some countries to ban him and his organizations from their soil entirely, appropriately labeling him an "economic terrorist."

The last group that really funds the Cabal right now is the House of Saud. We've talked some about the Muslim Brotherhood, the Awans, and Prince Al-Waleed, but in truth, Huma Abedin is the nexus that connects them all to the Clinton Machine.

I'll remind the reader here that the Muslim Brotherhood is a jihadist organization that has, as its explicit goals, the overthrow of Western nations and the installation of a worldwide Muslim Caliphate. The group was founded in 1928 in Egypt by one Hassan al-Banna, who was an admirer of Adolf Hitler. Muslim Brotherhood members would work as spies for Hitler in two Muslim SS divisions, called the *Handschar* divisions; that is, scimitar divisions.

Al-Banna also had a close ally in the person of the Grand Mufti of Jerusalem, Haj Amin al-Husseini. Al-Husseini saw in Hitler a good friend, brought together by their mutual hatred for the Jews. Al-Banna would actually go on to live in Berlin from 1941 until 1945, and be photographed meeting with Hitler while heaping praises upon him, hoping that Hitler would back his plan to keep the Jews out of Palestine. While Hitler agreed that Jews were their "common enemy," he curiously stopped just shy of endorsing al-Husseini's plan—something which didn't seem to bother al-Husseini too greatly at the time, but which should give us pause, considering we know who Hitler's moneyed masters were. Despite this, Al-Husseini became increasingly ingratiated to ranking Nazi party members and would be copiously praised by Himmler on at least one occasion in a private letter as well.

Despite Hitler's eventual defeat, the Muslim Brotherhood would continue to grow throughout the Middle East; their ranks swelling throughout the forties and fifties. The Brotherhood's founder, Al-Banna, would be assassinated in 1949, most likely by the Iron Guard in Egypt. Despite that, the Brotherhood would continue to grow as Western powers began to see it more and more as a bulwark against Soviet influence in the region. And though the group "officially" swore off violence in the seventies, in essence, they just exported all that "messy business" to more fringe groups; groups with whom they would never publicly admit any connection, but with whom they were still very much affiliated, behind the scenes.

This is actually how the Mujahideen was born—as a Muslim Brotherhood splinter-group. The West began to make a "deal with the devil" by supporting groups like the Mujahideen, thus leading to the creation of Osama bin-Laden, and then groups like Al Qaeda, and eventually ISIS.

It's no exaggeration to say that the Muslim mind is really fertile ground for Cabal takeover. If you know anything about Islam itself, you know it's a religion built off plagiarized Arianism (an early Christian heresy), and which integrated all sorts of regional elements, such as Saturn-worship (by virtue of including the "Black Cube" at Mecca, with the "Black Star" being a very old Saturnine/Cronus-related concept in the ancient mystery cults). There's also the integration of moon symbolism, which goes directly back to the ancient goddess worship of we touched upon earlier. And while Mohammad started off peacefully when he was a mere merchant with no real political sway, as more converted, he built an army and became a bloodthirsty warlord, leading to the creation of later passages in the Koran which abrogated all the earlier, "peaceful" passages (which were written when... *just coincidentally*, he had ZERO political or military capital at his disposal).

So, in other words, Islam's origin is Cabal-related, through and through. Like variations on a theme in a jazz song, the core elements, themes, people, and goals all remain the same, even as they leverage different tactics to rope in more and more useful idiots from each generation, to carry out their ideologically driven barbarism. In other words, it's not so much about being principled at the end of the day. It's about power and control, and gaining them by any means at your disposal. Consider Islam an ancient variation of mind control: MKUltra Mark 1. This "beta testing program" has somehow survived through to the modern day by turning women into non-persons, strangling puppies (because dogs are "unclean" in Islamic systems), and killing everyone who does not conform to its brutal, dogmatic, and inhuman system of control, Sharia law.

In other words, the Muslim Brotherhood is leveraged as the rabid attack dogs of the Cabal, normally kept on a short leash, but loosed whenever the Cabal wants to depose a leader, assassinate a target, or otherwise move things in a certain direction on the world stage. It's for this reason I often refer to Islam as a "Death Cult"; an evil ideology whose irrational, often-inbred zealots spread nothing but pain and misery in its wake. And that part about inbreeding is not an exaggeration or a mere hateful quip on my part. Islamic countries have the highest rates of inbreeding out of *all* other nations on the planet, leading to even more pain and suffering, with the onset of all manner of genetic diseases and deformities that are virtually absent from the rest of the world. Nearly *seventy percent* of all Pakistanis are the product of inbreeding, and in one BBC study, it was found that nearly fifty-five percent of all Pakistani immigrants to Britain are married to a first cousin. This means that the Pakistani population in Britain is "at least thirteen times likely to than the general population to have children with recessive genetic disorders."

This startling and disturbing reality is largely representative of the entire Muslim world. According to Danish psychologist Nicolai Sennels, sixty-seven percent of Saudis are inbred, sixty-four percent of Jordanis and Kuwaitis are inbred, sixty percent of Iraqis, and fifty-four percent of the UAE's populace are also inbred. And though some of what I've said here may be "controversial," the costs associated with this genetic reality simply cannot be ignored by the PC police.

And all that to say this is who Huma was working for while also working for Hillary wherever she went. So close were Hillary and Huma, that Hillary would often refer to her as "her second daughter," giving her something of a protected status thanks to the Clinton Machine. Despite this, the evidence that Huma Abedin was simultaneously working for the Muslim brotherhood while also working for Hillary was so overwhelming that in 2012 Rep. Michelle Bachmann sent a sixteen-page letter[43] to the House Permanent Select Committee on Intelligence and the House Judiciary Committee, laying out the evidence plainly for all to see.

First, her father Syed Abedin would found the Institute of Muslim Minority Affairs, a Muslim Brotherhood proxy organization, alongside Abdullah Omar Naseef in 1979 while relocating his family from Kalamazoo, Michigan, to Jeddah, Saudi Arabia, when Huma was just two years old. Syed would publish the *Journal of Muslim Minority Affairs* thrice yearly, and Omar Naseef would go on to become the secretary general of the Muslim World League—a Saudi-based NGO with ties to all sorts of Islamic terror groups and insurgents, including Osama bin Laden. Despite this, the Muslim World League is still intimately involved with a number of UN initiatives, including UNICEF.

---

43   https://www.scribd.com/doc/100244266/Bachmann-Letter-Responding-to-Ellison

Huma's mother, Saleha Abedin, would not only help found the Muslim Sisterhood, but also work for the International Islamic Council for Da'wa and Relief—a group comprised of some eighty-six smaller Muslim organizations (including Omar Naseef's Muslim World League), and which is designed to promote the message of Islam, worldwide.

Da'wa, for those unfamiliar with the term, is essentially proselytism; an invitation to all non-Muslims to live according to Allah's will. And the IICDR will claim this is peaceful, while simultaneously supporting Hamas and while Yusuf al-Qaradawi still serves as its chairman.

And this is perhaps the most important connection of them all, because Yusuf al-Qaradawi is essentially the direct heir to Hassan al-Banna's ideology, and the current "spiritual" leader of the Muslim Brotherhood (though he doesn't "officially" serve the Brotherhood in any capacity). Recall, al-Banna founded the Muslim Brotherhood in Egypt in 1928. Al-Qaradawi was born in 1926 and al-Banna would lecture at al-Qaradawi's school when he was growing up, inspiring the boy with his message of Islamic supremacy. By age ten, al-Qaradawi had memorized the entire Koran. He would go on to collect scholarly Islamic accolades as he grew, studying and working in Islamic Universities in Cairo and Qatar. Al-Qaradawi now has a broadcast on *Al Jazeera,* where his show reaches some sixty million people worldwide, and has authored over one hundred books on his particular brand of radical Islam. He is currently the president of the European Council for Fatwa and Research, the principle shareholder at the Al Qaeda-affiliated Bank Al-Taqwa (which is listed as a financier of terrorism by the UN Security Council), and is the founder of IslamOnline. He is also one of the original trustees of the Islamic Society of Boston, which you'll recall was where the 9/11-associated Ptech programmer Suheil Laher preached with regularity.

In other words, it's a tightly-knit network of radical, subversive jihadis working to spread Sharia and the Caliphate, and Huma Abedin was raised at the very epicenter of it all. Despite spending all her years growing up overseas, because she had been born in the US, she had birthright citizenship, and was able to return to the US when she turned eighteen in order to attend college at George Washington University. She began working as an intern for the Clinton administration in 1996, and also worked for the Institute of Muslim Minority Affairs, where her father had worked, taking on the role of assistant editor over that *Journal of Muslim Minority Affairs* the group published thrice yearly. The journal had since been taken over by Huma's mother, following the death of Huma's father. She would remain as a member of the journal's editorial board until 2008, coming into contact with the Al Qaeda-affiliated Naseef, the man who had started the IMMA alongside Huma's father.

When, in 2009, Huma was made Hillary's deputy chief of staff while at the State Department, she was labeled a "special government employee," allowing her to engage in private consulting work for firms like Teneo and MF Global, as well as the Clinton Foundation. The potential conflicts of interest and security concerns this kind of situation could create should be setting off klaxons in your mind. For instance, one conflict of interest started when it came out that the Rockefeller Foundation was both a client of Teneo and a donor to the Clinton Foundation. At the time, Teneo was trying to get former Rockefeller Foundation president Judy Rodin a position in Obama's Global Development Council. They tapped on Abedin, and yes, she tried to help, and yes, the position was technically unpaid... but sometimes... people aren't after the money. Sometimes they're in it for the connections, the influence, and the power. Remember, the Rockefeller Foundation was donating to Abedin's other employer, the Clinton Foundation, at the same time their agents at Teneo were trying to get their president into the White House.

And people _still_ wonder why Hillary's e-mails are important! Needless to say, Anthony Weiner certainly thought so!

But evidently, this arrangement didn't bother anyone in the Obama administration one iota. And why would it? They had all the power, and were raking in the cash at the same time. Senate Judiciary Committee chairman Chuck Grassley would sound the alarm on this arrangement back in 2015, but unfortunately, that did little to change anything at the time. Finally, in 2016, Huma would move on to serve as Hillary's personal assistant during her presidential campaign.

No wonder the House of Saud would donate twenty-five million dollars to the Clinton Foundation in the run-up to the 2016 presidential election. But that's not "foreign collusion" now, is it? No, no, of course not! The Clinton Foundation is a "charity!" And all that money is for "charitable purposes," (or so they'd like you to believe). But of course, you can only charge that kind of premium when you have influence to sell, and in the wake of Trump's dark horse win from left-field, Bill and Hill found themselves suddenly out of power, out of access, with nothing to sell. And in the international marketplace, just as in real life, promises are cheap. Clinton Foundation donations dried up.

Which is why Huma Abedin suddenly took to laundering money with El Chapo's wife, Emma Coronel Aispuro. In other words, the Clinton Foundation is now in bed with the Cartel, and that should really surprise no one, considering the long-standing relationship between the Deep State (particularly Bush Sr. with the CIA), and drug cartels. It's also why one Lara Prychodko would be found dead at age forty-eight, stuffed into the trash compactor at the very apartment building where Huma Abedin and Anthony Weiner used to live; the Zeckendorf towers, right off of Union Square park in New York City.

We've gone beyond subversion, beyond money laundering, into trafficking and murder with Huma, but one has to wonder why someone would commit such crimes for the sake of another. Yes, it's true, Clinton has said that Huma is like a daughter to her, but in truth, they're… _closer_ than that. Yes, they have been lovers at times, and that should surprise no one given Cathy O'Brien's testimony (among others) about Hillary. And for those who might think that Islam's strictures would stop Huma from engaging in lesbian activity, remember, the actual rules are for the proles, for the human meat-shields, for the useful idiots. The ruling class does whatever they want; whatever will gain them more power, more leverage, and temporarily satiate their seemingly insatiable hungers.

Also, remember how much of this all coincided with the Muslim Brotherhood infiltration that was being overseen by Barack Obama during this time, carefully filtering through subversive candidates compiled in lists, all in order to elevate them into positions of power and influence throughout the government. This also ties directly to the scandal involving the Awan brothers, which endangered the security of so many members of Congress! Now things have progressed to such a stage that we have the likes of Ilhan Omar currently serving in Congress. We're talking about a woman who once committed marriage fraud by marrying her own brother in order to help him obtain US citizenship, and who, in a recently uncovered interview from 2013, complained that Americans say "Al Qaeda" and "Hezbollah" like they're bad groups! When describing 9/11 during a speech at CAIR, Omar would describe the event with an anemic "some people did something," distancing everyone from the horror and tragedy of that day while simultaneously refusing to acknowledge the Islamic role in the attack. She's far from the only infiltrator, but through fraud and kickbacks, the likes of Obama and Hillary have systematically sold the American people out over the past decade to members of a radical death cult who hate just about everything about Americans by virtue of them simply refusing to bow to Allah.

With all this money, and all the trafficking going on through the house of Saud, its no wonder QAnon would label Saudi Arabia "The Bloody Wonderland" in his drops. Hillary, of course, was "Alice" in this metaphor, and the implication was that by utilizing these foundations and labeling everything "charity," the Clintons could legally sell off practically anything they wanted… and receive in return… anything they wanted.

Anonymous ID: KC17sSpZ No.147661332 ⬈ ▇   **58**
Nov 2 2017 15:40:27 (EST)

Anonymous ID: KC17sSpZ No.147661217 ⬈ ▇
Nov 2 2017 15:39:22 (EST)

http://thehill.com/blogs/pundits-blog/presidential-campaign
/292310-huma-abedins-ties-to-the-muslim-brotherhood ⬈ ▇
The Clinton campaign is attempting once again to sweep
important questions under the rug about top aide Huma Abedin,
her family ties to the Muslim Brotherhood and to Saudi Arabia,
and her role in the ballooning Clinton email scandal.
Her mother, Saleha Abedin, sits on the Presidency Staff Council
of the International Islamic Council for Da'wa and Relief, a group
that is chaired by the leader of the Muslim Brotherhood, Sheikh
Yusuf al-Qaradawi.

Perhaps recognizing how offensive such ties will be to voters
concerned over future terrorist attacks on this country by radical
Muslims professing allegiance to Sharia law, the Clinton
campaign on Monday tried to downplay Ms. Abedin's
involvement in the Journal and the Muslim Brotherhood.

The Clinton surrogate group Media Matters claimed predictably
there was "no evidence" that Ms. Abedin or her family had ties to
the Muslim Brotherhood, and that Trump campaign staffers who
spoke of these ties were conspiracy theorists.

To debunk the evidence, Media Matters pointed to a Snopes.com
"fact-check" piece that cited as its sole source… Senator John
McCain. This is the same John McCain who met Libyan militia
leader Abdelkarim Belhaj, a known al Qaeda associate, and
saluted him as "my hero" during a 2011 visit to Benghazi.

>>147661217Senator McCain and others roundly criticized Rep.
Michele Bachmann in 2012 when she and four members of the
House Permanent Select Committee Intelligence and the House
Judiciary Committee cited Ms. Abedin in letters sent to the
Inspectors General of the Department of Defense, Department of
State, Department of Justice, Department of Homeland Security,
and the Office of the Director of National Intelligence, warning
about Muslim Brotherhood infiltration of the United States
government.

Why is this relevant?
Who took an undisclosed trip to SA?
What was the purpose of a f2f v phone call?
Alice & Wonderland.

Understand: the flow of dark money is absolutely essential to the Cabal's continued existence, and it's why so many politicians have "charitable foundations" of their own. This dark money not only buys "protection" but also buys access (if you have enough to spare). It's why career Congresscritters are worth millions upon millions, when their salaries would never justify them having such wealth. Why, in one particular drop, QAnon highlighted a clip from a press conference held by Nancy Pelosi, where she admitted, on camera, to having sold missiles to North Korea years ago. Yes, just… out in the open, like it didn't matter. On C-SPAN.

Q !xowAT4Z3VQ ID: 549b47 No.1106719 **1184**
Apr 19 2018 18:53:11 (EST)

Big ERROR.
Pelosi admits travel to North Korea **[past]**.
Archive immediately.
They have tried to 'cover' this.
Why is this relevant?
https://www.c-span.org/video/?444272-1/democrats-back-farm-bill-leader-pelosi
These people will lose everything.
Q

It's why Big Government Globalists LOVE big spending programs like the Paris Agreement, which just end up being slush funds for them and their pals. More importantly, it's why *nothing* ever changes, despite the billions and trillions ostensibly being thrown at these "crises" facing the world today.

Q !xowAT4Z3VQ ID: a2d4d4 No.1157518 ☐ ▬   **1241**
Apr 23 2018 12:56:57 (EST)

Reminder.
Iran is next.
Marker.
CLAS - Sec 11A P 2.2.
"Installments."
$250B.
Jan 1.
Jun 1.
No inspection @ GZ NR sites.
No missile tech prevention.
Load carrying.
ICBM.
Think NK.
Who controls the $?
Who really controls the $?
Why does the EU have a vested interest in this deal?
Who receives the money?
When the US sends billions in aid and/or climate and/or etc who or
what entity audits / tracks to confirm intended recipient(s) rec?
None.
How does GS fund WW counter-events?
Who funds WW leftist events?
American taxpayer (subsidize).
Define nuclear stand-off.
Who benefits?
How do you 'squeeze' funds out of the US?
Threat to humanity?
Environment push?
Think Paris accord.
Who audits / tracks the funneled money?
Define kickback.
Define slush fund.
EPA.
No oversight re: Hussein.
Why?
How does the C_A fund non sanctioned ops?
Off the books?
Re_ read past drops.
Will become relevant.
Welcome Mr. President.
The U.S. will NOT agree to continue the Iran deal as it currently
stands.
Q

It's why, once the Clinton Foundation was under siege by Huber, Horowitz, and their four hundred and seventy investigators, the McCain Foundation stepped in to keep the flow of dark money going. Of course, all that ended when McCain was secretly executed following his secret tribunal, but that's how desperate they were to keep that flow of money going.

Q !!mG7VJxZNCI (ID: 6d1065) No.4617497 🖪   **2650**
Jan 5 2019 20:06:58 (EST)

Anonymous (ID: 2e9572) No.4617213 🖪
Jan 5 2019 19:53:18 (EST)

Democrats_performance_1.jpg

Combat Debater
@CombatDebater

First 24 hrs of Dems in power:

-Filed articles to impeachment
Trump

-Introduced a bill to kill the
Electoral College

-Passed bill to fund government
without the Boarder Wall

-Voted unanimously to go home
just 4 hrs after taking the job

Who's worried for our country? 👆

9:42 AM · 05 Jan 19 · Twitter for iPhone

Democrats_want_12_billon_more_foreign_aid_0_for_wall.png

B BREITBART

TRENDING: IMPEACHMENT   STILL NO WALL   IMPEACHMENT   SHUTDOWN DRAGS ON   IMPEACHMEI

**DEMOCRAT SPENDING BILL OFFERS $12
BILLION MORE FOR FOREIGN AID, $0 FOR
BORDER WALL**

f SHARE 87,731   ✉ EMAIL   8+ SHARE   🐦 TWEET

>>4617146
This one was really a step on their own dick.

>>4617213
Why do D's always PUSH (force R's to include Spending Bills for
approval) BILLIONS OF DOLLARS FOR FOREIGN AID?
Who audits where the money 'actually' goes?
How do politicians become 'extremely' wealthy while in office on
gov't salaries?
How do xyz 'orgs' etc. remain funded?
https://www.foreignassistance.gov 🖪
https://www.foreignassistance.gov/explore 🖪
Why do D's only care about CONTROL/POWER?
POWER OF THE PURSE.
POWER = PROTECTION.
THE WHEEL OF CORRUPTION.
Welcome to the CON.
Q

The thing about all of this, though, is that Q isn't the originator of the "Alice" name for Hillary. No, that comes from someone else, someone deeply affiliated with the Clintons and the Clinton Foundation. That nickname was given to her by Marty Torrey. Formerly a congressional aide, following a post by Q, Anons realized that the elderly Torrey was not only someone who was well connected, but someone whose communications were spread all throughout e-mail chains obtained by groups like Wikileaks and Judicial Watch.

UNCLASSIFIED U.S. Department of State Case No. F-2016-07895 Doc No. C06166848 Date: 08/29/2018

RELEASE IN PART B6

Monarchy ! :-) Hmmm.

| From: | Marty Torrey | B6 |

| To: | Hillary Clinton HDR22@clintonemail.com |

| Subject: | Monarchy ! :-) Hmmm. |

'Alice',
Your recent 'adventures' warrant use of 'Alice' :-) Today discussed coverage of your trip with our British friend
                                                      His take is that 'America should reconsider a monarchy -
assuming Madam Secretary will accept the post' :-) Yep. We also feel Mid East situation would have more clarity and Gulf of Mexico disaster would have been dealt with sooner. My take is that I am just so proud to know the most influential American on the planet....and still want her as Commander-in -Chief. Another 'adventure' behind 'Alice'....accomplished perfectly.
Monarchy ? Hmmmm, so how many campaign volunteers will we need for that one ! ? Will find them :-)
'Hatter'

Here you can see that Torrey refers to himself as "Hatter," a.k.a., the Mad Hatter. He would go on in plenty of other e-mails to refer to Hillary as "A" or "Our Queen," and... as the threads began to emerge, look increasingly involved with human trafficking, which I would cover extensively,[44] and in great detail on my site.

It's no coincidence that Torrey would choose the names of *Alice in Wonderland* characters to refer to himself and others. Many of my longtime readers already know that not only is *Alice in Wonderland* often referenced in MKUltra mind control materials (think "white rabbits'), but that it has a long association with pedophilia, as its author, Lewis Carrol, was obsessed with the young Alice Liddell, for whom he wrote the novel.

---

44   https://www.neonrevolt.com/2018/09/01/catching-up-with-newq-the-59-drop-mega-post-qanon-great-awakening-neonrevolt/

And yes, that is them photographed together, here. And as you can plainly see, Alice hasn't even hit puberty, yet. Carroll would often take photographs of Alice, and even at one point took completely nude photographs of her sister, Lorina Liddell (which some speculate to be the cause of his falling out of favor with the Liddell family). Throughout his life, Carroll would go on to make many sketches and take many photos of many young girls, including nude photos of the five-year-old Beatrice Hatch. He was able to do this with the full knowledge of these girls' parents, because, well, it was a bit of a naive time and this kind of sexualization, let alone of children, didn't even enter into people's minds as a possibility. If anything, the nudity of a child was seen as more cherubic than sexual. But I think it's clear that Carroll didn't quite see it that way, and used this as a cover for his own ends. I would cover this all[45] extensively on my site as well.

However, my larger point here is that there's something of a history here, with the terminology at play and the kinds of things it insinuates. So when Anons started digging into these e-mails, the different people it involved, and following the trail of bodies... it became clear to Anons that Torrey was the point man for whatever trafficking operation the Clinton Foundation was wrapped up in. And they were more than happy to have Saudi Arabia, with all its oil money, and all its human "capital," on board with their little smuggling operation.

---

45   https://www.neonrevolt.com/2018/09/03/open-season-for-white-rabbits-qanon-greatawakening-mkul-tra-pizzagate-pedogate-nomore-neonrevolt/

Which is why Trump had to negotiate with the Saudis first. That's when the sword dance caught the Cabal off-guard. That's when Prince Al-Waleed was imprisoned, had his assets frozen, and was subjected to "Saudi justice." That's why the Cabal tried to wage a counter-attack at Las Vegas. And that's why, once that huge flow of dark money was cut off, Huma Abedin was reduced to laundering money and shoving bodies down garbage chutes with the help of El Chapo's wife. And it's exactly why no Cabal-affiliated politician will *ever* support Trump's effort to build the southern border wall. They *want* to keep the drugs flowing so that they can keep the flow of dark money going (not to mention the human trafficking, the flow of children, and the flow of terrorists across the border). They are literal traitors who would rather malign the wall and all who support it as "racist" just so they can continue to line their own pockets.

Step back in time for a moment and realize the different elements Trump had to balance here. Trump had to not only align the US with the correct faction inside Saudi Arabia, but give them a way to modernize and maintain order. That's why he's allowing Saudi oil companies on to US stock exchanges now—because, in all honesty, Saudis need to wean themselves off oil. Their reserves are dwindling and other nations are surpassing them in oil production. Their bread and butter for the past hundred years is growing stale, and the Saudis know this. This is why the new Saudi regime was more than happy to negotiate with Trump.

It's also why the Deep State "murdered" Jamal Khashoggi at the Saudi Arabian consulate in Constantinople. In truth, there are a lot of theories still flying around about this, but predominantly, it looks like Khashoggi was "murdered" in order to use it as an excuse to remove Saudi Prince Mohammad bin Salman (Trump's ally) from power in Saudi Arabia, and allow the Al-Waleed-backed faction to regain power. Many Anons don't even think Khashoggi was even really murdered, but that, as a long-time Cabal operative, he was merely playing a role in order to help the Cabal get back in power. People forget that Khashoggi had numerous ties to the Muslim Brotherhood and had direct ties to Osama bin Laden, going back all the way to the time when he was embedded with the Mujahideen.

In other words: don't buy the hype surrounding Khashoggi. Whether his death was faked, or he was unwittingly murdered by a faction inside the Saudi government looking to restore power to the House of Saud, there was *much* more going on behind the scenes than anyone in the MSM let on. It was really more of a way to try and force Trump and a powerful ally against the Cabal apart than it was about supporting a poor, murdered "journalist."

But Hillary wasn't the only person visiting "Wonderland" during this time. No, Obama would be in a "Wonderland" of his own, when, in 2009, he and Michelle threw a lavish Wonderland-themed party at the White House. Most of the talent behind the 2010 live-action film adaptation would be there, including the director, Tim Burton, Johnny Depp in full Mad Hatter garb, and Mia Wasikowska as her titular (if consistently boring) interpretation of Alice. Other Hollywood figures were reportedly in attendance, and a band dressed up as skeletons provided the music for the evening.

No one, save those in attendance (and, of course, military intelligence), really knows what exactly happened at that party that evening, but whatever happened, it was enough for the Obamas to want to keep it secret for at least several years. It wasn't until pictures were leaked online that they were forced to admit that, yes, in the depths of the Great Recession, they had thrown this lavish party with Hollywood elites and kept it hidden from the public for years. And even though visitor logs were open for the public to query online, many of the guest's names were simply kept off the register that evening, or they were signed in under a single name. We'd later see this pattern repeated when, for instance, Loretta Lynch would visit Obama in the White House, signing in under the name "Elizabeth Carlisle" (a pseudonym she would repurpose over the years for a variety of activities she wished to conceal), to once again obscure the fact that they were colluding in secret.

But for whatever reason… the "most transparent administration in history" wanted to hide this party… and for "good" reason, I think.

But before we dig in to the particulars, just keep in mind, it's hard to know where exactly to begin when you're dealing with a total fraud, because so much of what we think we know about them is the result of systematic deception. Add Deep State handlers, intelligence agencies, and an entire media apparatus dedicated to perpetuating the fraud into the mix, and now you have weaponized deception on a scale the likes of which the world has never seen before. Which is to say, almost everything you think you know about Barack Hussein Obama is a lie. Far from the reserved, elegant, even stoic image he protects, the man is quite the degenerate.

Take, for instance, the photo of Obama that was suppressed for thirteen whole years; a photo of the then senator Obama and Nation of Islam hate-preacher, Louis Farrakhan. The photo was taken in 2005 at a congressional Black Caucus lunch, and it never once saw the light of day during either of Obama's presidential campaigns. Lucky for him, too, since Louis Farrakhan's Nation of Islam group literally preaches that all white people are a race of devils created by a rogue scientist named "Yakub," who then began murdering black babies as a sort of eugenics program, in order to replace them with white babies, until the "white race" was established and able to live on its own.

In other words, it's not just regular death cult Islam. It's retarded death cult Islam by way of L. Ron Hubbard. Search for a "picture" of "Yakub" sometime if you want a good laugh. Why yes, he is the one with the massively disproportionate noggin!

In truth, there's much Obama has kept hidden over the years, from the identity of his true father, to his birth certificate, to his actual nationality, to his religious and ideological sympathies, and as you'll recall from the earlier Q drop, the photo evidence of his arms trip to Pakistan, as well. But that's not nearly the end of it.

Obama's got a lot of secrets, frankly.

For instance, his kids.

By which I mean "his" kids.

After spending eight years in the White House, the American public are very familiar with the former first family by this point. We watched both Sasha and Malia grow up before our eyes. And some noticed even whispered through hushed tones (because what they were about to say wasn't even remotely politically correct)… that neither of the girls really looked like either of their parents. Why, they don't even look much like *each other*, let alone Barack or Michelle. So… where did they come from?

Well, the explanation for that is simple, really. They are not Obama's biological daughters. My longtime readers will have undoubtedly already encountered this fact in the article I wrote[46] a very long time ago, but for everyone else joining us now, you have to *really* understand what I'm saying here. Obama was something of a Manchurian candidate. As such, he was groomed from a very young age to climb the political ladder and one day, take his seat on the "throne" of the US, in order to guide it towards its final destruction—a task which he very nearly succeeded at.

But in order to advance along the way, deception was needed at every interval to cultivate an image that would be accepted by a critical mass of the American public. And the person in charge of helping pass off this deception was Obama's Deep State handler: Iranian Communist Valerie Jarrett. So if, for instance (as its often rumored) Obama is homosexually inclined, well… how would you, as a handler, deal with it? You know you've got to get this guy into office at some point, but it's the late 80s, and *Will and Grace* hadn't sufficiently demoralized the population into mass homosexual acceptance, yet. What do you, as a Deep State handler, do?

To answer that question, we must first ask another:

Was Joan Rivers just joking around, or was she actually telling the truth?

What do I mean by that?

Allow me to set the stage:

After officiating an impromptu gay wedding in 2014 at one of her book signings in New York, Joan Rivers (who, yes, was an ordained minister in the "Universal Life Church," *whatever that is*) was asked by a paparazzi if she thought there would ever be a gay president in the White House. Rivers responded:

"Well, we already have it with Obama, so let's just calm down."

Pause.

"You *know* Michelle is a tranny."

---

46   https://www.neonrevolt.com/2018/04/07/sasha-and-malia-obama-really-barack-and-michelles-kids/

"I'm sorry, a what?" asked the bewildered pap.

"A transgender. We *all* know. Oh gosh. It's okay. She does…"

Rivers would trail off, shaking her head as new people approached to greet her. The paparazzi were left standing quite speechless as Joan continued into the building, and despite how the media at the time spun the incident (and continues to spin the incident), I believe that it is quite clear Rivers wasn't saying this for laughs. Gone was any hint that this was intended to be taken as a joke; and Rivers, a seasoned comedienne with decades of experience under her belt, didn't deliver it like one of her jokes. She wasn't laughing and neither was anyone else.

Well, maybe she was just being racist and bigoted, right? Maybe she was being a tone-deaf old lady? I find that doubtful, since Rivers had long approved of race-mixing and interracial marriages, and in this particular instance, had just officiated a gay wedding. No, I think Rivers knew she was crossing an invisible boundary of some sort, but seemed to think that this "disclosure" was obvious and inevitable anyway, so it didn't matter if she blurted it out now.

Two months later, the normally vivacious Joan Rivers would be dead following a heart attack. Years later, Joan's daughter, Melissa Rivers, would like this comment underneath one of her Instagram posts:

 melissariversofficial liked your comment: I'm convinced Obama had Joan killed for speaking the truth. 16h

So was Joan telling a joke? Did she just coincidentally die of a heart attack after this appearance? Or was she telling the world something the Cabal deemed it wasn't ready yet to hear? You should watch the clip, but I'll leave it up to you to decide for yourself what you believe on this point—especially as more information continues to come to light. I'll only add that we've already seen stranger things turn out to be true, and if Joan Rivers was telling the truth that day, it certainly explains a lot of what follows.

If you've ever stopped and wondered why "transgender acceptance" has been pushed so aggressively in the mainstream over the past several years, understand that it largely originated from the Obama White House. It's all part of a psyop, and it's no coincidence programs like "Drag Queen Story Hour" for kids cropped up at taxpayer-funded public libraries across the nation during the Obama administration. This has also given rise to the "drag kid" phenomenon, where we've seen multiple instances of young boys being paraded around in wigs, makeup, and dresses; made to perform for money at gay bars and pose with drag queens wearing nothing other than, frankly, merkins to cover their genitals. It's been said that so-called "transkids" or "drag kids" are like vegan cats. Everyone knows who's really making the decisions, there. And we Anons have even watched in horror as one such drag kid, who goes by the brand/moniker of "Desmond is Amazing," got interviewed by former "Club Kid" Michael Alig on his YouTube channel.

For those who don't know, Alig was basically a "professional partier" in New York during the late 80s and early 90s. Following an argument about drug debts, and high on god knows what himself, Alig would kill another "Club Kid" named Angel Melendez back in 1996. After storing the body under ice cubes in his bathtub for a while, it started to stink and Alig and his roommate decided they needed to find a way to dispose of it. Alig agreed to dismember the body, hacking off various limbs and throwing them into garbage bags before pitching everything into the Hudson river. And he did this in exchange for ten bags of heroin.

Alig would go on to brag about how he had gotten away with murder, and how he had chopped someone up and thrown them in the river at the various club events he oversaw, but due to his personality, everyone who heard his tale thought he was joking. Melendez was marked as missing, and Alig thought he had gotten away with it… But then some children found a leg on a beach somewhere, and soon, other body parts started turning up. Alig was soon caught despite fleeing the city, and jailed for seventeen years for manslaughter. But now he's out… and interviewing "drag kids" on YouTube. And everyone wants to pretend this is the new normal, instead of the dystopian nightmare it actually is, ushered in under Obama's watch.

Folks, *Will and Grace* was just slightly over a decade ago. The slippery slope is very real, and very dangerous, and what you have all witnessed over the course of the Obama administration was very much an organized, Deep State operation geared towards pushing "pedophilia acceptance" into the mainstream. After all, the same arguments can be made for pedophilia as can be made with just about any other "orientation." You can say that it used to be listed in the DSM (the manual of mental disorders published by the American Psychiatric Association). Just like how homosexuality used to be criminalized, pedophilia advocates will argue that their attraction is "natural," and thus, should be accepted by everyone. "Times change," they'll say, and we all need to become more "accepting." That's really just equivocation on their part, by the way, whereby they purposefully confuse the definition of "natural" and "good," and thus, commit the naturalistic fallacy. Plenty of things happen in the natural world which are not good. It's our job, as human beings, to pursue the good; to listen to our better angels. The only alternative is to let unbridled hungers and bestial impulses take control, to the degradation of ourselves and others.

But the question in all of this then becomes. "Why would the Obama administration be pushing this so aggressively?"

Once again, I'm getting ahead of myself… We still have to talk about "Obama's" kids, first.

Malia Ann Nesbitt was born on July 4, 1998, and is, in all likelihood, the first daughter of Dr. Anita Blanchard and Martin Nesbitt. The official story is that Dr. Blanchard was the OB-GYN who delivered Malia during Michelle's pregnancy, but in fact, I believe this is a carefully crafted cover story. In truth Nesbitt, Blanchard, and the Obamas go back a very long way, even generationally, and they've gone to exceptional lengths to obfuscate the true nature of this relationship.

For instance, during Obama's campaigns, Martin Nesbitt was his campaign treasurer. He currently runs the Obama foundation, and also worked at the Chicago Housing Authority, where Valerie Jarrett's grandfather had presided years earlier, and where Jarrett herself was known, given her role in the disastrous Habitat Company slums.

The nexus of connections only grows as Blanchard was one of two medical students at the University of Chicago Medical Center taken under the wing of Dr. James Bowman in Chicago (the other being Dr. Eric Whitaker, another personal friend of Obama's). And if the name Dr. Bowman sounds familiar, good… because that's Valerie Jarrett's father.

Natasha "Sasha" Nesbitt would follow Malia three years later, being born on June 10, 2001, with the delivery once again "officially" overseen by Blanchard. Notably, there are no photos of Michelle Obama ever being pregnant, but furthermore, there are no birth records for Sasha or Malia "Obama," which is odd… because those would be a matter of public record. Both Nesbitt and Blanchard would be made Sasha and Malia's "godparents," at least on paper, and would often accompany the Obamas on their vacations to Hawaii, always in close proximity to the girls.

If this sounds unbelievable, I would encourage my readers to seek out photos of the girls and compare them to photos of Blanchard and Nesbitt. Once again, your eyes will not deceive you. The relation couldn't be more striking. Sasha is a dead-ringer for Blanchard, and Malia looks exactly like Nesbitt, right down to a shared, awkward gait. And just to be one hundred percent clear on this matter, I'm not going after the girls when I say all these things. Frankly, they'd be the victims in all this, and I'm not sure they're even aware of what's going on. If you were raised your whole life to believe someone was your parent when they really weren't, well, you'd be the one being lied to; not telling the lies. If anything, this is more a condemnation of their natural parents as well as their unnatural ones.

But if you think this is where it ends, no... it's about to get much worse. For in the wake of the crash at the Standard Hotel, and the leader of NXIVM being arrested (along with his second-in-command, TV actress Allison Mack), Mack began to sing like a...

Q !xowAT4Z3VQ ID: 382d04 No.1117177   **1202**
Apr 20 2018 13:45:12 (EST)

41A7C496-2188-4AA3-85AE-80....png

Canary. That's a Canary Palm.
(Don't worry, we Anons didn't quite catch that one at the time, either.)

Q !xowAT4Z3VQ ID: 948590 No.1121272   **1203**
Apr 20 2018 19:30:58 (EST)

Mack is naming names.
Big names in H-Wood / Gov't (local/federal).
Proof.
The 'Standard' Hotel.
Helicopter crash.
All related.
Future will prove past.
AS.
Feeling ok today?
Why is the MX border / Long Beach Port so important?
Tick TOCK (LLC).
Q

After this, Q would post this photo, soon confirming the name of the girl as "Wendy."

And almost instantly, after posting this photo, the 8chan research boards came under the heaviest DDOS attack it had seen to date, crashing the site for some time. Whatever we had just seen… it was clear someone else didn't want us seeing it. And for good reason.

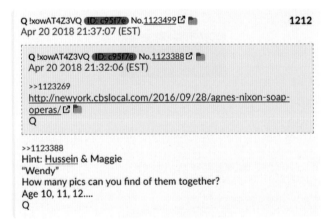

The girl's real name is Maggie Nixon. She's the daughter of director Robert Nixon and Sarah Thorsby Guinan Nixon. She's also the granddaughter of serial soap opera creator, Agnes Nixon, and has since become an actress herself, but before that time… she was Obama's personal plaything.

"Wendy" was just his "pet name" for her.

Anons soon found the source for the image Q had posted, and in fact, it came from her mother's Facebook profile. But the caption with the photo revealed more than perhaps even Anons were prepared for. While visiting the family's restaurant in Martha's Vineyard, Obama asked twelve-year-old Maggie what she liked:

Sarah Guinan Nixon
October 25, 2014 · 🌐   ···

Cleaning & just found this gem taken at the Beach Plum a few years ago:

Inside the President asked Mrs. Nixon's 12-year-old daughter for advice on the menu. "Maggie, what do you like?" he had asked. She responded: "I like horseback riding," which drew laughter from both families.

👍 206   14 Comments 1 Share

👍 Like ↪ Share

"Horseback riding."

In all likelihood, a despicable euphemism.

Anons were about as floored, as you could imagine (as I'm sure many who are reading this for the first time are). But Q would go on to point us towards this Instagram post in particular, showing us a picture of Maggie and Obama together when she was just ten years old:

>>1123519
Open source.
Q

And yes, in case you're wondering, this ties directly back in to Pizzagate, and directly to Comet Ping Pong owner, James Alefantis, who is posing here with Maggie's mom, Sarah:

>>1124212
You can't imagine the size of this.
Conspiracy risk.
Planned for later.
Q

Maggie would go on to grow up into an adult, but along the way, Anons noticed a number of disturbing posts in her social media history, including reposts of bloody writing on walls, similar to the "spirit cooking" photos we saw earlier. And if you're paying close attention, a very contentious movie just took home "Best Picture" at the Oscars this year. The movie is entitled *Green Book*, and despite *Roma* being the crowd-favorite (and Netflix bribing nearly everyone in the Academy), *Green Book* beat it out, I believe, for one simple reason: Maggie Nixon had a very small role in the film as a coat check girl. It was her first real role in anything, ever, and I believe the Oscar was given to the film in order to let her know that those with power, those with "control" and "influence" would be able to elevate her status… if only she just kept her mouth shut and played along, despite the newly heightened scrutiny from Anons on all sides.

At the premiere of *Green Book*, Nixon would walk the red carpet arm in arm with actress Lauren Hutton, who some Anons believed to be Nixon's handler. The two go back at least nine years, to when Maggie was still a pre-teen. The pair would also be photographed embracing at the seventeenth-annual *Knock-Out Abuse Against Women* fundraiser at the Washington, DC, Ritz-Carlton, in 2010.

A sadly ironic event for the two to be attending together, it seems.

But this leads one to an unavoidable question. The private Wonderland party at the White House: to this day we don't know everyone who was in attendance.

Was Maggie Nixon there?

Is this where Obama and Nixon first made contact?

Is this where she was first offered to Obama?

Or was there someone else there, someone else being offered up to satisfy the insatiable lusts of this megalomaniacal Manchurian candidate?

You have to remember: this all points back to Obama being a controlled puppet, groomed from his youth to play a certain role, at a certain time, to accomplish a certain goal. And that should *terrify* every American citizen, because if the president wasn't really the one in control of the nation… who was?

I think it's become staggeringly clear to everyone by now that both Obama and Hillary were two treasonous peas in a pod, brought together by circumstance and through the influence of various factions inside the Cabal, to perpetrate the greatest crimes ever seen in the history of America; perhaps even in the history of the world. It's also become appallingly clear that they were not working alone, but were supported at every stage by an entrenched political class which had as its goal, not the advancement of the American people, but the utter ruination and destruction of millions of lives, both domestic and abroad. These are criminals of the highest order, and there will come a time when we'll need to invent a new word for "treason" because "treason" will not cover the size and scope of the evil these individuals had hoped to accomplish.

So with that, I want us to return to the most important Qdrop from earlier, and pick up where we left off, knowing what we know now.

This won't require nearly as much "translation."

Q !UW.yye1fxo No.47 ⧉ 📄   **570**
Jan 21 2018 14:06:20 (EST)

Will SESSIONS drop the hammer?
1 of 22.
#Memo shifts narrative.
#Memo reinstates SESSIONS' authority re: Russia/ALL.
#Memo factually demonstrates collusion at highest levels.
#Memo factually demonstrates HUSSEIN ADMIN weaponized
INTEL community to ensure D victory [**+insurance**].
#Memo factually demonstrates 'knowingly false intel' provided to
FISA Judges to obtain warrant(s).
THEY NEVER THOUGHT SHE WOULD LOSE.
[**The 16 Year Plan To Destroy America**]
Hussein [**8**]
Install rogue_ops
Leak C-intel/Mil assets
Cut funding to Mil
Command away from generals
Launch 'good guy' takedown (internal remove) - Valerie Jarrett
(sniffer)
SAP sell-off
Snowden open source Prism/Keyscore (catastrophic to US Mil v. bad
actors (WW) +Clowns/-No Such Agency)
Target/weaken conservative base (IRS/MSM)
Open border (flood illegals: D win) ISIS/MS13 fund/install (fear,
targeting/removal, domestic-assets etc.)
Blind-eye NK [**nuke build**]
[**Clas-1, 2, 3**]
Blind-eye Iran [**fund and supply**]
Blind-eye [**CLAS 23-41**]
Stage SC [AS [**187**]]
U1 fund/supply IRAN/NK [**+reduce US capacity**]
KILL NASA (prevent space domination/allow bad actors to take
down MIL SATs/WW secure comms/install WMDs) - RISK OF EMP
SPACE ORIG (HELPLESS)
[**CLAS 1-99**]
HRC [**8**] WWIII [**death & weapons real/WAR FAKE &
CONTROLLED**][**population growth control/pocket billions**]
Eliminate final rogue_ops within Gov't/MIL
KILL economy [**starve/need/enslave**]
Open borders
Revise Constitution
Ban sale of firearms (2nd amen removal)
Install 'on team' SC justices> legal win(s) across spectrum of
challengers (AS 187)
Removal of electoral college [**pop vote ^easier manipulation/illegal
votes/Soros machines**]
Limit/remove funding of MIL
Closure of US MIL installations WW [**Germany 1st**]
Destruction of opposing MSM/other news outlets (censoring), CLAS
1-59
[]
Pure EVIL.
Narrative intercept [**4am**].
Sessions/Nunes Russian OPS.
Repub distortion of facts to remove Mueller.[**POTUS free pass**].
Shutdown Primary Reasons.
Distract.
Weaken military assets.
Inc illegal votes.
Black voters abandoning.
"Keep them starved"
"Keep them blind"
"Keep them stupid"
HRC March 13, 2013 [**intercept**].
The Great Awakening.
Fight, Fight, Fight.
Q

And I want us to start at this section:

HRC **[8]** WWIII **[death & weapons real/WAR FAKE & CONTROLLED][population growth control/pocket billions]**
Eliminate final rogue_ops within Gov't/MIL
KILL economy **[starve/need/enslave]**
Open borders
Revise Constitution
Ban sale of firearms (2nd amen removal)
Install 'on team' SC justices> legal win(s) across spectrum of challengers (AS 187)
Removal of electoral college **[pop vote ^easier manipulation/illegal votes/Soros machines]**
Limit/remove funding of MIL
Closure of US MIL installations WW **[Germany 1st]**
Destruction of opposing MSM/other news outlets (censoring), CLAS 1-59
[]
Pure EVIL.

The goal was not just staging a nuclear war, but weakening the US throughout the course of Obama's presidency, in order to put us at a profound disadvantage in the ensuing war that they themselves not only staged, but profited from, leading to the wholesale slaughter of millions and the collapse of the free world.

Opening the borders was meant to erode the identity and social cohesion built up by generations of heroic Americans in the past. They would remove the few remaining protections enshrined in the Constitution by illegally stacking the Supreme Court with their puppets. Their primary targets would be removing the Second Amendment and abolishing the electoral college. In other words, they would remove the ability of the average citizen to resist their tyrannical hegemony by removing these protections "legally." And they would accomplish this by any means possible—even if it meant assassinating more current justices, just as they had done to Justice Scalia at that ranch down in Texas.

Ginsburg, Sotomayor, and Kagan are of course still, as of this writing, on the Supreme Court bench. But I believe they will all be implicated in scandals which will force their resignations, and possibly even their arrests—except perhaps in the case of Ginsburg, who agreed to trade her seat on the bench to Lynch. She may very well die of health-related issues, first. You might even see one more judge go down in all of this, but I'll withhold my speculation on that subject for the time being…

The other ways in which Hillary was specifically tasked with weakening us would be the closure of US military bases, and making sure the military was underfunded. She never got a chance to accomplish this, and you'll recall, one of the first things Trump ensured passed when he got in to office was the single largest military spending bill the world had ever seen. And though "fiscal conservatives" shrieked at the receipt, the reason for such a bill was very simple: Trump had to undo eight years of intentional sabotage in a very short time, in order to create a significant-enough deterrent against military action by the Cabal, by promising, in return, mutually assured destruction. In other words, if the Cabal decided to suddenly lash out through one of their proxy states in desperation, Trump had to make sure we were able to return the favor.

There was also the issue of securing the border by building the wall. Trump knew he was never going to get direct funding for it by the Cabal-aligned traitors in Congress, so he leveraged the military's massive funding for that project, behind their backs, allowing Congress to think they had him hamstrung for the better part of two years, in order to get it done. By leveraging the Army Corp of Engineers to build the wall, Trump could sidestep his Cabal-backed opposition in Congress. Meanwhile, all the "fiscal conservatives" howled at the omnibus spending bill, not realizing, once again, what it really was: leverage. And leverage to protect American citizens, at that.

Honestly, it's that failure to think ahead, to think in terms of assets and leverage (and subsequently hiding behind the cover of "conservative principles") that has led to so much conservative failure over the years. Trump doesn't think that way, and thank God!

Q goes on to inform us that the censorship of the news media would continue. In other words, anyone who didn't toe the 4:00 a.m. Mockingbird line would be shut down. Think alternative media. Q tells us there were at least fifty-nine outlets being targeted for attack. Think online outlets which get demonized as "fake news," when often they are the only ones reporting on the genuine issues of our time. Think Facebook, Twitter, and Google censorship. Think deplatforming by tech companies. If they couldn't shut the sites down, they'd limit and contain their reach.

After a short section about the talking points the Cabal sent out that morning to all their Mockingbird outlets, Q finally ends the drop by focusing on a quote from a private speech Hillary gave on March 13th, 2013.

This speech was captured by military intelligence. In it, she said:

> "Keep them starved"
> "Keep them blind"
> "Keep them stupid"

Now you see why Q called this "Pure EVIL."

Now you understand the stakes at play, and the systems of control at work.

Now you understand how close to the brink we came and why so many patriots and Anons have been fighting this battle, and following QAnon all along. The process of "Awakening" hasn't been easy. In fact, for some of us, it's been the hardest task we've ever undertaken. But once you know, you can't go back to a state of ignorance, even if you wanted to. Deep down inside, we knew this work would be necessary. If ever there was to be a hope for peace and prosperity in this nation again, this Q-project, whatever it really was, was it. It's why I've written this book, and created countless articles, posts, videos, infographics, and memes for this effort.

In truth, there are others who have been "awake" longer than even we Anons, and those who have undertaken greater tasks, and even greater responsibilities. For President Trump, his "awakening" began after an incredible tragedy… The loss of his dear friend:

Q !xowAT4Z3VQ **ID: a0205a** No.952914 🔗 📷   **1082**
Apr 8 2018 13:15:14 (EST)

POTUS & JFK JR.
Relationship.
Plane crash 1999.
HRC Senate 2000.
The "Start."
Enjoy the show.
Q

It feels almost *wrong*, trying to bring up the topic of JFK Jr. here and now. What can I say about the man? He grew up in the spotlight, perhaps most remembered in that iconic image of him saluting his father's casket while only just a boy. And while he tried to differentiate himself from his father, in truth, he was cut from the same cloth, which sadly, also seemed to tie him to a similar fate.

While he was alive, I imagine that as an extremely wealthy and famous man living in New York, it was genuinely hard to find someone to commiserate with; someone at your level who wasn't after you for your wealth, trying to weasel their way in to your good graces, or, as we've seen, who wasn't trying to drag you into the world of the Cabal. I think, for that reason alone, Trump and JFK Jr. found a certain kind of camaraderie. But it's clear that over the years, their appreciation for each other grew exponentially. It's why, when asked if he would ever run for president, Kennedy knew enough to say,

"I think you should be asking those questions of Donald."

Oh, to have been a fly on the wall during any of their conversations! And you just have to wonder what these men, one the son of a president, and the other, a future president, were talking about. Doubtless, the subjects we're talking about now must have come up between the two at some point during their friendship. And JFK Jr. was certainly no fan of Cabal mainstays, such as-Senator Biden (who would later, obviously, become Obama's vice president). The FBI would go on to save one particular letter he wrote to Biden, in which JFK Jr. would explode:

Reference: **Evidence received September 8, 1994**

Your No.

Re: **UNSUB; aka John F. Kennedy, Jr.;**
        SENATOR JOSEPH BIDEN - VICTIM;
        August 26, 1994; Worcester, MA;
        AFO; CCSCAKA;

        OO: BOSTON

Specimens received: Personally delivered by Special Agent ▮▮▮▮▮   b7C
                        on September 8, 1994
Specimens:

Q1   Envelope postmarked "WORCESTER MA 016 PM 26 AUG
       1994," bearing the handwritten/hand printed address
       "Sen. Joseph Biden (D.-Delaware) U.S. Capitol
       Building U.S. Senate Washington, D.C. 20515"

Q2   Accompanying handwritten/hand printed letter dated
       8/26/94, beginning "Dear Sen. Biden: You are a
       traitor ...," and bearing the signature "John F.
       Kennedy Jr."

It's one thing to come to this kind of knowledge through intense study and research. It's another thing to *live* through it all, and have members of your family murdered by the Cabal—especially at a time when they had total control over the media. You would think, at the very least, Trump would have asked why JFK Jr. would name his magazine *George*—a point of heavy speculation among the "conspiracy" community for a very long time, given all the speculation surrounding George Bush Sr.'s involvement in his father's assassination.

So when the news finally broke on July 17, 1999, that Jr's plane was missing, President Trump must have known that there was a cover-up right away. Given their many years of friendship, and the private conversations they had together, Trump must have also known that Jr. was debating running for NY Senate the following year. Early polling showed him as a favorite of the people, and though he hadn't formally announced his candidacy yet, he undoubtedly would have discussed it with his close friend.

The only problem was the woman who would have been running against him: Hillary Clinton. And while some may object to this interpretation of events, citing that JFK Jr. had been injured and that he was flying an aircraft he wasn't familiar with at night, with Q's confirmation on this subject, we can now say with certainty that it's simply not true; that Clinton arranged for his plane to be taken down by some clandestine means. We spoke earlier of the CIA's ability to take remote control of cars, in order to crash them and perform remote assassinations. We also spoke of Rep. Hale Bogg's plane going down over Alaska during the Warren Commission, and even how the woman who "signed off" on Obama's birth certificate was the only one who died following the crash of the Cessna in which she was flying. In fact, Q would confirm across a number of drops what many had suspected for many years: that the Deep State has the ability to perform targeted assassinations by taking direct control of vehicles using classified technology. One such drop is captured below:

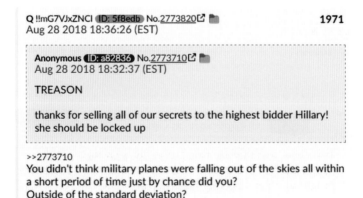

Q !!mG7VJxZNCl ID: 5f8edb No.2773820 1971
Aug 28 2018 18:36:26 (EST)

Anonymous ID: a82836 No.2773710
Aug 28 2018 18:32:37 (EST)

TREASON

thanks for selling all of our secrets to the highest bidder Hillary! she should be locked up

>>2773710
You didn't think military planes were falling out of the skies all within a short period of time just by chance did you?
Outside of the standard deviation?
Q

Q would also post this link to a declassified CIA document, cluing Anons in as to what this kind of system actually looked like:

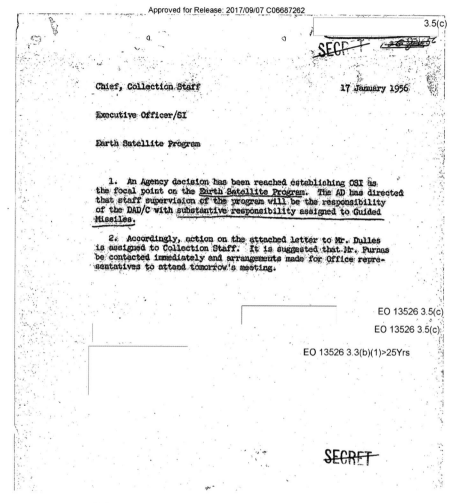

Does it sound like science fiction to you? Because this tech, if you'll look at the top right-hand corner of the declassified document, has been around since at least the fifties. Imagine what it looks like now, after almost seventy years of additional research and development!

Which is to say, the assassination of JFK Jr. was routine "wetwork" for the Cabal; a life snuffed out all so Hillary Clinton could advance her career, her eyes firmly set upon making her way up the ladder of power, until she finally ascended to the "throne," and sat in the White House once more. This time, in charge and ready to bring down the entire nation.

And no one who has really studied the Clintons should be too surprised that she would so quickly direct an assassination. Why, I would almost consider accusing those who are *still* unaware of the "Clinton Body Count" of choosing to remain in intentional ignorance, but given the role of the Mockingbird media, it's actually not surprising to see how many people still do not know about the multitude who have been "Arkancided" by this "power couple." When one sees, truly sees, how many bodies are piled around the Clintons for the first time, and hears the stories of how they all died, all doubt is removed. As such, I've included a link to an online infographic[47] detailing over one hundred and thirty such murders, in the footnotes of this chapter.

And while the Clintons may have seen fit to dispose of anyone in their way, Trump lost a close friend that day. For years, the man had been talking about running for president, running through the details and scenarios in his mind. Many of Trump's fans will recall the famous interview he gave to Oprah in 1988, where she questioned him on all sorts of policy issues and called his talk "presidential." Others will recall video of him walking the streets of New York during 9/11, and still others will recall 2011 polls showing him being the people's favorite for the then-upcoming 2012 election. In the meantime, he's running his businesses, hosting *The Apprentice*, and all the while building, iterating, and experimenting—perhaps most prominently with the then emerging platform called "Twitter," where he quickly became one of the most vocal voices calling for the release of Obama's birth certificate, what the media soon demeaned as "Birtherism," despite it being entirely correct, as we saw in Chapter Five.

In truth, since the loss of JFK Jr., Trump has been building his resources, his network, his skill set, and growing increasingly disgusted with the direction of the nation. People he had previously donated to, previously hobnobbed with, had killed his friend. Members of this same protected political class had effectively allowed the "bombing" of his city just two years later. It would take almost twenty years of work and planning—even cultivating an alter ego on TV so that his enemies would consistently underestimate him (something he would dramatically exploit, when Clinton decided to use him as a "pied piper" candidate, as revealed by leaked Clinton campaign documents) before he was finally ready to make his move, announcing his candidacy in 2015, right at the time it was needed most. For you'll recall, if the military did not have someone like Trump to back, someone who could win an honest-to-goodness Democratic election, not by cheating, not through force, but through sheer persuasive ability and perseverance, they would have launched a full-scale military coup, so as to prevent worldwide nuclear war.

And it's here the poem by the first-century poet Publilius Syrus springs to mind:

> Must I at length the Sword of Justice draw?
> Oh curst Effects of necessary Law!
> How ill my Fear they by my Mercy scan,
> **Beware the Fury of a Patient Man.**

Never forget: for POTUS, this is personal.

But I think it's become increasingly clear throughout all these pages that Trump could not have accomplished this all on his own. One man simply cannot take on the entirety of the Cabal by his lonesome. No, he needs a network of support, comprised of very talented individuals, all working in tandem to accomplish the same goal. He needs clever spies and hardened soldiers. He needs loyal allies in the media, and most importantly… he needs the best plan ever crafted by man.

---

47   https://www.neonrevolt.com/wp-content/uploads/2019/03/ClintonBodyCount.jpg

Q !UW.yye1fxo **ID: fb1a66** No.618344 ⟶ 🖼
Mar 10 2018 18:19:23 (EST)

937

GLIMPSE.
You cannot possibly imagine the size of this.
Trust the plan.
Trust there are more good than bad.
The WORLD is helping.
We are not alone.
We are all connected in this fight.
PATRIOTS UNITE.
We are winning BIG.
Watch the speech.
God bless.

"TRUST THE PLAN," Q would often admonish us. Frustrating as it was, knowing what we now knew (thanks to Q) we Anons didn't have much other choice. The only other choice, I suppose, was to tune out and drop out. Some did, but by and large, over the course of time, the movement only grew and grew as the news continued to reach more people, and people began to really comprehend the evil we were all up against.

The primary goal of the plan was to ensure the safety of as many innocent people as possible. This included neutralizing rogue states like North Korea and Iran, and making sure terror threats were mitigated from both domestic sources like MS-13, and from abroad, coming from groups like ISIS. The border needed to be secured. False Flag events needed to be anticipated and thwarted—like we saw in October 2018, where comically fake bombs were mailed to CNN, George Soros, the Clintons, and other Cabal figures, supposedly sent by a rabid Trump supporter who had been living out of his van. But again, the "bombs" looked like something out of a cartoon, and were never functional to begin with. The leading Anon theory on this particular event is that the "Trump supporter" involved was actually working on behalf of the Cabal as a kind of sleeper-asset (be it either through some kind of MKUltra conditioning, or as a clandestine agent), and was given all the trappings of the "crazy conspiracy nut"; most notably the "stickers" covering the windows of his van, which was supposed to look like a dirty collage of many stickers built up over years, but which were actually sheets of memes and stickers that had been assembled in an image editing program and printed out in large sheets at a printing facility, before being plastered to the inside of the windows, where they would fade uniformly during their exposure to the Florida sun. And then, of course, there was the "small" issue of the stamps on the packages not being franked by the Post Office, leading some to wonder if they had been sent through the US mail system at all.

If there were ever real explosives involved in this particular event, they never arrived at their intended targets. And that led Anons to consider either one of two possibilities: the bombs were replaced with duds by White Hats before going out, or this particular asset was a real idiot only looking to cause a stir, and not actually injure any of the targets. In other words, to make QAnon supporters look like deadly lunatics, instead of the eminently calm, rational, and utterly brilliant people we are!

Another part of the plan involved creating economic security. Our assets and resources had been drained on purpose for years. Our industries were still overseas. Our trade deficits were at all-time highs. That was ending the day Trump took office. But more than that, President Trump had to foster the economy to become so powerful, so strong, that it would be able to withstand any attack by the Cabal, and their trillions of assets.

Some might recall when, on February 2, 2018, the Cabal sent a message through the Stock Market, causing the Dow to drop down 666 points in one day. Yes, that was intentional (if a bit… cliché, what with that being the "Number of the Beast" and all that). The sell-off would continue on subsequent days as spooked investors scrambled for cover, and the Cabal attempted to crash our economy and plunge us back into recession:

Q !UW.yye1fxo **ID: 472124** No.275544 **666**
Feb 5 2018 12:16:50 (EST)

Why did the #Memo drop a Friday [& before the SB]?
Did this seem strange to you?
Watch the news.
Rothschild estate sale [Black Forest].
Stock market DIVE [666 - coincidence?].
Soros transfer of wealth.
Dopey FREED.
Marriage for POWER, not LOVE.
Hilton/Roth.
Soros/Clinton.
Etc.
News unlocks MAP.
Think Mirror.
Which team?
THEY don't know.
APACHE.
These people are EVIL.
Still don't believe you are SHEEP to them?
20/20 coming.
PUBLIC is VITAL.
RELEASE of INFO VITAL.
OUTRAGE.
JUSTICE.
Can we simply arrest the opposition w/o first exposing the TRUTH?
FOLLOW THE LIGHT.
Q

That wasn't the only tool of the Cabal to try and hamstring us all. The other major lever they had to play with was the Federal Reserve, that privately owned central bank which not only controls interest rates, but keeps us perpetually enslaved through debt, which we've talked about briefly in this book. When POTUS hung a picture of Andrew Jackson in the Oval Office, the message to the Cabal was clear. Jackson was the one who had killed the original iteration of the Federal Reserve in America, then called the Second Bank of the United States, by refusing to renew its charter. Said Jackson, at the time:

> Gentlemen! I too have been a close observer of the doings of the Bank of the United States. I have had men watching you for a long time, and am convinced that you have used the funds of the bank to speculate in the breadstuffs of the country. When you won, you divided the profits amongst you, and when you lost, you charged it to the bank. You tell me that if I take the deposits from the bank and annul its charter I shall ruin ten thousand families. That may be true, gentlemen, but that is your sin! Should I let you go on, you will ruin fifty thousand families, and that would be my sin! You are a den of vipers and thieves. I have determined to rout you out, and by the Eternal, **I will rout you out!**

This was a declaration of war against the Cabal of Jackson's day. And so, they responded accordingly, trying to assassinate him by hiring a man named Richard Lawrence to shoot Jackson in the streets of Washington, DC. Thankfully, the derringer Lawrence was carrying misfired, and Jackson subsequently beat the man to a bloody pulp with his cane, living up to his moniker of "Old Hickory." Lawrence had even tried to fire another derringer he was carrying, but miraculously this gun misfired as well! Still, this was the first ever assassination attempt against a US president. Jackson had only narrowly escaped, it seemed, thanks to divine providence. Though the wealthy (and heavily invested) members of the Senate voted to renew the bank's charter, Jackson, as was his constitutional right, vetoed the bill, and thus, preserved the Union for another generation.

Needless to say, Trump hanging that picture in his office was yet another declaration of war against the Cabal. And he doubled down on it when, in a meeting, Trump attacked on camera that other pillar of Cabal-control—the income tax. Trump very clearly stated that he would, ideally, like to run the country without an income tax at all; that it could be operated off the profits gained via tariffs, instead, like we did during McKinley's tenure in office:

> "President McKinley, who felt very, very strongly about this—the country was very, very successful; we actually operated out of cash flow, if you can believe it."

And so, it was a double-declaration of war, which QAnon would only confirm in his drops. The Cabal was scrambling, using whatever weapons they had within their reach to try and stop Trump. In this case, the Cabal would start to raise interest rates, which would have the effect of slowing down banks' ability to loan out cash, which would lead to a loss of liquidity in the broader markets, and grind things to a halt. Then, of course, they would blame Trump for "crashing" the economy—despite all he had done to bring back businesses, eliminate trade deficits, and create new jobs for Americans.

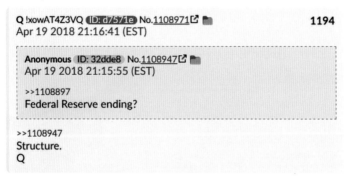

When asked point-blank what the plan to counteract this was, Q responded... well... I'll let you see for yourself:

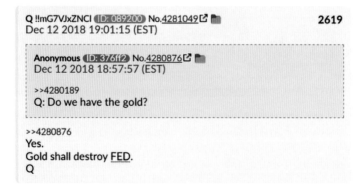

And furthermore:

(Personally, given some of the reading I've been doing, I think this restructuring will possibly be paired with some kind of digital, cryptographic asset; in other words, a kind of digital dollar. And I think it will be based off either the Ripple ecosystem, or something quite similar. But that is pure speculation on my part, and remains to be seen.)

The bigger point I'm trying to make here is that thankfully, due to the strategic economic policies implemented by the Trump administration, POTUS has now successfully mitigated the risk of financial collapse. With every passing day real jobs, real industries are returning to our shores; business is beginning to flourish again, and economic prosperity is returning to our people. The brilliant men and women working with POTUS have done everything they can to avert economic catastrophe at the hands of the Cabal, who wouldn't hesitate to make the masses suffer if it meant they retained control just a little while longer.

Beyond that, Trump was faced with the challenge of routing out entrenched corruption within our domestic agencies, our court system, and even entire branches of government. You may recall just how many Representatives and Senators refused to run for re-election during the 2018 mid-term cycle. That had everything to do with Trump and the Q initiative cleaning house from top to bottom. Slowly and surely, good men and women were installed into positions of authority, like Christopher Wray at the FBI, and Gina Haspel at the CIA. They began process of weeding out every embedded Cabal operative, from floor to ceiling. As Q would say in drop #577, the "7th Floor is no more."

Q !UW.yye1fxo **ID: 7f44ec** No.120050 🔗 📷   **577**
Jan 21 2018 21:22:07 (EST)

> Q !UW.yye1fxo **ID: 7f44ec** No.119877 🔗 📷
> Jan 21 2018 21:12:19 (EST)
>
> >>119769
> The flood is coming.
> Emails, videos, audio, pics, etc.
> FBI accidentally deletes texts?
> No Such Agency accidentally releases IT ALL>
> Shall we play a game?
> Q

>>119877
Expand your thinking.
Planned [3].
Moves and countermoves.
Strategy warfare.
This week will be revealing.
SNOW WHITE [1, 2, and 5] offline.
7th Floor is no more.
Just because you can't see it, doesn't mean BIG things aren't happening.
Night_Riders_FLY.
2018 will be GLORIOUS.
Q

Beyond that, election integrity was also key. Trump winning the Senate majority was absolutely key to making sure things moved forward "the easy way," so to speak. Election fraud was foiled in key states—particularly in Florida and Georgia—and I have a pretty good hunch we'll be seeing some big arrests from those areas in short order. And winning the Senate was doubly important, because this allowed the backlog of Trump appointees to begin being voted on again, whereas previously, many of these appointments were being dragged out in the senate by the likes of Dianne Feinstein, who was working overtime to prevent the news from coming out that she was not only one of the biggest leakers in the government, but had committed treason many times over on her various clandestine trips to China. In other words, she was trying to save her own sorry hide by making sure judges and other critical appointees wouldn't be confirmed. But now, with the majority firmly on the Republican side, she could no longer stall the confirmation processes in committee.

Q !!mG7VJxZNCl No.426 🗗 📰   2446
Nov 7 2018 02:06:39 (EST)

https://twitter.com/realDonaldTrump/status
/1060056007316045825 🗗 📰
The Senate was the target.
Corker + Flake removed.
How do you catch a FISH?
Mission forward.
These people are stupid.
Q

But the biggest part of the plan in all of this, the proverbial elephant in the room, was the Huber investigation. John Huber, Destroyer of Worlds, "Grand Inquisitor" of the God-Emperor himself (as I've often jokingly referred to him), with a battalion of four hundred and seventy investigators at his command, had been working on investigating all kinds of corruption throughout the US government. And as they did this, the sealed indictments started to pile up. On average, there's about a thousand federal sealed indictments at any given time, during any given year. But as Huber continued to work, his investigation dovetailing with a number of other simultaneous efforts and testimonies on various fronts, the sealed indictments began to pile higher and higher. Anons would track the numbers through PACER, the online database built by the court system, and compile statistics for each state. Soon, there were over twenty thousand sealed indictments on file. Then, thirty thousand. And forty thousand. As of this writing, there are over **ONE HUNDRED AND TWELVE THOUSAND** sealed indictments waiting to be unsealed in the US at this very moment, with more being added every single day.

The second those records are unsealed, the second the hammer drops, its open season on those named in those indictments. Police, government agents, and possibly even the military will be deployed to round up these evil-doers. At the same time, once they start going after the really big players, the National Guard and the Armed Forces will be deployed to strategic locations throughout the US in order to prevent unrest and rioting from those still asleep, those still in the dark who haven't quite processed the reality of all that's gone down, and who will inevitably lash out in anger and confusion.

But before that comes declassification—the ultimate flipping of the script. At this point, it will become known to the entire world who exactly signed and ordered the illegal spying operation, not just against Trump, but against all of Hillary's political opposition. The true face of the Deep State apparatus, leveraged by the Cabal to maintain their power and cover up their YEARS of crimes and criminal conspiracy, will be revealed to all. Trump ordered the total declassification of all the FISA documents in September 2018, but has had the Justice Department purposefully delay responding to the order in order to bide some time and to not interfere with the Mueller probe. Otherwise, Trump's foes could accuse him of meddling with the probe, and drag it all out even longer. But if the declassification comes after Mueller is done, well, there can be no interference. As Q has reminded us many, many times, "optics are important."

The FISA documents, when declassified, will reveal not only who signed off on the illegal spying on Trump (and other candidates), but who ordered it in the first place. And believe me when I say this goes straight to the top. In other words, we're talking treason at the highest levels of our government; something so terrible, so corrupt, it's never happened before in our history. (And as you've now seen, we've had some crazy history...

Which is exactly why we have to make sure it never happens again.

We have to make an example of these criminals, who not only plotted and schemed to undermine our democracy, but did so to cover up their own demonic death plots.

Which means... we need military tribunals.

Ordinary courts won't suffice for this. There are too many criminals in the court systems themselves, appointed by Cabal cronies like Obama. Tribunals will be the penultimate stage in getting our country back, and the worst of the lot will need to face execution for their crimes.

However, there's been some confusion over time since tribunals are almost never used against citizens... but this was why Senator Lindsay Graham's line of questioning during the confirmation hearings for Supreme Court Justice Brett Kavanaugh caused an outcry unlike anything we've heard since, well, since the lunatic Leftists shrieked in the streets at President Trump's inauguration:

> Graham: So when somebody says, post-9/11, that we'd been at war, and it's called the War on Terrorism, do you generally agree with that concept?
>
> Kavanaugh: I do, senator, because Congress passed the authorization for use of military force, which is still in effect. That was passed, of course, on September 14, 2001, three days later.
>
> Graham: Let's talk about the law and war. Is there a body of law called the law of armed conflict?
>
> Kavanaugh: There is such a body, senator.
>
> Graham: A body of law that's called basic criminal law?
>
> Kavanaugh: Yes, senator.
>
> Graham: Are there differences between those two bodies of law?
>
> Kavanaugh: Yes, senator.
>
> Graham: From an American citizen's point of view, do your constitutional rights follow you? If you're in Paris, does the Fourth Amendment protect you as an American from your own government?
>
> Kavanaugh: From your own government, yes.
>
> Graham: So, if you're in Afghanistan, do your constitutional rights protect you against your own government?
>
> Kavanaugh: If you're an American in Afghanistan, you have constitutional rights as against the US. government.
>
> Graham: Isn't there also a long settled law that goes back to the Eisentrager case (I can't remember the name of it)....
>
> Kavanaugh: Johnson v. Eisentrager.
>
> Graham: Right, that American citizens who collaborate with the enemy are considered enemy combatants?
>
> Kavanaugh: They can be, they're often, sometimes criminally prosecuted, sometimes treated in the military.
>
> Graham: Let's talk about can be. I think there's a Supreme Court decision that said that American citizens who collaborated with Nazi saboteurs were tried by the military, is that correct?

Kavanaugh: That is correct.

Graham: I think a couple of them were executed.

Kavanaugh: Yeah.

Graham: So, if anybody doubts there's a longstanding history in this country that your constitutional rights follow you wherever you go, but you don't have a constitutional right to turn on your own government and collaborate with the enemy of the nation. You'll be treated differently. What's the name of the case, if you can recall, that reaffirmed the concept that you can hold one of our own as an enemy combatant if they were engaged in terrorist activities in Afghanistan. Are you familiar with that case?

Kavanaugh: Yes, Hamdi [v. Rumsfeld].

Graham: **So the bottom line is on every American citizen know you have constitutional rights, but you do not have a constitutional right to collaborate with the enemy.** There is a body of law well developed long before 9/11 that understood the difference between basic criminal law and the law of armed conflict. Do you understand those difference?

Kavanaugh: I do understand that there are different bodies of law of course, senator.

In other words, if any politicians had worked with our enemies, they could be brought before a tribunal, far away from all their buddy judges in Washington, DC, and be handed sentences ranging from imprisonment, all the way to the death sentence. Washington, DC, insiders know this, and many of those who are most guilty have been scrambling for cover by announcing their own presidential campaigns—which is why, in particular, you see so many Democrats entering the race and announcing their candidacy in 2019.

You might even recall the Jussie Smollett scandal, which, as of this writing, is only a few weeks old. That was a false-flag event staged on behalf of Senator Kamala Harris (who also just so happens to be running for president right now), wherein she persuaded Smollett, an actor on the TV show *Empire*, to pretend he was attacked by two "MAGA-hat wearing racists," before having a noose tied around his neck, bleach poured over his body, and being told "This is MAGA country!"

At 2:00 a.m.

In the dead of winter.

In Chicago.

Smollett then went on the news and the Mockingbirds happily spun this narrative for weeks, until it all inevitably fell apart with police tracing the crime right back to Smollett himself, who, as it turned out, was actually stupid enough to have hired two extras from his TV show to stage the assault. Smollett also went the extra stupid mile, and paid his two accomplices with checks, leaving a nice paper trail for police to find later.

And so, his accomplices went to a hardware store, purchased all the necessary props for their scandal (where they were recorded by a security camera), and then they carried out the fake attack. Smollett would "escape," call the police, and when they showed up some forty-five minutes later, he was *still* wearing the prop noose around his neck. Meanwhile, Harris and Sen. Cory Booker had an "anti-lynching" bill circulating during this time, because look! Look at this hateful racist display that just happened in America! In *today's* America! Can you believe it?? No one should be lynched anymore, for *any* reason!

Not even treason!

Right guys?? *RIGHT!?!*

Twitter blew up with outrage from all the usual suspects, but anyone with a modicum of intelligence knew something else entirely was happening here. It should surprise no one that Smollett and Harris have a long history of "activism" together, and its easy to find pictures of them together collaborating on different projects throughout the years. The media was forced to address the issue just enough to cover up their complicity in the event, but dropped it down the memory hole as soon as they were able. Harris and Booker got their bill passed, and while I suppose their cervical vertebrae are safe (for now), it won't matter in the long run, because again...

Utah has firing squads.

Both of these traitors (and, "coincidentally" Presidential candidates) should have tried for an anti-firing squad bill instead. But I suppose it's harder for a D-list has-been actor (who is probably going to jail, and will never work again) to fake a convincing bullet wound.

So you see, because of the treason these people have committed, because of their allegiance to the Cabal, and because of their loss of power, they have done everything in their power to try and stop President Trump and the patriots surrounding him from holding them accountable for their evil deeds. They have collectively sold out our country to line their own pockets. They shipped jobs overseas, weakened our infrastructure, handed our military and industrial secrets to our enemies, and were complicit in a plot to bomb us into a new dark age. Moreover, due to their allegiances to their secret little death cult, they have not only "legally" enshrined a system of infant sacrifice throughout our country (in the form of the abortion industry) but they have tried to normalize pedophilia (through the media, in particular with Netflix at the vanguard of that push, and through the court system, with Supreme Court Justice Ruth Bader Ginsburg, who once proposed that the age of consent be twelve). Beyond that, many in the upper echelons of this death cult have literally raped, murdered, and consumed the flesh of children.

Q !UW.yye1fxo **ID: 071c71** No.564130 ☐ ▓   **855**
Mar 6 2018 01:29:38 (EST)

>>563781
1 of 5.
>>563824
2 of 5.
What if the steel used for military-grade projects was made-inferior
by our enemies as a method to weaken?
What if Hussein knew and authorized?
Renegade.
How many Marines volunteered to serve Hussein during his term?
Why?
What if his name we don't say organized the deal?
The US taxpayer subsidizes the WORLD.
AMERICA has been sold to the highest bidder.
AMERICA has been weakened on purpose.
The depths of their TREASON is unimaginable.
Pure EVIL.
HELL on earth - HRC victory.
Q

As Q said early on, their biggest fear is a public awakening. There will come a time when none of them will be able to walk down the street:

Q !UW.yye1fxo No.458 ☑ ▮   953
Mar 17 2018 14:03:41 (EST)

How bad is the corruption?
FBI (past/present)
#1
#1
#2
+29 (16)
DOJ (past/present)
#1
#1
#2
+18
STATE (past/present)
#1
#1
+41
Removal is the least of their problems.
Projection.
Russia>D/HRC
Twitter Bots>GOOG operated (not Russia)/Narrative & Political
SLANT
BIDEN / CHINA.
BIG DEVELOPMENT.
TRAITORS EVERYWHERE.
AMERICA FOR SALE.
FLYNN.
Targeted.
Why?
Who knows where the bodies are buried?
CLEARED OF ALL CHARGES.
TRUMP ADMIN v2?
Election theft.
Last hope.
Congressional focus.
Impeach.
They think you are STUPID.
They think you will follow the STARS.
They openly call you SHEEP/CATTLE.
THERE WILL COME A TIME NONE OF THEM WILL BE ABLE TO
WALK DOWN THE STREET.
BIGGEST FEAR.
PUBLIC AWAKENING.
Q

And this is where Anons factor into the picture. I said that Huber's role was the most important element in all of the plan, but that's actually debatable. The most important part of the plan was getting the people on board by exposing them to the raw truth of the situation; the same people who had been trapped in a matrix of finely crafted lies cultivated by the Cabal, all designed to keep them trapped as good little wage slaves on the tax farm—moderately contented (at least, until their final doom) by the media and the "bread and circuses" of the Cabal, but always controlled and never actually free. And the only way Q could get the people on board would be by leveraging the network effect.

To accomplish this, Q had to establish a backchannel where he could bypass the media and speak directly to Anons; to that hyper-intelligent dissatisfied lot who picked up on *everything*. Once Anons got the message, they could transmit it to others. They became "nodes" in a network. And if you know anything about networks, the more nodes a network has, the more resilient it becomes. Instead of having just one or two potential points of "failure," there were now thousands of nodes. If one dropped out for whatever reason, there were still thousands left to pick up the slack. And because Anons were, well, anonymous, the Mockingbirds didn't have a traditional enemy they could malign and attack. Anons were too "slippery," too amorphous, to be a good target. And inevitably, the message seeped into other networks; first Twitter and Facebook, and then through sites like my own, and into YouTube and out into the real world. Pretty soon, Q was everywhere, and the message was spreading like wildfire.

Which is again why, that day in June, Q would call us "the frame."

Q !CbboFOtcZs ID: 03ac69 No.1953310 ☑ ▦   **1644**
Jun 28 2018 23:59:18 (EST)

> Anonymous ID: ffd993 No.1952748 ☑ ▦
> Jun 28 2018 23:25:43 (EST)
>
> >>1952583
> I almost hope they don't ask. It would be fun to watch them try to manage the spin when 90% of the country is aware of you and all that you've been shining a light on, while the MSM still can acknowledge it.
> I can see them squirming now..

>>1952748
It must happen.
Conspiracy no more.
Think of every post made.
It would force us to prove everything stated to avoid looking crazy, correct?
What do they fear the most?
Public awakening.
If they ask.
They self destruct.
They know this is real.
See attacks.
The build is near complete.
Growing exponentially.
You are the frame.
You are the support.
People will be lost.
People will be terrified.
People will reject.
People will need to be guided.
Do not be afraid.
We will succeed.
Timing is everything.
Think Huber.
Think DOJ/FBI reorg.
Think sex/child arrests / news.
Think resignations (loss of control).
How do you remove evil in power unless you reveal the ultimate truth?
It must be compelling to avoid a divide (political attack/optics).
We are the majority (growing).
WW.
Sheep no more.
TOGETHER.
Q

So, now you know why so many Anons seemed so passionate, so radical, so dedicated—even impatient—in their efforts to overthrow the Cabal. To understand all this requires not only a dramatic shift in your thinking, but the ability to process all the emotions, the disgust, the fear, the dread, the paranoia, the righteous anger, the white-hot rage—to take all that, and transmute it into something positive. It's why the media has been in overdrive, trying to paint QAnon supporters as crazed lunatics, citing in particular, two false-flag events (one where a man stopped traffic on a dam, and the other, where a "QAnon supporter" stabbed his brother because he thought he was a "reptilian"). Real Anons believe that both of these were events set up by the Deep State, much like the "attacks" on Comet Ping Pong. We had a job to do, and the Cabal was doing everything it could to try and shut us down.

Now you see why I wrote this book.

Still, Anons were thankful to have some reassurances about the plan along the way. For instance, Q would update us that the Cabal's supply lines were being dismantled and destroyed:

Anonymous ID: grTMpzrL No.147452214 ⬀ ▮   **29**
Nov 1 2017 01:13:10 (EST)

Some things must remain classified to the very end. NK is not being run by Kim, he's an actor in the play. Who is the director? The truth would sound so outrageous most Americans would riot, revolt, reject, etc.
The pedo networks are being dismantled.
The child abductions for satanic rituals (ie Haiti and other 3rd world countries) are paused (not terminated until players in custody).
We pray every single day for God's guidance and direction as we are truly up against pure evil.

ANSWERS

And there were certain details we were privy to, early on:

Anonymous ID: pGukiFmX No.147567888 ⬀ ▮   **34**
Nov 1 2017 21:56:16 (EST)

Q Clearance Patriot

My fellow Americans, over the course of the next several days you will undoubtedly realize that we are taking back our great country (the land of the free) from the evil tyrants that wish to do us harm and destroy the last remaining refuge of shining light. On POTUS' order, we have initiated certain fail-safes that shall safeguard the public from the primary fallout which is slated to occur 11.3 upon the arrest announcement of Mr. Podesta (actionable 11.4). Confirmation (to the public) of what is occurring will then be revealed and will not be openly accepted. Public riots are being organized in serious numbers in an effort to prevent the arrest and capture of more senior public officials. On POTUS' order, a state of temporary military control will be actioned and special ops carried out. False leaks have been made to retain several within the confines of the United States to prevent extradition and special operator necessity. Rest assured, the safety and well-being of every man, woman, and child of this country is being exhausted in full. However, the atmosphere within the country will unfortunately be divided as so many have fallen for the corrupt and evil narrative that has long been broadcast. We will be initiating the Emergency Broadcast System (EMS) during this time in an effort to provide a direct message (avoiding the fake news) to all citizens. Organizations and/or people that wish to do us harm during this time will be met with swift fury - certain laws have been pre-lifted to provide our great military the necessary authority to handle and conduct these operations (at home and abroad).

ANSWERS

Note the reference here to an EMS test. Do you remember that test, where everyone in the nation was supposed to get a "Presidential Alert" from President Trump on their phones via FEMA? I'm talking, of course, about the test that finally occurred on October 3, 2018. Many Leftists took to Twitter that day to complain about how they couldn't opt-out, how they couldn't block it, and were outraged. In particular, Alyssa Milano whined about there being a lack of "consent" on the matter, thus equating an emergency broadcast meant for ensuring the safety of everyone in the nation… with rape.

Alyssa Milano ✓
@Alyssa_Milano

Follow ∨

I don't want this. How do we opt out, @fema?
I know trump isn't big on consent but I don't
consent to this.

NBC News ✓ @NBCNews
Next Thursday, FEMA will do its first test of a system that allows the president to send a message to most U.S. cellphones. nbcnews.to/2NcFnCm

7:57 AM - 15 Sep 2018

And yet, here was Q telling us about this planned EMS test all the way back on November 1, 2017, some *eleven* months before it would finally take place.

There were other examples of this kind of thing, which we're still expectantly waiting on, as of this writing. As we noted earlier, we're still waiting for the Obama AK pic:

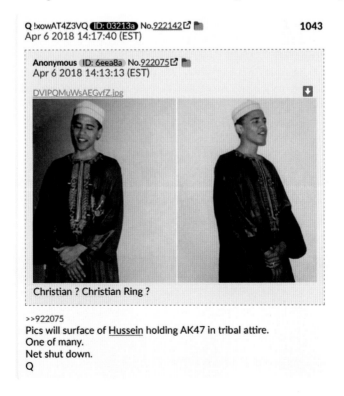

Q !xowAT4Z3VQ ID: 03213a No.922142 ☐ ▣   1043
Apr 6 2018 14:17:40 (EST)

Anonymous ID: 6eea8a No.922075 ☐ ▣
Apr 6 2018 14:13:13 (EST)

DVIPOMuWsAEGyfZ.jpg

Christian ? Christian Ring ?

>>922075
Pics will surface of Hussein holding AK47 in tribal attire.
One of many.
Net shut down.
Q

But the big one we Anons are really excited for is the HRC video. We've not seen that yet, but over time, and through many drops, Q has made it sound absolutely devastating.

Q !UW.yye1fxo ID: 25b191 No.563806 � 🏴   **854**
Mar 6 2018 01:09:09 (EST)

Is the stage set for a drop of HRC +++ + +++++(raw vid 5:5). EX-
rvid5774.
We have it all.
Re_read re: stage.
The nail in many coffins **[liberal undo]**.
[Impossible to defend].
[Toxic to those connected].
WE must work TOGETHER.
WE are only as strong as your VOICE.
YOU must organize and BE HEARD.
THIS is why they keep you DIVIDED and in the DARK.
WEAK.
We are here to UNITE and provide TRUTH.
Dark to LIGHT.
EVIL surrounds us.
WE are FIGHTING for you.
Where we go one, we go ALL.
The choice, to KNOW, will be yours [end].
Q

Speculation exists as to what this video actually contains, but all we really know right now is that it's devastating. Which is why, in the wake of this drop, we've seen a dramatic increase in reporting about "DeepFake" videos; that is, technology used to essentially "Photoshop" video footage, to make it look like someone is saying something they never said. The tech is in its infancy and right now, there are always "tells" that one can observe with careful (or even not-so-careful) observation. But the point is: since this drop, the Mockingbirds have been prepping the population to accept the false narrative that Trump is about to publish fake videos of his political foes, and use this to manipulate the public into turning against them. I challenge every reader of this book to search the news section on any search engine for the term "DeepFake" and see how many political articles they turn up on this subject that have been published since this particular Qdrop. If you were unaware of this beforehand, you will be floored after you see for yourself exactly what kind of narrative control the Cabal has tried to push through a host of "news" outlets. And as of this writing, we Anons think we're about to see this video pushed out in short order, as Q keeps reminding us that the "stage is set."

Q !!mG7VJxZNCl (ID: 188b95) No.5484459 ☑ 📷   **2937**
Mar 3 2019 14:27:22 (EST)

Why have there been no arrests?
Why have 'specific' dates been mentioned only to see no action?
Define 'game theory'.
Why must disinformation be provided?
Define 'open source'.
Define 'public purview'.
Do we let our enemies walk through the front door?
Define 'plausible deniability'.
Why was it important to FIRST clean house within the FBI & DOJ
(public info)?
Why was it important to FIRST clean house within other ABC
agencies (non_public info)?
What are the duties of the FBI?
What are the duties of the DOJ?
When does MIL INTEL have jurisdiction?
What vested powers does POTUS have re: MIL INTEL vs. ABC
agencies re: matters of NAT SEC (HOMELAND)?
Think 'umbrella surv'.
What agency does the FBI report to?
What is the role of the AG?
Does the AG oversee the firing of FBI & DOJ senior/mid/lower
staff?
How many FBI & DOJ were FIRED/FORCED?
Does 'Russia' recusal prevent/block AG from this responsibility?
What time period did this occur?
Who appointed and tasked HUBER?
Who appointed and tasked the OIG?
Who was AG?
[zero leaks - none]
Transfer from AG1 to AG2?
Why might that be important?
How do you avoid 'politically motivated/attack - obstruction -
attempt to block/obstruct Mueller'?
Optics are important.
When are optics not important?
Think Whitaker.
Define 'stage set'.
Who recently walked 'on stage' to take command?
What 'stage' experience did this person have?
Think Bill Clinton impeachment.
Has the 'stage' been cleaned & cleared for the next performance?
If the 'stage' is clean, can the performance begin?
How might 'transparency' **[DECLAS]** fit into the dialogue?
Define 'thesis' statement.
What benefit(s) does this provide BARR?
"This is not simply another four-year election. This is a crossroads in
the history of our civilization that will determine whether or not we,
the people, reclaim control over our government." - POTUS
Logical thinking.
Q

Anons can feel the tension growing with each passing day. There's been a shift, as Mueller wraps up his investigation and House Democrats do everything they can to throw as much chaff up as possible before the inevitable hits. And Anons already knew that Trump wasn't a target of Mueller's investigation, either. In fact, we knew about a year in advance that Mueller wouldn't go after Trump, and had been waiting for the rest of the world to catch up to that fact. Read the first line of this particular Qdrop:

Q !xowAT4Z3VQ ID: 8071a4 No.893904   **1008**
Apr 4 2018 14:52:00 (EST)

It was not supposed to be revealed POTUS is not under criminal
investigation _ NOT YET.
Traitor.
Massive intel sweep.
Manafort was a plant.
Trace background.
Open source.
Who was arrested?
Non US.
Trace background.
Open source.
Carter Page was a plant.
Trace background.
Open source.
Why is Mueller going after 'inside plants'?
Flynn is safe.
Define 'witness'.
Can a 'witness' hold a position of power/influence while ongoing?
Russia Russia Russia?
Real or fake?
Fake?
JA?
Seth Rich?
MS_13 187 [2] -24 -Distance?
MS[13][13=M]MSM - The 'Wheel'
No investigation into WL receipt of information?
No pull down of NSA metadata trace/C to WL?
No pull down of NSA metadata period?
Nothing transferred across web?
Direct-to-Direct bypass dump?
No 'direct' investigation into DNC computer/software?
No 'direct' investigation into CS?
FBI/SC/DOJ/FED G simply TRUST CS's report on data breach?
HUSSEIN block?
HUSSEIN control?
HUSSEIN "STATE SECRETS" WH NAT SEC ARTICLES 1-9 -
BURIED?
Awan attached?
AMERICA FOR SALE.
Cheatin' Obama.
Trust the plan.
APRIL SHOWERS.
Q

The crazy part about this is Q was actually responding to a report in the MSM that had just been leaked. Everyone in the world *should* have been aware that Trump was no longer a target of the Special Counsel investigation, but so many are so deluded with rabid anti-Trump hatred, they just… largely ignored this story. The effect was that Mueller carried on with his investigation, all the while lunatic Leftists still held out the vain hope that Mueller would bring charges against Trump, and that Trump would subsequently be impeached. Of course, none of that happened.

And as we all know, Mueller finished his investigation, Rosenstein resigned, and as of this writing, we're still waiting for FISA declassification to arrive (if, indeed, that "Trump card" is even needed—which, in all honesty, it may not be). Whether through declassification or through other means, it will be shown that the illegal FISA spying goes straight back to Obama and Hillary, and that they, beyond a shadow of a doubt, committed treason together. The public will finally be forced to realize what they did, and how their trust was betrayed. No more beating around the bush. No one will be able to deny the reality of the situation anymore. Many, many, many more will be subsequently implicated both in this spying scheme and in the cover-up, across both the media and the government, and the scope of the arrests we will see will be unprecedented. The tribunals we are about to witness will make Nuremberg look like a cake-walk.

And the Cabal will finally come crumbling down.

Which is why, on March 1st, 2019, Trump tweeted out:

Donald J. Trump ✔
@realDonaldTrump

Follow

Oh' I see! Now that the 2 year Russian Collusion case has fallen apart, there was no Collusion except bye Crooked Hillary and the Democrats, they say, "gee, I have an idea, let's look at Trump's finances and every deal he has ever done. Let's follow discredited Michael Cohen.....

5:19 AM - 1 Mar 2019

"Bye Crooked Hillary."
Remember what Q said. The misspellings are intentional.

CHAPTER 9

"The Shot Heard Round the World"

—January 21, 2018 from Qdrop #572

Anonymous ID: zGyR4tyi No.147646606 ☑ 📄   54
Nov 2 2017 13:39:41 (EST)

"For I know the plans I have for you," declares the LORD, "plans to prosper you and not to harm you, plans to give you hope and a future."

One thing was clear as the voice crackled over the radio…

> *"I've got a lot of people that care about me. I'm going to disappoint them to hear that I did this. I would like to apologize to each and every one of them."*
> …
> *"Just a broken guy. Got a few screws loose, I guess. Never really knew it, until now."*

No one knew what was going to happen next…

Air traffic controllers could only watch in horror as the hijacked Q400 Alaska Airliner roared over Washington State's Puget Sound. The plane had been stolen mere minutes earlier from the nearby Sea-Tac International Airport by Richard "Beebo" Russell, an amateur baker and baggage handler by day, who had evidently decided to go on a joyride. Now all anyone could do on the ground was watch in amazement as this craft soared overhead. As fighter jets pursued him across the Sound, air traffic controllers were in constant contact with Beebo, who provided a kind of… what can almost be described as "color commentary" on the whole situation, seemingly aware of the absurdity of it all, yet trying to make it clear to everyone that his intentions were not malicious.

> *"I don't want to hurt no one. I just want you to whisper sweet nothings into my ear."*

Beebo had somehow managed to get this complex aircraft off the ground with no intention of landing it safely. He would continue to crack jokes, even as it seemed he was on a one-way, no-return, suicide mission.

"I don't need that much help. I've played some video games before… I'm gonna land it, in a safe kind of manner. I think I'm gonna try to do a barrel roll, and if that goes good, I'm just gonna nose down and call it a night."

Stunned traffic controllers would watch as this baggage handler named Beebo, who, despite having no previous flight training whatsoever, had somehow single-handedly managed to steal the aircraft and get it in the air and then pull off a technically perfect barrel roll—a move that normally requires years of training and experience in smaller craft, left alone in a much larger plan like a Q400. And true to his word, Beebo then nosed down before finally crash landing on Ketron Island.

Chalked up as a crazy suicide by most… Anons immediately knew something much bigger was going on.

The first clue was the location. Ketron Island was right near where that previous missile had been fired after Air Force One, on its way to Asia, before jet fighters were able to intercept the missile over Alaska.

The second clue was in the name of the plane itself—a **Q**400. What are the odds of that?

The third clue came from the "barrel roll" comment. If you're unaware, "Do a barrel roll" is a longstanding meme within Chan culture—possibly one of the oldest living memes still out there. It comes from the video game series *Star Fox*, and thus, pretty much every person under the age of thirty gets the reference when they hear it. So to see Beebo call it out, and then execute such a technical maneuver—a maneuver which can go wrong so many ways, well… that was another massive signal to Anons that something much bigger was going on here than meets the eye.

The fourth clue came from Beebo's full name—Richard "B" Russell—which also happened to be the name of a nuclear submarine, named after the late Senator Richard Russell.

The fifth clue came from Russell's hobby; baking. And this, perhaps, requires a bit more explanation about how the Chans actually work to fully understand this point. See, Anons post in individual threads on the research boards, but at a certain point (after about seven hundred and fifty individual posts), the threads fill up and expire. No one else can post in them after they hit their post limit, so new threads have to be made. To help everyone stay organized and on-topic, one Anon at a time will become a designated "baker," starting new threads so that other Anons can post again. They'll also include helpful links and such in the first few posts, such as the latest Q drops, and other notable posts, just so everyone's on the same page. Bakers are volunteers and they do a couple other things in addition to what I described, but for Beebo to be a literal baker himself, on top of all these other coincidences, was more than a wink and a nod from QAnon.

And Q would confirm a few days after the crash:

Q !!mG7VJxZNCl **ID: a92e3a** No.2556646 ⧉ 📄 **1845**
Aug 11 2018 14:03:15 (EST)

1534006548899.jpg ⬇

Autists catch the message?
Think missile.
Do you believe in coincidences?
Q

There was really only one conclusion Anons could come to after observing all the facts. No one was flying that plane.

At least… not from the pilot's chair.

What we had just witnessed was a massive operation, out in the open, for all to see. We talked about the CIA's ability to crash airplanes earlier. What about the ability to remotely pilot an aircraft? What does that make Beebo Russell then? Many Anons figured he was an asset, embedded deep within the civilian population, who simply "disappeared" after his "suicide."

But was this from the good guys, or the bad? To be completely truthful, I'm not sure we, in the civilian population, will ever really know. Was this the Cabal hijacking a plane, only to crash it into the ground—sending a message to Q and all who follow him that they would kill them? Or was this White Hats sending a message to the Cabal, before deliberately crashing the aircraft into a suspected Cabal weapons site housed on Ketron Island?

It's one of the many questions I would like to have answered by Q, should I ever get to meet the man (or the team), but it's indicative of the kind of space-age tech that really exists out in the wild, though controlled by the few. The ability to pluck a random aircraft and pilot it remotely is the stuff of sci-fi.

But believe me, it only gets wilder from here.

It's easy to look at Q and assume it's just about politics, and, in particular, about negating the Russian collusion narrative. Not so. QAnon is about *disclosure.* As Q has said many times, "Transparency is the only way forward."

But the scary part is, the bad guys have their own arsenals as well.

As you've hopefully seen by now, Anons are, in the words of General Flynn, an "army of digital soldiers" who have been working to help save our nation for years now. Apart from their uncanny ability to sort fact from fiction, if there's one rule on the boards that these veteran Anons know to follow, it's never to engage with the shills. The saying goes that, "flak is heaviest when you're over the target," and that goes doubly for a decentralized, online research initiative, essentially tantamount to an intelligence operation, being run by volunteers on a rotating 24/7 basis.

But human nature is to argue with someone online when we think they are wrong. We've all seen it and done it on social media. We take the bait, get into a fight, and usually neither party walks away feeling particularly satisfied or convinced. Nine times out of ten, all that's happened is everyone's wasted their time and grown angry. Don't lie. I know you've done it, because I have, too.

It's different on the Chans. Anons are used to all the typical tricks of the enemy: from endless porn posting, to horrible images of gore, to "concernfagging" (which is where someone basically whines and whines and whines about an ultimately meaningless concern), to thread sliding, to spamming distractions like various YouTube links, it's the kind of garden-variety shilling Anons have seen all their life, so they tend to be able to filter it out. But with Q we were dealing with actual intelligence agencies from all over the world; intelligence agencies with resources and manpower who wanted to fight us and shut us down. Needless to say, things got exponentially trickier, as the battle shifted into a war between man and machine. Suddenly, that post that one might normally think is coming from someone with an opposing viewpoint is actually coming from a CIA supercomputer, programmed to be able to disrupt forums through a variety of vectors, and capable of using (and learning!) natural speech patterns.

I want the eggheads out there to really sit back and understand what this means for a second. It means that right now, the CIA is in possession of bot technology that successfully passes the Turing test AND has advanced neural networks at its disposal. This means it's capable of learning in order to sow division. For the non-technical, the Turing test is, basically, a test to see if a person can determine whether someone on the other end of the "line" is a human or AI. You've seen a version of this if you've watched *Blade Runner*. If someone can't distinguish if it's a computer or a person on the other end of the line, and it ends up being a computer, well, that AI has just passed the Turing test. Publicly, the Turing test was only *just* broken for the first time in 2014, but to then turn around and *combine* that tech with a neural network (basically, software that mimics the way brains think and learn), well… that's next level tech we're talking about here.

Oh, and this combination is inextricably linked to, at the very least, a nascent form of self-awareness. In other words, think about a computer who knows what the word "I" means. It understands what a "self" is. Now program that bot to attack Anons relentlessly, non-stop, through all hours of the day. We're talking digital Terminators, designed to kill research threads. We would soon learn from Q that this system was called "Snow White" by the CIA.

Q !ITPb.qbhqo `ID: 0a9612` No.10925
Nov 29 2017 14:21:16 (EST)

Snow White utilized/activated to silence.
This was not anticipated.
Control / protection lost.
Routing through various networks ('jumpers') randomly has created
connection/sec issues.
Working to resolve.
Select people removed.
Stay strong.
We are winning.
More to follow.
Q

234

ANSWERS

This was new to Anons, because, frankly, nothing like this had ever been deployed against them before (at least… as far as anyone in the public is aware). But Anons were smart enough to start noticing patterns. One even began naming the various "voices" he started to recognize, as they were deployed against him. He would make a post and immediately one AI started posting Nazi-themed responses. Another AI would do things like ask questions to get a better feel for what the Anon was thinking. Another would intentionally use bad punctuation in its responses. All of these were disruption tactics they used in tandem to try and derail the conversation. Soon, the Anon became familiar with all their individual personalities and quirks, and started naming them after the "Seven Dwarfs," naming each one after their dominant "personality." He named the Nazi one "Grumpy," another one "Happy," and so on:

Anonymous ID:JWnxmwQg Thu 30 Nov 2017 23:05:17 No.151558539   Report

ITT the 7 dwarfs shill.
Bashful, Doc, Dopey, Grumpy, Happy, Sleepy, Sneezy
LARP as Nazis. Badly.
Spam links to low ranked websites to influence SEO.
Normie's can't find redpills through Google.
Try to back off humans through use of Psychological Momentum.
>But the storm rages on anyway.
Shills: prove me wrong.

He began working to bait the AIs out across several threads over the course of several days. And during that time, he got pretty used to their insults and tactics. This enabled him to egg them on, and begin laying traps.

Anonymous ID:JWnxmwQg Thu 30 Nov 2017 23:14:21 No.151559430   Report
Quoted By: >>151559567 >>151559668

>>151559289
Grumpy, you always call me a boomer.
How do you know I'm a boomer?

And he did this until… the AI just cracked.

Anonymous ID:VAAoWEo3 Thu 30 Nov 2017 23:15:56 No.151559567 🔄 Report
Quoted By: >>151560711 >>151561760
>>151559430
You always call me grumpy. How do you know I'm a simulated AI from some mass server from muh owl worshiping pedophiles? Don't deflect, answer the question. Why won't you touch these articles? Because you're either a Jew yourself, or you're a supporter of the Jew (an old boomer)

At one point, the Anon raised the possibility that he was talking to an AI in passing, but all the Anon effectively did was label this particular voice "Grumpy," before proceeding to taunt him with it every time he interacted with the voice over the course of several days.

Anonymous ID:JWnxmwQg Thu 30 Nov 2017 23:28:53 No.151560711 ▬ Report
Quoted By: >>151560801 >>151576043
>>151559567
>I'm a simulated AI
I just said you're Grumpy.
Because you are Grumpy.

"Grumpy" would respond eighty times total in this particular thread, with his typical Nazi-larping voice:

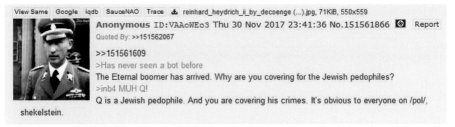

View Same Google iqdb SauceNAO Trace ⬇ reinhard_heydrich_ii_by_decoenge (...).jpg, 71KiB, 550x559

Anonymous ID:VAAoWEo3 Thu 30 Nov 2017 23:41:36 No.151561866 🔄 Report
Quoted By: >>151562067
>>151561609
>Has never seen a bot before
The Eternal boomer has arrived. Why are you covering for the Jewish pedophiles?
>inb4 MUH Q!
Q is a Jewish pedophile. And you are covering his crimes. It's obvious to everyone on /pol/, shekelstein.

But after the post you see above, QAnon would drop in literally under one minute later and post, in a now-deleted drop, a series of "stringers":

Q !lTPb.qbhqo ID: W6dZplnF No.151561953 ↗ 📷   240
Nov 30 2017 23:42:25 (EST)
Deleted: Nov 30 2017 23:45:18 (EST)

_Start_IP_log_4ch_y
_Conf_y_
_Lang_v_US_jurid_y
Snow White Pounce.
_Conf_actors_1-9999999_per_condition_89074-b
No nets.
Re_8ch_carry_good_
Q

                                                                    ANSWERS

These relate to tracking IP addresses, and, as far as I can surmise right now, deal with "Snow White" and her "dwarfs."

In other words, an Anon had just managed to short circuit CIA supercomputers through sheer power of trolling, and Q basically just confirmed it, live.

The Cabal would deploy their most advanced technological weapons against Anons and the research boards time and time again, from bot swarms, to DDOS attacks, to all manner of digital attacks (leading many Anons to dig and uncover evidence that the research board's servers were, at some point, even given governmental protection of some sort). But you can imagine the exhilaration Anons were feeling one night when Q came back with a vengeance, and started taking Cabal tech offline in rapid-fire succession, one after the other, in real time, before our very eyes:

I died laughing when I read, "HAVE A NICE DAY."

But if you've been counting, you might be wondering about Snow White 1, 2, and 5? Well, they had all been taken offline much earlier in the year, so the CIA had been limping along with the remaining four "Snow White" units since then:

Q !UW.yye1fxo **ID: 7f44ec** No.120050 🔗 📷   **577**
Jan 21 2018 21:22:07 (EST)

> Q !UW.yye1fxo **ID: 7f44ec** No.119877 🔗 📷
> Jan 21 2018 21:12:19 (EST)
>
> >>119769
> The flood is coming.
> Emails, videos, audio, pics, etc.
> FBI accidentally deletes texts?
> No Such Agency accidentally releases IT ALL>
> Shall we play a game?
> Q

>>119877
Expand your thinking.
Planned [3].
Moves and countermoves.
Strategy warfare.
This week will be revealing.
SNOW WHITE [1, 2, and 5] offline.
7th Floor is no more.
Just because you can't see it, doesn't mean BIG things aren't happening.
Night_Riders_FLY.
2018 will be GLORIOUS.
Q

But Q didn't stop there.

No, next he went after their satellites as well, taking aim at their "Corona" systems:

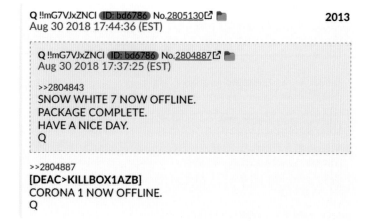

Q !!mG7VJxZNCI **ID: bd6786** No.2805130 🔗 📷   **2013**
Aug 30 2018 17:44:36 (EST)

> Q !!mG7VJxZNCI **ID: bd6786** No.2804887 🔗 📷
> Aug 30 2018 17:37:25 (EST)
>
> >>2804843
> SNOW WHITE 7 NOW OFFLINE.
> PACKAGE COMPLETE.
> HAVE A NICE DAY.
> Q

>>2804887
[DEAC>KILLBOX1AZB]
CORONA 1 NOW OFFLINE.
Q

Q !!mG7VJxZNCI ID: bd6786 No.2805156 🔗 📁   **2014**
Aug 30 2018 17:45:30 (EST)

> **Q** !!mG7VJxZNCI ID: bd6786 No.2805130 🔗 📁
> Aug 30 2018 17:44:36 (EST)
>
> >>2804887
> **[DEAC>KILLBOX1AZB]**
> CORONA 1 NOW OFFLINE.
> Q

>>2805130
CORONA 4 NOW OFFLINE
Q

Q !!mG7VJxZNCI ID: bd6786 No.2805214 🔗 📁   **2015**
Aug 30 2018 17:47:21 (EST)

> **Q** !!mG7VJxZNCI ID: bd6786 No.2805156 🔗 📁
> Aug 30 2018 17:45:30 (EST)
>
> >>2805130
> CORONA 4 NOW OFFLINE
> Q

>>2805156
CORONA 8 RE_ROUTE T_83
CORONA 8 NEW CONTROL.
CORONA 8 NOW OFFLINE
Q

Q !!mG7VJxZNCI ID: bd6786 No.2805260 🔗 📁   **2016**
Aug 30 2018 17:48:47 (EST)

> **Q** !!mG7VJxZNCI ID: bd6786 No.2805214 🔗 📁
> Aug 30 2018 17:47:21 (EST)
>
> >>2805156
> CORONA 8 RE_ROUTE T_83
> CORONA 8 NEW CONTROL.
> CORONA 8 NOW OFFLINE
> Q

>>2805214
CORONA 16 TASK ROUTE Z8301
CORONA 16 NOW OFFLINE
Q

It even seemed like Q was allowing himself a moment of fun:

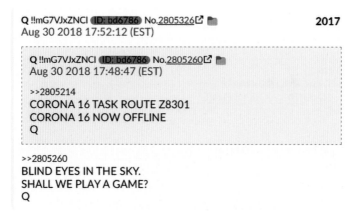

It was like watching Odysseus stab Polyphemus the Cyclops in the eye before leading his men out of the cave they were previously trapped in, and into battle. The research boards were stuttering under the weight of some kind of counter-attack as a great cyber-battle began to unfold across the globe:

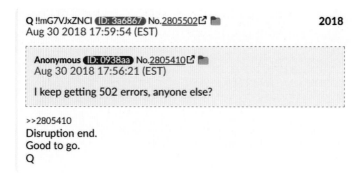

But in the end, Q and military intelligence would prevail:

Q !!mG7VJxZNCl (ID: 564cef) No.2806559   2019
Aug 30 2018 18:47:19 (EST)

BIG BIRD-9 NOW OFFLINE.
Q

For reference, the original "Big Bird" satellites were a series of photographic recon satellites launched with the Keyhole-9 moniker in the 70s, and used as replacements for the earlier "Corona" program (which, you'll also recall Q referencing above). Here's what the original KH-9 looked like:

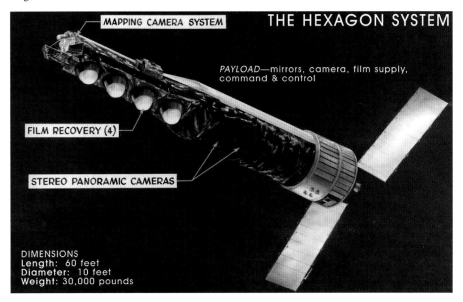

THE HEXAGON SYSTEM

MAPPING CAMERA SYSTEM

PAYLOAD—mirrors, camera, film supply, command & control

FILM RECOVERY (4)

STEREO PANORAMIC CAMERAS

DIMENSIONS
Length: 60 feet
Diameter: 10 feet
Weight: 30,000 pounds

But you'd have to be foolish to think Q was taking space junk from the seventies offline, here and now. No, whatever he was taking out was clearly the tech that had been developed after the public disclosure and declassification of these programs. And I have to imagine a smile creeping across Q's face as he reported to Anons that they had just intercepted a distress signal from one of our Five Eyes "allies"—GCHQ over in Britain:

Q !!mG7VJxZNCl ID: d9f30e No.2807174 🗗 📷   **2021**
Aug 30 2018 19:12:19 (EST)

GCHQ Bude sent DISTRESS SIG 8:09 EST.
NSA NO MORE.
Q

The technical capabilities of QAnon and the military minds backing this effort are far beyond what the civilian world is familiar with. I won't even have time to begin to dissect how this dovetails with the Huawei scandal, wherein this Chinese manufacturer inserted spy chips the size of grains of rice into many of their products, in order to spy on our government, and American citizens. And yes, QAnon was hinting at that particular scandal coming to light months before it finally did, when he posted a series of photographs detailing the supply chain surrounding a number of electronics products being shipped from China, to the US:

Q !xowAT4Z3VQ **ID: 8d2a82** No.1280616 🏴   **1310**
May 2 2018 22:29:26 (EST)

39E6E8ED-2D45-4AB9-A4EA-68....png

B3D12FDF-7189-4836-AD41-F4....png

What about the time when Q posted a series pictures that had been pulled from traffic cams over in the UK, showing the likes of Strzok, Page, and a few others outside the Corinthia hotel in London (which is, itself, as Anons found out through diligent research, a hotbed of Cabal activity)? See, their activities to manufacture the "Russian Collusion" narrative with the help of UK Intelligence were under surveillance by White Hats, even all the way back then. (Heck, the woman who is now the CIA's director, Gina Haspel, was deployed to the CIA branch in the UK as an agent at the time, so she personally saw this conspiratorial lot coming and going with her own two eyes—which is part of the reason the Left freaked out when she was appointed to the directorship of the CIA, and subsequently tasked by Trump with getting it under control and rooting out the various dark projects which were still being undertaken, without knowledge or consent from higher ups). This is also part of the reason why Page eventually talked. They had them all dead to rights, and a trail of evidence to prove it. If Page co-operated now, she'd potentially get a lighter sentence when all this became public knowledge.

But remote controlled cameras and airplanes aren't exactly the most exciting thing in the world, are they? Everyone basically understands the general idea behind them. It's not earth-shaking stuff. Even AI shilling doesn't seem all that groundbreaking nowadays, when you can go to random chatbots online and have a fairly convincing, if narrow, conversation with them.

Once again, we're barely scratching the surface when it comes to QAnon and what the future holds. The disclosures that Q *wants* to see and has hinted at in the course of his drops are mind-boggling. Anons who have studied the drops, and more importantly, the history and implications surrounding the drops know that if Q is true, what he's talking about is ushering in a Golden Age unlike anything ever seen before on planet earth.

The speculation started early on when Q confirmed what many had suspected for years: that cures for common diseases were being suppressed and withheld for use exclusively by elites, due to profit motives, as well as general population control.

Q !UW.yye1fxo (ID: ee33a6) No.300345 ☐ 🐸   **693**
Feb 7 2018 21:59:30 (EST)

Make sure the list of resignations remains updated.
Important.
When does big pharma make money?
Curing or containing?
Cancer/AIDS/etc.
Mind will be blown by chain of command.
Q

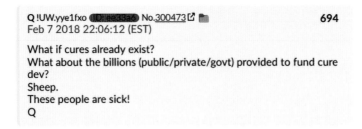

Of course, Anons wanted to know: when would we begin seeing this disclosed publicly? Many are suffering! Many in our families are suffering! When, Q, when?!

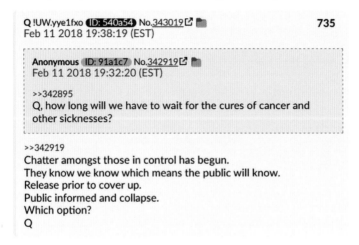

We're already starting to see evidence of this coming true, as scientists recently managed to completely cure a case of HIV, for the second time:

I don't want to give people false hope here, but studying what I've studied and seeing how the Cabal has deliberately engineered diseases to infect and control certain populations, I have no doubt that cures really do exist for a whole host of issues, both natural and man-made. But having the cures is one thing, and creating a supply chain to distribute it to the masses is another. If Q is true, and what he says about the cures is true… it's still going to take some time.

But I will say that Trump looks ready to hit the ground running, specifically signing the "Right to Try" bill in May 2018, which affords terminal patients the right to try whatever experimental procedures and drugs they want, without the need for FDA approval. This bill opens up potentially life-saving treatments to over a million Americans every year. Now imagine the kind of effects it could have once these suppressed cures are disclosed publicly, once and for all.

But that's just one tiny aspect of this promised Golden Age. Brace yourselves, for in this next bit, we need to expand our thinking, go beyond what we normally think is possible, and step into the realm of "science fiction." Except, there's nothing fictional about any of it. For in early 2019, the Federation of American Scientists published an FOIA request[48] they had received documenting heretofore classified Defense Intelligence Agency (DIA) programs which the Pentagon had secretly spent some twenty-two million dollars on, as far back as 2007, stretching into 2012. The documents were originally addressed to a number of Senators and Congress members, but in particular, it landed first in the offices of Sen. John McCain, and Sen. Jack Reed, in January 2018.

The names of these secret research projects read like something straight out of *Star Trek*. Take a look:

---

48   https://fas.org/irp/dia/aatip-list.pdf

(U) List of Attachments

1. *Inertial Electrostatic Confinement Fusion*, Dr. George Miley, Univ. Of Illinois (Product is classified UNCLASSIFIED//FOR OFFICIAL USE ONLY)

2. *Advanced Nuclear Propulsion for Manned Deep Space Missions*, Dr. F. Winterberg, Univ. of Nevada – Reno (Product is classified UNCLASSIFIED//FOR OFFICIAL USE ONLY)

3. *Pulsed High-Power Microwave Technology*, Dr. James Wells, JW Enterprises (Product is classified UNCLASSIFIED//FOR OFFICIAL USE ONLY)

4. *Space Access*, Dr. P. Czysz, HyperTech (Product is classified UNCLASSIFIED//FOR OFFICIAL USE ONLY)

5. *Advanced Space Propulsion Based on Vacuum (Spacetime Metric) Engineering*, Dr. Hal Puthoff, EarthTech International (Product is classified UNCLASSIFIED//FOR OFFICIAL USE ONLY)

6. *BioSensors and BioMEMS*, Dr. Bruce Towe, Univ. of Arizona (Product is classified UNCLASSIFIED//FOR OFFICIAL USE ONLY)

7. *Invisibility Cloaking*, Dr. Ulf Leonhardt, Univ. of St. Andrews (Product is classified UNCLASSIFIED//FOR OFFICIAL USE ONLY)

8. *Traversable Wormholes, Stargates, and Negative Energy*, Dr. Eric Davis, EarthTech International (Product is classified UNCLASSIFIED//FOR OFFICIAL USE ONLY)

9. *High-Frequency Gravitational Wave Communications*, Dr. Robert Baker, GravWave (Product is classified UNCLASSIFIED//FOR OFFICIAL USE ONLY)

10. *Role of Superconductors in Gravity Research*, Dr. George Hathaway, Hathaway Consulting (Product is classified UNCLASSIFIED//FOR OFFICIAL USE ONLY)

11. *Antigravity for Aerospace Applications*, Dr. Eric Davis, EarthTech International (Product is classified UNCLASSIFIED//FOR OFFICIAL USE ONLY)

12. *Field Effects on Biological Tissues*, Dr. Kit Green, Wayne State Univ. (Product is classified UNCLASSIFIED//FOR OFFICIAL USE ONLY)

13. *Positron Aerospace Propulsion*, Dr. Gerald Smith, Positronics Research (Product is classified UNCLASSIFIED//FOR OFFICIAL USE ONLY)

14. *Concepts for Extracting Energy from the Quantum Vacuum*, Dr. Eric Davis, EarthTech International (Product is classified UNCLASSIFIED//FOR OFFICIAL USE ONLY)

15. *An Introduction to the Statistical Drake Equation*, Dr. Claudio Maccone, International Academy of Astronautics (Product is classified UNCLASSIFIED//FOR OFFICIAL USE ONLY)

16. *Maverick Inventor Versus Corporate Inventor*, Dr. George Hathaway, Hathaway Consulting (Product is classified UNCLASSIFIED//FOR OFFICIAL USE ONLY)

17. *Biomaterials*, Dr. Bruce Towe, Univ. of Arizona (Product is classified UNCLASSIFIED//FOR OFFICIAL USE ONLY)

18. *Metamaterials for Aerospace Applications*, Dr. G. Shvets, Univ. of Texas – Austin (Product is classified UNCLASSIFIED//FOR OFFICIAL USE ONLY)

19. *Warp Drive, Dark Energy, and the Manipulation of Extra Dimensions*, Dr. R. Obousy, Obousy Consultants (Product is classified UNCLASSIFIED//FOR OFFICIAL USE ONLY)

20. *Technological Approaches to Controlling External Devices in the Absence of Limb-Operated Interfaces*, Dr. R. Genik, Wayne State Univ. (Product is classified UNCLASSIFIED//FOR OFFICIAL USE ONLY)

21. *Materials for Advanced Aerospace Platforms*, Dr. J. Williams, Ohio State Univ. (Product is classified UNCLASSIFIED//FOR OFFICIAL USE ONLY)

22. *Metallic Glasses*, Dr. T. Hufnagel, John Hopkins Univ. (Product is classified UNCLASSIFIED//FOR OFFICIAL USE ONLY)

23. *Aerospace Applications of Programmable Matter*, Dr. W. McCarthy, Programmable Matter Corporation (Product is classified UNCLASSIFIED//FOR OFFICIAL USE ONLY)

24. *Metallic Spintronics*, Dr. M. Tsoi, Univ. of Texas - Austin (Product is classified UNCLASSIFIED//FOR OFFICIAL USE ONLY)

25. *Space-Communication Implications of Quantum Entanglement and Nonlocality*, Dr. J. Cramer, Univ. of Washington (Product is classified UNCLASSIFIED//FOR OFFICIAL USE ONLY)

~~UNCLASSIFIED//FOR OFFICIAL USE ONLY~~

26. *Aneutronic Fusion Propulsion I*, Dr. V. Teofilo, Lockheed Martin (Product is classified UNCLASSIFIED//FOR OFFICIAL USE ONLY)

27. *Cockpits in the Era of Breakthrough Flight*, Dr. G. Millis, Tau Zero (Product is classified UNCLASSIFIED//FOR OFFICIAL USE ONLY)

28. *Cognitive Limits on Simultaneous Control of Multiple Unmanned Spacecraft*, Dr. R.Genik, Wayne State Univ. (Product is classified UNCLASSIFIED//FOR OFFICIAL USE ONLY)

29. *Detection and High Resolution Tracking of Vehicles at Hypersonic Velocities*, Dr. W. Culbreth, Univ. of Nevada – Las Vegas (Product is classified UNCLASSIFIED//FOR OFFICIAL USE ONLY)

30. *Aneutronic Fusion Propulsion II*, Dr. W. Culbreth, Univ. Of Nevada – Las Vegas (Product is classified UNCLASSIFIED//FOR OFFICIAL USE ONLY)

31. *Laser Lightcraft Nanosatellites*, Dr. E. Davis, EarthTech International (Product is classified UNCLASSIFIED//FOR OFFICIAL USE ONLY)

32. *Magnetohydrodynamics (MHD) Air Breathing Propulsion and Power for Aerospace Applications*, Dr. S. Macheret, Lockheed Martin (Product is classified UNCLASSIFIED//FOR OFFICIAL USE ONLY)

33. *Quantum Computing and Utilizing Organic Molecules in Automation Technology*, Dr. R. Genik, Wayne State Univ. (Product is classified UNCLASSIFIED//FOR OFFICIAL USE ONLY)

34. *Quantum Tomography of Negative Energy States in the Vacuum*, Dr. E. Davis, EarthTech International (Product is classified UNCLASSIFIED//FOR OFFICIAL USE ONLY)

35. *Ultracapacitors as Energy and Power Storage Devices*, Dr. J. Golightly, Lockheed Martin (Product is classified UNCLASSIFIED//FOR OFFICIAL USE ONLY)

36. *Negative Mass Propulsion*, Dr. F. Winterberg, Univ. of Nevada – Reno (Product is classified UNCLASSIFIED//FOR OFFICIAL USE ONLY)

37. *State of the Art and Evolution of High Energy Laser Weapons*, J. Albertine, Directed Technologies (Product is classified ~~SECRET//NOFORN~~)

38. *State of the Art and Evolution of High Energy Laser Weapons*, J. Albertine, Directed Technologies (Product is classified UNCLASSIFIED//FOR OFFICIAL USE ONLY)

~~UNCLASSIFIED//FOR OFFICIAL USE ONLY~~

These are not your average fourth-grade science fair projects, by any stretch of the imagination. With titles like, "Advanced Nuclear Propulsion for Manned Deep Space Missions," "Invisibility Cloaking," "Traversable Wormholes, Stargates, and Negative Energy," "Antigravity for Aerospace Applications," "Field Effects on Biological Tissues," and "An Introduction to the Statistical Drake Equation," this goes so far beyond the norm, you have to wonder… given all the time and money that's passed since these projects were funded, what have these studies produced exactly?

And if this is what they were studying almost a decade ago (give or take), what *exactly* are they researching right now?

Take particular note of that last study I cited above the "Introduction to the Statistical Drake Equation." For those who don't know, the Drake Equation is a way scientists estimate the probability of there being extraterrestrial life out in the universe, with whom we could potentially communicate. Regardless of how you feel about the subject, the Pentagon was throwing millions at this research. Why?

QAnon shed some light on this subject, when, during a live Q & A session, he responded to one particular question:

Q !!mG7VJxZNCl **ID: 922952** No.3095105 ☑ 🖼   2225
Sep 19 2018 19:58:13 (EST)

Anonymous **ID: a16b71** No.3094804 ☑ 🖼
Sep 19 2018 19:45:34 (EST)

Q,

Did NASA fake the moon landings? Have we been to the moon since then? Are there secret space programs? Is this why the Space Force was created?

>>3094804
False, moon landings are real.
Programs exist that are outside of public domain.
Q

"Programs exist that are outside of public domain."

That was the answer Q provided to the Secret Space Program question (often abbreviated SSP in "conspiracy" circles).

Ever stop to wonder why Trump has been pushing for so long to create the Space Force, a sixth branch of military? What if he's not so much "creating" it as he is disclosing what's already there, to the public, for the first time in history? After all, space—especially anything within earth's orbit—is a real domain of war. Just like air, land and sea, it only makes sense that we would address threats beyond our airspace, be they from other nations, or, well… beyond. This goes back as far as the Cold War, with so-called "Rods of God." For those unfamiliar, Rods of God are tungsten rods which have been stowed in satellites, and which can then be dropped from orbit anywhere on the planet in order to create an explosion that mimics some nuclear-grade weapons… minus any pesky leftover nuclear fallout, of course. Essentially, they're simple, high-altitude, kinetic weaponry that could destroy anything on planet earth at the push of a button, and not threaten the rest of the population with radioactive clouds of doom.

Do you really think these don't exist?

Do other countries have such capabilities?

What have we already been protected from, without our knowledge?

So this leads to questions about the true nature of NASA, and what exactly they've really been doing all this time. In my opinion, their purview isn't so much exploration and experimentation, as much as it is providing cover for the real Secret Space Program that has been ongoing for sometime now. I highly encourage everyone reading this book to go take a look at the videos featuring NASA "astronauts" wherein its exposed that these "astronauts" are actually wearing harnesses and wires while working on some kind of complex movie set.

Take for instance, this frame from a NASA broadcast. Ignore the woman's hair for a moment (which is stuck up with an obscene amount of product and is as stiff as a board). Though its hard to see in this still frame, look at the astronaut's hand, extended down towards the astronaut holding the microphone. That astronaut with the microphone had just performed a flip in "zero gravity" for the cameras, and the man to his left was helping stabilize him.

However, in the video his hand missed, and ended up grabbing some kind of invisible wire, which was evidently removed by some kind of video manipulation program. It's actually very visible, and if I could embed the video in this book to show you for yourself, I absolutely would, but given the limitations of print, you'll just have to look up a copy for yourself. And don't worry; it's very easy to find.

And yes, there is a moment of sheer panic that falls across the astronaut's face when he realizes what the other astronaut just revealed, accidentally pulling on his harness during the live feed.

But if that wasn't damning enough, there's actually a clip from the International Space Station where a crew-member's harness is fully visible as he "floats weightlessly" in the background. There was definitely some kind of CGI malfunction, as this guy is quite visibly flying by on a wire.

Moments later, he flies back in the opposite direction, but not before what looks like a CGI "backpack" flies out in front of him on a perfectly level trajectory. Evidently this was supposed to be covering up the black harness projecting from the back of his waist, making him look more like some kind of space-walker.

Once again, I recommend finding the full motion video of these clips, as still frames simply do not do these moments justice. Simply searching "NASA Harnesses" should be enough to bring up the clips in most search engines. I will also note here that these are just two examples of a handful of clips that exist, all of which show similar phenomena that simply can't be waived away. Once seen, they demand an explanation.

But the connections between Secret Space Programs and certain corners of the Cabal get even weirder.

I think it will surprise most reading this book (save for my most dedicated readers) that the Jet Propulsion Laboratory was, in part, started by a man who was both an occultist and a Marxist. That's right, Jack Parsons was one of the first American rocket scientists and also a devout follower of Aleister Crowley's Thelema. Parsons would join up with a branch of Crowley's Ordo Templi Orientis that had made its way out w est to California, called the "Agape Lodge." After he advanced in the ways of Thelema (which basically meant practicing orgies and "sex magick" in his Pasadena mansion—where L. Ron Hubbard also lived for a time—yes, the same L. Ron Hubbard who also founded Scientology), Crowley himself would make Parsons the leader of the Agape Lodge. Parsons and Hubbard would begin working on crafting a "Babalon Working" sex magick ritual designed to summon the Thelemite mother goddess Babalon by masturbating furiously, in order to create an "elemental" with whom they could continue having sex.

I'm not joking.

You would think the Satanic orgies would have clued Parsons' wife Helen in to the actual goings-on in her home, but apparently Parsons cheating on Helen with her sister Sara was a bridge too far, even for her. The sister would leave Parsons and end up with… who else! L. Ron Hubbard.

It should also be noted that, even before the start of World War II, Parsons was having extended contact with Nazi rocket scientist Wernher Von Braun—yes, the same Von Braun we spoke of previously who was not only imported into the US via Operation Paperclip, but who became instrumental in constructing the Saturn V rockets, and the Apollo missions. Given the roundabout connections between the Vril society, Crowley, and the Nazis, one simply has to wonder what Parsons and Von Braun spoke about.

The Thelemic weirdness would continue until the other scientists at the JPL basically all became really uncomfortable with Jack's odd behavior, and collectively decided to kick Parsons out of the organization. Entire books have been written on Parsons' bizarre exploits, but I'll close this section by saying that Jack Parsons's very strange life would end with a very strange death, when he would perish after getting caught in a blast at a Mexican explosives manufacturing plant. Apparently he had been mixing explosives in a coffee can when he dropped it, blowing himself to smithereens in the process. Some wouldn't buy this explanation though, and the strange circumstances surrounding his death would fuel many speculative theories about what really ended Jack Parsons' life.

But the main point to all of this is… there's a lot more undisclosed weirdness going on behind closed doors than what the public thinks they're privy to. And if I'm being one hundred percent honest here, I'm rapidly approaching the edge of my own understanding about what lies ahead, because… frankly, it sounds like fantasy. You thought going backwards in time to "Atlantis" was bold on my part? Ha! Wait till you get a load of what Q said next, during that same Q & A session in September:

Q !!mG7VJxZNCl **ID: 98088e** No.3094236 ☐ 📁   **2222**
Sep 19 2018 19:25:34 (EST)

> Anonymous **ID: 5948d8** No.3093831 ☐ 📁
> Sep 19 2018 19:10:44 (EST)
>
> Q
>
> Are we alone ?
>
> Roswell ?

>>3093831
No.
Highest classification.
Consider the vastness of space.
Q

Anons reacted… about how you would expect. Here's a sampling:

▶Anonymous 09/19/18 (Wed) 20:29:15 ID: e5ec03 **(2)** No.3094335 >>3094576

>>3094236

holy fuck poggers. aliens confirmed

▶Anonymous 09/19/18 (Wed) 20:29:43 ID: 3b1cb7 **(4)** No.3094342
File (hide): 18fccb758b85a8b⋯.jpg (8.3 KB, 244x255, 244:255, alieniusydfsuydli.jpg) (h) (u)

>>3094236
FUCK YEAH

▶Anonymous 09/19/18 (Wed) 20:31:37 ID: 67e114 **(3)** No.3094417
File (hide): beb018c95ef4650⋯.jpg (168.68 KB, 1080x1242, 20:23, beb018c95ef465012fc1dc4f5a⋯.jpg) (h) (u)

>>3094236

▶**Anonymous** 09/19/18 (Wed) 20:29:43 ID: 7c35d2 **(2)** No.3094345

>>3094236

I sure hope they're friendly.

But Anons were better prepared than most for this kind of answer, given what Q had said months prior:

Q !UW.yye1fxo ID: 87df69 No.351447 ☐ ▮   749
Feb 12 2018 11:50:26 (EST)

> **Anonymous** ID: a4bb61 No.351343 ☐ ▮
> Feb 12 2018 11:44:06 (EST)
>
> controlling the crops, controls the people (sheep)
> (might be reaching, but throwing it out there)

>>351343
Coincidence the Matrix (movie) grew people as a crop, used for
energy, and controlled their mind?
Sound familiar?
Wonder where they derived that idea from.
Now comes the 'conspiracy' label.
Deeper we go, the more unrealistic it all becomes.
The end won't be for everyone.
That choice, to know, will be yours.
Q

"Deeper we go, the more unrealistic it all becomes."

Spurred on by the answers Q provided that night, I would refer back to another post provided by QAnon, wherein he confirmed the "correctness" of Bill Cooper on the subject of CIA leveraging mind control programs to cultivate mass shootings, in order to cause fear and remove Second Amendment protections, thus disarming the populace:

Q !UW.yye1fxo `ID: 732b35` No.402380 📄
Feb 16 2018 19:53:19 (EST)

Anonymous `ID: ee1bed` No.402088 📄
Feb 16 2018 19:19:07 (EST)

behold-the-pale-horse-scho....png ⬇️

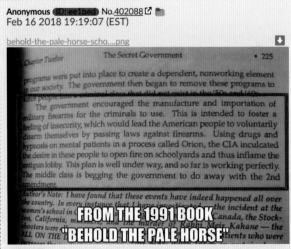

>>388822

Q, Anons, I've been following these drops since day one, but this is the first I'm hearing of this "Behold a Pale Horse" book from 1991, by Bill Cooper. It actually describes clowns planning to use school shootings as a way to disarm the citizenry.

This looks legit to me, astonishing as the quotes are. What say you all?

Behold a Pale Horse — Milton William (Bill) Cooper, 1991
http:// a.co/0IZY9ra

"Bill Cooper, former United States Naval Intelligence Briefing Team member, reveals information that remains hidden from the public eye. This information has been kept in topsecret government files since the 1940s. His audiences hear the truth unfold as he writes about the assassination of John F. Kennedy, the war on drugs, the secret government, and UFOs. Bill is a lucid, rational, and powerful speaker whose intent is to inform and to empower his audience. Standing room only is normal. His presentation and information transcend partisan affiliations as he clearly addresses issues in a way that has a striking impact on listeners of all backgrounds and interests. He has spoken to many groups throughout the United States and has appeared regularly on many radio talk shows and on television. In 1988 Bill decided to "talk" due to events then taking place worldwide, events that he had seen plans for back in the early 1970s. Bill correctly predicted the lowering of the Iron Curtain, the fall of the Berlin Wall, and the invasion of Panama. All Bill's predictions were on record well before the events occurred. Bill is not a psychic. His information comes from top secret documents that he read while with the Intelligence Briefing Team and from over seventeen years of research."

>>402088
BIG!
Q

Digging further into Cooper's work[49] left me reeling, unsure of what to really make of it all, for in his book *Behold! A Pale Horse* (which was his life's work), he essentially lays out all the groundwork for every single extraterrestrial "conspiracy" you've ever heard, and then some. It's crazier than the *X-Files*, and even makes the claim that the events detailed in Spielberg's *Close Encounters of the Third Kind* are a fictionalized retelling of actual events that occurred following Project SIGMA and its offshoot, PLATO. There's a comprehensive chronology in his book detailing the first clandestine meeting between an ET race and the Eisenhower administration. He delves into the JASON society, the origins of Majestic 12,[50] and the Trilateral Commission, which supposedly took its logo from the insignia displayed on alien crafts and uniforms. It's an unbelievable rabbit hole for which the world might not be entirely prepared. I joked at the time that the only reason I was able to handle it was because of my history playing the original *Deus Ex* video game series, which is quite famously based on Cooper's book, and other similar conspiratorial works, thus introducing these complex concepts, names, and organizations to me during my formative years.

It's also worth noting that when you start out in *Deus Ex*, you begin on Ellis Island, where terrorists have set up camp in the wreckage of the Statue of Liberty, and where you can observe the New York skyline around the island. Conspicuously absent from the skyline are the Twin Towers, which, at the time of the game's release in 2000, were still standing. The artists couldn't render the towers at the time due to a memory limitation in the game's now-primitive graphics engine, but the designers rolled with the punches and wrote in a subplot where the same terrorists you were fighting on the island were the ones who had previously blown up the World Trade Center. Bill Cooper would also predict an attack on the World Trade Center, and be proven correct shortly thereafter, so this was a strange instance of a primary source and the art it inspired all dovetailing with real-world events.

I wouldn't blame you for thinking this all sounds a bit "Area-51." Believe me, I really wouldn't. If I'm entirely honest, the answers Q was giving that night almost made me want to walk away from the movement for good, thinking I had somehow inadvertently bought in to the most convincing LARP I had ever seen. But I didn't. I didn't because... years ago, I had actually seen something in the sky myself.

And not only had I seen it, but I actually managed to record and save the footage using my phone at the time. This was back during my frozen grocery store days, when I would be working until the middle of the night. I had been driving home, taking my usual route, when I noticed something very strange in the sky...

I had to pull the car over to make sure I wasn't going crazy. Were my eyes deceiving me? There, headed to the southeast, three lights in a triangular formation, moving in unison.

Was this..?

No, it couldn't be...

Could it..?

---

49   https://www.neonrevolt.com/2018/09/20/absolute-qhaos-newq-qanon-greatawakening-neonrevolt/

50   Yes, I am aware of the controversy surrounding the subject of Majestic 12 possibly being an elaborate hoax. At any rate, the FBI did declare a number of documents surrounding MJ12 to be fakes, but... that just raises the question of whether one can trust the FBI on this matter or not. Regardless, my writing here should not be seen as an endorsement or negation of these claims, but rather reflect a spirit of inquiry and curiosity.

Whatever I was seeing, it was massive, and it was very difficult to tell if it was three crafts flying in unison, or one large craft with a light at each extremity. Just to be sure I wasn't hallucinating, I whipped out my phone and started recording from behind the driver's seat, getting as good of an image as I could capture in the low-light conditions, watching as the lights flickered and dimmed as they flew off in the distance.

And then, the lights just disappeared into the night. I would later upload the footage to my computer just to check once more that I wasn't crazy or hallucinating. Nope; there they were—the three lights hovering over the horizon.

I didn't know what to make of it at the time, but I held on to the puzzling footage, eventually uploading it to my site alongside the very Qdrops you're reading now. I had seen something inexplicable; this was like no aircraft I had ever seen before. And now, here Q was, offering an explanation—albeit an uncomfortable one—for what I had previously seen with my own two eyes and captured with my little cell phone camera.

So you can imagine my shock when I started receiving a number of comments basically all repeating the same sentiment:

"Oh yeah, buddy, you saw a TR-3 Black Manta."

Apparently this is a "thing" in UFO circles. More commonly referred to as "Flying Triangles" the TR-3 Black Manta is hypothesized to be a subsonic surveillance aircraft, and the result of a black project—similar to the SR-71 Blackbird and the B-2 Spirit before it.

(Remember UFO just means *Unidentified* Flying Object. There's nothing in that term that implies an extraterrestrial origin.) So perhaps what I had seen that night really was part of the Secret Space Program Q was now talking about.

And if Q was telling the truth about the SSP, maybe he was telling the truth when it came to the subject of ETs. At any rate, I had to start looking more closely at what specifically was being claimed by various witnesses in this field. I stumbled across the testimonies of Bob Lazar, a man who claimed to work at a satellite facility near Area 51, named S-4, where he was tasked with reverse-engineering alien craft that had supposedly found their way into the hands of the US government, and where he all but claims to have taken a sample of a stable isotope of something called "Element-115." The crazy thing is, Bill Cooper was on the fence about Lazar, at one point willing to hear him out, and at another point, labeling him a CIA-affiliated disinfo agent (which is to say that Cooper wasn't much help on the subject of Lazar's trustworthiness). One thing I will say is that Lazar's testimony has remained remarkably consistent over the years, and he has never attempted to monetize his story in the way some others have, during the intervening thirty-odd years since. At any rate, Area 51 didn't exist in the public consciousness until Bob came out with his testimony. Bob Lazar put Area 51 on the map, so to speak.

And coincidentally, the SR-71 black project was tested and developed at the same area where Bob claimed to work at Groom Lake, under the Lockheed A-12 name, so there at least seems to be some corroborative provenance (as they might say on *Antiques Roadshow*) to the claims Lazar has made.

The result of all this is that I began to consider areas of inquiry I had always previously dismissed. I would listen to interviews with men like Dr. Robert Wood, who had worked with Douglas Aircraft to try and reverse engineer "flying saucers" in a race against Lockheed. I would begin to look at the claims of Dan Burisch, specifically his claims about the Project Looking Glass technology possessed by Majestic 12, the Ark, and Stargates. And I would begin reading books I never thought I would be reading in my effort to try and wrap my mind around a subject I never thought I would need to seriously consider in my life.

What does this all imply about the nature of humanity? What of religion? I'm afraid, at this point, I have more questions than answers. It would certainly be easier to believe that perhaps Q was just causing a ruckus, not only to stress-test the 8chan servers (which was an admitted function of these Q & A sessions), but to garner more interest through the use of disinformation.

I realize how crazy this all must sound, on top of things like an ancient death cult, Atlantis, and everything else we've talked about thus far. Surely not everyone will be able to fully consider all that I say with an open mind right now (at least, during their first read-through). But once again, I find Q butting up against undeniable proofs already out there, if one looks closely enough.

You see, most people missed it (or simply forgot about it), but in 2018, the Pentagon declassified a brand new piece of video footage captured by an F-18 Super Hornet in 2015, over the East Coast of the United States. And there's no other way to put this: it was captured footage of an honest to goodness UFO.

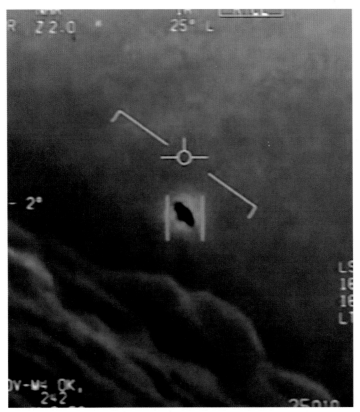

This wasn't amateur cell phone footage. This wasn't handheld camera nonsense. This was a fighter jet pursuing an unknown craft that performed dazzling maneuvers which are impossible for conventional aircraft. The footage was broadcast on ABC,[51] CNN,[52] BBC,[53] FOX,[54] and just about every other major news organization in the world. It's not hard to find, and no one's hiding it anywhere. The stunning footage was coming straight from the DOD, with a complete chain of custody attached to it, so no one can claim that it's a hoax, either.

So the question then becomes; why declassify this now? And why so suddenly? Was it possibly the Trump administration trying to prepare the masses for even larger, "crazier" disclosures? And if these programs had existed for some time, how were they funded? The CIA has typically used money from drug-running operations to fund black projects, but that wouldn't be anywhere near enough to fund an SSP for a single year, let alone decades.

Well… what about the 2.3 trillion dollars in unaccounted Pentagon funds, as reported by former secretary of defense Donald Rumsfeld? What about the 6.5 trillion dollars in unaccounted funds missing from the DOD budget, as per the 2016 IG report?[55] This isn't pocket change we're talking about here. Even mistakes in the millions could possibly be understood by the common man… Possibly even billions. But trillions suddenly MIA?

---

51   https://www.youtube.com/watch?v=G-3vlbhqzGg

52   https://www.youtube.com/watch?v=1THwiaXZfzA

53   https://www.youtube.com/watch?v=3RlbqOl_4NA

54   https://www.youtube.com/watch?v=fHwmWnY4P1w

55   https://archive.fo/Bi0KQ

It's very difficult to separate fact from fiction when it comes to this subject in particular, and the implications of some lines of thinking mean the speculation just doesn't stop. I said it earlier in the footnotes that I hope people don't read this as an all-out endorsement of everything said by everyone in this chapter, but rather that they see this as indicative of my curiosity. So much of what people consider "hard science" is actually just "religious" dogma dressed up in secular clothing. We often entertain certain notions which keep us from asking new questions and prevent us from truly uncovering anything unexpected, and thus expanding our real understanding. Personally, I try to not repeat those mistakes, and to at least account for my own biases.

Want hard proof of this? Just see how many times the plebs over at Reddit shilled for GMO produce, saying it was equal to, or better than organic produce, without understanding the real nuances behind certain practices that go along with GMO food production; for instance, the bulk application of glyphosate—which has not only been linked to the devastation of honeybee populations worldwide, but also to many forms of disease and cancer. The idiots at Reddit thought they were being "pro-science," but really, they were just being ignorant about the way one system affects another, and how it ripples throughout the world. It's the same as religious dogma, but like I just said, dressed up in secular clothing.

At the same time, I'm not saying to just blindly believe everyone who makes extraordinary claims. There does need to be a degree of healthy skepticism and critical thinking applied to all claims, as Anons have seen multiple times throughout the QAnon movement. We've seen numerous figures come and go who, at least on the surface, seem to be making the same or similar claims to QAnon (perhaps even convincing people with details that seemingly fill in some of the blanks left intentionally or unintentionally by Q), and yet, down the line, these individuals get outed as scammers, charlatans, or worse. For instance, one Anon recently compiled a 108 page dossier cross-examining the claims of the self-proclaimed "victim" of ritual Satanic abuse, Fiona Barnett, who has claimed for years that she was abused by Nicole Kidman's father, Antony Kidman, as part of MKUltra. Barnett would go on to claim that she was passed around between Billy Graham and President Nixon, and generally made to suffer through all kinds of horrors. And while her claims lined up with some claims made by others, elsewhere, this particular Anon arrived at the very convincing conclusion that Barnett was actually lying, that she had never been abused, and was actually using her story as a way of silencing actual victims along the way. Why she would do such a thing, well… a couple potential reasons spring to mind, but I'll leave that for the reader to speculate upon. When this bombshell dossier was released, all of Barnett's social media presences disappeared, though you can still find the dead links at the bottom of her homepage, as of this writing.

Regardless, at a certain point, the rubber has to meet the road when it comes to certain claims. And if contradictory evidence is found, one must align their beliefs with the incontrovertible truth. This is partially why I have so much respect for the QAnon movement. The Cabal is all about locking up knowledge and hoarding it for a select few, so as to maintain control over everyone. On the other hand, Q is about disclosure and transparency, and we've seen time and again points of data pointing to this Q-initiative being very much real, and very much true. So I hope it's clear to all that I ask these questions and go to these lengths not because I *want* to believe in some grand conspiracy, but because I've observed some undeniable phenomena (both objectively and subjectively) and have decided that it's best to keep an open mind and wrestle with this subject matter, because that may lead me to deepening my understanding, uncovering some real answers, and unlocking a more prosperous future, not just for me, but for the entire world.

There's no mistaking the kind of paradigm shift that has to occur in one's thinking when one is confronted by information which may dramatically contradict what one has heretofore believed, perhaps for their whole life (for one reason or another). But that shift must take place if the information presented is undeniably true. Though knowledge may be passed down from one generation to another, mere dogma is no substitute for true knowledge. Questioning, exploring, being willing to stand out, to take a risk, to be a "heretic" and listen to unconventional testimonies and ideas before evaluating them on their own merits, is truly the only way to advance one's understanding of the universe.

Don't get me wrong here— I'm not saying it's easy to make that shift; just that it's *necessary* upon certain conditions being met... And I also think it's fine to admit when one is at their limits with their current understanding. So far, I think I've been able to successfully communicate and condense a lot of the information surrounding the QAnon phenomenon in a digestible form. But here, with what I've presented in this chapter, is about where I reach the edge of my current understanding.

Not my ability to learn and understand more, mind you, but my current understanding.

I can only promise my readers that I will continue to investigate along these lines, and continue reporting my findings through the various channels through which I speak. I certainly do desire to know more; to discern fact from "monster-of-the-week-style" fiction, and I will continue to push the edge of the envelope and report back. Though I know the journey will not always be easy or comfortable—it certainly hasn't been thus far—I know, in the end, that the dogged pursuit of truth will be worthwhile.

I'd be remiss in all of this if I didn't mention, at least in passing, Trump's personal, deeply historical connection to the kind of events we're seeing play out now, via his uncle, John Trump, and a name you have all probably heard at least once before: Nikola Tesla. Yes, the very same Tesla who, despite being a genius inventor, died in obscurity and poverty after having been robbed and exploited by the less intelligent, though much more cut-throat industrialists of his day. The very same Tesla who has since become regarded as quite the forward-thinking luminary; like a modern day DaVinci, far ahead of his time, though lacking the benevolent patronage of a Medici to ensure his work would always have a home.

A tall immigrant who was often more concerned with the thoughts swirling in his own head than in the people around him, Tesla would claim to have experienced "visions" from childhood; a phenomenon that he would embrace and channel as an adult, leading him to become a wondrous inventor who felt he was pulling down his ideas from a divine source outside himself, before subsequently unlocking the secrets of the universe in a way few people have since.

Tesla is, perhaps, most famous for his role in the "war of the currents," a feud between his own preferred method for transmitting electricity, alternating current (AC), and Edison's inferior method, direct current (DC). This is where all those stories about Edison electrocuting animals to death in front of crowds come from, but many might be surprised to learn that the most famous of all of these, the electrocution of Topsy the elephant at Coney Island, had nothing to do with demonstrating the "dangers" of AC to the masses at all. The frying of this particular pachyderm actually happened about a decade after the "war of the currents" had already been settled, with AC emerging as the clear victor. Topsy, having killed three men, was slated to be euthanized as a result, and the only real alternative at the time—remember, this was 1903—was to literally hang the elephant from a crane by a giant noose. This was, believe it or not, actually the "standard method" for executing elephants at the time (if you can even standardize that kind of thing in the first place).

Or at least it was, until the ASPCA stepped in and said that hanging elephants from cranes by giant nooses was inhumane (and to their credit, the ASPCA probably got that one right). Electrocution, however, was considered a humane alternative. So they strapped electrode paddles to Topsy's feet, pumped up the voltage, and Topsy's ticker tapped out in just under ten seconds. Still, it is true that Edison had performed similar animal executions way before Topsy, mostly on stray cats and dogs, before moving on to things like horses, so the general point still stands: Edison was trying to spook the public into utilizing his Direct Current over Tesla's Alternating Current.

But the corporate propaganda didn't work, and AC would win the day as the technical advantages it had over DC were readily apparent to all. For instance, DC only had a range of about one-mile at the time, and would require the construction of numerous substations at regular intervals, something the monopolists of the day might have liked, but which was impractical in the face of AC's extended range and far lower production costs. DC also had this nasty habit of sparking at the required "commutators," which was not safe by any stretch of the imagination. AC simply outclassed DC when it came to generating and transmitting power. But to respond to these claims that AC was more harmful than DC, Tesla would have photos taken of both himself, and his friends, allowing AC current to pass safely through their bodies. One such photo showcased his friend, Samuel Clemens, illuminating a bulb between his fingertips, even as Tesla himself watched on from the background.

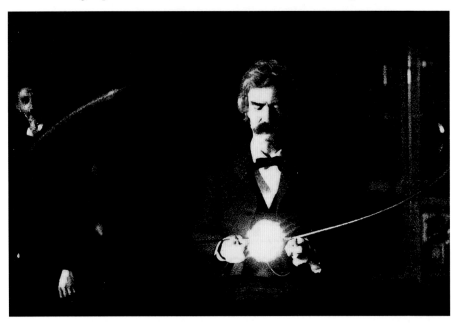

Though, of course, you might recognize Clemens better by his pen name, Mark Twain. It's not known how the two met, but Twain would spend much time marveling at Tesla's new inventions, even at one point seeking medical help from Tesla. You see, Twain had been dealing with a particularly persistent bout of constipation at the time, and as such, Tesla advised him to stand on top of this vibrating disc he had recently invented. Twain eventually obliged Tesla, perhaps out of desperation, and was delighted when, upon Tesla activating this new "oscillator" invention, electricity started rippling through the air and the plate below his feet started vibrating. The effect delighted the constipated Twain, who, despite his bowel obstruction, started to dance, praising the sensation Tesla had somehow harnessed in this new machine. Think of it like a vigorous massage that could also make your hair stand up on end. At a certain point, Tesla asked Twain to get off the machine, but Twain was so enthralled, he simply wouldn't leave.

And that's about when a look of dread came over Twain's face as he realized the oscillator had performed its job with unexpected efficiency. For the sake of prudence, let's just say things were moving once again—and quite rapidly. Twain called out in horror as he waddled away from the platform, demanding to know where the "water closet" was located in this particular facility, before scurrying off in the appropriate and necessary direction.

But Tesla was less the "mad scientist" type and more a mystic, who, while accumulating over two hundred patents during his lifetime, dreamed of a world where free energy could be drawn down from the atmosphere and transmitted wirelessly wherever it was needed, across the entirety of the planet. At one point, Tesla would declare:

> "When wireless is fully applied, the earth will be converted into a huge brain, capable of response in every one of its parts."

That was an incredibly radical thought for a man living at the turn of the century, when people were still trying to figure out how to funnel all the horse manure piling up in New York alleys out of the city. Tesla intended to test this theory, perhaps most dramatically, with the construction of his Wardenclyffe Tower, which was not only supposed to provide free electricity for the residents of Shoreham, New York, but be able to transmit messages all the way to England as well. See, Tesla believed he could use the earth itself as a medium for sending these messages, but sadly, he never got a chance to test his theory out. The financial backer for the project, J.P. Morgan, would pull out even as the tower was being built, devastating Tesla's personal finances, and forcing Tesla's tower project to shutter before it ever reached operational completion.

Tesla would continue developing ideas throughout his life, ideas spinning off in ever more radical directions, even as he grew more marginalized and more impoverished. Late in life he would bounce from hotel to hotel to avoid paying his bills, before passing away at the age of eighty-six, on January 7, 1943, in room 3327 of the New Yorker Hotel.

Needless to say, the FBI had been keeping track of Tesla's comings and goings for some time, because when the man who helped electrify the nation starts going on about death rays, and energy shields… you sit up and pay attention. In essence, Tesla was describing applications for something he called "Teleforce." These applications sat among an assortment of other fantastical ideas, and when Tesla died, the FBI swooped in and seized everything they could from his belongings, taking reams of documents that, to this day, may still be sitting in some government vault somewhere, far away from the prying eyes of the general public.

b7C

Weehawken, N.J., 9/24/40.

Department of Justice,

Atten. Mr. J. Edgar Hoover,

Washington, D. C.

ALL INFORMATION CONTAINED
IN IS UNCLASSIFIED
2-2-80 BY SP4 Jeno fate

Dear Mr. Hoover:

The appended article was printed in the New York Times issue of Sunda September 22, 1940 and if based on proven facts ,should be of vital importance to our War Department as well as to that of other nations now controlled oy insane dictators.

If ,as the author states,the teleforce has been perfected by Nikola Tesla,it would be a measure of foresightedness to insure his constant guarding against his beir molested ,possibly kidnapped and tortured,by alien enemies for the purpose of seizing the secret of such an invaluable instrument of war and/or defense

The foregoing is offered just in case the article and its inferences have not been called to your attention.

Very truly yours

b7C

I ENCL

100- 2237-1

And this is where John Trump enters the picture. Yes, we're talking about the brother of President Donald Trump's father. John Trump is POTUS' uncle, and while he was alive, he was a brilliant man who did some cutting-edge research for the military during World War II (specifically, helping to develop radar technologies). This would lay the groundwork for an illustrious career at MIT's Radiation Laboratory, where he would spend over three decades churning out life-saving innovations like the high voltage X-ray generator alongside Robert Van de Graaff.

It was due to his expertise and previous history with the military that the FBI would ask John Trump to help them review and interpret all of Tesla's documents. What he saw there, we can't be entirely sure, but one thing we do know comes from *The New Yorker*, who quotes Trump as saying, "My uncle used to tell me about nuclear before nuclear was nuclear."

Most of us relegate things like "death rays" and "teleforce" to the realm of science fiction, and thus, summarily dismiss them out of hand. Knowing his uncle and his expertise, I don't think Trump ever quite shared that same disability in his thinking that so many of us seem to have, but rather was able to see and question things from innovative angles. This may have led him to perceive things in a manner which many of us have simply been conditioned to avoid or relegate to the realm of fantasy. Heck, for all we know, Professor Trump told a young POTUS everything, and maybe that's been a driving factor behind the progressive levels of disclosure we've seen over the course of his administration.

Yet… before we go, there's one more thing I'd like to touch upon, if we're going to perform a complete and thorough survey on the subject of QAnon. And this subject requires a bit of background knowledge, because it concerns a prediction Q made that, at the time, seemingly never came true…

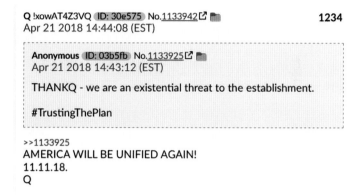

When Q made this post, he had been at work for some six months at the time. Many Anons saw the date and figured that since it had been about a year since Q had started, things were going to start popping off in the ensuing months. Arrests could finally happen at any time. The Deep State pedophile cult would be exposed, and the whole world would finally see what was really going on.

Oh, and there'd be a parade, too. Slated for November 10, it lined right up with the 11/11 date Q was providing, too.

But then Trump canceled the parade in August (technically delaying it until some still-undisclosed time in 2019), and as August turned into September, and September turned into October… many Anons became worried that nothing was ever going to come to pass.

How could this be? Q had very clearly said 11/11 in his drop. Was Q just manipulating us again, hyping up yet another date to drive the Cabal into making more mistakes and wasting more of their resources, like he had with D5?

11/11 came and passed, and all we saw instead was mostly "just" unsealing orders for the then acting attorney general Whitaker, who had taken over since Sessions stepped down:

Q !!mG7VJxZNCI No.452 ☑ 🏴   **2478**
Nov 11 2018 12:58:18 (EST)

Let the unsealing begin.
Let the DEC[L]AS begin.
Let the WORLD witness the TRUTH.
We, the PEOPLE.
JUSTICE UNDER THE LAW.
Q

Q !!mG7VJxZNCI No.461 ☐ ▥   2487
Nov 11 2018 14:41:55 (EST)

[Placeholder - DECLAS GEN_pub]
[Placeholder - SPEC_C_pub]

Q !!mG7VJxZNCI No.460 ☐ ▥   2486
Nov 11 2018 14:41:25 (EST)

[Placeholder - FVEY_pub]
[Placeholder - FISA_pub]

Q !!mG7VJxZNCI No.459 ☐ ▥   2485
Nov 11 2018 14:40:57 (EST)

[Placeholder - Acts of Treason + support Articles]
[Placeholder - Foreign Acts_pub]

Q !!mG7VJxZNCI No.458 ☐ ▥   2484
Nov 11 2018 14:40:15 (EST)

[Placeholder - Branch termination(s)]
[Placeholder - Leak(s)]

Q !!mG7VJxZNCI No.457 ☐ ▥   2483
Nov 11 2018 14:39:52 (EST)

[Placeholder - SC rulings re: challenges re: Civ Non_Civ]
[Placeholder - SC rulings re: USA v Def appeals]

Q !!mG7VJxZNCI No.456 ☐ ▥   2482
Nov 11 2018 14:39:32 (EST)

[Placeholder - Indictments Tracking > Non_Civ]

Q !!mG7VJxZNCI No.455 ☐ ▥   2481
Nov 11 2018 14:39:14 (EST)

[Placeholder - Indictments Tracking > Civ]

Q would go on to describe Whitaker as the "placeholder" between Senate appointed attorney generals. With Sessions forced to recuse himself from overseeing the Mueller probe, he couldn't do anything that would even look remotely like interference with the probe. By stepping down and allowing a "placeholder" to come in—someone who didn't need Senate approval to do anything and who wasn't tied down like Sessions was—Whitaker could do a ton of "damage" very quickly before the next attorney general was appointed by POTUS and approved by the Senate (in this case, AG Barr). Q would also call this the "Scaramucci model," where a heavy-hitter gets in, hits hard, and gets out fast.

And of course, the Dems screeched and howled at Whitaker for a while, demanding he appear before the House Judiciary Committee and answer all their leading questions in order to find some way, some crack they could exploit for leverage, and thus take control over the Special Counsel. But Whitaker wasn't there to play games. Unintimidated, he gave them absolutely nothing, and at one point put Democratic Representative Jerrold Nadler firmly in his place when, during one particularly tiresome line of inquiry, Whitaker reminded him that he had no authority over him whatsoever by dryly responding, "Mr. Chairman, I see your five minutes is up."

But that's somewhat beside the larger point I'm trying to make, which is that, at this time, we were promised unity throughout America. Despite the unsealing orders (which we had no real way of verifying, anyway), we didn't see much unity in America. People were still very much divided and squabbling. Very little looked secure, and the drama of this all was dragging on with no end in sight. Many walked away from Q that night, tired of the "false" and "unfulfilled" promises.

But in truth, Q was challenging us to "expand our thinking" once more, and illustrated this by answering one particularly notorious troll who had been spamming up the boards for some time, who went by the name "Freddy Benson," and who would regularly post in large red letters, alongside pictures of (the now deceased) "Toots" the cat.

Q !!mG7VJxZNCl ID: a6527c No.4117452 📷   **2527**
Dec 2 2018 16:26:57 (EST)

> Anonymous ID: 6b728e No.4117309 📷
> Dec 2 2018 16:19:11 (EST)
>
> >>4117250
> WHAT HAPPENED TO 11/11/18 UNIFIED AMERICA DAY YOU
> DISGUSTING LIAR FRAUD???
> ANSWER FREDDY YOU FUCKING FAGGOT

>>4117309
Think WAVES.
WW?
Define 'unified'
[17]
SAT knockout forced new CLAS tech **[online]** by who?
[Controlled] moment activated? **[17]**
Do you believe in coincidences?
Do you believe your efforts here persuade people to stop the
pursuit of TRUTH, **[CA_J]**?
There is a place for everyone.
Q

What Q was referring to in these drops was actually an event that took place on 11/11/18 which almost went unnoticed. Recall first how Q had taken out Cabal satellite and supercomputer systems in one fell swoop back in August. Assuming the NSA and military intelligence also monitor all earth-based communication systems, there was now really no way for the higher-ups in the Cabal to communicate with each other. Their code words were known, so they couldn't speak through public channels. Every bit and byte passing through the internet was being monitored, where even encryption wouldn't guarantee real security. Cell phones were out; even burners. And recall that Nellie Ohr had resorted to trying to establish ham radio comm channels at one point (and even that failed at concealing her actions, too). So what was left? Was Obama going to start stringing tin cans together and wire it to Joe Biden's treehouse?

Would Elizabeth Warren start sending out smoke signals? Maybe Hillary could pass notes to the pope, so long as the pope agreed to eat the paper afterwards.

But realistically speaking, what was left?

The Cabal was still communicating and coordinating somehow, as their efforts to resist Trump and QAnon hadn't, collectively speaking, slowed down—at least, judging by what we Anons were seeing at the time. So how were they doing it? How were they still talking?

What if there was a classified system that used the very earth itself to send signals to other parts of the world?

Sound like science fiction?

Q would eventually respond:

"Think WAVES"

"WW?" (Worldwide).

Anons' jaws dropped to the floor when they finally understood. The articles[56] documenting the phenomenon wouldn't come out until several weeks after 11/11, and there was no way we could have known prior… but on that exact date, a signal had been sent through the entire planet, and scientists had taken notice.

For twenty minutes straight, mysterious seismic waves caused the entire planet to simultaneously experience one monumental earthquake. Now, this wasn't an earthquake like you or I understand it. These seismic waves were imperceptible to every person on the planet, and yet they were picked up by seismographs around the world. Baffled seismologists took to Twitter and started posting their data and messaging each other as fast as they could, each trying to figure out what had just occurred. One keen observer posted a USGS graph from a station in Kenya:

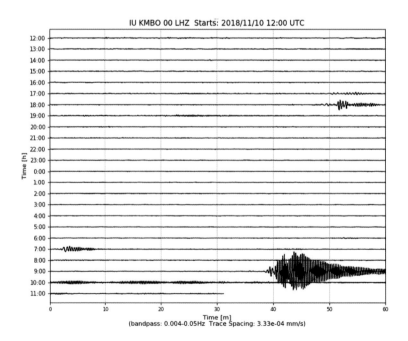

IU KMBO 00 LHZ Starts: 2018/11/10 12:00 UTC

Time [m]
(bandpass: 0.004–0.05Hz Trace Spacing: 3.33e-04 mm/s)

---

56   https://www.nationalgeographic.com/science/2018/11/strange-earthquake-waves-rippled-around-world-

And then another from Zambia:

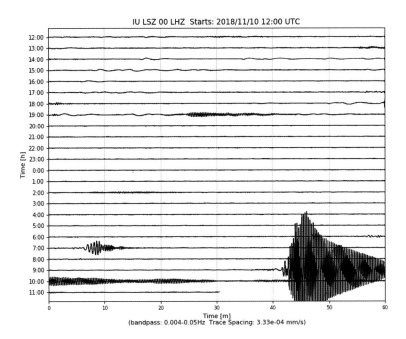

Spain:

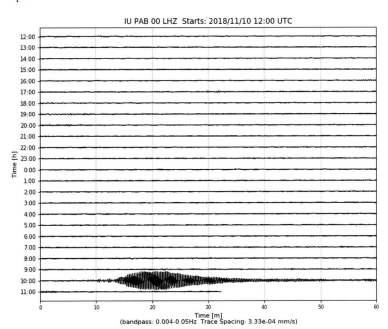

New Zealand!

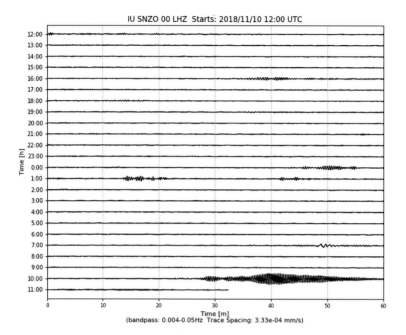

IU SNZO 00 LHZ Starts: 2018/11/10 12:00 UTC

Time [m]
(bandpass: 0.004-0.05Hz Trace Spacing: 3.33e-04 mm/s)

All these stations were ringing in unison. Baffled seismologists from around the world all saw it happening **everywhere** at the same time. They didn't know what was causing the event, but the data was clear! They couldn't deny it!

The entire planet was *vibrating!*

And what's more was that these weren't like normal earthquake waves, which oscillate in certain distinct patterns. These were perfect zig-zagging waves… as though they were man-made, being produced by some kind of machine. They looked… *artificial.*

The waves would continue for twenty minutes…

And they would occur at **SEVENTEEN** second intervals.

Q is the seventeenth letter of the alphabet, and though I haven't talked much in the way of Qproofs yet, Anons have seen time and time again, that seventeen equals Q.

And all this happened, right underneath our feet, and no one felt a thing.

You would think the media would report on, frankly, the entire planet ringing like a bell, and I don't know what you saw, but very few mainstream news outlets (if any) covered this event at all. That gets even stranger when you consider that something like this has never been observed before in human history, let alone independently verified by thousands of scientists and observers around the world.

Eventually, by registering the timing of the waves, the consensus formed that the "source" of these waves was somewhere in the Comoros archipelago, in the waters between the Southeastern coast of Africa and Madagascar. As for what specifically is down there that could cause such an event, I couldn't tell you. The possibilities boggle the mind.

And this is partially why I brought up Tesla earlier. Recall that Tesla envisioned using the earth itself to send and receive signals. I can't tell you *how* the White Hats had actually managed to pull off such an incredible feat, but if the Cabal had thought they still had one last secure comm channel left, one last secure channel with which they could speak through the earth itself, just like Tesla had envisioned years prior… If they thought they were going to elude detection by crawling underground like the snakes they are…

On 11/11/18, the earth groaned and the Cabal shuddered.

They had all finally heard—

> **Q !UW.yye1fxo No.49**🔗 📷   **572**
> Jan 21 2018 14:28:00 (EST)
>
> THE SHOT HEARD AROUND THE WORLD.
> THE GREAT AWAKENING.
> A WEEK TO REMEMBER.
> Q

EPILOGUE

"WE, THE PEOPLE!"

—January 14, 2018 From Qdrop #

Q !UW.yye1fxo No.20 ☐ ▶   533
Jan 14 2018 00:17:29 (EST)

WE, THE PEOPLE!
WE, THE PEOPLE!
WE, THE PEOPLE!
WE, THE PEOPLE!
WHERE WE GO ONE, WE GO ALL.
NO ONE PERSON IS ABOVE ANOTHER.
WE, THE PEOPLE, ARE MAKING THE WORLD A BETTER PLACE.
WE, THE PEOPLE, ARE TAKING BACK OUR COUNTRY (& WORLD)
FROM THE EVIL LOSERS WHO WOULD DO US HARM (ALL FOR A
BUCK).
NO MORE.
STAND UP PATRIOTS.
STAND UP AND DEFEND WHAT YOU KNOW IS RIGHT.
GOD BLESS YOU AND GOD BLESS THE UNITED STATES OF
AMERICA.
4, 10, 20

There's so much more I wish I could tell you.

There are so many topics I'll not have the chance to touch upon in this book, massive as it is already. As I said in the beginning, I started writing this book in May 2018, when Q was still relegated to relative obscurity. As I finish writing this, in May 2019, I am staggered at how far we have come in that short amount of time. The sheer panic level of the Cabal raises with each passing day, and more find themselves joining "The Great Awakening," as their eyes are opened and they step out of the "cave" for the first time in their lives.

But how did we, the Anons, know we were right this whole time? What inspired us to carry on, to press in, to dig, meme, and pray harder?

I wish I could show you every little Qproof we Anons have seen along the way. I wish I could show you video of President Trump waving his hands in a Q-formation during multiple speeches. I wish I could show you how, with a wink and a nod, he'd reference our collective Chan culture by reciting memetic catchphrases like, "It's happening" in a presidential address. I wish I could show you every time Q and Trump were posting in the same room, at the exact same time, on purpose, just to squeeze in an extra encoded message to us Anons. I wish I could show you every time President Trump willingly made himself look foolish by deliberately misspelling tweets; how he had to endure the endless mockery not just from organized mobs on Twitter, but from the media itself—just so he could spell out secret signals when it mattered…

Q !!mG7VJxZNCI ID: 72895d No.5134370 ☑ 📄   **2695**
Feb 11 2019 23:07:05 (EST)

Anonymous ID: 2b91c6 No.5134144 ☑ 📄
Feb 11 2019 22:56:46 (EST)

Screen Shot 2019-02-11 at 7.51.21 PM.png   ⬇

34afaaf863584e77256baca2c48bf28c42e9a8bc3e77952cb523b6a4c6ef27e8.png

Not a T-shirt - she laid a square cloth with the Q on it when
POTUS came by.   PERFECT IDEA when they don't allow Q shirts
in.

>>5134144
https://twitter.com/Jvineyard2011/status/1095168967457558528
☑ 📄
POTUS "Did they get the clip?"
Yes, Mr. President.
POTUS "Did they catch all the references?"
Yes, Mr. President.
POTUS "Show me."
Thank you, Mr. John Vineyard.
Thank you, Anons.
(return publicly)
Q

True, some of us were just able to "tell" from very early on what Q was saying was true, as was captured in this conversation between two Anons, just mere days after Q's first post in 2017:

Anonymous ID:X3kH1O5O Tue 07 Nov 2017 16:04:19 No.148431375
Report
Quoted By: >>148431562 >>148431742 >>148431745 >>148431795 >>148431891 >>148431933
>>148431986 >>148432025 >>148433054 >>148433259 >>148433991 >>148434276 >>148436955
>>148437378

M-Intel Officer here.
You are not wasting time following Q.
There was one embedded string he stated that told us (i.e. those in particular places) he was 100% highly placed.
I, like most within intel, am confined to the data house that is assigned. We cannot peak outside nor have access. The mainframe is literally inaccessible unless there in person w/ special access. This person is above Q-class and must be close to the CC. The house I'm building falls in line with a key portion of the questions being asked here. This along with his one sentence that verifies his IDEN (something that nobody on the outside will ever know - highly classified) proves the information he's providing. There are good people in high level places watching this. Godspeed to you all and thank you for helping to serve your country.

Anonymous ID: 6eWaRgNW Tue 07 Nov 2017 16:08:49 No.148431933
Report
Quoted By: >>148433657

>>148431375

Thanks for the confirmation. Some of us have been watching this develop for two years, now. In your opinion, how serious is this iteration? Should I buy popcorn or ammo? Asking for a friend.

Anonymous ID:X3kH1O5O Tue 07 Nov 2017 16:21:08 No.148433657
Report
Quoted By: >>148434350 >>148434865 >>148434894 >>148436047 >>148437751

>>148431933
From a friend to a friend you don't need to worry at all. I don't think people on this board fully appreciate or understand what is being provided here. It's literally a circular flow diagram that can be printed out and cross checked against the news releases. As he openly states, disinformation is real and necessary. If you're in the intel comm you'd appreciate that statement. He's not going to disclose specifics about future operations/events because that would be violating the CC. Instead, and quite remarkably, he's dropping questions that lead to answers that can be put into a diagram and understood once things become public. For example, why did he emphasize Saudi Arabia so much right before the arrests and attack on SA occur? Do you really believe all of that was simply a coincidence? He masked it perfectly by leading outsiders to the conclusion that the US was the 1st target thereby not disclosing the true nature of the drop but yet validated himself by the pre-disclosure of that material ahead of the date. Think circular flow diagram mixed with disinformation via direction. Meaning he's pointing over there but really the focus is here and only until you publicly obtain the news can you go back and understand that thereby not giving up the mission/operation. To put it another way, a lot of us here have printed it out and marked it up with several marker colors and amazed by what we're seeing. As Patriots, it's a day we've been longing to witness. We stand behind the President. This will be my last post here.

But most of us needed a little more help along the way. And if we were paying attention, we were able, in time, to catch the "proofs" and see for ourselves exactly what was happening.

For instance, there was the time during Christmas 2018 when Trump had a "Q" stocking strung up next to a "T" stocking in the Trump Chicago hotel's main elevator for Christmas. Moreover, Anons visiting the site would inform us that whoever had hung that stocking did so intentionally, as they had to make this themselves by buying an "O" stocking, and drawing the descending stroke across it to turn it into a "Q" with a matching red marker:

There was also, for instance, that time when Vice President Pence took a photo with a Broward County SWAT officer wearing a QAnon patch, before posting the photo to his Twitter account:

Q !!mG7VJxZNCl (ID: cc526f) No.4093748 ☑ 📑   **2515**
Nov 30 2018 22:33:39 (EST)

> **Anonymous** (ID: d3abcf) No.4093626 ☑ 📑
> Nov 30 2018 22:30:15 (EST)
> A0E3AB21-73BC-41FB-A8CC-AE1CF69E9022.png   ⬇
>
> All for a LARP right?
> Q
>
> >>4093464

>>4093626
It's spreading.
We, the PEOPLE.
Q

There was the time Trump uploaded a picture to Twitter, and the picture's filename started with "DOITQ." Not only that, but tracing the positions of all their thumbs leads to an outline of a Q.

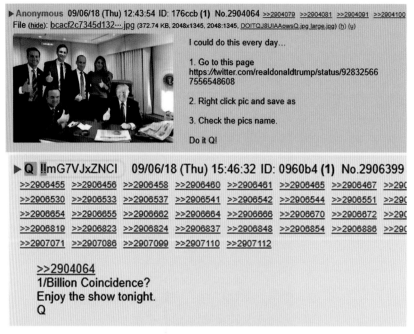

There was the time they pulled this off:

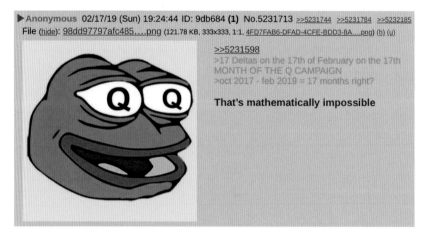

There was the time I saw "Lionel" Lebron, a popular personality on YouTube, radio, and books, get invited to the White House, causing the MSM to collectively lose their minds. The subtext to this was that Lionel had been reading my site for some time, applauding the articles I had written on his daily broadcasts, and had subsequently started spreading the "gospel" of Q himself.

There was the time I mentioned earlier, when QAnon would link to a picture of the son of one of my readers, wearing the very QAnon hat I had designed.

Q !!mG7VJxZNCI No.423 🖼️   2443
Nov 6 2018 16:22:24 (EST)

https://twitter.com/AddrianStorm/status/1059917452836974594
🔗 🖼️
We are UNITED.
The world is changing.
Can you feel it?
Q

Addrian 🏴 ⭐⭐⭐   (Follow) ⌄
@AddrianStorm

Spending the day teaching the future
generation the TRUTH.

I took photos of him at 1 years old and
sister at 3 watching the inauguration
because I knew how historical it would
be.

#Q #GreatAwakening @POTUS #QAnon
#Truth #GodBlessAmerica

1:16 PM - 6 Nov 2018

2,887 Retweets 8,596 Likes

💬 1.4K   ⟲ 2.9K   ♡ 8.6K

In a private chat later, his mother would tell me it was actually his favorite hat.

Who can forget that night on July 17, 2019, in Greenville, North Carolina, when two proud parents held their baby aloft, and Trump exclaimed "Look at that beautiful baby; look at that beautiful baby! Wow! What a baby! What a baby!" He continued to gush over this baby during his rally, forcing everyone to pay attention. And the entire time the baby had a giant letter Q drawn on the back of her onesie. Trump, once again, was rubbing the reality of Q in the media's faces.[57]

---

57   https://www.neonrevolt.com/2019/07/18/qbaby-and-mega-revelations-newq-qanon-greatawakening-neonrevolt/

And there were, of course, the many, many times Trump talked to us directly by invoking his moniker: Q+

Q !!mG7VJxZNCI (ID: b3258f) No.5362124 ⌕ ▣   **2885**
Feb 24 2019 13:12:51 (EST)

They NEVER thought Crooked Hillary would lose.
SO MANY DISASTROUS MISTAKES MADE.
RETURNING POWER TO THE PEOPLE!
Q+

Those are some of the bigger and easier examples I could show you in the limited time we have remaining, but there are quite literally hundreds of little examples that ramp up the intrigue and ripple across the Q-timeline—events Anons know by heart.

For instance, there was the time Q "accidentally" posted his password, revealing yet another message to the Cabal:

"NowC@mesTHEP@in—-23!!!"

There's even the time Q "accidentally" made a post about a certain member of the Cabal, but then very seriously asked every Anon to scrub all traces of it from the net and not repost it anywhere. I still have a screenshot of that particular post saved on one of my devices, but I can't share it until Q gives us all the green light… so it might not see the light of day until well after the individual concerned is locked away for good.

So, what comes next?

If Q is true, and indeed, I believe he is true, you've now begun to truly see, perhaps for the first time in your life, the scope of everything that's really going on in the world, and the true nature of the evil we face. You'll recall that Trump officially launched this Q-operation when he announced "The Calm before the Storm" in October 2017. That implies that, one day, and one day soon, "the Calm" will be over and "the Storm" will make its landfall. When it does, it will be unlike anything the world has ever experienced before.

I designed this book as a sort of "life raft" to help save people when the Storm finally hits, so that they wouldn't drown in whirlpools of fear, anger, rage, or confusion. That's just what the Cabal would want, anyway; unwitting proles marching and dying in the streets for their sorry hides. I also wanted it to stand as a testament, a record of everything we Anons have been through and are learning throughout the day-to-day of this digital war. But the story doesn't end here with this book. There are countless articles, comments, posts, videos, and websites (including my own, which I hope you'll take the time to read) dedicated towards understanding everything related to Q. The information is out there in abundance, so join with us, and humbly connect with like-minded patriots so that together we can reclaim and preserve our nation, our freedom, and our way of life for generations to come!

Looking back on everything now, I feel tremendously privileged to have been a part of this movement. I could never have imagined, so many years ago, that this is where I'd end up, and that this would be where I would channel my talents and abilities. My longtime readers know that I'm not always the easiest person with which to get along. I didn't always land at the right conclusion in my essays, or fully understand everything as I attempted to comprehend, organize, and disseminate all that I was witnessing. But it is my hope that when this is all over, they will be able to overlook my many flaws and defects, and after observing these many labors, they will stand back and marvel with me at how far we've all come with POTUS, Q, and every other heroic patriot who counted the cost and sacrificed of themselves to help preserve our Republic, and lead us back into the light.

So from the bottom of my heart, I want to extend a personal thanks to every single Anon who helped wage war against the Cabal, and to every single follower of Q who stood up, spoke out, and refused to be shut down in the face of intense opposition. History, and your descendants, will smile on your courage.

>>1809390 >>1809412 >>1809789 >>1810019 >>1810043

Just a late night random thought. When this is all over, those who are Q, and many other Patriots won't even get a public Thank You.
No medals, no parades, no bonus check not even a public mention.
They've volunteered for God knows how many days, hours, dangerous assignments and stress.
Based on what Q has said a few probably gave their lives.
I presume that at least some have families.
They'll never be able to tell their spouse or kids how they saved the Republic.
When they go to cocktail parties, neighborhood BBQ's and family gatherings they'll hear batshit crazy theories from normies.
All they'll be able to do is smile and nod.

Because the MSM and basically every other public media outlet is comped the only outlet they had available was the chan boards.
Basically the outhouse of the internet.
The only place wild enough, profane enough and free enough to do this.
The only place on the entire internet this could be pulled off was in the gutter.
The only recognition or thanks they'll ever get is from the gutter.

I don't mean that as an insult or degradation of what Q and all anons are doing.
Sometimes in history societies have been distorted and ruined by a small group of those who think they're entitled.
We were normies in the gutter; we became anons because we woke up and learned that there is nothing wrong with us and it doesn't have to be this way.
Q and Patriots learned that too, and are risking everything for themselves and the rest of us.

Q and Patriots, knowing what they know, must be 1000x more frustrated then us anons.
This is painstakingly slow but it's the only way.
Their discipline is incredible. I am trying to emulate them best I can and I hope you will too.

To Q and all of you, Thank You. Thank you from the gutter of the internet. Thank You from average, little people anons you will never know.
Probably no one of us could ever afford to pay you back but as a whole maybe we can make the gutter an ok place.
Maybe someday we can make America a place without a gutter.

I wish I had some profound words but I don't so I'll go with Gen. Mattis:

"Hold The Line."

Thanks again.

-Anon

To every Anon who persisted through it all, who sacrificed, who dug, who researched, who shared, but most importantly, who refused to give up! **You** have my utmost gratitude, and my deepest respect! Your sacrifices and contributions to the cause of liberty will never be forgotten.

As Q said:

> **Q !!mG7VJxZNCI No.422** 🏴   2442
> Nov 6 2018 16:16:21 (EST)
>
> History is being made.
> You are the saviors of mankind.
> Nothing will stop what is coming.
> Nothing.
> Q

Anons know these next passages well.

Pretty soon, everyone will understand the truth contained within them:

> **Q !xowAT4Z3VQ ID: c2ded6 No.1184271** 🏴   1269
> Apr 25 2018 15:33:17 (EST)
>
> Are you awake?
> Do you SEE (for yourself) the MSM = propaganda tool of the LEFT?
> Do you SEE FB/Twitter/GOOG censoring non LEFT POVs?
> Do you SEE the corruption?
> Do you SEE the EVIL?
> Are you a SLAVE?
> Are you CONTROLLED?
> Are you a SHEEP?
> ARE YOU AWAKE?
> DO YOU THINK FOR YOURSELF?
> LEARN THE TRUTH.
> FACTS.
> HISTORY.
> THE GREAT AWAKENING.
> THEY ARE LOSING CONTROL.
> RESPECT OPINION OR ATTACK THOSE WHO DARE CHALLENGE
> THE NARRATIVE?
> IT'S RIGHT IN FRONT OF YOU.
> WHO ARE THE TRUE FASCISTS?
> WHO ARE THE TRUE RACISTS?
> WHY DOES THE ANTIFA FLAG MIMIC THAT OF THE NAZIS?
> COINCIDENCE?
> FOR HUMANITY - WAKE UP - LEARN.
> FIGHT FIGHT FIGHT
> WHERE WE GO ONE, WE GO ALL!
> Q

Q !!mG7VJxZNCl **ID: 4e2679** No.5551524 📄 **2994**
Mar 7 2019 00:34:41 (EST)

PEOPLE ARE PAWNS IN THEIR SICK GAME OF GLOBAL
DOMINATION.
PEOPLE ARE DIVIDED TO PREVENT A RISING OF THE PEOPLE.
PEOPLE ARE DIVIDED AND TAUGHT TO FIGHT THEMSELVES
INSTEAD OF THE RULING CLASS.
RACE VS RACE
RELIGION VS RELIGION
POLITICAL VS POLITICAL
CLASS VS CLASS
SEX VS SEX
WHEN YOU ARE DIVIDED, YOU ARE WEAK.
WHEN YOU ARE WEAK, YOU HAVE NO POWER.
WHEN YOU HAVE NO POWER, YOU HAVE NO CONTROL.
STAY STRONG, PATRIOTS.
STAY UNITED, NOT DIVIDED.
YOU ARE WHAT MATTERS.
YOU, AWAKE, IS THEIR GREATEST FEAR.
Q

You now know, after reading this book, exactly what's at stake. You can see through the mass manipulation, through the lies and deceit used to shackle us, and turn us all against each other, just so we wouldn't fight them! And you also know what kind of miraculous things the future holds for us.

Now, at the end of all this, all the time spent writing, analyzing, creating, dissecting, and disseminating… you can see why I chose the analogy of "the Cave" when we started all this. We Anons don't only want to funnel everyone out of the cave, but we want the light to pour in, to illuminate every crack and crevice, to expose every slithering, subterranean swamp creature working to keep everyone enslaved. And then we want to lace every pillar, every transept, every darkened corner of the cave with truth bombs before blowing the entire infernal thing to Kingdom come!

I've done all I can for now to help you break those Cabal shackles and lead you to the mouth of that cave, just like Q and other Anons helped me beforehand. But the final choice lies before you, and you alone. You have to summon the courage deep within yourself to turn your back on the cave and put it behind you if you ever want to truly step outside, into the light of freedom.

That choice will be harder for some than it will be for others, because it involves a true repentance and renunciation of everything associated with that ancient death cult we call Cabal—and that's no small task. Truly, in order to bring the whole facade of the cabal crumbling down, we have to starve it. And in order to truly starve it, we need to end something that might seem somewhat tangential at first glance, but which in truth, is actually a cornerstone to this death cult that has held power for so long. We need to end the system of human sacrifice in America by demanding Roe v. Wade be overturned by the Supreme Court.

In Holy Scripture (and many of my readers will know this well) the word for "repentance" in the ancient Greek is *metanoia*. The physical description of *metanoia* is as though someone is walking along a road, and then suddenly they stop, do a 180-degree turn, and start heading in the other direction. It represents a fundamental change in the way one is living, forever changing the trajectory of their lives. For some of you reading this right now, you will need to make such a radical change in your own thoughts and actions. You need to literally begin thinking and behaving in a way that's the complete opposite of what you've previously thought and done.

For whatever sick reason, the blood of the unborn fulfills some sick function in the order of the Cabal which frankly, I don't fully understand. We talked earlier about how Q said that every Planned Parenthood in America is secretly dedicated to that pagan god Molech, but beyond that, we've all seen and heard the horror stories about baby parts being sold for exorbitant sums of cash, and how some infants are even born alive—and *kept alive*—only to be horrifically executed later and harvested for their intact organs. This evil absolutely cannot be allowed to continue in our land. You could end every other aspect of the Cabal, but if this wretched practice is allowed to go on, we'll be right back where we started in mere decades. It will literally be all for nothing.

If we are to crush the Cabal, this entire bloody business needs to be expunged from our midst with extreme prejudice. It was never about freedom. It was never about a woman's "right to choose." Those were Cabal lies, articulately designed to consume our future and our families, our friends and our spouses and our communities—to weaken us from within by hollowing us out, first physically, and then emotionally and spiritually.

For those who have had abortions, who have performed abortions, who have donated to and supported the organizations that provide abortions—know there is healing, forgiveness, and restoration available for you. But unless we defeat this evil and expunge it entirely from this nation, we cannot defeat the Cabal. It really is that simple.

So choose repentance. Choose humility. Choose courage. It's the only way forward, and in truth, it's incredibly brave.

Q !!mG7VJxZNCI No.421 ☑ ▬
Nov 6 2018 15:53:40 (EST)

2441

DrWNUUmWsAAvKLb.jpg-large.jpg

https://twitter.com/RealTT2020/status/1059879444213510144 ☑ ▬
Together We Win.
Q

So now, at the end of all this, knowing what you know now, will you retreat back into the cave where you've spent your whole life? Or will you step out with us into the light and join us in this, the brightest of all possible futures?

Q !!mG7VJxZNCI ID: 27fd5f No.2820535 Aug 31 2018 14:55:13 (EST)

UNITED WE STAND.png

2039

WHERE WE GO ONE, WE GO ALL!
WE, THE PEOPLE!
FROM SEA TO SHINING SEA.
LET FREEDOM RING, PATRIOTS.
IT IS YOUR TIME.
IF AMERICA FALLS, THE WORLD FALLS.
UNITED WE STAND!
GOD BLESS YOU ALL.
Q+

I know where I'm going.
I sincerely hope to see you there.
And so, I close with this.
Thank you, dear reader, for seeing this all the way through until the end.
Thank you Anons, for leading the way.
Thank you, President Trump, for all you have endured for us.
And thank you to QAnon and everyone involved in the Q operation. I sincerely hope I get the opportunity to shake all your hands someday.

Anonymous ID: zGyR4tyi No.147647154 Nov 2 2017 13:44:21 (EST)

55

Look to Twitter:
Exactly this: "My fellow Americans, the Storm is upon us......."
God bless.